THE HISTORY OF THE TECHNOLOGY AND CONSTRUCTION COURT ON ITS 150TH ANNIVERSARY

This collection marks the 150th anniversary of the Technology and Construction Court by presenting insights into its history and impact.

The contributors are current and retired senior judges, renowned academics and leading construction and technology lawyers. The book draws on their different perspectives and approaches to showcase different aspects of the Official Referees and the TCC from its origins in the Judicature Act 1873 through to its modern-day role as an international leader in dispute resolution through litigation, arbitration and adjudication.

Different essays consider the role of the TCC in procedural reform, the digital transformation of dispute resolution, and building safety. The book also looks at how the TCC has impacted on doctrinal English law.

The book also explores the lives and impact of notable Official Referees and TCC judges from the senior judiciary's perspective, with contributions by Lord Dyson on the transition from the Official Referees to the TCC, Sir Rupert Jackson on the Housing Grants, Construction and Regeneration Act 1996, Dame Finola O'Farrell on the TCC today, Sir Peter Coulson on Sir Brett Cloutman QC (a Senior Referee who was awarded a Victoria Cross) and Her Honour Frances Kirkham on the court's role in the regions.

The creation of a specialist dispute resolution forum for complicated engineering, construction and technological disputes is a foundational milestone in the legal history of construction law in England and Wales. This collection offers a unique insight from the judiciary, practising lawyers and academics into the significance and development of the court.

The History of the Technology and Construction Court on its 150th Anniversary

Rewriting the Rules

Edited by
Sir Peter Coulson
and
David Sawtell

•HART•
OXFORD • LONDON • NEW YORK • NEW DELHI • SYDNEY

HART PUBLISHING

Bloomsbury Publishing Plc

Kemp House, Chawley Park, Cumnor Hill, Oxford, OX2 9PH, UK

1385 Broadway, New York, NY 10018, USA

29 Earlsfort Terrace, Dublin 2, Ireland

First published in Great Britain 2023

A catalogue record for this book is available from the British Library.

A catalogue record for this book is available from the Library of Congress.

ISBN: HB: 978-1-50996-417-8
ePDF: 978-1-50996-419-2
ePub: 978-1-50996-418-5

Typeset by Compuscript Ltd, Shannon

CONTENTS

LIST OF CONTRIBUTORS

Rachel Ansell KC MA (Cantab) is the former Chair of TECBAR and is Joint Head of Chambers at 4 Pump Court. Her practice covers construction and engineering, energy, insurance, and professional negligence disputes. She is one of the pre-eminent construction silks at the bar with a global profile demonstrated by her involvement in some of the biggest disputes in the UK and abroad. Rachel is recognised as a leading practitioner in Chambers & Partners, Chambers Global, and Legal 500 and was awarded Construction Silk of the Year at the Chambers UK Bar Awards 2017 and International Arbitration Silk of the Year at the Chambers UK Bar Awards 2019.

Sir Peter Coulson is a Lord Justice of Appeal and the Supervising LJ for TCC appeals. He has been a judge since 2004, when he was the last person appointed as a Senior Circuit Judge to the TCC in London. He was formerly a Presiding Judge on the North Eastern Circuit between 2011 and 2014 and the Judge in Charge of the TCC between 2015 and 2018.

His Honour Stephen Davies is the permanent Judge of the Technology and Construction Court in Manchester following his appointment in October 2007. He has acted as an arbitrator and as a mediator, both as a barrister and as a judge. He is a course director on the Specialist Jurisdictions course at the Judicial College and has spoken at numerous seminars on construction-related matters.

Lord Dyson was a High Court Judge 1993–2000, Judge in Charge of the Technology and Construction Court 1997–2000, a Lord Justice of Appeal 2001–2010, a Justice of the Supreme Court 2010–2012, Master of the Rolls 2012–2016.

Hannah Fry LLB (QMUL), LLM (QMUL) is a barrister practising at 39 Essex Chambers, London, where she specialises in international and domestic commercial and construction disputes. Hannah regularly appears as sole counsel in the High Court and County Court and has appeared (led) in the Privy Council and Supreme Court. She also appears before international arbitral tribunals.

Nicholas Higgs MEng, MSc, CEng, MICE, FCIArb is a barrister practicing at 39 Essex Chambers, London, focusing on domestic and international construction and energy disputes in adjudication, litigation and arbitration. Prior to being called to the Bar of England and Wales he had a career as a chartered engineer with Ove Arup and Partners specialising in bridge design and in the procurement and delivery of large-scale infrastructure projects in the UK and overseas.

Sir Rupert Jackson was a High Court Judge from 1999 to 2008 and a Lord Justice of Appeal from 2008 to 2018. He served as Judge in Charge of the Technology and Construction Court from 2004 to 2007.

Aleksander Kalisz is a Research Associate at the Centre of Construction Law & Dispute Resolution at The Dickson Poon School of Law, King's College London. His academic interests are in construction disputes, arbitration and international economic law. He is involved in an empirical study of construction adjudication in the United Kingdom, parallel to his work on several other projects in the field of dispute resolution. He is also pursuing an MPhil/PhD in international arbitration at King's College London as a Nash Scholar.

Her Honour Frances Kirkham qualified as a solicitor in 1978. She was a construction and engineering law specialist, assisting professional and corporate clients with contract formation and dispute resolution. In 2000 Frances was appointed the designated TCC Judge in Birmingham, a post she held until her retirement from the bench in 2011. Frances is a Justice of the Qatar International Court and Dispute Resolution Centre, a Fellow of the Chartered Institute of Arbitrators and is a Chartered Arbitrator.

Michael Levenstein BA (Penn), MSc (Oxon), MA (Cantab), LLM, FRSA is a barrister practising at Gatehouse Chambers in Gray's Inn, specialising in construction and commercial litigation. He serves on the Executive Committee of the Technology and Construction Bar Association (TECBAR). In addition to his practice, he is a Visiting Lecturer and LLM supervisor at The City Law School, University of London. He has written, co-edited and/or contributed to multiple books, including *Construction All Risks Insurance, Construction Professional Indemnity Insurance* (both Sweet & Maxwell, 2018-present) and the British Constructional Steelwork Association's *Construction Contractual Handbook* (2019).

Dr Laura Lintott PhD (Cantab), MA (Oxon), LLM (PLP) works as a senior lawyer (Solicitor Advocate) in the City of London with a focus on both international and domestic construction dispute resolution. She is Visiting Fellow at King's College London teaching on the Construction Law and Dispute Resolution MSc programme and supervisor for undergraduates in land and private law at the University of Cambridge.

Juan Lopez LLB is a barrister practising at 39 Essex Chambers, London, specialising in infrastructure planning, domestic and international construction, and energy and environmental law, in litigation, adjudication and arbitration. His focus includes nationally and internationally strategic energy installations (all typologies) and major transportation schemes, from consenting through to construction, as well as energy supply, financing and procurement disputes.

Dr Douglas Maxwell LLB, MPhil (Cantab), PhD (Cantab) is a barrister practising at Henderson Chambers, London, where he specialises in health and safety, product liability, property law and public law. He is the author of *The Human*

Right to Property (Hart 2022). Prior to joining Henderson Chambers, Douglas was employed in research roles at the Law Commission and the Faculty of Law, University of Oxford.

Professor Renato Nazzini is Professor of Law and Director of the Centre of Construction Law and Dispute Resolution at King's College London. He is also a partner at LMS Legal LLP. An experienced arbitrator and counsel in international arbitration, he has a wide industry knowledge, from construction, oil and gas and infrastructure to IT and digital, from pharmaceuticals to consumer goods. He is dually qualified English Solicitor and Italian Advocate, a member of the ICC Arbitration and ADR Commission, Italy, a member of the ICC Task Force on Dealing with Corruption Issues in International Arbitration, a member of the Advisory Board of Africa Construction Law, and a Fellow of the Chartered Institute of Arbitrators. Renato published six books and more than 80 articles and book chapters on international arbitration or competition law and is General Co-editor or member of the editorial board of four leading international journals. He has been Visiting Professor at the University of Turin, the University of Zurich, and FGV of San Paulo, Brazil. He holds a PhD from the University of London and a PhD from the University of Milan.

Dr Elizabeth Norton PhD (KCL), MA (Cantab), MSt (Oxon), FRHistS is an historian and non-practising solicitor. A Fellow of the Royal Historical Society, she has taught History at King's College London. Her Ph.D research looked at the Blount family of the West Midlands in the sixteenth century, including researching their use of the Courts of Chancery, Common Law and Star Chamber.

Dame Finola O'Farrell DBE was called to the Bar in 1983 by Inner Temple and took Silk in 2002. Prior to her judicial appointment, Mrs Justice O'Farrell DBE had over 30 years' experience as a leading barrister in construction, engineering, energy, shipbuilding and information technology cases. She acted regularly as counsel or arbitrator in international arbitrations and is an accredited adjudicator and mediator. In 2007 she was appointed as a Recorder and in 2016 she was appointed as a Justice of the High Court (King's Bench Division), assigned to the Technology and Construction Court, part of the Business and Property courts. She was appointed as Judge in Charge of the TCC from 2 March 2020.

Dr Michael Reynolds PhD (LSE), LLM (QMUL), MSc (KCL), FCIArb, CArb is Solicitor and Chartered Arbitrator, Visiting Senior Research Fellow, London School of Economics, Senior Lecturer in Private international Law at the University of East London, and Module Leader in International Dispute Resolution and Arbitration at BPP University College, London. He is author of *Instruments of Peacemaking* (Hart Publishing, 2021).

David Sawtell MA (Cantab), MPhil (Cantab), MSc (KCL), FCIArb is a barrister practising at 39 Essex Chambers, London, where he specialises in international and domestic construction and real property disputes. He is a Bye-Fellow at

Peterhouse, University of Cambridge and College Teaching Associate for land law and equity. He is undertaking a PhD at the University of Cambridge, researching the taxonomic interface between land law and construction law; he was awarded a Francis Paterson Scholarship from the Society of Construction Law.

Dr Stacy Sinclair PhD, MSc, LLB, BS(Engineering), BS(Architecture), RIBA is a Solicitor, Architect, Partner and Head of Technology and Innovation at Fenwick Elliott LLP, Secretary of The Technology and Construction Solicitors' Association and Chair of FIDIC's Digital Transformation Committee.

Simon Tolson BA(Hons), CArb, FCIArb is a Solicitor, Chartered Arbitrator and Adjudicator, Senior Partner of Fenwick Elliott LLP, Honorary President of The Technology & Construction Solicitors Association (Past Chairman), visiting lecturer at King's College London on the MSc in Construction Law & Dispute Resolution.

TABLE OF CASES

TABLE OF STATUTES

TABLE OF STATUTORY INSTRUMENTS

Introduction

SIR PETER COULSON AND DAVID SAWTELL

The Judicature Act 1873 transformed civil justice in England and Wales. The old system of higher courts, which had existed in a recognisable form since the later medieval period, was swept away and replaced by the new Supreme Court of Judicature, itself divided into specialist divisional courts and the Court of Appeal. At the same time, the two separate legal systems of Law and Equity were fused. One part of that transformation has been less publicised, but has had equally long-lived consequences. By section 83 of the Judicature Act 1873, the office of the Official Referees was created. This office, re-cast as the Official Referees' Business by the Courts Act 1971 before finally becoming the Technology and Construction Court (TCC) of the High Court in 1998, has continued to the present day. The Official Referees, and then the judges of the TCC, have continued to hear highly complicated cases involving technical, scientific, technological and construction and engineering issues. Their decisions have helped shape the common law in general, and construction, technology and procurement law in particular. It is the 150th anniversary of the genesis of this office of the Official Referee and their business, continuing into the work of the TCC, that this book celebrates.

This book is a collection of pieces written by contributors from a range of backgrounds and experiences of the Official Referees and the TCC. Some of them are retired and current judges of the TCC; three of them have also sat in appellate courts from that Court's decisions. A number of the writers are practitioners with an extensive professional background, either as solicitors or members of the Bar, dealing with TCC business. This book also boasts chapters written by academics whose research into dispute resolution informs their analysis of the history of this institution. The writers bring not only their research, but their personal recollections and experiences of the Official Referees and the TCC, to their contributions, while also including the memories and accounts of their colleagues and peers. The book, therefore, reflects the different approaches, experiences and research methods of its contributors, and we believe it is very much the richer for it.

Mid-nineteenth century methods for dispute resolution involving factually or technically complicated evidence, such as bringing an action in the Queen's Bench or Court of Common Pleas or in the Court of Chancery, or referring a dispute to arbitration, were unsatisfactory. The common law courts still relied on juries as finders of fact. The use of special juries was unsatisfactory, but dispute resolution through especially qualified decision makers offered a clue as to what might be a better solution. Even if a dispute could be framed in such a form that it was possible to bring the matter in Chancery, the procedure was beset by delays. As Dr Elizabeth Norton discusses in the first chapter, there was scope for a new form of dispute resolution designed especially to tackle complicated disputes which were unsuitable for juries.

The first report of the Judicature Commissioners recommended the appointment of the Official Referees' office. A judge could refer a cause, or issues arising within it, to be tried by an Official Referee. These recommendations were implemented in the Judicature Act 1873. Dr Laura Lintott discusses the genesis and early history of the Official Referees in the second chapter in this book. These reforms were not, at first, well received; the Official Referees were initially charged on an hourly basis, while not all of the appointments were universally acclaimed. By the early twentieth century, however, the Official Referees had become an established part of the Supreme Court of Judicature, discharging work in a range of technically and factually complicated areas.

The Official Referees of the early part of the twentieth century were also pioneers in case management techniques. Dr Michael Reynolds discusses the innovations that they developed in the third chapter of this book. In particular, Sir Francis Newbolt, one of the Official Referees, brought forward a range of case management techniques that are now familiar to post-Woolf practitioners.

The history of the Official Referees and the TCC has, in a number of respects, been shaped by the individual contributions of a number of different people from a range of different backgrounds. With good reason, names (listed in chronological order) such as Alfred Hudson, Donald Keating QC, Edgar Fay QC, Lord Dyson, Sir Peter Coulson, and Sir Rupert Jackson resonate and recur throughout the different chapters in this book. We are fortunate that we count some of them among the contributors to this book. The fourth chapter, however, considers a man whose life and career counts among the most remarkable. Sir Peter Coulson relates the story of Sir Brett Cloutman, Victoria Cross, Military Cross, Queen's Counsel and ultimately Senior Official Referee. He was awarded the Military Cross and the Victoria Cross for his bravery on the Western Front during the First World War. He went on to the Bar, before serving again in the Second World War. His service is a notable example of the personalities and experiences of those who became Official Referees and Judges of the TCC.

As an Appendix to this book, Dr Norton has written a series of short biographies from the first Official Referees up to the early 1950s, with Dr Reynolds writing a biography of Sir Francis Newbolt KC.

The later Official Referees and judges of the TCC are within living memory. Sir Peter Coulson has brought together, in the fifth chapter of this book, a collection of those recollections from a number of distinguished practitioners, with assistance from David Sawtell. It gives an account of the Official Referees and the TCC from the late 1950s until the first part of the twenty-first century that would otherwise go unrecorded. It is rare indeed for there to be such a distillation of personal accounts of one court. All practitioners (whether or not they have appeared before the Official Referees or in the TCC) can relate to the tenor of the descriptions that Sir Peter has recorded.

The most notable moment in this recent history, of course, is the transformation of the Official Referee's Business into the Technology and Construction Court. After over 100 years of continuous existence as an adjunct of the High Court (including the formal dissolution in the Courts Act 1971, and the corresponding immediate reconstitution of 'Official Referee's Business' at the same time), the Official Referees were finally transmogrified into a fully established part of the Queen's Bench Division of the High Court. It is rare to have an eyewitness account of the birth of a court. Lord Dyson provides this in chapter six in this book. It came at a key juncture in construction law. The Housing Grants, Construction and Regeneration Act 1996 had just come into force. One of his first tasks was to shape the way in which the decisions of adjudicators, freshly minted by section 108 of the 1996 Act, would be enforced. It was a decision of the TCC (and subsequently upheld by the Court of Appeal) that meant that construction adjudication became a powerful force for rapid dispute resolution in construction.

Any history of an institution must also acknowledge the low points as well as the highlights. The first Official Referees were not universally well received, with the Solicitors Journal commenting that the appointments 'cast no lustre upon the office'.[1] The 1980s and the 1990s saw a number of excellent judges among the Official Referees, with Judge Thayne Forbes QC becoming a High Court Judge. The early 2000s, however, saw the publication of an infamous and devastating article in the magazine *Legal Business* about the TCC in 2004. Sir Rupert Jackson worked hard to restore the reputation of the Court, with the appointment of five full time High Court Judges (Sir Vivian Ramsey, Sir Robert Akenhead, Sir Peter Coulson and Sir Antony Edwards-Stuart becoming the 'Jackson Five').[2] One of the reasons that the Official Referees and then the TCC has been so long-lived has been its resilience and ability to change, as well as its utility.

Sir Rupert Jackson's name is also synonymous with the formative decisions in respect of Part II of the 1996 Act. His chapter (written with Nicholas Higgs and Hannah Fry) gives his account of the early years of the new regime of payment and dispute resolution. Any student of the 1996 Act would be well served to read this chapter of the book.

Sir Rupert Jackson's account brings us towards the modern day and the current workings of the TCC. Dame Finola O'Farrell (or Mrs Justice O'Farrell, as those of us current practising in the TCC would refer to her to our instructing solicitors) gives a comprehensive and detailed account of modern practice in the Court. The TCC's work today is primarily litigation of technically complex disputes. Much of

[1] *Solicitors Journal* (1875) 20 SJ 289; cited by E Fay, *Official Referees' Business*, 2nd edn (London, Sweet & Maxwell, 1988) 18.

[2] P Coulson, 'Lord Justice Jackson and the Evolution of the Technology and Construction Court' in J Bailey (ed), *Construction Law, Costs and Contemporary Developments: Drawing the Threads Together – A Festschrift for Lord Justice Jackson* (Oxford, Hart, 2018).

it arises from building, technology and engineering disputes. The TCC also has a busy workload arising from procurement challenges. Pro-active case management and the facilitation of ADR remains a central part of the Court's approach. This chapter discusses a number of the most important aspects of the TCC's procedure.

Part of the original purpose of the Official Referees was to facilitate local investigation. This aim has continued through to the modern day, with the TCC operating in a number of cities. Chapter nine focuses on the recent history of the TCC in Manchester, Birmingham, Liverpool and Leeds as examples of how the TCC outside London has developed. It has been written by Her Honour Frances Kirkham, who has long been associated with the TCC in Birmingham, His Honour Judge Stephen Davies, TCC Judge in Manchester and Michael Levenstein.

Having brought us up to the modern day, the next chapters draw the microscope back to consider a number of highly important issues that arise from the work of the Official Referees and the TCC.

Professor Renato Nazzini and Aleksander Kalisz, the Director of and a Research Associate at the Centre of Construction Law and Dispute Resolution in the Dickson Poon School of Law in King's College, London, analyse the contribution of the TCC to arbitration. The Centre of Construction Law and Dispute Resolution is one of the world's leading construction law research and teaching centres. The Centre itself has made highly significant contributions to the study of construction law and the resolution of disputes arising from construction projects. 2022 saw the 35th anniversary and celebration of its foundation. We are grateful to Professor Nazzini and Aleksander Kalisz for their magisterial and rigorous study of the leading decisions of the TCC in respect of arbitration.

The Official Referees and the TCC have long been at the forefront of procedural and technical innovation. This is brought to life by Stacy Sinclair and Simon Tolson in Chapter eleven, who give an account of the TCC's digital transformations and innovations from the 1990s to the present day.

One of the most important aspects of construction law is building safety. This was tragically demonstrated by the Grenfell Tower disaster in June 2017, which saw the death of 72 people in a fire in a high-rise residential building in west London. The work of academics such as Philip Britton, Sue Bright and Matthew Bell in highlighting the numerous legal issues that arise from unsafe or defective construction works has demonstrated the vital importance in ensuring that this area of the law is functionally effective. The Official Referees and the TCC have been active throughout their history in disputes arising out of construction defects and building safety. Rachel Ansell KC, the former Chair of TECBAR and Dr Douglas Maxwell review 150 years of fire safety in buildings in chapter twelve. They take a snapshot of the state of the law in 1873, 1923, 1973 and 2023, describing the prevailing regulatory and private law legal framework in each period. This legal historical study highlights the changing legal framework and context for building safety.

The Official Referees and the TCC have had significant influence on the development of construction law in particular, and the common law more generally.

A number of the most important cases in contract law and tort that form the basis of English doctrinal law today were considered at first instance in this Court. David Sawtell traces how the Official Referees and the TCC have contributed to this development. The first part of their history is difficult to find in the law reports: it was a regular complaint that the decisions of the Official Referees were not being reported, with a resultant impact on the growth of doctrinal construction law. The start of specialist law reporting was a green light to a far clearer contribution to English construction law.

The last substantive chapter in this book is by Juan Lopez. While the previous chapters explored the history of the TCC, he turns his attention to its future, and in particular, to energy and environment litigation. The UK energy sector is diversifying to nuclear, wind, solar, biomass, hydrogen geothermal, and tidal sources of energy, tilting away from oil and gas dependency. This poses a future challenge for the TCC and for other forms of dispute resolution. A series of recent cases have cast a light on what the issues in the future are likely to be. The ultimate conclusion of this chapter is that the TCC is well place to resolve the disputes that will no doubt arise.

One consistent theme that emerges from this book is the importance of excellence in the resolution of serious technical, construction, engineering and other complicated disputes. A court must be seen to be rigorous in its application of the law, but also its ascertainment and assessment of the facts, which are so very important in these types of disputes. The advantage of a specialist court is that a cadre of judges experienced in the technical, factual and legal challenges that this kind of work presents is more likely to be consistent in its decision making. At the same time, such a group of judges must also achieve excellence in their application of the law more generally. Disputes as to contractual or tortious liability, or the conduct of arbitration business, spans all of the parts of what is now the Business and Property courts. What a study of the last 150 years of the Official Referees and the TCC demonstrates is the qualities that go into making a court of this longevity. It must be able to change with the times; on a handful of occasions, the Official Referees undertook significant reform and transformation.

This book, therefore, presents more than a doctrinal or procedural legal history of the Official Referees. It offers different perspectives from different participants in its history, as well as academic insights into its nature. As is typical with construction law, there is a huge overlap between the practitioners, the scholars, and the judges involved. As the TCC looks ahead to the future of dispute resolution in complicated, technical and scientific disputes, the need for such a forum is just as strong, if not stronger, than it was in 1873.

Sir Peter Coulson
David Sawtell

1

The Antecedents to the Official Referees

DR ELIZABETH NORTON

Had he known what was to follow, Mr Macintosh may well have shied away from undertaking railway works on behalf of the Great Western Railway Company, for which sums became due to him in June 1838.[1] With the parties unable to agree payment, Macintosh filed a Bill of Complaint in the Court of Chancery in 1847, for work done and materials supplied by him in the construction of the defendant's railway. Eight years later, on 30 May 1855, the Bill finally received an official response, with Vice-Chancellor Stuart ordering an enquiry into:

> Whether anything and what remains due to the Plaintiff in respect of the works executed and the materials supplied or otherwise under the several contracts in the pleadings of this cause mentioned, having regard to the terms of the said contracts respectively and to the circumstances under which the Plaintiff carried out an executed the said works.

It was nearly another eight years before this enquiry was completed, with a certificate issued by the Court on 19 February 1863 holding that the plaintiff was to receive over £147,000, with nearly £70,000 of this interest due to the length of time since the sum owed had originally been due. This was not the end of the matter, with both parties attempting to either discharge or vary the certificate, motions that were refused by the Vice-Chancellor. The defendant then appealed, with the matter heard again in May 1863. Sixteen years after the Bill of Complaint was first issued, the Court allowed the defendant's appeal, effectively sending the matter right back to the start again. While *Jarndyce v Jarndyce* of Charles Dickens' *Bleak House* is usually namechecked when the inefficiencies of the nineteenth century Chancery are highlighted, observers need not look to fiction. *Macintosh v The Great Western Railway Company*, an all too real Chancery case, was far from an isolated example. By the nineteenth century, Chancery was renowned primarily for swallowing up fortunes in its never-ending procedure and processes.[2]

[1] *Macintosh v The Great Western Railway Company* S.C.3Sm. & G.146; 2 n.r.210; 32 L.J. Ch.412; 8 L.T.479; 11 W.R.788.

[2] JH Langbein, 'Fact Finding in the English Court of Chancery: A Rebuttal' (1974) 83 *Yale Law Journal* 1620, 1629.

The 'hydra-headed monster' of the Chancery courts, as one highly critical commentator put it in 1850, tends to draw observers' attention, but the nineteenth century Common Law courts were not without their faults.[3] Had Mr McIntosh instead have had cause to issue in the Court of the King's Bench, he might have come across several 'Guinea pigs' as he made his way into the building.[4] This scurrilous term for Special Jurors reflected the fact that the ability to request a 'Special Jury' from a considerably narrower pool of men was criticised for leading to a group of almost professional jurors in the nineteenth century, while the ubiquitous jury trial in the common law courts led to delay and inconsistent awards. As the nineteenth century progressed there were growing calls for reform in both the courts of Common Law and of Equity. Few would have denied that such change was badly needed.

The Official Referees who, of course, heard matters concerning technology, engineering and construction, had their origins in the general dissatisfaction with the civil courts of the common law and equity, as well as the limitations of arbitration, in the nineteenth century, with the concerns of Parliament, the judiciary, legal practitioners and the general public increasingly vocal in relation to civil matters as a whole as that century progressed. After nearly three quarters of a century of complaint and legislation, the Judicature Act of 1873 brought the Official Referees into existence 150 years ago, with the form taken and the procedure they were intended to follow very much built on what had worked, and what had very much not worked, in civil litigation in the centuries before. It is impossible to understand the rationale behind the Official Referees without delving into its antecedents in the courts of the common law, the courts of equity and of the process of arbitration, which became increasingly important as litigants sought, at all costs, to avoid the problems and delays of the courts of law.

I. The Common Law Courts

Although subject to less criticism than the courts of Chancery, the Common Law courts were widely considered to be in need of reform by the start of the nineteenth century, with criticism focussing on their centralised nature, the inadequacies of the assize system and the cost of bringing even the smallest of claims.[5] Indeed, the cost of litigation in the central courts doubled between 1680 and 1750, thanks to an increase in legal fees.[6] While not on the level of the Chancery courts,

[3] HM Weston, *Chancery Infamy: Or a plea for an Anti-Chancery League* (Effingham Wilson, 1850) 4.

[4] J Oldham, 'Special Juries in England: Nineteenth Century Usage and Reform' (1987) 8 *The Journal of Legal History* 148: 157. The name, a rather scurrilous one, comes from the fact that Special Jurors received a guinea per case, much higher than the shilling of eight pence due to an ordinary juror.

[5] P Polden, *A History of the County Court, 1846–1971* (Cambridge, Cambridge University Press, 1999) 7–8; W Swain, *The Law of Contract 1670–1870* (Cambridge, Cambridge University Press, 1999, 2015) 11.

[6] Swain (n 5) 11.

delays were complained of, with no courts sitting during the summer vacation and most business dealt with in the four terms, each of which were only three weeks in length. Certainly, by the 1820s, there were concerns that the King's Bench was unable to manage its workload effectively.[7] At the same time, the English court system was to some extent fragmented, with considerable overlap in business between the common law courts and the courts of equity, particularly in relation to disputes concerning land.[8]

Common law cases were heard before a jury, something which was not initially viewed negatively by commentators, with the anonymous author of *A Compendious Library of the Law*, which was published in 1740, considering that juries 'are incorporated with our Constitution and are the most valuable part of it; nay, may be termed the very vitals of it; without them no man's life can be impeached, no man's liberty or property ought to be taken from him'.[9] Sir William Blackstone, too, wrote favourably of juries, concerned that cases heard before Commissioners alone could result in 'petty tyranny'.[10] There were, however, concerns about the unpredictable results, particularly in relation to damages, that a jury could produce.

One innovation was particularly controversial. Special Juries were used from the seventeenth century, although they became particularly important in the late eighteenth century, largely through their use by Lord Mansfield.[11] Special Juries, which were jurors selected from a narrower pool than usual and for particular characteristics, such as professional expertise or social class, were used repeatedly by Lord Mansfield in the Court of the King's Bench in the 1770s and 1780s to shape commercial law.[12] He created 'merchant juries', drawn from the ranks of mercers, to sit in insurance cases or other cases involving bankers' customs regarding bills of exchange or promissory notes, with their expertise useful both to the Court and to the parties and to provide reassurance that the jury understood the subject matter before them.[13] That this was what Lord Mansfield intended is clear from his statement in the insurance case of *Lewis v Rucker*, in which he contended that 'the special Jury, (amongst whom there are many knowing and considerable Merchants,) … understood the Question very well, and knew more of the Subject of it than any Body else present; and formed their Judgment from their own Notions and Experience without much Assistance from anything that passed'.[14] Lord Mansfield did not, however, confine his special juries to commercial cases, as has been identified from studies carried out on his surviving notebooks which

[7] Polden (n 5) 9.
[8] Swain (n 5) 20–21.
[9] *A Compendious Library of the Law* (London, 1740) 122.
[10] W Blackstone, *Commentaries on the Laws of England*, Book the Third (Clarendon Press, 1768) 82.
[11] Oldham (n 4) 148; Swain (n 5) 25–6.
[12] Oldham (n 4) 148.
[13] ibid.
[14] (1761) 2 Burr. 1167, 1168.

suggest that only 27 per cent of the 600 special jury cases noted were for purely commercial disputes.[15]

Special juries remained a frequent feature of nineteenth century commercial cases, commonly being requested by parties in an attempt to obtain a higher status jury. There were also concerns that they were requested as a delaying tactic by parties, as well as drawing criticism from the fact they were drawn from a small pool of jurors, leaving the courts open to accusations of jury rigging.[16] A newspaper editor who was unsuccessful in a libel claim, made such claims in print, complaining

> that Special Juries have been packed for special purposes has been long suspected. The subserviency they have evidenced has been the ground of this suspicion; and the public opinion has been further strengthened by the circumstance that when the Special Jurors have *not attended*, and common jurors have supplied their places, acquittals have almost always followed in cases of libel.[17]

He made his feelings very clear in the title to his work: *An Appeal to the Citizens of London Against the Alleged Lawful Mode of Packing Special Juries*. Amidst this criticism it is unsurprising, but likely fair, that there were claims of professional jurors who made a good living off the cases.[18] The guinea paid to each juror was certainly an incentive for an individual to want to sit multiple times a year. The Juries Act of 1870 hoped to solve some of these problems, for example requiring that a juror could serve no more than once a year, but calls for reform continued. The earlier County Juries Act of 1825 had similarly taken some steps, requiring a random, anonymous selection of jurors to be made from a larger list prepared by the sheriff. Neither of these statutes overcame all of the criticism, however, with continuing calls for reform. Special juries were finally mostly abolished in 1949, although there have been occasional calls for the reintroduction of a jury of experts in some cases, most notably fraud trials.[19]

Calls from Parliament and the judiciary for the reform of civil court juries were initially muted, with concerns in the seventeenth and early eighteenth century about the possibility of judicial subservience, particularly given that until 1689 judges held their offices at the pleasure of the Crown.[20] The position improved over the course of the eighteenth and nineteenth centuries, with the judges of the mid-nineteenth century generally above such criticism.[21] There were also growing calls

[15] Oldham (n 4) 150.

[16] ibid 152; C Hanly, 'The Decline of Civil Jury Trial in Nineteenth-Century England' (2005) 26 *The Journal of Legal History* 253–278, 274.

[17] T Wooler, *An Appeal to the Citizens of London Against the Alleged Lawful Mode of Packing Special Juries* (London, 1817) 2.

[18] Oldham (n 4) 155 notes in a Select Committee report to the House of Commons and City of London in 1817 that some special jurors served in almost half of the 114 cases investigated, while nine (out of a total of 274) serve on one-third of the cases surveyed.

[19] Oldham (n 4) 159.

[20] Hanly (n 16) 255.

[21] ibid 257.

from within Parliament for the removal of jury trials in at least some civil matters, with Henry Brougham MP, for example, suggesting in Parliament in 1830 that jury trials were simply not required in many matters, stating that:

> If the parties themselves are willing to admit that [the case] should not be referred to a jury, then I say no mischief can be done by allowing the Judge and the parties to dispose of the case in a manner which may seem most agreeable to them.[22]

In 1833 the Common Law Commissioners recommended that actions for less than £5 should be decided in 'a summary way without a jury'.

There was actually strong precedent for civil trials held without juries in the Court of Requests, which was first established in London in the reign of Henry VIII. Initially the Court, which sat at London's Guildhall, heard debt matters below the value of 40 shillings, with similar courts established throughout England and Wales at various times by Act of Parliament over the centuries, making it a relatively familiar forum of justice, with the impetus for these localised courts usually coming from the petitions of local merchants or the municipal authorities.[23] While the Court of Requests was initially a court of Equity, from at least 1830 they increasingly applied the common law. Courts of Request were inexpensive to run and were notably faster than other forms of justice, with no jury sitting and no judge. Instead, the Court was presided over by a Commissioner who initially had no legal background, although this changed as the Common Law came to be applied more frequently.[24] Their jurisdiction, which varied from court to court, was also increased, with the courts commonly able to hear matters worth up to £5 or more. They were popular and widespread by the eighteenth century. They could be extremely busy with 200,000 suits initiated in the Court of Requests across England in 1830, rising to 400,000 a year by 1840.[25] This far outnumbered the suits initiated in the superior courts, which stood at around 90,000 claims per year by the late 1820s. As Conor Hanly has noted in his work on the decline of the civil jury trial, by the middle of the nineteenth century 'the majority of civil cases in England were adjudicated in non-jury courts. A mode of summary civil trial had become familiar to litigants, especially those involved in the recovery of small debts'.[26]

The popularity and success of these local juryless courts almost certainly provided the impetus, along with growing calls for reform, for the County Courts Act of 1846, which created a new system of county courts which gave litigants the choice of whether or not to have a jury trial. Many of the new county courts were also created by converting existing Courts of Requests, while the matters

[22] *Parliamentary Debates*, second series, vol 24, cols 243–279, 264 (1830).
[23] Hanly (n 16) 267.
[24] Polden (n 5) 11.
[25] Hanly (n 16) 267; Polden (n 5) 11, although he notes that the application of the common law could be patchy: 'although some later Acts expressly required the court to adhere to the common law, their own lack of legal knowledge, the rarity of legal representation in the court and the want of an effective appeal meant that the commissioners had a pretty free hand'.
[26] Hanly (n 16) 268–69.

they heard had usually been previously within the jurisdiction of the Court of Requests, both factors which likely also helped associate the new county courts with them – and their lack of juries – in the parties' minds. Certainly, it quickly became apparent that there was little appetite for trial by jury, with the vast majority of county court cases proceeding without one.[27] As has been noted, 'this fact was seized upon by commentators as proof that the civil jury need not be mandatory and could be safely removed from the superior courts. The County Courts Act of 1846 therefore represents a crucial step in the decline of the civil jury'.[28]

With mounting criticism, as well as the precedent set by the success of the (mostly) juryless county courts, it is unsurprising that change was enacted in relation to civil juries in the superior courts, with the Common Law Procedure Act of 1854 making a jury trial optional for civil cases in the Westminster courts.[29] This was a significant change since the Act allowed parties to consent in writing to the judge alone deciding the issues of fact, although it was also necessary for the Court to consider such a cause of action appropriate, measures which have been described as 'timid' by one modern commentator.[30] The superior courts attracted higher value and more complex claims, such as in construction cases, which have always been notable for their length, factual complexity and the requirements for expert evidence.[31] Probably as a result of this, the decline in jury trials in the superior courts was less dramatic than in the county courts, with a jury still sitting in approximately 80 per cent of cases by 1883.[32] However, these numbers continued to fall and, by the 1950s juries sat in only around two–three per cent of cases.[33] The Court of Appeal case of *Ward v James* effectively sounded the civil jury's death knell, with it decided that, in personal injury cases, it was only in extraordinary circumstances that a case should be heard by a jury.[34] This was confirmed by the House of Lords in *Williams v Beesley* in 1973, rendering civil jury trials all but extinct.[35]

II. The Courts of Equity

Few aspects of the law excited more critical comment, from politicians, practitioners and laymen, than the Chancery courts in the nineteenth century. According to

[27] Hanly (n 16) 271 notes that in the first eight months of county courts' existence they dealt with 267,445 cases, of which only 800 were heard before juries.

[28] Hanly (n 16) 267.

[29] ibid 253.

[30] E Fay, *Official Referees' Business* (London, Sweet & Maxwell, 1988) 10.

[31] ibid 136.

[32] Hanly (n 16) 277.

[33] ibid 278.

[34] [1965] 1 All ER 563. In court Lord Dennning MR noted that the role of juries in personal injury trials had become almost negligible, in any event, while he hoped that requiring judges to decide damages would improve the uniformity and predictability of awards.

[35] [1973] 1 WLR 1295.

William Carpenter, a journalist and the author of a treatise advocating Chancery Reform, which was published in 1850, 'The Court of Chancery is universally admitted to be an instrument of the most intolerable exaction and oppression'.[36] He considered that its reach was universally negative, since the Chancery Court:

> 'devours widows' houses,' withholds the property of the orphan, and reduces to poverty, pauperism, or the miseries of a prison, multitudes of the twenty thousand who have the ill-fortune to be annually brought within its jurisdiction. No one can be found to stand forward in its defence. Its judges and officers, its solicitors and barristers, who grow wealthy by its practice, have lifted up their voices against it.

Indeed, he considered:

> To get into Chancery is deemed one of the greatest calamities that can befall an individual; to get property out of Chancery, when it is once laid hold of by the powers of the Court, is a feat almost beyond human skill; even the residue, after the bulk of it has been eaten up by fees and costs, can seldom be recovered during the life-time of the original suitor or rightful owner.

He may have exaggerated that some suits had been 'pending for upwards of a century', but certainly decades was not unusual. It is all-but impossible to find any contemporary commentators saying anything positive about the early nineteenth century Chancery, with the Court very far from the innovative body that it had once been. Much of the criticism was political in nature, but there was also a great deal of truth in the accusation, with even purely administrative work, such as the appointment of a trustee or a guardian, being treated procedurally as though it was a litigation dispute.[37]

The rigidity of Chancery's procedures by the nineteenth century was very far from the original intention behind the courts of Equity. Equity, as administered through the courts of Chancery, was intended to give more flexibility than the Common Law, allowing judges to decide what was an equitable outcome rather than being bound by the weight of their case law.[38] As such, Chancery proved wildly popular when it first emerged in England and Wales, with a noticeable decline in business brought before the Common Law courts from the mid-fifteenth century until the mid-sixteenth century.[39] This is often characterised as evidence of the popularity of equity and the growing use of trust structures.[40] Trusts, however, made up only a small minority of Chancery business in the period, with

[36] W Carpenter, *Chancery Reform: The Equity Jurisdiction of the Court of Chancery; A Lecture* (London, 1850) 30.

[37] M Lobban, 'Preparing for Fusion: Reforming the Nineteenth-Century Court of Chancery, Part I' (2004) 22(2) *Law and History Review* 392. Interestingly, in spite of the intense criticism in print, the Chancery received little attention from the general public in the nineteenth century, with work towards reform increasingly coming from lawyers (M Lobban – 'Preparing for Fusion: Reforming the nineteenth-Century Court of Chancery, Part II' (2004) 22(3) *Law and History Review* 565–599).

[38] Lobban, 'Preparing for Fusion Part I' (n 37) 391.

[39] M Blatcher, *The Court of the King's Bench 1450–1550* (London, Bloomsbury, 1978) 14.

[40] ibid 22.

civil disputes – previously the business of the common law – making up the bulk of cases.[41] The sixteenth century has rightly been characterised as a litigious age, with individuals from all levels of society prepared to resort to litigation over often fairly insignificant matters and it may therefore have been the procedure of the Chancery courts that appealed. While in theory the Chancery courts were central institutions in the same way as the Court of the King's Bench which sat at Westminster, in practice the Lord Chancellor, who was the Chancery's only judge, delegated the management of cases, which followed a largely written process and meant that parties and witnesses did not necessarily need to leave the localities to pursue their suits.[42]

The advent of Chancery in England and Wales was an immediate success, but it quickly became bogged down in its own case law, while forum-shopping, with litigants hedging their bets by issuing in multiple courts was a problem of the sixteenth century courts and later.[43] There was a large amount of overlap between the early Chancery and the Common Law courts, with the sixteenth century Chancery prepared to accept contractual disputes, with the subject matter as mundane as a dispute over a piece of broad cloth[44] and the return of cups and glasses that had been lent to a defendant.[45] While most construction disputes were dealt with in the common law courts, since Chancery actions frequently concerned land, there could be some overlap. For example, the late fifteenth century/early sixteenth century Chancery case of *Bunnyng v Lacy* concerned fire damage to a messuage in Bury St Edmunds which was caused by a chimney built by the defendant.[46] *Humfrey v Spaldyng*, a Chancery case from the early fifteenth century similarly dealt with a construction dispute over a chimney. In this case the defendant, a skinner, built a chimney in Norwich to the annoyance of the claimant's tenants.[47] *Coke v Ludgater*, a further Chancery case from the 1550s, concerned the failure of a chimney that had been (it was alleged) inexpertly built of earth and chalk at Felpham in Sussex.[48] Construction matters were at issue in the early courts of Chancery relatively frequently, something that was likely due to the convenience of a court that did not require the parties to travel to London and the Chancery's popularity relative to the common law courts at the time. As the sixteenth century progressed, Chancery judgments became more rigid as the body of case law built

[41] WJ Jones, 'Due Process and Slow Process in the Elizabethan Chancery' (1962) 6 *American Journal of Legal History* 123–150, 149; A Televantos, *Capitalism Before Corporations: The Morality of Business Associations and the Roots of Commercial Equity and Law* (Oxford, Oxford University Press, 2020) 176–77.

[42] WJ Jones, *The Elizabethan Court of Chancery* (Oxford, Oxford University Press, 1967) 12–13.

[43] For example, *Ballard v Purslowe* involved the claimants' issuing in both the Court of Chancery and the Court of the King's Bench in the hope of achieving a favourable outcome in one of them (The National Archives [TNA] C2/Eliz/B17/51 and TNA C2/Eliz/B19/52).

[44] TNA C1/168/55.

[45] TNA C1/1141/4.

[46] TNA C 1/11845.

[47] TNA C 1/5/195.

[48] TNA C 1/1412/43-44.

up, but it remained a popular forum. The surviving records suggest that the vast majority of Bills of Complaint were settled or abandoned before progressing to judgment, suggesting that in many cases litigation was used as a way of prompting settlement rather than with the aim of securing a judgment.[49]

It is in later centuries that problems really arose in the Chancery Court. To all intents and purposes, it was a one judge Court, something which unsurprisingly led to delays mounting as the Court's workload increased.[50] The Court's judicial personnel only significantly increased towards the end of the nineteenth century.[51] As John H Langbein has noted in an article confirming the fact finding powers of the Court of Chancery, 'at least since the 16th century, the Chancellor had a jurisdiction vastly larger than his resources. To administer it required massive delegation'.[52] This is evident in the examples from early cases where the bulk of the Chancery procedure was carried out in the localities with local commissioners. It is even more apparent during the seventeenth and eighteenth centuries when the Chancery began to refer increasing numbers of cases to common law trial as a means of delegating factual disputes that it simply did not have the time or resources to deal with.[53] Nonetheless, it reserved equity, borrowing resources, but not ceding jurisdiction in these delegated matters.[54] Such delegation, in any event, did little to speed up the workings of the Chancery as it moved into the nineteenth century.

III. Arbitration

Given the considerable concerns about both the Chancery courts and the Common Law courts in the late eighteenth and early nineteenth centuries, it is no surprise that would-be litigants explored other means through which to settle

[49] J Sharpe, 'The People and the Law' in B Reay (ed), *Popular Culture in Seventeenth-Century England* (London, 1985) 244–270, 253; R Cust and A Hopper, 'Duelling and the Court of Chivalry in Early Stuart England' in S Carroll (ed), *Cultures of Violence: Interpersonal Violence in Historical Perspective* (Basingstoke, Palgrave Macmillan, 2007) 156–171, 169; RB Outhwaite, *The Rise and Fall of the English Ecclesiastical Courts, 1500–1860* (Cambridge, Cambridge University Press, 2006) 2; S Hindle, 'The Keeping of the Public Peace' in P Griffiths, A Fox and S Hindle (eds), *The Experience of Authority in Early Modern England* (London, Bloomsbury, 1996) 213; C Brooks, *Lawyers, Litigation and English Society Since 1450* (London, Bloomsbury, 1998) 12; E Norton, 'The Blounts in the Long Sixteenth Century' (Unpublished PhD thesis, King's College London, 2019); this has also been observed in nineteenth century cases, as identified by Lobban, 'Preparing for Fusion Part I' (n 37) 399–400.

[50] Technically, it had two judges – the Lord Chancellor and the Master of the Rolls, but until 1829 the Master of the Rolls only sat when the Lord Chancellor was not sitting. Even when a new office of Vice Chancellor of England was created by legislation in 1831, this just meant that the Lord Chancellor ceased to hear cases, perpetuating the court's problem of lack of judicial personnel (Lobban, 'Preparing for Fusion Part I' (n 37) 393). Common law judges could effectively delegate decision making to juries, Chancery's officials had to handle all matters before the court.

[51] Langbein (n 2) 1629.

[52] ibid.

[53] ibid.

[54] ibid 1620, 1630.

their disputes, with arbitration becoming increasingly widely used in commercial disputes.[55] Arbitration is, of course, ancient, with Frank D Emerson, writing on the history of arbitration in the US, tracing its roots all the way back to the Biblical King Solomon.[56] Certainly, arbitration was already an established legal institution in England by the fifteenth century, with a high number of mercantile disputes settled by arbitration tribunals in which the parties would agree to submit their dispute to arbitration under the common law before taking court action.[57] There were advantages to this approach, particularly in relation to matters which crossed jurisdictions, something particularly applicable to merchant disputes, while arbitration tended to be cheaper and provide a faster judgment than going through the court system. Arbitration had become well enough established by the seventeenth century to attract treatises from legal theorists, most notably John March's *Actions for Slander and Arbitrements*, which was first published in 1648 and went through several editions.[58] March, a barrister from Gray's Inn, considered that 'Arbitrements were never more in use than now. And most men either have been or may be Arbitrators; or at least have done, or may submit themselves to the Arbitration of others.'[59] He considered that 'As long as Differences and Contentions arise among men, which be to the Worlds End, certainly the learning of Arbitrements will well deserve our Knowledge', suggesting that he considered arbitration to be of considerable importance to his practice and the practice of others. An anonymous treatise which was published in 1694 called *Arbitrium Revivum: Or the Law of Arbitration* also stressed its importance to seventeenth century dispute resolution.

Standard forms of arbitration agreements and awards also appear in the seventeenth century, indicating its use, particularly in relation to construction and insurance. Indeed, 90 building agreements survive for the Grosvenor Estate in Mayfair, dating to between 1720 and 1730, with almost all containing arbitration clauses.[60] Later that century, Blackstone included arbitration in his Commentaries on the Laws of England (1765–69).[61] In the US, too, arbitration found 'a foothold in chambers of commerce as early as 1768 in New York, 1794 in New Haven, and 1801 in Philadelphia', although it was not widely accepted as a means of dispute resolution in the US until the twentieth century.[62] There was considerable suspicion of arbitration amongst the English courts too, between the seventeenth and

[55] Fay (n 30) 9.
[56] FD Emerson, 'History of Arbitration Practice and Law' (1970) 19 *Cleveland State Law Review* 155: engagedscholarship.csuohio.edu/clevstlrev/vol19/iss1/19 (accessed 11 October 2022).
[57] S Brekoulakis, 'The Historical Treatment of Arbitration under English Law and the Development of the Policy Favouring Arbitration' (2019) 39(1) *Oxford Journal of Legal Studies* 124–50, 127.
[58] J March, *Actions for Slander and Arbitrements* (London, 1674 edition).
[59] ibid 149.
[60] Brekoulakis (n 57) 128.
[61] Blackstone (n 10) 16–17.
[62] Emerson (n 56) 159–160.

nineteenth centuries, although Stavros Brekoulakis has recently argued that the extent of this hostility is overstated, characterising the relationship as one of 'cautious trust'.[63]

A major difficulty in parties using arbitration as a means of avoiding either the Chancery or Common Law courts was the fact that the courts traditionally considered that agreements to arbitrate a dispute could not oust the jurisdiction of the English court, something which meant that they were revocable at will by either party right up until the arbitrator's decision was given.[64] Initially, arbitration appears to have been conceived of as an informal procedure, aimed at eradicating disputes at a local level which threatened community resolutions, in much the same way as early use of the Chancery courts to promote an out of court settlement.[65] As such, arbitrators tended to be prominent members of the local community rather than lawyers or professional arbitrators.

This of course changed in later centuries, although arbitration remained a cheaper and faster means of obtaining justice in most cases, while, since participation was based on consent, tribunals could assume jurisdiction over disputes relating to different regions, giving it a potentially broader application than the Common Law courts.[66] The principle that arbitration awards were revocable at will under the common law remained a major problem throughout the eighteenth century and into the nineteenth, with this principle established in *Vynior's Case*,[67] which involved an action brought in the Court of Common Pleas in 1609 by one Robert Vynior against William Wilde whom (it was claimed) had failed to pay a bond of £20 to secure an arbitrator's decision. Wilde's claim that he was not under an obligation to pay since he had withdrawn from the arbitration before the arbitrator reached his decision was accepted by the Court, while later case law also confirmed that arbitration agreements were freely revocable. It was only in 1856 in *Scott v Avery*[68] that this position changed, with the House of Lords ruling that, while an agreement to submit to arbitration remained potentially revocable, they should be given effect unless exceptional circumstances, such as illegality or fraud, applied. The decision in *Scott v Avery* revolutionised arbitration, as other jurisdictions slowly came to note. In 1920 the State of New York, for example, enacted a law-making agreements to arbitrate any arising disputes included in contracts binding on the parties and legally enforceable.[69]

In addition to the mid-nineteenth century courts ruling on the enforceability of arbitration agreements, the Common Law Procedure Act of 1854 also provided the courts with the power to require arbitration, something which demonstrates a

[63] Brekoulakis (n 57) 125.
[64] ibid.
[65] ibid 130.
[66] Brekoulakis (n 57) 129; Fay (n 30) 9.
[67] (1609) 77 ER 597, 8 Co Rep 80a.
[68] (1856) 5 HL Cas 811.
[69] Emerson (n 56) 161.

recognition of the increasing importance of arbitration, particularly in relation to complex commercial disputes. In section 3, the Act required that:

> if it be made to appear at any time after the issuing of the writ to the satisfaction of the court or a judge upon the application of either party that the matter in dispute consists wholly or in part of matters of mere account which cannot conveniently be tried in the ordinary way it shall be lawful for such court or judge upon such application if they or he think fit … to order that such matters either wholly or in part be referred to an arbitrator appointed by the parties or to an officer of the court … and the award or certificate of such referee shall be enforceable by the same process as the finding of a judge upon the matter referred.

Edgar Fay, in his work on the Official Referees considered that in this statutory provision, with its 'compulsory arbitration', 'was sown the seed of the official referees' courts'.[70] There was, however, still criticism of the way that arbitration was carried out in England and Wales, particularly in relation to the fees charges by arbitrators and the fact that it was difficult to call them into account if they erred in law. In truth, by the mid-nineteenth century it was widely recognised that none of the potential ways to resolve commercial disputes – the common law, Chancery or arbitration – were entirely fit for purpose, with growing calls for reform.

IV. The Antecedents of the Official Referees' Court

For all their criticism, Special Juries, at least in the form of Lord Mansfield's Merchant Juries, did play a potentially important role, since 'it had long been apparent that some issues of fact of a scientific or technical or detailed nature could not satisfactorily be tried by a jury'.[71] While it was initially hoped that the answer to this was arbitration, as can be seen in the provisions of section 3 the Common Law Procedure Act of 1854, it soon became apparent that more was required. In 1867 the government appointed a Royal Commission headed by Lord Cairns, the future Lord Chancellor, who was then a Judge of Appeal in Chancery, to determine how change in the judicature could be effected. Their first Report noted, amongst other things, the problem of how complex issues of fact should be tried, since

> it has long been apparent in the practice of the courts of common law that there are several classes of cases litigated in those courts to which trial by jury is not adapted and in which the parties are compelled – in many cases after they have incurred all the expense of a trial – to resort to private arbitration. Until the Common Law Procedure Act of 1854 the parties could not be compelled to go to arbitration, and the power given by that Act is limited to cases where the dispute relates wholly or in part to matters of mere account of where the parties have themselves before action agreed in writing to refer the matter in difference to arbitration.[72]

[70] Fay (n 30) 10–11.
[71] ibid.
[72] First Report of the Judicature Commissioners, 25 March 1869, 25 Parliamentary Papers 1868/69 (No 41340)12.

Such complex and technical cases included, of course, those concerning technology, construction and engineering, with the inadequacies of the common law courts and arbitration in relation to these matters laid bare.[73] The Commission recommended that, for such matters:

> we think there should be attached to the Supreme Court officers to be called Official Referees and that a judge should have the power at any time after the writ of summons and with or without pleadings and generally upon such terms as he may think fit to order a cause, or any matter arising therein, to be tried by a Referee; and that whenever a cause is to be tried by a Referee such trial should be by one of these Official Referees unless the judge otherwise orders.[74]

The proposed Official Referees were, effectively a type of 'subordinate judge', with the Commission considering that 'the Referee should, unless the judge otherwise directs, proceed with the trial in open court *de die in diem*'.[75] Essentially, the Commission recommended incorporating compulsory arbitration into litigation, but placed within a judicial setting, overcoming the disadvantages identified in independent arbitration.

The Commission's recommendations were incorporated into the Judicature Act 1873, which received Royal Assent on 5 August 1873. With its fusion of the old courts of common law and chancery into one Supreme Court, it effectively overcame much of the criticism of the old, separate system: the possibility of further 'guinea pig' special jurors or a *Jarndyce v Jarndyce* were swept away.[76] Section 83, too, confirmed that 'there shall be attached to the Supreme Court permanent officers to be called Official Referees for the trial of such questions as shall under the provisions of this Act be directed to be tried by such Referees'. Section 56 set out the role of these Official Referees:

> subject to any rules of court and to such right as may now exist to have any particular cases submitted to the verdict of a jury, any question arising in any cause or matter (other than a criminal proceeding by the Crown) before the High Court of Justice or before the Court of Appeal may be referred by the court or by any Divisional Court or judge before whom such cause or matter may be pending, for inquiry and report to

[73] Indeed, R Burrows, 'Official Referees' (1940) 56(4) *Law Quarterly Review* 504–513, 511 in a study from 1940, nearly 70 years after the Official Referees were established, has noted that 'The work of an Official Referee is of a most varied description. In practice it is usual to refer for trial all cases arising out of building contracts and claims for possession upon a forfeiture for breach of covenant to repair with claims for damages for breach of covenant. These cases generally involve masses of important detail, particularly in actions between landlord and tenant where there are long schedules of dilapidations and conflicts of evidence between the architects and surveyors for the parties about the condition of the premises and the question of damages', demonstrating the very real need identified for the Official Referees.

[74] First Report of the Judicature Commissioners, 25 March 1869, 25 Parliamentary Papers 1868/9 (No 41340)13–14.

[75] MP Reynolds, *Caseflow Management: A Rudimentary Referee Process, 1919–70* (Unpublished PhD thesis, The London School of Economics and Political Science, 2008) 29.

[76] Calls for fusion came out of court reforms of the mid nineteenth century, which had generated the question 'whether it was necessary to have separate courts of law and equity, or whether there should be a fusion of judicatures' Lobban, 'Preparing for Fusion Part I' (n 37) 390.

> any official or special referee and the report of such referee may be adopted wholly or partially by the court and may (if so adopted) be enforced as a judgment of the court.

Section 57 confirmed that:

> in any cause or matter (other than a criminal proceeding by the Crown) before the said High Court in which all parties interested who are under no disability consent thereto, and also without such consent in any such cause or matter requiring any prolonged examination of documents or accounts, or any scientific or local investigation which cannot in the opinion of the court or a judge conveniently be made before a jury or conducted by the cuurt through its other ordinary officers, the court or judge may at any time on such terms as may be thought proper, order any question or issue of fact or any question of account arising therein to be tried either before an official referee, to be appointed as hereinafter provided, or before a special referee to be agreed on between the parties.

With this, the framework for the Official Referees was born.

2

The Early History of the Official Referees from 1873 to 1960

DR LAURA LINTOTT

I. Introduction

Judicial innovation of procedure, with the aim of case management efficiency and consistency, was one of the main driving forces in the Victorian era behind creating the office of Official Referees in 1873 when the Judicature Acts were passed by Parliament (in 1873 and 1875 respectively).

The creation of a specialist dispute resolution procedure for complicated cases (eventually focusing on engineering, construction and technological cases) was a foundational milestone in the legal history of construction law in England and Wales. The reform was prompted by scandalous delays of jury trials that involved complex factual issues.[1] The specialist knowledge and expertise of Official Referees catered for cases with high-volume documentary evidence and where conflict of expert opinion arose. To begin with, their jurisdiction initially extended further covering cases in relation to dilapidations, textile manufacturing, commission cases and matters involving prolonged examination of documents, scientific data and local investigations from areas of business, commerce and industry.[2]

At the time, it became clear that a reform was necessary to cater for the diverse and sophisticated needs of different branches of law in different courts. This marked the start of an exciting evolutionary process with the aim of ensuring that technical and complex issues were tried and dealt with at a highly competent level giving the respective cases the time and attention to detail that they deserved.

As time progressed, the stand-alone legal area of construction and engineering crystallised. The office of Official Referees initially consisted of mainly King's or Queen's Counsel, sat in the High Court as circuit judges and section 83 of the Judicature Act 1873 gave the Official Referees additional powers similar to those of High Court judges compared to the previous legislation. In addition,

[1] E Fay, 'Official Referees' Business' (1984) 49(3) *Arbitration* 264, 265.
[2] E Fay, *Official Referees' Business*, 2nd edn (London, Sweet & Maxwell, 1988) cover page.

rather than being bound only to London, they were to sit outside London when necessary.[3]

The purpose of this chapter is to look at the emergence of the Official Referees, their roots and connection to the TCC as well as the main motivators behind setting up the office of Official Referees and how the initiative has shaped caseflow management between 1873 and 1960.

II. What Led to the Formation of the Office of Official Referees?

In the mid-nineteenth century, all questions in the common law courts were tried by jury. Law and equity were in the grip of an antagonistic spasm. While county courts set up in 1846 were aimed at providing some relief, originally their jurisdiction was limited to claims for debt or damage of up to £20. Where a claim was for a sum of over £5, any of the parties had a right to ask for a trial by jury. This obsolete legal system led to unnecessary expense, delay and uncertainty. These were all characteristics of litigation of commerce and industry that businessmen in all areas of commercial life complained about. They started to follow the typical trend of the time, to withdraw their custom from courts and opt for arbitration instead, also incorporating arbitration clauses into their contracts. While this seemingly aided expediency and avoided technicalities, the arbitration practice itself was developing flaws of its own. To improve the legal services provided by courts, the Common Law Procedure Act 1854 allowed a common law judge to try a question of fact without the need for a jury. This was however somehow limited as all the parties and the relevant judge had to agree to this to start with.

The origins of arbitrators and Official Referees are very different. Litigants invented arbitrators with the idea in mind of circumventing the 'courts' oppression'. On the other hand, the office of Official Referees was created by courts to circumvent 'litigants' oppression'.[4]

> Whether the inducement was the practice of arbitration or litigation, a new model was created: a court officer and a subordinate judge with a referral jurisdiction to deal with matters of enquiry and report, reference for a preliminary issue, and the taking of an account.[5]

As the title suggests, the focus of this chapter is on the timeframe between 1873 and 1960. There are several key pieces of legislation noted in this chapter that form part of the evolution of the office of Official Referees.[6]

[3] E Fay, 'The Alexander Lecture 1980' (1980) 46(2) *Arbitration* 74–81.
[4] Fay (n 1) 264, 265.
[5] M Reynolds, 'Caseflow Management: A Rudimentary Official Referee Process 1919–70' Ph.D Thesis (London School of Economics, 2008) 43.
[6] ibid 296–298.

Section 3 of the Common Law Procedure Act 1854 stated that a judge was able to refer a matter of account to an arbitrator or officer of the court termed a 'Referee'.

> It was this extended use of arbitration by the courts which induced the Judicature Commissioners to recommend and the Judicature Acts to create the office of official referees.[7]

On the other hand, Sir Roland Burrows QC (Lord Birkenhead's former private Secretary) noted: 'The reason for the recommendation is to be found in the practice of the Court of Common Law and of Chancery.' This essentially led to the creation of a new model where referral jurisdiction was bestowed onto a court officer and a subordinate judge to deal with matters of enquiry and report, reference for preliminary issue and the taking of an account.[8] Such a referee's award or certificate was then enforceable as if it was a finding of a jury. It was the taking of account that was one of the main and earliest duties that Official Referees had. For about 20 years after the office of Official Referees had been set up, taking accounts formed the main part of Official Referees' work.[9]

In 1867, the government appointed the Royal Commission (consisting of Judicature Commissioners) headed by Lord Hugh Cairns (Judge of Appeal in Chancery and soon to become Lord Chancellor at the time). The purpose was to devise a plan about judicature.

The first report of the Judicature Commissioners[10] ('First Report') recommended the appointment of the Official Referees office. It also replaced old courts of common law and equity with one Supreme Court with its Court of Appeal and High Court.[11] It was the First Report that set the basis for the Judicature Act 1873. The main focus of the First Report was on the difficulties of the dual system of equity and common law and on easing the way in which complex issues of fact were tried. The Commission recommended the following:[12]

> We think there should be attached to the Supreme Court officers to be called Official Referees and that a judge should have the power at any time after the writ of summons and with or without pleadings and generally upon such terms as he may think fit to order a cause, or any matter arising therein, to be tried by a Referee; and that whenever a cause is to be tried by a Referee such trial should be by one of these Official Referees unless the judge otherwise orders. … The judge should have power to direct where the trial shall take place and the Referee should be at liberty … to adjourn the trial to any place which he may deem to be more convenient. The Referee should, unless the judge otherwise directs, proceed with the trial in open court de die in diem.

[7] W Holdsworth, *History of English Law*, Vol XIV, 198.

[8] Reynolds (n 5) 43.

[9] Fay (n 2) 113.

[10] First Report of the Judicature Commissioners, 25 March 1869, Parliamentary Papers 1868/69 (No 41340).

[11] Fay (n 2) 11.

[12] First Report (n 10) 12.

The office of Official Referees was specifically tied to England. The First Report recommended that attached to the Supreme Court should be the Official Referees office with a decision of an Official Referee to be treated on par with a jury's verdict.[13] The Judicature Commissioners pointed out that certain cases were unfit for jury trial, which meant that in those cases parties in dispute felt forced to go to arbitration instead. The Commissioners recommended that the judge trying such cases did this with assessors they selected or alone without a jury (unless the parties explicitly asked for a jury). The Commissioners also suggested support from scientific assessors would be of benefit during the whole or part of the proceedings. A consideration was also given to referrals under the Common Law Procedure Act 1854 in relation to disputes referred to a barrister or an expert. It was concluded that barristers could not devote the continuous attention to matters that they deserved. On the other hand, experts were not ideal either as they lacked the relevant knowledge of the law of evidence and procedural rules.[14]

The originators of the office of Official Referees were mainly Lord Chancellors Hugh Cairns and Roundell Palmer, First Earl of Selborne, who were influenced by the statutory referral jurisdiction formerly given to the Chancery Masters, judges and officers of the common law courts through the Common Law Procedure Act 1854 and also the Chancery Amendment Act 1858. The provisions of those pieces of legislation enabled macro-management in the courts at the time in that they reduced the judges' lists. The aim was that the office of Official Referees would produce a similar benefit and by reducing the list further make the whole system more efficient.[15]

For the avoidance of doubt, when referring to 'micro' and 'macro' caseflow management in this chapter, these terms refer to Official Referees making their work more efficient and effective (micro level) and to the Judicature Commission and superior judiciary facilitating the more efficient delegation of work (macro level).[16] Section 3 of the Chancery Amendment Act 1858 also provided that the Court of Chancery could make provision for assessing damages or any questions of fact that would arise in any action or proceedings to be tried by a special or common jury.

On 13 February 1873, Lord Selborne gave a speech in the House of Lords on the second reading of a third Judicature Bill in which he introduced the concept of Official Referees to the public. Lord Selborne confirmed that the idea stemmed from Parliament and the judiciary. According to him, the reform emanated from society's advancement, increase in legal business and separation of the superior courts. The goals of the Bill were aimed at a more efficient macro-management by unifying legal and equitable jurisdictions thereby creating one consolidated jurisdiction resulting in greater cost efficiency, simplicity and procedural uniformity. In Lord Selbourne's view, if actioned, the reform would mean that judges could transfer cases to Official Referees (while Official Referees would not be able to do

[13] R Burrows, 'Official Referees' [1940] *Law Quarterly Review* 504, 504.
[14] Reynolds (n 5) 44.
[15] M Reynolds, 'Of Civil Procedure and Settlement' (2010) 29(2) *Civil Justice Quarterly* 194–204.
[16] Reynolds (n 5) 56–57.

the same amongst themselves at this point in time) to alleviate the judges' workload, leading to greater business efficiency.[17] On the new office of Official Referees, Lord Selborne noted:[18]

> It is proposed to retain trial by jury in all cases where it now exists, except in one particular. Your Lordships know that there is a class of cases which the parties may take to the Assizes, and in some instances must take there, and which are yet totally unfit to be tried by a jury at all. The result is that the parties are compelled to take such cases out of court and submit them to arbitration; and as no provision has been made by law for the conduct of these arbitrations, the consequence is that very great expense frequently arises out of them. It was a very valuable recommendation of the Judicature Commission that public officers to be entitled 'Official Referees' should be attached to the court, to deal with cases of this kind, and to whom such cases should be sent at once without the useless expensive form of a jury trial. The Bill proposes that such cases should be sent to reference, even if the parties do not consent, and it also provides for the appointment, where the parties may desire it of special referees. The proposal in the Bill is that they shall determine all questions of fact or account, leaving questions of law to be determined by Divisional Courts. I venture to think that will be found a valuable and important provision.

In summary, Lord Selborne advocated that the office of Official Referees was implemented, which at the time would have a subordinate jurisdiction but would benefit from the advantage of a flexible process assisting courts with their workload and aiming for seamless caseflow management. Other objectives included avoiding unnecessary expense of referrals to arbitration and to assist the High Court judges by relieving them of detailed factual examinations.[19]

Section 58 of the Judicature Act 1873 meant that Official Referees were given the same power as officers of the court. This also had the consequence that a judgment by an Official Referee could be set aside as if it was a verdict of a jury.

> In all cases of any reference to or trial by Referees under this Act the Referees shall be deemed to be officers of the Court, and shall have such authority for the purpose of such reference or trial as shall be prescribed by Rules of Court or (subject to such Rules) by the Court or Judge ordering such reference or trial; and the report of any Referee upon any question of fact on any such trial shall (unless set aside by the Court) be equivalent to the verdict of a jury.

III. Emergence of the Office of Official Referees

Section 83 of the Judicature Act 1873 created the Official Referees' office. Essentially, this meant that scientific, technical or detailed issues were to be referred for inquiry or trial to Official Referees in the capacity as judicial officials.[20]

[17] ibid 49–50.
[18] Hansard, HC (series 3) Vol 214, col 346 (13 February 1873). The Hansard reports here are in indirect speech.
[19] Reynolds (n 5) 49–51.
[20] R Jackson, 'Denning Lecture 2006 – The Tower of Babel: What Happens When a Building Project Goes Wrong?' (2008) 24(2) *Construction Law Journal* 87–94.

Section 56 of the Judicature Act 1873 ensured that any question in any civil cause in the High Court or the Court of Appeal could be referred to a referee. Although such a reference involved a judicial inquiry, it meant that the referee would report to the judge eventually making the order. If the judge did not adopt the referee's report, the report would have no force. The judge was free to adopt the report in its entirety or in part or reject it. The judge could also refer the issue to the same or different referee. This meant that a report was not equivalent to the verdict of a jury.[21] Having said that, once the report was adopted, it was capable of enforcement as if it were a judgment or an order.[22]

Section 57 of the same act meant that any matter of fact or account in a civil case before the High Court could be referred to a referee for trial either if all relevant parties agreed to this (not being under disability) or without such consent where a case needed a 'prolonged investigation of documents or accounts or such scientific or local investigation as could not in the opinion of the Court or a judge conveniently be made before a jury or conducted by the Court through its other ordinary officers.'[23]

According to section 57 of the Judicature Act 1873, a referee's report on any question of fact was equal to a jury's verdict. Where a matter had been referred for trial under section 57, resulting in a definite decision, such a decision could not be set aside (similarly to a jury's verdict) or ignored by the judge who made the order. If a judge wanted the decision to be set aside, an application had to be made on motion to the Divisional Court.[24] While the power to refer a matter to a referee under the Judicature Act 1873 applied to all issues falling under section 57,[25] it was not possible to refer the whole action[26] and the Official Referee had no power to make a judgment or to make any order as to costs.[27]

In summary, there is an important distinction to be made between sections 56 and 57. Where a reference was made under section 56, it would result in the referee reporting to the judge who made the actual order.[28] On the other hand, a reference for a trial under section 57 would result in a definite decision, which could not be set aside or disregarded by the judge who made the order.[29] The effect of these two sections at macro-level was that the process became more efficient and effective as the office of Official Referees helped alleviate the volume of cases in High Court. Judges could therefore hear their cases sooner. The next aim was to ensure that the micro-process would be made also more efficient and effective.[30]

[21] *Wenlock v River Dee Co* (1887) 19 QBD 155.
[22] Burrows (n 13) 505.
[23] ibid.
[24] *Cooke v Newcastle and Gateshead Water Co.* (1882) 10 QBD 332.
[25] *Wood v Pilley* (1880) 5 QBD 427; *Knight v Coates* (1887) 19 QBD 296.
[26] *Longman v East* (1877) 3 CPD 142.
[27] Burrows (n 13) 505, 506.
[28] ibid 505.
[29] *Cooke v Newcastle and Gateshead Water Co.* (n 24).
[30] Reynolds (n 15) 194–204.

The higher court system, which has been in place since the Middle Ages, was reorganised in its entirety by the Judicature Acts 1873 and 1875 respectively. We saw earlier that the Judicature Act 1873 was a judicial-reform measure pioneered by Lord Selborne. The measure meant that the English court system moved from a duality of common law and chancery (equity) to a single hierarchy of courts.

The first Lord Chancellor to operate under the new court system was Lord Cairns, who was successful in macro-managing the unification of equity and common law and managed to codify procedural law. His strong view was that referees should replace arbitrators.[31] Below is an example from 12 November 1875 showing Lord Cairns' strong support of the office of Official Referees.

> I am directed by the Lord Chancellor to enclose for the information of the Lords of the Treasury the opinion and determination of the Lord Chancellor and of the Heads of the Divisions of the High Court of Justice as to the numbers, qualifications, and tenure of office of the Official Referees in pursuance of Section 83 of the Judicature Act 1873 and have to ask the sanction of the Treasury …. that these Official Referees should be substituted for arbitrators pro hac vice, that the number of Official Referees will not be sufficient and that a greater number will be required: but they (Presidents of Divisions) think that within first instance the experiment may be tried with four Referees, that is to say one for each of the four Divisions, Chancery, Queen's Bench, Common Pleas and Exchequer. The salary of these Official Referees has to be fixed under Section 85 by the Treasury with the concurrence of the Lord Chancellor. The Lord Chancellor is of the opinion that looking to the judicial character of the functions which these Referees will have to perform, to the circumstances that they will have to give up all private practice and that their work will be ejusdem generis with but certainly higher than that which the Masters who receive £1,500 a year now perform. The salary specified ought not to be less than £1,500 and competent men cannot be got for less, and this opinion is held very strongly by the Presidents of the Divisions. The Lord Chancellor understands that upon references to Masters of the Common Law Courts of matters of account it has been the practice to charge a fee for each hour of the Master's time occupied, which fee went into the general revenue. The Lord Chancellor thinks it would be open to the Treasury to consider whether some charge should be made to the suitors to the reference for the time of these Official Referees that may be occupied and that this whole charge of the Official Referees may be lightened. The Lord Chancellor would be obliged to Their Lordships if they would give the subject of this letter their immediate attention as it is highly desirable that the Official Referees be appointed as soon as possible there being already cases which have been referred to them and are now waiting for trial before them.

It is obvious that there was some uncertainty as to the number of Official Referees and their salary. The Treasury responded acknowledging the higher status of the office of Official Referees on 19 November 1875.

Notably, while the Judicature Act 1873 came into force on 2 November 1874, there was a significant delay in relation to the appointment of Official Referees.

[31] Letter. H.J.L. Graham. Principal Secretary to L.C. to William Laws, H.M. Treasury. 12 November 1875. LCO 1/73. [HPIM0445-0448.].

For a whole year, not a single Official Referee was appointed showing the typically human aversion to change, no matter how positive. In its issue of 13 November 1875, the *Law Times* criticised this lack of action.[32]

> … since the clauses giving power to make such appointments are some of the clauses of the Judicature Act from which considerable practical advantage may reasonably be expected to be derived, it seems somewhat desirable to call public attention to the fact that they have not yet been put into operation. … The consequence of the defects of the present system is that in cases of moment in this at present inevitable delay the parties have hitherto generally preferred appointing and paying an arbitrator selected by themselves to having their cases heard by the Masters of the courts. Now the proposed system of the appointment of official referees seems admirably adopted to supplement the weak points of the present system and to provide reasonably speedy cheap and efficient tribunals. If men of standing and practical experience in whom the parties can have confidence are appointed and compelled where the parties require it to hold sittings in the place where the question in dispute arises or where the parties and their witnesses reside, one of the chief objections to the present references before Masters is met, and if their sittings are held de die in diem, as the Act contemplates, another great objection to the present system, that of the delay consequent on the matter being referred to a Master, is also obviated. The sittings of the official referees de die in diem will also tend, apart from any question of expense, to make a trial before one of them a more favourite mode of trial than a reference to an arbitrator chosen by the parties; unless indeed such arbitrators abandon their present usual methods of proceedings which consists of adjourning from time to time as may suit their own convenience or that of counsel on either side.

Eventually, Lord Cairns was successful in obtaining the funds to secure an appointment of four Official Referees[33] and the authorities selected four barristers (two of them were silks) who were appointed as full-time Official Referees on 15 February 1876 – James Anderson QC, George Dowdeswell QC, Charles Roupell and Henry Verey (whose time at the office of 44 years was never exceeded).[34]

On 24 February 1876, Lord Cairn's proposal for Official Referees to be able to appoint their own clerks as clerks of the High Court was accepted by the Treasury.[35] The idea was for these Official Referees to sit continuously at a location convenient to the parties and to make decisions without the help of a jury. There were two types of decisions to be had, under sections 56 and 57 of the Judicature Act 1873. As for the Official Referees' status at this point in time, they were subordinate to the High Court judiciary. This shows that the Judicature Commissioners' recommendation to give authority to Official Referees to enter final judgment on trying the whole case was not reflected in the Judicature Act 1873.[36]

[32] (1875) 60 *Law Times* 30.
[33] Lord Selborne suggested three referees with one of them to be appointed to the Chancery Division.
[34] (1876) 62 *Law Times* 310.
[35] Reynolds (n 5) 56–57.
[36] Fay (n 2) 15.

As a consequence of the Judicature Acts 1873 and 1875, higher courts were abolished and a new Supreme Court of Judicature was introduced, which comprised of the High Court of Justice and the Court of Appeal. The High Court was then further divided into five specialist divisional courts. The House of Lords had the role of the highest court of appeal in the land, which was enshrined in the Appellate Jurisdiction Act of 1876.[37]

IV. The Scandal of Innovation

Innovative changes sometimes need time to prove themselves. The innovation of arbitration within the litigation process was underwhelming. As noted above, the Judicature Act 1873 failed to give Official Referees the authority to try entire cases. This diminished their status in the judicial hierarchy. The scale of fees for the services provided by Official Referees simply copied the practice of arbitrators, which again had the effect of discouraging recourse to the office of Official Referees. In addition, a scandal ensued on appointment of the first four Official Referees. According to the *Law Times*:[38]

> … the outcry against the proposed appointment of the gentlemen selected to fill the office of official referee ought to open the eyes of the government to the mistaken policy which has been adopted by them. It is evident that men of greater reputation than any of the gentlemen nominated (with the exception perhaps of Mr. Dowdeswell Q.C.) are clearly required both by the public and the profession.

Innovation requires patience for new inventions and ideas to be implemented, tested, tweaked and eventually reluctantly accepted and embraced by the system and the public. The same applies to the introduction of the office of Official Referees. At this point, Official Referees were still not contributing enough to shift the work from the courts.

Parliament reacted on 10 March 1876 focussing on the issue called by Sir Henry James MP 'a grave and important scandal'.[39] The debate was initially postponed but resumed on 26 May 1876. The vote in relation to the four appointments was passed but the negative publicity did not improve the standing of the new court. The House of Commons then reformed the fee system. For example, the hourly fees were channelled into the Consolidated Fund instead of the Official Referees' pockets.[40] The hourly fee was abolished and replaced by a nominal fee per case. Another debate followed in the House of Commons in 1880. A concern was raised that the salary of the four official referees was too high considering their

[37] www.parliament.uk/about/living-heritage/transformingsociety/laworder/court/overview/judicatureacts.

[38] (1876) 60 *Law Times* 654.

[39] Fay (n 2) 18.

[40] ibid 19.

work was too light. This argument was rebuffed by the Solicitor General (Sir Farrer Herschell):[41]

> … during the present year the four official referees had been fully occupied, almost all of them having sat on every day during the legal year except in the vacations and some having been unable to get through the amount of work provided for them. … In consequence of the amount of work which now came before the official referees it would be impossible to dispense with the serves of any one of them without causing delay to the discharge of business.

This is a prime example of the relatively slow yet unfettered success in the innovative progress of Official Referees. The House of Commons did not turn its sight again to the issue of Official Referees until 1884.

In the 1880s, Official Referees' courts began to be adequately used showing that there was appetite for their work.[42]

V. The Office of Official Referees vs. Arbitration

Section 9 of the Judicature Act 1884 introduced an amendment, which meant that a whole cause could be referred to an Official Referee by consent. Official Referees were given power to direct how judgment would be entered and make orders as to costs. It was an important step marking the development of Official Referees from subordinate officers into judges of valuable actions. However, Official Referees were only able to try actions as permitted by law and as by order were referred to them with the Official Referee's decision lacking authority for other cases.[43] Section 11 of the Judicature Act 1884 allowed parties to an arbitration to refer a dispute to an Official Referee by consent.

The Arbitration Act 1889 repealed a number of the relevant sections of the Judicature Acts with the most pertinent sections being section 3 (power to agree on an Official Referee as an arbitrator), section 13 (reference for inquiry and report), section 14 (reference for trial) and section 17 (Court of Appeal's power to refer for trial). All of these sections bore a striking resemblance to those of the Judicature Act 1925 introduced later on. The Arbitration Act 1889 allowed the parties to an arbitration agreement to ask an Official Referee to act as an arbitrator.

To show the sentiment at the time in relation to 'ordeal by litigation', below is a quote from *The Times*.[44]

> … the mercantile public is not fond of law, if law can be avoided. They prefer even the hazardous and mysterious chances of arbitration in which some arbitrator who knows

[41] ibid 20.
[42] Fay (n 2) 20.
[43] Burrows (n 13) 506.
[44] Anonymous article on the Judicature Acts, said to be by Lord Bowen, *The Times*, 10 August 1892; Fay (n 2) 11.

> as much of law as he does of theology, by the application of rough and ready moral consciousness, or upon the affable principle of dividing the victory equally between both sides, decides intricate questions of law and fact with equal ease.

The point is that although alternatives to litigation, such as arbitration, were flawed resulting in substantial fees with varying availability of arbitrators (who did not shy away from disregarding principles of natural justice) and a lack of appeal on law, such alternatives were still often preferred by members of the public to the 'ordeal by litigation'.[45]

VI. Sir Newbolt's Scheme, Transfer of Cases between Official Referees, the Scott Schedule and the Joint Expert

A separate chapter is devoted to *Procedural reform and innovation*, which analyses the scheme devised by Sir Francis George Newbolt ('Scheme') in depth. In the context of this chapter, the Scheme is therefore mentioned only briefly but is mentioned nevertheless as it forms an important, if not revolutionary, part of the early history of the Official Referees.

In the 1880s, the Rules of the Supreme Court were heavily amended. Order 36 focussing on Official Referees was also amended so it gave them power to hold trial at any place,[46] order discovery and production of documents,[47] order costs at interlocutory and judgment stages[48] and a power to give orders on directions after reference.[49]

It was this specific power that made it possible for Sir Newbolt to create his Scheme incorporating innovative informal discussions in chambers.[50]

Sir Newbolt's thought process was summarised in one of his articles:[51]

> A true function of the Court, it is submitted, is especially in the commercial cases under consideration, not to conciliate or exhort the parties, as is sometimes suggested much less to hurry them, or to deprive them of a perfect freedom of action, but to use the available machinery of litigation to enable them to settle their disputes according to law without grievous waste and unnecessary delay and anxiety: and in particular to show them how this, if desired, may be accomplished. The only so called concessions which the parties can be said to make are made not only voluntarily, but in their own direct pecuniary interest. This has little, or nothing, to do with the common place saying of ordinary life that a man loses nothing in the long run by forbearance, fair dealing or generosity.

[45] Fay (n 2) 11–13.
[46] Order 36 Rule 48 RSC 1883.
[47] Order 36 Rule 50 RSC 1883.
[48] Order 36 Rule 5 RSC 1883.
[49] Order 30 RSC 1883. Referees gave directions soon after the referral.
[50] Reynolds (n 5) 31.
[51] F Newbolt, 'Expedition and Economy in Litigation' (1923) 39 *Law Quarterly Review* 440, 427.

The early evolution of caseflow management was enshrined in the role of Official Referees and their multi-faceted role. As mentioned above, section 3 of the Arbitration Act 1889 essentially gave parties to a case the power to appoint an Official Referee as an arbitrator by consent, using such consent to extend the Official Referee's powers. The parties could also by consent waive the Rules of the Supreme Court and by party agreement, an Official Referee was able to sit in chambers and resolve a case formally. This revolutionary step was reflected in Sir Newbolt's Scheme and his rationale behind the benefits of having 'friendly business discussions'.[52] Judges at the time never contributed to settlement discussions so as not to be seen to prejudice their impartiality and independence.[53]

In 1888, it became possible for Official Referees to transfer cases between each other. In 1889, the Senior Official Referee (the most senior serving referee with no specific authority over the rest of the Official Referees with the exception that his clerk on his advice allocated cases by rota) had to make a return of cases to the Lord Chancellor and Lord Chief Justice. The reason for this was for the work to be monitored.[54] According to the Judicature Act 1894, appeals had to go to the Divisional Court at the time. In the same year, the number of Official Referees was reduced from four to three.

By 1890, Official Referees' business reached a recognisably modern pattern. In 1892 they were provided with premises of their own in Portugal Street, behind the Royal Courts of Justice on the Strand. This meant that they were no longer scattered across several chambers. While Official Referees had an abundance of work, they still needed to work on their reputation. The next two appointments were still viewed with suspicion. G W Hemming QC was appointed in 1877 followed by Sir Edward Ridley appointed in 1886, who upon promotion was later replaced by Mr Edward Pollock in 1897 (knighted in 1922).[55]

In 1893, Official Referees were granted the power to inspect property, which proved to be a vital case flow management tool.[56]

The main point of Official Referees' interlocutory management in 1920s following Sir Newbolt's Scheme focussed on their ability to control the process. This resulted in faster trials and earlier settlements, which supported the efficiency of a continuous judicially managed process.[57]

It was in 1920, when Lord Birkenhead appointed two referees who brought innovation and modernisation for Official Referees: George Scott and Sir Francis Newbolt. They were appointed at the time of the acquisition of the non-jury Queen's Bench list trebling the workload of the Official Referees in two years (1919–21). George Scott introduced the 'Scott Schedule' (referred to later in this book), while Sir Newbolt introduced his Scheme (also referred to later in

[52] Letter: Sir Francis Newbolt to Lord Birkenhead's Secretary Sir Claude Schuster. 15 February 1922. LCO 4/152 [HPIM 0592].
[53] Reynolds (n 5) 72, 73.
[54] Order 47A RSC 1883. (December 1888).
[55] Fay (n 2) 21–23.
[56] *McAlpine v Calder* [1893] 1 QB 545.
[57] Reynolds (n 5) 90.

this book). The Scott Schedule summarised the pleadings setting out the items in dispute, their value, description of the contract or the works, the remedial work and its cost with columns in the schedule for the parties' comments and the Official Referees' decision. The purpose was to aid early settlement through defining the issues of fact and quantum early and in a way can be considered part of Sir Newbolt's Scheme.[58]

It was to Sir Newbolt's credit that the caseflow management of Official Referees became more efficient and effective. Before his Scheme emerged, the trend was that the judge was to have no part in settlement. The responsibility of any settlement fell on the parties to each case. The judge's case management was minimal if any at all. Sir Newbolt experimented with a rudimentary form of micro-case flow management 78 years before the Civil Procedure Rules were implemented in 1998.[59] He had a very pragmatic and practical approach. His strategy was utilising an early First Summons for directions the moment a case was referred to him and giving directions for the further conduct of the case as well as making enquiry about the case and the issues that needed to be tried. This approach differed from that of Masters in the King's Bench at the time who would focus only on giving directions for further conveyance of the case. Sir Newbolt's focus was on the complexity of each case and how long it would take at trial hearing with the aim of setting a trial date at the directions hearing. By being a step ahead and establishing what the issues were in each case right from the beginning, Sir Newbolt was sometimes successful in encouraging earlier resolution by being more involved in discussing the merits and value of the relevant claim with representatives of the relevant parties.[60]

It was the avenue of the practical and commercially minded discussions in chambers that led to Sir Newbolt's cost and time effective case management. This actually echoes Lord Selborne's aim of procedural simplicity. Sir Newbolt was pragmatic in his approach and had a known rapport with solicitors appearing before him – traits that allowed his Scheme to emerge, which was nothing else but a practice of subordinate judicial power outside the traditional scope of the power exercised by a judge or a Master. This approach was simply aimed at saving time and cost of litigation and essentially provided the foundation on which the modern judicial case management built on later.[61]

Sir Newbolt's Scheme was recorded for the first time in his private and confidential report to Lord Birkenhead in May 1920.[62] Sir Newbolt put forward ideas how to improve the practice of the court, which included:[63]

(a) Adopting more expeditious and economic procedures tailored proportionately to meet the value of the claim by, for example, discussing issues with solicitors representing the parties to the case at the first directions hearing.

[58] ibid 31.
[59] ibid 28, 29.
[60] Newbolt (n 54) 439.
[61] Reynolds (n 15) 197, 198.
[62] National Archive, LCO 4/152 letter from Sir Francis Newbolt KC to Lord Birkenhead (5 May 1920).
[63] Reynolds (n 15) 194–204.

(b) Not referring cases involving an aggregate of £100 to the High Court due to costs of such proceedings being disproportionate.[64]
(c) Encouraging rapport between Official Referees and solicitors appearing before them.
(d) Abolishing the Official Referees' policy of conciliation and non-interference, which prolonged cases.
(e) Ensuring that Official Referees had the requisite expertise in interpreting accounts and knowledge of technical aspects of construction so that 'unqualified' Official Referees would not have to rely so heavily on expert evidence.
(f) Introducing the idea of a single joint expert nominated by the parties to the case or the court instead of each party having their own expert, which in some cases proved to be inefficient.
(g) Sending appeals to the Court of Appeal directly instead to the Divisional Court of the King's Bench Division with the aim of Official Referees' status to be placed between that of High Court and County Court judges (a change that took 12 years to implement).

Sir Newbolt's practical mind and sensitivity formed the basis behind his successful case management technique, which was 'discussion in chambers' on an informal basis with the parties' representatives.[65] In his own words: 'It is by friendly business discussions over the table that simplification is offered.'[66]

While there is no definition to be found of what constitutes 'discussion in chambers', clarity is offered in one of Sir Newbolt's articles,[67] where he discusses one of his cases. The main point is establishing the core facts of the dispute and then taking an active role in promoting potential for settlement. Sir Newbolt focussed on the importance of costs of any further proceedings and proving the case. He also highlighted the potential 'terrific punishment' defendants could endure if they failed to make an offer:[68]

> The great error in the ordinary honest Defendant's course is that he fails to pay enough into Court. So in all cases immediately under consideration the Defendant must pay in something: the punishment is terrific if he does not, as he is entirely at the mercy of the Plaintiff, and in general has to pay most, or all of the costs of both sides in any event.

When Sir Newbolt wrote to Lord Birkenhead after July in 1921, he stated:[69]

> I have devised means of enabling the parties to have their disputes decided cheaply and rapidly and my efforts in this direction have been widely approved by the profession.

[64] A claim of £100 in 1920 would equal £4,250 in 2008.
[65] Reynolds (n 15) 194–204.
[66] National Archive, LCO 4/152 letter Sir Newbolt to Lord Birkenhead.
[67] Newbolt (n 54) 432.
[68] ibid 486.
[69] National Archive LCO 4/152. The letter is undated, but appears on Lord Chancellor's file after July 1921 correspondence.

Essentially, Sir Newbolt's approach is the earliest appearance of the operation of rudimentary form of judicial case management in England, years before Lord Woolf's reforms in 1998.[70] The Scheme was effective and hard to find fault with.[71]

As for Sir Newbolt's approach to experts, he preferred to make an order for an expert who was appointed by the relevant parties to the dispute by consent. However, he ensured that such appointments would take place in cases where he thought that one expert of one discipline would be sufficient for both parties.

The main advantage of this strategy was that the independent expert would provide a copy of their report to both parties long before the preparation for the trial began. Based on the report, the parties could then discern the likely outcome of a court hearing (based on the expert's assessment of facts, not law). This often resulted in cases not even progressing to trial. Another advantage of having one expert only was that they focussed on the facts in case and were not distracted by combative strategies (as opposed to where there were two experts, and their reports were being compared against each other). The main point was timing. By having the expert report well in advance of the trial, the parties could assess what their likelihood of success was, what they were prepared to offer/accept in potential settlement and agree the terms of settlement. This was more likely to result in satisfied parties than having to go to trial where a decision would be issued on terms that may not suit either of the parties.[72]

Sir Newbolt's case management techniques pre-date other courts' and jurisdictions' attempts of this kind in interlocutory practices. However, the process of preliminary issues was advocated back in 1867 in the First Report.[73]

It is not unusual for a visionary to be overlooked, and while Sir Newbolt prepared the ground for a reform as to case management and use of expert evidence in the framework of settlement discussions, it took decades for his vision to be echoed properly in Lord Woolf's reforms.

It could be suggested that Sir Newbolt's initiative led to a change in 1934 when courts were empowered to appoint such experts. Another procedural innovation and case management function that has an impact even today is the use of second summons for directions, which is nothing else but a pre-trial hearing or further case management conference. All of this demonstrates Sir Newbolt's aim of a tighter continuous judicial control to modernise caseflow management.[74]

VII. Proceedings before Official Referees

Aside from an arbitration under section 3 of the Arbitration Act 1889, under the Judicature Act 1925 a matter could be referred to an Official Referee either for

[70] Reynolds (n 15) 194–204.
[71] Reynolds (n 5) 29.
[72] Reynolds (n 15) 194–204.
[73] First Report (n 10) 13.
[74] Reynolds (n 5) 92.

enquiry and report under section 88 or trial under section 89. A reference for inquiry and report was an ancillary jurisdiction. The court had the option to refer any question that arose in any action to a referee (subject to the right to a jury). The inquiry was judicial in nature and included witnesses.[75] The referee addressed their report to the court or judge who referred the matter to then form a judgment. Interestingly, in matters of account, the report set out the facts as found by the referee and listed items that were allowed and disallowed[76] while not providing the actual reasons for the findings.[77] The court could however ask the Official Referee to provide explanations, which the referee provided in their capacity as an officer of the court rather than a witness.[78]

A reference for trial was an option in any civil action where all of the relevant parties consented (if not under disability), where the action required 'any prolonged examination of documents or any scientific or local investigation which cannot in the opinion of the Court or a judge conveniently be made before a jury or conducted by the Court through its other ordinary officers'[79] or where the disputed issue was wholly or partly a matter of account.

There was no clear definition of what 'prolonged examination of documents' meant, whether in statute or in case law.[80] In *Ormerod v Todmorden Mill Co.*,[81] Brett LJ formed the view that the intention was 'a prolonged examination of such documents as is necessary to inquire into in order to enable the judge to leave … the questions of fact'.

His view was also that this did not include examination that was necessary only for the judge to make a determination on a question of a legal right. It was also not entirely clear what would amount to a 'scientific or local examination'.[82] As for 'matters of account', these did not include cases where liability was disputed in their entirety. However, there was a matter of account where liability had been established.[83]

The question is, when should the court have made an order referring a matter to an Official Referee. In *Hurlbatt v Barnett*,[84] Lord Esher M.R. stated that 'The matter … giving the jurisdiction should not be incidental or subordinate to the other questions in dispute but should be a substantial element to be decided in the action.'

Another question is what proceedings before an Official Referee looked like. The answer is simple in that they followed the ordinary course of proceedings in

[75] *Wenlock v River Dee Co.* (n 21).
[76] *Burrard v Callisher* (1882) 30 WR 321.
[77] *Dunkirk Colliery Co. v Lever* (1878) 9 Ch. D. at 28.
[78] Burrows (n 13) 507.
[79] ibid 507, 508.
[80] *Green v Barrett* [1874] WN 204.
[81] (1882) 8 QB.D 677.
[82] *Leigh v Brooks* (1877) 5 Ch D. 292; *Saxby v Gloucester Wagon Co.* [1880] WN 28.
[83] Burrows (n 13), 508.
[84] [1893] 1 QB 80.

an ordinary non-jury action. When it came to interlocutory matters, these were decided in chambers. This was similar as before a Master with the caveat that in chambers, there was no appeal to the judge.[85] As for hearings, these were located in the law courts or, depending on where the trial took place, in London or locally in a convenient place.

On trial of issues, reports under the Judicature Act 1873 and trial of actions wholly referred under the Judicature Act 1884 (section 9), the Arbitration Act 1889 (section 14) or the Judicature Act 1925 (section 89) could be appealed in the Chancery Division to the judge who made the actual initial order and in the King's Bench Division to the Divisional Court.[86] The effect was that the court would review the decision in its entirety and would be able to replace its own determination in relation to both issues of fact and law.

Sections 88 and 89 of the Supreme Court of Judicature (Consolidation) Act 1925 respectively meant that a court or judge could refer any question arising in any cause or matter to an Official Referee for inquiry or report (with such report being capable of being adopted and enforced by the court or judge as a judgment or order). A court or judge was also enabled to order the cause or matter to be tried before an Official Referee (except for criminal proceedings).

Section 1 of the Administration of Justice Act 1932 made it possible for an Official Referee's decision (for references of actions under section 89 of the Judicature Act 1925) to be appealed directly to the Court of Appeal. We are talking about any decision of an Official Referee on a legal point. This meant that an Official Referee's decision was in a much stronger position than a decision issued by a judge without a jury. This is because a decision of such a judge in relation to findings of fact could be challenged unlike an Official Referee's decision. Official Referees would usually provide a formal judgement so that the parties and the Court of Appeal, where necessary, would understand the reasons behind a decision. However, such a decision did not have the authority of a High Court decision. An Official Referee had the jurisdiction to set aside their own decision.[87] Section 11 of the Arbitration Act 1950 provided that where an Official Referee was called upon to act as an arbitrator in a private arbitration, they needed to take up their role.[88] While this section was not made much use of, the Arbitration Act 1950 also provided (replacing section 56 of the Judicature Act 1873) that either an issue or the whole case could be ordered to be tried before a special referee or an arbitrator that the parties agreed on or by an Official Referee. The effect was that Official Referees became nearly indistinguishable from judges (however not having the title 'judge' until 1972).[89]

[85] *Conway v Henwood* [1934] 50 TLR 474.

[86] Burrows (n 13) 509; s 1(5) of the Supreme Court of Judicature (Procedure) Act 1894 provided that an Official Referee's judgment could be appealed to a Divisional Court.

[87] Burrows (n 13) 510.

[88] Fay (n 2) 8.

[89] Fay (n 3) 74–81.

VIII. Sir Eastham and Further Modernisation of Case Management

Sir Newbolt was succeeded by Sir Michael Eastham as Senior Official Referee, who sent a memorandum on 13 July 1954, after his retirement from the Bench to the Lord Chancellor.[90] Eastham's agenda focussed on how to further modernise case management and substantially diminish non-jury actions. He was also of the view that candidates to be appointed as High Court judges should have experience of conducting long non-jury cases. He thought that in the 1950s, High Court judges were not as efficient as they lacked specialist experience at the bar in long non-jury actions. In addition, he advocated for diminishing delays by trying cases within weeks of referral, supporting caseflow management at interlocutory stage. This was a modern idea (in line with Sir Newbolt's Scheme) as at the time, in the majority of cases, there was a period of at least ten months between the date of setting down for trial and the hearing. The delays in fixing a trial date in ordinary Queen's Bench actions were circumvented by Official Referees.[91] Finally, he supported the view that a judge should be more active as part of case management in the trial due to their knowledge and experience with long non-jury cases.[92]

The office of Official Referees was subsequently abolished by section 25 of the Courts Act 1971 (coming into force on 1 January 1972), which was when Official Referees were transformed into Circuit judges. However, prior to the section coming into force, the jurisdiction which Official Referees exercised was preserved and called 'Official Referees' business'.[93]

The Courts Act 1971 made it clear that 'Official Referees' business' should be addressed by Circuit judges (as the Lord Chancellor should determine). Now 'Official Referees' business' is known as 'Technology and Construction Courts' business.

IX. Who were Official Referees and What did they do?

Having set out the historical evolution of the office of Official Referees above, the question arises, what was it that Official Referees actually did. As the Common Law Procedure Act 1854 developed, the Judicature Commissioners recommended the appointment of Official Referees. As noted earlier, their role was to primarily alleviate the courts' burden of voluminous inquiries and investigations and not to focus only on matters of account but also on issues of fact. Such issues of fact would need scientific or local scrutiny. The Common Law Procedure Act 1854 set out two precedents. The first one focussed on the Court of Chancery

[90] 4 LCO 4/417. Official Referees. Appointment of Deputies and Question of Temporary Assistance.
[91] LCO 2/5976 [HPIM0939].
[92] Reynolds (n 5) 105–106.
[93] Fay (n 2) 3.

practice of referring matters to officers of the Court or alternatively individuals with specific qualifications to inquire and report. The second one then focussed on the practice of issuing arbitration consent orders.[94] The idea was that Official Referees' work would concentrate on scientific inquiries, therefore not including issues on any point of law. At the time it was therefore not contemplated whether Official Referees need to be lawyers or not. Section 83 of the Judicature Act 1873 creating the office of Official Referees stated:

> There shall be attached to the Supreme Court permanent officers to be called Official Referees, for the trial of such questions as shall under the provisions of this Act be directed to be tried by such Referees. The number and the qualifications of the persons to be so appointed from time to time, and the tenure of their offices, shall be determined by the Lord Chancellor, with the concurrence of the Presidents of the Divisions of the High Court of Justice, or a majority of them (of which majority the Lord Chief Justice of England shall be one), and with the sanction of the Treasury. Such Official Referees shall perform the duties entrusted to them in such places, whether in London or in the country, as may from time to time be directed or authorized by any order of the said High Court, or of the Court of Appeal; and all proper and reasonable travelling expenses incurred by them in the discharge of their duties shall be paid by the Treasury out of moneys to be provided by Parliament.

The section makes it clear that the Lord Chancellor could decide what qualification, number and tenure of office Official Referees should have. Considering that what Official Referees were asked to produce was essentially a judicial determination and specific knowledge and experience was needed, it naturally followed that Official Referees were eventually expected to be lawyers.[95] The Lord Chancellor determined in the end that an Official Referee should be either a barrister or a solicitor. Section 9 of the Judicature Act 1884 was aligned with this view:

> In any cause or matter (other than a criminal proceeding by the Crown) now pending or hereafter commenced before the High Court of Justice or Court of Appeal, in which all parties who are under no disability consent thereto, the Court or a Judge may at any time, on such terms as may be thought proper, order the whole cause or matter to be tried before an Official Referee, who shall have power to direct in what manner the judgment of the Court shall be entered, and to exercise the same discretion as to costs as the Court or Judge could have exercised.

This meant that Official Referees could be required to make decisions on questions of law as well as on questions of fact. Schedule 4 of the Supreme Court of Judicature (Consolidation) Act 1925 further confirmed what qualifications were required at paragraph 1 in that an Official Referee is to be:

> (i) A practising barrister of not less than ten years' standing; or
> (ii) A master, King's Bench Division; or
> (iii) A master in lunacy.

[94] Burrows (n 13) 510, 511.
[95] ibid 511.

Issues that could be referred to Official Referees were no longer just matters of account but could be any issues by consent of the parties. Another category of issues that could be referred to Official Referees were where matters needed any prolonged examination of documents or accounts or any scientific or logical investigations that could not be made conveniently before a jury or in court.[96]

The duties and responsibilities of Official Referees included referrals for trial of disputes that would emanate from building contracts, as well as claims for possession upon a forfeiture for breach of covenant to repair with claims for damages for breach of covenant. Cases of this nature would usually be complex and include voluminous amounts of detail. This would be particularly the case in relation to disputes of conflicts of evidence between architects and surveyors for relevant parties in relation to the condition of premises and damages and also disputes between landlord and tenant as to long lists of dilapidations. The work of Official Referees became quite varied and was no longer focussed only on assessment of damages (where liability had been already decided) or taking accounts. Instead, Official Referees moved on to long non-jury actions where their work was equal to that of a High Court judge in cases of this nature. The position and status of Official Referees was recognised by Warrant under His Majesty's Royal Sign Manual on 17 December 1938 declaring that 'the Official Referees of the Supreme Court of Judicature shall each be called, known and addressed by the style and title of "His Honour" before his name and shall have place and precedence next after Knights Bachelor'.[97]

By 1910, the pattern of Official Referees' work became consistent and would comprise of very few cases for inquiry and report or for arbitration with most cases linked to buildings or engineering works.

From the 1920s,[98] Official Referees started to enjoy a more prominent reputation as noted by Sir Roland Burrows in 1940:[99]

> … they commenced as subordinate officers and have developed into judges of important actions. … The official referees are no longer merely assessing damages where liability has been decided or taking accounts but are now trying a large number of non-jury actions and doing the same work as a High Court judge in such cases. This change has been brought about gradually and successfully and it seems likely as time goes on that more and more actions will be referred to them for trial.

An interesting situation arose at the time in that Official Referees had an unprecedented position in the judicial hierarchy. While they had the powers of High Court judges, they lacked the status. Their office was pseudo-functionary covering a variety of roles including that of a Master, arbitrator, judge and jury. This all

[96] Fay (n 3) 74–81.
[97] Burrows (n 13) 512, 513.
[98] In the 1920s, there were three Official Referees, Sir Edward Pollock, Sir Francis Newbolt and Mr G Scott.
[99] Burrows (n 13) 512.

was against the backdrop of the rising practice of a rudimentary form of judicial case management by Official Referees in the King's Bench Division. The office of Official Referees was in essence set up to replace the jury trial in complex technical factual cases and to rid the system of the abuses caused by references to arbitrators under the Common Law Procedure Act 1854.[100] An observation on this was voiced in *The Times*:[101]

> The especial scandal of the Common Law – we mean the system of compulsory arbitration, so often imposed at the eleventh hour upon the unwilling suitor because the judge will not, or cannot, entertain his case – is to be removed, and official and other referees will act under the court.

In addition, Commissioners were aware of problems caused by arbitration:[102]

> The Arbitrator thus appointed is the sole judge of law and fact, and there is no appeal from his judgement, however erroneous his view of the law may be, unless perhaps when the error appears on the face of his award. Nor is there any remedy, whatever may be the miscarriage of the Arbitrator, unless he fails to decide on all matters referred to him, or exceeds his jurisdiction, or is guilty of some misconduct in the course of the case.

The system of compulsory arbitration was often imposed at the last minute where the judge would not or could not address the case. The aim was to abolish this measure so that Official Referees could act instead.[103]

Between 1876–77, there were 78 referrals. Between 1879–80, there were 139 referrals and between 1897–98, there were 262 showing the rise in the popularity of referrals to Official Referees.[104] The annual number of cases was between 200 and 300 up until 1914. Understandably, during the First World War the number of cases declined, however business boomed after the war and peaked at 507 cases in 1921, after which the number dwindled back to below 300. In 1949, the number of cases went up again to 400 cases and reached 465 cases in 1951 to then drop back again.[105]

> There was a time when life in the official referees' courts was leisurely. The courts did not sit until 10.15 a.m. when summonses were taken first and then trials. There were not many construction cases, so that official referees spent much of their time sitting in the Queen's Bench Division or as Commissioners of Assize. A case in 1953 (Fox v. Fox) lasted for 36 days and was the longest there had been since the creation of the courts in 1876. There was no vacation official referee.[106]

[100] Reynolds (n 15) 194–204.
[101] *The Times* (22 April 1869) 8, issue 26418, col F.
[102] First Report (n 10) 13.
[103] ibid; *The Times* (22 April 1869) 8, Issue 26418, col F.
[104] Reynolds (n 15) 194–204.
[105] Fay (n 2) 24.
[106] J Newey, 'The Preparation and Presentation of Cases in the Official Referees Courts' (1990) 6(3) *Construction Law Journal* 216–224.

However, this trend changed significantly over the years that followed and the 1,000 cases mark was passed in 1985 showing the resilience and popularity of the office of Official Referees.[107]

In 1942, the House of Lords decided that alleged professional negligence cases should not be tried by Official Referees as there was no right of appeal on fact.[108] Parliament quickly reacted by conferring a right of appeal in cases of this nature. Cases around negligence actions against architects, engineers and surveyors became a substantial part of work of Official Referees. The evolutionary process of the role of the Official Referees' office progressed to a stage where Official Referees slowly became fully fledged judges. The Administration of Justice Act 1932 ensured that appeals were to go directly to the Court of Appeal and in 1938 the Official Referees' status was uplifted by way of a Royal Warrant so that their title became 'His Honour'.[109]

This was followed by the Evershed Report when the Committee on Supreme Court Practice and Procedure (Evershed Committee) reviewed the Official Referees' courts and reflected as follows:[110]

> In recent years the ambit of the maters referred to official referees has greatly increased and today a large variety of matters are tried before them, in particular heavy and complicated cases involving matters of detail, e.g. cases arising out of building contracts, claims for possession of leasehold premises upon forfeiture for breach of covenant to repair and damages for breach, and claims for commission where a servant or agent is remunerated by commission. … We are satisfied that in these and other special types of cases there may be considerable advantage to the litigant in having the matter referred to an official referee. The hearing is less formal and, due to the great experience of the official referees in the special types of case usually heard by them, more expeditious. Further in necessary cases the official referee sits outside London in some court or room conveniently near the subject matter of the dispute so that a great saving of costs is achieved where there are a number of local witnesses.

Evershed also recommended that the claimant could apply to the Master for a dispensation of pleadings where the claimant gave appropriate notice after the entry of an appearance by the defendant. In addition, Evershed's view was that any additional summons for directions should be heard by the same Master if possible. Importantly, Evershed advocated robust summons for directions to limit the issues to be tried and the cost of proof. This is very much in line with Sir Newbolt's philosophy. Finally, Evershed came up with the idea that the judge should have the pleadings to hand before they came to court.[111]

The Evershed Committee was also aware of the growing number of cases and suggested that the number of Official Referees is increased from three back to four, which materialised in 1948. The Committee also felt that the Official Referees'

[107] Fay (n 2) 24.
[108] *Osenton & Co. v Johnston* [1942] AC 130.
[109] Fay (n 2) 25.
[110] Final Report of the Committee on Supreme Court Practice and Procedure, 1953 (CMD. 8878).
[111] Fay (n 2) 252–253.

jurisdiction should be widened. This was reflected in sections 88 and 89 of the Judicature Act 1925 (bringing forward the content of sections 13 and 14 of the Arbitration Act 1889):

88. Reference for report.

(1) Subject to rules of court and to any right to have particular cases tried with a jury, the Court or a judge may refer to an official or special referee for inquiry or report any question arising in any cause or matter, other than a criminal proceeding by the Crown.

(2) The report of an official or special referee may be adopted wholly or partially by the Court or a judge and if so adopted may be enforced as a judgment or order to the same effect.

89. Reference for trial.

In any cause or matter, other than a criminal proceeding by the Crown,—

(a) If all the parties interested who are not under disability consent; or

(b) If the cause or matter requires any prolonged examination of documents or any scientific or local investigation which cannot in the opinion of the Court or a judge conveniently be made before a jury or conducted by the Court through its other ordinary officers; or

(c) If the question in dispute consists wholly or in part of matters of account; the Court or a judge may at any time order the whole cause or matter, or any question or issue of fact arising therein, to be tried before a special referee or arbitrator respectively agreed on by the parties, or before an official referee or officer of the Court.

The Committee's recommendation was that, apart from consent cases, the cases should not be limited to prolonged examination of documents and scientific and local investigations and accounts. Instead, a general power should be given to remit whenever deemed appropriate on the basis of convenience, economy, expedition or for any other reason.[112]

By section 14 of the Arbitration Act 1889, Official Referees obtained the power to try the whole of a case. The trial procedure proved to be superior to the inquiry and report procedure, which throughout latter years become less and less popular. This was a substantial departure from the original procedure laid for Official Referees in 1873, when holding of an inquiry into facts and the production of a report to the court was one of their main duties.[113]

Another fundamentally important recommendation introduced by the Committee was to enable cases to be transferred among the Official Referees:[114]

> We desire to draw attention to the fact that cases are now allotted to the official referee. Once a case has been assigned, it can only be transferred by consent of the parties or by

[112] Final Report of the Committee on Supreme Court Practice and Procedure, 1953 (Cmd. 887, paras 107 and 108).

[113] Fay (n 2) 120.

[114] First Interim Report of the Committee on Supreme Court Practice and Procedure, 1944 (Cmd. 7764, para 108.

> order of the Lord Chancellor. This sometimes results in one official referee having too much work and another having no work at all. Accordingly, we recommend that it be made possible to transfer cases between official referees without the present restrictions.

This recommendation was implemented successfully and proved to be a substantial administrative improvement contributing to a balanced workload of the individual Official Referees.

Section 9 of the Administration of Justice Act 1956 provided that the Crown were to appoint Official Referees on the recommendation of Lord Chancellor. Official Referees also had to take the judicial oath on appointment and their time in office was subject to a retiring age of 72 (which could be extended under section 17(2) of the Courts Act 1971 to up to 75). Section 15 of the Administration of Justice Act 1956 widened the Official Referees' jurisdiction transferring the relevant provisions into the Rules of the Supreme Court. Another important point was brought about by the new Order 36A on 1 October 1957, which gave effect to section 15 of the Administration of Justice Act 1956. The Order abolished the right of the parties to choose their referee by consent and from then onward all cases were to be allocated by rota (rule 5(3) of Order 36).

> The most distinctive characteristic, and many believe the principal advantage, of the ORs' Courts is that each case is allocated to a named OR, who deals with all interlocutory proceedings in it and, if available, tries it. This has been the practice since 1876, when ORs were created. Since 1884, the Rules of the Supreme Court have required that the allocation should be by rote, so preventing 'forum shopping'.[115]

In 1956, the number of Official Referees was again reduced from four to three, which persisted until 1983 when a fourth Official Referee was appointed again. In 1982, litigants acquired the right to start their actions in the court of Official Referees meaning Official Referees were judges of a specialised court within the High Court (a tribunal one could compare with the Commercial Court in terms of status).[116]

In 1900, the office of Official Referees moved from Portugal Street to the west wing of the Royal Courts of Justice, in 1965 the office moved to Victory House in Kingsway and in 1969 the office returned to the Royal Courts of Justice.[117]

The Report of the Royal Commission on Assizes and Quarter Sessions 1969 (Beeching Report) expressed concern over Official Referees services being too much confined to London:[118]

> We are anxious that similar facilities to those existing in London should be available at the main centres of court activity in the provinces. It is for this reason that we recommend that Circuit Administrators should regard it as one of their functions to ensure

[115] J Newey, 'The Official Referees' Courts Today and Tomorrow' (1994) 10(1) *Construction Law Journal* 20–27.
[116] Fay (n 2) 25.
[117] Fay (n 2) 26–27.
[118] Cmd. 4153.

> that arrangements are made for the services of official referees to be available when required. It might simplify the arrangements if each of the present three official referees assumed responsibility in this respect for two circuits.

While the last suggestion was not adopted, part-time provincial Official Referees emerged. By section 25 of the Courts Act 1971, Official Referees' business was to be transacted by Circuit judges.[119] This meant that, additionally to London Official Referees, the Lord Chancellor also appointed Circuit judges in the provinces to act as part-time Official Referees.

The types of cases included initially matters of property, commercial, marine, employment, patents, tort, dilapidations, actions on account in money lending transactions, matters on account as to administration of an estate and construction and engineering cases. With time, construction and engineering cases became the core of the office of Official Referees jurisdiction in the late twentieth century.[120] From the inception of the office of Official Referees, most of the work however focussed on the construction industry and all its layers.

X. Conclusion

The office of Official Referees was created in response to a substantial procedural reform, meaning that the procedural and administrative system was unified and codified by the Judicature Commissioners between 1867 and 1869.

The Judicature Commissioners aimed for a way to alleviate the case load burden of the courts and provide a faster and cheaper way of resolving a certain type of dispute. Jurisdiction of the courts had been realigned, provision for equitable remedies in the courts of common law had been made and the courts of Common Pleas and Exchequer were abolished. Exchequer Chambers were replaced with the Court of Appeal. This marked a new period in legal history. The reform included the creation of the office of Official Referees. In essence, the office of Official Referees came about to put a stop to problems in cases of referrals under the Common Law Procedure Act 1854. Official Referees were akin to arbitrators with the added benefit of being court officers under the supervisory jurisdiction of a High Court judge. The aim was that this would stop the abuse of delay caused by adjourned hearings.

The office of Official Referees had been brought about at the same time as the essential procedural reform unifying the administrative system. The Judicature Commission recognised the need to alleviate the courts' workload leading to greater cost and time efficiency with the right type of expertise. The Official Referees adopted to some extent the old Chancery practice of reference to a Master

[119] Repealed by s 152(4) and Sch 7 of the Supreme Court Act 1981 and replaced by s 68 of the same Act.

[120] Reynolds (n 15) 194–204.

or chief clerk or alternatively to an arbitrator under the Common Law Procedure Act 1854. Official Referees also replaced lay juries. They disposed of the non-compulsory referral deficiency in the Common Law Procedure Act 1854 and cut the cost of having to refer back to the court where faulty arbitration awards needed to be corrected. Simple caseflow management was introduced to the outdated trial system, which had conflicting remedies in different courts with separate jurisdiction and an overflow of cases, some of which involved complex factual issues of a scientific or technical nature. As the office of Official Referees developed, note must be taken of the Official Referees' striving for ongoing innovations. The subordinate nature of the office of Official Referees made it possible for Sir Newbolt to then introduce a more informal and flexible process to some extent.[121]

Official Referees were ahead of their times when it came to procedural development and case management in particular. The Scheme introduced by Sir Newbolt was a revolutionary concept introducing a more active role of the judge in the settlement discussion between the parties of a case, encouraging more informal discussions between the judge and the parties' representatives, promoting settlement and use of experts (and a joint expert in particular) to encourage and expedite settlement. The Scheme was a highly pragmatic, logical and practical concept with the aim to assist both the judicial system, by alleviating its case load, and litigants, who were encouraged to settle to save money and time for them as well. It was not uncommon before the Scheme for the value in dispute to be substantially less than the cost of litigation. The hypothesis is that the Scheme's 'rudimentary process may have been used in up to a quarter of all referrals or used in some facet in 5,404 cases and was capable of producing an 80 per cent saving in expert witness costs in Newbolt's time'.[122]

With the creation of the office of Official Referees, referrals to arbitrators under the Common Law Procedure Act 1854 were avoided by the Judicature Commissioners recommending compulsory referrals. Where a case was technically complex or scientific in nature, or where a court came to the conclusion that a case should be referred to an Official Referee, the Judicature Commission considered the jury trial to be unsuitable. The Supreme Court was created in 1873 as a result of the need to update an administration of justice that was causing a backlog of cases in the High Court and an inefficient system of non-compulsory references.

Section 56 of the Judicature Act 1873 made enquiry and report by Official Referees compulsory, which paved the way to a referee caseflow management. Section 57 made provision for parties to agree to a referral with the referral otherwise being compulsory if the case was technical or scientific. Cases were usually referred to Official Referees, where they needed investigation and understanding of highly complex technical and scientific matters – usually being actions in contract and tort. Sir Newbolt interpreted his role as Official Referee by challenging the idea of a detached judge that should not be concerned with settlement.

[121] Reynolds (n 5) 241.
[122] ibid 38.

Considering that the Judicature Commission's aim was to facilitate a faster and cheaper process of dealing with judicial business in courts, this aim was furthered by Sir Newbolt's Scheme of an active approach of judges in encouraging settlement. The Judicature Commission's recommendations for Official Referees to visit the scene or the site (something a judge would not do) in relation to the relevant case further supported their role and the need to utilise their technical and scientific expertise. The visits often had the effect that they led to cases settling. The consequence of Official Referees bringing together the roles of judges, experts and assessors led to Sir Newbolt having created improved ways of utilising experts in a case managed role. As we know, the Judicature Commission brought about a reform of the judicial system as a whole, which included the creation of the office of Official Referees.[123]

At macro-case management level, the Commission achieved its objective to establish a subordinate judicial level of the office of Official Referees that were able to act more informally. As a result, the creation of Official Referees led to less pressure on the superior court judiciary. Referrals to Official Referees led to circumventing expensive jury trials in the nineteenth century and non-jury list cases in the 1920s. The High Court list was also relieved. The Evershed Committee recognised the benefit to parties in referral of matters of account, forming a substantial section of the Official Referees' work.[124]

At micro-case management level, during Sir Newbolt's time (while the number of referrals doubled) disposal rates were efficient. There was a tripling of disposals before trial. The different Official Referees managed to keep the backlog at a certain limit. After the war, the backlog decreased proportionately from 80 per cent of referrals in 1947 to 65 per cent of referrals in 1960.

Sir Newbolt usually exercised the modern powers with the parties' consent so that time and money could be saved in litigation. He also advocated for the cases to be brough in as soon as possible as that meant that these could be considered for directions by the Official Referee. His view was that the trial judge should take their own summonses for directions, similarly to Official Referees practice. At the first directions hearing in chambers, Sir Newbolt would then conduct 'mere discussions' with the parties' legal representatives shortly after the referral. The purpose was to understand the main issues and for him to then promote an effective process or settlement. He then suggested that a second summons be taken before trial, a practice that Eastheam (Sir Newbolt's successor) followed as well. In essence, what it meant was that the court exercised more control over the process.[125]

Another of Sir Newbolt's contributions was his use of experts, again resulting in cost and time savings for the litigants. One could argue that his efficient initiatives were curbed by the fact that at the time of his appointment there was the acquisition of the non-jury list, which tripled references between 1919 and 1921.

[123] Holdsworth, *History of English Law*, Vol XIV, 198.
[124] ibid 238–239.
[125] ibid 243.

Considering that two cases from the list took 18 months to reach trial, one can understand Sir Newbolt's recognition of the need to speed up the process. As a result of the Scheme, cases were often tried within a few weeks from the point of referral.[126] As for interlocutory modernisation brought about by Official Referees, this resulted in more efficient conduct of business recognised by the Evershed Committee on Supreme Court Practice and Procedure appointed on 22 April 1947. The purpose was, again, cost and time efficiency. Evershed advocated for a greater use of the power under Order 37A to appoint a court expert, in line with Sir Newbolt's idea in the 1920s. In essence, Official Referees helped courts with a backlog of cases, saved High Court judges time and jury trials and encouraged and facilitated settlement early on in the process. This saved both time (of about 50 to 80 per cent at trial) and cost for the litigants. As the evolution of the role of the office of Official Referees progressed from 1873, the tribunal that was set up to provide a mode of trial alternative to jury trial morphed into a valuable specialist office (and eventually court) focussing on construction litigation emanating from one of the largest industries in the world – the construction industry.

[126] LCO 2/5976. [HPIM 0936].

3

Rudimentary Prototypes in Case Management Techniques (1919–49)

DR MICHAEL REYNOLDS

In his treatise on *The Common Law*,[1] Oliver Wendall Holmes stated that: 'The life of the law has not been logic: it has been experience.' In this chapter the contribution of Sir Francis Newbolt KC is considered and if any judgement can be placed on that it is that of Holmes. His work demonstrated that it was very possibly his procedural 'experiments', lost to history, that gave birth to this distinct court and the innovative approach of its judiciary. In researching the story of the Official Referees' Court, I found that its particular procedural characteristics had been created through the experience of the judges and especially so by the creativity of Sir Francis Newbolt.[2] Thus in this chapter we explore by reference to the contemporaneous documentary evidence relating to the invention of a rudimentary form of case management techniques as practised by Sir Francis Newbolt in the 1920s.[3] Here we focus on micro-management aspects of Newbolt's 'Scheme' and the reasons for it; an assessment of its impact, and the extent to which it promoted earlier settlement and saved costs.

I. Sir Francis Newbolt

Like Lord Selbourne, Newbolt came from a religious background being the second son of the Vicar of St Marys in Bilstone, born 21 November 1863. He was educated

[1] Little, Brown, and Company 1881 (1909), Boston, 1881.

[2] KC 1914; Hon. R.A.; J.P., M.A., F.C.S., A.R.E. Hon. Professor of Law in the Royal Academy. Publications included: *Sale of Goods Act 1893*; *Summary Procedure in the High Court*, and *Out of Court*. Official Referee 1920–1936.

[3] This chapter is based on my earlier doctoral research at the National Archives, the House of Lords Library, and the Library of the London School of Economics and also on my recent articles in *Amicus Curiae* M Reynolds, *Caseflow Management: A. Rudimentary Referee Process 1919–1970* PhD Thesis., (London: London School of Economics,2008); M Reynolds, 'In Chancery: The Genesis of Micro-Caseflow Management' (2020) 1(2) *Amicus Curiae* 165–200; M Reynolds, (2020) 'Judicial Experiments in Caseflow Management 1920–1970' (2020) 1(3) *Amicus Curiae* 389–417; M Reynolds 'Reflections on the Judicial Case Management Experiments of Sir Francis Newbolt' (2022) 3(3) *Amicus Curiae* 490–516.

at Clifton, and later at Balliol College Oxford where he read Natural Science (Chemistry) obtaining honours in 1887. He read law with Sir Thomas Wilkes Chitty, his brother-in-law, and a leading authority on Common Law procedure. He was called to the Bar by the Inner Temple in 1890 and joined the Western Circuit. He remained in Wilkes Chitty's Chambers for ten years but did not enjoy an extensive practice. He took Silk in 1914. While at the Bar he continued his interest in science and gave over 1,000 experimental science lectures in boarding schools. He became Recorder of Doncaster in 1916, and a Chancellor of the Diocese of Exeter and Bradford and Chairman of the Devon Quarter Sessions. He became a referee after Sir Henry Verey's resignation in 1920. He was President of the Norwegian Club from 1920 to 1926 and an honorary member of the Land Agents Society. He was also an accomplished etcher and the author of a number of books in law, art and literature.[4]

A. The Court

The Court Newbolt joined was established to alleviate some of the symptoms of systemic failure in the pre-1873 system as recommended by the Judicature Commissioners. The Court adopted the old Chancery practice of reference to a master or chief clerk, or to an arbitrator under the Common Law Procedure Act 1854. It was also intended as a substitute for a lay jury. It was invented to overcome the deficiency in the Common Law Procedure Act 1854 of non-compulsory referral, and needless expense of referral back to the Court to correct erroneous awards of commercial arbitrators. Newbolt's colleagues were Sir Edward Pollock, George Scott, Sir William Hansell – the last said to be very capable.[5]

II. Sir Edward Pollock

Sir Edward was one of 24 children of Lord Chief Baron Pollock born 1 February 1841.[6] In 1863 he became a member of the Royal College of Surgeons and subsequently a Fellow. He was called to the Bar by Inner Temple in 1872. He enjoyed a varied commercial practice and was responsible for the 8th Edition of *Russell on Arbitration and Award* published in 1900. He was a member of a Committee of Experts appointed by the Foreign and Colonial Office in 1910 to review the work of international commercial arbitration and to ensure that British commerce enjoyed the same privileges as foreign commerce in respect of enforcement of awards abroad.[7] *The Times* said that Pollock made an excellent referee and was

[4] *The Times* (9 December 1940) 7; Issue 48794: col E.
[5] In post 1927–31.
[6] *The Times* Obituary (16 April 1930) 16; Issue 45489: col C.
[7] *The Times* (6 June 1910) 10; Issue 39291: col D.

remarkably quick in seizing on all the essential facts and figures of a case. His geniality made it a pleasure to appear before him. He was also a member of the Royal Institution and the Anglo Finnish Society.[8]

III. Sir William Hansell

Sir William was educated at Charterhouse and Christchurch Oxford and took honours in the Classical Schools graduating in 1880. He was called to the Bar by Inner Temple and devilled for Roland Vaughn Williams the future Lord Justice. He assisted Vaughn Williams with the textbook *Williams on Bankruptcy*. Hansell was the virtual author of its later editions. He became the leading authority on this branch of the law and took up a standing appointment as Counsel to the Board of Trade in bankruptcy matters. Hansell was a high churchman. He did some ecclesiastical work and had a good general practice. In 1917 he became Recorder for Maidstone. He took Silk in 1927 at the age of 71. A few weeks later on the retirement of Sir Edward Pollock (age 86) Lord Cave appointed Hansell to fill Pollock's vacancy. Hansell was in post until 1931 and a year later was appointed as a Commissioner of Assize for the North-eastern Circuit. In 1933 he was elected Treasurer of the Inner Temple. He died in 1937.[9] It may be significant that in Lord Sankey's time[10] Bosanquet sent a Memorandum compiled by Pitman[11] and himself (both appointed as referees by Sankey). That stated:[12]

> For many years the work of the Official Referees' Courts was of comparatively small importance but following upon the appointment of Mr (afterwards Sir) Edward Pollock in 1897, and later during the tenure of office of Sir William Hansell, the work of these Courts has steadily developed and increased in amount and importance.

IV. George Scott KC

George Scott served as a referee from 1920 to 1933 and is noted as being the inventor of the Scott Schedule.[13] This schedule was adapted from the surveying practice of dilapidations schedules and utilised for cases of defective work giving descriptive details of the works, the cost of remedy and description of the repair required.

For all of these referees, salary and numbers[14] remained a grievance as they saw these elements as dissuading more successful barristers from applying

[8] *The Times* (15 December 1923) 11; Issue 43525: col B.

[9] *The Times* (20 April 1937) 22; Issue 47663: col D.

[10] 1929–35.

[11] Official Referee 1933–1945.

[12] National Archives LCO 4/152.

[13] E Fay, *Official Referees' Business*, 2nd edn (London, Sweet & Maxwell, 1988) 70.

[14] Lord Cairns and the Heads of Divisions had considered that they would need at least four referees but the Treasury would not agree. LCO 4/152.

for such posts.[15] During the early part of his tenure Newbolt as Senior Referee was aware of this problem and corresponded with the Lord Chancellor, Lord Birkenhead, who was sympathetic to the challenges Newbolt and his colleagues faced.

V. Lord Birkenhead

It was the Lord Chancellor, FE Smith, Lord Birkenhead who appointed Newbolt and with whom Newbolt first corresponded about his 'Scheme'. Birkenhead was an energetic Lord Chancellor and scholar of Wadham College, Oxford. He is said to have been a model of 'sober correctness'[16] who never pretended knowledge which he did not have. Birkenhead supported the reform of civil procedure and land law. He attempted to reform the outdated circuit system undertaking some preliminary work on the Supreme Court of Judicature (Consolidation) Act 1925. He improved the tenure of county court judges paving the way for the County Courts Act of 1924.[17] His research assistant was Sir Roland Burrows who later wrote an article about the work of the referees in the *Law Quarterly Review* in 1940.[18]

A. Newbolt's 'Scheme'

What caused Newbolt to invent a rudimentary form of case management was the outmoded trial system, the divergent remedies in different courts of separate jurisdiction, and the backlog of cases some of which involved complex factual matters of a scientific or technical nature. What facilitated this was the subordinate nature of the referee's office permitting Newbolt to adopt a more flexible and informal process in some areas. What he invented to overcome the delay and backlog in his list was a 'Scheme' which may be identified from his account in *Expedition and Economy in Litigation* and from his reports to the Lord Chancellor.[19]

The elements of his 'Scheme' may be identified more specifically as:

(a) special procedures in chambers enabling informal referee resolution and early settlement;
(b) judicial intervention at various stages of the process to effect settlement;
(c) the use and invention of the single joint expert/court expert;

[15] Referees' salaries were then £1,500 and had not been increased since 1873. The number of cases referred had quadrupled after the First World War. When Lord Cairns wrote to the Treasury on 12 November 1875 to request the Treasury to suggest referees might be paid more than £1,500 the proposal was rejected by the Treasury.

[16] RFV Heuston, *Lives of the Lord Chancellors 1885–1940* (Oxford, Clarendon Press, 1964) 382.

[17] R Burrows, 'Roland *Official Referees*' (1940) 56 *LQR* 504–513.

[18] ibid.

[19] F Newbolt, 'Expedition and Economy in Litigation' (1923) 39 *LQR* 427.

(d) the use of a proportionate approach to costs so that the costs of the case should have some reasonable relationship to the value of the item in dispute;
(e) the invention of special forms of submission such as a Referees' Schedule;
(f) the formulation of preliminary issues or questions for the court;
(g) flexibility as to the place of hearing at more economic locations and attendances on site.

All these elements contributed to a more effective and efficient mode of working and represented a form of judicial activism, sometimes interventionist, in order to accelerate the proceedings. By this means being a combination of formal and informal court processes Newbolt and his colleagues resolved certain types of complex technical disputes earlier saving time and cost. These elements of rudimentary case management and referee alternative resolution are examined in more detail subsequently to explain how and why all this came about in the 1920s in this court pre-dating notions of case management and proportionality as well as semblances of ADR by more than half a century.[20]

B. Events Leading to the Invention of Case Management and Judicial Settlement

The architects of the 1873 judicature reforms declared their intention to replace commercial arbitration with a court managed referee system. The referral of cases from the Queen's Bench and Chancery Divisions to referees was a form of macro-case management, realised through Section 3 of the Common Law Procedure Act 1854. Newbolt played a pivotal role in what may be described as a procedural revolution.

The philosophy underlying Newbolt's 'Scheme' was clearly set out in his seminal article and his concluding remarks in the *Law Quarterly Review*:[21]

> The true function of the Court, it is submitted, is especially in the commercial cases under consideration, not to conciliate or exhort the parties, as is sometimes suggested much less to hurry them, or to deprive them of a perfect freedom of action, but to use the available machinery of litigation to enable them to settle their disputes according to law without grievous waste and unnecessary delay and anxiety: and in particular to show them how this, if desired, may be accomplished. The only so called concessions which the parties can be said to make are made not only voluntarily, but in their own direct pecuniary interest. This has little, or nothing, to do with the common place saying of ordinary life that a man loses nothing in the long run by forbearance, fair dealing or generosity.

[20] ADR did not really establish itself as an alternative to litigation until after 1976, regarded by some as a turning point in legal history. That was the year of the Pound Conference at St Paul, Minnesota on: *Perspectives on Justice in the Future* and Chief Justice Warren Burger's pejorative as to whether there was not a better way.

[21] Newbolt (n 19) 440.

But the essence of this early evolution of case management lay in the function of the referee, his multi-function role being derived from: that of a master to whom matters were referred under the Common Law Procedure Act 1854; a judge of the High Court in terms of powers subsequently conferred after 1876; an arbitrator in terms of the referees' early use of directions after issue of the writ, and finally a juryman's role where he would deal with trials of fact as 'a jury'.[22] It may be argued that the utility of Section 3 Arbitration Act 1889 enabling parties to appoint a referee as an arbitrator by agreement was decisive in terms of using consent as a means to extend the referees official formal power.[23] By consent of the parties the *Rules of the Supreme Court* could be waived and by party agreement the referee could sit in chambers and informally resolve the case. This revolution is clearly demonstrated in Newbolt's correspondence with Lord Birkenhead,[24] in particular, his reference to 'friendly business discussions' and in his article, where he refers to 'an informal discussion in Chambers'.[25] This was an extraordinary process for these times and quite unconventional because judges never entered the arena, believing that if they did so they would be perceived to prejudice their impartial and independent position. It was a high-risk strategy for Newbolt which caused Birkenhead some concern.

For present purposes, it is only necessary to record what the development was and why it occurred in the context of the contemporaneous literature. In many respects the referee was a multi-functionary who bridged the void between a traditional Anglo-Saxon judicial culture based on the adversarial process, and the laissez faire business approach of the commercial man. The point was that adjudicating cases in a traditional manner was just not cost effective with the type of issues before the Court and the voluminous evidence that referees had to analyse. What Newbolt worried about was the time spent on the case in proportion to its overall commercial value.

In the twentieth century the referees' role became more clearly defined. Their status was slightly increased by the acquisition of the non-jury list, and the abolition of rights of appeal on matters of fact. The referee's multi-function role was self-evident from sections 88 and 89 of the Judicature Act 1925.[26] A considerable

[22] Eastham's notebooks for the period 1940–49 reveal numerous illustrations of case management features especially in the period 1944–48. Cases included matters of account, disputes as to matrimonial property, war damage claims, dilapidations cases, building and engineering cases and questions of costs. The entries also reveal that this judge frequently sat outside London and was requested on some occasions to exercise power 'as a jury'.

[23] To effect such appointment the arbitration agreement had to be lodged with the nominated referee's clerk and then entered in his list unless it was given a special appointment for hearing. The Award was published on payment of a court fee. Sch 1, s V, Supreme Court Fees Order 1924.

[24] Letter: *Newbolt to Lord Birkenhead's Secretary Sir Claude Schuster* (15 February 1922). LCO 4/152.

[25] Newbolt (n 19) 438.

[26] Section 88 provided that where any case was to be tried with a jury the court could refer the matter to an Official or Special Referee for enquiry and report. Any question arising in any cause or matter other than a criminal proceeding by the Crown and further the report of an Official or Special Referee could be adopted wholly or partly by the court or judge and if accepted could be enforced as a judgment or order to the same effect. Section 89 Supreme Court Judicature Act 1925 applied where any cause or

increase in referrals occurred in the 1880s and 1890s as may be seen from the following table.

Table T.1 Annual referrals 1876–98

Year	Referrals
1876–77	78
1877–78	70
1878–79	91
1879–80	139
1888–89	277
1889–90	313
1896–97	267
1897–98	262

Source: Returns of Judicial Statistics 1876–98.

The abolition of a right of appeal from referees to the Divisional Court also added to their status as a court of first instance. Opportunity was afforded for case management at an early stage of the proceedings because referees had developed the practice of giving directions on an early summons for directions taken out after the issue of the writ and before close of pleadings. Crucial to this development in the early 1920s was the acquisition of the non-jury list from the Queen's Bench Division which radically increased referee workload by 65 per cent in the years 1919 to 1922.

C. Newbolt's Invention

It is argued that the introduction of this rudimentary form of case management in the 1920s, coupled with referee encouragement for settlement, positively affected the outcome of referrals. It is probable that were it not for Newbolt's approach and that of his colleagues there would have been much delay in the trial of cases and higher cost. If it is the case that Newbolt practised case management, the question has to be asked whether that accounts for the apparent effect on caseflow in the period between 1919–36. If it survived Newbolt's era, does it have any marked effect in the period 1947–70 for which periods judicial statistics are available?[27] If we consider the 18 years (inclusive) of the Newbolt period, the average percentile

matter other than criminal proceedings could be tried by a referee, officer of the court, special referee or arbitrator if the cause or matter required any prolonged examination of documents or any scientific or local investigation.

[27] MP Reynolds *Case Management: A Rudimentary Referee Process, 1919–70*, Appendix, Civil Judicial Statistics Analysis: Official Referees: 1919–70. (Thesis: London School of Economics, 2008).

of disposals and settlements from 1919 to 1936 was 28 per cent of the referrals. If we take a similar period after the war 1947–64 the average settlement and disposal rate before trial is 19 per cent of the referrals. What these results tend to suggest is that the Newbolt era was a more activist time in terms of settlement and the post war period less activist.

A further detailed study and analysis of these periods, and the Minute Book analyses 1959–62 and 1965–67, confirm that there was a marked difference as a result of these measures in the respective periods.[28]

It is strange perhaps that whilst there is clear direct contemporaneous evidence from the Lord Chancellors' files, the judges Minute Books and the judges note-books at the National Archive as to the existence of this phenomenon and the effects of it, there is no corroborative evidence in the most likely place – the *Rules of the Supreme Court* themselves save what may be inferred. The *Annual Practice* of 1930 at pages 640–641 headed *Notes on the practice before the Official Referees* states:

> Once an order for reference to an Official Referee has been made the Solicitor's clerk shall enter the case with the Official Referees Clerk with the Writ and the Order for reference from the Queen's Bench Division or the Chancery Division. Directions will be given by the Official Referee and *all interlocutory proceedings given by him in his Chambers*[29] including the issuing of Summonses, drawing up and dealing with orders and filing of documents. Summonses and applications will be heard by the Referee at 10.30am each day. Appeals against Interlocutory Orders will be referred to a Judge in Chambers.

Whilst there is no reference to any form of rudimentary case management process the note confirms that the referee was master of *all interlocutory proceedings*.[30] That being the case the referee would have had every opportunity, in theory and in practice, for bringing some order to the case and encouraging a time and cost-saving timetable as well as a process tailor-made for the particular case. In the absence of any express reference to Newbolt's 'Scheme' in the RSC discussed here reliance may be placed upon the contemporaneous reports made by Newbolt and Sir Tom Eastham to Sir Claude Schuster KC,[31] the Lord Chancellor's Permanent Secretary, and Eastham's surviving notebooks.[32]

[28] ibid 155–208.

[29] Emphasis added.

[30] Emphasis added.

[31] Sir Claude Schuster KC was appointed by Lord Haldane because of Lord Haldane's other urgent duties. Lord Haldane contemplated that Schuster would be the right man to set up a Ministry of Justice. Schuster played a pivotal role regarding micro-case management aspects. Schuster was the conduit through which the Lord Chancellor communicated with the Law Society, The Bar Council and the Bench as well as both Houses of Parliament. Schuster had a particular interest in what Newbolt was doing because of Schuster's involvement with a more efficient County Court procedure.

[32] J114/1-8.

D. Evidence of Newbolt's Procedural Experiments and Innovations

The best evidence of Newbolt's novel forms of process in the 1920s is a report that Newbolt made to Lord Birkenhead in July 1920. Newbolt's letter enclosing it, and the report itself, formed the basis of what Newbolt later described as his 'Scheme.'

Newbolt's covering letter to Schuster dated 5 July 1920 enclosing a report to the Lord Chancellor stated:

> Dear Claude,
>
> Here is the Report. It is cut down to its extreme limits to make itself read. I have shown it to no one.
>
> I cannot, of course, say that any of the defects [in the system] are due to individuals, but I feel some surprise that my very simple expedients have not occurred to anyone before.
>
> Today after I signed the report I had a case where the parties gladly agreed to have commission accounts examined by an independent accountant, this saving more than half of the time of trial.
>
> Do please try and do something to improve our status more definite and dignified.
>
> Yours,
>
> F. Newbolt.[33]

Here Newbolt tells the Lord Chancellor's Secretary that the Court has a problem with traditional procedures and the way to overcome it involves what today we would term case management measures. His report is revolutionary in the same sense as was said at the time of the creation of the referees' office. Despite this, Birkenhead's eventual reply in February 1922, referred to subsequently, cautioned about pressure from the Bench in settlement, but one can also infer Birkenhead's concern for what he called: 'the waste of public time.'[34]

Newbolt's full report is as follows:[35]

Confidential	**Official Referee's Court**
5th July 1920	**No. 195**
	Royal Courts of Justice

> I was appointed an Official Referee in April 1920 and had long been aware that there were serious defects in the business connected with this office. I am now informed that a brief report on the matter would be acceptable.
>
> The defects fall under 3 heads:
>
> 1. Those which are noticeable in all litigation in the courts;

[33] LCO 4/152.
[34] LCO 4/152 *Letter: Schuster to Newbolt. 21 February 1922.*
[35] LCO 4/152.

2. Those which are due to the personality of the Referees, and their want of status procedure and position; and
3. Those which are due to the present practice in this Court.[36]

The result of all these combined is that the volume of the business is not what it should be, and a vast number of disputes go to private arbitration instead of any to the Courts.

The reasons given generally for preferring a lay arbitration are that (1) it is a much cheaper tribunal; and (2) much more expeditious; (3) a lay arbitrator is chosen who belongs to the particular trade in which the dispute arises, or is an experienced solicitor or chartered accountant; and there is practically no appeal.

Here I say incidentally suggest that it is an anomaly that the appeal from a referee may go as of right to the Court of Appeal, and the House of Lords, but it must first pass through the Divisional Court. It seems difficult in these days to justify this extra proceeding in appealing against the decision of one who has all the powers of a High Court judge.

From the legal and logical point of view, indeed from almost any point of view, a lay arbitration is open to the gravest objections. Whenever a motion to set aside an award is made gross irregularities, often amounting to a denial of justice, are disclosed. These are well known, and indeed not enlarged upon, but the fact remains that the attraction of a cheap and speedy decision is so great that more important matters are overlooked. The natural desire to have a judge who understands trade customs will be dealt with later.

The first question then is how the present procedure can be cheapened and accelerated.

There is much room for improvement. I am informed that the list left to me by my predecessor will occupy my Court for a year, and some of the cases which I have already dealt have been over a year-one or two over a year and a half-on the way to trial.

During the last few days 3 cases have been referred to me after reaching trial before a judge, and in many cases the order or agreement to refer comes too late.

Solicitors are slow to take the initiative, and though it is not possible to generalise on many points it may be confidently stated that a strong tradition has grown up in the profession that a 'good reference,' when once the order is made, is a windfall for counsel and solicitors; it is long, lucrative and leisurely affair with great inducements to keep it alive, without fear of judicial censure.

The result of this tradition is that heavy and unmerited loss falls on almost every litigant, whether successful or not.

Connected with this great grievance is one of a more subtle nature. Many genuine disputes properly referred owing to the details of the claim, and involving in the aggregate £100 cannot be satisfactorily tried in the High Court at all on the present system.

The cost per hour is out of all proportion to the value of the items. It is a negation of business methods to spend even half an hour on an item valued at £2 or £3 and in a great many cases it is evident from an early period that the costs will probably fall upon the defendant and this has a great tendency to lengthen the case and penalise him. *This is hardly explained to him.*[37]

[36] ibid.
[37] Written in Newbolt's handwriting, the rest of the report being typed. Emphasis added.

While upon this question of expense I should point out that a great deal of unnecessary time has been taken up in the past owing to the traditional attitude of the referee which can only be explained by his want of some more definite status. He has endeavoured to make up for his want of authority by a policy of conciliation and non-interference, especially when leaders of the Bar have appeared before him, and this attitude always tends to lengthen a case very considerably. I recollect one, which although it might well have been tried in about 10 days actually took 22 days, and the referee listened without comment to the speeches of counsel which occupied no less than 22 hours. The costs amounted to £5,000 and owing to an incomplete judgement the trial proved abortive.

Lastly it is clear that a referee is not a member of a trade; he for instance cannot be so expert at accounts as an accountant, or so familiar with building as a builder; and so he has to listen to contradictory evidence on many questions which would create no difficulty if he were a member of the particular trade or business. By comparison to a lay arbitrator this adds to expense.

As to these points I can best put my 2 first suggestions for improvement in the form of examples:

(1) In an action on a mortgage the defendant desired to take an account over 12 years. Accountants were to be called on both sides and the case was expected to last 2 or 3 days. On a summons before trial I suggested that only one accountant should be employed an independent man nominated by agreement or by me. This was accepted. I named an accountant and he was engaged for one day. Upon his report the defendant capitulated. No briefs were delivered.

The same accountant is now by consent in another case, investigating the accounts of sales of goods amounting to £12,000 the amount in dispute being only a small balance less, I should think, than the costs of a 2 day trial. There will be an immense saving of expense here.

(2) In an action for damages for bad workmanship in decorating a theatre it was intended to call expert witnesses on both sides. On a summons, I suggested that one independent expert should examine and report, and this was accepted and his report was received. It will very greatly reduce the time of the trial and the extra expense of witnesses and increase the probability of a satisfactory decision.

There is no compulsion, and counsel and solicitors seem well aware of the advantage of the parties of the introduction of these changes, which are made possible by the fact that, at any rate, after the order of reference, all the summonses come before the judge who is to try the case. He can always, if he likes, get seisin of the case, and save much of the expense incurred by leaving the solicitors to carry it on in the usual way.

There remains the fundamental difficulty of status and to improve this, and so obtain the best candidates for this responsible position, clothed as it is with all the powers of a High Court Judge I venture to suggest (1) that the Referee should take precedence of County Court judges (2) that all appeals from their decisions should go direct to the Court of Appeal leave being required to appeal from a decision on a summons; (3) that the recognised form of address to a Referee should be 'My Lord' a title of respect allowed to a Commissioner of Assize and even to a junior barrister when he sits as a recorder or deputy recorder of a city like Bradford (4) that the salary and allowances should be increased and their pensions be at least on the same scale as those of County Court judges.

> These suggestions hardly seem to require much argument but I may illustrate them by the following examples:
>
> Some little time ago, in order to help an old friend who was ill I sat for 3 days as a Deputy County Court Judge and in my last case, in which no solicitor or counsel appeared I gave judgment for £5. In my first case here I gave judgment £17,700.
>
> Counsel of the first rank sometimes appear on references and it is essential to the proper speedy and economical conduct of the judicial business, whether heavy or light, that the referees should occupy a position which enables them not only to possess but to exercise all the powers of a judge in the most effective manner. Otherwise the old tradition will revive. I have endeavoured to compress my observations into the smallest possible compass, but in connection with this part of my report I cannot help wondering what a judge of the King's Bench Division would say if after adjourning a part heard case for the convenience of the plaintiff's leading and junior counsel, he found that neither of them appeared at the time arranged owing to engagements which they considered more important. In a Referee's Court such an incident carries no penalty, except for the plaintiff.
>
> F. Newbolt.[38]

This report is important because in it Newbolt identified the deficiencies in the referral process and is direct evidence of his conception of micro-case management or the 'Scheme' described above which had at its core the expeditious and economic resolution of disputes by conventional and unconventional means. In the absence of evidence to the contrary it is the first real and direct evidence of a rudimentary form of case management in this court. Here Newbolt recognised the issue and tells the Lord Chancellor how he overcame practical problems by his form of case management.

Newbolt used experts sparingly and proportionately. They had no right of audience. There was no provision in the *Rules of the Supreme Court* for a court expert. This did not come about until 1934 when Order 37A was amended.[39] It appears that Newbolt may have invented the idea of a court expert and there is some evidence of it. He did it to expedite the process and save money: saving half the trial costs clearly demonstrated its success.

To Birkenhead the first issue he raised was of great concern to him and his colleagues – the question of status and judicial ranking. Judges like arbitrators must have command of the hearing not in telling counsel what to do but in commanding respect for their office and function. In that sense the personality of the referee was important, particularly where the referee was of an equal professional standing to those appearing before him. Difficulty arose where the leaders of the Bar appeared before a referee whom the leaders considered had equal or lesser standing. Referees continued to complain about their status for decades because of this. Whilst it is arguable that subordination had advantage in terms of informality, it could be detrimental where a referee might have difficulty

[38] LCO 4/152.
[39] RSC (No.2) 1934.

in encouraging a leader to settle where there was always the tension as between the rights of parties to their day in court and the limited resources available to the Court in terms of time allocation and cost, not just of the parties, but of the tax payer in the context of Treasury policy.[40]

Second, Newbolt warns about 'cheap and speedy' arbitration and the dangers of injustice through irregular awards, but at the same time he advocates reducing the costs of time spent in court and recommending what today we might interpret as elements of case management: expediting referrals from masters to referees and a use of independent experts. Significantly he identifies lawyers as a problem and suggests that a 'good reference' militates against efficiency. In the same vein he attacks disproportionate cases where the legal costs are out of all proportion to the value of the claim.[41] Newbolt clearly understood and demonstrated his overriding commitment to cost effective case management which today is perceived as one of the key features of judicial case management.

Third, he perceived that there was a perceived disadvantage of appeals to the Divisional Court;[42] they took time and added further unnecessary cost to the appellate procedure. The figures given in the *Annual Returns* gave an average of 7 per cent of cases were appealed.[43] But, not all referees agreed with Newbolt. For example, Hansell did not agree with the abolition of all appeals.[44] From Newbolt's point of view it would have made things far more efficient and given the referees more credibility and status.

In this context, the passing of the Administration of Justice Act 1932 must be considered a triumph in terms of Newbolt's attempts to improve both the procedure of the Court and the recognition of the referees' role. The reason for this success was due to Lord Sankey, the Lord Chancellor, who wrote a memorandum to the Cabinet in September 1932 regarding several legal reforms 'which experience has shown to be desirable'.[45]

[40] These were years of austerity and restraint following the First World War when the economy suffered from loss of productivity due to the adjustment and reorganisation of industry from a wartime basis to a peacetime one, and reorganisation of international trade and finance following wartime disruption as well as a flu pandemic that killed millions around the world. There followed mass unemployment among demobilised servicemen and widespread strikes took place. In April 1920 a severe slump accompanied by mass unemployment was caused by an austerity budget that severely reduced government spending, together with a deflationary rise in interest rates. A return to the gold standard presaged stagflation reducing exports and increasing unemployment. This placed obvious pressure on the Treasury to reduce spending on civil justice which was further increased by the effects of a General Strike in 1926 and later by the Wall Street Crash of 1929 and a deepening depression in 1932.They were also years of growing European and international tension.

[41] Newbolt reported a case to the Lord Chancellor where the Plaintiff's costs exceeded the damages awarded. He gave the example of a case of five eggcups at three pence each and two pie dishes at one and sixpence. This case took as long as a case where the damages involved were £20,000. LCO 4/152.

[42] LCO 4/152.

[43] Between 1928–31 there were 31 appeals which occupied the Divisional Court for 51 days, each appeal taking an average of eight hours. Five were further appealed to the Court of Appeal taking another four days in court. LCO 4/152.

[44] National Archives LCO 4/152.

[45] LCO 2/1710 *Lord Chancellor to Cabinet.*

Lord Sankey advised the cabinet:[46]

> … This reform has been duly considered by the Council of Judges of the Supreme Court, and its achievement calls for legislation since it is not within the competence of the Supreme Court Rule Committee.

Although Newbolt was in favour of the legislation Hansell and Bosanquet[47] approached the question of appeals differently from Newbolt.[48] Bosanquet wrote to Lord Sankey in November 1932 saying:[49]

> OFFICIAL REFEREE'S COURT
>
> No. 691
>
> Royal Courts of Justice
>
> November 2nd, 1932.
>
> My Dear Paterson,
>
> I have been reading with interest the clause in the Bill which the Lord Chancellor is introducing dealing with appeals from Official Referees. I should much like to have an opportunity of putting my views-which incidentally were those of Hansell him (*sic*). Which of his Secretaries is concerned with this hand of the business? The view which we both hold is that while we entirely agree that the appeal should go straight to the Court of Appeal, we think that having regard to the complexity of the matters which come before us the procedure by Special Case would be cumbersome, and in many cases quite unworkable. Of course, Hansel's view is deserving of much more respect than mine. I know that it is in conflict with Newbolts-but then the latter would like to abolish appeals from Official Referees altogether-and has stated to me that in his view the proposed method would in effect do so!
>
> Yours ever
>
> S.R.C. Bosanquet.

However, Newbolt seems to have won the day by sending a Memorandum to Lord Sankey:[50]

> Administration of Justice Act, 1932
>
> MEMORANDUM
>
> What further Rules of Court are necessary.
>
> In my opinion it would be to the advantage of suitors, and for necessary alterations in the Rules of Court to be made this term. If this is not generally acceptable, I suggest that the order should be made direct Jan. 1st, 1933, as the day, and the alterations, which seem slight and not controversial could be considered and settled in a brief period, this term.

[46] ibid.

[47] Sir Ronald Bosanquet KC Official Referee 1931–54.

[48] Senior Official Referee 1927–1931.

[49] LCO 2/1710 Sir Ronald Bosanquet KC *Letter to Lord Chancellor, 2 November 1932.*

[50] LCO 2/1734 *Appeals from referees: question of altering rules consequent on the Administration of Justice Act, 1932 (s.1); Rules of the Supreme Court (No.4, 1932; Appeals from Official Referee's Order, 1932*, Memorandum from Sir Francis Newbolt QC to Lord Chancellor, November 1932.

The points requiring consideration are-

(1) Cases sent to the Referee for enquiry and report, under Section 88 of the principal Act;[51]
(2) Interlocutory appeals on questions of law;
(3) Trial of any question or issue of fact under Section 89 of the principal Act, which implies that the action remains in the jurisdiction of the Judge making the order of reference.

As to (1) the practice in this respect has become almost obsolete. I cannot remember having had such a case in 13 years, and I am informed by the Rota Clerk that only one such case has come into the office, certainly during the last 3 or 4 years.

Such a report when adopted, wholly or partially, becomes a judgement automatically and the appeal, if any, is an appeal against the decision of the Judge.

(2) Almost every interlocutory order is discretionary, and without appeal, but in a rare case a point of law might be decided. But I have formed the opinion which is shared by all those whom I have consulted that the Act forbids interlocutory appeals to the Court of Appeal or otherwise.

(3) Trials by Official Referees merely of issues of fact, except the estimation of damages are now unknown. Apart from damages, it is the invariable practice of the Judges to refer the whole cause or matter.

…

(Sgd) Francis Newbolt

Senior Official Referee

19.11.32.[52]

Newbolt's comment that High Court judges had adopted the practice of sending the *whole cause or matter* to a referee is significant. It goes beyond what Lord Selbourne said in the House of Lords in February 1873 that referrals would be confined to matters of fact and account.

One of the advantages of not having a jury was that the judge could order a short adjournment for the parties to consider settlement. The parties frequently requested trials on liability only without any reference to damages.[53]

Newbolt noted that the draft new rules recognised the referees' position by extending Rule 19A of the *Rules of the Supreme Court*.[54] This gave a right to appeal a decision of a referee on a point of law to the Court of Appeal, instead of to the Divisional Court of King's Bench.

[51] LCO 2/1734. Newbolt had certainly not had any such case in 15 years and were to all intents defunct.

[52] LCO 2/1734 *Memorandum Newbolt to Lord Chancellor.*

[53] ibid.

[54] LCO 2/1734 *Memorandum: Supreme Court Rule Committee on Rules of the Supreme Court (No.4) 1932.*

Rule 19A applied to appeals from the Railway and Coal Commission and the Railway Rates Tribunal.

On 13 December 1932 Albert Napier[55] sent the Lord Chief Justice, Lord Hanworth an advance copy of the new procedure. Hanworth endorsed the letter:[56]

> Yes. I have gone through them and agree
>
> Hanworth[57]

Appeals direct to the Court of Appeal was perhaps the high-water mark of Newbolt's efforts to raise the standing of the referees. Newbolt's July 1920 report was the catalyst for Newbolt's 'Scheme' and whether officially supported or not it became the foundation for practice in the referees' court. The November 1932 Memorandum and Newbolt's views as to appeals gave the Court a greater standing. Lord Sankey's action brought the referees' court into line with the other Queen's Bench courts so that their judgments were not capable of review by High Court Queen's Bench judges. The significance of the measure meant in effect that the judgment of the referee became a judgment of the High Court.[58]

Newbolt's 'Scheme' was the prototype of case management and informal referee resolution and provides the basis for the exposition of the theory that case management and informal referee resolution created a more efficient court. We further examine this 'Scheme' by a literature review and qualitative analysis of contemporaneous archival material and Newbolt's publications. From this review the following analysis of the principal features of rudimentary case management emerge.

VI. Elements of Rudimentary Official Referee Case Management

A. Informal Procedural Discussions

Newbolt's article in the *Law Quarterly Review*,[59] 'Expedition and Economy in Litigation', described various case-types including building and dilapidations cases, matters of taking account, local examination of building, machinery and farms and other subject matters. His central critique was aimed at cost inefficiency and delay. Newbolt wrote that defendants incurred unnecessarily burdensome costs

[55] Napier was assistant secretary in the Lord Chancellor's office and Deputy Clerk of the Crown in Chancery from 1919 to 1944 when he became Permanent Secretary to the Lord Chancellor and Clerk of the Crown in Chancery. He has been described as a 'brake not an accelerator'.

[56] LCO 2/1734 *Letter from Lord Chancellor to the Master of the Rolls, Ernest Murray Pollock, Lord Hanworth*. (1923–1935). Rules effective as at 1 January 1933.

[57] LCO 2/1734.

[58] LCO 2/1710 *Note on the Administration of Justice Bill by Lord Chancellor's Assistant Secretary Napier*.

[59] Newbolt (n 19) 434.

in preliminary proceedings which were not 'always deserved'.[60] This loss deterred parties from litigation.

As Newbolt said:

> The interlocutory proceedings before reference may be so extravagant and dilatory as to defeat justice.

Newbolt significantly developed a practice at First Summons for Directions stage of not only giving directions for the further conduct of the case, but also made it his practice to discuss the merits, issues and value of the claim with the solicitors who appeared before him. In the course of this he took the opportunity of questioning by what means time and cost could be saved. In Newbolt's words he had 'friendly business discussions' during the interlocutory process with those appearing before him. It was this business-like approach and his rapport with solicitors that facilitated his 'Scheme'. This was a characteristic that seems to have continued in practice to the benefit of the Court and practitioners alike. Newbolt certainly considered his approach effective so much so that in his last letter to Birkenhead as Lord Chancellor he wrote:[61]

> 13th Feb 1922
>
> My dear Lord Chancellor,
>
> I have from time to time sent in reports of the work in my Court, beyond the official returns, showing how I am able to prevent delay, simplify procedure and reduce expense. Now at the suggestion of two of the judges, I wish to draw attention specially to a case in which I delivered judgment yesterday as it is a striking example of what I am fighting against.
>
> The judgment is in writing, and if you so desire, I will send you a copy.
>
> A dispute arose between a builder and a building owner and a writ was issued in October 1920: the case only came before me for trial.
>
> The interlocutory proceedings during the previous 16 months was open to the most severe criticism and when I reserved judgment after a three day trial I ascertained by courtesy of the solicitors that the plaintiff's total costs were estimated at £497, including about £125 for counsel's fees and the defendant's costs at about £400. Total about £900. The plaintiff recovered £122, ordered by previous payment set off to £27.
>
> I gave judgment for £27.
>
> If the case had come before me on the delivery of the Statement of Claim indorsed on the writ it could have been disposed of in a few weeks at small cost.
>
> On a hint from one of the judges, I only desire to add that in my scheme for cheapening and expediting litigation nothing is done without consent. It is by friendly business discussions over the table that the simplification is offered.

[60] ibid 435.

[61] LCO 4/152.

In no case has any decision of mine in Chambers been overruled and the only appeal against a decision of the court was emphatically dismissed today by the Divisional Court.

I respectfully suggest that after 2 years trial this is a satisfactory answer to any enquiry.

Yours truly,

Francis Newbolt

The Rt Hon.

The Lord Chancellor

This letter is significant first, because it confirms Newbolt's 'Scheme' in particular his 'friendly business discussions in Chambers' undertaken with the support of the parties. Second, because the decisions he reached as a result and his practice were never appealed or overruled. It is quite revolutionary in its content for those times, as is the fact that another judge suggested that Newbolt disclose his 'friendly business discussions'.

Birkenhead clearly felt some unease about this because of the judicial function and questions of judicial independence and impartiality which were essential to counter any suggestion of bias or prejudice. Descending into the arena of such discussions was undoubtedly a hazard as it would be for any judge or arbitrator. Thus, the last reply from Birkenhead's Permanent Secretary, Sir Claude Schuster, to Newbolt is an important caution in this regard although there is no evidence that such discussions ever made cause for complaint or appeal:[62]

21 February 1922

Dear Frank,

The Lord Chancellor asks me to reply to your letter of the 13th February.

He is very glad to read it. He had always anticipated from his long acquaintance with you that you would dispense justice with expedition and equity and that in so doing you would have special regard to the interests and the pockets of the litigant.

There is only one point upon which he has felt some uneasiness. He has now sat as a judge himself for three years and his experience during that time has confirmed the opinions which he formed at the bar as to the judicial conduct of litigation. It is no doubt desirable that the advantages to be obtained by settling instead of fighting should be present to the mind of the lay client and of his professional advisers. But the Chancellor himself has seen so much of the dangers which arise from any undue pressure towards a settlement exerted from the Bench that he himself is most careful ever to avoid such action. There are cases which are better fought out and there are clients who desire to fight even more than they desire to win. And there are others who, though their principal object is victory, are better content with defeat than an inglorious peace. So strongly does the Chancellor hold these views that he always deems it desirable to impress them upon all who administer justice, but he thinks that they are specially to

[62] LCO 4/152.

be borne in mind by anyone who, like yourself, is eager for justice and justly impatient of the waste of public time.

Yours sincerely,

(Sgd). Claude Schuster

Sir Francis Newbolt K.C.

Birkenhead's unease about settlement discussions goes to the heart of a dilemma here: on the one hand, the referees wanted to have the status of High Court judges which Newbolt felt they were 'all but in name'. On the other hand, Newbolt wanted to dispense justice informally (which he undoubtedly found quicker) because this was the only way he could expedite his list. Newbolt's approach might be reconciled to the Commissioners objective of a process being 'capable of adjusting the rights of the litigant parties in the manner most suitable to the nature of the questions to be tried'.

Whilst Birkenhead's letter of reply was ambiguous in that Birkenhead thought that Newbolt should have special regard to 'the interests and the pockets of the litigants', he also felt some 'uneasiness' in that there were dangers in judges 'exerting any undue pressure towards a settlement'. On the other hand, he was alive to 'the waste of public time'. Birkenhead could not sanction the 'Scheme' because of his unease in the light of his own experience in sitting as a judge and anxiety over 'undue pressure' from the Bench. On the other hand, Birkenhead and Schuster undoubtedly recognised Newbolt's initiative and to an extent whilst the letter is cautious it is also some acknowledgement for Newbolt's work. It is fortunate that Newbolt's early experimentation in this field coincided with Birkenhead's tenure and that Birkenhead did not ignore Newbolt's reports, his experimentation, or the 'Scheme' although Birkenhead would have been unlikely to have adopted such practice or to have encouraged it for the reasons he gave.

What is significant is that in the absence of any other contemporaneous evidence of fact Newbolt's 'experiments' may be considered as the first attempt by a judge to use alternative processes of dispute resolution in England in a court setting.

Newbolt was not deterred by Schuster's response of 21 February 1922 and there is no evidence to suggest that Newbolt altered his practice, because some time after July 1921 he wrote again to Birkenhead intimating support from the profession:[63]

> I have devised means of enabling the parties to have their disputes decided cheaply and rapidly and my efforts in this direction have been widely approved by the profession …

This suggests that Newbolt's informal discussions with the solicitors for each party were supported by them just as today many practitioners see sense in mediation saving time and costs. Newbolt's approach may have been like an early neutral

[63] LCO 4/152. The letter is undated but appears on the Lord Chancellor's Office file after the July1921 correspondence.

evaluation giving each side a reality check on what costs might be incurred and whether that bore a proportionate relationship to the value of the claim.

A further extract from Newbolt's article gives a good example of the benefit of Newbolt's approach here:[64]

> The Defendant who often has good reason to complain of some overcharge, of defective work, swears a vague affidavit, and obtains leave to defend as to part, or all, of the claim. But he may have, in fact, no case.
>
> If a few days after an order on the summons before the Master the parties met before the Referee and discussed the position such a miscarriage of justice as appears in the cases described would be impossible. The main source of avoidable waste of money is the occupation of time in Court which a little thought and discussion in Chambers would save, and does save. In matters of account, in kindred cases, much money has been thrown away in the past by discussing in open court matters of pure arithmetic, or the contents of business books which turn out not to be in dispute, or not material to the issue, or fatal to one parties contention. Many other examples might be given. In one case evidence was taken before and also at the trial on both sides to prove the market price of goods at a foreign port. *If a preliminary discussion had taken place*[65] none of this evidence would have been gone into as it was not relevant to any issue on the pleadings. Another instance will strikingly illustrate the point. A mortgagor claimed an account of matters extending over many years: the case was expected to last for a fortnight. After *an informal discussion in Chambers*[66] the parties agreed that an independent accountant should examine the books before trial, as a witness for both sides, and report on the points in difference: so that the issue between the parties should be defined and tried. He reported that having explained the figures to both the Plaintiff and the Defendant there were no points in difference and there was nothing to try. *This is not arbitration or conciliation or concession, but an intelligent use of a Court of justice by business men.*[67] They spent perhaps £50 or less in arriving at a result which would in the ordinary course have cost ten times that sum, and would have worried them for a year.

What is crucial here are Newbolt's explicit references to 'preliminary discussion', 'informal discussion in Chambers', and 'use of a Court of justice by business men'. The fact that this article was published a year or so after his correspondence with the Lord Chancellor reveals his commitment to an anticipatory form of procedure akin to a form of evaluative mediation perhaps bypassing formal process. His illustrations relate to matters of account and do not appear to require forensic investigation. In such cases there does not appear to be justification for full disclosure as required for trial and the resolution may be based on preliminary discussions and limited disclosure with consequent saving of time and costs.

Newbolt's 'Scheme' was not applied in all his cases but in a limited number which excluded dilapidations and damage to property claims.[68]

[64] Newbolt (n 19) 438–439.
[65] Emphasis added.
[66] Emphasis added.
[67] Emphasis added.
[68] Newbolt, *Further Report to Lord Chancellor*, June 1921.

As proof that this 'Scheme' worked Newbolt's article included the following figures for the recovery of damages in the immediate post first world war period which appear in the following table:

Table T.2 Amounts recovered

Year	Cases	Amount Recovered
1920	100	£76,536
1921	150	£81,482
1922	171	£171,079

Source: Expedition and Economy in Litigation.[69]

According to Newbolt, less than a quarter per cent of the cases were subject to any appeal. What is interesting about his figures is that there appears a 100 per cent increase in recovery at the time Newbolt confirms that the 'Scheme' was in operation. Newbolt sent a copy of this article to Lord Haldane,[70] Lord Cave, Lord Justice Atkin,[71] and Sir Wilkes Chitty.[72]

Lord Haldane was more appreciative than Lord Cave as Schuster, on behalf of Haldane, wrote:

9th May 1924.

Dear Frank,

The Lord Chancellor has asked me to thank you for your letter of the 2nd May and for the copy of the Law Quarterly Review which accompanied it. He has read your article with much interest and has considerable sympathy with many of the suggestions you make.

He will be very glad to discuss any proposals which may be made with the Solicitor General in due course.

Yours sincerely

(sgd) Claude Schuster

Sir Francis Newbolt, K.C.

Unfortunately, in this matter we cannot judge how far Lord Haldane's sympathy might have resulted in any reform as Haldane's party was defeated in the general election of October 1924, following a motion of no confidence in the House of Commons. But despite what might have been at official level we know that following Newbolt's retirement in 1936 this informal process was continued as a matter of referee practice by his successors. This was demonstrated by a number of

[69] Newbolt (n 19) 439.
[70] LCO 4/152 Letter: *Newbolt to Napier* undated.
[71] Newbolt's book: *Out of Court* was dedicated 'by his friend the author' to Lord Justice Atkin in 1925.
[72] Newbolt's former Head of Chambers.

matrimonial property disputes which were referred to the referees after the war.[73] One such example was *Johnson v Johnson*.[74] Here the costs were grossly disproportionate. Damages were assessed for the plaintiff at £1 on the claim and for the defendant at £6 10 shillings on the counterclaim with costs on the County Court Scale. On an adjourned application the plaintiff was ordered to pay the defendant all the defendant's costs of £100. These terms were agreed between counsel at an adjourned hearing before the referee in chambers to avoid further cost.

B. Elements of Newbolt's Scheme

The interlocutory management in the 1920s as advocated by Newbolt centred on the referee having control of that process. It is argued here that Newbolt's 'Scheme' resulted in more expeditious trials, if not earlier settlement, which promoted his 'Scheme' of a continuous judicially managed process whether that was under the *Rules of the Supreme Court* or ad hoc or an informally managed consensual process.

C. Experts

i. Use of Single Joint Expert/Court Expert

Presaging the civil justice reforms of the 1990s by more than 70 years, Newbolt pioneered the use of court experts. He saved time and costs by the proper and necessary employment of experts. In his report of 5 July 1920[75] Newbolt tells Lord Birkenhead about his experiments with expert evidence citing the accountancy expert example.

What is interesting here is that Newbolt was experimenting, not only with a case management process at least 14 years before the *Rules of the Supreme Court* were augmented by Order 37A,[76] but he was directly intervening in the action in order to reduce cost and delay and procure by these means a quicker solution and settlement. This is therefore a good example of judicial management and 'interventionism'.

There is no evidence that Newbolt's practice encouraged the parties to incur further costs of instructing their own party experts. From the archives it appears

[73] These are included in the notebooks J114/1-8 and refer to assessment of value of matrimonial property, and disputes over ownership. Evidence from the second comparative period 1947–1070 is contained in ch 4 in this volume.

[74] J114/1 21 October 1946.

[75] LCO 4/152, 5.

[76] Under *Rules of the Supreme Court* (No: 2) 1934, Order 37A each party had the right to call an expert or experts with leave with regard to the 'issue for the expert'. This enabled the Court in non-jury actions to appoint an independent Court expert to 'enquire and report upon any question of fact or opinion not involving questions of law or construction'.

that the court expert was the only expert engaged as there are no references to the parties' own experts.

The important point here is that the initiative came from the judge, not the parties; the judge taking control away from the lawyers to actively caseflow manage the proceedings more economically.

On the same theme, just over 10 years later, Newbolt wrote to the editor of *The Times* about methods of saving expense:[77]

> … Since the war there has naturally been a great stream of cases brought by landlords against tenants about dilapidations, and by builders, contractors, and decorators, and others against building-owners about the price of work done, and in all these cases at least the parties are very anxious to avoid unnecessary expense, and eagerly fall in with the idea that only one expert witness should be employed. He is not an assessor or arbitrator, but a witness. The saving of money, especially to defendants, is surprising.
>
> The plan has a double advantage, as the independent expert gives both parties a copy of his proof long before the expensive preparation for the trial, and from its perusal they can predict the result of a hearing in Court, apart from questions of law, so accurately that in many cases no formal trial takes place at all. … If only one witness is employed he is single minded, and paid to be truthful and helpful, and not combative. He is chosen by the parties, by some professional institution, or by the Court, and can naturally be cross-examined by both sides, though this has very rarely happened. The same procedure can be pursued in many other cases, particularly those involving accounts, inspection of books, vouchers, &c. A report by one independent accountant of the contents of these, before any proceedings are taken beyond the writ, saves a startling percentage of the costs of the action.
>
> There are many other ways of saving expense, which, when offered, are eagerly agreed to by litigants, but as they are not compulsory or according to old routine they are not so often suggested as they might be. Space does not permit me to suggest how the apparent difficulty about fixing trials can be met, or *how the suggested second summons for directions before the Judge would be most beneficial*,[78] or how arbitration, with all its convenience and finality can be obtained in the Law Courts for the ordinary Court fees.
>
> Yours truly,
> FRANCIS NEWBOLT

Not only does this letter advocate the utility of the single joint expert but it has wider implications for Newbolt's 'Scheme' and an activist approach. It may well be that because of Newbolt's practice in this sphere the rules were changed in 1934 to empower the Court to appoint such experts.[79] The other important procedural

[77] *The Times* (4 September 1930) 11: Issue 45609; col F.

[78] Emphasis added.

[79] RSC (No. 2), 1934. applied to non-jury cases in which any question for an expert witness was involved. Maugham LJ regretted such witness had not been appointed in *Fishenden v Higgs and Hill Ltd.* (1935) 153 LT 128 CA. Apart from this statutory power, the court could appoint an expert at Common Law under its inherent power *Kennard v Aslam* (1894) 10 TLR 213; *Henson v Ashby* [1896] 2 Ch 1. 26; *Coles v Home and Colonial Stores Ltd* [1904] AC 179, 192 and *Badische v Lewisham* (1883) 24 Ch Div 156.

innovation and case management function we would recognise today is the use of that 'second summons for directions'. This translates today to a pre-trial hearing or further case management conference. It is also further evidence of a tighter continuous judicial control: another facet of modern case management.

In *Expedition and Economy in Litigation* Newbolt advocated the use of experts to deal with particular matters which could save time in the interlocutory process:[80]

> What the commercially minded Defendant, willing to pay his debts, wishes to do is to show why and in what respects he objects to paying the whole of the claim, and this he does by giving particulars of the items which he says are not chargeable, or are overcharged. Every case must be treated on its special circumstances and not upon any rule which is not a Rule of Court, but there are some large classes of cases with common features: the greatest saving has been effected by the introduction of the independent expert witness and the attendant reduction of interlocutory proceedings which are rendered unnecessary, and of the expensive hours of trial in Court.

ii. Use of Experts

Newbolt's 'Scheme' appears to have encompassed several experiments with experts as investigators. One example he reported to Birkenhead in November 1921 was in the form of a letter from a member of the Bar, Mr S A. Merlin. Mr Merlin told Newbolt that his initiative in the case had been:

> One of the most practical means of reform of our jurisprudence as shown for years, as I know how costly were these actions in the past.

In the case, Newbolt ordered the surveyor/expert to view the premises. The expert took his instructions from Newbolt not from the parties. The plaintiff claimed £349 damages. £300 was paid into Court, but the Surveyor opined that the claim was worth £185. This produced an expeditious settlement, saving costs without the need for a trial.[81] This innovation was ground-breaking because Newbolt himself selected and instructed the expert.

In *Expedition and Economy in Litigation*[82] Newbolt gives two further examples of the use of experts which are contradictory.

> Number 13 – Writ issued March 1921, action eventually referred. An accountant nominated in 1922 to make a report and in January 1923 after a two day trial Plaintiff recovered about £140. 22 months from issue of Writ to trial. Costs exceeded £400, accountants were not independent and their appointment was made before the case was referred.
>
> Number 14 Dilapidations case – Defendant put in a substantial defence and paid £300 into Court less than half the amount of the claim. After several days hearing the Plaintiff accepted the Defendant's offer of £500 including costs. The Plaintiff's costs were taxed

[80] Newbolt (n 19) 427.
[81] LCO 4/152.
[82] Newbolt (n 19).

> at £577. The assistance of an independent witness was refused, had it been accepted in all probability it would have saved the Defendant a sum not much less than his whole legal liability under the covenant.'

Example 13 suggests that such partisan experts did not reduce delay or costs whereas, in example 14, the Court appointed expert may have facilitated considerable savings. The important point here is how they may be managed by the judge, not the parties. Newbolt seemed very aware of this. Whilst the lawyers undoubtedly helped facilitate some settlements, in others 'enjoying a good reference' was another matter. In such cases, case management was a means of making the process cost effective and less attractive to those who might want to protract the proceedings.

iii. Advantage of Independent Experts

Newbolt's objective, as explained in his article, was focussed on questions of damages and costs:

> … that in a *discussion in chambers* on date and mode of trial both parties agree that one expert engaged and paid by both sides is preferable, and for the following secondary reason, even more than for the most obvious one. The great error in the ordinary honest Defendant's course is that he fails to pay enough into Court. So in all cases immediately under consideration the Defendant must pay in something: the punishment is terrific if he does not, as he is entirely at the mercy of the Plaintiff, and in general has to pay most, or all of the costs of both sides in any event.[83]

The dilemma was how the defendant was to estimate the measure of payment in. To pay in too little was useless. He had to act on the advice of his expert. According to Newbolt, such experts calculated the figures upon rash assumptions assuming their evidence would be accepted on every single point. Newbolt gave warning about this:

> When he comes into Court he hears the Plaintiff's experts swear to a claim not only larger, but in some cases twice, three times, five times or even ten times as large. A recent decision was for six times the Defendant's figure, although it only amounted to one quarter of the Plaintiff's figure. In another the estimate of a reliable expert was 10% of that of his opponent.

Understanding expert evidence was one of the key problems for referees who might have had little knowledge of the technical issues before them, hence Newbolt's attention to the proper use of experts in his court:

> An independent witness surveys the subject matter unbiased and estimates that the amount due before any of the great expense of the trial is incurred, with any necessary reservations, where questions of law may arise, and gives proof to both sides, and receives half his fee from each, both halves being made costs in the cause. He may be

[83] Emphasis added.

> cross examined by both parties if either calls him at the trial, which he attends only if required: and both parties retain the right to call any amount of evidence to contradict him, a right which in practice, however, is not often exercised. The advantage to both parties can easily be perceived, but to the Defendant it cannot be over-estimated. He knows in time what to pay into Court, and in general is able to agree the facts with the Plaintiff, and to narrow the issue to something which occupies the Court for perhaps one fifth of what used to be considered the normal time. The layman who has had this properly explained to him, and prefers the old method, and what is called a fight to a finish regardless of costs, can hardly be said to exist.[84]

We have already seen the utility of judicial intervention in the appointment of court experts, but in this context, what is particularly interesting here is the linkage in Newbolt's analysis of an independent expert's role and settlement. Newbolt saw a credible expert as playing a useful role in estimating or calculating the damages which could facilitate early settlement. The expert was in court to assist the court, not to advocate the parties' case. More importantly Newbolt refers to saving 'perhaps one fifth of what used to be considered the normal time' by such means.

D. The problems of Delay and Need for Proportionate Approach to Costs

In his critique *Expedition and Economy in Litigation*,[85] Newbolt criticised the waste of time and money in the traditional adversarial procedural system. Whilst not directly advocating his scheme of a concurrent consensual referee resolution process, he acknowledged the fundamental principle that allowed 'every citizen to make or resist a claim in the courts with perfect freedom'. He then considered the citizen's complaint:

> No one complains that his case is impatiently tried, or decided against him by a dishonest, biased or incompetent tribunal: and yet every litigant complains.

Reading the article, it is clear that his experience as a referee led him to these views. He focused upon delay and expense as being the subject of very wide complaints. As he wrote:

> They overlap to a certain extent, as delay causes expense and actual loss of money in more ways than one: unnecessary proceedings not only cause expense, but also delay. In all discussions between those who desire to see a serious grievance mitigated or removed a difficultly always arises because the actual relevant facts are not ascertained or agreed. I shall therefore try to avoid this, by first inviting perusal of the briefest précis of a small number of recent cases, referring to them afterwards only by their numbers. The points to bear in mind are (a) time from writ to judgement; (b) amount of expenses of litigation in comparison with money obtained or in dispute; (c) payment into Court;

[84] Newbolt (n 19) 437
[85] Newbolt (n 19) 427.

> (d) the assumed desire of one or both litigants for a fight to the finish regardless of expense; (e) the urgent necessity especially at the present time for encouraging litigation and not starving it, or diverting it towards the quicksands of arbitration.[86]

From the same article Newbolt gives illustrations of disproportionate costs and some practical examples 'so extravagant and dilatory as to defeat justice'.[87]

The first was that of a builder who issued proceedings by writ in October 1920 against the building owner for the balance of account. After interlocutory proceedings lasting 16 months the case was referred and judgment was given for the plaintiff in the sum of £27. The trial lasted three days and the plaintiff's costs including £125 for counsel amounted to £490. The defendant's costs were approximately £410. The defence was dated nine months after the Statement of Claim. £900 was spent pursuing a £27 claim. The costs were 33 times the amount of claim.[88]

His second illustration was a claim for damages for dilapidations worth £100. £10 was paid into court. It took almost three years to come to trial. The referee gave time to settle and negotiate without result. Judgment was given for the plaintiff for £16. Costs were awarded on the County Court Scale.

Another illustration (Number 9) concerned a schedule of dilapidations and a claim for damages for £162. Proceedings were issued in January 1922. The defendant refused consent to a referral and wanted the High Court to decide on a matter of title. He lost that preliminary issue in January 1923 and a reference for an assessment of damages was taken in April 1923. At trial, in June 1923, the value of items was reduced from £95 to £81. The plaintiff's taxed costs were £129; the defendant paid that and the costs of the reference. Newbolt commented that the liability of £81 was increased to about five times that amount by the contest which lasted for 18 months; without the help of an independent expert witness the defendant's losses would have been much greater.

To be a success Newbolt's 'Scheme' required continual management of the process by the judge and avoidance of such examples as this. His publications and reports suggest that Newbolt would have enquired not only into merits, but also into costs in proportion to the value of the case.

In Eastham's report to Lord Jowitt on 28 January 1947 and in the report's appendix he cited the case of an ex-London Sheriff who sued his architect and his quantity surveyors for negligence claiming £35,000 in respect of an extension and alteration of his country house.[89] The trial lasted 22 days. Four King's Counsel were instructed with one brief marked at 350 guineas. The referee gave judgment for the plaintiff in the sum of £4,214 with costs. The taxed costs in this case were over £3,500.

[86] ibid.

[87] ibid 435.

[88] Interestingly in 2005 the Court of Appeal dealt with a similar situation in the *Burchell* case where legal costs were 37 times the damages awarded.

[89] Lord Chancellor 1945–51. LCO 4/153. *Appendix to Report of Sir T Eastham to Lord Jowitt, Lord Chancellor* (28 January 1947).

Eastham's notebooks have numerous entries dealing with costs. Eastham was innovative in this area; his orders being more in keeping with the second millennium than the mid-twentieth century. In *Harris v Mac Rex Foods Limited*,[90] for example, a claim for defective works to a boiler, judgment was given for the plaintiff who was not fully paid, and an order was made against the defendant for payment out. Both solicitors agreed that the judge could make a 'fractional order' on costs on a four-fifths basis.[91] In *Plant Machinery v HP Thomas Limited* an order was made for payment of monies out of £200 to plaintiff's solicitors without further authority and the trial was adjourned until May 1947. Each party was ordered to pay half the court fees of the application for adjournment.[92]

In *Zenith Skin Trading Co Ltd v Frankel*[93] there is a good example of a modern costs order such as more lately seen under the *Civil Procedure Rules*. Here the plaintiff's costs of the first day of trial were borne 70 per cent by the defendant, and 30 per cent by the plaintiff. The defendant paid all subsequent costs to the plaintiff.

It seems the referees were ahead of their times because there is further evidence of a more modern type of costs order, for example, an entry on 31 January 1949 for the adjourned hearing of *Jayes Limited v Home Foods Limited*.[94] The Order entered provided that the defendants be granted two-thirds of the costs of the hearing. What is demonstrated here is the referee's modern approach to costs, what we call today 'proportionality', and its application as a basis for the award of costs.

E. Invention of Special Pleadings

In *Expedition and Economy* Newbolt criticised formal pleadings considering that a mere formal denial by way of defence was totally unnecessary and burdensome.[95] It was merely a 'dilatory step in the proceedings'.

In his eleventh example concerning a claim for dilapidations the parties nominated a surveyor as a joint expert.[96] There were no pleadings, no summonses, nor was a trial appointment fixed. Newbolt dispensed with pleadings and ordered Statements of Case being a summary of the claim with the relevant documentary evidence. In other cases, he often found that the defendants demanded particulars which had already been received before the action, but were not given to the solicitor. He also found that defendants often put in defences alleging work not done, excessive charges and bad workmanship, without adequate or any particulars.

[90] J114/2, 92.
[91] Considering the year is 1948 this is a very modern type of costs award where costs are not awarded as to each party's case, but one order is made taking into account the other side's result. This saved time and cost in taxing two bills, one for the claim and another for the counter claim.
[92] J114/2.
[93] J114/4.
[94] J114/6, 67–105.
[95] Newbolt (n 19) 430 and 435–436.
[96] Newbolt (n 19) 430.

Newbolt considered that these defendants acted unthinkingly without regard to the fact that they would have to pay for these further proceedings. Newbolt was critical of those who spent time 'making costs' and went to trial 'rashly' as opposed to those who employed experts properly. Such persons were excluded so far as he was able.[97]

F. Preliminary Issues and Questions for the Court

In his article, Newbolt considered the advantages of the new Order 30 RSC[98] regarding the summons for directions procedure.[99] He opposed this for referees because of the advantage of dealing with directions early. He saw the Summons for Directions as arbitrators saw preliminary meetings: a business meeting to discuss the agenda for resolving the dispute. There was no point in leaving issues to be defined too late if it could be avoided, as he wrote:

> Without venturing upon any general criticism of legal procedure, it may safely be said that there is no greater check on wasteful expenditure than the arrangement by which the Trial Judge takes his own summonses, especially if he makes notes of them upon the file ... *the mere discussions across a table which costs nothing in comparison with the costs per minute in Court,*[100] discloses what issue it is exactly that the parties wish to try, and eliminates the very source of the litigants grievances. Where the case is referred too late the mischief is already half done, but in time this will remedy itself, and all cases which must eventually be referred will be referred on the issue of the Writ, or at any rate on the hearing of a summons under Order 14.[101]

Again, the focus here is upon informal discussions at the summons hearings and what they could achieve. This would be lost by adherence to Order 30. Newbolt reiterates his views contained in his letter dated 15 February 1932 to Lord Sankey.[102] He confirms his informal resolution practice and indicates how important it is to caseflow manage the process so that issues between the parties are identified early to save the Court time and party costs. The former procedure had been to issue a Summons for Directions before pleadings were exchanged.[103] The new Order 30 (ignored by the referees in practice) provided that such summons could only be issued after service of the Reply.

[97] ibid 435–437.

[98] RSC 1883 as amended by RSC (No.1) 1933. Under the 1883 rules the taking out of the summons for directions was optional; under the 1933 amendment it had to be taken out within seven days of close of pleadings.

[99] Newbolt (n 19) 437.

[100] Emphasis added.

[101] Newbolt (n 19) 437–438.

[102] LCO 4/152 Lord Sankey was appointed Lord Chancellor from the High Court Bench in 1929 and served as Lord Chancellor until 1935, the only Commercial Court judge to have become Lord Chancellor.

[103] RSC amendments to RSC 1875 (May and August 1897, and July 1902).

G. Geographic and Economic Factors

One of the novelties of the Judicature Acts was that the referee was empowered to sit at a convenient location. It was not unusual for referees to sit elsewhere. In fact, in 1925, Newbolt sat in Manchester.[104]

The following correspondence confirms that Newbolt also sat in Lancaster. The endorsement by Lord Cave rejected Newbolt's request for a meeting.

> Much more complicated
>
> impossible now[105]
>
> 12 March 1925
>
> Confidential
>
> OFFICIAL REFEREES' COURT
>
> No. 195
>
> Royal Courts of Justice
>
> W.C. 2
>
> Dear Lord Chancellor,
>
> Augustine Sherman is reported as having stated at Assizes that there ought to be an Official Referee for Lancashire as many cases arise there suitable for such a Court as witnesses cannot conveniently travel to London. This is so misleading that, if allowed, I should be glad to explain the position to you privately, and invoke your assistance.
>
> I should be able to explain to you, and cannot do so in a letter, why cases are "specially referred", so as to avoid the Rota.
>
> Why References mistakenly go first to Assizes with enormous loss to the litigants is easily explained: but to begin at the beginning, Lancashire witnesses need not come to London to attend the Court of an Official Referee. Except, very rarely, by consent, they never do so, as the Referees travel to Liverpool and Manchester when necessary. I have myself been to the latter even to take the evidence of a witness going abroad. ….

Subsequently Eastham recorded that he sat at the Town Halls in Leeds[106] and Henley.[107] He also sat in the Magistrates Court at Tunbridge Wells.[108] Another example in the post Second World War decade is a note by John Trapnell KC[109] in *Agnew v Maycock*[110] who notes that proceedings took place in the Town Hall in Leeds. Also in *Plaehet v Stormond Engineering Corporation Limited* Sir Derek

[104] LCO 4/152. Letter to Lord Cave, 12 March 1925.

[105] LCO 4/152 Lord Cave's handwritten note endorsed on letter.

[106] J114/1. Entry for 12 November 1944.

[107] J114/2 29 January 1946, *Davis v Solomon*. Dilapidations case. Judgement for defendants for £70 with costs and leave to enforce.

[108] J114/8, 9–10.

[109] Official Referee 1943–1949. Formerly appointed Judge Advocate of the Fleet while holding his post at the Bar. He was also Recorder of Plymouth. *The Times* (21 July 1933) 16: Issue 46502; col D. He was also a Commissioner of Assizes appointed on the Midlands Circuit in July 1948. *The Times* (10 July 1948) 3: Issue 51120; col C.

[110] J114/6, 15. This was for an account of partnership debts.

Walker Smith agreed with the referee that there would be no formal disposition, and that evidence could be taken at the plaintiff's premises.[111]

In Eastham's report to Lord Jowitt[112] he describes an action by the plaintiff, the owner of land in Durham, who claimed damages from the defendant a colliery company for subsidence caused to the plaintiff's land by mining operations. Liability and damages were tried by the referee at Newcastle for the convenience of the parties.

Such sittings at the convenience of the parties must be considered a time and cost saving exercise.

H. Preliminary Assessment of the 'Scheme'

Having analysed the instances of rudimentary caseflow management in the inter war years it is interesting to consider the impact of Newbolt's experiments by way of a preliminary survey of the court's overall effectiveness. This survey covers the Pollock court between 1920 and 1927 as illustrated in Tables T.3.1–T.3.2[113] and the Newbolt court 1928–36 illustrated in Table T.3.3.

What is significant in the context of the hypothesis is the marked effect the 'Scheme' may have had between 1921 and 1929. Comparing Tables T.3.2 and T.3.3 we find an increase of 22 per cent in the rate of disposals to referrals in those years from 19 per cent in 1921 to 41 per cent in 1929 and 1931.

Table T.3.1 Total referrals and trials

Year	**1919**	**1920**	**1921**	**1922**	**1923**	**1924**	**1925**	**1926**	**1927**
Total references	210	393	649	593	470	376	389	400	389
Tried	86	159	296	291	184	181	168	157	155
Percentage tried	41%	40%	46%	49%	39%	48%	43%	39%	40%

Source: Civil Judicial Statistics 1919–27.

Table T.3.2 Total cases withdrawn and disposed of and percentages of same

Year	**1919**	**1920**	**1921**	**1922**	**1923**	**1924**	**1925**	**1926**	**1927**
Withdrawn or otherwise disposed	44 21%	91 23%	127 19%	118 20%	144 31%	76 20%	105 27%	136 34%	115 30%

Source: Civil Judicial Statistics 1919–27.

We also observe that before the war it would appear that Pollock's court was more efficient in terms of resolving matters at trial.

[111] J114/8, 205. Here the parties managed to arrive at a settlement. This was produced in the form of an order of settlement. Evidence taken 18 January 1949.

[112] Lord Chancellor 1945–51. LCO 4/153. *Appendix to Report of Sir T Eastham to Lord Jowitt, Lord Chancellor* (28 January 1947).

[113] Percentage values throughout the text have been rounded up from decimal to whole integers. These figures rounded up from figures in the Civil Judicial Statistics Analysis: Official Referees: 1919–70.

During Newbolt's time as Senior Official Referee, 1928–36, the corresponding figures were:

Table T.3.3 Percentage of trials and disposals

Year	1928	1929	1930	1931	1932	1933	1934	1935	1936
Tried	130	121	105	109	96	102	134	139	179
Percentage of referrals tried	39%	33%	31%	32%	31%	32%	40%	40%	48%
Withdrawn or otherwise disposed	118	148	133	140	107	102	75	86	70
Percentage of referrals withdrawn or otherwise disposed	36%	41%	40%	41%	35%	32%	22%	24%	19%

Source: Civil Judicial Statistics 1928–36.

Newbolt's court appears more resourceful in encouraging parties to resolve matters either by withdrawal or settlement before trial thus saving the time and costs of a court hearing. Such a difference in approach may be the dividing line between an activist and a passive approach to case management or it may simply suggest that Newbolt alone adopted this approach.

VII. Conclusions

The interesting question here is whether Newbolt's 'Scheme' was efficient and effective. Calculating the average percentage of disposals and trials we find that in the period 1919–1927 Sir Edward Pollock resolved most of his cases at trial amounting to 43 per cent of his list and 25 per cent of his cases were otherwise resolved before trial. In Newbolt's case, 32 per cent of his cases were resolved before trial and 36 per cent at trial.[114] Comparison is difficult because the nature and type of case is not given but broadly speaking this shows some tendency to suggest that Newbolt's approach had an effect as he indicates in his correspondence with Lord Birkenhead and in his published article and letters,

Table T.3.4 Average percentage of referrals resolved before and at trial

Management stage	1919–27-Pollock	1928–36-Newbolt
Resolved before trial	25%	32%
Resolved at trial	43%	36%

Source: Tables T.3.2.–T.3.4 of M Reynolds, Caseflow Management: A Rudimentary Referee Process, 1919–70 (London School of Economics, Thesis, 2008).

[114] This is a preliminary analysis and is quantified in far more detail in ch 5 of MP Reynolds, *Caseflow Management: A Rudimentary Referee Process, 1919–70* (London School of Economics Thesis, 2008).

Here we may conclude:

First, the earliest direct evidence of micro-case management in the Court was Newbolt's Report in July 1920 to Lord Birkenhead. Second, that Newbolt recognised the utility of expert determination more than half a century before the benefit of such expedient was perceived by the legal profession. Third, that Newbolt experimented with the idea of a court expert. Fourth, that Newbolt pioneered effective cost saving devices such as identification of preliminary issues; early case directions; referral to an agreed expert and use of experts to examine other experts, as well as dispensation of formalities such as formal pleadings in certain cases. Fifth, he advocated the proportionate use of time and related the value of the claim to the costs of the case. Sixth, the referees' case managed through an early summons for directions process and pre-trial summons giving the parties more opportunity to consider settlement.

Finally, they acted flexibly like their predecessors in sitting at locations convenient to the parties and visiting the site of the claim.

In summary Newbolt and his colleagues demonstrated a rudimentary form of case management which included an informal settlement process through what he termed 'an intelligent use of a court of justice by businessmen'.[115] Beyond that it can be hypothesised that Newbolt's 'Scheme' may have been employed in 25 per cent of the referee cases in the following order:

Table T.4 Statistical Analyses.

During Newbolt's time as Senior Official Referee, 1928–36, the corresponding figures were:

Table T.4.1 Percentage of trials and disposals

Year	1928	1929	1930	1931	1932	1933	1934	1935	1936
Tried	130	121	105	109	96	102	134	139	179
Percentage of referrals tried	39%	33%	31%	32%	31%	32%	40%	40%	48%
Withdrawn or otherwise disposed	118	148	133	140	107	102	75	86	70
Percentage of referrals withdrawn or otherwise disposed	36%	41%	40%	41%	35%	32%	22%	24%	19%

Source: Civil Judicial Statistics 1928–36.

Newbolt's court appears more resourceful in encouraging parties to resolve matters before trial thus saving the time and costs of a court hearing. Such a difference in approach may represent the dividing line between an activist and a passive approach to case management.

[115] Newbolt (n 19) 438–439.

Table T.4.2.

If we hypothesise the analysis of the judicial statistics, court records and clerks diaries we may find the following:

Period	Referrals	Hypothetical Average percentile	Hypothetical Number of cases case managed
1919–1938	7,683	25%	1,921
1947–1970	13,932	25%	3,483
1919–1970	21,615	25%	5,404

Source: Judicial Statistics 1919–70 as calculated in Appendix C.5 Spreadsheet.[116]

These statistics present an extraordinary claim and discovery which may help to explain why the procedure in the Court was unique and, in many respects, ahead of its time. A lead many of us who practised in the Officials Referee's Court can happily attest to and acknowledge the outstanding contribution they made to civil justice. It is no surprise therefore that the TCC today continues in the footsteps of Newbolt and others whose judges have reached the highest places in the judicial hierarchy.

[116] See also: ch 5 of M Reynolds, *Caseflow Management: A Rudimentary Referee Process, 1919–70* (London School of Economics, Thesis, 2008) 208.

4

Sir Brett Cloutman: The Last VC of the Great War

SIR PETER COULSON

I. Introduction

His full title was His Honour Sir Brett MacKay Cloutman VC, MC, QC. My researches have not thrown up anyone else with that incredible set of decorations and appointments. He was the Senior Official Referee between 1954 and 1963, and was by all accounts a distinguished and kindly man, in an age when kindness was not perhaps the typical attribute of a judge. In the photograph that used to hang on the fourth floor of St Dunstan's House, and now adorns the chambers of Fraser J in the Rolls Building, he looks up with a smiling and open face, his arm round his dog. But he is not wearing judge's robes or a barrister's pin-stripe: he is in military uniform. And that, perhaps, gives the main clue to the formative experiences of his life because, in 1918, serving in France with the Royal Engineers, Brett Cloutman won the very last Victoria Cross awarded in the First World War.

II. Early Life and the Outbreak of War

Born in Muswell Hill, in North London, on 7 November 1891, he was the son of Alfred and Clarissa Jane. His father had begun his working life as a junior assistant at the furniture company, Maples, but went on to become Governing Director, and later Life Governor, of the firm. Cloutman had two elder brothers: Wolfred, the brother to whom he was closest, had been born the previous year, in 1890. A few years later, the family moved out to Hemel Hempstead in Hertfordshire and Cloutman was educated at Berkhamstead School (where he played the clarinet in the school orchestra), and then Bishop's Stortford College. Both schools were relatively close to home. He then went to London University, where he read modern languages, and where he was a member of the Officer's Training Corps, as part of the Royal Engineers contingent.

In 1911, having left university, he worked as a house furnisher for Maples and lived in Crouch End, the part of North London to which his parents had returned. It appears that at that point, he was unsure what he wanted to do with his life. Of course, in August 1914, he may have felt that destiny had taken that decision out of his hands. Within a month, he had enlisted as a Rifleman in the 12th Battalion, London Regiment. Incredibly, he was originally refused a commission because of his poor eyesight. He had reached the rank of Lance-Corporal before the authorities relented, and he was commissioned as a lieutenant into the Kent (Fortress) Royal Engineers on 3 March 1915. By July he had been promoted to captain.

Wolfred had also joined the Royal Engineers as a lieutenant. He went up the line sometime in the spring of 1915 when the new recruits who had enlisted in the summer of 1914 were pushed into a series of bloody and unsuccessful encounters with the Germans, such as Neuve Chappelle and, later in the year, Loos. The waste was such that Rudyard Kipling's only son, John (who had also been refused a commission in a number of regiments because of his bad eyesight), was killed within hours of disembarking from the train that had brought him to the Front. Wolfred came through the spring battles unscathed but, on 21 August 1915, he died from gas poisoning near Albert. It appears that he had gone out to try and rescue a sergeant who had become trapped in a mining operation that had gone wrong. Wolfred was just 25 years old.

Between 1916 and 1918, Cloutman also served principally on the Western Front, where the attrition rate, particularly for young officers, was so appallingly high. It must have been something of a respite when, on leave in 1916, he married Margaret Hunter. Although she was from Chiswick, the couple decided to make North London their home. All too soon, Cloutman was back on the Western Front. Somehow, he survived the grim attrititional battles of 1917, taking an active part in the attacks at Vimy Ridge and Passchendaele. He was also involved in the German Spring offensive of 1918, which broke through the Line in many places, came within a few miles of Amiens, and almost broke through to the sea.

III. The Military Cross

By the autumn of 1918, the tide of war was turning in favour of the Allies. The German break-out of the spring had led to a serious over-stretching of their resources. From early August they were chased back north-eastwards through the old battlefields of the Somme, and further back still, until the Third Army was on the verge of pushing the Germans out of France altogether. But there remained a large number of formidable obstacles right across the north-eastern corner of France, behind which the Germans were able to create a series of strong defensive positions.

Major Cloutman (as by then he was) was closely involved in those last days. On 30 September 1918, he undertook a personal reconnaissance of the Canal d' Escaut at Banteux, to investigate the possibility of bridging it. He went alone, deliberately leaving his men under cover. He was under heavy machine gun fire throughout. He made the necessary observations and then returned to his men. His 'conspicuous gallantry' earned him the Military Cross. But that was only a rehearsal for the main event.

IV. The Victoria Cross

Just over a month later, on 4 November 1918, there began the second battle of the Sambre, when the allies attacked on a 30-mile front, from Valenciennes to just north of Oisy. It was to be the last major offensive action of the war. One obstacle was the Sambre canal near Ors, where Wilfred Owen was killed on 4 November as he endeavoured to get his men across the water in the teeth of shells and machine gun fire. And another was the River Sambre itself, where the Germans lay on the far bank, having destroyed all the bridges across the river.

All the bridges but one. At Pont-sur-Sambre, the Quartes Bridge, which was a single span girder bridge on stone abutments, had been wired for demolition but had not been destroyed. On 6 November, Major Cloutman saw the charges and their leads, and realised that, if he could cut the leads, the bridge could be saved and used to get a large part of the Third Army across the river. Again, leaving his men under cover, he went forward alone, and, under persistent machine-gun fire, jumped into the freezing river and swam under the bridge. Not only was he at risk from the machine guns, but of course the charges could have been detonated at any time. Once under the bridge, he was able to cut the leads from the charges, and then swim back, in water described by the citation as 'swept by shell and machine-gun fire'. Miraculously, he arrived back unscathed.

Cloutman was, in that way so typical of the young officers of his generation, enduringly modest about his exploit. He observed in the 59 Field Company War Diary that, after nightfall, the Germans were able to set fresh charges and blow up the bridge. He hinted that his earlier efforts had all been rather academic. But, as he was doubtless to realise when he became an Official Referee, the devil was in the detail: the charges laid by the Germans would have destroyed the abutments as well as the bridge itself, whilst the subsequent damage they caused was relatively easy to make good because the abutments were undamaged. Their survival meant that the engineers had the bridge working again relatively quickly, and the advance continued. Just a week later, the Armistice was signed and the war was over.

© National Portrait Gallery, London.

It was for this extraordinary exploit that Cloutman won the last Victoria Cross awarded during the Great War. He was promoted to Lieutenant-Colonel. His VC was gazetted on 31 January 1919 (with the MC being gazetted the following day). It was presented to him by King George V at an investiture on 13 February the same year. The medal can now be found in the Royal Engineers Museum in Chatham, Kent where it is displayed with the numerous other medals Cloutman was awarded across two World Wars. What is more, the Quartes Bridge over the River Sambre, its abutments still intact, remains in use to this day.

V. The Bar

After the War, Cloutman briefly returned to work at Maples before deciding he was going to be a barrister. He joined Gray's Inn and was called to the Bar in 1926. The only record relating to him in the Pension Minute book was the Inn's refusal, in December 1925, to exempt him from four terms of dining due to his war service. Even allowing for the dangers of hindsight, that seems an astonishingly mean-spirited response to his request: in the Twenties, it was a common complaint by those who had served in the War that those who had not done so made no allowances for what they had experienced. Siegfried Sassoon memorably said that he vehemently wished that the fat, smug civilians who had stayed behind were themselves subjected to the horrors of the Front. Cloutman would have been quite justified in feeling the same way.

Cloutman joined chambers at 1, Garden Court. He built up a varied practice, mainly on the Western Circuit, and mainly in civil work. Like many young barristers, he wrote a book to encourage solicitors to instruct him in a particular field of practice. *The Law Relating to Authors and Publishers* was published in 1927. Although rather stodgy in style, it is, at 145 pages, a pretty brisk treatment of this complex area of the law. Perhaps Cloutman came to realise that it might have been a bit too brisk: there was a second edition two years later which was more than twice as long. It is difficult to gauge the success or otherwise of the book, although it should be noted that any eager reader of the work had to wait another 20 years for the third and final edition.

Extensive research has failed to turn up any reported case in which Cloutman appeared between 1926 and 1939. Unlike today, when the judgments of any judge are immediately available on the internet, usually with a neutral citation number, and counsel widely advertise their appearances in even the most mundane case, in those days only a tiny proportion of cases were reported. So we cannot hold it against him that his name cannot be found in the Law Reports. It is not perhaps too unfair to summarise his career at the Bar to say that, whilst his practice cannot have been of the highest order, there is no reason to suppose that it was not entirely satisfactory.

By 1935, as part of what appears to be an attempt to live in every part of North London, he was living with Margaret in Bow Lane, in Finchley. They had two daughters, Mary and Jill.

VI. The Second World War

When war was declared in 1939, Cloutman joined up with the Royal Engineers again. Although he was by then 48, it seems that either he or the powers that be, or more likely both, concluded that a desk job was not for him. He once more saw active service overseas, including Syria, and Egypt. He was Chief Engineer in the Levant Engineer Battalion. As 1943 turned into 1944, he was in Italy, part of the slow advance north following the Italian surrender. It must have reminded Cloutman uncomfortably of the slog of the Western Front; even the weather was bad that winter. He was mentioned in despatches (*London Gazette* 4 January 1944) as a result of his 'gallant and distinguished services' in the Middle East.

In all Cloutman was awarded four medals in the First War and five in the Second, his War Medal 1939–1945 decorated with the oakleaf to reflect his mention in despatches. He was on any view an astonishingly brave man.

Furthermore, it might be said that the Royal Engineers have done rather better in honouring his memory than the law has so far managed. Tony Harking, who was the Under-Treasurer of Gray's Inn from 2015 to 2022, had previously commanded the Royal School of Military Engineering. He was delighted to tell me that the main headquarters building of the part of the School in Minley, in Surrey, is named after Cloutman. Appropriately, that is where they teach combat engineering, including building demolitions.

VII. Subsequent Legal Career

Cloutman returned to civilian life and even took silk in 1946. But he obviously felt that, after all he had seen and done, his heart was no longer in the life of a barrister. So the following year, he became the Senior Chairman of the War Pensions Tribunal. It was an obvious fit for him; I can only imagine – and hope – that the claimants who appeared in front of him were treated with all possible generosity.

In 1948, he was appointed as an Official Referee. This was reflected on the title page of the third edition of his book, where he is referred to as 'His Honour Brett Cloutman VC MC KC'.

Cloutman became one of four Official Referees: the others were Sir Tom Eastham (the Senior Official Referee), Sir Ronald Bosanquet, and Lionel Leach, who was appointed at the same time as Cloutman.

Since 1900, the Official Referees had worked on the third floor of the West Wing of the Royal Courts of Justice. It was known as the Official Referee's Corridor and, apart from an unsuccessful foray to Victory House on Kingsway in the mid-1960's, it was where the Official Referees stayed until 1988, when they moved to St. Dunstan's House on Fetter Lane. The Corridor always had a cozy, calm atmosphere that stood in contrast to other parts of the RCJ, but it was not easy to find if you had not been there before and it was not easy to access: the choice was a long climb up three flights of stairs or a very rickety lift.

What sort of work would Cloutman have been doing in that quiet backwater of the RCJ? The statistics show that he would have done somewhere between 50 and 75 trials each year, although most such trials would not have extended beyond two or three days. As to the specifics, regrettably none of his notebooks from this period survive. However, the notebooks of his colleague, Sir Tom Eastham have survived in the National Archives. They show that, in addition to the typical fare of building defects and disputed final accounts, Cloutman would have been undertaking assessments of damages and referrals from the War Damages Commission, and deciding claims for repairs to properties and cars, disputes over commissions and fees, landlord and tenant disputes (particularly dilapidation claims), claims on guarantees, and claims arising out of the termination of building contracts.

VIII. Senior Official Referee

In 1954, after lengthy terms of service, both Sir Ronald Bosanquet and Sir Tom Eastham retired, and Cloutman became the Senior Official Referee. Although it appears to have been delayed until the Queen's Birthday Honours of 1957, he received the customary knighthood that, in those days, went with the position.

In those days, before the Building Law Reports and the Construction Law Reports, it was rare for the decisions of Official Referees to be reported, and it is thus difficult to find a judgment of Sir Brett Cloutman in the law reports. However, one exception is the case of *Collins v Flynn*,[1] in which, in a careful and elegantly reserved judgment, he ruled that a tenant's repairing covenant did not render him liable for failing to undertake extensive foundation and rebuilding work, because such work was necessitated by an inherent defect in the building.

An interesting footnote is that the successful tenant in that case was represented by a thrusting junior called Donald Keating, after whom the leading construction set of chambers is named. What is more, Donald's advocacy must have been good because, in the subsequent decision in *Ravenseft Properties v Davstone (Holdings) Ltd*, Forbes J said that Cloutman had misdirected himself and that *Collins* was therefore of 'doubtful' authority.[2]

Frustratingly, although it appears that some of the notebooks of Sir Walker Kelly Carter QC (who was an Official Referee between 1954 and 1971) have found their way into the National Archives, none of Sir Brett Cloutman's notebooks for this period have survived.

What was he like to appear in front of? Incredibly, we know. Anthony Butcher KC, the doyen of the Construction Bar, can recall appearing before Sir Brett when he was the Senior Official Referee, and remembers it as something of an anodyne experience. I suppose that if you had spent your youth being shot and shelled at, building defects are unlikely to get the pulses racing. At least he did not shout.

Inexplicably, given the distinguished nature of his military record and his other achievements (amongst other things, he was a member of the Athenaeum), he was never elected to the Bench at Gray's Inn. It might be said that, until recently, Gray's had a poor record of electing circuit judges to the Bench, and the snobbery about construction work prevalent in those days would also have worked against him.

[1] [1963] 2 All ER 1068.
[2] [1978] EWHC QB 1.

IX. Retirement and Death

The year before he retired, on 17 July 1962, Sir Brett Cloutman attended a Garden Party at Buckingham Palace for all the surviving recipients of the VC. Following his retirement in 1963, he lived quietly in a flat in Highgate (in the same block as the actress Margaret Rutherford), although it appears that the lure of the Official Referees remained reasonably strong. He continued to sit from time to time in retirement, and there is a notebook of his in the National Archives dating from 1966. It appears that on 26 July 1966, Cloutman sat on the case of *Vincent Murphy & Co Ltd v South Eastern Joinery Works (1950) Ltd* which he described as 'a claim as to the price of building materials'. The outcome of this less-than-glamorous litigation is not recorded. Perhaps it settled.

Sir Brett Cloutman VC, MC, QC died on 15 August 1971. His obituary notice appeared in *The Daily Telegraph* two days later. He was cremated in Golders Green Crematorium. His name is on the Memorial Plaque that records the 14 – yes, 14 – recipients of the Victoria Cross who were cremated there. There is also a memorial stone to Cloutman at the Hornsey War Memorial.

Reproduced with kind permission of Steve Lee.

But, even after so many years, the Western Front laid a final claim to Cloutman: at his request, his ashes were interred at Wolfred's grave at the leafy Norfolk Cemetery, at Bercordel-Becourt, two miles east of Albert. So, can I recommend that, the next time you are in France, tearing down the A1 motorway to Paris and beyond, you try and find time to get off at junction 13.1, drive across the Somme countryside, where almost every village name is itself a monument to heroism and futility, and seek out the small Norfolk Cemetery? Like every cemetery maintained by the Commonwealth War Graves Commission in that part of France, it is very beautiful and unbearably moving.

A distinguished part of the story of the TCC lies buried there.

5

The Later Official Referees and Judges of the Technology and Construction Court

SIR PETER COULSON (WITH DAVID SAWTELL)

I. Introduction

The purpose of this chapter is to describe the later Official Referees and judges of the Technology and Construction Court in London: to identify briefly their legal careers; the notable cases with which they were involved (either as barristers or judges); and to give at least some flavour of what they were like as a judicial tribunal. That last element explains how far back in time I have been able to go. Sir Walker Kelly Carter QC served as an Official Referee between 1954 and 1971. He is the first Official Referee that senior members of the Construction Bar can recall, so our historical review starts with him.

I should at the outset acknowledge all the assistance that I have received in producing this chapter from, amongst others, Sir Patrick Garland, John Uff KC, John Blackburn KC, Phillip Boulding KC (whose anecdote about Judge Fox-Andrews wins the prize for the best true story), Marcus Taverner KC and Rosemary Jackson KC. Particular thanks must go to Richard Fernyhough KC, Richard Wilmot-Smith KC and Paul Darling KC for their fair and affectionate tributes, many of which I have cited below. The decision as to what material to use and what not was entirely mine, and apologies are due to anyone whose anecdotes missed the cut.

This is a story with four parts: (II) the steady growth in the reputation of the Court from the late 1950's to the 1980's; (III) the period in the 1990's, remembered as something of a golden age for the new TCC; (IV) an extremely difficult time at the end of the 1990's and at the start of this new century; and (V) the complete turnaround in the fortunes of the court, thanks to a number of recently retired senior judges. But it is perhaps appropriate to start with an entirely fictional Official Referee.

Henry Cecil published *Brothers In Law* in 1955.[1] Between pages 25 and 39 there was an extended scene in which the young barrister hero Roger Thursby is left to fend for himself in front of an Official Referee called Sir Hugo Cramp. By the time of the film, two years later, the scene had been re-written, although most of the humour still comes from the fact that Thursby, played by Ian Carmichael, does not have a clue what he is doing. The Official Referee, on the other hand, most certainly does: nicely underplayed by John Welsh, the Official Referee ignores Carmichael's stunned silences and gaping mouth, and conducts a lengthy debate with himself about the finer points of abatement and set-off. One important thing, however, is retained from the book. When the judge discovers that there are over 50 items in dispute, and no Scott Schedule, he expresses his surprise and annoyance with a series of 'tut tuts' and informs the parties that he will rise, and when he comes back in an hour he expects to be told that the case had settled.

The scene demonstrates that by the late 1950s, Official Referees had a reputation for knowing the law. It also demonstrates that, even then, settlement was the wisest option.

II. The Steady Growth in Reputation: 1960–1985

A. Sir Walker Kelly Carter QC 1954–1971

Sir Walker Kelly Carter was born on 7 July 1899, the son of Walter Carter CBE and Annie Carter. He attended Repton School before going up to Sidney Sussex College, Cambridge. He was called to the Bar in 1924 by Inner Temple; he became a Bencher in 1965. He was a member of the Reform Club.

He took silk in 1951. He served as Chairman of the East Midlands Agricultural Land Tribunal from 1948 to 1954. Between 1964 and 1971, he sat as Chairman of the Criminal Injuries Compensation Board. He also sat as the Chairman for Quarter Sessions for Parts of Lindsey in 1945–1967, and for Parts of Kesteven in 1961–1967. He retired as Senior Official Referee in 1971.

He died on 29 March 1985.

He appeared as junior counsel in the case of *R v Grant*, which concerned the admissibility of the evidence by one prisoner against another jointly charged with the same offence.[2]

Judge Kelly Carter's Minute Books are preserved in the National Archives. Sadly, all of his decisions are unreported.

Judge Kelly Carter practised on the Midland Circuit and really wanted to be appointed to a rural county court on that circuit. Instead, as he once remarked to Geoffrey Lane, a friend who went on to be Lord Chief Justice, 'they gave me short

[1] H Cecil, *Brothers in Law* (Michael Joseph, 1955).
[2] [1944] 2 All ER 311.

trousers and a whistle'. Sir Patrick Garland recalls that, in defects or dilapidations cases, instead of ploughing through the interminable detail, Judge Kelly Carter would say to counsel for the plaintiff: 'Let's try a couple of specimen issues so I can get the flavour of the case.' As Patrick remarked, 'you can see where that led …'.

B. Percy Lamb QC 1959–1969

Percy Lamb was born on 26 September 1896, the son of Thomas Lamb and Bertha (née Poole).

He was Chancellor of the Diocese of Rochester from 1954 to 1971. He was Recorder of Faversham from 1948 to 1950, and Recorder of Rochester from 1950 to 1959. He was the first, and only, Chairman of the Inns of Court Executive Council from 1962 to 1967. He was a Commissioner of Assize on the Oxford Circuit in 1965 and the Midland Circuit in 1966.

Percy Lamb was called to the Bar by Gray's Inn in 1923, becoming a Bencher in 1947. He took silk in 1949. Judge Lamb was the Treasurer of Gray's Inn in 1962 when, amongst others, he called Malcolm (later Lord Justice) Pill to the Bar.

He was co-author of *The Law of Town and Country Planning* (1950), *A Guide to Rating Practice and Procedure* (1951; 2nd edn, 1956; 3rd edn, 1963); and *Lamb's Encyclopædia of Housing* (1957).

He died on 28 October 1973.

Judge Lamb decided the important landlord and tenant case of *Silvester v Ostrowska*.[3] He held that the reference to a non-existence covenant in a notice given under section 146 of the Law of Property Act 1925 did not destroy its efficacy. He was also the first instance judge in *Harrison v Wells*, which concerned tenancy by estoppel.[4] His judgment was overturned by the Court of Appeal.[5] The Court of Appeal's decision was later considered to be wrongly decided *per incuriam* by Lord Denning MR in *Industrial Properties (Barton Hill) Ltd v Associated Electrical Industries Ltd*:[6] contrary to the decision of Judge Lamb and the Court of Appeal's decision in *Harrison v Wells*, it was held that the rule that a lessee was estopped during the currency of the lease from disputing his lessor's title continued to operate after the expiry of the lease, unless after the termination of the lessee's possession a claim was made against him by title paramount in respect of some part of the period of the lease.

Judge Lamb was apparently the judge in *Peak v McKinney*, although he is, perhaps understandably, not referred to by name in the law report.[7] In that case, McKinney, as nominated sub-contractors, carried out defective piling which required remedial works that took six weeks to complete. However, the overall

[3] [1959] 3 All ER 642.
[4] [1966] 2 All ER 171.
[5] [1967] 1 QB 263.
[6] [1977] QB 50.
[7] (1976) 1 BLR 111.

delay to the project as a whole was 58 weeks because of Liverpool Corporation's delay in deciding what should be done about the problem. Peak claimed the entirety of the 58-week delay against McKinney, a claim upheld by Judge Lamb, who concluded that it was reasonable in all the circumstances that work was suspended for 58 weeks in all.

McKinney appealed, but their principal difficulty was that Judge Lamb's conclusion was a matter of fact and in those days there could be no appeal from an Official Referee on a finding of fact. However, the Court of Appeal said that the rule did not extend as far as a conclusion which was not based on any evidence or upon a view of the facts which could not reasonably be entertained. They concluded that Judge Lamb's conclusion was 'quite insupportable' and the appeal was allowed.

It appears that this was only one of a number of decisions in which it was felt that Judge Lamb may not have reached the right conclusion. Indeed, in Official Referee terms at least, I am told that he was the starting point for the old joke: 'My Lord, this is an appeal from Judge Lamb, sitting as an Official Referee, but there are other grounds …'.

C. Sir Norman Richards QC 1963–1977

Norman Richards was born on 29 December 1905, the son of LM Richards and Gertrude Richards. He was educated at Charterhouse and at Trinity College, Cambridge. During the Second World War, he was mentioned in despatches twice, and was awarded an OBE. He was called to the Bar by Inner Temple in 1928; he became Master of the Bench in 1961. He took silk in 1955.

He was Recorder of Merthyr Tydfil from 1960 to 1963, and was Deputy Chairman of the Middlesex Assizes from 1962 to 1965. He was President of Her Majesty's Council of Circuit Judges in 1973.

He was a member of Brooks's, Portland, and the MCC. He died on 29 December 1977.

His decision in *Hollebone v Midhurst and Fernhurst Builders Ltd*,[8] where he determined that the cost of reinstatement was the appropriate measure of damages despite being more than the difference in value before and after the fire that caused the damage, is an important decision on the correct approach to damages for remediation.

He is described as 'sometimes an irascible judge' by Richard Fernyhough KC. But he remembers that, if counsel settled a case before lunch on the first day, they were always rewarded with a glass of sherry.

John Blackburn KC recalls that Judge Richards was an excellent lawyer but agrees with Richard that he could be somewhat intimidating to young counsel. For John, this pattern reached its nadir when he was doing a case against Roger Toulson (as he then was). John's version of the expert's report was favourable to his client,

[8] [1968] 1 Lloyd's Rep 38.

but, unbeknownst to him, a very different version had been sent to the other side which was much more critical. Every young barrister's worst nightmare came true when John referred to his version of the report, and Roger politely explained to Judge Richards that there was another, rather different version. Judge Richards was not impressed but, on the other hand, he patiently heard out John's valiant attempt to win the case on the basis of an unhelpful report he had never seen. Although that attempt was to no avail, John recalls that, after that, his lack of confidence in those matters listed before Judge Richards fell away and he found appearing before him a pleasure. When they cannot get any worse, things usually get better.

D. Sir William Stabb QC 1969–1985

William Stabb was born on 6 October 1913, son of Sir Newton Stabb OBE and Lady EM Stabb. He was educated at Rugby and at University College, Oxford. He was called to the Bar in 1936 by Inner Temple, and became Master of the Bench in 1964 and Treasurer in 1985. He took silk in 1968.

He was Junior Counsel to the Ministry of Labour in 1960 and Prosecuting Counsel to the Board of Trade from 1962 to 1968. He served as Deputy Chairman from 1961 to 1969, and then as Chairman from 1969 to 1971, of the Bedfordshire Quarter Sessions.

Judge Stabb was Senior Official Referee from 1978 to 1985. He died on 19 December 2003.

Judge Stabb was the first instance judge in *Sutcliffe v Thackrah*.[9] The House of Lords held that, in issuing interim certificates an architect did not, apart from specific agreement, act as an arbitrator between the parties; but that he was under a duty to act fairly in making his valuation and was liable to an action in negligence at the suit of the building owner; Judge Stabb's judgment was restored. The notorious rule in *Chambers v Goldthorpe* was therefore overruled.[10]

Judge Stabb was the first Official Referee that many of us first appeared in front of 40 years ago. He was kindly and patient with nervous, gibbering young barristers and, if he thought a junior member of the Bar showed promise, he would ring their Head of Chambers to say so. A small thing, perhaps, but remembering the profound effect it had on me all those years ago, it is something I try and do to this day.

He always tried to make junior barristers feel at home in his court. At the end of those big multi-party directions hearings in the 70's and 80's that so often took place in the large but ill-lit court in Alexander House, on Kingsway, the only thing the junior had to do was to stand up and ask for a certificate for two counsel. Judge Stabb would peer into the gloaming and say: 'Well, Mr Coulson, I had no idea I had the benefit of your wise counsel this afternoon, but now that I know,

[9] [1974] AC 727.
[10] [1901] 1 KB 624.

of course you can have the certificate for which you ask.' I did not flatter myself; he said it to all of us.

Richard Fernyhough KC also regarded Judge Stabb – uniformly known as 'Willy' – as 'the doyen of the OR's and a wonderful judge'. Richard remembers his clever stratagem to keep counsel to the point 'by making a manuscript note using a short, fat fountain pen and going at a speed which an arthritic snail would have been proud of. That gave counsel plenty of time to prepare his next question and shortened the evidence significantly.'

Judge Stabb died in 2004. His originality shone out even then. He had a memorial service with a magician. And at the end of his funeral service, in his home village of King's Langley in Hertfordshire, the congregation was told to stay in their seats until the organ voluntary had finished. 'You will then applaud', we were instructed. 'It is what Sir William always did.'

E. Edgar Fay QC 1971–1980

Edgar Fay was born on 8 October 1908 and was educated at Pembroke College, Cambridge. He was called to the Bar in 1932 and joined the Western Circuit in 1934. Seventy-four years later, in October 2008, when he was a hundred years old, he accepted life membership of the Western Circuit 'with optimism'.

His father, Sir Sam Fay, was managing director of the Great Central Railway. Judge Fay joined 3 Paper Buildings because it was the leading chambers for railway law and he spent much of his time at the Bar appearing before the Railway Rates Tribunal and Transport Tribunal, usually seeking fare increases on behalf of railway companies.

In 1959, he was asked by the Minister of Aviation to conduct an independent review into the Munich air crash which killed eight of the all-conquering Manchester United side known as 'the Busby Babes'. The West German inquiry had blamed the aircraft's captain and, although Fay did not go that far, he did conclude that the captain had not done enough to satisfy himself that the plane was free of ice. However, in 1968, Fay was invited to reopen his enquiry when it was discovered that the German investigation had supressed evidence from an official who had inspected the wings immediately after the crash and seen no ice upon them. His subsequent report in June 1969 dealt in detail with this suppression of evidence, and it upset the West German Government a good deal. Sadly, the captain was never fully exonerated.

He was head of chambers at 3 Paper Buildings from 1956 to 1971, when he became a judge. In 1974, he was also asked to conduct an enquiry into the collapse of the Crown Agents in 1974 with debts of £212 million. Judge Fay's damning 203-page report, published in 1977, found that the Crown Agents had embarked on a seven-year spending spree of reckless lending without qualified staff. He certainly did not mince his words: 'catastrophe', he said was 'not too strong a word for the Crown Agent's risk-taking, incompetence, folly and euphoria'.

Judge Fay was a diligent Official Referee who was described as having a 'radar-like intellect'. He was not, however, known for his sense of humour. The only recorded occasion when he laughed openly in court was during a lengthy opening of a very dull case by Bruce Mauleverer. The case was being heard in Alexander House in Kingsway in the summer. It was very hot and stuffy, so some of the windows had been opened. Judge Fay was concerned that Brian Knight, counsel for one of the many defendants, was sitting by an open window with the traffic rumbling by. The judge said: 'Mr Knight, you would be able to hear much more of what Mr Mauleverer is saying if you close the window.' Brian Knight immediately retorted: 'If your Honour is offering me a choice between hearing what Mr Mauleverer is saying or staying cool, I will respectfully opt to keep the window open.' Apparently Judge Fay broke with tradition and hooted with laughter.

He once told John Uff KC that one of his pet hates was counsel saying to him 'Your Honour could not find that …' or 'Your Honour could not conclude that …'. Apparently, Judge Fay used to think to himself: 'Oh, couldn't I? You just watch!'

Following his retirement, he wrote an extremely useful book entitled *Official Referees' Business*, first published in 1983, with a second edition in 1988. He became a busy and popular arbitrator. He died on 14 November 2009, aged 101.

F. Lewis Hawser QC 1978–1990

(Cyril) Lewis Hawser was born on 5 October 1916, the son of Abraham and Sarah Hawser. He died on 25 July 1990. He was educated at Cardiff High School before going up to Balliol College, Oxford. He was called to the Bar in 1953 and took silk in 1959. He was made a Bencher of Inner Temple in 1966, and became Treasurer in 1987. He was Recorder of Salisbury from 1967 to 1969, and Recorder of Portsmouth from 1969 to 1971; he was a Recorder of the Crown Court from 1972 to 1978. He was Senior Official Referee from 1985 to 1990.

HHJ Lewis Hawser QC, together with Sir William Stabb QC and Edgar Fay QC, was one of a group of judges in the 1970s and early 1980s who helped to build up the reputation of the Official Referees' Court.[11] A number of his decisions were reported, including *Twins Transport Ltd v Patrick & Brocklehurst (trading as H. V. & C. Patrick Estates Developers)* on the effect of an exclusion clause,[12] *Bramall & Ogden Ltd v Sheffield City Council* on whether leave to appeal should be granted in respect of an arbitrator's award under the Arbitration Act 1979,[13] and *Secretary of State for the Environment v Essex Goodman & Suggitt* on the accrual of the cause of action against a surveyor.[14]

[11] *Fenice Investments Inc v Jerram Falkus Construction Ltd* [2009] EWHC 3272 (TCC) at [33] per Coulson J (as he then was).

[12] (1983) 4 ConLR 117.

[13] (1983) 1 ConLR 30.

[14] [1986] 1 WLR 1432.

Such was his reputation at the Bar that it was an enduring mystery why Judge Hawser never made the High Court Bench. Indeed, his under-appointment was so obvious that there was even a story about it in *Private Eye* (a publication not known for its interest in the ORs). Some said it was because he was a conscientious objector during the war; others that it was as a result of anti-Semitism; some even suggested that it was because his client got a shorter sentence then many of the others at the end of the Great Train Robbery trial. But the High Court Bench's loss was definitely the TCC's gain.

Richard Fernyhough KC recalls one occasion when a silk from Wales was seeking to set aside an arbitral award. Lord Diplock had recently said that such applications should not exceed half an hour so, after half an hour, with the Welsh silk only just getting started, he apologised for overrunning his allotted time. The judge was puzzled. Once it was explained to him what Lord Diplock had said, Judge Hawser told the silk that 'we are not all masters of the common law like Lord Diplock, so take as long as you need'.

When he became the Senior Official Referee following the retirement of Sir William Stabb, Judge Hawser became the first person to occupy that position not to be offered a knighthood. It appears that the Establishment's mysterious vindictiveness even extended to that humiliation, a fact remarked on at his memorial service. To make matters worse, this meant the end of the convention whereby the Senior Official Referee received a knighthood, a justifiable disappointment to his successor, Judge Newey.

There were perhaps two special features of Judge Hawser's time as an Official Referee. One was his kindness to youngsters. The other was that he was almost always accompanied by his genial wife who sat unobtrusively, but concentrating hard, throughout any hearing. You never knew whether to make your submissions to him or to her.

G. John Newey QC 1980–1993

John Newey was born on 20 October 1923. He was educated at Dudley Grammar School and Ellesmere College, before going up to Queens' College, Cambridge. He was called to the Bar by Middle Temple in 1948, where he became a Bencher in 1977. He held numerous legal and judicial posts.

As a junior, John Newey was standing counsel to the Post Office which meant that he was involved in some of the great cases of the 1960s, including those that brought about the end of Pirate Radio. In silk, he did a good deal of planning work.

He died on 19 May 1994.

A number of Judge Newey's decisions have been reported. One of the most significant might well be *Perry v Tendring DC, Thurbon v Tendring DC*.[15] In that case, he held that there is no claim against a builder for breach of a statutory duty

[15] (1984) 30 BLR 118.

for failure to comply with the building regulations. This became one limb of the decision of the House of Lords in *Murphy v Brentwood* when the principle in *Anns v Merton* was finally overturned.[16]

Without any question, the most famous case that Judge Newey ever tried, at least on an anecdotal basis, involved not one, not two, but three unusual interventions by Paul Darling KC (as he then was not). Whilst being led by Richard Fernyhough KC, Paul became agitated during Richard's cross examination of a witness. He whirled his arms about so emphatically that he knocked Richard's wig and his glasses off his head, which then fell onto a jug a water which spilled all over Richard's papers. The late, great John Slater, who was on the other side, told the judge that it appeared that Mr Fernyhough had been assaulted by his junior. Subsequently Richard got his own back by calling the same Paul Darling as a witness, to seek to show that an alleged oral agreement as to quantum had been reached by experts outside the Court during an adjournment. Paul remains one of the very few members of the Construction Bar to have given evidence in the courts in which he regularly appears. Happily, his evidence was not disbelieved.

And still Paul was not done. Another witness had to be called and Judge Newey's wonderful usher, Betty, had disappeared. As the nearest junior to the witness box, Paul was required to swear the witness in. Judge Newey remarked: 'Mr Darling has been of the greatest help to the court: Counsel, Witness and now Usher!'

Rosemary Jackson KC recalls oversleeping and rushing to court, where she was appearing in front of Judge Newey. Everyone was white-faced and worried because they thought she had been involved in a train crash that had occurred that morning. There was a chilly atmosphere when she told the truth. But, she said, Judge Newey remained his usual polite self, simply wringing his hands and advising her to get a new alarm clock. She said she was never late for court again.

Judge Newey's son, Guy, is of course now Lord Justice Newey. In *Mears Ltd v Costplan Services (South East) Ltd*, I sat with him in a case about the precise definition of practical completion, often an important issue in building cases because of the limitation position.[17] I wrote the lead judgment and identified two decisions of his father's that were both bang on point and indisputably correct (see [65] and [75]). I think Guy took particular pleasure in agreeing with my judgment in that case.

H. David Smout QC 1983–1987

David Smout was born on 17 December 1923, son of Sir Arthur Smout and Hilda Smout (*née* Follows). He attended the Leys School, before going up to Clare College, Cambridge, and reading for his LLM at Birmingham University. He was

[16] *Anns v Merton* [1978] AC 728; *Murphy v Brentwood District Council* [1991] 1 AC 398. The decision in *Murphy* is discussed in ch 13 in this volume.

[17] [2019] EWCA Civ 502, [2019] 4 WLR 55.

called to the Ontario Bar in 1949, and was a lecturer at Osgoode Hall Law School in Toronto from 1949 to 1953. He was called to the English Bar by Gray's Inn in 1953. He took silk in 1975. He was a member of the Garrick Club.

David Smout's practice was originally in Canada. He was junior counsel for the respondent in *Ponoka Kalmar Oils Limited v OF Wakefield Co.*,[18] the last Canadian case to go to the Privy Council. He was paid the princely sum of 10 guineas for his efforts.

In practice, he specialised in contractual disputes, and was one of the editors of *Chitty on Contracts.*

When he was appointed as an Official Referee, Judge Smout was an unknown quantity but, as Richard Wilmot Smith KC rightly recalls, it did not take long before the Bar came to realise that he was a proper lawyer, well at home with construction disputes, who quickly evolved into 'something special'. He was kind, lucid, practical, hard-working, and an effortless lawyer. His analysis was always crisp, clear and succinct. As Richard put it: 'We liked him.'

He was also quietly efficient. In *Kimbell v Herts DC*,[19] he managed the case, at a time of long lists on the Official Referees' corridor, to a trial just 17 months after the case had started. He heard the case over seven days, when many thought it would take two or three times that long. The last day of the trial was 31 July and his judgment was handed down on 21 August. That judgment is a simple model of its kind. He addressed the facts, the evidence, the relevant citations, quantum and contribution. All in eight pages.

As an Official Referee, Judge Smout dealt with a number of important cases, including *Design 5 v Keniston Housing Association Ltd* (on the relevance of a claimant's insurance arrangements to a defence of no loss),[20] and *Kensington and Chelsea and Westminster Area Health Authority v Wettern Composites Ltd* (on apportionment of damages).[21]

However, he did not escape the more mundane aspects of work as an Official Referee. *Lovell v Penrose* was a classic building dispute, about an extension to a smart house in Surrey, with the contractor wanting the final payment due on his account, and the householder cross-claiming for defects. The dispute was worth just £20,000 and there was a long Scott Schedule.

Marcus Taverner KC, for whom this was his first ever building case, had to cross-examine the other side's expert on every item in the Scott Schedule. He began with item 19, the door-bell. He cross-examined furiously and without interruption. After about 20 minutes, the expert could take no more and made a concession. 'So', crowed Marcus, 'you admit that the door bell had scratches on it?' Judge Smout, who Marcus remembered for 'his wonderful twinkly smile' looked again at item 19 in the Schedule. 'Mr Taverner', he observed, 'that's £2.95 in the bag.'

[18] [1960] AC 18.
[19] (1986) 9 ConLR 119.
[20] (1984) 34 BLR 92.
[21] [1985] 1 All ER 346.

Judge Smout's promising career as an Official Referee was tragically cut short by his illness and early death, on 7 May 1987.

I. Esyr Lewis QC 1984–1998

Esyr Lewis was born on 11 January 1926, of the Reverend TW Lewis, a Congregationalist Minister, and Mary Jane May Lewis (*née* Selway). He attended Salford Grammar School and Mill Hill School,[22] before going up to Trinity Hall, Cambridge, taking both his degree and his LLM (known as an LLB at that time in Cambridge); he stayed on as a supervisor in law at Trinity Hall from 1950 to 1955. He joined Gray's Inn and was called to the Bar in 1954. He joined Farrar's Building in the Temple, undertaking mostly personal injury work.

He took silk in 1971. He sat as a Recorder from 1972 to 1984, and as a deputy High Court Judge from 1978 to 1984.

Judge Esyr Lewis QC heard the first instance decision in *Murphy v Brentwood*.[23] He also heard *Tesco Stores Ltd v The Norman Hitchcock Partnership Ltd*, which concerned design and supervision liability for fire damage by vandals.[24]

He was a member of the Garrick Club and Old Millhillians and was the Treasurer of Gray's Inn in 1987.

He was the last judge to hold the post of Senior Official Referee, before Mr Justice Dyson (as he then was) became Judge in Charge of the TCC.[25]

Judge Lewis often appeared vague and mildly baffled by the case in front of him. But this was almost always an act: he was an excellent lawyer with a good grasp of what mattered in any particular case. Although he could sometimes be a little slow, not only did he get there in the end, but he inevitably got the right answer. I am unaware of any major case in which Judge Lewis was ever successfully appealed. Given the size and weight of the cases with which he routinely dealt, that was a major accolade in itself.

It is, however, fair to say that he was rather less at home with cases about technology. Lord Justice Stuart-Smith remembers doing a case about a malfunctioning bespoke computer system (aren't they all?). Patrick Twigg QC spent three days opening it and, towards the end of the third day, referred to 'the operating system'. Esyr looked up innocently and said 'Ah Yes, Mr Twigg: the operating system. Is that hardware or software?' It appears that the parties settled the case the next day.

[22] During his five years there, because of the war and the school's evacuation to the country, he never actually attended a single class in its famous North London grounds.

[23] (1988) 13 ConLR 96; see ch 13 in this volume.

[24] [1997] 56 ConLR 42.

[25] For a fuller description of Esyr Lewis QC and his life, see Colin Reese QC's obituary in the Autumn 2011 edition of TECBAR Review.

J. John Davies QC 1984–1993

John Davies was born on 15 April 1921. He was educated at Pontardawe Grammar School and University College of Wales, Aberystwyth, as well as Trinity Hall, Cambridge. He was an Assistant Law Lecturer at Leeds University from 1946 to 1948. He was called to the Bar by Middle Temple in 1948, and became a Bencher in 1973 (and Emeritus Bencher in 1993). He took silk in 1967. He was a Recorder from 1974 to 1984. He died on 4 December 2005.

As a barrister at Fountain Court, John Davies had been Mrs Thatcher's pupil master. A clever man and a kindly judge, with a wide range of interests (he once showed me a large Pissarro which he had bought in the 1950's for 100 guineas and had been recently valued at £750,000), the sort of grinding detail that formed a natural part of the Official Referee's lot was not really to his taste. As a consequence, he was perhaps better at the shorter points of law than the long, drawn-out trials.

A number of his decisions were reported. In *Amantilla Ltd v Telefusion plc*,[26] Judge John Davies QC sitting on Official Referees' Business held that a builders' claim for a quantum meruit was a claim within section 29(5) of the Limitation Act 1980. One well-known decision was *McAlpine Humberoak Ltd v McDermott International Inc*,[27] where he sat with two expert assessors. The case concerned the changes and numerous variations to the design and construction of the main deck of a new oil rig. John Uff KC cross-examined the claimant's main witness for some weeks (those were the days!) and managed to get him to concede large parts of the claim. However, Judge Davies had other ideas. Despite being asked not to in firm terms by the claimant's leading counsel (who was to become Sir Anthony May, the President of the Queen's Bench Division), the judge held that the volume of changes had frustrated the contract so as to make the thing undertaken a thing different in kind from that contracted for. The claim was allowed almost in full. The decision was overturned on appeal.[28]

Judge Davies was a very proud Welshman which inevitably included an enormous enthusiasm for rugby. Phillip Boulding KC, who was a double rugby blue at Cambridge and played for Bedford, often found himself on the winning side in front of Judge Davies. The Judge, who was known for his lively pursuit of red herrings, would often quiz Phillip about the finer points of the game, and even the names of particular commentators. The moral was: never appear against Boulding in front of Judge Davies.

Judge Davies was also a smoker. This led him to take regular breaks. Although he always said that this was for the benefit of the short-hand writer, the wisps of smoke that would appear from under his door told a different story.

[26] (1987) 9 ConLR 139.

[27] (1990) 24 ConLR 68.

[28] (1992) 28 ConLR 76. See the discussion in D Sawtell, 'Enrichment-based Claims for a Quantum Meruit in Construction Disputes' [2019] *International Construction Law Review* 101, 118–19.

Because of our shared interest in art, Judge Davies was unfailingly kind to me when I was very young. I recall one huge pre-trial review with about 20 counsel, including some of the grandest silks of the day, when I was for the fourth third party to the third defendant's counterclaim, or some such minor role. The judge came into court and as leading counsel for the plaintiff was clearing his throat, the judge said: 'Before we start, I should just like to say: Mr Coulson, that's a very nice tie!'

In the end, he decided that he had had enough, and retired abruptly. He became the first judge I have ever known who failed to attend his own valedictory. Apparently, he decided that he would prefer to walk the dog.

III. 'The Golden Age'

The reputation of the Official Referees had, thanks to the efforts of the judges identified above, slowly but surely increased during the 1970s and the first part of the 1980s. But there then came a period when new appointments, allied to the judges already there, increased that reputation exponentially. In particular, the arrival of Judge John Hicks QC and Judge Thayne Forbes QC (who later became Mr Justice Forbes), gave rise to what many users of the Court of a certain vintage still refer to as 'the golden age'.

A. James Fox-Andrews QC 1985–1994

James Fox-Andrews was born on 24 March 1922. He was educated at Stowe and then at Pembroke College, Cambridge. He was called to the Bar by Gray's Inn in 1949, where he became a Bencher in 1971. He took silk in 1968. He was Deputy Chairman of the Devon Quarter Sessions from 1970 to 1971. He was Recorder of Winchester in 1971, and Honorary Recorder from 1972 to 2000. He was a Recorder of the Crown Court from 1972 to 1985. He was a member of the Hurlingham Club. He died on 15 September 2002.

Judge Fox-Andrews tried the dispute about the Catholic Cathedral in Liverpool which, like many award-winning buildings of the era, looked great but could not keep the rain out. He attended the site view, and agreed to have a closer look at the roof from a viewing cradle hoisted into place by a crane. When he was about 40 foot or so in the air, inspecting a balcony over a public thoroughfare, the judge peered over the edge of the cradle. He must have looked suitably apprehensive, because a passer-by noticed his expression and sought to comfort him from the safety of the ground. 'Don't jump, mate', he shouted. 'The Giro's in the post!'

There are few judgments of Judge Fox-Andrews in the law reports. This was partly due to the fact that, having set out the documents and submissions at some length, the decision itself was often confined to a paragraph, or even a sentence.

In *Ossory Road*,[29] the *ratio* was in one subordinate clause. But it was mainly due to the fact that he brokered a deal in so many of his cases before they got that far. The truth is that Judge Fox-Andrews invented mediation long before it was trendy and fashionable; indeed, at a time when it did not even have a name. He would take the opportunity in interlocutory proceedings of pointing out the strong and the weak parts of the claimant's case, and then the strong and the weak parts of the defendant's defence. He would not indicate what he thought the answer was but he had such a clear eye for identifying the key elements of each side's case (particularly those parts which you wanted to keep hidden) that the parties usually found some way of settling the case shortly after the hearing.

B. Peter Bowsher QC 1987–2003

Peter Bowsher was born on 9 February 1935. He attended St George's School at Windsor Castle, then Ardingly; he went on to Oriel College, Oxford. He was called to the Bar by Middle Temple in 1959, becoming a Bencher in 1985. He took silk in 1978. He had a number of judicial appointments, including sitting as a Deputy High Court Judge in the Queen's Bench and the Chancery Divisions in 1985 to 1987.

He was a member of Brooks's Club and the Royal Automobile Club.

Judge Bowsher's decisions were frequently reported. These include *Secretary of State for Foreign and Commonwealth Affairs v Percy Thomas*,[30] on the incorporation of arbitration clauses; and *Sahib Foods Ltd (in liquidation) v Paskin Kyriakides Sands (a firm)*.[31]

Judge Bowsher was an extremely efficient tribunal. He was, to the best of my recollection, the first Official Referee to undertake his own typing. Furthermore, he often produced a typed judgment within days of the end of the trial.

Sometimes this thirst for efficiency got the better of him. On one occasion, Rosemary Jackson KC was doing a case in front of him. On her return to court, she became stuck in the lift at St. Dunstan's House, together with at least one other member of the Bar. There was a phone in the lift. She got through to Judge Bowsher's court and explained her predicament. Judge Bowsher ordered that she continue her cross examination of one of the witnesses from the lift. Rosemary does not recall that as a particularly successful piece of case management.

Much more successful was the case of *John Mowlem and Co. Plc v Eagle Star Insurance* in 1995.[32] The construction press described this as the 'case of the century' not because of the luminaries involved (Charlie Falconer, David Steel and Richard Wilmot Smith, amongst others) but because it was the first paperless trial in a significant case. The trial lasted for nearly four months, although the

[29] *Ossory Road (Skelmersdale Ltd) v Balfour Beatty Ltd* [1993] CILL 882.
[30] (1998) 65 ConLR 11.
[31] (2003) 87 ConLR 1; [2003] EWCA Civ 1832, 93 ConLR 1 (on appeal to the Court of Appeal).
[32] This case is further discussed in ch 11 in this volume.

judicial timetabling exercise still caused some controversy. Charlie Falconer said he needed a day and a half to cross-examine witness X. Judge Bowsher graciously allowed him 20 minutes. At the end of the trial, Judge Bowsher, in his typical way, promptly produced a draft judgment and the case then settled.

C. John Loyd QC 1990–1997

John Loyd was born on 18 July 1933. He was educated at Wycliffe College, before going up to Gonville and Caius College, Cambridge. He was called to the Bar by Gray's Inn in 1958, becoming a Bencher in 1994. He took silk in 1981. He sat as a Recorder from 1985 to 1990. He died on 1 May 2002.

Judge Loyd gave the first instance decision in *Linden Gardens Trust Ltd v Lenesta Sludge Disposals Ltd*.[33] The case went all the way to the House of Lords.[34] It is one of the most important cases on the assignment of causes of action and third party losses.

Judge Loyd was the first professional negligence specialist to become an Official Referee. Because of the range of professional negligence cases that the Court dealt with, involving architects, engineers and quantity surveyors, his expertise was invaluable in building up the reputation of the court.

Ian Pennicott KC and Paul Darling KC were once battling in front of Judge Loyd about the proper interpretation of a standard form tri-partite arbitration clause. On the afternoon of the second day, Ian cheerfully informed the judge that he had met the man who had drafted the clause in the street at lunchtime. 'What a dreadful confession for a man to have to make' said the judge.

D. John Hicks QC 1993–2000

After National Service, he trained as a solicitor and qualified in 1952. He was a partner in Burchells from 1955 to 1965. I imagine that at some point even such a diffident man as John realised that he was instructing barristers with half his brains, and that he really could and should do it himself. He read for the bar and was called in 1966. He was in chambers at 4, Pump Court, taking silk in 1980, and serving as Head of Chambers for three years. He was a fountain of help and advice to all. His first love in law was real property, on which he wrote articles for *The Conveyancer* – but he had encyclopaedic knowledge and understanding across the whole spectrum of law and professional conduct and ethics.

In 1988 he became a county court judge. In 1993, he became a judge of the Technology and Construction Court, sitting in St Dunstan's House in Fetter Lane. There can be no doubt that John was eminently fitted for this work. He was

[33] (1990) 25 ConLR 28.
[34] [1994] 1 AC 85.

ruthlessly analytical and never frightened of hard work. He was also a first-class mathematician.

One of John's great successes at the Bar was *Street v Mountford*:[35] an important case at the time on distinction between tenancy and licence in relation to residential accommodation. It was a case from the West Country which went all the way to the House of Lords. The appeal involved persuading Sidney Templeman – a famously ferocious Law Lord – to re-establish the traditional view that an occupier of land for a term at a rent is a tenant if granted exclusive possession and to overrule a decision of Lord Denning which had stood for years. John succeeded, resulting in these memorable words from Lord Templeman:

> … the consequences in law of the agreement, once concluded, can only be determined by consideration of the effect of the agreement. If the agreement satisfied all the requirements of a tenancy, then the agreement produced a tenancy and the parties cannot alter the effect of the agreement by insisting that they only created a licence. The manufacture of a five-pronged implement for manual digging results in a fork even if the manufacturer, unfamiliar with the English language, insists that he intended to make and has made a spade.[36]

When he was Lord Chief Justice, Nick Phillips told me that John Hicks was the opponent he most feared at the Bar. This was unsurprising: Judge Hicks had a formidable intellect combined with a disarmingly calm and polite manner. When you were in front of Judge Hicks, you read the papers, prepared the case, and then did it all over again, just to be on the safe side.

In *Holbeck Hall Hotel v Scarborough BC*,[37] most of the Hotel had unfortunately fallen down a cliff. The Hotel's insurers sued the local authority as adjoining landowners, and also ground investigators. The case featured geotechnical issues of inordinate complexity involving slip circle analysis and a coefficient of friction, or something like that.

No-one could have tried it better than Judge Hicks. He brought with him a slide rule, calculator, tables, pencils and paper, and pitched into the geotechnical issues with enthusiasm.

During the trial, the three geotechnical experts eventually agreed what the coefficient of friction was. When this was announced, Judge Hicks invited them to the front of the Court and into a 'hot tub', long before that became fashionable. He explained politely that they were all wrong about the coefficient of friction, and, in detail, why. The explanation sailed way above the heads of all the barristers acting in the case. The geotechnical experts retreated crestfallen. The next day they agreed that his calculations were right and theirs were wrong.

It was brilliant judging, to which even the Court of Appeal paid tribute (although they did reverse him on a point of law).[38]

[35] [1985] AC 809.
[36] ibid, 819E-F.
[37] (2000) 69 ConLR 1.
[38] [2000] 2 WLR 1396.

My favourite Judge Hicks story was another occasion when I was present. It was a relatively impenetrable case about defective steelwork. He was, as ever, courteous and engaged. Suddenly, whilst counsel of no importance was droning on about something or other, it became apparent that Judge Hicks was not listening and was instead deeply engrossed in something of his own, pulling out files, making notes and the like. Counsel stopped talking and the Court sat quietly. After many minutes Judge Hicks looked up, gave his genial beam, and said: 'If someone could give me the thermal co-efficient of steel, I think I have worked out this case.' They just don't make judges like that anymore.

E. Thayne Forbes QC (later Mr Justice Forbes) 1990–1993

Thayne Forbes was born on 28 June 1938. He attended Winchester College and Wolverton Grammar School, before going on to University College London for his LLB and LLM. He served in the Royal Navy from 1963 to 1966, before being called to the Bar by Inner Temple in 1966. He took silk in 1984. He was an Official Referee from 1990 to 1993, before going on to the High Court Bench as a judge of the Queen's Bench Division from 1993 to 2009. He was Judge in Charge of the TCC from 2001 to 2004.

Judge Forbes perhaps epitomised the growing reputation of the Court because he was the first ever Official Referee in modern times to be appointed to the High Court Bench.[39] He went on to become a Presiding Judge on the Northern Circuit and, in 2001, he came back to be the judge in charge of the TCC. From 2004, he was Chair to the Working Group set up by the Judges' Council to report on judicial welfare.

In his role as a Presiding Judge, Forbes J tried Harold Shipman, the doctor who killed over 100 of his elderly patients. Lady Justice Davies, who was leading counsel for the defence, said 'he was simply the best judge we could have had for that case'.

He retired from the High Court Bench in January 2009 and is a member of the Garrick Club.

Because Judge Forbes had known us all at the Bar, he was very knowledgeable about our particular characteristics. When the other side were trying to cure the absence of notices by serving them during the hearing, Paul Darling KC said a rude word. Judge Forbes, who had doubtless heard all, said, 'Mr Darling, I think you said something *sotto voce*.' Darryl Royce pointed out that Paul had never said anything *sotto voce* in his life. The judge, who was also a bit fed up with Darryl's clients, said, 'Well, this time he is entitled to be loud.'

[39] Sir Edward Ridley was the only previous Official Referee to be promoted to the High Court Bench but, since he was widely regarded as inept, this promotion could only be ascribed to his brother, who was conveniently Home Secretary at the time. It was another century before the Judicial Appointments Commission was created.

F. Cyril Newman QC 1994–1998

Cyril Newman was born on 2 July 1937. He died on 15 January 2000.

He attended Sacred Heart College, Droitwich, and Lewes County Grammar School for Boys, before going up to Merton College, Oxford. He was called to the Bar by Middle Temple in 1960. He took silk in 1982. He sat as a Recorder from 1982 to 1986, and as a Circuit Judge from 1986 to 1994. His most notable decision was probably *Birse Construction Ltd v Haiste Ltd and Derek Bradford Associates and Newton*, which considered what the meaning of 'same damage' is under section 1 of the Civil Liability (Contribution) Act 1978.[40]

Judge Newman was another kindly, patient judge, always anxious to get it right.

Unfortunately for Judge Newman, he acquired a reputation of always finding in favour of the person who addressed him last. Wily performers in the TCC spotted this quickly, and would regularly seek to have the last word, whether they were entitled to it or not. I have been provided with countless anecdotes to support this theory and even now it is possible to discern the pride and frustration of those who respectively managed to get the last word, and those who did not. There were refinements too. I recall that the trick became to save your second-best point until your planned open 'last word' which, if loosed off at the right moment, could well prove decisive.

G. Richard Havery QC 1993–2008

Richard Havery was born on 7 February 1934. He attended St Paul's, before going to Magdalen College, Oxford; he later undertook his MSc at Imperial College, London. He was called to the Bar by Middle Temple in 1962, becoming a Bencher in 1989. He sat as an Assistant Recorder from 1982 to 1986, and as a Recorder from 1986 to 1993. He later edited a book, *History of the Middle Temple*,[41] a collection of interesting and important chapters and articles on one of the Inns of Court.

In the technical cases that he did at the Bar, you underestimated him once and never, ever again. They say that his cross-examination as a junior in *IBA v EMI*[42] at first instance, about the oscillation of the television mast at Emley Moor prior to its collapse, was the best anyone had ever seen.

Judge Havery could appear a little dry but he was, in fact, a brilliant judge with a razor-sharp mind, who concentrated hard, always understood the facts and the technical issues, and was fair, courteous and very rarely wrong. If you were not properly prepared, Judge Havery and Judge Hicks made a formidable pace attack, a bit like Lillee and Thompson: if one did not get you, the other one would!

[40] (1995) 44 ConLR 17.

[41] R Havery, *History of the Middle Temple* (Oxford, Hart Publishing, 2011).

[42] *Independent Broadcasting Authority v EMI Electronics Ltd and BICC Construction Ltd*: in the Court of Appeal at (1978) 11 BLR 29 and the House of Lords at (1980) 14 BLR 1.

When the House of Lords overturned the Court of Appeal's decision in *Marcic v Thames Water Utilities Ltd*, and reinstated Judge Havery's judgment at first instance,[43] they had some relatively disobliging things to say about the principal judgment in the Court of Appeal,[44] delivered by Phillips LJ (as he then was).[45] It was noticeable that, when Judge Havery retired, not only was his valediction presided over by Phillips as the Lord Chief Justice, but he made a point of telling that story against himself.

In his own speech on that occasion, Judge Havery said that, as a judge, you still had 'that Monday morning feeling' you had had at the Bar, 'but it was one of anticipation, not apprehension'. Those words have always stayed with me. They eloquently summarise one of the best features of life as a judge.

IV. The Difficult Years

It was, I suppose, inevitable that by the mid-late 1990s, the reputation of the Court had increased so much that some sort of recalibration was inevitable. That was not necessarily the fault of the judges in the Court at the time, although there was a period when there were too many successful appeals against TCC decisions in the Court of Appeal, and some of the adverse comments made there were meant to (and doubtless did) sting hard. These difficulties reached their nadir in the edition of Legal Business for November 2004, which included an article about the TCC entitled *Courting Criticism* which was extremely critical of many of the judges in the court. The article was exaggerated and many of the criticisms were unfair, but that was not the point: the article reflected the perception of court users and, in the dispute resolution business, perception is all. The judges in the Court over this period faced an uphill battle to restore the court's reputation.

A. Humphrey Lloyd QC 1993–2005

John Lloyd was born on 16 November 1939. He went to Westminster and then to Trinity College, Dublin. He was called to the Bar by Middle Temple in 1963, becoming a Bencher in 1985. He took silk in 1979. He sat as a Recorder from 1990 to 1993. He has held an impressive number of academic and editorial positions, predominantly in construction law. He practised out of Atkin Chambers. He is a member of the Reform Club.

It is very difficult to even attempt to list his notable cases. A practitioner in this field is always returning to his decisions, as statements of the law, examples

[43] [2002] QB 929.
[44] [2002] EWCA Civ 64, [2002] QB 929.
[45] [2003] UKHL 66, [2004] 2 AC 42 at [68]–[70] per Lord Hoffmann.

of its application, or where they are cited with approval in subsequent decisions. One decision, in particular, that has stood the test of time is *ERDC Group Ltd v Brunel University* on the effect of letters of intent.[46] He was also a founder of the Society of Construction Law.

Judge Lloyd was the first out-and-out construction law specialist to become a judge of the TCC. That sounds odd: why did the job not attract specialists in the field prior to Judge Lloyd? The answer was a combination of the financially rewarding nature of the work at the Construction Bar, and the relatively low status of the Official Referees in the hierarchy of the judiciary as a whole. For example, I can remember a great debate about whether the judges of the TCC were senior to the Old Bailey judges; since nobody could provide a definitive answer to that question, there used to be an unseemly amount of pushing and shoving in the procession at Westminster Abbey for the opening of the legal year.

It made a huge difference to appear in front of a judge who had, until recently, been doing the same work as you. Judge Lloyd had a formidable knowledge of construction law which was reflected in his many judgments in the law reports. Following his service as a judge of the court, he went on to become a highly respected construction arbitrator.

B. Anthony Thornton QC 1994–2015

Anthony Thornton was born on 18 August 1947. He went to Eton College and then Keble College, Oxford. He was called to the Bar by Middle Temple in 1970, becoming a Bencher in 1992. He took silk in 1988. He sat as a Recorder from 1992 to 1994. From 2009 to 2015, he sat as a Deputy Judge of the Administrative Court and the Queen's Bench Division, and a Judge of the Crown Court; he retired in 2015.

Judge Thornton followed Judge Lloyd from Atkin Chambers to the TCC. It was another positive sign that construction specialists were being appointed to the Bench. That was particularly true in the case of Judge Thornton because he had an encyclopaedic knowledge of the law. He was always a pleasant and courteous tribunal.

Perhaps his difficulty was that because he was himself so clever, he expected it in others. That meant, amongst other things, that he acquired a reputation for sometimes over-complicating matters which, so it was thought by the Bar, were relatively straight-forward. He was also sometimes over-solicitous of the parties' comments when they received his draft judgments; he would make changes to the draft as a result of the comments made, which then led to a further round of comments and a further round of changes. In that way, it might be said that he was too nice to be a TCC judge in those rather strained days.

[46] [2006] EWHC 687 (TCC), 109 ConLR 114.

C. David Wilcox 1998–2012

David Wilcox was born on 8 March 1939. He went to Wednesbury Boys' High School, and then to King' College, London. He was called to the Bar by Gray's Inn in 1962. He was in practice in the Midland and Oxford Circuits, becoming Head of Chambers at College Street Chambers in Nottingham. He was a Recorder of the Crown Court from 1979 to 1985, and then a Circuit Judge from 1985 to 1998.

Judge Wilcox had not done construction work before he came from the Midland circuit to sit as a TCC judge. Unlike some of his predecessors, he always gave the impression that he was pleased and proud to be sitting as a TCC judge. Moreover, his background in criminal and general common law gave him an unrivalled eye for the merits of any dispute: if, on a fair view of the matter, right was on your side, then Judge Wilcox was too.

This quality is perhaps best summarised by Marcus Taverner KC. Marcus said of him:

> I just thought he was wonderful; kind and surreal in his instinct for a case. He never gave the impression of having over-taxed himself before the start of a case. But he had some sort of mystical sixth sense. He was always right. He just latched on to the one, possibly two, points in a case that mattered.

Would that all judges were the subject of such praise.

D. John Toulmin QC, CMG 1997–2011

John Toulmin was born on 14 February 1941. He attended Winchester College before going up to Trinity Hall, Cambridge; he went on to the University of Michigan. He was called to the Bar by Middle Temple in 1965, becoming a Bencher in 1986 and Senior Bencher in 2011. He took silk in 1980. He sat as a Recorder from 1984 to 1997, and as a Deputy High Court Judge from 1994 to 1997.

John Toulmin read law at Cambridge where he was part of an impressive group of young men who went on to run the Conservative Party: Michael Howard, Kenneth Clarke and John Selwyn Gummer, among others. He and Michael Howard formed a doubtless intimidating debating team and toured the US whilst they were still undergraduates.

The major part of his junior practice was medical defence work, both in the claims and disciplinary fields. He was junior counsel to Phillip Otton QC (later Lord Justice Otton) in the Normansfield Inquiry into misconduct at a psychiatric hospital which had led to a nurse's strike. He subsequently joined the hospital management committees of the Bethlem and Maudsley Hospitals and became a Trustee of the Institute of Psychiatry. When that merged with Kings College London, he became a member of the College Council and later chair of its governance committee. He also found time to become an English member of the EU Council concerned with the harmonisation of lawyers and legal qualifications, work which became the basis of Directive 98/5/EC and led to his appointment to CMG (which he called his 'Sound of Music' decoration). He was subsequently a Trustee of the Academy of European Law in Trier, Germany and chaired the Board of trustees for 13 years.

Judge Toulmin also had possibly the best hinterland, as it is now called, of any judge I have known. He bought a derelict house in Burgundy and restored both the house and its vines. Along with his wife Carolyn and his children, the house in France (and the wine he made there, Clos Toulmin) was the greatest love of his life. He also loved the Temple Church and did much to promote it and the services held there as well as the quality of the music. It was fitting that his funeral took place there.

Judge Toulmin heard the trial of the preliminary issues in the famous *Factortame* litigation, which considered damages for breaches of European Community law.[47]

Judge Toulmin was clever and, as his judgments in the bigger cases showed, a judge able to handle difficult points with precision and aplomb.

Perhaps his principal difficulty was that he found the mundane TCC work much less engaging and there were times when he would not hide his impatience. That was a particular sadness to me because, outside court, he was an extremely supportive and entertaining colleague. When I started as a judge, Judge Toulmin was very often my first port of call whenever I had a question or a concern.

Judge Toulmin could also garner mixed reviews in relation to his promotion of women at the Bar. Some women, I know, found him difficult. But if he thought that the female barrister in question was good, he was rigorous in his promotion of her and unstinting in his praise for her efforts. Sarah Hannaford KC was one such barrister who I know Judge Toulmin admired enormously. Another was Fiona Sinclair KC. Lord Justice Stuart-Smith remembers standing up to open a big case in which the written opening had been prepared by him as the leader, and Fiona, as his junior. As Jeremy stood up, Judge Toulmin said: 'Could I just say, Ms Sinclair, that is a very impressive written opening?' Credit where it was due, perhaps?

He was one of those most personally affected by the changes subsequently introduced by Jackson J, with the bigger cases being given to High Court judges, not the Senior Circuit judges. It caused him great upset and hurt. But he never let that affect his friendships. He remained on excellent terms with Paul Darling KC even though Paul, as Chair of TECBAR, was vigorously supporting the reforms. And he said to me, long before it happened, that one of the good things about the changes was that I would probably become a High Court Judge.

E. Richard Seymour QC 2000–2015

Richard Seymour was born on 4 May 1950. He attended Brentwood School, and went on to Christ's College, Cambridge. He was called to the Bar by Gray's Inn

[47] [2001] 1 WLR 942.

in 1972. He took silk in 1991. He sat as an Assistant Recorder from 1991 to 1995, and then Recorder from 1995 to 2000. He was a Judge of the TCC from 2000 to 2005; he was then assigned to the Queen's Bench Division from 2005 to 2015.

There is no getting away from the fact that Judge Seymour divided opinion. He could sometimes be difficult and he certainly had strong views about particular aspects of the law (if the offer or the acceptance were a bit murky, he would tell you that you did not have a contract, even if the parties had behaved for years as if there was one). He was possibly the most prepared judge that any of us had appeared in front of: on the morning of the first day, I often felt that he knew more than anyone else in the room about the case. But of course, sometimes this worked against him.

Famously, in the *Brompton* case, it was Judge Seymour who persuaded the defendants to strike out the claimant's case during the opening. Judge Seymour then allowed the application that he had himself instigated, only to be reversed in trenchant terms by the Court of Appeal.[48]

He enjoyed old-fashioned cross-examination but he was aware of the proper limits. At one point, he interrupted Marcus Taverner KC in the middle of his cross-examination to observe: 'This is not cross-examination. It is intimidation!' Marcus bowed graciously and said 'Well, thank you my Lord.' Judge Seymour looked puzzled and said: 'That wasn't necessarily a compliment, Mr Taverner.'

F. Peter Coulson (2004–Present)

In June 2004, I was the last person appointed as a senior circuit judge to sit in the TCC in London. It is for that reason that I can lay some claim to the title 'The Last Official Referee'. Beyond that, it is doubtless better to draw a discreet veil over my (enormously enjoyable) time as a judge of the TCC.

V. The Redemption

The TCC had a history of having eminent judges in charge of the court. Between 1998 and 2000, Dyson J (as he then was) was the judge in charge, immediately before he went to the Court of Appeal. He was succeeded by Forbes J who was, as I have already noted, the first Official Referee in modern times to be promoted to the High Court Bench. In 2004, he was succeeded by Jackson J (as he then was). The article in Legal Business suggested that this was a good appointment but that Mr Justice Jackson 'has his work cut out to rescue the reputation of the TCC'.

But that was precisely what Mr Justice Jackson went on to do. It was not easy, and there was a certain amount of upset, even anger, amongst the judges as his changes took effect. Some judges were moved out of the Court altogether.

[48] *Royal Brompton Hospital National Health Service Trust v Hammond (No. 5)* [2001] EWCA Civ 550, 76 ConLR 62.

Mr Justice Jackson's principal innovation, which plainly ought to have happened years before, was the decision to ensure that all the bigger cases were tried by High Court judges. This led to the creation of a small group of judges, inevitably known as the Jackson Five, who undertook that work. The existing judges of the Court continued to hear cases, but they were no longer dealing with the significant disputes.

It is impossible to overstate the workload that this change imposed on Mr Justice Jackson himself. Many of the other designated High Court judges were otherwise engaged, so he undertook the majority of those trials himself. He would then produce lengthy *extempore* judgments, and move on immediately to do the next trial. It was a working life that would have broken most people. Mr Justice Jackson thrived, and so, inevitably, did the court.

Over the years, Mr Justice Jackson encouraged a number of first class silks to apply to become judges of the High Court. They were Mr Justice Ramsey, Mr Justice Aikenhead, and Mr Justice Edwards-Stuart. Each went on to become the judge in charge of the TCC. I succeeded the last of that trio in that role in 2015. Between them, those three judges built on the work done by Mr Justice Jackson and created the reputation which the TCC enjoys today. Amongst other things, they created a huge body of adjudication law and brought public procurement work to the TCC. Their contribution can still be seen in the vital role that the TCC plays in the Business and Property Courts, in the Rolls Building on Fetter Lane and across the country.

It is perhaps appropriate to end this review at that point. Many of the subsequent appointees to the TCC, such as Mr Justice Fraser, Mrs Justice Jefford, and Mrs Justice O'Farrell, were former specialist practitioners at the Construction Bar. They have been ably assisted by other High Court judges including in particular Lady Justice Carr and Lord Justice Stuart-Smith (as they now are) and Mr Justice Waksman. However, they are all sitting judges, and whilst it would be fun to subject them to the same scrutiny as, say, Sir Walker Kelly Carter QC at the start of this chapter, that should properly wait for another book.

6

The Birth of the Technology and Construction Court

LORD DYSON

It came as a complete surprise to me to be asked in 1997 to become the first High Court Judge in charge of the Official Referees ('ORs'). How did this come about? I had practised at the Bar from 1968 until I was appointed as a judge of the Queen's Bench Division of the High Court in 1993. Until 1986, I was at 11 King's Bench Walk which later moved to 10 Essex Street and later still and after my time became known as 'Keating Chambers'. In 1986, I moved to become Head of Chambers at 2 Garden Court which later moved to 39 Essex Street and is now known as '39 Essex Chambers'.

For much of my 25 years at the Bar, I specialised in Construction Law. Keating Chambers and Atkin Chambers were the two sets that specialised in Construction Law. Construction disputes were determined either by arbitration or by litigation in the courts. Most of the litigation was allocated to the High Court. This was because it involved sums that exceeded the jurisdiction of the County Court at that time. But almost none of the cases were issued in the Queen's Bench Division (whether in the Commercial List as it was called or the general QB list) or in the Chancery Division. Although they were High Court cases, they were allocated to the ORs.

I hope that I avoid covering the ground that is traversed by other contributors to this book. But even if I do cover some of the same ground as one or more of the other contributors, I wish to highlight a number of features of the way in which the ORs conducted their business and of the procedures that they adopted. The first is the procedure that they adopted for managing their cases. Each case was allocated to an individual OR, who took the case 'from cradle to grave': he (it was always a 'he' when I was in practice at the Bar) managed the case from inception to trial and then conducted the trial himself. This was very different from the system usually adopted in the High Court, where cases were managed from inception to trial by procedural judges who were called Masters and tried by a High Court Judge or a Deputy High Court Judge. In cases which involved more than one procedural hearing, it was not uncommon for more than one Master to be involved; and usually, the trial judge knew nothing about the case until very shortly before it was allocated to him for the conduct of the trial. The advantage of the 'cradle to grave' approach was that the OR imposed his stamp on the case from the very outset and the parties knew what to expect from him. This ensured a consistency of judicial approach. It was also efficient because, if properly applied, it meant that by the time the case came on for trial, the OR knew what the case was all about. It was not necessary to open a case at trial by explaining the facts and issues in the case. Judges schooled in the traditional way of doing things thought that it was an advantage to know nothing about the case they were trying until it was opened to them. In this way, they approached the case with a completely open mind. I recall one case which I was about to open and the judge said to me: 'now Mr Dyson, what's this case all about?'

Second, the ORs adopted a number of procedures for managing cases both before and at trial which were imaginative and ahead of their time. A number of these were the inspiration for some of the civil procedure reforms that were recommended by Lord Woolf and which formed the basis of the Civil Procedure Rules 1998, which applied to all cases commenced after 26 April 1999. One that I recall vividly was what is now called 'hot tubbing'. This term was unknown at the time. Sir Walker Kelly Carter, who was a master exponent of the procedure, would not have understood what the term meant and would certainly not have approved of its use. The idea of having two witnesses (usually expert witnesses) giving evidence at the same time in a procedure largely conducted by the judge would have been anathema to the traditional judge. Practitioners who only appeared before the ORs rarely must have been bemused by this strange procedure. But it was particularly useful in complicated technical cases; and there is now widespread acceptance of it.

But the ORs' innovative approach to litigation should not be exaggerated. Although skeleton arguments transformed the conduct of much of the work, I do not believe that they were first introduced into our system of litigation by the ORs. Moreover, during my years in practice, cases before the ORs (and elsewhere) would last for what would now be regarded as unacceptably long periods. A hearing which would now take one week could take three or four. Openings could last one or two weeks. Major changes were made to accelerate things, but I don't think that that they were initiated by the ORs, although they were embraced by them.

The OR cases were heard in what was called 'the Official Referees' Corridor', which was on the second floor of the West Green Building in the Royal Courts of Justice. The courts rooms were off this corridor and access to it was by means of a rickety lift. It was almost as if the courts were a hidden secret, far away from the main courts. For the uninitiated, they took some finding. The courts were later moved to St Dunstan's House, Fetter Lane.

The cases allocated to be tried by the ORs usually involved technical issues and often much detail. Until the age of the computer, in practice most of them were about building and engineering disputes. The arrival of the computer generated complex technical litigation about both hardware and software. The ORs' corridor was the natural home for such disputes. So they were added to the class of cases that were routinely tried by the ORs.

So both before and during my early years at the Bar, construction disputes were dealt with in London in rooms off a distant corridor on the second floor in the RCJ by judges who were not called 'judges', but 'Official Referees'.

On the whole, those who practised at the Commercial and Chancery Bar thought that OR work was tedious and lacking in legal importance or interest. These practitioners rarely appeared in the Official Referees' Corridor. They had a low regard for OR work. Somehow, the work of the Commercial Court and Chancery Division was seen as being far more important, interesting and intellectually challenging. Their views were reinforced by the fact that the ORs were not High Court judges, although almost all of the work they did was High Court work. Many of the cases involved very large sums of money. But it did not help that the ORs were not even called judges although, in fact, after the enactment of the Courts Act 1971, they were Senior Circuit judges. They were called referees.

It was, therefore, not at all surprising that none of the inhabitants of Lincoln's Inn or Essex Court were interested in becoming an OR. Perhaps more surprising was the fact that remarkably few practitioners from the specialist Construction Bar were interested either. During my early years at the Bar, there were only two sets of chambers that proclaimed themselves as specialist Construction Chambers. These were Keating Chambers and Atkin Chambers, although they did not bear these illustrious names until much later. In the past 50 years or so, increasing numbers of barristers and solicitors have been doing construction law work. Until the 1980s, no members of the two specialist chambers had become judges at all. They preferred to satisfy such appetites as they had for dispute resolution by sitting as arbitrators, staying in smart hotels in sunny climes and continuing to enjoy the fruits of their lucrative practices. A few specialist practitioners were appointed as ORs, but they were a rarity. It was only after High Court judges started to be appointed on a fairly regular basis to the Technology and Construction Court ('TCC') (as the ORs' court had now become) that specialist practitioners began to sit as judges in that court. The appointment of High Court judges to the TCC, which in my view was long overdue, encouraged specialist practitioners to want to sit there; it also raised the standing of the Court to a position on a par with that of the Commercial Court and Chancery Division.

So most of the ORs who were sitting when I was at the Bar had been barristers who were general practitioners. Notable examples were His Honour Judge William Stabb QC, His Honour Judge Edgar Fay QC, His Honour Judge Lewis Hawser QC, His Honour Judge Newey QC, His Honour Judge Esyr Lewis QC, His Honour Judge Peter Bowsher QC, His Honour Judge John Hicks QC, His Honour Judge Cyril Newman QC and His Honour Judge Thayne Forbes QC (who later became Forbes J). I had regularly appeared before all of them. The best of them were extremely good judges. None of them had specialist practices in the field of Construction Law. The attraction of being an OR must have been that the work was challenging, was High Court work and, on the whole, the quality of the advocates was high. Being a senior circuit judge trying this kind of work was more prestigious than being an ordinary circuit judge trying criminal cases or county court cases. I suspect that those who were drawn to being an OR would have hoped to be appointed to the High Court Bench, but did not quite make it. In my view, some of them were at least the equal of, if not better than, many of the High Court judges before whom I appeared as a barrister.

When I was appointed as a judge to the Queen's Bench Division of the High Court in 1993, I did not expect to try any Construction or Computer cases. And I did not do so. My contact with the ORs ceased. I no longer read the Building Law Reports or the Construction Law Journal. I had moved into what felt like a different world. I was trying heavy criminal cases, hearing criminal appeals, trying a wide range of general civil cases and, above all, hearing a large number of public law cases. My practice at the Bar had not equipped me for any of this.

One day late in 1997, I was told by the clerk to Lord Bingham, the Lord Chief Justice, that he wanted to see me. I was not told why and had been given no clues by anyone as to what he wanted to discuss. It did not occur to me that he might have wanted me to assume some responsibility for the ORs. I went into his room with a degree of trepidation. He was friendly and tried to put me at my ease immediately by starting: 'I'll come straight to the point.' He said that he was concerned about the ORs. Some of them were not performing well enough and there was a particular problem of delayed judgments. As a result, some litigants were not issuing OR proceedings in London, preferring instead to issue elsewhere, such as in Birmingham. Lord Bingham asked me whether I would be willing to be the judge in charge of the ORs in the hope that I might be able to improve the situation and that the presence of a High Court Judge might enhance the standing of the ORs' court. He did not say what improvements I might recommend or make. He did not say for how long he wished me to serve in this new position. He did, however, say that he hoped that, when my term came to an end, I would be able to recommend one of the serving ORs to be my successor as the judge in charge and that my successor would be appointed to the High Court Bench. In this way, over time High Court judges would be appointed to sit in the ORs' court. So my job specification was rather vague. It seems to have been to identify problems that were facing the Court and to recommend improvements.

Lord Bingham's approach came as a complete surprise to me. I was not aware that there had been any disquiet about the performance of all or any of the ORs as individual judges or about the court system and its processes. Since 1993, I had not given the ORs much thought. I had not been aware of any general dissatisfaction with the ORs when I was in practice. On the whole, their reputation had been very good.

Lord Bingham was my judicial hero. I had no hesitation in casting aside whatever reservations I might have had about undertaking this task and agreed to take it on. I was then asked to see Lord Irvine of Lairg QC, the Lord Chancellor. Before the passing of the Constitutional Reform Act 2005, the Lord Chancellor was Head of the Judiciary and was responsible for running the entire Justice System, including the ORs. Lord Irvine thanked me for agreeing to become the judge in charge of the ORs. He did not say precisely what he had in mind, but he clearly thought that I might suggest some changes because his parting shot was '*Festina lente*' (move things along, but not too fast). I took this to mean that I should try to make the ORs' court more efficient, but take my time and certainly not cause a sudden revolution.

There had been talk for some years about the possibility of the ORs becoming High Court judges, but there was considerable opposition to this idea from some of the senior judiciary. It was clear that some of them did not have a high opinion of the ORs or the work that they did. From what he said, Lord Bingham gave me the impression that, to some extent, he shared this view. I am sure that, when he was at the Bar, he did not practice in the Official Referees' Corridor; and that when he was a first instance judge, he did not try any construction cases. He may have heard a few appeals in construction cases, but this was hardly a good basis from which to form an accurate view of what the ORs did.

He seemed to think that the ORs' diet was mainly resolving tedious disputes which were the subject of Scott Schedules or delay and disruption claims (known to the *cognoscenti* as 'buggeration' cases). I tried to disabuse him by pointing out that some of the most significant recent common law cases had started out life as OR cases. I doubt whether I convinced him. But this important fact has often been overlooked. A few examples will suffice.

In *Anns v Merton London Borough Council*,[1] a local authority was held by the House of Lords to be liable in negligence for failing to carry out a proper inspection of the foundations of a building and failing to see that the builder had not complied with relevant statutory building regulations. Lord Wilberforce enunciated a two stage test for establishing whether a duty of care existed: first, whether there was a sufficient relationship of proximity or neighbourhood between the person who had suffered damages and the defendant such as to give rise to a prima facie duty of care; and if so, second whether there were any considerations which ought to negative or limit the scope of the duty, or the class of persons to whom it is owed or the damages to which a breach of it may give rise. Until it was criticised in *Caparo Industries plc v Dickman*,[2] this famous statement was subsequently applied in many negligence cases, and by no means only in construction cases. The first instance decision in *Anns* was given by Judge Edgar Fay QC sitting as an OR.

Peabody Foundation Fund v Sir Lindsay Parkinson and Co Ltd[3] was another OR case which was appealed ultimately to the House of Lords. It too laid down principles which were of general application to the law of negligence and went far beyond construction law.

[1] *Anns v Merton London Borough Council* [1978] AC 728 (HL).
[2] *Caparo Industries plc v Dickman* [1990] 2 AC 605 (HL).
[3] *Peabody Foundation Fund v Sir Lindsay Parkinson and Co Ltd* [1985] AC 210 (HL).

The principles stated by Lord Wilberforce in *Anns* were revisited by the House of Lords in *Murphy v Brentwood District Council*,[4] where it was held that *Anns* had been wrongly decided. This is not the place to examine the reasoning of Lord Keith in *Murphy*. It is sufficient to point out that the first instance decision in this case was given by His Honour Judge Esyr Lewis QC.

Another important case which was issued in the ORs' court was *Lamb v London Borough of Camden*.[5] This was a leading decision on remoteness of damage and the test of reasonable foreseeability of damage, especially where the damage has been caused by third parties. The plaintiff had left her house unoccupied at a time when the defendant authority negligently allowed a sewer to fracture causing damage to the plaintiff's property. While the property was awaiting repair, it was invaded by squatters who caused further damage. The OR refused her claim for damages from the authority. Her appeal to the Court of Appeal was dismissed. The mere fact that, as found by the OR, it was reasonably foreseeable that strangers might invade the house and cause damage was not enough to fix the authority with liability for the damage so caused. Once again, an important decision of general application.

I mention these cases because they give the lie to the general misconception that still persisted when I arrived in 1998 that the ORs did little else than hear long tedious cases involving Scott Schedules: all fact and no law.

After that diversion into the scope of the cases that were heard by the ORs/TCC Judges, I return to the situation that faced me when I arrived in 1998 to be judge in charge of the court. It was clear that a wholesale upgrade of the ORs to the High Court Bench was a non-starter. The resistance to this from some of the most senior judges was deep-rooted. Their view was coloured by the fact that the judges were referees (ie not proper judges) who heard cases in the Official Referees' Corridor and later at the top of St Dunstan's House in Fetter Lane and that the subject-matter of the cases that they tried was boring and not worthy of the attention of High Court judges. To accord the status of High Court Judge to Official Referees would devalue the High Court brand.

Lord Bingham's solution was something of a compromise. The introduction of a High Court Judge to be the judge in charge of the ORs was an innovation. For the first time, a High Court Judge would sit in the ORs' court and try OR cases. This would go some way to acknowledge the importance of the ORs and what they did. But in my view (and that of many others), it was irrational not to have this important class of High Court cases tried by High Court judges.

Lord Bingham told me that he had spoken to the ORs (there were about six of them) and informed them of his plan. Judge Esyr Lewis QC was the senior OR and therefore the OR in charge of the Court at the time. He was due to retire in 1998. The convention of the Court was that the OR in charge was the senior OR. Judge Bowsher was the second most senior OR and was expecting to succeed Judge Lewis in the usual way. My arrival would defeat that expectation.

[4] *Murphy v Brentwood District Council* [1991] AC 398 (HL).
[5] *Lamb v London Borough of Camden* [1981] QB 625 (CA).

Although senior judges, who knew little or nothing about the ORs and what they did, believed that they still operated from the ORs' Corridor, in fact they had moved out of the RCJ to occupy the top two floors at St Dunstan's House in Fetter Lane. This was an improvement on a remote corridor in the RCJ, but still somewhat out of the way. The lower floors were occupied by the Commercial Court.

So it was that in 1998, I moved from my room in the RCJ to a room on the top floor at St Dunstan's House. My arrival was heralded by a visit by Lord Irvine and Lord Bingham and an event in court to which some of the regular users of the ORs' court were invited. Such was the excitement generated by this visit that a red carpet was laid on the floor of the lift.

I was a little apprehensive about how my arrival would be received by my new colleagues. I had appeared before some of them when I was at the Bar. They knew me quite well and it must have been reassuring to them that I was familiar with the work that they did. I believe that most of them were quite pleased that I had come. If they were not themselves to be made High Court judges, it was at least a step in the right direction of promoting the importance of the work that the ORs did that a High Court Judge was appointed to be in charge of the court.

Immediately after my arrival, I went to speak to each of the ORs individually. I knew that Peter Bowsher would be upset. He had been an OR for about 10 years. I had appeared before him many times. He had always treated me well and I thought he was an efficient and good judge. But he was very senior and I had occasionally seen him speak sharply to those who appeared before him. I believed that he must have been looking forward to assuming the role of Senior Official Referee. He was my first port of call. I found him polite in an icy way. This was entirely understandable. He made it clear to me that he was unhappy about what had happened. I explained that I had not sought the job, but had felt it my duty to take it on. I said that I hoped he would give me the benefit of his huge experience and help me to make a success of my new role. It is measure of the man that over the next few years, he did precisely that. He was enormously supportive and caused me no difficulties. I was extremely grateful to him for all the help he gave me.

My initial conversations with the other ORs were easier, although my subsequent dealings with some of them were to prove quite difficult.

I did not have a particular vision for the Court and none had been suggested to me by Lord Bingham or Lord Irvine. My ideas developed slowly. I was concerned by what I discovered about the delays of some judges in delivering their judgments. This was bad for the litigants who were having to wait too long for their judgments. It was also bad for the reputation of the Court and not fair to the excellent ORs who were not slow in producing their judgments. But I did not think that this problem could be solved by any systemic changes. The problem lay with the individual ORs themselves. Regretfully, I came to the conclusion that some of these judges were not up to the job. But I was powerless to do anything to remedy the problem. All I could do was to cajole and try to persuade and to make sure that all judges had sufficient time to write their judgments. They were given ample time and I was, frankly, appalled at how long two of them in particular took. One of them accused me of putting him under such pressure that he was in danger of having a nervous breakdown and had had to consult his doctor. The other was chaotic as well as slow. He would sometimes fix a trial date and start a long trial before he had completed an outstanding judgment in another big case. He also had a penchant for imposing case management directions on the parties which were contrary to what they had agreed. I certainly did not believe that judges were obliged to make consent case management orders merely because the parties had agreed them. That would have been a dereliction of judicial responsibility. But if parties, seemingly represented by competent solicitors and counsel, had reached an agreement as to how a case should proceed, my view was that there had to be cogent reasons not to give effect to their agreement. All the more so in a complex case where the parties were bound to have a better grasp of the issues than the judge could reasonably be expected to have. All of that seemed to me to be obvious. It must have been frustrating for parties, who had probably spent considerable sums on legal fees in arriving at an agreement, only to find that their agreement was unravelled by the judge who was determined to make directions that the parties did not want and which differed from the directions that they had agreed that they did want.

A further concern I had was that, if there was a marked disparity between the approaches of the judges as to the way in which litigation should be conducted, this would not reflect well on the reputation of the Court as a whole. To some extent, it is inevitable that some judges are considered to be, and are in fact, better than others. But maverick judges are bad for the system.

Cases were allocated to judges for management and eventually for trial by a rota system. This was the system that I inherited and with one qualification I maintained it. I thought that it would have been wrong in principle for a court official to allocate cases to judges other than by strict rotation; and also wrong that judges could indent for cases that they wanted to take on, whether because they thought they would be interesting or for any other reason. The one qualification was that, as the judge in charge, I thought it appropriate that I chose some of the cases that I wanted to hear. This was for two reasons. First, if there was a particularly important case, it was right that I as the sole High Court Judge should hear it. It was for that reason that I heard the first cases under the Housing Grants, Construction and Regeneration Act 1996 ('HGCRA'). Second, I avoided trying very long cases. This was because I did not think it right that a disproportionate amount of my time should be devoted to one case. I confess that I was not attracted by the prospect of trying a very long case either. But that was not the principal reason for my taking this course. So far as I am aware, the policy that I applied for the allocation of cases caused no resentment or other difficulties among my fellow judges or the users of the court.

Allocating cases by rotation works well if the subject-matter of the cases is broadly uniform. That was certainly the case with the work of the ORs/TCC judges. And by background and experience at least, all the judges of the Court were equally well qualified to deal with the cases that comprised the main diet of work. So the subject-matter of the cases did not warrant a departure from the rota system. But the quality of the judges varied and regular users of the Court were aware of this. The practitioners talked to each other and knew who the good judges were and who were to be avoided, if possible. I understand that parties resorted to various stratagems to ensure that their case was not allocated to a particularly bad judge or judges. Generally speaking, therefore, there was no reason to depart from the rota system for the allocation of cases. If there was a problem, it lay with the quality of one or two of the judges.

I found it difficult to know how to deal with the problems that I have described, especially the problem of delayed judgments. The nuclear option would have been to report them to the Lord Chief Justice, but that was a course I was reluctant to take and never did take. Somehow, we muddled through. These problems highlighted the importance of appointing good judges in the first place and the limited powers a supervising judge enjoys to control and manage those whom they supervise.

It was not long before I decided that something had to be done to assimilate the ORs fully into the court system, especially the High Court. It seemed to me to be anomalous that these judges were still being referred to as 'Referees' when they were judges whose role was in principle no different from that of any other judges. No other judges were called 'Referees', a title that must have been puzzling to litigants who were unfamiliar with the system. The subject-matter of many cases was such that they could just as readily have been issued in the Commercial Court or Chancery Division as in the ORs' court. They were predominantly commercial contract cases. They did not differ in kind from other commercial cases. The main difference was that their subject-matter was construction. It struck me as particularly odd that shipbuilding disputes were issued in the Commercial Court because their subject-matter was the construction of ships rather than of buildings. It was an accident of history that the judges of the ORs' court were still referred to as ORs. I thought that this should be changed. Some litigants must have wondered why their cases were being tried by referees and not proper judges. Surely referees were for sporting contests, not court cases. Moreover, retaining the title of OR gave fuel to the belief that the ORs' court and the work that they did was less important than, and inferior to, that of the Commercial Court and Chancery Division. Perception was important and I thought that it was necessary to remedy the situation.

The first thing to do was to change the name of the court. I was keen not simply to call it 'the Construction Court'. First, the ORs did not only try construction cases. Second, many shared Lord Bingham's belief that OR cases were all about Scott Schedules or, I would add, delay and disruption claims. One way of emphasising that the ORs did not only try construction cases was to expand or change the name of the court. I first thought of 'Construction and Technical Court', but I believed that in no time this would be shortened to 'CAT' and the Court would be perceived to be yet another tribunal rather than a mainstream court. And the word 'Technical' seemed inappropriate. It might suggest that the Court itself engaged in technical activities and would not indicate the type of disputes that were referred to it.

I thought 'Technology' sounded more modern and cutting-edge, and that idea would be further promoted by 'The Technology and Construction Court' rather than 'The Construction and Technology Court' (even though at that time most of the work was construction). It did not occur to me that in no time at all 'The Technology and Construction Court' would become known as 'The TCC'.[6] When I told Lord Bingham that I would like the Court to be renamed and that I preferred 'The Technology and Construction Court' to 'The Construction and Technology Court', he teased me. He did not think it mattered, but I thought that it did.

In retrospect, it is hard to believe that it took so long for the change of name to come about. In 1998, some seasoned users of the Court still referred to it as 'the ORs' corridor'. I believe that the change of name and, in particular, the inclusion in it of the word 'Court' was a most important milestone in the history of the Court and its integration into the mainstream of the court system. The ORs were pleased with the change of name and I believe that the users of the Court were too.

There were two other changes that I introduced with the approval of Lord Bingham. The first was that the ORs should be addressed under the style of 'my Lord' and 'your Lordship'. This is the style of address for High Court judges (and above). It is also the style of address for judges who sit in the Central Criminal Court (the Old Bailey) even though they are not High Court judges, but senior circuit judges. I could see no reason why these judges should be addressed 'my Lord', but the ORs, who were also senior circuit judges, were addressed 'your Honour' like all circuit judges of whatever rank. This may have seemed to be a mere cosmetic change, but I thought it was more significant than that. It was another indication that the judges of the TCC should be treated as equivalent in standing to High Court judges. The TCC judges loved this change. Although they might not have admitted it, they enjoyed being addressed as 'my Lord'.

The second change that I introduced was also symbolic in a sense. The Daily Cause list was published to show the cases that were due to be heard each day in the Royal Courts of Justice and St Dunstan's House. At the top of the List appeared the names of the cases that were listed to be heard that day in the Court of Appeal, followed by those that were listed to be heard in the High Court. Lower down the List were other cases including those to be heard by Masters and Registrars. Right at the bottom of the List were the cases due to be heard by the TCC judges. It seemed to me that this was quite wrong. It was almost as if these cases were an afterthought and barely worthy of mention at all. This was consistent with the ORs' corridor having been in a remote part of the RCJ and later at the top of St Dunstan's House. As a result of my intervention, the TCC cases were listed after the Commercial Court and Chancery Division cases.

I believe that these changes helped to enhance the standing of the TCC. But the breakthrough that was really needed was that some or all of the TCC judges should be High Court judges. This change did not occur during my time as judge

[6] 'Official Referee's Court is now TCC', *The Times*, 13 October 1998.

in charge of the TCC. But I believe that the changes that I introduced were an important stepping stone along the way. There was no justification for treating the TCC as inferior to the Commercial Court and the Chancery Division.

Another innovation that I introduced was to hold regular periodic meetings with all the judges. These were a useful medium for the exchange of ideas and for me to impart information to them and hear any of their complaints directly from them. It was surprising that such meetings had not previously taken place. I had the impression that each of the judges had been something of an island to himself (there were no female judges at that time). Although it was important to respect the independence of the judges, it seemed to me that we could learn from each other and a degree of uniformity of approach was desirable. This was especially desirable in relation to the approach to procedural matters such as what kind of directions to give at case management conferences.

I believe that innovations of this kind did something to develop an *esprit de corps* in the court. I also tried to foster collegiality by taking trouble to deliver valedictory addresses to retiring judges. I recall the valedictory I gave for Judge Esyr Lewis when he retired in 1998. Members of his family were present. He was held in great affection by his colleagues, the staff and those who appeared before him. I tried to reflect this in my speech. I recall saying that I had been searching for an amusing anecdote about him, but had found nothing. Not even a youthful peccadillo in the Brecon Beacons. It was good to try occasionally to lighten the mood in what was essentially a rather serious court.

It was not only the changes that I introduced that enhanced the standing of the court. I believe that my arrival as the first High Court judge to sit in the ORs' court/TCC itself contributed to raise the profile and standing of the court. I heard some TCC cases myself. On the whole, I chose cases which I thought were important and difficult.

Until I arrived in the court, I had not heard of a statute which rejoiced in the name of the HGCRA. As is now well known, this statute introduced adjudication in construction disputes. The history of the adjudication litigation is an important subject that is dealt with elsewhere in this book. In this chapter, it is sufficient if I describe how, in February 1999, I came to decide the first adjudication case that was litigated in our courts.[7] It was entirely appropriate that this case was issued in the TCC. Disputes arose in relation to an interim application for payment, which Macob referred to adjudication. The adjudicator decided that Morrison should pay a sum in excess of £300,000. Morrison refused to comply with the decision and Macob applied for a mandatory injunction to enforce the adjudicator's decision. Morrison defended the application on the basis that the adjudicator's decision was wrong on the merits and also that the contract contained a valid arbitration clause. As for the first point, I decided that a decision whose validity was challenged on the merits was nevertheless a 'decision' within the meaning of the HGRA and was

[7] *Macob Civil Engineering Ltd v Morrison Construction Ltd* [1999] EWHC 254 (TCC) 0, [1999] BLR 93.

therefore enforceable. Second, I refused to accept that, just because the dispute was subject to a separate reference to arbitration, the adjudicator's decision should not be enforced. I said that the HGRA had not abolished arbitration and litigation of construction disputes. It had merely introduced an intervening provisional stage in the dispute resolution process. Crucially, it had made it clear that the decisions of adjudicators were binding and had to be complied with until the dispute was finally resolved.[8]

The background to my decision in this case was that claimants in construction cases who alleged that they were owed money were often confronted with defences which, though dubious, were sufficient to prevent the claimants from obtaining summary judgment in respect of the debts that were owed to them, thereby compelling them to engage in expensive and protracted litigation or arbitration. This was a problem which was faced, in particular, by subcontractors who were seeking payment of debts owed by more muscular main contractors. The problem was particularly acute in cases where the subcontract contained a clause which provided that an arbitration between the main contractor and subcontractor could not be commenced until the main contract works had been completed, at any rate unless the main contractor decided otherwise. This was a mischief that the adjudication scheme was intended to address. It seemed to me that, if it was open to a defendant to resist the enforcement of an adjudicator's decision by saying that the decision was not a decision within the meaning of the HGRA because it was erroneous in fact or in law, the aims of the scheme would be frustrated and adjudication would rapidly become a dead letter. My decision was described in some quarters as 'robust'. It set the tone of what was to follow. Surprisingly, Morrison did not appeal.

It was not long before claimants' attempts to enforce the decisions of adjudicators by summary proceedings were being resisted on all manner of grounds. The next adjudication case that I heard did go to the Court of Appeal.[9] The adjudicator had awarded a sum which, it was common ground, he had arrived at by making a simple arithmetical error. He had erroneously awarded £207,741 in favour of Dahl-Jensen and it was common ground that he should have awarded £141,254 in favour of Bouygues.[10] I held that it was inherent in the scheme that injustices would occur, but that these would be subsequently corrected by litigation, arbitration or agreement. If a defendant could resist a claim for summary judgment to enforce an adjudicator's decision by alleging that the decision was arguably erroneous in fact or in law, the scheme would fail.[11] I therefore held that the courts would not refuse to enforce an adjudicator's decision on the grounds of error, even an obvious error that was admitted to be such by the defendant. It would only refuse to enforce a decision if it was arguable that there had been a fundamental jurisdictional error

[8] ibid, para 14.

[9] *Bouygues (UK) Ltd v Dahl-Jensen UK Ltd* [2000] BLR 49 (TCC); [2000] EWCA Civ 507, [2001] 1 All ER (Comm) 1041 (Court of Appeal).

[10] ibid (TCC), [11].

[11] ibid, [34]–[35].

or serious procedural unfairness.[12] The defendants' appeal was dismissed by the Court of Appeal and I believe that this approach has been robustly and consistently applied in subsequent case law.

Various practitioners told me at the time that they disagreed with my decisions. I recall one saying that Lord Denning would not have allowed the courts to become a tool for injustice in this way. Of course, I saw the force of the argument that to require a defendant to comply with an adjudicator's decision that was manifestly incorrect is unfair and produces injustice. But I believed that it was necessary to interpret and apply the 1996 Act in a manner which would promote the policy objectives of achieving justice for contractors who were being starved of cash-flow by being forced to sue for their money in expensive, drawn-out arbitration and litigation. The statutory solution to this problem was to devise a scheme which provided for decisions by adjudicators which had only temporary binding effect. If occasionally this meant that an adjudicator's decision which was obviously incorrect was nonetheless enforceable, that was a price that had to be paid in the interests of preserving the integrity of the scheme as a whole.

During the years since I ceased to be involved with the TCC at the end of 2000, when I was appointed to the Court of Appeal, the enforcement of adjudicators' decisions has formed an important part of the court's diet of work. The approach that I adopted in *Macob* was refined and developed in the following years. But I believe that these early decisions have formed the bedrock of the court's jurisprudence in this area of the law. I always found it surprising that the adjudication scheme, suitably adapted, has not been applied outside construction contracts.

As I approached the end of my period as the judge in charge of the TCC, I had to consider whether I could conscientiously fulfil Lord Bingham's hope that I recommend one of the then serving ORs to be appointed as my successor and thereby a High Court Judge. I reluctantly came to the disappointing conclusion that none of them had the necessary qualities. Instead, I suggested that Thayne Forbes J be appointed. He had been a High Court Judge since 1993, having been an OR from 1990 to 1993.

In what I said so far, I have focused on the ORs/TCC in London. But I should not conclude without referring to the Senior Circuit judges who decide OR/TCC cases outside London. In recent decades, the specialist Circuit judges who sit in the large regional Civil Justice Centres have played an increasingly important role in trying these cases. Their contributions have been invaluable.

I look back on my time as judge in charge of the TCC with considerable satisfaction. I believe that the arrival of a High Court Judge and the changes that were made during my time there contributed to the enhancement of the status of the court. My appointment was the first step along the road to establishing the TCC as a court in which High Court judges routinely tried what used to be known as OR cases. The standing of the TCC is now on a par with that of the Commercial Court and the Property and Business Court.

[12] ibid, [36].

7

The TCC and the Housing Grants, Construction and Regeneration Act 1996

SIR RUPERT JACKSON, NICHOLAS HIGGS AND HANNAH FRY

I. Introduction

The interpretation and application of the Housing Grants, Construction and Regeneration Act 1996 ('the HGCRA' or 'the Act', as later amended by the Local Democracy, Economic Development and Construction Act 2009), has been part of the core work undertaken by the TCC since the Act came into force in 1998. An entire text book could be written on the subject (as Sir Peter Coulson has ably demonstrated) so to do this subject justice in one short chapter will require a somewhat sweeping overview of the Act and subsequent litigation.

The most significant change brought in by the Act was a statutory right to adjudicate a dispute under a construction contract 'at any time'. Adjudication is a private dispute resolution mechanism involving a neutral third party acting under an agreed process and reaching a decision on a dispute, or on specified issues.[1] Adjudication quickly became established as a means for resolving many construction disputes. It has largely displaced domestic arbitration in the construction field.

The statutory right to adjudication was introduced following Sir Michael Latham's 1994 report *Constructing the Team*.[2] This chapter briefly considers the genesis of the reforms proposed in Sir Michael's report, and the history of the Act which placed them upon a statutory footing. It then examines the key role that the TCC played in establishing the scope of the Act's application and, importantly, the means of enforcement of the 'temporarily final but binding' decisions made by adjudicators under the Act's powers.

From the early TCC decisions such as *Macob Civil Engineering Ltd v Morrison Construction Ltd*,[3] *Bouygues UK Ltd v Dahl-Jensen UK Ltd*[4] and

[1] S Blake, J Brown and S Sime, *The Jackson ADR Handbook*, 2nd edn (Oxford, OUP 2016) 2.08.
[2] Sir M Latham, *Constructing the Team* (HMSO 1994).
[3] *Macob Civil Engineering Ltd v Morrison Construction Ltd* [1999] BLR 93.
[4] *Bouygues UK Ltd v Dahl-Jensen UK Ltd* [2000] BLR 49.

Carillion Construction Ltd v Devonport Royal Dockyard Ltd,[5] to the more recent interventions of the Supreme Court such as in *Bresco Electrical Services Ltd (In Liquidation) v Michael J Lonsdale (Electrical) Ltd*,[6] the unique role of the TCC in the development of adjudication jurisprudence is reviewed, together with its impact on other jurisdictions.

The introduction of statutory adjudication coincided with the formation of the TCC, as described by others elsewhere in this work. Thus, adjudication work was woven into the fabric of TCC jurisprudence from the outset. This took on particular importance following the resolution in 2004 that TCC business in London would be heard exclusively by High Court judges. In the period from 2004 to 2007, adjudication issues came to occupy approximately 25 per cent of the time of the judge in charge of the TCC.

II. The Genesis of the HGCRA

The author of *Constructing the Team* had been a Conservative MP, but at the time of the commissioning of the review in July 1993 he was no longer sitting in Parliament, having stood down in 1992. The sur-title of Sir Michael's report was 'Final Report of the Government/Industry Review of Procurement and Contractual Arrangements in the UK Construction Industry'. He was at pains to stress that the review was a joint enterprise between government and industry with Sir Michael being 'an independent, but friendly observer'. His brief had been to make 'recommendations to Government, the construction industry and its clients regarding reform to reduce conflict and litigation and encourage the industry's productivity and competitiveness'. It seems somewhat remarkable that the final report was published just a year after the announcement of the review, in July 1994. It contained a comprehensive set of recommendations together with proposals for swift implementation.

The contemporary problems of the construction industry were well known and longstanding. The industry had been the subject of a number of similar prior reports: the Simon Report in 1944,[7] the report by Sir Harold Emmerson in 1962[8] and the Banwell Report in 1964.[9] It could be said that relatively little had changed

[5] *Carillion Construction Ltd v Devonport Royal Dockyard Ltd* [2005] EWHC 778 (TCC) [2005] BLR 310.

[6] *Bresco Electrical Services Ltd (In Liquidation) v Michael J Lonsdale (Electrical) Ltd* [2020] UKSC 25, [2020] Bus LR 1000.

[7] Report of the Central Council for Works and Buildings, chaired by Sir Ernest Simon, *The Placing and Management of Building Contracts* (HMSO 1944).

[8] Report prepared for the Minister of Works by Sir Harold Emmerson, *Survey of Problems Before the Construction Industries* (HMSO 1962).

[9] Report of the Committee prepared for Ministry of Public Building and Works, chaired by Sir Harold Banwell, *The Placing and Management of Contracts for Building and Civil Engineering Work* (HMSO 1964).

since Brunel's day:[10] aggressive tendering, low productivity and poor economic outcomes, particularly for sub-contractors. The consequences of these structural problems, and the accompanying litigiousness, were familiar territory in the Official Referees' courts and elsewhere:

> The Courts are aware of what happens in these building disputes; cases go either to arbitration or before an official referee; they drag on and on and on; the cash flow is held up. In the majority of cases, because one party or the other cannot wait any longer for the money, there is some kind of compromise, very often not based on the justice of the case but on the financial situation of one of the parties. That sort of result is to be avoided if possible. In my judgment it can be avoided if the Courts make a robust approach, as the Master did in this case, to the jurisdiction under O. 14.[11]

The call by Lawton LJ in the above passage to adopt a more robust approach to resolving building disputes, whilst not acceded to without qualification by his fellow Lord Justices, perhaps presaged the approach which would later be taken to the enforcement of adjudication following Latham's report.

To describe the Latham report as a whirlwind hitting the industry is no exaggeration.[12] In contrast to the earlier studies there seemed to be a general consensus that, this time, the recommendations needed to be put into practice. Latham was both practical and wide-ranging in the steps he saw as needing to be taken to shake the construction industry from its stupor. His mission was to engender a new, more collaborative and cooperative culture. Numerous of his recommendations are still recognisable today, although their genesis may not be acknowledged or remembered. The CICS scheme for certification of construction workers flowed from the recommendations for training and registration made by Latham. The Considerate Contractor's scheme was initiated following the recommendations for improvements in the public perception of the industry. The proliferation of the NEC forms of contract may have occurred in any event, but it was Latham who recommended their adoption for all public sector projects and promotion to private sector clients.

The elements of Latham's report of most significance to the legal profession were those encompassed within his proposed 'Construction Contracts Bill'. The call to place some of his reforms onto a statutory basis was answered by government, albeit being made through the HGCRA rather than as a standalone construction Bill. This was not a wholesale adoption, however. There were a number of proposed reforms in the Latham Report which did not make their way into the Bill. Latham included proposals for, essentially, decennial liability accompanied by mandatory defects insurance and changes in the liability of suppliers. Whilst a working group developed these proposals in some detail they were then passed to

[10] See, eg, *Ranger v The Great Western Railway Company* (1854) 10 ER 824.

[11] *Ellis Mechanical Services vs. Wates Construction Limited* [1978] 1 Lloyd's Rep 33, (1976) 2 BLR 57 (Lawton LJ).

[12] Mr Justice Jackson, '2006 Denning Lecture' (28 November 2006) www.filewiz.co.uk/bacfi/denning_lecture_2006.pdf (accessed 28 July 2022).

the Law Commission and progressed no further. His proposal for a project trust fund did not even make it as far as the Law Commission, although, as recently as September 2022, the government have promoted a policy of the use of project bank accounts in construction projects.[13]

The key recommendations which were incorporated into the HGCRA were provisions in respect of payment and adjudication. Sir Michael had envisaged a similar regime to the unfair contract legislation providing statutory backing to standard form contracts such as the NEC and the JCT. His proposal was that amendments to the standard forms which interfered with certain rights of payment, set-off or immediate adjudication would be deemed invalid by statute. His recommendations for adjudication were as follows:

> 9.14 I have already recommended that a system of adjudication should be introduced within all the Standard Forms of Contract (except where comparable arrangements already exist for mediation or conciliation) and that this should be underpinned by legislation. I also recommend that:-
>
> 1. There should be no restrictions on the issues capable of being referred to the adjudicator, conciliator or mediator, either in the main contract or subcontract documentation.
> 2. The award of the adjudicator should be implemented immediately. The use of stake holders should only be permitted if both parties agree or if the adjudicator so directs.
> 3. Any appeals to arbitration or the courts should be after practical completion, and should not be permitted to delay the implementation of the award, unless an immediate and exceptional issue arises for the courts or as in the circumstances described in (4) overleaf.
> 4. Resort to the courts should be immediately available if a party refuses to implement the award of an adjudicator. In such circumstances, the courts may wish to support the system of adjudication by agreeing to expedited procedures for interim payments.
> 5. Training procedures should be devised for adjudicators. A Code of Practice should also be drawn up under the auspices of the proposed Implementation forum.[14]

The approach taken in drafting the Housing Grants, Construction and Regeneration Bill was slightly different. It followed the approach of, for example, the Supply of Goods and Services Act 1982 in providing for statutorily implied terms. The slight twist was the mandating of a minimum standard to be provided for in contracts, with a statutory scheme as a fall back if the contract were deficient. This approach was explained as follows by the Construction Minister during the second reading of the Bill:

> Our provisions provide a right to refer construction disputes for adjudication. We expect that entitlement to be met normally by the construction industry deciding, as a matter

[13] The Cabinet Office, *The Construction Playbook* (Version 1.1, HMSO September 2022).
[14] Latham (n 2) 91–92.

> of course, to include adjudication arrangements in its contracts. The Government are challenging the industry to take action to improve its contractual practice and to introduce the sort of adjudication arrangements that best suit it. The best outcome must be that there is no need for a fall-back.
>
> However, we have a view about the minimum standards that contractual adjudication clauses must satisfy. They relate to speed of decision, impartiality, and the freedom for an adjudicator to investigate disputes and reach his own conclusion. In another place we added the necessary provision to give adjudicators protection from personal liability so long as they act in good faith.
>
> The Government are conscious that one party to a contract may think that it can tip the scales in its favour if it strikes out the adjudication clause. That is the industry's experience until now. If there is no adjudication provision in a contract, or the clause is defective in any way, we shall provide a fall-back adjudication mechanism in our scheme for construction contracts, to be made by statutory instrument.[15]

The minimum standards required by the Bill applied, as Sir Michael had recommended, in respect of payment provisions and adjudication. The fall-back referred to by the minister was introduced as secondary legislation in the form of the Scheme for Construction Contracts (England and Wales) Regulations 1998 ('the Scheme').

The HGCRA duly received Royal Assent in July 1996 and the relevant sections came into force on 1 May 1998.[16]

The work of Sir Michael in gaining sufficient consensus amongst the disparate vested interests of the construction industry, and in such a short period of time, is remarkable; although the Construction Minister's prediction that the verb '*Lathamisation*' would enter the English lexicon proved somewhat hyperbolic.[17] As the parliamentary records show, much compromise was required in order to reach a final version of the Bill and subsequently of the Scheme.

As the industry, and the courts, implemented the Latham recommendations and the requirements of the HGCRA and the Scheme, the compromise nature of the Act became evident as its boundaries were tested. Indeed, Sir Michael somewhat distanced himself from the Act, hoping that it might remain in the background and, rightly, suggesting that it might need further consideration after a reasonable period of operation.[18] Various aspects proved open to abuse by those members of the industry who had perhaps not adopted the spirit of Latham's reforms, merely adherence to the letter.

[15] The Minister for Construction, Planning and Energy Efficiency (Mr Robert B Jones) *Hansard*, HC Deb Vol 277, cols 45–54 (07 May 1996).

[16] The Housing Grants, Construction and Regeneration Act (England and Wales) (Commencement No. 4) Order 1998.

[17] *Hansard*, HC Deb, Vol 281, col 80 (8 July 1996).

[18] Writing in the foreword to M Wood, *The Construction Act: A Practical Guide* (Oxford, Chandos Publishing (Oxford) Limited, 1999): 'The Act sprang from the Report. I personally was in no way involved in the drafting of the Bill, nor with its changes as it progressed through Parliament. There are sections of it which I find disappointing or in need of further consideration after a reasonable period of operation. Nevertheless, the Act was a necessary compromise between conflicting pressures on the previous Government and this one.'

In response, the government legislated again, this time in the form of the Local Democracy, Economic Development and Construction Act 2009 ('the LDEDCA'). This was, again, something of a hodgepodge of an Act with the provisions in relation to construction having little to do with the Act's other provisions. The significant changes which this introduced to the HGCRA were: inclusion of oral contracts, outlawing of '*Tolent*' clauses, codification of the slip rule, clarification of suspension rights and amendments to the payment notice regime.

It had been suggested that the limitation of the HGCRA to written contracts was influenced by its coincidence with the Arbitration Act 1996 and a desire to align adjudication and arbitration. Given the proliferation of oral contracts in the construction industry, particularly further down the supply chain, this had denied some parties access to statutory adjudication. The amendments of the LDEDCA removed this fetter.

So called '*Tolent*' clauses had been a controversial feature of adjudication since the decision of HH Judge Mackay in the Liverpool District Registry in April 2000 in *Bridgeway Construction Ltd v Tolent Construction Ltd.*[19] In that case there was a provision in the contract that the party serving a notice to adjudicate should bear all of the costs and expenses incurred by both parties in relation to the adjudication, including but not limited to all legal and experts fees, together with the adjudicator's fees and expenses. The claimants in that case argued that the relevant clauses were void because they tended to inhibit the contracting parties from pursuing their lawful remedies by way of adjudication. HH Judge Mackay disagreed.

Parliament sought to make such clauses of no effect through the changes introduced by the LDEDCA. Due to various last minute interventions at the Bill stage, there was some controversy over whether the drafting that was eventually incorporated would achieve the desired aim.[20] The controversy was rendered moot by the decision of Edwards-Stuart J in *Yuanda (UK) Co Ltd v WW Gear Construction Ltd.*[21] That case concerned a contract which included the following clause:

> Clause 9A: The adjudication procedure will be the TeCSA Adjudication Rules (amended to require nomination by the RICS and joining of the members of the professional team in a multi-party dispute situation). Notwithstanding the provisions of the above procedure and regardless of the eventual decision in the adjudication or in any subsequent litigation the Trade Contractor agrees that should he make a reference to Adjudication under the terms of this contract then he will be fully responsible for meeting and paying both his own and the Employer's legal and professional costs in relation to the Adjudication.

Edwards-Stuart J held that it was not contrary to the HGCRA to provide the adjudicator with the power to make an award as to how the parties' costs should

[19] *Bridgeway Construction Ltd v Tolent Construction Ltd* (2000) CILL 1662.

[20] See the discussion in D Helps, 'Construction Act Review (October): Outlawing Tolent Clauses and the LDEDC Act 2009 – the Denouement of Section 108A' (2011) 27(7) *Construction Law Journal* 575–593.

[21] *Yuanda (UK) Co Ltd v WW Gear Construction Ltd* [2010] EWHC 720 (TCC), [2011] 1 All ER (Comm) 550.

be borne. However, in *Yuanda* the practical effect of Clause 9A would be to deprive the contractor, if successful, of his remedy save to the extent that it exceeded the amount of the employer's costs. This, he found, would be contrary to the purpose of the Act allowing adjudication 'at any time'. The judgment was given before the coming into force of the LDEDCA. Although the learned judge referred to the incoming provisions he was clear that his decision would have been the same in any event.

Similarly, the amendments to provide for a slip rule codified what was already the position in case law. *Bloor Construction (UK) Ltd v Bowmer and Kirkland (London) Ltd*[22] had set the precedent that where a contract was silent there would be an implied term that the adjudicator could correct his decision in respect of arithmetical or other obvious errors. Section 140 of the LDEDCA provided the adjudicator with a statutory power to do so. The accompanying amendments to the Scheme provided a time limit of five days.

The other amendments, particularly in relation to payment notices, were more extensive. A new nomenclature of 'pay less notices' replaced 'withholding notices' and contract administrators were required to review their procedures to ensure they complied with the new regime.

The amendments made by the LDEDCA did not receive universal acclamation,[23] and it was questioned whether many of the amendments were required at all. The judges of the TCC had been given the task of making the Act work. It was a task they approached with enthusiasm tempered by their considerable experience of disputes in the construction industry. It would be an interesting exercise to consider whether the changes introduced by the LDEDCA might have all been effected, other than the change to extend adjudication to oral contracts, through the developing jurisprudence of the TCC in any event. Another book could probably be written on that subject alone.

The immediate question for the judges of the TCC, when the Act first came into effect, was how adjudication decisions would be enforced. This is the topic we now turn to consider.

III. The HGCRA and Enforcement

The intent of the government incorporating adjudication into the HGCRA was explained by the Minister for Construction during the Parliamentary debate on the Bill as follows:

> The Bill promotes a clear system of dispute resolution called adjudication. The industry is clear about what it means by that: it wants a mechanism that produces a fast and impartial resolution of a dispute and allows the contract to continue. The industry does

[22] *Bloor Construction (UK) Ltd v Bowmer and Kirkland (London) Ltd* [2000] BLR 314.

[23] See, eg, the discussion in P Sheridan and D Helps, 'Construction Act Review (October)' (2008) 24(7) *Construction Law Journal* 572–589.

> not want the decision necessarily to be the final one. It wants to ensure that disputes are tested at the time, on the spot and are resolved quickly to the parties' satisfaction.[24]

As indicated above, the HGRCA achieves this aim by requiring construction contracts (as defined within the Act) to contain effective provisions for adjudication. These minimum effective provisions are contained in section 108 of the Act. They include a right to give notice of a reference to adjudication at any time, to provide for a timetable for securing an adjudicator's appointment and for the subsequent decision and impose a duty on the adjudicator to act impartially. In the event that the mandatory requirements are not met then the adjudication provisions of the Scheme are applied. The Scheme contains detailed provisions for adjudication, adding flesh to the bones of the section 108 minimum requirements.

One lacuna in the HGCRA, however, is the means by which an adjudicator's decision, once obtained, is to be enforced. One of the requirements of section 108 is as follows:

> (3) The contract shall provide in writing that the decision of the adjudicator is binding until the dispute is finally determined by legal proceedings, by arbitration (if the contract provides for arbitration or the parties otherwise agree to arbitration) or by agreement.
>
> The parties may agree to accept the decision of the adjudicator as finally determining the dispute.

The provisions of the Scheme which will be implied if a construction contract fails to meet the requirement of section 108(3) are as follows:

> 23.—(1) In his decision, the adjudicator may, if he thinks fit, order any of the parties to comply peremptorily with his decision or any part of it.
>
> (2) The decision of the adjudicator shall be binding on the parties, and they shall comply with it until the dispute is finally determined by legal proceedings, by arbitration (if the contract provides for arbitration or the parties otherwise agree to arbitration) or by agreement between the parties.

The Scheme then goes on to provide that that section 42 of the Arbitration Act 1996 applies to the Scheme with the necessary modifications: that is that a court may make an order requiring a party to comply with a peremptory order made by the tribunal (oddly, the Scheme replaces 'tribunal' with 'adjudicator' elsewhere but not in the first subparagraph of section 42). The intention of the Scheme appears to have been to provide parties with recourse to the courts to enforce an adjudication decision by applying for a section 42 order. The oddity is that this provision would only be available under the Scheme, if a construction contract was compliant with section 108 of the HGCRA then there is no equivalent provision under the Act.

[24] The Minister for Construction, Planning and Energy Efficiency (Mr Robert B Jones) *Hansard*, HC Deb Vol 277, cols 45–54 (07 May 1996).

It is somewhat unclear, therefore, why section 42 of the Arbitration Act was incorporated into the Scheme[25] and the mechanism whereby Parliament intended that adjudication decisions should be enforced. It is one thing for the Act to provide that a decision is binding, but what is to be done if a party refuses to be so bound? Plainly some form of state sanction to enforce adjudicator's awards was required, but the detail is not present within the Act. As will be seen, the suggestion that an application under section 42 of the Arbitration Act may be the correct route is hampered by its absence from the Act and from the practical difficulties which such an application faced. The rationale for enforcement had been clearly stated by Parliament, even if the mechanism had not been:

> We intend to propose that parties be required to abide by an adjudicator's decision until practical completion of the contract, but that thereafter they may reopen the dispute. I re-emphasise the remarks by my noble Friend Lord Lucas during debate in the other place. We do not intend that adjudication should be used simply to postpone resolving disputes. We have had enough of disputes within the construction industry. Government, the industry and its clients want to see an end to them: they are expensive and damaging to the industry's productivity and reputation. We want to see the industry using the opportunity that we are giving it to improve its payment record and to resolve disputes quickly, without dragging them into arbitration or before the courts.[26]

Although Parliament seemed to be inferring that resolution may be achieved without recourse to the courts, it was not long before the first adjudication enforcement case came before the newly-formed TCC in London. Thus Dyson J was faced, in *Macob v Morrison*[27] with charting a route through the somewhat confused territory which the Act and the Scheme presented for those seeking to enforce this novel statutory adjudication decision.

Macob concerned a payment dispute which was referred to adjudication, Macob being ordered by the adjudicator to pay their sub-contractor, Morrison, approximately £300,000. Macob gave notice to Morrison that any dispute over the decision should be referred to arbitration, pursuant to the arbitration provisions in the sub-contract. When Morrison applied to the TCC to enforce the decision Macob applied to stay the dispute to arbitration pursuant to section 9 of the Arbitration Act 1996.

In making his decision the adjudicator had given permission to apply to the Court under section 42 of the Arbitration Act, as modified by the Scheme, for an order requiring compliance by the recalcitrant party. Macob contested the decision as being incorrect on the merits and arrived at in breach of the rules of natural justice. Three important issues therefore arose for determination: 1) whether there was a binding and enforceable adjudication decision; 2) whether there should be a stay to arbitration; and 3) how the adjudication decision should be enforced.

[25] Dyson J expressed similar uncertainty in *Macob* (n 3), discussed further below.

[26] The Minister for Construction, Planning and Energy Efficiency (Mr Robert B Jones) *Hansard*, HC Deb Vol 277, cols 45–54 (07 May 1996).

[27] *Macob* (n 3).

In determining how he should proceed, Dyson J relied upon the intention which Parliament had expressed during the passage of the Bill. He summarised that intention as follows:

> It is clear that Parliament intended that the adjudication should be conducted in a manner which those familiar with the grinding detail of the traditional approach to the resolution of construction disputes apparently find difficult to accept. But Parliament has not abolished arbitration and litigation of construction disputes. It has merely introduced an intervening provisional stage in the dispute resolution process. Crucially, it has made it clear that decisions of adjudicators are binding and are to be complied with until the dispute is finally resolved.[28]

As to the first question, Dyson J held that a decision whose validity is challenged is nevertheless a decision within the meaning of the Act and the Scheme. A challenged decision was still therefore binding on the parties until finally determined by litigation or arbitration.

As to the second question, a stay to arbitration was refused. The judge found that a party could not contend for a decision to be determined in arbitration without also recognising that it was a decision under the Act. The decision therefore had to be complied with rather than enforcement being stayed to arbitration.

The final question was enforcement. An order under section 42 of the Arbitration Act would have required a mandatory injunction ordering payment. Dyson J considered that it could not have been Parliament's intention that the consequences of breach of an injunction (contempt of court) would be more serious than of a failure to pay a money judgment.

Although in *Macob* there was no application for a money judgment, Dyson J concluded that:

> Thus s42 apart, the usual remedy for the failure to pay in accordance with an adjudicator's decision will be to issue proceedings claiming the sum due, followed by an application for summary judgment.

This means of enforcement was swiftly endorsed as other cases came before the TCC judges. In April 1999, a groundworks contractor sought to enforce an adjudication award in its favour for £12,212 worth of works at Borough Market in London in *Outwing Construction Ltd v H Randell and Son Ltd.*[29] Although payment was made of the decision amount on the return date for the application, HHJ Humphrey Lloyd QC nevertheless confirmed summary judgment as being the correct route for enforcement, following *Macob*, and awarded Outwing their costs (£750) of bringing the action.

As the jurisprudence developed, parties sought to test the grounds upon which an adjudicator's decision might be resisted at the enforcement stage. However, without Dyson J's clear-eyed appreciation of the role for which adjudication was

[28] *Macob* (n 3) 97.
[29] *Outwing Construction Ltd v H Randell and Son Ltd* [1999] BLR 156.

instituted it might be wondered whether it would have proceeded upon as sure a footing as his decision in *Macob v Morrison* placed it.

Not all commentators were quite so enthused with the developing jurisprudence on adjudication enforcement. Ian Duncan Wallace QC, writing in the Construction Law Journal,[30] was critical of aspects of Dyson J's reasoning in *Macob*. In particular he was concerned that it should not stand as authority that an adjudicator could proceed contrary to the rules of natural justice and yet have a decision enforced (as to this question, refer to the following section). To say that Duncan Wallace was not a fan of the HGCRA is possibly an understatement. His prediction of widespread injustice being done through 'erroneous awards' produced under 'impractical time limits' subsequently proved to be overly gloomy. As readers may know, adjudication soon became both accepted and relied upon by the industry as a swift method of resolving disputes, ranging from payment failures through to actions for damages due to professional negligence. One measure was the number of reported cases in the Building Law Reports: by 2000 there were already 13 adjudication enforcement cases reported, up from four in 1999.

By 2006, after eight years of the Act, the new regime had settled in and adjudication enforcement comprised about 20 per cent of the new claims launched in the London TCC.[31] Not all judges welcomed the wide ambit of adjudication: in *AWG Construction Services Ltd v Rockingham Motor Speedway Ltd* HH Judge Toulmin CMG QC lamented that adjudication had 'developed into an elaborate and expensive procedure which is wholly confrontational'.[32] Adjudication has, nonetheless, become the de-facto method of dispute resolution in construction, almost entirely replacing domestic arbitration.

Whilst it may be thought that the law regarding enforcement is now settled, there continue to be attempts to circumvent the 'pay now, argue later' rationale for enforcement of adjudication developed by the TCC. As recently as May 2022, HHJ Hodge QC sitting in the Manchester TCC heard detailed argument as to whether enforcement of an adjudication decision should be stayed to arbitration, pursuant to section 9 of the Arbitration Act 1996. Taking *Macob* as the touchstone for his dismissal of a stay, and the granting of summary judgment, the judge neatly summarised the position after over two decades of TCC decisions on the subject:

> Given that practical completion of this construction project was certified almost 15 years ago, I recognise that the 'pay now, argue later' policy that underlies the adjudication provisions of the Construction Act has something of a hollow ring in the present case. However, in this court, hard cases do not make bad law.[33]

[30] IND Wallace, 'HGCRA Adjudicators' Errors and Enforcement' (2000) 16(2) *Construction Law Journal* 102–113.

[31] 74 out of 392 in the year ending 30 September 2006. TCC Annual Report: www.judiciary.uk/wp-content/uploads/JCO/Documents/Reports/tcc_2nd_ann_report.pdf (accessed 27 July 2022).

[32] *AWG Construction Services Ltd v Rockingham Motor Speedway Ltd* [2004] EWCH 888, [2004] TCLR 6 [122].

[33] *The Metropolitan Borough Council of Sefton v Allenbuild Limited* [2022] EWHC 1443 (TCC) [90].

IV. The HGCRA and Natural Justice

The concerns over natural justice in adjudication developed into a consideration of whether breach of natural justice principles may act as a ground to refuse enforcement of an adjudicator's decision. The HGCRA and the Scheme do not contain a requirement to comply with natural justice, nor do they define natural justice or state in detail its requirements. However, section 108(2)(e) of HGCRA and paragraph 12(a) of the Scheme, as well as many of the standard form contracts, impose a duty on the adjudicator to act impartially.

There are inherent features of the adjudication process which may create a risk of the rules of natural justice being breached. First, the timeframe within which the adjudication must be completed. Section 108(2)(c) of the HGRCA requires the adjudicator to reach a decision within 28 days of referral or such longer period as is agreed by the parties after the dispute has been referred. Section 108(2)(d) of the HGRCA allows the adjudicator to extend the period up to 14 days with the consent of the referring party. This timeframe aims to ensure prompt and rapid decisions by the adjudicator. However, it also puts pressure on the adjudicator to fully and fairly digest the parties' arguments and reach a decision.

Second, section 108(2)(a) of the HGRCA enables a party to give notice 'at any time' of their intention to refer a dispute to adjudication. This can lead to complex disputes being referred to arbitration several years after the completion of the projects.

Third, section 108(2)(f) of the HGRCA and Part I, paragraph 13 of the Scheme permits the adjudicator to take the initiative in ascertaining the facts and the law. The adjudicator therefore may conduct an entirely inquisitorial process or invite representations from the parties. Therefore, as the adjudicator may take the initiative, there is a greater risk that the rules of natural justice might be breached.

This inevitable tension has long been recognised by the TCC. HHJ Toulmin summarised the issue as follows:

> As disputes referred to adjudication have become ever more complex, and referrals are made (in contrast to the original purpose of the legislation) long after the relationship between the parties is at an end, there might be a conflict for an adjudicator between reaching a decision within the stringent time limits under ss.108 and 109 of the Housing Grants Construction and Regeneration Act 1996 (the Act), and the adjudicator's duty under the Act to act impartially.[34]

The meaning of natural justice in the context of adjudication and the extent to which it can be used as a potential ground to refuse enforcement has evolved over the history of the TCC. When the Act came into force in 1998, there was doubt and ambiguity over whether natural justice principles may act as a ground to refuse enforcement of an adjudicator's decision.

[34] *Rockingham* (n 32) [11].

In *Macob v Morrison*, Dyson J made it clear that a mere procedural error should not invalidate an adjudicator's decision.[35] The defendant in this case argued that the adjudicator's decision was invalid and unenforceable on grounds that the adjudicator had made a procedural error in conducting the adjudication in breach of the rules of natural justice. Dyson J held that if an adjudicator's decision is wrong 'whether because he erred on the facts or the law, or because in reaching his decision he made a procedural error which invalidates the decision, it is still a decision on the issue'.[36]

Adjudication decisions have been upheld on this basis, even where the adjudicator has been shown to have made an error. In *Bouygues UK Ltd v Dahl-Jensen UK Ltd*, the Court of Appeal held that the adjudicator's determination would be binding if they asked the right question but answered it in the wrong way and a nullity if they asked the wrong question.[37] In that case, the adjudicator answered the question put to him but in making calculations to answer the question of whether the payments so far made under the subcontract represented an overpayment or an underpayment, he overlooked the fact that the assessment should be based on the sum presently due for payment, ie, the contract sum less the retention, rather than the gross contract sum. That was an error made when the adjudicator was acting within his jurisdiction and therefore the award was enforceable.

The TCC clarified in later cases that natural justice may be an effective ground to refuse enforcement of an adjudicator's decision, although it would be restricted in scope.

In *Discain Project Services Ltd v Opecprime Development Ltd (No.1)*, the defendant relied upon the fact that the claimant had had telephone conversations with the adjudicator which had not been communicated to it and in these conversations, submissions concerning the adjudication were alleged to have been made.[38] HHJ Bowsher refused to enforce the adjudicator's decision summarily and gave leave to defend on the basis that it was arguable that there had been a breach of the rules of natural justice. Regarding natural justice, HHJ Bowsher held:

> I do understand that adjudicators have great difficulties in operating this statutory scheme, and I am not in any way detracting from the decision in Macob. It would be quite wrong for the parties to search around for breaches of the rules of natural justice. It is a question of fact and degree in each case, and in this case the adjudicator overstretched the rules.
>
> [...]
>
> That Scheme makes regard for the rules of natural justice more rather than less important. Because there is no appeal on fact or law from the adjudicator's decision, it is all the more important that the manner in which he reaches his decision should be beyond reproach. At the same time, one has to recognise that the adjudicator is working under

[35] *Macob* (n 3).
[36] ibid, [19].
[37] *Bouygues* (n 4).
[38] *Discain Project Services Ltd v Opecprime Development (No.1)* [2000] BLR 402.

> pressure of time and circumstance which makes it extremely difficult to comply with the rules of natural justice in the manner of a court or an arbitrator. Repugnant as it may be to one's approach to judicial decision-making, I think that the system created by the Housing Grants Construction and Regeneration Act can only be made to work in practice if some breaches of the rules of natural justice which have no demonstrable consequence are disregarded.[39]

This passage was cited with approval in *Balfour Beatty Construction Ltd v The Mayor of Burgesses of the London Borough of Lambeth* whereby HHJ Lloyd commented that, 'it is now well-established that the purpose of adjudication is not to be thwarted by an overly sensitive concern for procedural niceties'.[40]

The judges of the TCC have been cognisant of the ease with which a party can mount a challenge based on an alleged breach of natural justice and the potential for the floodgates to be opened.[41] Judges have navigated this problem by requiring that the breach of natural justice must be material in order to refuse enforcement on a summary basis.

Building on *Discain*,[42] HHJ Lloyd in *Balfour Beatty Construction Ltd v The Mayor of Burgesses of the London Borough of Lambeth* held that an alleged breach of the rules of natural justice must be material or significant:

> In determining whether a party has been treated fairly or in determining whether an adjudicator has acted impartially, it is very necessary to bear in mind that the point or issue which is to be brought to the attention of the parties must be one which is either decisive or of considerable potential importance to the outcome and not peripheral or irrelevant. It is now clear that the construction industry regards adjudication not simply as a staging post towards the final resolution of the dispute in arbitration or litigation but as having in itself considerable weight and impact that in practice goes beyond the legal requirement that the decision has for the time being to be observed. Lack of impartiality or of fairness in adjudication must be considered in that light. It has become all the more necessary that, within the rough nature of the process, decisions are still made in a basically fair manner so that the system itself continues to enjoy the confidence it now has apparently earned.[43]

In *Carillion Construction Ltd v Devonport Royal Dockyard Ltd* Jackson J at first instance held that where an adjudicator declines to consider evidence which on his analysis of the facts and law is irrelevant, that is not a breach of the rules of natural justice.[44] He held that it will only be in an exceptional case that an adjudicator's failure to put his provisional conclusions to the parties will constitute such

[39] ibid, [10], [74].

[40] *Balfour Beatty Construction Ltd v The Mayor of Burgesses of the London Borough of Lambeth* [2002] EWHC 597 (TCC), [2002] BLR 288 [27].

[41] *Macob* (n 3) [18].

[42] *Discain* (n 38).

[43] *Balfour Beatty* (n 40) [29].

[44] *Carillion Construction Ltd v Devonport Royal Dockyard Ltd* [2005] EWHC 778 (TCC) [2005] BLR 310.

a serious breach of the rules of natural justice that the Court will decline to enforce his decision. The Court of Appeal expressly approved this proposition and added that it would only be in the plainest cases that a challenge could be mounted on the basis of breach of the rules of natural justice.[45]

Adjudication continues to be used for high value complex final account claims and TCC judges have questioned whether adjudication was intended to resolve such disputes. For example, HHJ Lloyd commented in *Balfour Beatty*:

> This is yet another case in which adjudication has been launched after completion of the works and in which the dispute attracts a simple description but comprises a highly complex set of facts and issues relating to the performance of a contract carried over many months. It may well be doubted whether adjudication was intended for such a situation.[46]

Further, Chadwick LJ in *Carillion Construction Ltd v Devonport Royal Dockyard Ltd* made the following observation:

> The scheme was not enacted in order to provide definitive answers to complex questions. Indeed, it may be open to doubt whether Parliament contemplated that disputes involving difficult questions of law would be referred to adjudication under the statutory scheme; or whether such disputes are suitable for adjudication under the scheme.[47]

Carillion was a post-completion dispute over which Carillion sought payment of over £10 million. An arbitration or litigation of the same matter might have been expected to take many months (if not years) with a hearing of at least several weeks.

The TCC have set out clear guidelines to deal with natural justice concerns arising from the nature and size of the claim. In *CIB Properties Ltd v Birse Construction Ltd* HHJ Toulmin held that the test is not whether the dispute is too complicated to refer to adjudication but whether the adjudicator was able to reach a fair decision within the time limits allowed by the parties.[48]

In *Amec Group Limited v Thames Water Utilities Ltd*, Coulson J summarised the principles applied by the TCC in this area:

> (a) The mere fact that an adjudication is concerned with a large or complex dispute does not of itself make it unsuitable for adjudication: see CIB v. Birse.
> (b) What matters is whether, notwithstanding the size or complexity of the dispute, the adjudicator had: (i) sufficiently appreciated the nature of any issue referred to him before giving a decision on that issue, including the submissions of each party; and (ii) was satisfied that he could do broad justice between the parties (see CIB v. Birse).
> (c) If the adjudicator felt able to reach a decision within the time limit then a court, when considering whether or not that conclusion was outside the rules of natural

[45] *Carillion Construction Ltd v Devonport Royal Dockyard Ltd* [2005] EWCA Civ 1358, [2006] BLR 15 [84]–[87].

[46] *Balfour Beatty* (n 40) [30].

[47] *Carillion* (n 45) [86].

[48] *CIB Properties Ltd v Birse Construction Ltd* [2004] EWHC 2365 (TCC), [2005] 1 WLR 2252 [26].

> justice, would consider the basis on which the adjudicator reached that conclusion (HS Properties).[49]

As parties have tested the boundaries of when an adjudication decision may be resisted, the judges of the TCC have made clear that natural justice has an important, albeit subordinated, role in adjudication. The TCC has dealt with the challenges posed by the inherent features of the adjudication process by introducing clear guidelines concerning materiality of breach of natural justice principles and the size and nature of the claim. This has allowed adequate safeguards to be imposed to uphold natural justice without driving a cart and horse through the Act's original intentions to create a speedy interim dispute resolution mechanism.

V. The HGCRA and Insolvency

There have been important questions raised before the TCC concerning the compatibility of the adjudication of construction disputes and insolvency. In particular, if there are cross-claims between the parties to a construction contract and one of them is in liquidation, can there be an adjudication of any dispute between them about those cross-claims?

Rule 14.25 of the Insolvency (England and Wales) Rules 2016 (SI 2016/1024) makes provision for automatic set-off of cross-claims between a company in liquidation and each of its creditors, giving rise to a single net balance between them to be ascertained by the taking of an account:

> 14.25. (1) This rule applies in a winding up where, before the company goes into liquidation, there have been mutual dealings between the company and a creditor of the company proving or claiming to prove for a debt in the liquidation.
> (2) An account must be taken of what is due from the company and the creditor to each other in respect of their mutual dealings and the sums due from the one must be set off against the sums due from the other.
> (3) If there is a balance owed to the creditor then only that balance is provable in the winding up.
> (4) If there is a balance owed to the company then that must be paid to the liquidator as part of the assets. [...]

The TCC has traditionally been wary about awarding summary judgment arising out of an adjudication involving cross-claims between parties where one of them is in liquidation. In *Bouygues (UK) Ltd v Dahl-Jensen (UK) Ltd*, Chadwick LJ commented on the effect of the Insolvency Rules, then the 1986 Rules, on cross-claims:

> In circumstances such as the present, where there are latent claims and cross-claims between parties, one of which is in liquidation, it seems to me that there is a compelling

[49] *Amec Group Limited v Thames Water Utilities Ltd* [2010] EWHC 419 (TCC) [60].

> reason to refuse summary judgment on a claim arising out of an adjudication which is necessarily, provisional. All claims and cross-claims should be resolved in the liquidation, in which full account can be taken and a balance struck. That is what rule 4.90 of the Insolvency Rules 1986 requires.[50]

Chadwick LJ did not come to a final conclusion regarding the effect of the liquidation in terms of jurisdiction of the adjudicator because the point was not taken before the trial judge or embraced with any enthusiasm on appeal. Accordingly, the appeal against the grant of summary judgment was dismissed, although a stay of execution was granted which 'substantially negated' the effect of the summary judgment.

Further, in *Hart Investments Ltd v Fidler*,[51] HHJ Coulson agreed with Chadwick LJ's ruling in *Bouygues*,[52] that insolvency is a compelling reason to refuse summary judgment. He considered that the essential point was that to enter judgment in that case might amount to an inaccurate assertion of the parties' substantive rights because the judgment would be based upon a decision which is only temporarily binding.

The question of whether and in what circumstances insolvent companies have the right to use adjudication proceedings came before the TCC in *Michael J Lonsdale (Electrical) Limited v Bresco Electrical Services Limited (In Liquidation)*.[53] Fraser J framed the central question as whether a company in liquidation can refer a dispute to adjudication when that dispute includes (whether in whole or in part) determination of a claim for further sums said to be due to the referring party from the responding party?

First, Fraser J held that the sums claimed to be due between the parties fell within the definition of 'mutual dealings' as set out in rule 14.25 of the Insolvency Rules 2016.

Second, he held that by operation of the Insolvency Rules, when a liquidator was appointed, claims and cross-claims ceased to be capable of separate enforcement and therefore, in this case the adjudicator did not have jurisdiction to determine the claim. In conclusion, he held that a company in liquidation cannot refer a dispute to adjudication when that dispute includes (whether in whole or in part) determination of any claim for further sums said to be due to the referring party from the responding party.

The TCC's decision was appealed to the Court of Appeal.[54] In terms of the jurisdiction argument, Coulson LJ could see no reason why, purely as a matter of jurisdiction, a reference to adjudication should be treated any differently to a reference to arbitration. If the contractual right to refer the claim to arbitration is not

[50] *Bouygues* (n 4) [35].

[51] *Hart Investments Ltd v Fidler* [2006] EWHC 2857 (TCC) [2007] BLR 30.

[52] *Bouygues* (n 4).

[53] *Michael J Lonsdale (Electrical) Limited v Bresco Electrical Services Limited (In Liquidation)* [2018] EWHC 2043 (TCC), [2018] BLR 593.

[54] *Bresco Electrical Services Ltd (In Liquidation) v Michael J Lonsdale (Electrical) Ltd* [2019] EWCA Civ 27, [2019] 3 All ER 337.

extinguished by the liquidation, the underlying claim must continue to exist. The fact that a reference to adjudication may not result in a final and binding decision cannot mean the claim is somehow extinguished.

However, Coulson LJ went on to stress the incompatibility of the two regimes:

> I consider that there is a basic incompatibility between adjudication and the regime set out in the Rules. The former is a method of obtaining an improved cashflow quickly and cheaply. The latter is an abstract accounting exercise, principally designed to assist the liquidators in recovering assets in order to pay a dividend to creditors. Rule 14.25 envisages the taking of a detailed account as between the company and the creditor, and the careful calculation of a net balance one way or the other, or quantifying the company's net claim against a creditor. By contrast, adjudication is a rough and ready process which Dyson J said in Macob Civil Engineering Ltd v Morrison Construction Ltd [1999] BLR 93 was 'likely to result in injustice'. They are therefore very different regimes.[55]

In terms of the futility argument, Coulson LJ held it would only be in exceptional circumstances that a company in liquidation facing a cross-claim could succeed in an adjudication, obtain summary judgment, and avoid a stay of execution. Even though an adjudicator might technically have jurisdiction, any decision would be incapable of enforcement and therefore futile. The solution to the incompatibility was to grant an injunction to restrain the continuation of the adjudication, and the trial judge in this case had been correct to do so. Therefore, whilst technically a company in liquidation can start an adjudication, there may be strong prospects of obtaining an injunction to restrain that adjudication.

The Supreme Court unanimously allowed Bresco's appeal on the futility issue and dismissed Lonsdale's cross-appeal on the jurisdiction issue.[56] First, Lord Briggs commended the utility of adjudication under the Act:

> It was designed to be, and more importantly has proved to be, a mainstream dispute resolution mechanism in its own right, producing de facto final resolution of most of the disputes which are referred to an adjudicator. Furthermore, the availability of adjudication as of right has meant that many disputes are speedily settled between the parties without even the need to invoke the adjudication process.[57]

Regarding jurisdiction, Lord Briggs held that the starting point was the Act and the Scheme. A claim submitted to adjudication would nonetheless confer jurisdiction to determine everything which might be advanced against it by way of defence, and that would necessarily include every cross-claim which amounted to, or was pleaded as, a set-off. The existence of a cross-claim operating by way of insolvency set-off did not mean that underlying disputes under the construction contract melted away so as to render them incapable of adjudication. The argument that they were replaced by a dispute in the insolvency wrongly assumed that the claims and cross-claims which fell within the insolvency set-off lost their separate identity for all purposes.

[55] ibid, [37].
[56] *Bresco* (n 6).
[57] ibid, [13].

Regarding futility, the starting point was that the insolvent company had a statutory and a contractual right to pursue adjudication as a means of achieving resolution of any construction contract dispute to which it was a party. It would ordinarily be inappropriate for the Court to interfere with the exercise of those rights. Injunctive relief might restrain a threatened breach of contract but not, save very exceptionally, an attempt to enforce a contractual or statutory right. That steep hurdle was not surmounted either generally, in the context of insolvency set-off, or on the facts of the instant case.

Therefore, as a result of the Supreme Court's judgment, judgment liquidators will be able to pursue claims through adjudication. However, the Supreme Court made clear that the TCC would continue to have discretion regarding the precise circumstances in which enforcement would be appropriate and the extent to which the Court would insist on undertakings or impose conditions.

> In many cases the liquidator will not seek to enforce the adjudicator's decision summarily. In others the liquidator may offer appropriate undertakings, such as to ring-fence any enforcement proceeds: see the discussion of undertakings in the Meadowside case 186 Con LR 148. Where there remains a real risk that the summary enforcement of an adjudication decision will deprive the respondent of its right to have recourse to the company's claim as security (pro tanto) for its cross-claim, then the court will be astute to refuse summary judgment.[58]

In adopting this view, the Supreme Court considered the TCC's recent judgment in *Meadowside Building Developments Ltd v 12-18 Hill Street Management Co Ltd*,[59] which held that enforcement of an award in the context of an insolvent liquidation may not be futile where the adjudication would determine the final net position between the parties under the contract and satisfactory security was provided in respect of: (a) any adjudication award successfully enforced; and (b) any adverse costs order against the company in liquidation.

In the first TCC case after *Bresco*,[60] *John Doyle Construction Ltd (In Liquidation) v Erith Contractors Ltd*, Fraser J gave helpful guidance on the use of summary judgment for enforcement of an adjudicator's decision where the claimant was a company in liquidation:

1. Whether the dispute in respect of which the adjudicator has issued a decision is one in respect of the whole of the parties' financial dealings under the construction contract in question, or simply one element of it.
2. Whether there are mutual dealings between the parties that are outside the construction contract under which the adjudicator has resolved the particular dispute.
3. Whether there are other defences available to the defendant that were not deployed in the adjudication.
4. Whether the liquidator is prepared to offer appropriate undertakings, such as ring-fencing the enforcement proceeds, and/or where there is other security available.

[58] ibid, [67].
[59] *Meadowside Building Developments Ltd v 12-18 Hill Street Management Co Ltd* [2019] EWHC 2651 (TCC), [2020] Bus LR 917.
[60] *Bresco* (n 6).

5. Whether there is a real risk that the summary enforcement of an adjudication decision will deprive the paying party of security for its cross-claim.[61]

Applying such principles, the claimant failed on the final principle as the security offered was inadequate to reassure the defendant that it would be able to repay the sum awarded if the adjudicator's decision was overturned. The claimant's intention to apply for security by advancing a letter of intent rather than a letter of credit or similar were not a sufficient safeguard and its ATE policy could potentially be avoided. Therefore, in the circumstances, summary judgment was refused.

The claimant appealed to the Court of Appeal, who upheld the TCC's judgment.[62] The Court of Appeal held that any undertaking or security offered must be 'clear, evidenced, and unequivocal' and the burden of demonstrating these requirements fell on the insolvent claimant who in this case 'failed to follow that simple course'.[63]

It is evident from the authorities discussed that there remains a complex relationship between the adjudication under the Act and insolvency. The Supreme Court in *Bresco* has made clear that insolvent claimants are able to pursue claims through adjudication.[64] The future development of the law in this area is likely to concern the TCC's discretion whether to enforce adjudicator's decision in such circumstances and the extent of the necessary undertakings and conditions as seen in *Meadowside* and *John Doyle*.[65]

VI. The HGCRA and Payment Notices

The relevant statutory provisions relating to payment under the Act are sections 109 to 111. Under the LDEDCA, sections 110 and 111 were heavily amended. Section 109 sets out a system of payment by instalments or stage payments. Section 110 sets out when payments become due and the requirement for payment notices. Section 111 sets out the requirement to pay a notified sum and that a payer must give notice of its intention to pay less.

As noted by the Court of Appeal in *Rupert Morgan Building Services (LLC) Ltd v Jervis and another*,[66] section 111 of the Act was directed at the mischief identified in the Latham Report which noted that main contractors were abusing their position to wrongfully withhold payment from sub-contractors who were in no

[61] *John Doyle Construction Ltd (In Liquidation) v Erith Contractors Ltd* [2020] EWHC 2451 (TCC), [2021] 2 All ER (Comm) 955 [54].

[62] *John Doyle Construction Ltd (In Liquidation) v Erith Contractors Ltd* [2021] EWCA Civ 1452, [2022] 2 All ER (Comm) 379.

[63] ibid, [32]–[33].

[64] *Bresco* (n 6).

[65] *Meadowside* (n 59), *John Doyle* (n 61) (n 62).

[66] *Rupert Morgan Building Services (LLC) Ltd v Jervis and another* [2003] EWCA Civ 1563, [2004] 1 WLR 1867 [14].

position to make any effective protest. The provision is directed at immediate payment and cashflow:

> I characterise the payment obligation as 'immediate' because section 111 of the HGCRA was, and section 111 of the Amended Act is, a provision concerned with cashflow and immediate payments. The Court of Appeal made that plain in relation to the HGCRA in Rupert Morgan. As discussed in Part 5 above, none of the changes made to section 111 in the Amended Act change the character of that provision. It is still a provision dealing with cashflow and immediate payments. If the employer fails to make a payment required, the contractor can enforce payment by adjudication, litigation or (if there is an arbitration clause) arbitration.[67]

Section 111 of the Act has led to a series of disputes before the TCC regarding 'smash and grab adjudications'. This term refers to an adjudication where the contractor claims for payment of the sum claimed in the relevant payment application where a valid and timely payment notice and/or pay less notice has not been given. If the adjudicator decided that the relevant notice was not valid or issued within the prescribed period, then the contractor would be entitled to immediate payment of the sum applied for regardless of the true value of the works.

This position was confirmed by the Court of Appeal in *Rupert Morgan*.[68] Jacob LJ held that in the absence of a withholding notice, then the contractor was entitled to be paid the sum due right away. However, he also stated that, 'It does not preclude the client who has paid from subsequently showing he has overpaid. If he has overpaid on an interim certificate the matter can be put right in subsequent certificates. Otherwise he can raise the matter by way of adjudication or if necessary arbitration or legal proceedings.'[69]

In *Harding (t/a MJ Harding Contractors) v Paice*, Edwards-Stuart J held that although in the absence of valid pay less notice, the employer must pay the amount stated in the contractor's account, it is open to the employer to have determined, either by adjudication or litigation, the question of what sum is properly due in respect of the contractor's account.[70] The decision was upheld by the Court of Appeal.[71] It was noted that in two more recent TCC cases, *ISG Construction Ltd v Seevic College*[72] and *Galliford Try Building Ltd v Estura Ltd*[73] discussed below, Edwards-Stuart J took a 'somewhat different line'.[74] However, the Court of Appeal in *Harding* stated that they did not need to decide whether or not they were correct as they involved interim payments rather than a final payment as in the present case.[75]

[67] *S&T(UK) Ltd v Grove Developments Ltd* [2018] EWCA Civ 2448, [2019] Bus LR 1847 [88].
[68] *Rupert Morgan* (n 66).
[69] ibid, [14].
[70] *Harding (t/a MJ Harding Contractors) v Paice* [2014] EWHC 3824 (TCC), 157 Con LR 98 [35]–[36].
[71] *Harding (t/a MJ Harding Contractors) v Paice* [2015] EWCA Civ 1231, [2016] 1 WLR 4068.
[72] *ISG Construction Ltd v Seevic College* [2014] EWHC 4007 (TCC), [2015] 2 All ER (Comm) 545.
[73] *Galliford Try Building Ltd v Estura Ltd* [2015] EWHC 412 (TCC), [2015] BLR 321.
[74] *Harding* (n 71) [68].
[75] ibid [69].

In *ISG Construction*, Edward-Stuart J held that if the employer failed to serve a payment notice or pay less notice in response to a contractor's interim application for payment, the employer had to be taken to have agreed the value stated in the application.[76] In this case, in an interim application the contractor claimed £1,097,696 was due. The employer failed to serve a timeous payment notice or pay less notice. The adjudicator made a declaration that the contractor was entitled to be paid the sum claimed. The contractor then launched a second adjudication, seeking a declaration as to the contractual value of the work as at the date of the interim application which the adjudicator found to be £615,450. The adjudicator mistakenly believing that the employer had complied with the first award, ordered the contractor to repay the overpayment. The employer then claimed the benefit of the second adjudication award. Edwards-Stuart J granted a declaration that the second adjudication award was invalid for want of jurisdiction. The first adjudicator must be in principle taken to have decided the question of the value of the work carried out by the contractor for the purposes of the interim application and the employer could not raise the matter again in a second adjudication.

Similarly, in *Galliford Try*, Edwards-Stuart J held that the employer could not bring a second adjudication to determine the value of the work at the valuation date of the interim application in question.[77] *Rupert Morgan* was cited to the judge in *Galliford Try*,[78] although was not in *ISG*.[79] Edwards-Stuart J held:

> There is nothing to prevent the employer challenging the value of the work on the next application, even if he is contending for a figure that is lower than the (unchallenged) amount stated in the previous application. If this was not made clear by my judgment, then it should have been, and it is certainly made clear by the decision of the *Court of Appeal in Rupert Morgan Building Services (LLC) Ltd v Jervis [2004] 1 WLR 1867*, in particular the passage from paragraph [14] that is set out in paragraph 30 below. My judgment in ISG v Seevic was not intended to go behind that.[80]

The practical difficulty with this result, as noted by the Court of Appeal in *S&T(UK) Ltd v Grove Developments Ltd*,[81] was that it was a large sum claimed in the interim application, namely £4 million, and there may have been no opportunity to correct any error in later interim certificates. Therefore, judgment was enforced only to the extent of £1.5 million and the enforcement of the balance stayed until further order.

The approach in *ISG Construction* and *Galliford Try*,[82] was followed in subsequent TCC cases,[83] until *Grove Developments Ltd v S&T(UK) Ltd*.[84] Coulson J

[76] *ISG Construction* (n 72).
[77] *Galliford Try* (n 73).
[78] *Rupert Morgan* (n 66), *Galliford Try* (n 73).
[79] *ISG Construction* (n 72).
[80] *Galliford Try* (n 73) [20].
[81] *Grove Developments* (n 67) [74].
[82] *ISG Construction* (n 72), *Galliford Try* (n 73).
[83] *Kilker Projects Ltd v Purton* [2016] EWHC 2616 (TCC), [2017] Bus LR 418; *Kersfield Developments (Bridge Road) Ltd v Bray and Slaughter Ltd* [2017] EWHC 15 (TCC), 170 Con LR 40.
[84] *Grove Developments Ltd v S&T (UK) Ltd* [2018] EWHC 123 (TCC), [2018] 2 All ER (Comm) 925.

held that an employer whose payment notice or pay less notice was deficient or non-existent could pay the contractor the sum stated to be due in the contractor's interim application but was then free to commence adjudication proceedings to dispute that the sum paid was the 'true' value of the works for which the contractor had claimed.

As to first principles, under the Act and the Scheme there was no limitation on the nature, scope and extent of the dispute which either party could refer to an adjudicator. Further, the dispute which the employer would wish to raise in a further adjudication was a different dispute to that determined in the previous adjudication, which concerned the question of whether the payment notice or pay less notice was deficient or out of time, not detailed matters of valuation. In his view, an analysis of the Court of Appeal authorities, such as *Rupert Morgan* and *Harding* all pointed the same way and supported his conclusions.[85] Coulson J did not agree with Edward-Stuart J's analysis in *ISG Construction* or *Galliford Try*.[86] He stated that the principal reason for those decisions was the judge's conclusion that, by failing to serve a valid notice, the employer must be deemed to have agreed that the amount claimed was the 'true' value of the interim application.[87] There is usually no basis in fact for the alleged agreement and no basis for deeming any such agreement.

The decision was upheld by the Court of Appeal.[88] Accordingly, an employer who had failed to serve a payment notice or a pay less notice was nevertheless entitled to adjudicate to determine the true value of an interim application. However, the Act could not sensibly be construed as permitting the adjudication regime to trump the prompt payment regime under section 111. Therefore, the Court of Appeal concluded that the employer was prohibited from embarking on an adjudication to obtain a re-valuation of the work before it had complied with his 'immediate payment obligation'.[89]

Shortly after the Court of Appeal's decision in *Grove Developments*, *M Davenport Builders Limited v Greer* came before the TCC.[90] In this case, the contractor submitted an application for payment of its final account. The employers having failed to pay the sum demanded by the final payment date, the claimant commenced adjudication proceedings for an order for payment. The adjudicator held that in the absence of a payment notice or a pay less notice, the contractor was entitled to recover the full sum demanded. Without paying the amount awarded, the defendants commenced a second adjudication to establish the 'true value' of the final account. In those proceedings the adjudicator held that no sum was payable by the employers to the contractor. On the contractor's application for

[85] *Rupert Morgan* (n 66), *Harding* (n 71).
[86] *ISG Construction* (n 72), *Galliford Try* (n 73).
[87] *Grove Developments* (n 84) [114]–[115].
[88] *Grove Developments* (n 67).
[89] ibid [107].
[90] *M Davenport Builders Limited v Greer* [2019] EWHC 318 (TCC), [2019] Bus LR 1273.

summary judgment to enforce the first award, the defendants sought to rely on the second adjudicator's award by way of set-off or counterclaim.

The TCC held that the defendants had not discharged their immediate obligation to pay the sums ordered in the first adjudication, so they could not rely on the subsequent decision. Stuart-Smith LJ stated:

> The decisions of Coulson J and the Court of Appeal in the Grove Developments Ltd case are clear and unequivocal in stating that the employer must make payment in accordance with the contract or in accordance with section 111 of the Amended Act before it can commence a "true value" adjudication. That does not mean that the court will always restrain the commencement or progress of a true value adjudication commenced before the employer has discharged his immediate obligation: see the decision of the Court of Appeal in Harding's case [2016] 1 WLR 4068. It is not necessary for me to decide whether or in what circumstances the court may restrain the subsequent true value adjudication and, in these circumstances, it would be positively unhelpful for me to suggest examples or criteria and I do not do so.[91]

In the latest case of *Bexheat Limited v Essex Services Group Limited*,[92] the TCC has made clear that an employer cannot even rely on an earlier adjudication which determines the true value of the works before complying with its immediate payment obligations. O'Farrell J helpfully summarised the applicable principles:

> Thus, it is now clear that:
>
> i) where a valid application for payment has been made, an employer who fails to issue a valid Payment Notice or Pay Less Notice must pay the 'notified sum' in accordance with section 111 of the 1996 Act;
> ii) section 111 of the 1996 Act creates an immediate obligation to pay the 'notified sum';
> iii) an employer is entitled to exercise its right to adjudicate pursuant to section 108 of the 1996 Act to establish the 'true valuation' of the work, potentially requiring repayment of the 'notified sum' by the contractor;
> iv) the entitlement to commence a 'true value' adjudication under section 108 is subjugated to the immediate payment obligation in section 111;
> v) unless and until an employer has complied with its immediate payment obligation under section 111, it is not entitled to commence, or rely on, a 'true value' adjudication under section 108.[93]

The TCC and the Court of Appeal have provided clarity in this area that if the employer has failed to serve a payment notice or a pay less notice they can still bring an adjudication to determine the true value of the works, however, only after it has complied with its immediate payment obligation. In light of Stuart-Smith J's comments in *M Davenport Builders*,[94] there may remain scope for parties to argue

[91] ibid, [37].
[92] *Bexheat Limited v Essex Services Group Limited* [2022] EWHC 936 (TCC), 202 Con LR 190.
[93] ibid, [76].
[94] *M Davenport Builders* (n 90).

whether and what circumstances the TCC may restrain the subsequent true value adjudication.

VII. The HGCRA and Other Jurisdictions

It was not only the UK which was concerned about the efficiency and litigiousness of its construction industry. The need to provide a framework for swifter resolution of construction disputes was being felt worldwide. In Hong Kong, very similar sentiments were being expressed as Latham had highlighted in his report:

> The Government believes that an efficient and competitive industry benefits the wider … community as well as those whose livelihoods depend on it. When industry participants are distracted or starved of funding by disputes or late payments, hardship can result and projects can suffer delays and falling standards.[95]

A selection of the countries where similar legislation has been introduced are described below.

A. New South Wales

Adjudication and security of payment provisions were introduced to New South Wales by the Building and Construction Industry Security of Payment Act 1999. As in the UK regime, the NSW Act prohibits parties from contracting out of the Act and the legislation generally binds government. Any 'pay when paid' clause is unenforceable, a default payment regime is 'imported' into the contract if one is not contractually agreed, and the contractor has a right to progress payments. An unpaid party also has the right to suspend works. The adjudication regime covers disputes about interim and final payments. It does not extend to other disputes between the parties. On 22 August 2018, New South Wales Fair Trading released the Building and Construction Industry Security of Payment Amendment Bill 2018 (NSW) proposing a number of changes to the 1999 Act. Key changes include the introduction of a statutory entitlement to progress payments at least once per month, and the introduction of liability for directors and other individuals who have contravened the Act.

B. Other Australian States and Territories

Queensland, Victoria, and South Australia have introduced legislation which broadly follows the NSW model. See the Building and Construction Industry

[95] Hong Kong Development Bureau, *Report on Public Consultation on Proposed Security of Payment Legislation for the Construction Industry* (April 2016) 1. Quoted in Bell, Ennis, Juddoo, Rajoo, Reynolds and Vogel, 'Security of Payment in the Construction Industry: Does International Experience Provide a Crystal Ball for North America?' (2018) 34(8) *Construction Law Journal* 601–632.

Security of Payment Act 2002 (amended in 2006) in Victoria and the Building and Construction Industry Payments Act 2004 in Queensland. In western Australia and the northern territory, the legislation permits a wider range of disputes to be referred to adjudication: for example, extension of time claims and claims for damages. The two regimes have been broadly categorised as the western and eastern Australian models, the former being more closely analogous to the provisions of the HGCRA.

C. New Zealand

In New Zealand, adjudication was introduced through the Construction Contracts Act 2002, as amended by the Construction Contracts Amendment Act 2015. When the UK 1996 Act was amended by the Local Democracy, Economic Development and Construction Act 2009, many of the changes to that UK 2009 Act were already features of the New Zealand Act.

A similar approach has been taken in New Zealand to the enforcement of adjudication as has the TCC in the UK:

> We are satisfied that the necessary analysis must be undertaken with the purpose of the Act in mind. The purpose provision of the Act includes the fact that the Act was 'to facilitate regular and timely payments between the parties to a construction contract'. The importance of such regular and timely payments is well recognised. Lord Denning (quoted in Gilbert-Ash (Northern) Ltd v Modern Engineering (Bristol) Ltd [1973] 3 All ER 195, 214 (HL) Lord Diplock) said: 'There must be a "cashflow" in the building trade. It is the very life blood of the enterprise'.[96]

It has been reported that, as in the UK, most of the disputes which are adjudicated in New Zealand end once a decision has been provided. Very few then go onto enforcement or further dispute.[97]

D. Malaysia

The Construction Industry Payment and Adjudication Act 2012 applies to all construction contracts made in writing after 22 June 2012, including those entered into by the Government of Malaysia. The adjudicator has 45 working days after issue of the response to the claim (or a reply) in order to issue a written decision.[98]

[96] *George Developments Limited v Canam Construction Limited* [2005] NZCA 244/04 (12 April 2005) [41].

[97] T Kennedy-Grant, 'Adjudication: The New Zealand Position' (2008) 24(5) *Construction Law Journal* 382–409.

[98] MEC Munaaim, 'Statutory Adjudication Around the World' (2020) 36(2) *Construction Law Journal* 132–163.

E. Singapore

Construction adjudication was introduced into Singapore by the Building and Construction Industry Security Payment Act 2004, which came into force on 1 April 2005.[99] Adjudication is widely used.[100]

An interesting feature of the Singapore regime is a provision for an adjudication review procedure, unique to the Singapore 2004 Act, section 18(2) of which states:

> … where a respondent to whom this section applies is aggrieved by the determination of the adjudicator, the respondent may, within 7 days after being served the adjudication determination, lodge an application for the review of the determination with the authorised nominating body with which the application for the adjudication had been lodged under section 13.

Only the responding party can make use of the procedure which will result in either a substituted decision or a refusal of the review and an upholding of the original decision. It appears that the Singapore courts will require a party to exhaust this process before challenging enforcement in the courts, although not if new evidence has come to light that was not before the original adjudicator.[101]

F. Summary

In all, at least fourteen overseas jurisdictions have introduced legislation based on the HGCRA or the amended HGCRA. Under many of the overseas statutes, disputes about the supply of building materials or goods are included in the adjudication regime. In the UK, section 105(2)(d) of the amended HGCRA excludes such disputes from the regime.

The nature of statutory adjudication means that case law from other jurisdictions is necessarily dependent upon the legislation from which it was birthed. The scope for influence across jurisdictions is therefore somewhat limited. However, the development and application of different approaches to the problems which beset the construction industry around the world will be followed with interest. There will doubtless be lessons which we may learn from other jurisdictions, and it is hoped some helpful jurisprudence from the TCC may be of value overseas in this sphere.

[99] www1.bca.gov.sg/regulatory-info/security-of-payment/building-and-construction-industry-security-of-payment-act (accessed 29 July 2022).

[100] For a comprehensive review of the recent Singaporean case law, see S Magintharan 'Recent Developments in Construction Adjudication in Singapore' (2020) 36 *Construction Law Journal* 219–290.

[101] N Todd and EC Ezeani, 'Adjudication Costs under the Housing Grants, Construction and Regeneration Act 1996: the Attractions of Singapore's Building and Construction Industry Security of Payment Act 2004' (2016) 4 *Jurists Review* 315–336.

VIII. Conclusion

Overall, the statutory adjudication system in construction has been remarkably successful. Its adoption overseas is evidence of that. Doubtless, part of that success can be attributed to the dedication of the judges of the newly-formed TCC in ensuring that Parliament's intention in passing the HGCRA was applied in practice. There is a scope for adopting a similar system in other fields of commercial litigation.

One example is professional negligence. There can be problems in resolving professional negligence claims through adjudication because of reputational implications and because, in practice, adjudicated disputes are very seldom re-litigated in the courts. Despite the difficulties the Professional Negligence Bar Association has introduced a voluntary adjudication scheme.[102] In *Beattie Passive Norse Ltd & Anor v Canham Consulting Ltd*, Mr Justice Fraser lamented the parties' failure to use the scheme. As he said: 'It would have been far quicker, and much more economical, than conducting a High Court trial which lasted over three TCC weeks, with all the costs to the parties that such a trial entails.'[103] Such an encouragement to adjudicate echoes the early days of construction adjudication in the TCC. Perhaps now is the time for the success of construction adjudication to be repeated elsewhere.

[102] See pnba.co.uk/pnba-adjudication-scheme (accessed 9 September 2022).

[103] *Beattie Passive Norse Ltd & Anor v Canham Consulting Ltd* [2021] EWHC 1116 (TCC), [2021] TCLR 5 [152].

8

The TCC Today

DAME FINOLA O'FARRELL

In 1873, the provisions empowering the Court to order that any matter requiring any prolonged examination of documents or accounts, or any scientific or local investigation, be tried by an official referee were intended to improve the administration of justice; in particular, to remedy the twin vices of delay and expense that plagued the legal system.[1]

When introducing the second reading of the Judicature Bill in Parliament, Sir John Coleridge, the Attorney General, stated:

> Another important provision in the bill was the power of appointing official and regularly constituted referees. It was proposed that the judge in chambers or the court should be able at any stage of the case, if it clearly appeared not to be a case fit for trial in court or for adjudication by a judge and jury, to refer it by an order. There would be attached to the courts certain official referees, who would take those references as part of their regular duty. He hoped that portion of the bill would be found satisfactory, and get rid, in working, of one of the justest causes of complaint that existed … In general, it was an attempt to initiate a more sensible and intelligible mode of procedure – to get rid, if possible, of the defects both of Chancery and Common Law procedure, and to produce something in the shape not of pleading, but procedure, that should be at once sensible and satisfactory.[2]

Since 1873, the TCC has been at the vanguard of innovation and increased efficiency in civil litigation. A sensible and intelligible mode of procedure, designed to promote access to justice without delay or undue expense, whilst facilitating alternative forms of dispute resolution, remains at the heart of the operation of the Technology and Construction Court (TCC) today.

I. The Work of the TCC

The TCC is part of the High Court, King's Bench Division, but falls under the umbrella of the Business and Property Courts of England and Wales (BPC).

[1] Supreme Court of Judicature Act 1873, ss 56–59.
[2] *Hansard* HC Deb. Vol 216, cols 652–54, 9 June 1873.

The BPC at the Rolls Building in London is the largest specialist centre for financial, business and property litigation in the world.

The TCC is a specialist court which deals primarily with litigation of technically complex disputes. Although, as its name suggests, much of the court's work arises in the field of technology and construction, it covers a wide range of disputes.

Notable building and engineering claims include the decade of litigation arising out of the development of the iconic Wembley Stadium.[3] Completed in 2007, the arena can seat 90,000 people for sporting events and, when built, was the largest covered stadium in the world with the longest unsupported roof structure. The roof is retractable, with moving panels so that it can be closed in bad weather but sun can reach all parts of the pitch. The roof weighs 7,000 tonnes, supported by a lattice arch of steel that is 133 metres high, 315 metres long and spans 220 metres across the stadium bowl. The arch is connected to the rest of the structure by cables anchored into a perimeter prismatic truss which distributes the horizontal loads to the legs. Construction of the novel design had to be modelled on computers to predict how the structure would behave during and after construction. It was an engineering triumph but the costs and duration of the works spiralled out of control, giving rise to multiple disputes, fought and resolved over many years through adjudication, arbitration, mediation and litigation in the TCC and Court of Appeal.

The TCC has many years of experience in dealing with building safety issues and fire claims, including technical issues such as the cause of the fire, means of fire spread, and property damage, together with contractual, factual and legal issues concerning allocation of responsibility for, and quantification of, the remedial works and associated costs.[4] Following the Grenfell Tower tragedy, in which 72 people lost their lives and the Grenfell Tower was engulfed by flames and destroyed within

[3] There are numerous Wembley decisions at first instance and on appeal, including: *Multiplex Constructions (UK) Limited v Cleveland Bridge UK Limited (No.1)* [2006] EWHC 1341 (TCC); *Multiplex Constructions (UK) Limited v Cleveland Bridge UK Limited (No.2)* [2007] EWHC 145 (TCC); *Multiplex Constructions (UK) Limited v Cleveland Bridge UK Limited (No.6)* [2008] EWHC 2220 (TCC); *Cleveland Bridge UK Limited v Multiplex Constructions (UK) Limited v* [2007] EWCA Civ 443 (CA); *Cleveland Bridge UK Limited v Multiplex Constructions (UK) Limited v* [2007] EWCA Civ 1372 (CA); *Cleveland Bridge UK Limited v Multiplex Constructions (UK) Limited v* [2010] EWCA Civ 449 (CA); *Honeywell Control Systems Limited v Multiplex Constructions (UK) Limited (No.1)* [2007] EWHC 390 (TCC); *Honeywell Control Systems Limited v Multiplex Constructions (UK) Limited (No.2)* [2007] EWHC 447 (TCC); *Brookfield Construction (UK) Limited v Foster & Partners Limited* [2009] EWHC 307 (TCC); *Brookfield Construction (UK) Limited v Mott Macdonald Limited* [2010] EWHC 659 (TCC).

[4] Many fire claims settle before a full trial but decided cases include: *John F Hunt Demolition Ltd v ASME Engineering Ltd* [2007] EWHC 1507 (TCC); *Biffa Waste Services Ltd v Machinenfabrik Ernst Hese GmbH* [2008] EWHC 6 (TCC); *Trebor Bassett Holdings Ltd v ADT Fire & Security plc* [2012] EWCA Civ 1158 (CA); *Howmet Ltd v Economy Devices Ltd* [2016] EWCA Civ 847 (CA); *Goodlife Foods Ltd v Hall Fire Protection Ltd* [2018] EWCA Civ 1371 (CA); *2 Entertain Video Limited v Sony DADC Europe Limited* [2020] EWHC 972 (TCC); *Martlet Homes Ltd v Mulalley & Co Ltd* [2022] EWHC 1813 (TCC).

a few hours,[5] the TCC has seen a significant increase in the number of building safety and fire claims issued. Some of the claims are for damages for the removal and replacement of defective cladding, comprising components similar to those used on Grenfell Tower. However, there are also many other claims in respect of buildings where the cladding, structural stability or other fire protection measures have been questioned following Grenfell and defects identified as a result of intrusive investigations.

A significant portion of TCC work concerns procurement challenges. UK Statutes and Regulations implemented the EU Directives in this area and set out the requirements for public procurement contracting and remedies for breaches, namely: the Defence and Security Public Contracts Regulations 2011;[6] the Public Contracts Regulations 2015;[7] the Concession Contracts Regulations 2016;[8] and the Utilities Contract Regulations 2016.[9] The grounds for most challenges raise issues of equal treatment, non-discrimination, transparency, proportionality, manifest error and irrational decisions. Remedies available to the Court include a declaration that the contract award is unlawful, an order setting aside the decision, remission of the decision to the contracting authority and damages where the breach is sufficiently serious.

Harmon v House of Commons[10] was one of the first high profile procurement challenges brought in the TCC. It concerned a claim by an unsuccessful tenderer for breach of the Public Works Contracts Regulations 1991 arising out of the development of a new building for Members of Parliament and their staff. The Court found that the contract had been awarded unlawfully on the basis that incorrect award criteria had been applied, giving rise to a preference towards UK companies. Over the years that followed, the TCC developed a body of case law which, together with its existing technical expertise and accumulated experience, have made it the specialist court for procurement challenges, which often raise a unique combination of private and public law, domestic and EU legal principles, and technically complex disputes.[11]

[5] *Report of the Public Inquiry into the Fire at Grenfell Tower on 14 June 2017*: Phase 1 Report (2019); www.grenfelltowerinquiry.org.uk.

[6] SI 2011/1848; the Procurement Bill, when enacted, will introduce one consolidated set of regulations governing public procurement exercises.

[7] SI 2015/102.

[8] SI 2016/273.

[9] SI 2016/274.

[10] *Harmon CFEM Facades (UK) Ltd v Corporate Officer of the House of Commons* (1999) 67 Con LR 1; [1999] 10 WLUK 904 (TCC).

[11] *Energy Solutions EU Limited v Nuclear Decommissioning Authority* [2016] EWHC 3326 (TCC); [2017] UKSC 34 (SC); *Ocean Outdoor UK Limited v Hammersmith and Fulham LBC* [2019] EWCA 1642 (CA); *Bombardier Transportation UK Limited & Others v London Underground Limited* [2018] EWHC 2926 (TCC); *Stagecoach East Midlands Trains Limited v SS Transport* [2019] EWCA Civ 2259; [2020] EWHC 1568 (TCC); *R (Good Law Project Ltd & Another) v SS Health and Social Care* [2022] EWHC 46 (TCC); *Camelot UK Lotteries Ltd v The Gambling Commission* [2022] EWHC 1664 (TCC).

The experience of the TCC in dealing with the full range of engineering expert evidence makes it the natural forum for determining energy disputes, including renewables, and IT disputes,[12] where issues of design, construction, implementation or operation of the systems arise.[13]

As envisaged when the specialist jurisdiction was set up in 1873, much of the TCC business requires the Court to grapple with vast volumes of data, whether documents, facts, variations, defects, parties, claims or the subject matter of the dispute. Extensive experience in dealing with such complex disputes enables the Court to case manage environmental damage claims and other group litigation[14] without undue delay or expense and so as to achieve a just and proportionate determination of the same.

The TCC's approach to arbitration claims and adjudication is supervision and support, including swift and robust enforcement of awards with limited grounds for review.[15]

II. Dispute Avoidance

Construction projects are rarely limited to a simple transaction or group of transactions. Usually, they involve a web of inter-connected contracts, many long-term (up to 30–40 years in the case of PFI contracts), with great uncertainty and complexity. It is impossible to make provision for every detailed step in the project or to foresee the impact of every contingency at the outset, even with the benefit of the sophisticated software programmes now available. As a result, situations often arise that are not clearly addressed by the contract, which can lead to disputes. This can be mitigated by the use of contractual risk procedures, clear and comprehensive provisions governing payments and change control, and the use of dispute resolution boards and adjudication to determine disputes that arise during the project. However, it is not surprising or unusual that some intractable disputes arise out of construction projects.

Although parties should always be encouraged to avoid litigation where possible, litigation may be appropriate in cases such as: disputes raising difficult points

[12] *BskyB Limited v HP Enterprise Services UK Limited* [2010] EWHC 86 (TCC); *SAP UK Limited v Diageo Great Britain Limited* [2017] EWHC 189 (TCC); *Soteria Insurance Limited (formerly CIS General Insurance Ltd) v IBM United Kingdom Ltd* [2021] EWHC 347 (TCC); [2022] EWCA Civ 440 (CA); *IBM United Kingdom Ltd v LZLABS GmbH & Others* [2022] EWHC 2094 (TCC).

[13] *Fluor Limited v Shanghai Zhenhua Heavy Industries Limited* [2016] EWHC 2062 (TCC); *Essex County Council v UBB Waste (Essex) Limited* [2019] EWHC 819 (TCC); *Equitix EEEF Biomass 2 Limited v Fox* [2021] EWHC 2531 (TCC).

[14] *The Corby Group Litigation* [2008] EWHC 619 (TCC); [2009] EWHC 1944 (TCC); *The Bodo Community & Others v The Shell Petroleum Development Company of Nigeria Limited* [2014] EWHC 1973 (TCC); *Vedanta Resources plc v Lungowe & Others* [2019] UKSC 20 (SC); *Ocensa Pipeline Group Litigation* [2016] EWHC 1699 (TCC); *Okpabi & Others v Royal Dutch Shell plc* [2021] UKSC 3 (SC); *Municipio de Mariana v BHP Group (UK) Limited* [2022] EWCA Civ 951 (CA).

[15] Adjudication is dealt with in detail in ch 7 in this volume.

of law or a test case, where a clear legal precedent is required; multi-party disputes, where there are a number of parties without adequate provision for joinder, contracts with different governing laws or disputes spanning different jurisdictions; cases that require a hearing with substantial factual and expert evidence, or allegations of fraud or dishonesty; where the main remedy sought is injunctive relief; and to enforce adjudication, expert determination and arbitration awards.

Some contracts contain tiered dispute resolution procedures that must be followed before substantive proceedings may be started. Alternative Dispute Resolution (ADR) is any process through which the parties attempt to resolve their disputes without a formal third party determination. The main forms of dispute resolution as an alternative to third party determination by litigation, arbitration or expert determination, are commercial negotiation and mediation.

In the TCC, before initiating proceedings, parties are required to comply with the Pre-Action Protocol for Construction and Engineering Disputes.[16] The purpose of the Protocol is to encourage the frank and early exchange of information about the prospective claim and any defence to it; to enable parties to avoid litigation by agreeing a settlement of the claim before the commencement of proceedings; and to support the efficient management of proceedings where litigation cannot be avoided.

The Court discourages any use of the Protocol as a tactical device to secure an advantage for one party or to generate unnecessary costs. In lower value TCC claims (such as those likely to proceed in the county court), the letter of claim and the response should be simple and the costs of both sides should be kept to a modest level. In all cases the costs incurred at the Protocol stage should be proportionate to the complexity of the case and the amount of money which is at stake. The Protocol does not impose a requirement on the parties to produce a detailed pleading as a letter of claim or response, or to marshal and disclose all the supporting details and evidence, or to provide witness statements or expert reports that may ultimately be required if the case proceeds to litigation. Where a party has serious concerns that the approach of the other party to the Protocol is not proportionate, then it is open for that party to issue a claim form and/or make an application to seek the assistance of the court.

A claimant does not have to comply with the Protocol if the claim: a) is to enforce the decision of an adjudicator; b) is to seek an urgent declaration or injunction in relation to adjudication (whether ongoing or concluded); c) includes a claim for interim injunctive relief; d) will be the subject of a claim for summary judgment pursuant to Part 24 of the CPR; e) relates to the same or substantially the same issues as have been the subject of a recent adjudication or some other formal alternative dispute resolution procedure; or f) relates to a public procurement dispute (for which there is a separate pre-action protocol). A further reason for not complying with the Protocol is if, by so doing, the claim may become time-barred

[16] The Construction and Engineering Protocol was first introduced in 2000, now in its 2nd Edition, and can be found at Section C-5 of the *White Book*.

for limitation.[17] In those circumstances, a claimant should commence proceedings without complying with the Protocol and must, at the same time, apply for directions as to the timetable and form of procedure to be adopted. The Court may order a stay of those proceedings pending completion of the steps set out in the Protocol. This can be of particular value where there are a number of potential parties to the claims but there is a real prospect that not all ultimately will be joined as necessary parties, or where further investigations are required before the parties are ready to plead their respective cases.

In all cases, the costs incurred at the pre-action protocol stage should be proportionate to the complexity of the case and the amount of money at stake. The Protocol does not mandate the parties to marshal and disclose all supporting details and evidence that may ultimately be required if the case proceeds to litigation. In appropriate cases, the parties may apply to the Court for an order that the parties are relieved from the obligation to comply or further comply with the Protocol.

The shape of the pre-action protocol exercise is a letter of claim, response by the defendant(s), opportunity for reply and a without prejudice meeting. The letter of claim must contain a clear and concise summary of the facts on which each claim is based; the basis on which each claim is made; and details of the relief claimed, including a breakdown showing how any damages have been quantified. The claimant must also provide the names of experts already instructed and on whom reliance is intended.

Each defendant has 14 days to acknowledge the letter of claim and 28 days (from receipt of the letter of claim) either to take any jurisdictional objection or to respond in substance to the letter of claim. The parties may agree an extension of the 28-day period up to a maximum of three months. In any case of substance, it is quite usual for an extension of time to be agreed for the defendant's response. The letter of response must state which claims are accepted, which claims are rejected and on what basis. It must set out any counterclaim to be advanced by the defendant. The defendant should also provide the names of experts who have been instructed and on whom reliance is intended. If the defendant fails either to acknowledge or to respond to the letter of claim in time, the claimant is entitled to commence proceedings without further engagement or warning.

A significant feature of the Pre-Action Protocol for Construction and Engineering Disputes is that, unlike other protocols, it requires the parties to meet, on a without prejudice basis, at least once, in order to identify the main issues and the material causes of their disagreement on those issues. The purpose of the meeting is to see whether, and if so how, those issues might be resolved without recourse to litigation or, if litigation is unavoidable, what steps should be taken to ensure that it is conducted in accordance with the overriding objective. The meeting provides an invaluable opportunity for the parties to hold preliminary commercial negotiations and explore options for settlement before substantial

[17] Contractual limitation period or statutory limitation period under the Limitation Act 1980.

costs are incurred. At or as a result of the meeting, the parties should consider whether some form of ADR would be more suitable than litigation and if so, they should endeavour to agree which form of ADR to adopt. Although the meeting is 'without prejudice', any party who attended the meeting is at liberty to disclose to the Court at a later stage that the meeting took place; who attended and who refused to attend, together with the grounds for their refusal; and any agreements concluded between the parties.

The Protocol does not contemplate an extended process and it should not be used as a tool of oppression. Thus, the letter of claim should be concise and it is usually sufficient to explain the proposed claim(s), identifying key dates, so as to enable the potential defendant to understand and to investigate the allegations. Only essential documents need be supplied, and the period specified for a response should not be longer than one month without good reason. In particular, where a claim is brought by a litigant based outside the UK it will generally be appropriate to confine the steps to the time limits provided by the Protocol and, in many cases, to hold a virtual meeting or even dispense with the meeting.

Because the purpose of the Protocol is to attempt a resolution of the dispute before substantial costs are incurred, if compliance with the Protocol results in settlement, the costs incurred will not be recoverable from the paying party, unless this is specifically agreed. If compliance with the Protocol does not result in settlement, then the costs of the exercise cannot be recovered as costs of the litigation, unless: a) those costs fall within the principles stated by Sir Robert Megarry V-C in *Re Gibson's Settlement Trusts*;[18] or b) the steps taken in compliance with the Protocol can properly be attributable to the conduct of the action: see the judgment of Coulson J in *Roundstone Nurseries v Stephenson*[19] where he held at [48]: '… as a matter of principle, it seems to me that costs incurred during the Pre-Action Protocol process may, in principle, be recoverable as costs incidental to the litigation: see *McGlinn v. Waltham (No. 1)* [2005] 3 All ER 1126'.

The Court encourages the parties to use ADR and will, whenever appropriate, facilitate the use of such a procedure. In most cases, ADR takes the form of inter-party negotiations or a mediation conducted by a neutral mediator. Alternative forms of ADR include early neutral evaluation (ENE), either by a judge or some other neutral person, who receives a concise presentation from each party and then provides his or her own evaluation of the case.

Where one or more parties unreasonably refuse to take part in ADR, the Court will consider giving directions for specific steps to be taken, such as letters of claim

[18] *Re Gibson's Settlement Trusts* [1981] Ch 179 – Sir Robert Megarry, Vice Chancellor, decided that on an order for taxation of costs, costs that otherwise would be recoverable are not to be disallowed by reason only that they were incurred before action brought. He also made plain that the words 'incidental to' extended, rather than reduced, the ambit of any order, although he said that it was important to identify what the proceedings were in any case and how and why the costs claimed were incidental to those proceedings. As to costs incurred before the proceedings commenced he said: 'Of course, if there is no litigation there are no costs of litigation. But if the dispute ripens into litigation, the question then arises how far the ambit of the costs is affected by the shape that the litigation takes.'

[19] *Roundstone Nurseries v Stephenson* [2009] EWHC 1431 (TCC).

and response, disclosure and meetings of the parties or their experts. Further, the Court will consider imposing cost penalties on the defaulting party, having regard to all the circumstances of the particular case. In *Halsey v Milton Keynes General NHS Trust*,[20] the Court of Appeal identified six factors that may be relevant to any such consideration: a) the nature of the dispute; b) the merits of the case; c) the extent to which other settlement methods have been attempted; d) whether the costs of the ADR would be disproportionately high; e) whether any delay in setting up and attending the ADR would have been prejudicial; f) whether the ADR had a reasonable prospect of success.

Where the parties identify a specific issue that prevents settlement, the Court may assist by ordering a preliminary issue to be tried or by directing ENE to break the stalemate. ENE may be carried out by any appropriately qualified person whose opinion is likely to be respected by the parties. In an appropriate case, and with the consent of all parties, a TCC judge may provide an ENE either in respect of the full case or of particular issues arising within it. Unless the parties otherwise agree, the ENE will be produced in writing and will set out conclusions and brief reasons. Such an ENE will not, save with the agreement of the parties, be binding on the parties.

III. Case Management

The TCC uses pro-active case management to ensure that the complex claims before it are dealt with efficiently and in a cost-effective manner. This includes early case management hearings, cost budgeting, disclosure, the witness statement practice direction and expert witness control.

The general approach of the TCC to case management is to give directions at the outset for the conduct of the case up to trial and then as necessary throughout the proceedings to serve the overriding objective of dealing with cases justly and at proportionate cost.

Case management in the TCC allows the parties at the first case management conference to know the timetable for all steps of the proceedings up to and including the trial date. The case management bundle provided to the Court for this case management conference includes the documents produced by the parties in complying with the Protocol. This allows the Court to review whether there should be an opportunity, by way of stay or timetabling, for the parties to reach a settlement either by negotiation or ADR. Equally where the dispute between the parties cannot be settled, the case management conference allows the Court to consider how a determination of that dispute can be dealt with in the most appropriate way, taking into account the overriding objective of the Civil Procedure Rules (CPR).[21]

[20] [2004] EWCA Civ 576; [2004] 1 WLR 3002.

[21] CPR 1.1 sets out the overriding objective of enabling the court to deal with cases justly and at proportionate cost, including: (a) ensuring that the parties are on an equal footing and can participate

The TCC has very wide powers generally under the CPR to manage cases. Central to effective case management is identification of the key issues that the Court will be required to determine. The parties are encouraged to prepare at an early stage a list of issues, in neutral terms (or, at least, a balanced summary of the position held by opposing parties) agreed, if possible. Such a document can be treated as a working document during the procedural stages of the proceedings and finalised once the key issues in dispute are identified. However, usually it is not necessary to have a lengthy list of issues and, in some cases, no list is required because the primary issues are clear from the pleadings. It is important that parties do not become distracted by valiant but failed attempts to reach agreement, particularly where one party seeks to produce a high-level list of generic issues, whilst another seeks to produce a comprehensive list of every question the Court must consider.

At the first CMC, the Court usually orders a timetable which will allow for the fair and prompt resolution of the action. It is important that the timetable is realistic from the outset of the proceedings, so that the parties can plan an efficient deployment of resources to ensure compliance with the same. The parties are required to confirm that there is in place a suitable protocol for conducting e-disclosure (a matter that should have been discussed by the parties during the Protocol stage). In document heavy cases the parties will be invited to consider the use of an electronic document management system; it is important that this is considered at an early stage because it will be closely linked to e-disclosure. Further, the parties are required to have completed the list of issues for disclosure and, where extended disclosure is required, identified which model of extended disclosure is sought for each issue, in accordance with Practice Direction 57AD.

A specific feature of case management conferences in the TCC is that the trial date is fixed at the first CMC, with a time estimate for the trial duration. At this stage, the Court endeavours to take account of the parties' requests for early trial dates and the availability of witnesses and legal representatives but the parties' wishes are not determinative; in particular, they are subject to the Court lists and available judicial resources. The parties are encouraged to consider a reasonable estimate for the trial together with a realistic estimate for judicial reading time as these can be listed in the CE-file diary and included in the order for directions at the CMC. The parties are required to notify the Court as soon as possible if there is any slippage in the timetable, or the estimate for the trial is discovered to be insufficient, or the trial date is in jeopardy but it is only in exceptional cases that the trial date will be moved once fixed.

fully in proceedings, and that parties and witnesses can give their best evidence; (b) saving expense; (c) dealing with the case in ways which are proportionate – (i) to the amount of money involved; (ii) to the importance of the case; (iii) to the complexity of the issues; and (iv) to the financial position of each party; (d) ensuring that it is dealt with expeditiously and fairly; (e) allotting to it an appropriate share of the court's resources, while taking into account the need to allot resources to other cases; and (f) enforcing compliance with rules, practice directions and orders.

A detailed timetable for the procedural steps to trial together with a fixed date for the start of the trial has proven to be an effective tool in controlling the twin vices of delay and costs in litigation. It enables the parties to anticipate points at which cost intensive preparation will be required and to plan ADR accordingly. Significantly, it can provide a catalyst for settlement as the date of judgment looms.

IV. Cost Budgeting

In December 2009 Sir Rupert Jackson produced his *Review of Civil Litigation Costs: Final Report*.[22] A significant feature of the recommendations was a departure from the position that costs were proportionate if they were necessarily incurred, with the introduction of a definition of proportionate costs:

> Costs are proportionate if, and only if, the costs bear a reasonable relationship to: (a) the sums in issue in the proceedings; (b) the value of any non-monetary relief in issue in the proceedings; (c) the complexity of the litigation; (d) any additional work generated by the conduct of the paying party; and (e) any wider factors involved in the proceedings, such as reputation or public importance.

The policy underlying the changed approach is that cost benefit analysis is a material factor in the conduct of civil proceedings, even in high value commercial disputes. If parties wish to pursue claims or defences at disproportionate cost, they must do so, at least in part, at their own expense. Factors that contribute to excessive costs include the size and complexity of the case, preparation of witness statements and expert reports, volume of material subject to disclosure, particularly given that most communications and records are now in electronic form, ineffective case management and late settlement.

The principles of cost budgeting are that: (a) the parties prepare and exchange litigation budgets; (b) the Court records the agreed budgets or reviews and revises the disputed parts of the budgets; (c) the Court manages the case so that it proceeds within the agreed or approved budgets; (d) at the end of the litigation, the recoverable costs of the winning party are assessed in accordance with the approved budget. In practice, it acts as both a floor and ceiling for the costs recoverable by the successful party.

The rules concerning cost budgeting are set out in CPR 3 and Practice Direction 3E.[23] The rules do not apply where the value of the claim is over £10 million, to litigants in person or where the Court otherwise orders. However, in any case, the parties may agree to apply the rules and the Court retains broad discretion to require compliance with part or all of the cost budget rules.[24]

[22] R Jackson, *Review of Civil Litigation Costs: Final Report* (The Stationery Office, 2010).

[23] Introduced by the Civil Procedure (Amendment) Rules 2013 (SI 2013/262) and amended by the Civil Procedure (Amendment No.4) Rules 2014 (SI 2014/867), the Civil Procedure (Amendment) Rules 2016 (SI 2016/234) and the Civil Procedure (Amendment No.3) Rules 2020 (SI 2020/747).

[24] CPR 13(3); *CIP Properties (AIPT) Ltd v Galliford Try Infrastructure Ltd* [2014] EWHC 3546 (TCC) per Coulson J (as he then was) at [16]–[24].

Rule 3.12(2) states that the purpose of costs management is that the Court should manage both the steps to be taken and the costs to be incurred by the parties to any proceedings so as to further the overriding objective, namely to deal with cases justly and at proportionate cost.

The rules require each party to file a costs budget in the prescribed form at the outset of the litigation, 21 days before the first case management conference.[25] Precedent H is the prescribed form for a costs budget. This divides the litigation into different phases, and the parties must set out the amount of the fees and disbursements for each phase separately. Parties must take care to ensure that they comply with the deadline for service of their budgets, failing which they are at risk of having their costs limited to the Court fees unless the Court orders otherwise or grants relief from sanction.[26] Seven days before the first case management conference, the parties are required to serve Precedent R Cost Budget Discussion Reports, setting out the figures which are agreed, which are not agreed, and a brief summary of the grounds of dispute.[27] The parties are encouraged to continue to discuss cost issues between them so as to try and narrow or remove any outstanding issues.

At the first costs and case management conference (CCMC) the Court considers the costs budgets. If the estimated future costs are agreed, the Court will make an order recording the extent to which the budgets have been agreed.[28] Where a budget or parts of a budget for estimated future costs are not agreed, the Court will consider the budget and make such revisions as it thinks fit. These are then recorded in a Costs Management Order.[29]

The approach taken by the Court generally is a broad brush assessment of the reasonable and proportionate costs for each phase to ensure that the overall costs are properly controlled and reflect the value of the issues to the parties and their respective financial positions. The exercise is not intended to require a detailed scrutiny of each item in the budget unless, exceptionally, the overall costs are considered to be disproportionate in all the circumstances.[30]

The Court has no power to approve any costs which are incurred, rather than budgeted, but may take those costs into account when considering the reasonableness and proportionality of all budgeted costs.[31] The Court may also record any comments it has about the incurred costs. In *CIP Properties (AIPT) Ltd v Galliford Try Infrastructure Ltd*,[32] the claimant filed a budget totalling almost £9.5 million

[25] CPR 13(1).

[26] *Mitchell v News Group Newspapers Ltd* [2013] EWCA Civ 1537; [2014] 1 WLR 795; *Denton v TH White Ltd* [2014] EWCA Civ 906; [2014] 1 WLR 3926.

[27] CPR 13(2).

[28] CPR 3.15(2)(a).

[29] CPR 3.15(2)(b).

[30] For a case where the budgeted costs exceeded the sum claimed in a case that had no features of complexity and therefore were considered to be disproportionate, see *GSK Project Management Limited v QPR Holdings Limited* [2015] EWHC 2274 (TCC).

[31] CPR 3.17(3).

[32] *CIP Properties (AIPT) Ltd v Galliford Try Infrastructure Ltd* [2015] EWHC 481 (TCC); [2015] BLR 285.

of which about £4.3 million had already been incurred. Coulson J (as he then was) considered that the costs budget was an unreliable document and that the figures placed in the 'Incurred' columns and the 'Estimated' columns were disproportionate and unreasonable. In his judgment there were four available options for the Court to consider: (i) order the claimant to prepare a new budget; (ii) decline to approve the claimant's costs budget; (iii) endeavour to set costs budget figures on a phase by phase basis, looking primarily at estimated rather than actual costs; or (iv) simply refuse to allow anything more in the costs budget beyond that which had already been spent. In the circumstances of that particular case, the judge decided that only the option of endeavouring to set costs budget figures on a phase by phase basis was workable, subject to modification to arrive at a better approximation to justice. He reduced the total budget from £9.5 million to about £4.3 million, roughly the amount said to have been already incurred, recording against each phase of the budget the amounts which he considered it had been reasonable for the claimant to have already incurred.

It is emphasised that the appropriate order to be made in each case turns on the particular circumstances of the case. There may be a good explanation for costs to be higher than usual, such as where there are international elements of the claim, jurisdictional challenges, multiplicity of parties and claims, or the sheer size of the case. Costs budgeting is not intended to be a rod with which to beat the parties. It is intended to assist them in keeping litigation costs to a reasonable and proportionate level.

Following a costs management order, a party must revise its budget upwards or downwards if significant developments in the case warrant such revision.[33] In *Persimmon Homes v Osborne Clarke*,[34] the High Court outlined a two-stage process to be adopted when dealing with applications to vary costs budgets under CPR 3.15A. The applicant first must satisfy the Court that it has met the mandatory requirements of CPR 3.15A(2)–(4) by establishing: (a) that there has been a significant development in the litigation since the last approved or agreed budget which warranted a revision; and (b) that the particulars of the variation has been submitted promptly to the other parties and the court. If the applicant meets those mandatory requirements, the Court will then consider whether to exercise its discretion to vary the figures.

Once approved, the costs shown in each phase of the costs budget will usually be recoverable on a detailed assessment if they have been incurred. Recovery will not usually be permitted where a party has overspent its budget for a particular phase, even though it may have underspent on another phase. The Court will not depart from the approved figure in the budget unless satisfied that there is good reason to do so: see CPR 3.18. Guidance as to the extent to which a court assessing costs can depart from the figures in an approved budget was given by the Court of Appeal in *Harrison v University Hospitals Coventry & Warwickshire*

[33] CPR 3.15A.
[34] *Persimmon Homes v Osborne Clarke* [2021] EWHC 831 (Ch).

NHS Trust.[35] In respect of budgeted costs, the assessing court should not make any departure, whether upwards or downwards, unless there is some good reason to do so. However, incurred costs, unlike budgeted costs, fall outside the ambit of CPR 3.18(b) and, accordingly, the assessing court has an unfettered discretion as to what, if any sums to allow.

The TCC has embraced the concept of cost budgeting as a successful tool for controlling the costs of litigation to a reasonable level proportionate to the case. The inconvenience of the time and cost required to prepare, discuss and decide the budgets is far outweighed by the advantages. Costs budgets enable the parties to carry out their own cost benefit analysis of the litigation, having transparency of the costs attributable to each phase of the proceedings, court guidance on the reasonableness of those costs and visibility of the costs to be incurred by the other parties. Early exchange of costs information equips the parties for mediation and commercial negotiations, which often become stalled over the allocation of costs rather than the substantive claims. For these reasons, the parties (if not the legal representatives or the judges carrying out the budget reviews) appreciate the value of costs budgeting.

V. Disclosure

Disclosure is a major source of the overall costs in conducting commercial litigation. In the Jackson Costs Review,[36] Sir Rupert Jackson adopted the general view that had been expressed amongst commercial practitioners and judges during the consultation period, namely, that in large commercial and similar cases a menu option should be introduced, including the option of ordering disclosure on an issue by issues basis to ensure that disclosure would be proportionate to the circumstances of the case. The primary difficulty arose from the vast increase in the volume of data available for disclosure, in particular electronic data. The wide range of alternative orders under CPR 31.5 were not, in practice, used by the courts or the legal profession; standard disclosure remained the default order in most cases. Searches were often far wider than necessary and disclosure orders were not sufficiently focused on the key issues. There was insufficient engagement between the parties and their advisers prior to the first CMC regarding disclosure and the CPR 31 procedure was conceptually based on paper disclosure, a mode of disclosure that had become dwarfed by electronic disclosure.

Further pressure for the system to change came in 2016 at the GC100 disclosure seminar, where widespread concerns were expressed by court users over the excessive costs, scale and complexity of disclosure. In 2016 a working group was

[35] *Harrison v University Hospitals Coventry & Warwickshire NHS Trust* [2017] EWCA Civ 792; [2017] 3 Costs LR 425.

[36] Jackson (n 22) ch 37.

established by the Chancellor of the High Court to address these concerns in the context of the BPC.

The working group, chaired by the then Vice-President of the Civil Division of the Court of Appeal, The Rt. Hon. Dame Elizabeth Gloster DBE PC, comprised a wide range of lawyers, experts, judges, representatives of professional associations and users of the BPC. The task of the working group was to identify the problems and propose a practical solution on the basis that it might in due course be extended beyond the BPC to other jurisdictions. It consulted with a range of interested parties and received extensive feedback. Several versions of a proposed new practice direction were produced by the drafting subcommittee between February and November 2017. Feedback was given by users, the legal profession, judiciary and e-disclosure specialists. The proposed Disclosure Review Document (DRD) was subjected to a 'road-testing' exercise over the summer of 2017 by a selection of law firms and users. Draft versions of the proposed Practice Direction and DRD, and a guidance note, were posted on the judiciary website on 2 November 2017, the public consultation phase continued until 28 February 2018, and revised versions of the practice direction and DRD were approved by the Civil Procedure Rule Committee on 13 July 2018.

The disclosure pilot started on 1 January 2019 in the BPCs across England and Wales, including the TCC, initially running for two years and extended until introduction of the new Practice Direction 57AD.[37] It must be recognised that there were a number of difficulties identified during the pilot; in particular, the procedure was seen as too cumbersome, entailing heavy front-loading of costs. Following extensive consultation and feedback, changes were made to address the major concerns identified but the consensus was that the pilot was a success.

Approved on 15 July 2022, Practice Direction 57AD is substantially in the form of PD 51U and replaces PD 51U as from 1 October 2022. The principle behind the current approach is that in TCC cases (and other cases in the BPCs) there is no automatic entitlement to search based disclosure. The Court will only make an order for extended disclosure where there has been full engagement between the parties prior to the CMC. Any order for extended disclosure will be tailored to the issues in the claim and must be reasonable and proportionate to the circumstances of the case.[38] This new approach to disclosure has required a cultural shift in practice. Standard disclosure is no longer seen as the default option. Parties have a duty to co-operate in finding a reasonable and proportionate solution to disclosure. There is an express duty to preserve documents and a duty to disclose known adverse documents.[39]

[37] PD 51U.

[38] For a discussion as to the approach to disclosure under the new practice, see: *UTB LLC v Sheffield United Limited* [2019] EWHC 914 (Ch) at [75]–[79]; *McParland & Partners Limited v Whitehead* [2020] EWHC 298 (Ch) at [3]–[4], [44]–[54] and [58].

[39] For a consideration of the ambit of the requirement to disclose adverse documents, see: *Castle Water Limited v Thames Water Utilities Limited* [2020] EWHC 1374 (TCC) per Stuart-Smith J (as he then was).

The parties are required to serve with each statement of case key documents by way of Initial Disclosure, namely, documents relied on, including those referred to in statement of case, and documents necessary for the other parties to understand the case they have to meet.[40]

One of the prominent features of PD57AD is that prior to the first CMC, the parties must file a joint DRD, listing the main issues in the case for the purpose of disclosure and any matters of common ground, setting out any agreed or competing proposals for extended disclosure, and providing information as to how documents are stored and how they might be searched and reviewed, including the use of appropriate technology assisted review (TAR) tools, such as predictive coding.[41]

The Court has complete discretion as to the disclosure order to make, if any,[42] but usually approves the agreed order proposed by the parties or selects the appropriate model from the menu of options:[43] Model A – disclosure limited to known adverse documents; Model B – disclosure limited to documents on which a party relies plus adverse documents (without any search required); Model C – request-led, search-based disclosure whereby the parties disclose specific documents or classes of document relating to defined disclosure issues; Model D – search-based disclosure by reference to the disclosure issues (with or without 'narrative' documents); and Model E – a wider search, including 'train of inquiry' documents, generally reserved for cases where allegations of fraud or serious breaches of trust have been made.

In all cases, an order for Extended Disclosure must be reasonable and proportionate having regard to the overriding objective including the following factors:[44] (1) the nature and complexity of the issues in the proceedings; (2) the importance of the case, including any non-monetary relief sought; (3) the likelihood of documents existing that will have probative value in supporting or undermining a party's claim or defence; (4) the number of documents involved; (5) the ease and expense of searching for and retrieval of any particular document (taking into account any limitations on the information available and on the likely accuracy of any costs estimates); (6) the financial position of each party; and (7) the need to ensure the case is dealt with expeditiously, fairly and at a proportionate cost.

The Practice Direction does not apply to Part 8 claims unless the Court orders otherwise; a party seeking disclosure in a Part 8 claim must file a list of issues for disclosure and the models to be adopted.

Although the Court has power to impose sanctions, such as adjournments or costs penalties, for non-compliance with the Practice Direction, it is rarely required. The parties and their legal advisors have been quick to adopt the new procedures and appreciate the substantial savings in time and cost in drafting

[40] Paragraph 5, PD57AD, para 5.
[41] ibid, para 7.
[42] ibid, paras 6.8–6.11.
[43] ibid, para 8.
[44] ibid, para 6.4.

issues for disclosure at an early stage in the litigation so as to avoid production of documents not relevant to the issues in dispute.

VI. Witness Statement Practice Direction

Prolix witness statements are a particular problem in construction litigation. Every construction project generates a mass of contemporaneous documents, evidencing every stage and nuance of the project – from the initial concept or outline design, through detailed design, budgets, tenders, contract formation, enabling works, main works, testing and commissioning, ancillary works and final account process. There are also drawings and computer models, meeting minutes, risk registers, scope change/variation orders, interim applications for payment and payment notices, site instructions and claims.

BPC users, including those in the TCC, recognised that witness statements had become unnecessarily long, and too often were used to provide a narrative account of events by detailed reference to and/or paraphrasing of documents in respect of which the witness was not able to give direct evidence, having not created or received the documents at the time, and having no direct involvement in the issues discussed in the documents. This problem was inefficient, caused a huge waste of time (in preparation, reading and responding to the statements) and increased costs with no benefit.

In March 2018 the Witness Evidence Working Group was formed to address concerns on the part of the judiciary that factual witness statements were often ineffective in performing their core function of achieving best evidence at proportionate cost in trials. Initially limited to the Commercial Court, it was extended to cover all trials in the BPC, including the TCC. In December 2019, the BPC Board accepted the recommendations in the Working Group's final report and on 22 October 2020 the Working Group's implementation report was accepted. In January 2021, Practice Direction 57AC and Appendix (Statement of Best Practice) were published, applicable to all trial witness statements signed on or after 6 April 2021.

A trial witness statement should contain only: a) evidence as to matters of fact that need to be proved at trial by the evidence of witnesses in relation to one or more of the issues of fact to be decided at trial; and b) the evidence as to such matters that the witness would be asked by the relevant party to give, and the witness would be allowed to give, in evidence in chief if they were called to give oral evidence at trial.

Under PD57AC, a witness statement must set out only matters of fact of which the witness has personal knowledge that are relevant to the case, and must identify by list what documents, if any, the witness has referred to or been referred to for the purpose of providing the evidence set out in their trial witness statement. Unless otherwise directed by the court, witness statements should not have annexed to them copies of other documents, save where a specific document needs to be annexed to the statement in order to make that statement reasonably intelligible.

The witness statement should be as concise as possible without omitting anything of significance, refer to documents only where necessary and should not quote at any length from any document to which reference is made; seek to argue the case, either generally or on particular points; take the Court through the documents in the case or set out a narrative derived from the documents, those being matters for argument; or include commentary on other evidence in the case (either documents or the evidence of other witnesses).

The witness must verify the statement by a statement of truth and confirm compliance with PD57AC. The witness statement must be endorsed by a certificate of compliance by the legal representative, confirming compliance with PD57AC. Sanctions for non-compliance include an order to produce a fresh witness statement, adverse cost orders and exclusion of the witness statement from evidence.

The purpose of the Practice Direction is not to change the law as to the admissibility of evidence at trial;[45] rather it is to eradicate the improper use of witness statements as vehicles for narrative, commentary and argument. The Practice Direction explains that the purpose of trial witness statements is to further the overriding objective by helping the Court to deal with cases justly, efficiently and at proportionate cost, including by helping to put parties on an equal footing, saving time at trial and promoting settlement in advance of trial. The Statement of Best Practice sets out the rules that should be followed to produce compliant statements.

Paragraph 5.2 of PD57AC empowers the Court to impose sanctions for any failure to comply with the Practice Direction, including striking out the offending parts of the witness statement.[46] However, as with PD57AD, the purpose of the Practice Direction is to change the culture of the conduct of litigation, to ensure that all steps taken are necessary for a fair resolution of the dispute, reasonable and proportionate to the circumstances of the case.

VII. Expert Witnesses

Expert evidence is evidence as to matters of a technical or scientific nature and will generally include expert opinion evidence. The quality and reliability of expert evidence will depend upon: (a) the experience and the technical or scientific

[45] *Mad Atelier International BV v Manes* [2021] EWHC 1899 per Sir Michael Burton GBE, sitting as a Judge of the High Court, at [9].

[46] For examples of the court's management of witness statements where applications have been made in respect of the PD57AC see: *Mansion Place v Fox Industrial Services* [2021] EWHC 2747 (TCC) – O'Farrell J; *Blue Manchester v Bug-Alu Technic GmbH* [2021] EWHC 3095 (TCC) – HHJ Stephen Davies; *Noksel Celik Boru Sanayi AS v Bemaco Steel* [2022] EWHC 68 (Comm) – Andrew Baker J.

qualifications of the expert; (b) the availability of evidence for the expert to consider (such as intrusive inspections, materials for testing and source code for analysis); and (c) the accuracy of the factual material that is used by the expert for his assessment.[47]

Expert evidence is frequently needed and used in TCC cases. Experts are often appointed at an early stage. Most types of case heard in the TCC involve more than one expertise and some, even when the dispute is concerned with relatively small sums, involve several different expert disciplines. Such disputes include those concerned with building and engineering failures and defects, delay and disruption, dilapidations, chemical and other environmental contamination, the supply and implementation of software systems, and quantum. However, given the cost of preparing such evidence, the parties and the Court must, from the earliest pre-action phase of a dispute until the conclusion of the trial, seek to make effective and proportionate use of experts. The scope of any expert evidence must be limited to what is necessary for the requirements of the particular case.

The Court considers in each case whether it is appropriate for the parties to rely on expert evidence; if so, what disciplines of experts should give evidence, on what issues, and whether any issues can be conveniently dealt with by single joint experts. This may be coupled with an order relating to the carrying out of inspections, the obtaining of samples, the conducting of experiments, or the performance of calculations. The parties must be aware that, in accordance with the overriding objective, the judge will only give the parties permission to rely on expert evidence if it is both necessary and appropriate, and, even then, will wish to ensure that the scope of any such evidence is limited as far as possible.

A distinctive feature of TCC case management is a requirement for the experts of like disciplines to meet, at least once, before preparing their reports and, thereafter, as often as proves necessary. The primary purpose of such meetings is to narrow any differences and to reach agreement on as many 'expert' issues as possible. However, such meetings also offer additional opportunities: to provide to the expert any written questions from the parties, which the expert must answer in writing; to define a party's technical case and to inform opposing parties of the details of that case; to clear up confusion and to remedy any lack of information or understanding of a party's technical case in the minds of opposing experts; to identify the issues about which any expert is to give evidence; to assist in providing an agenda for the trial and for cross examination of expert witnesses; and to limit the scope and length of the trial as much as possible.

Following the experts' meetings, and pursuant to CPR 35.12 (3), the judge will almost always require the experts to produce a signed statement setting out the issues which have been agreed, and those issues which have not been agreed, together with a short summary of the reasons for their disagreement. In any TCC

[47] Expert evidence is dealt with in detail in CPR Part 35 ('Experts and Assessors') and in the Practice Direction supplementing Part 35.

case in which expert evidence has an important role to play, this statement is a critical document and it must be as clear as possible.

Single joint experts are not usually appropriate for the principal liability disputes in a large case, or in a case where considerable sums have been spent on an expert in the pre-action stage. They are generally inappropriate where the issue involves questions of risk assessment or professional competence. However, single joint experts can often be appropriate in low value cases,[48] where technical evidence is required but the cost of adversarial expert evidence may be prohibitive; where the topic with which the single joint expert's report deals is a separate and self-contained part of the case, such as the valuation of particular heads of claim; where there is a subsidiary issue, which requires particular expertise of a relatively uncontroversial nature to resolve; or where testing or analysis is required, and this can conveniently be done by one laboratory or firm on behalf of all parties.

The TCC adopts a flexible approach to the presentation of expert evidence according to the needs of each case. Where a single joint expert has been appointed, or where the experts are in substantial agreement, it may be sufficient for the expert evidence to be in writing, without the need for any oral evidence. However, in many cases that get to trial, the Court is likely to benefit from the opportunity to hear from the experts and test the basis of their conclusions. Often, it is helpful for the parties to call all factual witnesses before any expert evidence, so that the factual foundation of the case is apparent. It is also helpful for experts in like disciplines to be called back-to-back, so that the technical arguments and the experts' responses can be compared more easily. In some cases, it may be appropriate for the experts for all parties to be called to give concurrent evidence, colloquially referred to as 'hot-tubbing'. When this method is adopted, there is generally a need for experts to be cross-examined on general matters and key issues before they are invited to give evidence concurrently on particular issues. If the questioning of the experts is to be carried out by the judge, it is necessary for the experts to produce very clear, comprehensive joint statements, setting out the basis of disagreement, and additional time needs to be set aside for preparation by the court.

VIII. Management of Complex Cases

On one view, almost every case in the TCC could be described as complex, given that technical complexity is a ground for issuing proceedings in the TCC. However, it is generally accepted that within the TCC a case is considered to be complex where any of the following features arise, particularly where more than one feature is present, namely, great numbers of parties, great numbers of experts and expert disciplines, great numbers of connected issues and claims, and very high value claims.

[48] For example, see the tailored approach taken to modest value cases set out in *The Sky's the Limit Transformations Ltd v Mirza* [2022] EWHC 29 (TCC) per HHJ Stephen Davies at [6]–[9].

The starting point for the Court in managing a complex case is to define the scope of the dispute. In *Building Design Partnership Limited v Standard Life Assurance Limited* at [39],[49] Coulson LJ confirmed that the basic ingredients of a statement of case were as summarised in his earlier judgment of *Pantelli*:[50]

> CPR 16.4(1)(a) requires that a particulars of claim must include 'a concise statement of the facts on which the claimant relies'. Thus, where the particulars of claim contain an allegation of breach of contract and/or negligence, it must be pleaded in such a way as to allow the defendant to know the case that it has to meet. The pleading needs to set out clearly what it is that the defendant failed to do that it should have done, and/or what the defendant did that it should not have done, what would have happened but for those acts or omissions, and the loss that eventuated. Those are 'the facts' relied on in support of the allegation, and are required in order that proper witness statements (and if necessary an expert's report) can be obtained by both sides which address the specific allegations made.

A pleading must set out clearly the grounds of claim and facts relied on, as explained by Teare J in *Towler v Wills* at [18]:[51]

> The purpose of a pleading or statement of case is to inform the other party what the case is that is being brought against him. It is necessary that the other party understands the case which is being brought against him so that he may plead to it in response, disclose those of his documents which are relevant to that case and prepare witness statements which support his defence. If the case which is brought against him is vague or incoherent he will not, or may not, be able to do any of those things. Time and costs will, or may, be wasted if the defendant seeks to respond to a vague and incoherent case. It is also necessary for the Court to understand the case which is brought so that it may fairly and expeditiously decide the case and in a manner which saves unnecessary expense. For these reasons it is necessary that a party's pleaded case is a concise and clear statement of the facts on which he relies …

All the case management tools referred to above may be used in this regard, including schedules (where necessary, Scott Schedules) setting out the detailed allegations of breach, delay, defects, remedial works and quantum; and lists of issues that distil all such information into the most essential questions to be determined by the court.

Once the scope of the case has been ascertained, the parties and the Court are in a position to consider the most efficient and cost effective method of determining it. Options include preliminary issues (especially points of law that could determine the claim or a substantial part of it), staged trials (dividing the case into manageable parts) and split trials (such as liability and quantum). Caution is always required when considering the appropriateness of preliminary issues.

[49] *Building Design Partnership Limited v Standard Life Assurance Limited* [2021] EWCA Civ 1793.

[50] *Pantelli Associates Limited v Corporate City Developments No.2* [2010] EWHC 3189 (TCC) at [11]; the pleadings should set an agenda for trial: *Wharf Properties v Cumine* [1991] 2 WLUK 304; (1991) 52 BLR 1 (PC).

[51] *Towler v Wills* [2010] EWHC 1209 (Comm).

Suitable preliminary issues can avoid the need for an expensive trial and provide the parties with a final determination of their dispute with expedition. However, if they are ordered inappropriately, they can have adverse effects: a) evidence may be duplicated; b) the same witnesses may give evidence before different judges, in the event that there is a switch of assigned judge; c) findings may be made at the preliminary issue hearing, which are affected by evidence subsequently called at the main hearing; d) the prospect of a preliminary issue hearing may delay the commencement of ADR or settlement negotiations; and e) two trials are more expensive than one.

One of the areas in which the TCC has particular experience is in using sampling and extrapolation as a tool by which the parties and the Court can organise the evidence and try the issues in a proportionate way.[52] In a very substantial case, this approach can be used in staged sub-trials, so that the issues in dispute are resolved or refined in tranches, increasing the prospects of settlement or at least determination of the material issues at an early stage in the litigation.

IX. Case Management of Adjudication Claims

Adjudication was introduced in 1998 by the Housing Grants, Construction and Regeneration Act 1996[53] as statutory dispute resolution for construction contracts. As explained in greater detail in chapter seven, under the Construction Act, parties have the right to refer disputes to adjudication at any time. There is a 28-day timetable for the adjudicator to issue their decision (subject to limited or agreed extensions of time). The adjudicator's decision is binding on the parties on an interim basis and can be enforced through the courts on a 'Pay now, argue later' basis.

The TCC has a special expedited procedure for adjudication enforcement. The enforcement claim is usually issued by a Part 7 Claim. Directions are given within about three days, whereby time for service is abridged and an expedited timetable is fixed for evidence, bundles and skeletons. A date for a summary judgment hearing is fixed (usually within four to six weeks of the directions for a remote hearing if no longer than half a day).

The TCC takes a robust approach to the enforcement of adjudication decisions. If the adjudicator has answered the right question, albeit in the wrong way, the decision will be binding. If the adjudicator has answered the wrong question, the decision will be a nullity: *Bouygues (UK) Ltd v Dahl-Jensen (UK) Ltd*.[54] The Court will enforce the adjudicator's decision unless it is plain that the question decided was not the question referred or the adjudicator's approach was obviously unfair.

[52] *BDP v Standard Life* (n 49) per Coulson LJ.

[53] Amended by the Local Democracy, Economic Development and Construction Act 2009, together referred to as 'the Construction Act'.

[54] *Bouygues (UK) Ltd v Dahl-Jensen (UK) Ltd* [2000] EWCA Civ 507.

It should only be in rare circumstances that the courts will interfere with the decision of an adjudicator: *Carillion v Devonport*.[55]

The limited grounds on which the Court will refuse summary judgment, are where the adjudicator did not have jurisdiction and a valid reservation of jurisdiction was made;[56] where there was no construction contract or the dispute was not subject to adjudication; where the dispute was already determined in another adjudication; breach of the rules of natural justice (such as a failure to consider a party's case or failure to allow representations) and apparent bias.

Insolvency poses a difficulty for the Court in ensuring that the philosophy of the Construction Act is maintained without causing a serious risk of injustice to the challenging party. This dilemma was grappled with by the Court of Appeal in *John Doyle Construction Ltd v Erith Contractors Ltd* where the Court held that the insolvency of a referring party did not preclude that party pursuing adjudication and obtaining an award but on enforcement such insolvency would be a material factor for the Court to take into account when deciding whether to refuse summary judgment or order a stay of execution.[57]

Part 8 may be appropriate for adjudication enforcement where no monetary relief is sought and a decision is required on a question that is unlikely to involve a substantial dispute of fact. However, the expedited adjudication enforcement procedure does not automatically apply to a Part 8 claim that is made as a defence to an enforcement claim and it should not delay the enforcement hearing. Competing Part 8 and Part 7 claims may be listed to be heard together if the parties agree or there is a short and self-contained issue which arose in the adjudication, it requires no oral evidence and the issue is one which, on a summary judgment application, it would be unconscionable for the Court to ignore: *Hutton v Wilson*.[58]

There has been a significant increase in adjudication claims – between 2020 and 2022 the number of adjudication claims issued in the TCC doubled. Most such claims settle before the enforcement hearing but, even where the adjudicator's decision is not accepted by one of the parties, the process of adjudication assists the parties in achieving a speedy resolution of their disputes. As recognised by the Supreme Court in *Bresco Electrical Services Ltd v Lonsdale*,[59] statutory adjudication has been successful, not only in improving cash flow within the construction industry, but also as a relatively fast, inexpensive and effective form of dispute resolution.

X. Managing Procurement Claims

One of the material challenges in managing procurement claims is the very tight time limits within which any challenge is required to be brought. An unsuccessful

[55] *Carillion v Devonport* [2005] EWCA Civ. 1358.
[56] *Bresco v Lonsdale* [2019] EWCA Civ 27.
[57] *John Doyle Construction Ltd v Erith Contractors Ltd* [2021] EWCA Civ 1452.
[58] *Hutton v Wilson* [2017] EWHC 517 (TCC).
[59] *Bresco Electrical Services Ltd v Lonsdale* [2020] UKSC 25; [2020] Bus LR 1000.

tenderer has 30 days from knowledge of the material facts to make a challenge. There is a standstill period of ten days (depending on mode of notice) after the notification of the decision before the authority can enter into the contract. If proceedings are issued and notified before the contract has been executed, there is an automatic suspension in respect of the contract award. The TCC Procurement Pre-Action Protocol applies.[60]

The TCC procedure is that the Claim Form and POC must be served within seven days after date of issue. Confidential information in pleadings should be redacted; the unredacted form should be served in an envelope marked confidential, with a letter seeking a court order for access to the file to be restricted. If, as is common, a parallel claim for judicial review is issued alongside the procurement claim, the Part 7 claim is issued in the TCC and the judicial review claim is issued in the Administrative Court. In most cases the judicial review claim is transferred to the TCC, where it can be case managed with the Part 7 claim and heard by a TCC judge who is also a designated judge of the Administrative Court.

Case management by the TCC will usually require the Court to consider whether an expedited trial is required (subject to the urgency and practicability of the same); any application to lift the suspension;[61] disclosure (confidentiality ring to deal with sensitive documents); joinder and participation of interested parties (notice should be given to those affected); and costs budgeting (parties can make written applications to the Court to change time or avoid need to file cost budgets).

Procurement reforms are in train as set out in the Procurement Bill.[62] They are intended to reform the UK's public procurement regime, making it quicker, simpler, more transparent and better able to meet the UK's needs while remaining compliant with its international obligations. Once the details of the final version are established, it will be necessary to revise the procedural rules for procurement claims. The Court is always open to new ways to improve the way in which claims can be conducted, to better serve the interests of justice, and is eager to make the new system work.

XI. COVID-19 Legacy

The COVID-19 pandemic saw the state's imposition of the greatest restrictions on individual freedom since the Second World War. It has had a profound and lasting impact on society, including the approach to civil litigation. The courts were

[60] At the time of writing this, the Procurement Protocol is contained in the TCC Guide at Appendix H but reform is ongoing to the procurement system, including remedies and procedure.

[61] Subject to changes to be introduced by the Procurement Bill when enacted, the applicable principles for determining such an application are set out in *American Cyanamid v Ethicon* [1975] AC 396 per Lord Diplock at 407G–408H; *National Commercial Bank Jamaica Limited v Olint Corporation Limited* [2009] UKPC 16; [2009] 1 WLR 1405 per Lord Hoffmann at [17]–[18]; *Covanta Energy Ltd v Merseyside Waste Disposal Authority* [2013] EWHC 2922 per Coulson J (as he then was) at [34] and [48]; and summarised in *Alstom v Network Rail Infrastructure Ltd* [2019] EWHC 3585 (TCC) at [29].

[62] As at September 2022 the Procurement Bill is in committee stage in the House of Lords.

quick to demonstrate that they could adapt their procedures to keep the wheels of justice turning but, throughout the extensive lockdowns and restrictions, high regard remained for the paramountcy of the principle of open justice.

On 19 March 2020 the message by the Lord Chief Justice was that events were moving so fast that detailed guidance on how to sustain the administration of justice would be overtaken by developments very quickly:

> We have an obligation to continue with the work of the courts as a vital public service, just as others in the public sector and in the private sector are doing. But as I have said before, it will not be business as usual. We are making arrangements to include those working in the courts within the scope of key workers who will be able to continue to send their children to schools. Further information about that will come later.

By 23 March 2020, the Lord Chief Justice stated:

> Events have continued to move at great speed. I indicated during the course of last week that we would keep them under review. As the Prime Minister has been telling the country, the spread of COVID-19 has continued to accelerate. The clear message from Government is to take all precautions to avoid unnecessary contact. A review of the arrangements in our courts is called for. This short statement comes to judges, and others, to provide some clarity for the coming few days … Hearings requiring the physical presence of parties and their representatives and others should only take place if a remote hearing is not possible and if suitable arrangements can be made to ensure safety.

On 25 March 2020 the Coronavirus Act 2020 was enacted, granting the government emergency powers to handle the COVID-19 pandemic, including power to close or restrict access to premises, including construction sites, to prevent gatherings and events taking place, failure to comply with which constituted a criminal offence punishable by a fine.[63] This was followed on 26 March 2020 by the Health Protection (Coronavirus, Restrictions) (England) (Amendment) Regulations 2020.

On 26 March 2020, a new Practice Direction 51Y made provision in relation to audio or video hearings during the period to which the material regulations remained in force; where the Court directed that proceedings were to be conducted wholly as video or audio proceedings and it was not practicable for the hearing to be broadcast in a court building, the Court had power to direct that the hearing must take place in private where necessary to do so to secure the proper administration of justice.

The TCC response to the evolving crisis was swift. Anticipating the lockdown, by 23 March 2020, the day on which lockdown was announced in the UK, the TCC had issued template orders and started sending out letters to the parties for remote hearings. By 26 March 2020, there was a Protocol for Remote Hearings for use across all jurisdictions of the High Court. In the TCC, a small number of trials were adjourned for COVID-19 reasons (where parties were isolating, based in areas of lockdown or NHS providers) but these were heard during the summer

[63] Sections 51–52; Schs 21 and 22.

vacation of 2020 or re-listed for an early hearing thereafter. Otherwise, all hearings went ahead as originally listed, save that they were remote, mostly video link hearings. As from June 2020, in person or hybrid hearings were offered in court, although the Court continued to offer remote hearings for court users who were unable or reluctant to travel to the courts. Impressive co-operation and flexibility was shown by the parties, legal representatives, judges and court staff to ensure that the wheels of justice kept turning.

The legacy of COVID-19 has been to demonstrate the resilience, agility and adaptability of the courts during challenging circumstances. The primary benefit of the experience was the acceleration of the use of technology to improve the efficiency and cost of legal proceedings without compromising justice. There has been a significant shift in favour of electronic working and greater use of remote hearings, whilst continuing to recognise the value of retaining in person hearings where appropriate.

Under the current scheme in the BPC, the default position for hearings under half a day is that such hearings take place remotely, including the Friday procedural hearing lists and adjudication enforcement hearings. The above position does not apply in Manchester and Leeds, where the default position for Friday applications is an 'in person' hearing. All other hearings are a matter for decision by the judge – the general position is that hearings with an estimate of more than half a day will be 'in person' subject to the circumstances of each case.

The TCC has adopted the BPC Protocol for Remote and Hybrid Hearings.[64] It is important to note that remote or hybrid trials require additional preparation and co-operation; any practical issues should be discussed and resolved at the PTR. No person may access a remote or hybrid hearing remotely without the court's permission (although not specifically addressed in the Protocol, this would include remote observation).[65] A party calling a witness located outside the jurisdiction must ensure that any necessary permission is obtained.

The TCC has embraced the technological progress, having started electronic working as early as 20 July 2009; indeed, the first claim to be issued in any jurisdiction under the electronic working pilot scheme was issued in the TCC. The TCC uses the CE-filing system and PD 51O applies. For a party who is legally represented, electronic working is mandatory for the commencement of proceedings and any subsequent claims or applications. For a party who is not legally represented, electronic working is optional.

The number of electronic applications has increased dramatically over recent years and currently stands at 1,800 per annum, most of which are dealt with in writing without a hearing. Parties in a TCC case are encouraged to deal with applications in writing, whenever practicable. Applications for abridgments of time, extensions of time and to reduce the trial time estimate can generally be dealt with in writing, as well as all other variations to existing directions which are wholly or

[64] Appendix K to the TCC Court Guide 2022.
[65] The Police, Crime, Sentencing and Courts Act 2022, s 198.

largely agreed. Disputes over particular aspects of disclosure and evidence may also be capable of being resolved in this way.

Before issuing an application, the applicant should send a draft to the other party, inviting a response within three days or other specified time. The responding party should indicate whether they consent to the application; if not, whether they agree to it being dealt with on paper and whether they wish to serve evidence or submissions in response. If agreed, a draft consent order can be filed. If opposed, the parties should try to agree whether it is suitable for determination on paper or by hearing, the timetable for submissions and evidence and estimate for any hearing.

The TCC has been at the forefront of the use of technology throughout the court process, from the use of CE-filing, electronic applications, TAR in disclosure, electronic bundles, to the use of computer models for analysis of complex engineering issues and presentations in court.

The legacy of the court's experience during the COVID-19 pandemic is that it demonstrated the success that came with co-operation and agility of the legal profession to adapt to new circumstances. It established the need for the evolution of legal processes to serve the interests of justice. Above all, it accelerated the introduction and use of technology to improve the efficiency and cost of legal proceedings without compromising justice.

XII. The Future

Looking to the future, the nature of disputes and disputes resolution is changing. Building Information Modelling (BIM), the use of computer-based models in a shared digital space, is revolutionising the construction industry. BIM will enable not just a 3D model of a project to be produced but will also facilitate the addition of costs, sequencing, management of the asset through its life, energy use and sustainability. The integration of BIM with smart contracts, digital contracts with embedded code for automated actions, when integrated with blockchain technology and crypto-assets, will generate automated responses to events throughout the design, construction and operation of projects. Such comprehensive project execution and asset management tools will change the nature of disputes and dispute resolution. As in the past, the TCC is ready to adapt and evolve to meet the challenge.

9

The TCC in the Regions

HER HONOUR FRANCES KIRKHAM, HIS HONOUR JUDGE STEPHEN DAVIES AND MICHAEL LEVENSTEIN

I. Introduction

The TCC has operated in a number of cities outside London. This practice has in fact predated the creation of the TCC itself, with the predecessors of TCC judges – the Official Referees and other suitable circuit judges – authorised to hear construction disputes outside London. The introduction of dedicated TCC Judges began in October 1998, at which point (and for the first time) a designated High Court Judge was assigned to be in charge of the TCC.

Practice Direction 60 provided that TCC cases brought in the High Court outside London could be issued in any District Registry but made clear that it was preferable wherever possible that these should be issued in Birmingham, Bristol, Cardiff, Chester, Exeter, Leeds, Liverpool, Manchester, Mold, Newcastle upon Tyne or Nottingham, 'in which a TCC judge would usually be available'.[1] The Practice Direction also provided that a TCC claim could be issued in the County Court hearing centres in each of the above-mentioned locations, in addition to the Central London County Court. The Practice Direction also refers to the TCC Guide, the second edition of which followed extensive input from not only various professional bodies, but also from TCC user committees in Birmingham, Cardiff, Liverpool, Leeds and Manchester. Many of the judicial contributors to this book provided invaluable contributions to publication of the TCC Guide.

This chapter is not the history of the TCC in all of these courts outside London. Instead, it is principally an account of some of the events taking place in four of those centres. It focuses on developments in Manchester, Birmingham, Liverpool and Leeds as examples of how the TCC outside London has developed. It is likely that other regional centres will have many stories to tell. Of course, important work has been undertaken in other cities, which deserved mention and recognition but are beyond the scope of this chapter. We apologise to judges and practitioners in other cities for not having written about their experiences. We hope that this

[1] PD 60, para 3.3.

brief account will be representative of the way in which the TCC has operated and developed outside London.

To a limited extent the TCC in London is a court of choice. In the regions, however, such choice is a significant feature. First, parties are able to choose whether to begin proceedings in or outside London. Some of the implications of this are discussed in more detail below. Second, in the recent past (and before the development of the Business and Property Courts) the overlap between the scope of the work of the Chancery Division, the Mercantile (now Circuit Commercial) Court and the TCC meant that in those cities where judges sat in all three divisions parties were often able, in effect, to choose their judge by deciding in which of the three specialist courts to launch their cases.

It has been necessary for TCC judges outside London to gain the confidence of the local community to attract work. Some of the consequences of that are discussed later in this chapter.

II. Manchester

This section contains His Honour Judge Stephen Davies' personal account of some of the developments in the TCC in Manchester.

The two underlying themes behind the development of the TCC in Manchester have been first, the presence for much of the period of two permanent full-time TCC Judges sitting in well-equipped court centres and second, the increasing number of specialist local counsel who practice full time or at least to a significant extent in TCC work.

Before 1992, TCC cases were dealt with by judges who did not sit full time on TCC work in a small court room within the old Manchester County Court. The workload of the TCC was small as a result with few local specialist counsel. Things changed significantly after the appointment of HHJ David Gilliland QC as a full-time TCC Judge in 1992, at the same time as the TCC moved to a very spacious court in a converted office building at the end of the M602 motorway in Salford.

HHJ Gilliland QC was immediately able to convert his experience as a QC specialising in real property disputes into expertise as a TCC Judge.[2] He was hugely intelligent and hard-working, firm and decisive in his judgments. This occasionally came as a surprise to the losing party, given his quiet and reserved manner during the hearings themselves. His dedicated clerks, who loyally supported him, used to say that the only time they knew he was irritated was when they heard a gentle but insistent tapping of his foot under the bench. Counsel who appeared regularly before him came to listen for that sound as well. He rarely reserved judgment in interlocutory hearings, preferring instead to deliver ex tempore judgments. London practitioners appearing before him – not to mention their

[2] As he and his contemporaries then were prior to the accession of King Charles III in September 2022.

instructing solicitors and clients – were pleasantly surprised to receive impressively detailed judgments delivered the same day. Sometimes they were less impressed when they discovered the difficulty of getting a taxi back from Salford to Piccadilly train station in Manchester at 6pm on a cold, wet, dark Friday evening; it is a shame that the extended Manchester tram service to Media City and beyond came too late to save them!

The volume and quality of work steadily increased. High-value substantial cases began to be issued in Salford. Judge Gilliland tried a number of such cases, including several lengthy trials, one a case about defects and delays in the Royal Exchange building in Manchester, another a claim about fraud in the IT industry and a third being a group litigation claim concerning main sewage replacement works in Preston city centre. Another case, about the inter-relationship between extensions of time, deduction of liquidated damages and termination in relation to a contract for the construction of apartments, eventually went to the House of Lords (*Reinwood v Brown & Sons*),[3] as did a flooding damage case which brought into question the continued existence and scope of the rule in *Rylands v Fletcher*.[4]

Eventually, the volume of work was such that in 2001 another full-time TCC Judge, HHJ Philip Raynor QC, was appointed to sit in Salford alongside Judge Gilliland. In the same way as with David Gilliland, Philip Raynor was immediately able to convert his own experience as a QC specialising in commercial litigation into expertise as a TCC Judge. Philip Raynor had the same qualities as David Gilliland, although he was also often a successful exponent of an informal but fair early neutral evaluation (ENE) discussion at the start of a hearing which usually enabled the parties to reach a sensible settlement. He was the embodiment of informality, sitting in shirt sleeves (and encouraging everyone in court to do the same) whenever the large glass windows in his court made the temperature uncomfortable and putting everyone at ease with his shrewd and common-sense approach. That easy informality belied his ability to understand and deliver incisive judgments in the cases which came his way. At the start of one lengthy trial, concerning a fire in a sugar beet factory in Bury St Edmunds caused by defects in a steam turbine generator, he cheerfully announced that the parties had been unlucky in drawing him as their judge since his wife complained that he had never changed a fuse in a plug in all their married life! Needless to say, he delivered a judgment at the end of the trial which disclosed his mastery of the case and which was subsequently upheld in the Court of Appeal (*British Sugar v Cegelec*).[5]

No other regional court centre has ever had two full-time TCC Judges. It is likely that the success of the Manchester TCC was due to the presence of two well-regarded, full-time TCC judges and an increasingly strong Manchester construction dispute professional sector. In addition to the number of major regional solicitor practices, Manchester – unlike other regional court centres – had

[3] *Reinwood Ltd v L Brown & Sons Ltd* [2008] UKHL 12, [2008] 1 WLR 696.
[4] *Transco v Stockport MBC* [2003] UKHL 61, [2004] 2 AC 1.
[5] *British Sugar plc v Cegelec Ltd* [2004] EWCA Civ 1450, [2004] 10 WLUK 165.

a growing specialist Bar. Three local QCs specialised in TCC work to a significant degree and also sat as TCC deputy judges in the Manchester TCC: the late Giles Wingate-Saul QC, Stephen Grime QC and Michael Black QC. There were also a number of junior barristers in the larger chambers who undertook a significant amount of TCC work. There was a well-established and well-attended TCC users' committee which put on seminars at which TCC High Court judges from London, as well as the local TCC judges and local practitioners, would speak.

In 2007, the TCC returned from Salford to Manchester with the opening of the iconic Manchester Civil Justice Centre. Judge Gilliland QC had been heavily involved with the design of the courts, which included a number of 'supercourts', two of which were assigned for use by the TCC judges and which could accommodate significant multi-party TCC trials. Sadly for him, the inevitable construction overrun meant that the opening of the Manchester CJC coincided with his retirement, so that he sat only once in one of the courts which he had helped design.

I replaced David Gilliland as the second TCC Judge, working alongside Philip Raynor. I was a local Manchester practitioner who, like others, had come to specialise in TCC disputes whilst remaining in practice in Manchester. The work of the Manchester TCC continued to remain vibrant, with one trial, concerning competing claims and counterclaims (including claims based on sampling and extrapolation) arising out of a long-term highways maintenance contract, lasting for almost three months and being the first of its kind to use a full electronic trial document management system outside of London (*Amey v Cumbria CC*).[6]

There were two particular advantages of the TCC moving to the Manchester CJC. The first was that it made it easier for other specialist Business and Property Courts judges to sit on TCC cases, increasing the opportunity for cases to be listed far more quickly than had been the case. The second was that it enabled High Court TCC judges to sit in Manchester to undertake general civil work but to hear TCC cases where possible whilst sitting there. Since the Manchester CJC opened, Coulson LJ, Stuart-Smith LJ, Akenhead J, Fraser J and O'Farrell J have all done so.

The Manchester TCC is also notable in that the replacement for Judge Raynor QC, another regional practitioner, HHJ Stephen Eyre QC, was subsequently appointed as a High Court Judge sitting in the TCC in London, illustrating that the TCC work in the regions could be of suitably high quality to justify the appointment of a TCC Circuit Judge of sufficient calibre to the High Court bench. One such case which Stephen Eyre QC case managed after it had been issued in Liverpool by the claimant's solicitors was a major multi-party claim involving claims for flooding following the collapse of a dam in Brazil (*Municipio de Mariana v BHP Group*).[7] His appointment follows the earlier elevation of HHJ David Waksman QC who had sat on TCC cases whilst at Manchester and who also sits as a High Court Judge in the TCC in London.

[6] *Amey LG Ltd v Cumbria CC Ltd* [2016] EWHC 2856 (TCC), [2016] 11 WLUK 333.
[7] *Municipio de Mariana v BHP Group plc* [2020] EWHC 928 (TCC), [2020] BLR 421.

Notwithstanding the ravages of the COVID-19 pandemic, the caseload in the Manchester TCC has remained fairly constant, in fact increasing during the past year. One reason for the Court's resilience lies in its willingness, alongside that of its users, to embrace new technologies such as video-conferencing software to facilitate remote hearings where necessary. Of last year's caseload in the Manchester TCC, the overwhelming majority – over 87 per cent – was allocated to the High Court.[8]

III. Birmingham

This section contains Her Honour Judge Frances Kirkham's personal account of some of the developments in the TCC in Birmingham.

My involvement began as a user, and convener of a users' committee. I was later appointed the designated TCC Judge in Birmingham.

When I first became involved with the TCC the civil courts in Birmingham were housed in poor quality buildings. All the civil courts needed better facilities but the TCC felt like the Cinderella of the Court Service. At that time, Judge John Toyn (an excellent TCC Judge) sat in a cramped and uncomfortable basement court. The poor environment did not prevent Judge Toyn providing a good service and giving good judgments.

The civil justice centre was later moved into a former department store. Court users remembered visiting the zoo and Father Christmas on the top floor before the Court moved in: maybe that was an unconscious attraction to use the TCC in Birmingham? The TCC users' committee in Birmingham was invited to comment on the plans for the new court. We recommended that the refurbishment work include running ducting within the court room allocated to the TCC to enable computers to be used in court: better to do it at that stage than wait until the need for this became obvious. The official response (echoed by the then judge responsible for TCC work) was astonishment that anyone should think the use of computers necessary. No provision was made for it at that stage.

The new court room was also fitted with an old-style witness box, which was wholly unsuitable. I succeeded in replacing the box with a large table which had room for files and (later) laptops.

The TCC in Birmingham was very conscious that it was a court of choice. We recognised that we were there to serve the parties and their representatives. We needed to be accessible and to gain the trust of local users.

We were blessed with the TCC clerk (Peter Duke during my tenure) and the other support staff for the specialist courts. They responded quickly and efficiently to questions from users. The excellent relationships between specialist judges and support staff resulted in the efficient running of the Court and providing a good

[8] Annual Report of the TCC 2020–2021, para 6.6.

service to users. Queries were answered quickly and, I hope, constructively. After all, the Court was there for the parties, and not for us.

The TCC in Birmingham, no doubt like those in other cities, aimed to create a fairly informal environment. Legal teams are (usually) comfortable in court. Most clients are not, especially those for whom this was a first experience of a court. It was important that the parties themselves felt that they were fully engaged with the process. They needed to understand what was being said and done in their name. Party representatives and judges needed to use language which the clients could understand. It was important that the clients did not feel they were in such an alien world that they were powerless. I felt that the formality of a conventional court created a gulf between judge and the parties.

Throughout my time as a judge, I never felt it sensible to wear a wig and gown. I did so when it was really difficult to refuse, but was not robed when dealing with TCC cases (or indeed Mercantile Court or Chancery Division cases). Legal representatives quickly learned that I did not require them to be robed: that was the default position on which they could rely. Carrying heavy books, files and laptops was enough without adding formal dress to that burden. This informality caused one visiting Senior Presiding Judge serious concern when he looked through the window into my court and saw us all having an unrobed discussion.

Informality was (unintentionally) enhanced by the practical arrangements in the court room. In the TCC we almost never had an usher. While the TCC clerk usually sat in court during hearings there were occasions when he was unable to be there. It was thus my task to navigate the court furniture when walking around to start the tape recorder and stop it at the end of the hearing.

We developed a big workload. That kept Peter Duke and others busy. To assist them I did not expect the clerks to draft orders but did this myself if the advocates had not provided usable drafts.

At an early stage I invited users to form a users' group. They did so enthusiastically. It was important to listen to their concerns and to address them whenever possible. I had been a solicitor in practice, so had first-hand experience, and understanding, of the needs and demands of clients. I made sure that the TCC clerk attended the meetings. We discussed openly and constructively where improvements could be made and those which were simply not possible within the system.

From the beginning I recognised that while there were excellent solicitors in the Midlands specialising in TCC work, there were few such specialists at the Birmingham Bar. Parties in substantial disputes would want to instruct specialist construction barristers, but not all of them would want to travel to and from Birmingham for a case management conference (CMC). So, from the beginning of my time as a TCC Judge, I encouraged telephone hearings which would accommodate party representatives from outside the area. We also found that work was coming in from other parts of the country. Use of telephone hearings was helpful to solicitors who were not based in the Midlands.

Under the TCC regime judges are not obliged always to sit in a court room. When we discussed a case involving parties from outside the area I would often raise the possibility of sitting somewhere other than the Birmingham court room. It became clear that finding a court room in another court centre would be difficult. So, we explored the use of other locations convenient to parties. In one case, we reached the end of the last day fixed for a full hearing, but had not finished the evidence. We discussed practical arrangements for completing the case. Diaries were consulted. No weekdays were possible for some weeks ahead, nor were there any Saturdays free. So, all agreed that we would sit on a Sunday only a week or so ahead. It would not be possible to use the court room, so all agreed that we would sit in the offices of one of the solicitors involved with the case. This we did. We made it clear that we were in effect in a court room. Everyone took it seriously. We completed the evidence and submissions. We avoided a long, and undesirable, delay. I hope that Peter Duke will forgive me for saying that he rather liked that arrangement: it was triple time for him on a Sunday.

During my time as TCC Judge in Birmingham, Caroline Alton was the Mercantile judge. Caroline Alton was a first-class judge. She had been the TCC Judge before me, during which time she enhanced the reputation of the TCC and laid the groundwork on which I could develop the Court. Caroline and I each had the luxury of running our own lists. Not only did that give us very welcome autonomy, but also it enabled us to juggle cases, impose realistic timetables and take a guess (insofar as that is ever possible) as to whether or not a case was likely to run to trial or settle.

The Birmingham TCC was an early user of early neutral evaluation (ENE). As Caroline Alton was sitting in the same building and had extensive TCC experience, she was the ideal judge with whom to partner for an ENE. Caroline and I would discuss which of us should undertake the ENE and which would take up the case if the ENE failed. My approach to an ENE was to invite the parties to say how they would like to deal with it. If they wanted to come into court, I would offer them a day or maybe half a day in a small case. They could make submissions, invite experts to give explanations, run through relevant documents, give PowerPoint presentations – whatever they thought might be most useful. The aim of course was to help their respective clients to understand how the case might be decided and so deal with settlement discussions realistically. In one ENE I could see the faces of the legal team for one party: it looked as though the comments I was making about the likely prospects of success mirrored advice which they had given their client, but which he had not accepted. There was only modest uptake of ENE. I could understand that: if the judge at an ENE suggested that one party was likely to be successful that could have the effect of making it more difficult to settle the case.

We adopted hot-tubbing at an early stage, and I think before other TCC judges tried this. I conducted a hearing in which two QSs were giving expert evidence. Their reports had shown markedly different opinions. They sat together at the witness table. They and I ran through the (seemingly endless) list of items in dispute. After a short time, the two QSs began to agree with each other, the pace increased and we ended up with only a small number of disputed items. I found it much easier to grasp the reasons for disagreement by listening to each in turn giving his opinion then listening to the discussion which ensued between the two of them.

Sensible and constructive legal teams appeared for a CMC in a high-value ground conditions case. The experts disagreed. The lawyers had found someone who was likely to have the answers and whom all could trust. They made a joint application that this person be appointed as an expert to assist both parties. We discussed the practicalities. I suggested that he be appointed an assessor (under CPR 35.15). After more discussion we had a break to enable the lawyers to approach the person concerned with that proposal. I was told he would be pleased to act as an assessor. The lawyers prepared a detailed scheme to enable this to happen. An early step which was agreed was to be an informal discussion between the assessor and experts which the parties could observe but in which they could not participate. To my real disappointment they (of course) settled. I had been looking forward to sitting with a person of such standing in his field.

On one occasion I was so frustrated by the lack of preparation in a case that I took a chance. I was fortunate that it did not backfire. A small case was due to come on for trial within the next few weeks. The experts had not filed a joint statement. At a pre-trial review I guessed (though one can never be sure) that one expert had not been instructed properly or indeed may have been instructed not to agree anything. I ordered the two experts to attend court a couple of days later. They arrived. I explained that I had arranged a room for them, in which they were to discuss the issues and prepare a joint statement; they would not be allowed to leave the building without my permission. At lunch time they asked to see me. They said that they had made excellent progress and promised to prepare their statement and send this to the Court within the next couple of days – oh, and please could they leave the building?! It worked.

My attempt to develop a vibrant County Court TCC was largely unsuccessful. Small disputes are the most difficult to manage. Often parties are unrepresented. If there is representation this is usually by inexperienced practitioners. It is very difficult to run a small, complex construction dispute proportionately.

There are excellent solicitors with specialist TCC practices in the Midlands. I was disappointed that we were unable to encourage the Birmingham Bar to develop TCC specialist practices. Birmingham has always suffered from its proximity to London as counsel have generally been willing to travel the comparatively short distances to meet clients and to appear in Birmingham. And, somewhat bizarrely, the Birmingham Bar could be more expensive than specialist London counsel.

The specialist courts in Birmingham (Chancery, Mercantile and TCC) introduced what we described as the shared list. At that time Alastair Norris QC was the Chancery Judge in Birmingham, and I have already mentioned Caroline Alton. We were each cross-ticketed to sit in the other two courts. Each of the three of us, as specialist judges, kept in our own list those cases which required the particular expertise needed for cases in that division. But there were cases in which that special expertise was not needed or where the issues might arise in more than one of the divisions. We agreed that those cases would be listed in the shared list. Thus, we ran four lists for three judges. In practice many cases settled before trial. As a result, every case in the shared list kept its allocated trial date. The system worked well, and for a number of reasons. The first is because the three of us trusted each other in the choice of cases to be put in the shared list. For example, I would not have asked either of my two colleagues to try an extension of time or prolongation case. And in the early days of adjudication enforcement, when the jurisprudence was developing, I did not put such cases into the shared list. The second is because the practitioners trusted us to choose carefully which cases could be allocated to the shared list. We would canvass this with parties and listened carefully to any objections. The parties co-operated with us in ensuring that a judge with the necessary skill and experience would try their case. It gave us, as judges, the opportunity to expand our experience and feel confident to deal with cases outside our primary areas of expertise. This was a major innovation. It inspired and led to the creation of the Business and Property Court (BPC).

As the TCC is a court of choice, it was necessary to play an active role in marketing the Court. I was grateful for the enthusiastic support of professional societies such as the Society of Construction Law (SCL), the Technology and Construction Bar Association (TECBAR), the Technology and Construction Solicitors' Association (TeCSA) and the Chartered Institute of Arbitrators (CIArb) which arranged events which showcased the Court, and incidentally gave me the opportunity for informal discussions, from which I could learn about any difficulties which needed to be resolved or improvements which might be made.

The judge in charge of the TCC played an important part in assisting the growth of the TCC in Birmingham. During my time in Birmingham, Sir Rupert Jackson was the first-class judge in charge. He recognised the need to ensure that the regions were operating well. He was hugely supportive: he visited regions regularly, spoke at conferences, seminars and other events outside London and which were important for the TCC. He attended users' meetings. He listened carefully to views and concerns expressed. Users could see that the local judge was valued by London and the local court well supported.

Indeed, Rupert demonstrated his confidence by introducing his civil litigation costs reforms in Birmingham. In May 2009 the TCC and Mercantile Court in Birmingham were chosen to take part in a pilot scheme to precede the national implementation.

Rupert took time to encourage deputies (most of whom were from London chambers) to sit in Birmingham, and I really appreciated the support of those who did come.

The work of the TCC in Birmingham increased. At that time, the TCC in London was thought to be a little in the doldrums. I hope that the increase in work outside London also reflected the efforts we made to offer the parties and their representatives a reliable and first-class service. An increase in quality work appears to be a trend which continues to the present, the last year seeing 37 of the 52 new TCC claims issued in Birmingham brought in the High Court.[9] The increase of the work in Birmingham meant that we could justify the appointment of an additional judge. To my huge delight Stephen Davies was appointed and joined me in Birmingham. It was a great pleasure working with him. Later on, Manchester was fortunate to be able to welcome him.

IV. Liverpool

In a similar way to Manchester, the reputation of the Liverpool TCC was enhanced when HHJ John Stannard was appointed as principal TCC Judge at around the same time as HHJ Gilliland QC was appointed in Manchester. The work and reputation of the Liverpool TCC increased. For example, Judge Stannard gave an oft-cited judgment in 1990 about the impact on a damages claim for defective work of the employer's non-notification of defects under the JCT defects liability clause and its decision to appoint remedial works without affording the contractor the opportunity to do so first (*William Tomkinson v Parochial Church Council of St Michael*).[10]

He was succeeded by HHJ David Mackay who continued in the role until his retirement in 2012. David Mackay had a genial manner and was, like Philip Raynor QC, a successful exponent of informal ENE. Judge Mackay also developed the idea of having a regional TCC liaison district judge, an innovation which has since been provided for in the TCC Guide, and extended across court centres nationwide. When Judge Mackay had to try cases, he was a well-respected judge, trying substantial matters including major insurance claims, fire damage cases and a case about defective milking machine equipment. Sadly, after his retirement the decision was taken not to replace him with a specialist TCC Judge which led to a diminution in the TCC work undertaken in Liverpool. This is a good illustration of the vulnerability which the regional TCC court centres have when there is no specialist TCC Judge in place for any length of time.

Even so, the Court has continued to remain active, in fact increasing its caseload in the last year (most of which was heard in the High Court)[11] and amidst the zenith of the COVID-19 pandemic. More recently the attraction of Liverpool as a TCC centre has been revitalised by the appointment of HHJ Neil Cadwallader as a full-time specialist BPC Judge sitting in Liverpool, undertaking TCC work as well as Chancery and Circuit Commercial Court work.

[9] Annual Report of the TCC 2020–2021, para 6.1.

[10] *William Tomkinson & Sons v Parochial Church Council of St Michael* (1990) 6 Const LJ 319.

[11] Annual Report of the TCC 2020–2021, para 6.5.

V. Leeds

Until the appointment of HHJ Mark Raeside QC as a full-time TCC Judge in 2013, Leeds had not had a full-time TCC Judge and, although it had always had a principal TCC Judge, the amount of time which the judge could devote to TCC cases was, like in Liverpool, limited. Judge Raeside's role was to promote the Leeds TCC as a vibrant court centre undertaking High Court work and focusing on the needs of court users, especially the strong regional solicitor practices based, or with offices, in Leeds. The profile of the Leeds TCC was enhanced as a specialist court centre upon becoming part of (and distinct from the other specialist courts within) the Business and Property Courts, located in the Leeds Combined Court Centre.

As well as hearing interlocutory matters by telephone he regularly reported back to court users and introduced what has become an annual SCL conference in Leeds.

Following his return to London he has been replaced by HHJ Siobhan Kelly, a local-based former barrister and District Judge who continues the development of the Leeds TCC as a specialist centre.

VI. The Future of the TCC Outside London

There is a shared fear that the future of the TCC outside London may be precarious, especially in the smaller regional TCC court centres where there are good transport links to London. The draw of London should not be underestimated. London has always enjoyed the benefit of specialist counsel practising from London chambers, whereas specialist counsel are rarer outside London. The introduction of electronic filing has made it much easier for solicitors in the regions to file in London. This has the potential to increase the tendency for cases to be drawn into London and away from the regions. To sustain a vibrant TCC in the regions, active encouragement from London-based judges is needed. The future of the TCC outside London is very dependent upon the willingness of judges in London to provide the support that is needed. There are a number of steps which might be taken.

London judges should ensure that cases which begin in London but have their roots in the regions are transferred from London to the relevant regional centre. This is so even where the parties are agreed that the case should remain in London, unless there is some other good reason for it to remain in London. The fact that counsel are both based in London should not be a good reason. Too many cases remain in London by default, especially where the first case management of such cases is often undertaken by deputies who may not necessarily be alive to the need to challenge the reason for the case remaining in London.

Deputies are willing to sit in London. They should actively be encouraged to sit in regional centres where they are needed.

The judge in charge of the TCC has an important role to play. They may decide that a case begun in a regional centre should be transferred to London (eg, because of its complexity or the sums in issue). Alternatively, they might decide that a senior High Court Judge should travel to the regional centre to try the case. For some time such a step has been seen as an attraction, providing one way in which parties might be encouraged to use the regional courts more frequently. But both actions have the potential to undermine the authority of the local judge. The judge in charge must liaise sensitively with the local judge and tread carefully.

The judge in charge also has an important part to play in marketing the TCC outside London and must recognise that users in regional centres may have different views as to how the Court might meet their needs. One size does not fit all. The judge in charge should actively encourage local user groups, and indeed should take time to travel to attend meetings of local users.

Ending on a positive note, it may be seen that the drawing of the TCC into the umbrella of the BPCs has had a very positive impact in relation to those TCC centres where there is a BPC, which include Bristol, Cardiff and Newcastle as well as Birmingham, Leeds, Liverpool and Manchester. In addition to the support of the judge in charge of the TCC, the TCC centres also now have the support of the BPCs supervising High Court Judge for the region in question as well as the overall support of the Chancellor of the High Court as the judge with overall responsibility for the BPCs nationally. All of the regional TCC centres have benefitted from this additional support. For example, both the previous Chancellor, Sir Geoffrey Vos, and the previous Vice-Chancellor, Mr Justice Richard Snowden (as he then was prior to his appointment to the Court of Appeal), put their full support behind the proposal for the appointment of a full-time BPC Judge in Liverpool as described earlier in the section on that city.

Although it is true that some BPC judges do not have the same breadth and depth of experience as full-time or permanent TCC judges, as has been noted in relation to Birmingham there is often a considerable overlap between the BPCs jurisdictions in cases involving the development or management of real property and in relation to IT disputes. The expertise and skills of most BPC judges enable them to try such TCC cases without difficulty. Flexible listing allows such TCC cases to be listed much earlier than would otherwise be the case, especially adjudication enforcement cases where there is nothing in the history of the adjudication which suggests that there is a difficult point about jurisdiction or similar to be determined. A further benefit of having TCC District Judges in the regional court centres is that small value cases, including adjudication enforcement cases, can be released to the TCC District Judge.

It is to be hoped that the TCC outside London will continue to play an important – and indeed increasing – role in the resolution of TCC disputes of all kinds in the UK.

10

Construction Law, the Arbitration Act 1996 and Beyond: The Contribution of the Technology and Construction Court to Arbitration

PROFESSOR RENATO NAZZINI AND ALEKSANDER KALISZ

I. Introduction

Construction contracts are inherently susceptible to disputes.[1] When they arise, they generally involve significant complexity and intricacy.[2] The Technology and Construction Court (TCC or 'the Court') and its predecessor, the Official Referees Court, were established with the primary purpose of providing a specialist forum in which such disputes could be effectively and efficiently litigated and decided. They have also been instrumental, however, to the development of the other dispute resolution mechanisms available in construction. Among them is arbitration where the TCC has made a visible contribution since the establishment of the Court in 1998.

Notwithstanding the success of adjudication and the attractiveness of the TCC as a dispute resolution forum in itself, arbitration is still important to parties in the construction, engineering and energy sectors. At the International Chamber of Commerce, the most frequently selected arbitral institution for administering arbitrations,[3] the construction sector accounts for the largest proportion of cases at 38 per cent.[4] Construction arbitrations also account for seven per cent of the

[1] *Pegram Shopfitters Ltd v Tally Wiejl (UK) Ltd* [2003] EWCA Civ 1750 [2] (May LJ).

[2] Sir V Ramsey, 'Construction Law: The English Route to Modern Construction Law Symposium: Construction Law in the Legal Academy: Keynotes' (2022) 75 *Arkansas Law Review* 251, 288.

[3] Queen Mary University of London, '2021 International Arbitration Survey: Adapting arbitration to a changing world' (Queen Mary University of London, White & Case 2021) arbitration.qmul.ac.uk/media/arbitration/docs/LON0320037-QMUL-International-Arbitration-Survey-2021_19_WEB.pdf (accessed 15 August 2022).

[4] ICC, 'ICC Dispute Resolution Statistics: 2020' (ICC, 2021) iccwbo.org/publication/icc-dispute-resolution-statistics-2020/ (accessed 30 June 2022).

caseload of the London Court of International Arbitration, taking fourth place behind banking and finance, energy and resources and transport and commodities industries.[5] A 2019 survey focused on construction arbitration identified London as the most common seat in these disputes.[6] These statistics suggest at the outset that the TCC jurisdiction spans a considerable share of the world's construction arbitrations.

Construction contracts themselves appear to favour arbitration. FIDIC forms include a default dispute resolution clause that refers all disputes to arbitration under the rules of the International Chamber of Commerce.[7] Arbitration clauses are included in the JCT contracts[8] and NEC4 contract.[9] Construction cases may be also subject to arbitration rules designed for this sector specifically: the Construction Industry Model Arbitration Rules,[10] the Institution of Civil Engineers Arbitration Rules[11] or the Rules of the Institution of Chemical Engineers.[12] It can be truly said that the construction sector has fully embraced arbitration. So much so that arbitration and litigation are now considered the two main forms of final dispute resolution available to parties in construction cases.[13]

Although the TCC and arbitral tribunals are sometimes said to be competitors,[14] the relationship is rather one of symbiosis. Arbitration is not a self-standing system that can function entirely without the intervention of the courts. First, arbitration rests on a valid arbitration agreement. It is only as effective as the courts' enforcement of the arbitration agreement that obliges the parties to arbitrate, rather than litigate, their disputes. Second, while arbitrators may be performing exactly the same function as courts, they lack the authority of the state that underpins the exercise of jurisdiction by judges. As a result, their powers lack any direct coercive effect vis-à-vis the parties and any direct and even indirect coercive effect vis-à-vis third parties. Therefore, the courts need to lend arbitral tribunals their support in order for arbitration to be truly as effective as litigation. Finally, English law, as most legal systems around the world, give the courts the ultimate power to ensure that arbitrators have acted with jurisdiction and that the procedure has been fair.

[5] LCIA, '2021 Annual Casework Report' (LCIA 2022) www.lcia.org/lcia/reports.aspx (accessed 15 August 2022).

[6] Queen Mary University of London, '2019 International Arbitration Survey: International Construction Disputes' (Queen Mary University of London, Pinsent Masons 2019) www.pinsentmasons.com/thinking/special-reports/international-arbitration-survey (accessed 15 August 2022).

[7] Clause 21.6, 2017 FIDIC Conditions of Contract (Second Edition).

[8] Art 8, JCT Design and Build Contract 2016; Art 8, JCT Standard Building Contract 2016. Equivalent provisions exist in most other JCT contracts.

[9] Options W1, W2 and W3, NEC4.

[10] 'CIMAR' published by the Joint Contracts Tribunal, currently in their 2016 version. See here: www.jctltd.co.uk/docs/JCT_CIMAR_2016.pdf.

[11] 'ICE Arbitration Procedure', currently in their 2012 version. See here: myice.ice.org.uk/ICEDevelopmentWebPortal/media/Documents/Disciplines%20and%20Resources/09-2-ICE-Arbitration-procedure-2012-04-30.pdf.

[12] 'IChemE Arbitration Rules', also known as 'The Pink Book', currently in their 2019 version. See here: www.icheme.org/knowledge/forms-of-contract/dispute-resolution/.

[13] J Bailey, *Construction Law*, 3rd edn (London, London Publishing Company, 2020) 1988.

[14] ibid 141.

English law goes further and, in certain circumstances, gives the courts the power to decide whether the award is correct as a matter of English law.

This chapter examines the contribution of the TCC to arbitration since the establishment of the Court in 1998. The Arbitration Act 1996 (the 'Act') came into force on 31 January 1997 and repealed most of the previous legislation concerning arbitration. While the Act is not a code in the civil law sense, it does set out a clear and structured regime of arbitration in England, Wales and Northern Ireland. Therefore, most of the analysis in this chapter will relate to case law interpreting, clarifying and applying provisions of the Act. This does not mean that the TCC has not made contributions beyond the statutory regime, for example in relation to the duties of experts.

For the purposes of this chapter, the authors considered almost 200 TCC judgments relating to arbitration, rendered since the establishment of the Court in 1998 until May 2022. The analysis is timely, as it comes after a quarter century of TCC experience in interpreting and applying the Act and at a time when the Law Commission is conducting consultations exploring its possible reform.[15]

This chapter is structured as follows. First, it discusses how the TCC construes and enforces arbitration agreements. Second, it examines the TCC's supportive powers in favour of the arbitration. Third, it analyses the TCC's supervisory powers over arbitration. Finally, conclusions are drawn.

II. Construing and Enforcing Arbitration Agreements

The existence and scope of an arbitral tribunal's jurisdiction rests on the arbitration agreement. As the Supreme Court explained in *Dallah Real Estate & Tourism Holding Co v Pakistan*,[16] if a party has not consented to being bound by an arbitration clause, they are not obliged to participate in any arbitration brought against them.[17]

A significant number of arbitration-related TCC judgments relate to the stay of legal proceedings.[18] A stay of proceedings order works akin to a specific performance order as a method for the courts to enforce the arbitration agreement.[19] A stay of proceedings may be granted pursuant to: (i) section 9 of the Act; or (ii) the inherent jurisdiction of the Court.[20] Under section 9, however, the Court has no discretion. A stay must be granted provided that the matter subject to the application falls under the terms of an arbitration agreement between the parties and that arbitration agreement is not null and void, inoperative, or incapable of being

[15] Law Commission, *Review of the Arbitration Act* (Law Com No 257, 2022) paras 5.27–5.35.

[16] *Dallah Real Estate & Tourism Holding Co v Pakistan* [2010] UKSC 46.

[17] ibid, [23–4].

[18] The empirical analysis conducted for the purposes of this chapter identified 17 TCC judgments relating primarily to an application to stay legal proceedings since 1999.

[19] *Channel Tunnel Group v Balfour Beatty Ltd* [1993] AC 334.

[20] *Aectra Refining And Marketing Inc. v Exmar N.V.* [1995] 1 Lloyd's Rep. 191.

performed.[21] However, even if a particular arbitration agreement is not one that falls under the Act[22] or the stay application falls short of section 9, the Court can nonetheless stay proceedings under its inherent jurisdiction.

A. What is an Arbitration Agreement?

A point that may arise on an application for a stay is whether the dispute resolution clause relied upon by the applicant is an arbitration agreement at all.

In *British Telecommunications Plc v SAE Group Inc*, Ramsey J had to construe the following dispute resolution clause:[23]

> 17.1 All disputes or differences which shall at any time hereafter arise between the parties hereto in respect of the construction or effect of this agreement or the rights, duties and liabilities of the parties hereunder or any matter or event connected with or arising out of this agreement (a 'Dispute') shall be referred to such independent third party (the 'Third Party') as the parties shall jointly nominate.
>
> 17.2 If the parties hereto shall fail to nominate a Third Party within [fourteen] days of the date of the occurrence of the Dispute then the Third Party shall be nominated at the request of any of the parties hereto by the President for the time being of the [Institute of Electrical Engineers].
>
> 17.3 The Third Party (whether appointed under Clause 17.1 or 17.2 above) shall act as an expert whose decision (including as to costs) shall except in the case of manifest error be final and binding upon the parties hereto.

Ramsey J had no hesitation in concluding that the clause in question was not an arbitration clause for three reasons. First, the reference to the third party acting 'as an expert' is a clear reference to expert determination and is inconsistent with arbitration. Second, the language to the effect that the decision 'shall except in the case of manifest error' be final and binding is a provision applicable to an expert determination rather than to arbitration. Third, there was no express obligation on the third party to hold a judicial inquiry, hear each party's case and evidence and there was no indication that this was intended.[24]

A more complex issue arose in *Turville Heath Inc v Chartis Insurance UK Ltd (formerly AIG UK Ltd)*,[25] where Edwards-Stuart J considered a complex dispute resolution clause in an insurance policy that provided that, in the event of a dispute, each party was to select an independent appraiser and that each appraiser would appraise the loss and submit any differences to an arbitrator. A decision agreed to by the two appraisers or either appraiser and the arbitrator would be binding.[26]

[21] Arbitration Act 1996, s 9(4).
[22] ibid, s 6.
[23] *British Telecommunications Plc v SAE Group Inc* [2009] EWHC 252 (TCC) [41].
[24] ibid, [45].
[25] *Turville Heath Inc v Chartis Insurance UK Ltd (formerly AIG UK Ltd)* [2012] EWHC 3019 (TCC).
[26] ibid, [5].

It was undisputed in the case that the clause was enforceable and capable of being invoked to resolve disputes concerning the amount of loss. The issue, however, was whether the clause constituted an arbitration agreement under section 6 of the Arbitration Act, allowing a party to apply for a stay of proceedings under section 9.[27] The Court held that it was not.[28] The main reason for this finding was that the arbitrator was not the sole decisionmaker, which is the requirement under the Arbitration Act pursuant to section 1 (mentioning 'an impartial tribunal') and section 33 (clarifying that the tribunal must 'act fairly and impartially').[29] Edwards-Stuart J emphasised that the arbitrator could be overruled if both the appraisers were in agreement.[30] Under the Arbitration Act, the arbitrator must be the sole decisionmaker on all the matters put before them.[31] On the other hand, the Court noted that the clause was valid and operable, despite not being an arbitration clause,[32] and granted a stay of proceedings under its inherent jurisdiction given that the ADR mechanism agreed by the parties had already progressed significantly.[33]

B. Competence-Competence and the Courts' Inherent Jurisdiction to Stay Proceedings

The principle of competence-competence, now considered a truly international principle in arbitration, ensures that an arbitral tribunal has the power to rule on its own jurisdiction. The Act codifies this principle in section 30. However, under the Act, although a tribunal may well have the first word on their jurisdiction, the courts have the last.[34] Furthermore, under section 9, the courts can determine jurisdiction before any tribunal has had the opportunity to do so when, on an application for a stay, the claimant argues that the arbitration clause is null and void, inoperative or incapable of being performed.

The principle of competence-competence and the then new section 30 of the Arbitration Act came under scrutiny by the TCC and subsequently the Court of Appeal in *Al-Naimi (t/a Buildmaster Construction Services) v Islamic Press Agency Inc.*[35] The parties signed a JCT minor works contract containing an arbitration clause. The issue was whether that arbitration clause extended to a subsequent oral

[27] ibid, [6].
[28] ibid, [60].
[29] ibid, [53].
[30] ibid, [54].
[31] ibid, [56].
[32] ibid, [64].
[33] ibid, [72]. *British Telecommunications Plc v SAE Group Inc* [2009] EWHC 252 (TCC) is another interesting case in which the TCC construed a dispute resolution clause and concluded that it was an expert determination clause rather than an arbitration clause.
[34] *Great Ormond Street Hospital NHS Trust v Secretary of State* (1997) 56 Con LR 1 [16].
[35] *Al-Naimi (t/a Buildmaster Construction Services) v Islamic Press Agency Inc* [1998] 10 WLUK 52.

agreement between the parties relating to certain additional works. The claimant commenced litigation for payment under the oral agreement. The defendant applied to the TCC to stay these proceedings under section 9 of the Act. The claimant contended that the arbitration clause under the JCT contract did not apply to the dispute concerning payment under the subsequent oral agreement. The issue before the TCC was whether, under the principle of competence-competence, the Court should determine the point itself or refer the issue to the tribunal and stay current proceedings.

In *Al-Naimi*, the Court stayed the proceeding and referred the jurisdictional issue to the tribunal.[36] HHJ Bowsher QC held that a stay would not only be granted where the particular cause of action pleaded falls within the terms of an arbitration agreement, but also where there is a dispute concerning the arbitration agreement itself. In doing so, he understood the principle of competence-competence to mean not only that the tribunal has the power to rule on its own jurisdiction, but also that the tribunal is the primary decisionmaker on its jurisdiction.[37]

The Court of Appeal took a different approach in the case.[38] The Court did not disagree with the principle that section 9 of the Act had not abolished the inherent jurisdiction of the court to stay proceedings so that a court retains the power, under its discretion, to stay proceedings without first ruling on the validity of the arbitration agreement. However, Waller LJ held that, in the instant case, the HHJ Bowsher QC should not have left the issue of jurisdiction to the tribunal but should have decided the issue himself because of the risk of the matter returning to the court as a challenge to the arbitral award under section 67. To save cost and time, the Court of Appeal held that the issue could be decided immediately, allowing the arbitrator to resolve the case on its merits only.[39] In doing so, the arbitration agreement was found to apply to the oral agreement and the Court referred the case to arbitration for determination on the merits.[40] Waller LJ also made several observations in relation to staying proceedings in favour of arbitration under the inherent jurisdiction of the Court. That power would be exercised if to rule on the jurisdiction of the tribunal would require a trial with oral evidence, the outcome of which was likely to be that the tribunal did have jurisdiction or if the tribunal would be a 'short step' away from determining the jurisdictional issues.

The TCC in *Al-Naimi* adopted a strong pro-arbitration approach, based on a robust interpretation of the competence-competence principle. The Court of Appeal, however, was guided by a pragmatic view of efficiency, predicated on the idea that if there is a jurisdictional dispute between the parties, then it is better for

[36] ibid, [18].
[37] ibid, [16–7].
[38] *Ahmad Al-Naimi (T/A Buildmaster Construction Services) v Islamic Press Agency Inc* [2000] CLC 647.
[39] ibid, 651.
[40] ibid, 653.

the court to decide it at the earliest opportunity, a view that prevailed in subsequent cases.[41]

C. Incorporation of Arbitration Agreements

Section 6(2) of the Act provides that the reference in an agreement to a written form of arbitration clause or to a document containing an arbitration clause constitutes an arbitration agreement if the reference is such as to make that clause part of the agreement. This is essentially a question of contractual interpretation.

In *Crest Nicholson (Eastern) Ltd v Western*,[42] the Westerns bought a house constructed by Crest Nicholson under the National House Building Council (NHBC) Scheme pursuant to which Crest Nicholson gave certain undertakings for defects and damage. A dispute arose in relation to professional fees that the Westerns incurred as a result of building defects. They commenced proceedings to recover these fees before a sole arbitrator appointed by the Royal Institution of Chartered Surveyors (RICS). The claimant, Crest Nicholson Ltd, however, sought a declaration from the TCC that the arbitrator had no jurisdiction.[43] The Court granted the declaration on the ground that there was no arbitration agreement in the purchase contract. There were references to arbitration on the NHBC's website relating to the Scheme both in the rules of the Scheme and in the claims charter. However, the arbitration clause in the rules of the Scheme applied only between the Council and the builder or developer. The fact that some of the provisions of the Scheme required the house builders to do things for the benefit of the owners did not have the effect of incorporating the arbitration clause into the purchase contract between the builder and the owners.[44] The references to arbitration in the claims charter were purely informative, indicating that arbitration was an option to resolve disputes between a builder and an owner.[45] This case emphasises the principle that arbitration agreements must be sufficiently certain, particularly when incorporated by reference to another document.[46] The Court looked closely at the relevant documents to determine whether the parties had intended to incorporate the clause in question into their contract and found that they did not.

[41] *European Film Bonds A/S v Lotus Holdings LLC* [2019] EWHC 2116 (Ch); *Hashwani v OMV Maurice Energy Ltd* [2015] EWCA Civ 1171; *Excalibur Ventures LLC v Texas Keystone Inc* [2011] EWHC 1624 (Comm); *TXM Olaj-Es Gazkutato Kft v Claxton Engineering Services Ltd* [2011] EWCA Civ 410; *Claxton Engineering Services Ltd v TXM Olaj-Es Gazkutato Kft* [2010] EWHC 2567 (Comm); *Midgulf International Ltd v Groupe Chimiche Tunisien* [2009] EWHC 963 (Comm); *Albon (t/a NA Carriage Co) v Naza Motor Trading Sdn Bhd* [2007] EWHC 665 (Ch); *El Nasharty v J Sainsbury Plc* [2003] EWHC 2195 (Comm); *T&N Ltd v Royal & Sun Alliance Plc* [2002] EWHC 2420 (Ch).

[42] *Crest Nicholson (Eastern) Ltd v Western* [2008] EWHC 1325 (TCC).

[43] ibid, [6–7].

[44] ibid, [42].

[45] ibid, [47].

[46] The Hon Sir V Ramsey and S Furst QC, *Keating on Construction Contracts*, 11th edn (London, Sweet & Maxwell 2021) para 17-012.

Preservation of party autonomy as the bedrock of arbitration was the guiding principle in the case.

The principle of party autonomy, which requires a close analysis of the parties' intention, was also the guiding principle in *Hackwood Ltd v Areen Design Services Ltd*.[47] A dispute arose out of a letter of intent, which stated that 'the basis of the contract will be the JCT Standard Form Contract with Contractor's Design 1998 Edition', which contained an arbitration clause. The works began after the letter of intent, but no JCT contract was ever executed. The respondent requested several extensions of time. They also initiated adjudication arguing that they were entitled to the extensions.[48] The adjudicator declined to grant the extensions of time and the case was referred to arbitration by the respondent.[49] The applicant argued that they were not a party to an arbitration agreement since the JCT contract was never incorporated into the contract and requested a declaration pursuant to section 72(1)(a) of the Arbitration Act to that effect. The TCC refused the application, finding that the JCT contract containing the arbitration clause was incorporated into the interim contract represented by the letter of intent. It was open to the parties to enter into a subsequent, replacement contract, but they had not done so. This did not make the incorporation of the terms of the JCT contract any less effective.[50]

D. Multi-Tiered Dispute Resolution Clauses

Since construction contracts tend to generate disputes, there has been a strong drive in the UK towards dispute avoidance, away from any formal dispute resolution procedures such as arbitration and litigation.[51] This, in turn, contributed to the popularity of multi-tiered dispute resolution clauses in construction contracts where parties agree to attempt to resolve disputes amicably and through several tiers of alternative dispute resolution leading to litigation or arbitration only if, and to the extent that, the other ADR mechanisms have failed.[52]

There are three main issues that arise from multi-tier dispute resolution clauses: (i) whether this method of dispute resolution is sufficiently defined to give rise to enforceable rights; (ii) whether each of the steps in the dispute resolution process is mandatory or voluntary; and (iii) whether failure to follow one of the

[47] *Hackwood Ltd v Areen Design Services Ltd* [2005] EWHC 2322 (TCC).

[48] ibid, [4].

[49] ibid, [5].

[50] ibid, [19–20].

[51] Sir M Latham, *Constructing the Team: Final Report of the Government/Industry Review of Procurement and Contractual Arrangements in the UK Construction Industry* (HMSO, 1994); J Bennett and S Jeyes, *Trusting the Team: The Best Practice Guide to Partnering in Construction* (London, Thomas Telford, 1995).

[52] See, eg, FIDIC Conditions of Contract for Construction (2017), clause 21.

steps precludes a party from proceeding to the next step.[53] The TCC has engaged with all of the above issues.

Whether a step in a multi-tier dispute resolution clause is enforceable at all depends on whether the purported condition precedent is such that its fulfilment can be objectively verified and does not represent an open-ended 'agreement to agree'. In *Holloway v Chancery Mead Ltd*,[54] Ramsey J, obiter, laid down a three-step test:

> It seems to me that considering the above authorities the principles to be derived are that the ADR clause must meet at least the following three requirements: First, that the process must be sufficiently certain in that there should not be the need for an agreement at any stage before matters can proceed. Secondly, the administrative processes for selecting a party to resolve the dispute and to pay that person should also be defined. Thirdly, the process or at least a model of the process should be set out so that the detail of the process is sufficiently certain.[55]

Ramsey J's holding was applied by the Court of Appeal in *Sulamérica Cia Nacional De Seguros S.A. and others v Enesa Engenharia S.A. and others*.[56] One of the issues in *Sulamérica* was whether under the multi-tiered dispute resolution clause in the contract, mediation was a condition precedent to arbitration. Moore-Bick LJ held that it was not a condition precedent as it did not set out a defined mediation process nor referred to a procedure of a mediation provider. For these reasons, the mediation clause was not certain enough as to form a condition precedent to commencing arbitration and *Holloway* was distinguished.[57]

If a given step in a multi-tier clause is enforceable, the question then arises if it is a condition precedent to the following step. *JT Mackley & Co Ltd v Gosport Marina Ltd*[58] concerned a contract applying the ICE sixth edition standard form.[59] The defendant sought to reopen two adjudicators' decisions by referring the disputes to arbitration. The issue was that the ICE conditions in clause 66 provided for a tiered dispute resolution process whereas arbitration only became available following a decision by the engineer, which had not been made. For that reason, the claimant sought a declaration that the arbitration notice was invalid.[60]

[53] Sir V Ramsey, 'Multi-tier Dispute Resolution Clauses in Construction Contracts' in R Nazzini (ed), *Transnational Construction Arbitration* (London, Informa Law, 2017) 27.

[54] *Holloway v Chancery Mead Ltd* [2007] EWHC 2495 (TCC). Decision applied in *Sulamérica Cia Nacional De Seguros S.A. and others v Enesa Engenharia S.A. and others* [2012] EWCA Civ 638; *Ohpen Operations UK Ltd v Invesco Fund Managers Ltd* [2019] EWHC 2246 (TCC).

[55] ibid, [81].

[56] *Sulamérica Cia Nacional De Seguros S.A. and others v Enesa Engenharia S.A. and others* [2012] EWCA Civ 638.

[57] ibid, [36].

[58] *JT Mackley & Co Ltd v Gosport Marina Ltd* [2002] EWHC 1315 (TCC).

[59] ibid, [10].

[60] ibid, [3]. The application had been made under s 32 of the Act and under Pt 8 of the CPR. In the end, the Court only decided the case under Pt 8 and did not determine, therefore, whether the non-fulfilment of a condition precedent gave rise to an issue of jurisdiction or admissibility. In *Republic of Sierra Leone v SL Mining Ltd* [2021] EWHC 286 (Comm), Burton J held that the issue was one of admissibility.

The Court held that the engineer's decision was a condition precedent to arbitration and the arbitration notice was invalid.[61] The defendant argued that the effect of clause 66 was to stay the arbitral proceedings. The Court labelled this argument as 'palpable nonsense'[62] as it would 'make a mockery out of the procedure set out in clause 66'.[63] Furthermore, the requirements of clause 66 of the ICE conditions also applied when arbitration was commenced in order to reopen adjudication decisions.[64] The Court said:[65]

> [A]rbitration is only available as a means of challenging the decision of an adjudicator if the relevant contract so provides or an ad hoc arbitration agreement is made. Where it is sought to rely on an arbitration clause in the relevant contract, it seems to me to be obvious that the ability to do so, and the terms upon which such may be done, fall to be determined under the relevant arbitration clause.

The issue of failure to fulfil a condition precedent in a multi-tier clause arose in *Al-Waddan Hotel Ltd v Man Enterprise SAL (Offshore)*.[66] The contract incorporated the 1987 FIDIC Conditions of Contracts for Works of Civil Engineering Construction, fourth edition.[67] Clause 67.1 required the parties to submit a dispute to an engineer for expert determination before resorting to arbitration.[68] The engineer had 84 days to decide the case.

The applicant attempted to appoint an engineer to resolve a dispute relating to non-payment. However, the applicant's nominee informed the parties that their contract had expired, so he could not accept the appointment.[69] The respondent initiated arbitration and obtained an award in their favour without any previous engineer's decision.[70] The applicant sought to challenge the award pursuant to section 67 on the grounds that the parties should have first obtained a decision from the engineer and that the purported engineer's reply concerning the expiry of the contract did not amount to a decision.[71]

The TCC held that a decision of an engineer was indeed a condition precedent to arbitration.[72] The reply of the engineer did not amount to a decision pursuant to clause 67.1.[73] However, the refusal by the engineer to carry out his function was analogous to a breach of contract with a clear refusal to act.[74] It did clearly signal that the engineer would not render a decision within the timeframe provided for

[61] *JT Mackley & Co Ltd v Gosport Marina Ltd* (n 58) [38].
[62] ibid, [37].
[63] ibid.
[64] ibid, [36].
[65] ibid.
[66] *Al-Waddan Hotel Ltd v Man Enterprise SAL (Offshore)* [2014] EWHC 4796 (TCC).
[67] ibid, [12].
[68] ibid, [21–2].
[69] ibid, [38].
[70] ibid, [5–7].
[71] ibid, [2].
[72] ibid, [60].
[73] ibid, [67].
[74] ibid, [58].

by the contract.[75] The onus was thus on the applicant to appoint another engineer. Therefore, according to the Court, the applicant's failure to make another appointment disentitled it from insisting on performance of the condition precedent in the arbitration agreement.[76] Raeside J said:

> It is and must be conceded that if a party desires to rely on the non-performance of a condition precedent he must do nothing to prevent the condition from being performed, and if there is anything that must be done by him to render possible the performance of the condition, a failure by him to do what is required disentitles him from insisting on performance of the condition.[77]

As a result, the section 67 challenge failed, and the Court upheld the award.[78] The *Al-Waddan* judgment on this point was recently applied in the Scottish case *Graeme W Cheyne (Builders) Ltd v Wilson*[79] to uphold the validity of an application for interim payment that, under the construction contract, had to comply with a condition precedent that had not been fulfilled because of the conduct of the party invoking it.

E. Multi-Contract Cases and Apparently Conflicting Dispute Resolution Clauses

Where the contract contains more than one dispute resolution clause, generally, courts are reluctant to treat such clauses as directly conflicting.[80] Instead, they are interpreted as multi-tiered dispute resolution provisions,[81] optional choice of arbitration or court provisions,[82] or as applying to different streams of the contractual relationship to be subject to different dispute resolution clauses.[83]

In *Costain Ltd v Tarmac Holdings Ltd*,[84] the parties entered into two contracts: one incorporating the NEC3 Framework Contract and the other on the terms of the NEC3 Supply Short Contract. Under the NEC3 Framework Contract, disputes are ultimately referred to court proceedings, whereas the NEC3 Supply Short Contract contains an arbitration clause. A dispute arose concerning the supply

[75] ibid, [69].
[76] ibid, [53].
[77] ibid, [53].
[78] ibid, [72–3].
[79] *Graeme W Cheyne (Builders) Ltd v Wilson* [2021] SAC (Civ) 24.
[80] R Garnett, 'Coexisting and Conflicting Jurisdiction and Arbitration Clauses' (2013) 9(3) *Journal of Private International Law* 361.
[81] *Ace Capital Ltd v CMS Energy Corporation* [2009] Lloyd's Rep IR 414.
[82] *Lobb Partnership v Aintree Racecourse Company Ltd* [2000] 1 BLR 65; *NB Three Shipping Ltd v Harebell Shipping Ltd* [2004] EWHC 2001 (Comm).
[83] *Paul Smith Ltd v H & S International Holding Inc* [1991] 2 Lloyd's Rep 127; *Shell Petroleum Co Ltd v Coral Oil Ltd* [1999] 1 Lloyd's Rep 72; *Ace Capital Ltd v CMS Energy Corporation* [2009] Lloyd's Rep IR 414.
[84] *Costain Ltd v Tarmac Holdings Ltd* [2017] EWHC 319 (TCC); [2017] 1 C.L.C. 491. Case was applied or considered in: *Surrey CC v Suez Recycling and Recovery Surrey Ltd* [2021] EWHC 2015 (TCC); *Bridgehouse (Bradford No.2) Ltd v BAE Systems Plc* [2019] EWHC 675 (Ch).

of concrete. The respondent issued court proceedings and the applicant sought to stay them pursuant to section 9 of the Arbitration Act. The respondent argued, under section 9(4), that the arbitration clause in the NEC3 Supply Short Contract did not apply to the dispute, which had to be litigated under the choice of court clause in the NEC3 Framework Contract.[85]

The Court held that there was an operative arbitration agreement – an arbitration agreement can govern a specific element of party's relationship if there is no discrepancy with another dispute resolution clause.[86] The NEC3 Framework Contract and the NEC3 Supply Short Contract terms related to different parts of the relationship. Since the dispute arose under the Supply Contract, it had to be arbitrated.[87]

The case also clarified the 'mutual trust and cooperation' obligation under clause 10.1 of the NEC3 Supply Short Contract. The respondent relied on the clause to argue that the applicant was estopped from pursuing arbitration since they had replied to the letter of claim, implying that they will not pursue arbitration.[88] This would have allowed the respondent to contend that the arbitration agreement was inoperative pursuant to section 9(4). Coulson J found that the clause aims at preventing one party exploiting the other but does not create an obligation to act fairly or abandon self-interest. Rather, the obligation is not to mislead the other party as to own actions.[89] In this case, the applicant made no such misleading representations and the clause cannot be used to 'somehow turn an otherwise unsuccessful assertion of estoppel (…) into a successful one'.[90]

F. Interaction between Adjudication and Arbitration

Under section 108 of the Housing Grants, Construction and Regeneration Act 1996 (the 'Construction Act'), as amended, a party has a statutory right to refer to adjudication disputes arising under a construction contract, as defined in the Act and subject to any exclusions provided for in the Act itself. Not surprisingly, the TCC made a significant contribution to clarifying the relationship between adjudication and arbitration. *JT Mackley & Co Ltd v Gosport Marina Ltd*,[91] discussed above, is a good example. The Court in that case held that even though an adjudicator's decision can be referred to arbitration under the Construction Act, the contract must provide for it or there must have been an ad hoc arbitration agreement. That contract may also place a condition precedent on bringing the case to arbitration and, if it does so, the condition precedent must be fulfilled before a valid reference may be made.

[85] ibid, [1–6], [13].
[86] ibid, [37].
[87] ibid, [142].
[88] ibid, [109].
[89] ibid, [123].
[90] ibid, [124–5].
[91] *JT Mackley & Co Ltd v Gosport Marina Ltd* (n 51).

Under the Construction Act, there is a right to refer a construction dispute to adjudication at any time. However, an adjudication decision is not a condition precedent to arbitration or litigation, unless the parties so provide in their contract. In *Price v Carter (t/a Ian Carter Building Contractors)*,[92] the contract incorporated the JCT Minor Works Building Contract.[93] The applicant argued that adjudication was a condition precedent to arbitration, so that the arbitrator lacked jurisdiction under section 67. The contract stated:

> Where Article 7 applies [the arbitration clause], then, subject to Article 6 [the adjudication clause] (…), any dispute or difference between the Parties of any kind whatsoever arising out of or in connection with this Contract (…) shall be referred to arbitration.[94]

The Court found that the above wording gave the parties a right to elect between adjudication and arbitration so that one party could refer the dispute to arbitration and the other to adjudication, bringing about parallel proceedings.[95] The Court said:

> There are, of course, forms of contract which provide that the reference of a dispute to adjudication is a necessary prerequisite of the right to refer that dispute to arbitration, but these usually do so in clear terms. There is no such clarity of language here.[96]

A different issue arises in relation to the enforcement of an adjudication decision. If the construction contract contains an arbitration clause, are disputes concerning the enforcement of the adjudication decisions matters to be referred to arbitration under section 9 of the Act? It was decided in *MBE Electrical Contractors Ltd v Honeywell Control Systems Ltd*[97] that section 9 cannot be used to undermine the interim finality of an adjudicator's decision and refer the case to arbitration.[98] While the merits of their dispute could be arbitrated, this did not apply to the jurisdiction of the adjudicator. Jurisdiction formed part of the enforcement proceedings before the court instead.[99] A different outcome would be contrary to the 'pay now, argue later' principle stemming from the Housing Grants, Construction and Regeneration Act 1996,[100] the Scheme for Construction Contracts (England and Wales) Regulations 1998,[101] and case law.[102] Langan J said:

> Sir Peter Coulson, writing extra-judicially, has said that it 'would make a nonsense of the adjudication process if the losing party could avoid the consequences of an adjudicator's decision by claiming that he disputed the decision and that that dispute should be referred to arbitration.' I respectfully agree.[103]

[92] *Price v Carter (t/a Ian Carter Building Contractors)* [2010] EWHC 1451 (TCC).
[93] ibid, [4].
[94] ibid, [10].
[95] ibid, [14].
[96] ibid, [15].
[97] *MBE Electrical Contractors Ltd v Honeywell Control Systems Ltd* [2010] EWHC 2244 (TCC).
[98] ibid, [31].
[99] ibid.
[100] ibid; Housing Grants, Construction and Regeneration Act 1996, Pt II.
[101] Paragraph 21 of the Schedule, The Scheme for Construction Contracts (England and Wales) Regulations 1998.
[102] *Macob Civil Engineering Ltd v Morrison Construction Ltd* [1999] C.L.C. 739, [1999] 2 WLUK 258.
[103] ibid, [34].

In clarifying the relationship between adjudication and arbitration, the TCC was guided by two policies: giving effect to the adjudication process as envisaged in the Construction Act, while, at the same time, respecting the parties' intention in choosing their preferred dispute resolution mechanism, to the extent allowed by the Construction Act itself. The above cases demonstrate that adjudication and arbitration can coexist efficiently and that, even within the statutory regime, parties still enjoy a significant degree of autonomy, for example by making adjudication a condition precedent to arbitration or choosing to allow both adjudication and arbitration to proceed concurrently.

G. Arbitrating Consumer Disputes

Arbitrating consumer disputes is highly controversial, to the extent that, in certain jurisdictions, it is almost entirely prohibited.[104] In England and Wales such arbitrations are restricted by the operation of primary and secondary legislation, currently the Consumer Rights Act 2015, implementing EU law, and the Unfair Terms in Consumer Contracts Regulation 1999. The substance of the Act and the Regulation have not been affected by Brexit at the time of writing, as it forms part of retained law.[105]

Zealander v Laing Homes Ltd was one of the earliest cases relating to consumer arbitration following the entry into force of the Arbitration Act 1996.[106] The case concerned an alleged breach of contract arising out of construction defects before the TCC. The defendant applied for the case to be stayed pursuant to section 9 of the Arbitration Act. The claimant argued that he was unaware of the arbitration clause since the Build Mark Agreement that contained it was only supplied to him after the agreements were signed.

The TCC held, relying on the now repealed Unfair Terms in Consumer Contracts Regulation 1994, that the arbitration clause was unfair and hence unenforceable.[107] Havery J found that the consumer had no knowledge of the clause before signing the contract.[108] In addition, the clause created a significant imbalance between the parties as it was restricted in scope only to matters arising in respect of construction. The claimant would have to initiate two separate proceedings – arbitration for his claims relating to construction defects and court proceedings in relation to matters arising out of the contract for sale. The Court viewed this as vexatious and emphasised that in order to assess the unfairness of such clauses, the courts should pay attention to the circumstances as a whole.[109]

[104] See, eg, in Australia *Dialogue Consulting Pty Ltd v Instagram, Inc* [2020] FCA 1846; in Canada see s 7(2), Consumer Protection Act 2002; in Germany see s 36, German Consumers' Dispute Settlement Act 2016.

[105] L Conway, 'Briefing Paper: Brexit UK consumer protection law' (*House of Commons*, 21 May 2021) researchbriefings.files.parliament.uk/documents/CBP-9126/CBP-9126.pdf (accessed 17 August 2022).

[106] *Zealander v Laing Homes Ltd* [1999] 3 WLUK 377.

[107] ibid, 730–1.

[108] ibid, 728.

[109] ibid, 731.

Further, the Regulation contained a 'grey list' of clauses that may be regarded as unfair in its Annex.[110] It expressly listed clauses that oblige the consumer to arbitrate disputes.[111] At the time, commentators were split as to the meaning of this schedule, arguing that the list contained clauses that are, in most circumstances, void or that the list creates a mere rebuttable presumption of unfairness to the consumer.[112] The TCC in *Zealander* clarified that the list constitutes mere guidelines,[113] and the Court must consider all the circumstances.[114]

The *Zealander* judgment was followed and expanded upon in *Mylcrist Builders Ltd v Buck*,[115] a decision that is still the leading authority for arbitrating consumer disputes in the construction sector and beyond. The question was whether the arbitration clause was unfair to the consumer pursuant to the Unfair Terms in Consumer Contracts Regulations 1999.[116] The clause was contained in the builder's standard terms. The 1999 Regulation contains a similar grey list schedule as its predecessor, the 1994 Regulation.[117]

The TCC held that the arbitration clause was unfair to the consumer, taking into account the nature of the work (here construction), the circumstances at the conclusion of the contract and the terms of the contract itself.[118] Ramsey J pointed to several factors in the case that led him to arrive at the conclusion that the clause caused an imbalance between parties' rights and obligations to the detriment of the consumer.

The starting point was that the clause was not individually negotiated. Instead, it was included in the builder's standard contract terms.[119] Second, the Court noted that upholding the arbitration clause would, coupled with section 9 of the Arbitration Act, deprive the consumer of alternative methods of dispute settlement.[120] Third, the Court looked at the costs of arbitration. It noted that the extent of arbitrator's fees that the consumer would be obliged to pay supported the finding of an imbalance between the parties, particularly given its proportion to the claimed amounts.[121] Fourth, the clause was insufficiently brought to the attention of the consumer – a layperson. The applicant should have made the respondent more alert to the importance and effects of the clause.[122] If that had taken place, she would have most likely objected, particularly given that she had no professional advisers involved in contracting.[123]

[110] Sch 3, Unfair Terms in Consumer Contracts Regulation 1994.
[111] ibid, para 1(q).
[112] S Bright, 'Winning the Battle Against Unfair Contract Terms' (2000) 20(3) *Legal Studies* 331, 349.
[113] *Zealander v Laing Homes Ltd* [1999] 3 WLUK 377, 729.
[114] ibid, 730.
[115] *Mylcrist Builders Ltd v Buck* [2008] EWHC 2172 (TCC).
[116] Now repealed by the Consumer Rights Act 2015.
[117] Sch 2, Unfair Terms in Consumer Contracts Regulations 1999.
[118] *Mylcrist Builders Ltd v Buck* [2008] EWHC 2172 (TCC) [59].
[119] ibid, [40].
[120] ibid, [54].
[121] ibid, [55].
[122] ibid, [56].
[123] ibid, [57–8].

However, *Mylcrist* does not lay down an absolute presumption of unfairness. This is illustrated in *Heifer International Inc v Christiansen*,[124] a case concerning a contract for the refurbishment of a property in Surrey. The employer, a BVI company owned by the Russian owner of the Surrey property, claimed damages for defective works against the applicants, Danish architects and Danish sub-contractors, who in turn applied for a stay under section 9 of the Act relying on arbitration clauses in their contracts. The claimant argued that the clauses were not binding by virtue of the Unfair Terms in Consumer Contracts Regulations 1999.[125] The Court found that the clauses were not individually negotiated but that nevertheless the claimant, advised by a leading Danish firm, had been able to influence the substance of their terms and, in any event, the clauses were not against good faith or inherently unfair.[126]

A material factor was that the consumer in *Heifer* was a company advised by a leading Danish firm. In contrast with individuals, companies have more resources, such as lawyers, to alert them to the risks of unfair contract terms. The *Heifer* case demonstrates that arbitration agreements with consumers are not necessarily always unenforceable. The TCC applies the Regulations flexibly and pragmatically, protecting consumers but also recognising that in certain circumstances consumers can be fairly bound by an arbitration agreement.

III. The TCC's Supportive Powers

A. Conditions for the Exercise of Supportive (and Supervisory) Powers: Links to the Jurisdiction

Section 2(1) to (4) of the Act sets out the scope of the application of the provisions in Part 1 of the Act, including provisions conferring supportive or supervisory powers on the English courts. It reads as follows:

> (1) The provisions of this Part apply where the seat of the arbitration is in England and Wales or Northern Ireland.
>
> (2) The following sections apply even if the seat of the arbitration is outside England and Wales or Northern Ireland or no seat has been designated or determined—
>
> (a) sections 9 to 11 (stay of legal proceedings, &c.), and
>
> (b) section 66 (enforcement of arbitral awards).

[124] *Heifer International Inc v Christiansen* [2007] EWHC 3015 (TCC).
[125] ibid, [5].
[126] ibid, [304].

(3) The powers conferred by the following sections apply even if the seat of the arbitration is outside England and Wales or Northern Ireland or no seat has been designated or determined—

(a) section 43 (securing the attendance of witnesses), and
(b) section 44 (court powers exercisable in support of arbitral proceedings);

but the court may refuse to exercise any such power if, in the opinion of the court, the fact that the seat of the arbitration is outside England and Wales or Northern Ireland, or that when designated or determined the seat is likely to be outside England and Wales or Northern Ireland, makes it inappropriate to do so.

(4) The court may exercise a power conferred by any provision of this Part not mentioned in subsection (2) or (3) for the purpose of supporting the arbitral process where—

(a) no seat of the arbitration has been designated or determined, and
(b) by reason of a connection with England and Wales or Northern Ireland the court is satisfied that it is appropriate to do so.

In *Braes of Doune Wind Farm (Scotland) v Alfred McAlpine Business Services*,[127] the applicant sought to challenge an arbitral award before the TCC. The respondent sought a declaration that the court had no jurisdiction as the arbitration was seated in Scotland.

The Court made a clear distinction between the seat of the arbitration and the venue of the arbitration. The arbitration agreement in this case contained wording that the 'seat of the arbitration shall be Glasgow, Scotland'.[128] However, at the same time, the agreement specified that English courts had exclusive jurisdiction to hear any disputes, subject to the arbitration clause.[129] Further, the proceedings were to be conducted under the Construction Industry Model Arbitration Rules (CIMAR) that only apply to arbitrations seated in England and Wales.[130]

Akenhead J held that the use of the word 'exclusive jurisdiction' meant that the English courts were intended to have jurisdiction over the arbitration. The references to the Arbitration Act supported that conclusion. As a consequence, the reference to Glasgow referred to the venue for the arbitration, rather than the juridical seat of the arbitration. A different conclusion would render pointless many of the provisions in the arbitration agreement.[131] This was a rare case in which the TCC demonstrated that the use of the word 'seat', while apparently clear, may not be conclusive if the construction of the overall agreement shows that the parties' intention was not reflected in the word used. It is important to emphasise here that the Court was neither rewriting the agreement for the parties,[132]

[127] *Braes of Doune Wind Farm (Scotland) v Alfred McAlpine Business Services* [2008] EWHC 426 (TCC).
[128] ibid, [6].
[129] ibid.
[130] ibid. See clause 1.6, CIMAR.
[131] ibid, [15].
[132] *Food Corp of India v Achilles Halcoussis (The Petros Hadjukyriakos)* [1988] 2 Lloyd's Rep 56.

nor modifying the arbitration agreements to reflect their purely subjective intentions.[133] It was simply construing the agreement in light of the parties' intention. The parties clearly intended to give control over the arbitration to a specific jurisdiction and that jurisdiction was England. That meant that the seat must also have been intended to be in England. Several subsequent cases applied the judgment in determining the seat of the arbitration.[134]

The application of section 2(4) was discussed in *Chalbury McCouat International Ltd v PG Foils Ltd*.[135] The case concerned an English company and an Indian company that was contracted to dismantle a manufacturing facility in the Netherlands. A dispute arose in relation to payment. The English company sought to arbitrate the case in England. However, the Indian company refused to give consent to the appointment of the tribunal, instead requesting that the arbitration be brought in India. The English company applied to the TCC for the appointment of the tribunal under section 18.[136] The contract provided for arbitration, but did not specify its seat, merely noting that 'if the issue is not resolved (…) the same will be referred to arbitration as per prevailing laws of European Union in the Europe'.[137]

First, Ramsey J applied the seminal *Channel Tunnel Group v Balfour Beatty Ltd*[138] case and held that, if there was a seat, the application for appointment of an arbitrator should have been made to the courts of the place where the arbitration is seated.[139] Although the seat was not expressly identified in this case, he added that England, rather than India, was the more likely seat of arbitration based on the above wording of the arbitration clause referring to 'laws of European Union in the Europe'.[140]

Second, Ramsey J looked to the proper law of the contract as a relevant connecting factor.[141] Here, there was no such determination, the only guidance offered being the reference in the arbitration clause itself to 'the laws of the European Union'.[142] Ramsey J applied the Rome Convention and held that it pointed to English law rather than the law of any other jurisdiction as the most likely governing law.[143]

Third, the Court gave weight to the fact that the payment under the contract took place in England.[144] Accordingly, the TCC held that the requirements of

[133] *Film Finance Inc v The Royal Bank of Scotland* [2007] EWHC 195 (Comm).
[134] *Shagang South-Asia (Hong Kong) Trading Co Ltd v Daewoo Logistics* [2015] EWHC 194 (Comm); *Shashoua v Sharma* [2009] EWHC 957 (Comm); *Enercon GmbH v Enercon (India) Ltd* [2012] EWHC 689 (Comm).
[135] *Chalbury McCouat International Ltd v PG Foils Ltd* [2010] EWHC 2050 (TCC).
[136] ibid, [3–7].
[137] ibid, [2].
[138] *Channel Tunnel Group v Balfour Beatty Ltd* [1993] AC 334 at 357H.
[139] *Chalbury McCouat International Ltd v PG Foils Ltd* [2010] EWHC 2050 (TCC) [21].
[140] ibid, [29].
[141] ibid, [22].
[142] ibid, [25].
[143] ibid, [28–9].
[144] ibid, [29].

section 2(4) for the connection of the arbitral process with England and Wales or Northern Ireland were met and exercised its power under section 18. The Court ordered for the LCIA to make the appointment to the tribunal, rather than the President of the Law Society as requested by the claimant.[145]

Given the popularity of London as a seat of construction arbitrations and the international nature of disputes referred to arbitration in London, the TCC case law clarifying the territorial links that trigger or may trigger the English courts' exercise of their supportive and supervisory powers under the Act is of particular significance. The TCC has construed and applied section 2 of the Act in a commercial manner, giving effect to the parties' intention, thus recognising once again that arbitration is a creature of party autonomy.

B. Extensions of Time for Giving Notice of Arbitration

Construction contracts often provide for time bars for starting arbitration. Pursuant to section 12 of the Arbitration Act, a party may apply to the court for an extension of time for commencing arbitration. Waller LJ in *Harbour General Works Ltd v Environment Agency*[146] held that section 12 is worded so as not to allow the courts to interfere with party bargains. However, he noticed an exception to this general rule. If the circumstances of the case are such that the parties, at the time of entering into the agreement, would have contemplated that the time bar might not apply, the court may intervene.[147]

In *Anglian Water Services Ltd v Laing O'Rourke Utilities Ltd*,[148] the parties engaged in the construction of sewage treatment facilities. The second edition (1995) NEC Engineering and Construction contract provided for arbitration if brought within four weeks of notification of the adjudicator's decision.[149] The referral took effect when received at the last address notified by the relevant party. The claimant forwarded the referral to arbitration to the defendant's solicitors who were, according to the defendant, only authorised to accept service in relation to the earlier adjudication. The defendant's solicitors acknowledged receipt and forwarded the documents to the defendant. Meanwhile, the four-week time limit expired.[150]

The defendant alleged that the notice of referral to arbitration was ineffective. The claimant sought a declaration from the TCC to the contrary and, in the alternative, applied for an extension of time under section 12 of the Arbitration Act.[151]

[145] ibid, [34].
[146] *Harbour General Works Ltd v Environment Agency* [2000] 1 Lloyd's Rep 65.
[147] ibid, 71.
[148] *Anglian Water Services Ltd v Laing O'Rourke Utilities Ltd* [2010] EWHC 1529 (TCC). Case applied in *Transport for Greater Manchester v Kier Construction Ltd (t/a Kier Construction – Northern)* [2021] EWHC 804 (TCC); *Fraserburgh Harbour Commissioners v McLaughlin & Harvey Ltd* [2021] CSOH 8.
[149] ibid, [2–4].
[150] ibid, [5–9].
[151] ibid, [10].

The Court noted that the defendant accepted any documentation relating to the adjudication to be served at the offices of its solicitors. The Court held that, as a result, this applied to the notice to refer the adjudicator's decision to arbitration because, despite the arbitration clause being separate to the clauses relating to adjudication, the two were connected.[152] Hence, the notification of the referral was valid.

The TCC also turned to the alternative argument relating to section 12, finding that such application would be allowed.[153] The relevant facts were that the claimant had no reason to believe that the service was ineffective, particularly since the receipt was confirmed by defendant's solicitors in this case and on earlier occasions. Therefore, holding the claimant to the strict notice provisions would have been unjust.[154]

C. Appointment of Arbitrators and Multi-Party Disputes

It is well known that construction disputes are often multi-party. In the case of *City & General (Holborn) Ltd v AYH Plc*,[155] a dispute arose under the JCT Standard Form of Building Contract of 1998 where the CIMAR applied. The CIMAR allowed for a joinder of related arbitral proceedings with the consent of the parties if the proceedings related to the same project, even if the parties are not the same.[156] The arbitration clause in the case permitted the arbitrator to decide whether to consolidate parallel arbitrations.

The TCC had little trouble in finding that section 18 should be triggered in principle since the subject matter of the case substantially fell within the ambit of the arbitration clause.[157] However, the Court spent significant time elaborating how the Court should exercise its discretion under that section. Jackson J noted that there was an existing, parallel arbitration between the claimant and a third-party contractor relating to substantially the same or connected issues.[158] The Court also considered that the purpose of the arbitration clause was to avoid the multiplicity of proceedings, with a view of reducing costs and avoiding the risk of inconsistent decisions. Given the above, the Court exercised its discretion to appoint the same arbitrator as in the parallel arbitration.[159] The TCC thus exercised its supportive powers to facilitate consolidation, taking into account both the connection between the disputes and the rules on consolidation chosen by the parties.

[152] ibid, [68].
[153] ibid, [90].
[154] ibid, [88–90].
[155] *City & General (Holborn) Ltd v AYH Plc* [2005] EWHC 2494 (TCC).
[156] CIMAR, rule 3.9.
[157] ibid, [31], [36–9].
[158] ibid, [53].
[159] ibid, [57].

D. Court Powers to Issue Interim Measures in Support of Arbitration

Pursuant to section 44 of the Act, English courts have broad powers by which they can support an arbitration. In particular, they can grant interim measures even if the seat of arbitration is not in England and Wales or Northern Ireland, unless it would be inappropriate to do so.[160] Furthermore, the power of the court to grant injunctions under the Senior Courts Act when it would be just and convenient to do so is independent of the Arbitration Act, provided it is exercised with due regard to the scheme of the Arbitration Act.[161]

In *Permasteelisa Japan KK v Bouyguesstroi*,[162] the defendant was contracted to construct office buildings in Russia. The claimant was one of the subcontractors on that project. The terms of the subcontract provided the defendant with a performance bond. The defendant requested the bank to pay them the full amount guaranteed under the bond. The claimant in turn sought an injunction from the TCC to halt the transaction or to freeze the proceeds.[163]

The claimant's argument for the section 44 injunction was that the defendant was not entitled to call the bond. They argued that the injunction was aimed at preserving assets until the arbitral tribunal had been appointed and could decide on the request for interim measures.[164] The defendant argued instead that an order preventing them from calling on the bond could be granted only in cases of a serious risk of fraud. Further, the claimant had not established a serious risk of dissipation to justify the granting of an order freezing the proceeds.[165]

Ramsey J clarified, first, that cases concerning the calling of a bond come within section 44(3) as they are generally urgent and relate to the preservation of assets.[166] As regards the interim injunction preventing the defendant from calling on the bond, Ramsey J held that the test that applied in respect of arbitration was the same as that which applies when the merits are to be determined in court proceedings. Although the claimant had a seriously arguable case that the defendant breached the subcontract by failing to meet the preconditions for calling in the bond, there was no seriously arguable case that the defendant could not honestly believe in the validity of the call.[167] Therefore, the application failed. As regards the application for a freezing order, there was no evidence of a serious risk of dissipation of

[160] Arbitration Act 1996, s 2.

[161] Senior Courts Act 1981, s 37; *AES Ust-Kamenogorsk Hydropower Plant LLP v Ust-Kamenogorsk Hydropower Plant JSC* [2013] UKSC 35.

[162] [2007] EWHC 3508 (QB). Decision applied in *MW High Tech Projects UK Ltd v Biffa Waste Services Ltd* [2015] EWHC 949 (TCC); *Palmerston Hotels & Resorts BV v Brocket Hall (UK) Ltd* [2016] EWHC 2018 (Comm).

[163] ibid, [2–7].

[164] ibid, [11–2].

[165] ibid, [13–4].

[166] ibid, [43].

[167] ibid, [52–8].

assets. In fact, it was doubtful that the defendant – an international construction company – would risk the reputational loss if they failed to pay monies owed.[168]

The case is an important clarification of the circumstances in which the TCC will or will not intervene under section 44(3) of the Act to halt a party from calling on a performance bond or to freeze the proceeds, a matter of great relevance to the construction industry.

In *Travelers Insurance Co Ltd v Countrywide Surveyors Ltd*,[169] the claimant sought disclosure of documentation from the defendant.[170] The main dispute fell under the terms of an arbitration clause in an insurance policy. The application was made under the CPR 31.16[171] and under section 44(3) of the Act. Coulson J refused the application. Pre-action disclosure under the CPR did not apply as the applicant was unlikely to be a party in subsequent proceedings in the TCC, as required by the Senior Courts Act 1981, section 33(2).[172] After all, there was a valid arbitration clause so the pre-action disclosure process in the TCC would be ancillary to the process in arbitration.[173] Turning to section 44(3), Coulson J emphasised that it can only be triggered in exceptional circumstances. The example he gave was the evidence being permanently lost, destroyed or damaged.[174] Therefore, the section should not be triggered in what he called 'standard cases' where the arbitrator could make the exact same order once the proceedings have commenced.[175] The case is important in two respects. First, it clarifies the relationship between arbitration and pre-action disclosure under the CPR. A valid arbitration agreement would in most circumstances make such application unavailable since the applicant is unlikely to be a party to litigation. Second, Coulson J analysed section 44(3), noting that the Court would be reluctant to exercise a power that was available to the arbitrator as well.

A similar outcome was reached in *Company 1 v Company 2*,[176] where the applicant sought an order for production of documents after the arbitration was commenced but before the constitution of the tribunal. The order for production of documents was refused because there was no evidence of risk that the documents would be destroyed.[177] *Mi-Space (UK) Ltd v Lend Lease Construction (EMEA) Ltd*[178] was also about pre-action disclosure. The applicant sought to litigate a dispute concerning their subcontract and requested pre-action disclosure from the respondent. The respondent argued that the dispute should be arbitrated. The dispute resolution clause in the subcontract envisaged that arbitrators would

[168] ibid, [54].
[169] *Travelers Insurance Co Ltd v Countrywide Surveyors Ltd* [2010] EWHC 2455 (TCC).
[170] ibid, [3].
[171] ibid, [8].
[172] ibid, [17–8].
[173] ibid, [20].
[174] *Travelers Insurance Co Ltd v Countrywide Surveyors Ltd* [2010] EWHC 2455 (TCC) [27–8].
[175] ibid, [27].
[176] *Company 1 v Company 2* [2017] EWHC 2319 (QB).
[177] ibid, [77–9].
[178] *Mi-Space (UK) Ltd v Lend Lease Construction (EMEA) Ltd* [2013] EWHC 2001 (TCC).

be selected from among the members of a Dispute Review Board. The parties had made no appointments to the Dispute Review Board. Akenhead J held that, as long as machinery exists through which a dispute could be referred to arbitration, the arbitration agreement meets the requirements of section 6 of the Arbitration Act.[179] Therefore, His Lordship refused to order pre-action disclosure and held that the arbitration agreement was enforceable as the parties could simply appoint members of the DRB. Failure to do so by one party would amount to a breach of contract and the other party could seek specific performance.[180]

Section 44(5) of the Act provides that the court shall act only if or to the extent that the arbitral tribunal, and any arbitral or other institution or person vested by the parties with power in that regard, has no power or is unable for the time being to act effectively. Therefore, there is potential friction between an application to a court under section 44 and emergency arbitrator procedures that provide for the appointment of an arbitrator for the purpose of determining an application for interim measures before the constitution of the arbitral tribunal. The TCC suggested, obiter, in *Seele Middle East FZE v Drake & Scull International SA Co*,[181] that the availability of emergency arbitration could possibly preclude the court from granting an interim injunction, although the issue was left open.[182]

Subsequent authorities expanded on this reasoning, suggesting that the courts have no power to grant interim relief where it could be granted by an expedited or emergency arbitrator in a timely manner. In *GigSky APS v Vodafone Roaming Services Sarl*,[183] a case also concerning the ICC arbitration rules, HHJ Waksman QC (as he then was) held that the appropriate time for determining whether the Court or an emergency arbitrator should grant interim relief is the time of the application to the Court. In this case, it would have taken 11 days to appoint an emergency arbitrator and hold a hearing. Therefore, it was faster for the Court to deal with the application.[184] By contrast, in the more recent *Gerald Metals SA v Timis* case,[185] the applicant applied for, and was refused, emergency arbitration by the LCIA. Leggat J held that the Court would not exercise its power under section 44 of the Act.[186] In this case, however, it was beyond question that the LCIA could act in a timely manner, so much so that an application to the LCIA had been made before the application to the Court. There was no doubt therefore that the institution could act effectively but had refused to do so, probably because the defendant had given adequate undertakings that addressed the alleged risk of dissipation of assets pleaded by the claimant.

[179] ibid, [35].
[180] *Mi-Space (UK) Ltd v Lend Lease Construction (EMEA) Ltd* [2013] EWHC 2001 (TCC) [25].
[181] *Seele Middle East FZE v Drake & Scull International SA Co* [2013] EWHC 4350 (TCC).
[182] ibid, [14].
[183] *GigSky APS v Vodafone Roaming Services Sarl*, 16 October 2015, unreported.
[184] ibid, [32–5].
[185] *Gerald Metals SA v Timis* [2016] EWHC 2327 (Ch).
[186] ibid, 17–8.

IV. The TCC's Supervisory Jurisdiction

A. Powers of the Court to Remove Arbitrators

The Arbitration Act empowers English courts to appoint arbitrators under section 18, but also remove them under section 24. Since this is a highly interventionist, potentially disruptive move, the order would not be made lightly by the courts.[187] In *Damond Lock Grabowski v Laing Investments (Bracknell) Ltd*,[188] the removed arbitrator was labelled as 'eccentric, autocratic and obsessive' in mistreating one of the parties, thus demonstrating the high threshold for a successful section 24 application.

An application to remove an arbitrator failed in *Benaim (UK) Ltd v Davies Middleton & Davies Ltd (No.2)*.[189] The applicant sought to remove the arbitrator under section 24 and challenged the award under section 68. The two applications were made on similar grounds.[190] There were ten different allegations against the arbitrator, including his alleged failure to act fairly and give each party the opportunity to present its case, failure to deal with all the issues that were put to him, and failure to provide reasons for the decision.[191]

Coulson J (as he then was) carefully analysed each of the grounds, concluding that neither the section 24 removal nor the section 68 application could be upheld.[192] He said in relation to section 24:

> [The applicants] need to demonstrate that in this case the Arbitrator failed to conduct the hearing properly, either because he did not give them an opportunity to present their case, or because he failed to deal with the issues put to him, and that a substantial injustice has resulted in consequence. In addition, so it seems to me, [the applicants] must show that his failure and its consequences are so serious that setting aside the Award under s.68 is not sufficient remedy, and that the only appropriate remedy is his removal as Arbitrator pursuant to s.24.[193]

Coulson J held that arguments supporting a section 68 application do not automatically support a section 24 application.[194] His Lordship added that 'with one exception, none of the complaints relied on under s.68 could, even if they were upheld, justify the removal of the Arbitrator under s.24 in any event'.[195] That one

[187] *Dredging & Construction Co Ltd v Delta Civil Engineering Co Ltd* (2000) 2 TCLR 438; *Groundshire v VHE Construction* [2001] BLR 395 where HHJ Bowsher QC described removal as a 'most serious step'; *Sinclair v Woods of Winchester Ltd* [2005] APP LR 07/14.

[188] *Damond Lock Grabowski v Laing Investments (Bracknell) Ltd* (1992) 78 BLR 132.

[189] *Benaim (UK) Ltd v Davies Middleton & Davies Ltd (No.2)* [2005] EWHC 1370 (TCC). Decision applied in *A v B* [2018] EWHC 2310 (Comm).

[190] ibid, [2–3].

[191] ibid, [51].

[192] ibid, [159–60].

[193] ibid, [26].

[194] ibid, [49].

[195] ibid, [27].

exception is when an arbitrator makes a finding on causation after the parties specifically requested him not to do so.[196]

The TCC further clarified, in *Goel v Amega Ltd*,[197] the relationship between the duty of an arbitrator to act fairly and his duty to act expeditiously. In this case, after the tribunal was constituted, the respondent in the arbitration failed to participate in the preliminary hearing, which had already been postponed to accommodate them, informing the arbitrator one day before the hearing date. The arbitrator, however, went ahead with the hearing and drafted a procedural timetable, inviting comments from both parties.[198] The respondent then changed their legal representation and requested an extension to comment on the procedural timetable, which the arbitrator granted. However, before the extended deadline expired, they notified the tribunal that the deadline would not be met.[199] The arbitrator offered a second procedural meeting, which was also rejected by the respondent. Instead, the respondent demanded a stay of proceedings. The arbitrator declined the request, which resulted in respondent's application under section 24, alleging breach of arbitrator's duties under section 33 on the grounds of bias.[200]

Coulson J refused the application although he held that substantiating a section 24 application may be informed by the arbitrator's exercise of his duties under section 33.[201] However, His Lordship found that the respondent had been given reasonable opportunity to present their case. One of the duties of an arbitrator under section 33 is to conduct the proceedings without unnecessary delay or expense. In case of party default, the arbitrator was right to minimise delay and expense by compel compliance with the procedural orders and progress the case.[202] The arbitrator acted fairly in the face of what he deemed to be a 'considerable provocation'.[203]

Nonetheless, the TCC is ready to intervene where circumstances justify it. In *Wicketts v Brine Builders*,[204] the claim concerned the construction of a house. A quantity surveyor was appointed to arbitrate the dispute and issued 19 different directions in the course of the proceedings. Although hearings took place, he did not address any of the points put to him by the parties in relation to his directions nor liability issues.[205] Moreover, these directions included exorbitant security for the arbitrator's fees and prohibited the parties to settle unless that security was paid. The TCC removed the arbitrator under section 24 describing the directions as 'outrageous'.[206] For example, the Court emphasised that although arbitrators

[196] ibid, [28].
[197] *Goel v Amega Ltd* [2010] EWHC 2454 (TCC).
[198] ibid, [7].
[199] ibid, [10–1].
[200] ibid, [11].
[201] ibid, [30–3].
[202] ibid, [31].
[203] ibid, [57].
[204] *Wicketts v Brine Builders* [2001] 6 WLUK 684.
[205] ibid, [3].
[206] ibid, [52].

have the power to request security under section 38(3) of the Act, such a power can only be used where there is credible evidence that the relevant party would be unable to pay the costs if it was ordered to do so. In the instant case, the arbitrator's order was based on speculation.[207] In this case, the Court also ordered the arbitrator to pay the costs of the court application.[208]

The TCC's approach to section 24 has been respectful of the arbitrator's discretion in matters of procedure and supportive of robust exercise of case management powers. On the other hand, the TCC has not hesitated to intervene to remove arbitrators when circumstances so required.

B. Settlements and Tribunal Jurisdiction

Settlements raise an important point in relation to their impact on the tribunal's jurisdiction. Typically, the arbitrator become *functus officio* once he determines all the matters referred by the parties.[209] *In Dawes v Treasure & Son Ltd*,[210] the dispute arose out of a construction project under the JCT Standard Form of Prime Cost Contract. The parties entered into a settlement in the course of an arbitration.[211] Subsequently, the claimant issued a new arbitration claiming additional remediation costs. The defendant applied to the first arbitrator for determination on whether the claimant can refer the costs of remediation to another arbitration, given the settlement. The arbitrator agreed with the defendant, finding that a separate claim could not be brought.[212] The issue before the TCC was whether the first arbitrator retained any jurisdiction over the dispute after the settlement and, if he did, whether he was right to conclude that the settlement compromised the further claims for defects.[213]

[207] ibid, [54].

[208] ibid, [62]. On this case, see Law Commission, *Review of the Arbitration Act* (Law Com No 257, 2022) paras 5.27–5.35, where the case is considered potentially problematic on the point of arbitrators' cost liability. The Law Commission appears to say that the Court should not have awarded costs against the arbitrator for not having adjourned the hearing before him because s 24(3) of the Arbitration Act allows the arbitrator to continue with the proceedings pending an application for their removal and, in any event, s 29 of the Act provides for arbitrators' immunity, which, in the Law Commission's view, should apply to any costs of the application to remove him. While the Court did not have the benefit of full arguments on these two points, it is worth noting that the mere fact that an arbitrator has a power or discretion to do something does not mean that any exercise of that power or discretion is unobjectionable. Therefore, while it is clear that an arbitrator who is challenged under s 24 may continue the proceedings, this does not mean that proceedings cannot be stayed in appropriate circumstances and that failure to do so may not be a breach of the arbitrators' duties. On the other hand, it does seem that s 29 would confer on the arbitrator immunity from any liability, including liability in costs, for anything done or omitted in his discharge of his functions as an arbitrator, including failure to stay proceedings. Quite a different matter is whether such an immunity extends to conduct of the arbitrator before a court, which was the other basis on which the Court awarded costs against the arbitrator in *Wicketts*. These points may be clarified in future amendments to the Act.

[209] *Prince v Carter* [2010] EWHC 1451 (TCC) [61].

[210] *Dawes v Treasure & Son Ltd* [2010] EWHC 3218 (TCC).

[211] ibid, [11], [13–4].

[212] ibid, [19–20].

[213] ibid, [25].

The TCC held that the initial arbitrator did retain unqualified jurisdiction even after the settlement.[214] The Court noted that a final award would usually signal the moment in which an arbitrator's jurisdiction ends.[215] However, the jurisdiction would be revived if a part of the award was remitted to the arbitrator.[216] Further, the Arbitration Act in section 51 suggested that even if a dispute is settled, the arbitrator retains some jurisdiction to determine issues of costs or any other matter remaining in dispute.[217] For example, the arbitrator could decide whether a settlement agreement existed or not. This post-settlement jurisdiction was unlimited unless restricted by the implied or express terms of the settlement or other contract.[218]

This case clarifies the point at which an arbitrator becomes *functus officio* number of elements: (i) meaning of a settlement under section 51 of the Act; (ii) the applicable arbitration rules; (iii) the conduct of the parties; and (iv) the terms of the settlement. The TCC made a novel point of law in this case. The decision was echoed later by the Singapore High Court in *Doshion Ltd v Sembawang Engineers and Constructors Pte Ltd*.[219] Choo Han Teck J held that an arbitrator may have jurisdiction to render an award as to the existence of a settlement between the parties.[220]

C. Determination of Preliminary Points of Law

Under section 45 of the Act, the court may determine a question of law arising in the course of the proceedings if the following conditions are met:

(i) the question is a question of law;
(ii) which substantially affects the rights of the parties;
(iii) which is being referred to the court either with the agreement of the parties or with the permission of the tribunal; and (if the latter):
(iv) the determination of the question is likely to produce substantial savings in costs; and
(v) the application is made without delay.[221]

In *Secretary of State for Defence v Turner Estate Solutions Ltd*,[222] the dispute concerned a design and construction contract. As Coulson J acknowledged '[t]here are surprisingly few authorities relating to s.45.'[223] The contract was a maximum price target cost contract, which provided for cost adjustment in the event of changes up to a maximum amount.[224] The defendant brought an arbitration,

[214] ibid, [32].
[215] ibid, [27].
[216] ibid.
[217] ibid.
[218] ibid, [29].
[219] *Doshion Ltd v Sembawang Engineers and Constructors Pte Ltd* [2011] SGHC 46.
[220] ibid, [4].
[221] *Secretary of State for Defence v Turner Estate Solutions Ltd* [2015] EWHC 1150 (TCC) [7].
[222] ibid.
[223] ibid, [8].
[224] ibid, [1].

claiming that the costs had exceeded the maximum amount stipulated by the contract. They alleged that the parties had departed from the cost adjustment procedure by conduct and that such procedure should, therefore, be disregarded. Conversely, the claimant counterclaimed for overpayment as the price cap had been exceeded. The issues before the TCC were: (i) whether the target cost could be adjusted after completion in respect of a change which should have been the subject of an adjustment during the design and construction period; and (ii) if not, whether the final price payable under the contract was to be calculated only on the basis of the costs actually incurred and without having regard to the contractual provisions concerning the calculation of actual costs and the maximum price cap as defined in the contract. The defendant's argument was that the parties had abandoned the cost adjustment procedure and that meant that the entire price calculation mechanism and price cap had to be disregarded.[225]

Coulson J noted that the issues raised were significant as the defendant's whole claim in arbitration assumed that they were entitled to ignore the maximum price target costs provisions of the contract. For that reason, the answer to the application would conclude the defendant's entire arbitration claim, limiting the arbitration to the claimant's counterclaim.[226] Coulson J hence noted that considering the preliminary point of law would substantially affect the rights of both parties and would lead to a significant savings in costs.[227]

In relation to the referred points of law, the Court applied business common sense, noting that it would be anomalous if the commercial bargain between the parties could be altered by a failure to comply with the cost adjustment procedure during the design and performance phases.[228] Furthermore, the Court applied the principle of interpretation that, insofar as possible, all parts of the contract should be given effect.[229] If the defendant's arguments were followed, the Court would have to disregard some parts of the contract.[230] As a result, turning to the questions raised in the section 45 application, the Court held that the target cost could still be adjusted even after the actual completion of the works. Second, the Court decided that the final price had to be calculated pursuant to the relevant contractual clauses.[231]

D. Enforcement of Arbitral Awards

As regards the enforcement of arbitral awards rendered by tribunals seated outside the UK, section 103 gives effect to the New York Convention 1958 and lists the

[225] ibid, [9].
[226] ibid, [13].
[227] ibid, [15], [21].
[228] ibid, [56].
[229] ibid, [62].
[230] ibid, [62–4].
[231] ibid, [109–11].

grounds upon which the court may refuse to enforce an award set out in Article V of the Convention. In *Honeywell International Middle East Ltd v Meydan Group LLC*,[232] the parties contracted to conduct refurbishing works at a Dubai racecourse and the dispute concerned Meydan Group's alleged failure to pay monies owed for the works. The Dubai-seated tribunal rendered an award in Honeywell's favour that then sought enforcement in the UK. The applicant Meydan Group sought to set aside an order to enforce the award mainly on the ground that the underlying contract, and hence the arbitration agreement, was procured by bribery. This allegedly made the award contrary to UAE law (ground under section 103(2)(b)) and contrary to UK public policy (ground under section 103(3)).[233]

The TCC held that the applicant had no real prospects of establishing that the bribery invalidated the arbitration agreement as to defeat summary enforcement of the award under section 103(2)(b). The allegation could have been dealt with in arbitration, as the applicant provided no new evidence.[234] The Court also noted that even if the bribery was established, that would not affect the arbitration agreement due to the principle of separability.[235] Turning to the UK public policy ground under section 103(3), the Court noted that contracts which have been procured by bribes were not unenforceable, unlike contracts that provide for bribery. Instead, the innocent party had the opportunity to avoid such a contract at its election.[236]

This judgment takes a pro-enforcement approach that prioritises legal certainty and finality even in the face of an allegation as serious as bribery, an approach that has since been confirmed by the Commercial Court and the Court of Appeal.[237]

E. Challenging an Award on the Grounds of Lack of Jurisdiction

The Arbitration Act lists three grounds pursuant to which an arbitral award[238] may be challenged in sections 67, 68 and 69. The result of a successful challenge is that an arbitral award can either be set aside, declared of no effect or remitted to the arbitrator, in whole or in part. For that reason, judgments concerning challenges to arbitral awards are particularly significant.

[232] *Honeywell International Middle East Ltd v Meydan Group LLC* [2014] EWHC 1344 (TCC). The leading case at that time was *Westacre Investments Inc v Jugoimport SPDR Holding Co Ltd* [1999] 3 WLR 811, CA.

[233] *Honeywell International Middle East Ltd v Meydan Group LLC* [2014] EWHC 1344 (TCC) [72], [159].

[234] ibid, [88–9], [94].

[235] ibid, [93].

[236] ibid, [184–5].

[237] *RBRG Trading (UK) Ltd v Sinocore International Co Ltd* [2018] EWCA Civ 838; *National Iranian Oil Co v Crescent Petroleum Co International Ltd and another* [2016] EWHC 510 (Comm).

[238] It must be an award, not a procedural order: see *ZCCM Investment Holdings Plc v Kansanshi Holdings* [2019] EWHC 1285 (Comm).

Section 67 gives a dissatisfied party the right to challenge an award for lack of substantive jurisdiction.[239] The reference to 'substantive jurisdiction' is a reference to section 30(1) and the applicant is confined to the grounds therein.[240] These matters are: (i) the validity of the arbitration agreement; (ii) the proper constitution of the tribunal; and (iii) whether matters have been submitted to arbitration in accordance with the arbitration agreement. A section 67 application will receive a full rehearing in court.

In *AMEC Civil Engineering Ltd v Secretary of State for Transport*,[241] the TCC grappled with the claimant's challenge to an arbitrator's interim award. The arbitration, in this case, concerned a contract implementing ICE Conditions of Contract.[242] A dispute relating to alleged defects was first decided by an engineer in favour of the defendant. The defendant then brought the case to arbitration since the claimant did not comply with the engineer's decision. In the arbitration, the claimant raised objections to the engineer's jurisdiction and alleged irregularities. The arbitrator rejected the claimant's objections in an interim award. These proceedings concerned the claimant's section 67 challenge to that interim award on three grounds:

(i) No dispute existed which was capable of being referred to the Engineer under the contract. Therefore, there was no valid Engineer's decision and hence nothing capable of being referred to arbitration.
(ii) If that is wrong, the Engineer's decision was invalid because the Engineer did not reach it by a fair process.
(iii) If there was a valid Engineer's decision, the arbitrator's jurisdiction was nevertheless limited to the three defects expressly identified in the Engineer's decision whereas the arbitrator had gone further.[243]

On the first point, the Court found that there was a dispute. The defendant had clearly set out its claim in correspondence. The parties had a meeting where they disagreed on who bore responsibility for defects.[244] At that time, the dispute crystallised, also for the purposes of the limitation period.[245]

With regards to the second ground, the claimant raised several allegations relating to the procedural unfairness of the engineer's decision.[246] The Court dismissed them noting that an engineer did not have to comply with natural justice in rendering a decision pursuant to the ICE conditions dispute resolution clause, although he did have to act independently and honestly.[247]

Turning to the third issue, the TCC held that the ICE Conditions must have intended for the entire claim submitted to the engineer to be arbitrable in a single

[239] *LG Caltex Gas Co Ltd v China National Petroleum Corpn* [2001] 1 WLR 1892.
[240] *Union Marine Classification Services LLC v Government of the Union of Comoros* [2015] EWHC 508 (Comm).
[241] *AMEC Civil Engineering Ltd v Secretary of State for Transport* [2004] EWHC 2339 (TCC).
[242] ibid, [13].
[243] ibid, [24].
[244] ibid, [32–3].
[245] ibid, [35].
[246] ibid, [37].
[247] ibid, [49].

procedure – rather than just a claim confined to the three defects identified by the engineer. Otherwise, the contract would have required the service of two notices of arbitration in the current case. As Jackson J (as he then was) noted, 'I cannot believe that the contracting parties intended to create such a bizarre procedure.'[248] The Court of Appeal affirmed the TCC judgment in this case on all three issues above.[249] In particular, it warned against construing arbitration clauses with legalistic rigidity that could impede the parties from starting timely arbitration.[250]

In *Michael John Construction Ltd v St Peter's Rugby Football Club*,[251] the issue concerned the scope of an arbitrator's jurisdiction. The case concerned a contract incorporating the JCT Intermediate Form of Building Contract and a dispute relating to payment under that contract. That contract contained an arbitration clause.[252] Following adjudicators' decisions and summary judgment proceedings, the applicant enforced the decisions on the respondent's trustees. In these proceedings, the Court also determined who the parties to the underlying contract were.[253]

The respondents then attempted to bring an arbitration, contrary to the finding of the Court that they were not parties to the contract.[254] The arbitrator agreed with the respondents and found that he had the authority to decide who the contracting parties were, despite the TCC's earlier judgment.[255] The applicant argued that the issue had already been decided in litigation and sought to challenge the decision under section 67 of the Arbitration Act before the TCC.[256]

The TCC held that the arbitrator made an error in law by permitting the respondent to adduce further material relating to a point that was already decided in earlier litigation. Therefore, the arbitrator exceeded jurisdiction by redetermining which party was a signatory to the contract and hence bound by the arbitration agreement. The Court also noted that the respondent misled the arbitrator as to adjudication, suggesting that its provisional nature extended to the subsequent enforcement proceedings before the Court.[257] Wilcox J added:

> It can only be in the most exceptional circumstances that a party may be permitted to bring forward further material relevant to the issue already decided by a court, in subsequent proceedings. The arbitrator in this case, in permitting the defendants to adduce further evidence failed to consider whether it was material which could not by reasonable diligence have been adduced in the earlier proceedings. Clearly it could have been.[258]

[248] ibid, [115].
[249] *AMEC Civil Engineering Ltd v Secretary of State for Transport* [2005] EWCA Civ 291.
[250] ibid, [31].
[251] *Michael John Construction Ltd v St Peter's Rugby Football Club* [2007] EWHC 1857 (TCC).
[252] ibid, [1].
[253] ibid, [28–31].
[254] ibid, [36].
[255] ibid, [39].
[256] ibid, [34].
[257] ibid, [38].
[258] ibid.

Hence, the section 67 challenge succeeded and the TCC ordered the award to be varied to the effect that there was no arbitration agreement between the applicant and respondent.[259] This case clarifies two important points. First, a court determination as to the jurisdiction of the arbitral tribunal in separate proceedings, even if not conducted under the Arbitration Act and its sections 32 or 67, has a *res judicata* effect in the arbitration. Second, the provisional nature of an adjudicator's decision does not mean that a court judgment concerning that decision in enforcement proceedings is not as final as any other judgment of the court on the issued that have been decided.

F. Challenging an Award Pursuant to a Serious Irregularity

Section 68 allows the applicant to challenge an award on the ground that it is affected by serious irregularity. It is mainly aimed at procedural failings 'in extreme cases where the tribunal has gone so wrong in its conduct of the arbitration that justice calls out for it to be corrected'.[260] The list of circumstances in section 68(2) was deemed a closed list in *Lesotho Highlands Development Authority v Impregilo SpA*.[261] At least one of the circumstances listed in subsection 2 must have then caused or will cause a 'substantial injustice' to the applicant. This means that the procedural failing significantly exceeded what could reasonably be expected in an arbitration so as to justify court intervention.[262]

In *Weldon Plant Ltd v Commission for the New Towns*,[263] the parties contracted, incorporating the ICE Conditions of Contract (sixth edition), for the construction of a water reservoir.[264] The contract was varied and the contractor commenced arbitration claiming for the fair valuation of the variation under clause 52.1, including additional overheads and profits. The arbitrator rendered an award in favour of the contractor but did not award overheads and profits. The contractor sought, inter alia, the remission of the award to the arbitrator.

The applicant argued that the incorrect assessment of the sums due amounted to a serious irregularity.[265] Judge Humphrey Lloyd QC concluded that while there was unfairness caused by failure to include overheads and profits in the valuation, this did not amount to a breach of the arbitrator's duty under section 33 and to serious irregularity under section 68. The Court expressly noted that section 68 should not be used as an indirect method of appealing a point of fact or law, other than in an exceptional case.[266] Further, under section 68(2)(d) the applicant's arguments

[259] ibid, [48].

[260] Departmental Advisory Committee on Arbitration, 'DAC Report on Arbitration Bill 1996' (DAC February 1996) [280]; *Lesotho Highlands Development Authority v Impregilo SA* [2005] UKHL 43 [27].

[261] *Lesotho Highlands Development Authority v Impregilo SpA* [2005] UKHL 43.

[262] *Stern Trustees v Levy* [2009] EWHC 14 (TCC) [23].

[263] *Weldon Plant Ltd v Commission for the New Towns* [2001] 1 All ER (Comm) 264.

[264] ibid, [1].

[265] ibid, [6–7], [11].

[266] ibid, [28].

were not put to the arbitrator clearly enough that these were issues to be decided upon. This ground for challenge cannot be used as a means of launching a detailed inquiry into the manner in which the tribunal considered various issues.[267]

A similar point was emphasised by the TCC in *Claire & Co Ltd v Thames Water Utilities Ltd*.[268] The claimant attempted to challenge an arbitrator's award pursuant to section 68, in a dispute concerning the level of compensation for loss of profits. The defendant commenced construction works outside the claimant's premises, making it impossible for the business to function. The defendant conceded liability and the arbitrator was requested to decide the level of compensation.[269] The arbitrator applied a 22 per cent profit margin in the award, significantly lower than what the claimant requested.[270] The claimant hence argued that the arbitrator applying such an egregiously low profit margin breached section 33 and hence section 68. The claimant also argued that the higher profit margin (at 75 per cent) was conceded by the defendant's expert accountant in cross-examination. The arbitrator's consideration of the point hence exceeded his jurisdiction under section 67.[271]

The TCC first noted that there was no agreement between the parties that the profit margin should be higher than 22 per cent. Therefore, the section 67 challenge was rejected.[272] Further, in relation to section 68, the arbitrator was entitled to use his own expert knowledge when assessing the appropriate profit margin.[273] Even if the lower margin was erroneous, that did not amount to a breach of section 33 or section 68. The Court emphasised that a challenge to the award cannot be used as a method of appealing a finding of fact. On this point, the Court pointed to the tribunal's authority to weigh facts under section 34 of the Act.[274] The judgment makes clear that the Court will be reluctant to revisit an arbitrator's finding of fact for the purposes of section 33 or 68 of the Arbitration Act, even if the finding was probably incorrect.[275]

The issue of serious irregularity under section 68 was later discussed in depth by the House of Lords in *Lesotho Highlands Authority v Impregilo SpA*.[276] The judgment resembles closely the reasoning in *Weldon* and *Claire* in distinguishing an arbitrator's errors of law from breaches of section 68, though these two TCC cases were not cited by the House of Lords. Lord Steyn gave the example that if parties specifically requested the arbitrator to apply simple interest and the

[267] ibid, [31].
[268] *Claire & Co Ltd v Thames Water Utilities Ltd* [2005] EWHC 1022 (TCC).
[269] ibid, [15–22].
[270] ibid, [23–8].
[271] ibid, [29–30].
[272] ibid, [42–4].
[273] ibid, [45].
[274] ibid.
[275] It is now well established that s 68 cannot be used to disguise a challenge to the arbitrator's findings of fact or law: *Protech Projects Construction (Pty) Ltd v Mohammed Abdulmohsin Al-Kharafi & Sons* [2005] EWHC 2165 (Comm); *Ameropa SA v Lithuanian Shipping* [2015] EWHC 3847 (Comm); *Shaw v MFP Foundation & Pilings Ltd* [2010] EWHC 1839 (TCC).
[276] *Lesotho Highlands Authority v Impregilo SpA* [2005] UKHL 43.

arbitrator awarded compound interest, that could be the basis of a successful challenge under section 68.[277] Therefore, the *Weldon*, *Claire* and *Lesotho* judgments point to the importance of the source of the arbitrator's alleged serious irregularity. If the arbitrator acted contrary to party instructions, the challenge might be successful. However, an arbitrator's incorrect or unfair application of law or facts would not suffice. Lord Steyn in *Lesotho* emphasised that section 68 requires the applicant to satisfy a high threshold,[278] as Judge Humphrey Lloyd QC had done in *Weldon Plant*.

In *London Underground Ltd v Citylink Telecommunications Ltd*,[279] both parties challenged the arbitral award under section 68. One party also brought a section 69 challenge. The dispute related to delays in a construction project. The arbitrator found that the defendant was entitled to an extension of time caused by the claimant's delays. The arbitrator treated the allegation as a global claim. The claimant argued that the arbitrator breached section 33 and hence section 68(2)(c) by adopting a global claim reasoning despite neither party pleading it.

The TCC refused the applications from both parties.[280] An arbitrator can make findings of fact that depart from the pleadings of the parties. A finding of serious irregularity was a matter of degree taking into account all relevant circumstances.[281] In the analysis of the serious irregularity element, the Court must consider the nature of global claims, ie, that issues of causation were based on inferences often derived from expert evidence and the facts.[282] The process, in this case, was hence not unfair and did not require the arbitrator to seek further submissions from the parties.[283] Therefore, there was no serious irregularity under section 68 and, even if there had been some irregularity, it had not caused substantial injustice to the parties.[284] The section 69 challenge also failed because there was no question of law to pursue and, even if there was, there was nothing obviously wrong with the arbitrator's approach.[285]

In the above judgments, the TCC noted the exceptional circumstances in which an award may be challenged pursuant to section 68 of the Arbitration Act. The Court also emphasised that such a challenge cannot be used as a method of re-hearing the dispute. In *L Brown & Sons Ltd v Crosby Homes (North West) Ltd*,[286] the applicant based their section 68 challenge on evidence that could have been put to the arbitrator, but was not. The dispute concerned the design and building of residential apartments in Manchester. The contract followed the standard JCT form with Design.[287] Several adjudications and two arbitrations followed.

[277] ibid, [29].
[278] ibid, [28].
[279] *London Underground Ltd v Citylink Telecommunications Ltd* [2007] EWHC 1749 (TCC).
[280] ibid, [337].
[281] ibid, [37].
[282] ibid, [142].
[283] ibid, [159–60], [167].
[284] ibid, [207].
[285] ibid, [320].
[286] *L Brown & Sons Ltd v Crosby Homes (North West) Ltd* [2008] EWHC 817 (TCC).
[287] ibid, [2].

The applicant argued that some of the documents disclosed in the second arbitration should have been disclosed sooner in the first proceedings. These documents allegedly evidenced that the respondent's director committed perjury in the first arbitration.[288] The applicant brought an application challenging the awards under section 68 and applied for an extension of time to making the application as it had been submitted 66 days late.[289]

The Court dismissed the application extension of time application.[290] The time limits in the Arbitration Act were strict and reflected the policy of section 1 of the Act. The provision expressly mentions that the object of arbitration is to decide disputes without unnecessary delay.[291] The applicant relied mainly on the strength of their section 68 challenge to argue for an extension, but this was not a primary consideration for the Court. Instead, weight would have been given to the length of the delay, its cause and the reasonableness of the party's conduct. In this case, the applicant had no good reason for the delay.[292]

Turning to the strength of the section 68 challenge, the deliberate non-disclosure of documents may be a breach of public policy under section 68(2)(g) if there is evidence of fraud or reprehensible conduct. Conduct is less likely to be fraudulent or reprehensible if the documents have not been requested by the arbitral tribunal. In any event, the Court noted that the case was weak, and the allegations of perjury were difficult to substantiate.[293] The TCC emphasised that if evidence could be deployed before an arbitrator, the courts would be reluctant to allow a losing party to rely upon the same material in their section 68(2)(g) application, save in exceptional circumstances. The Court refused to define these exceptional circumstances.[294]

In *F Ltd v M Ltd*,[295] the tribunal awarded the claimant significantly less than was claimed since the claim was made out under an incorrect term of the contract and applied a £1 million credit in favour of the defendant. One of the arbitrators provided a dissenting opinion that the majority's decision exceeded the tribunal's jurisdiction. The claimant argued that the tribunal acted unfairly and decided the case relying on matters that were not pleaded. The dissenting opinion was used as evidence to support a section 68 challenge.[296]

On the relevance of the dissenting opinion, the Court held that it could be relevant, but unlikely to be determinative.

> A comment or observation in a dissenting opinion, to the effect that an important point has been decided by the majority without reference to the parties, will be a factor to

[288] ibid, [5].
[289] ibid, [5–6], [37].
[290] ibid, [81].
[291] ibid, [26], [31].
[292] ibid, [32], applying Colman J in *Kalmneft v Glencore International AG* [2001] 2 All ER (Comm) 577 [59].
[293] ibid, [36].
[294] ibid, [71].
[295] *F Ltd v M Ltd* [2009] EWHC 275 (TCC).
[296] ibid, [6].

> which the court will attach weight in dealing with an application under section 68. Depending on the circumstances, such an observation may have considerable weight, although it is unlikely that it could, on its own, prove determinative.[297]

Further, the TCC noted that in this case, according to the tribunal, the contract clause relied upon by the claimant did not allow the claimed recovery.[298] This point was not expressly argued but the arbitral tribunal was still entitled to find that the clause in question did not support the claim.[299] There was neither serious irregularity nor substantial injustice as required by section 68.[300] However, the tribunal had no basis for finding the £1 million credit in favour of the defendant. It was neither pleaded nor admitted. The parties were not consulted on the point and hence the tribunal exceeded its powers under section 68(2)(b).[301] The risk of substantial injustice was significant in these circumstances and hence the award was remitted to the tribunal on the point.[302]

In *Secretary of State for the Home Department v Raytheon Systems Ltd*,[303] the TCC considered that remitting an award that was successfully challenged under section 68 might not always be adequate. The arbitration arose out of a purported contract termination. The arbitrator found in favour of the defendant but failed to address issues of fault and responsibility attributable to the defendant that were relevant to quantum. That led to the award being successfully challenged by the claimant under section 68. Since remitting the award would have required the same arbitrator to hear the same case twice, the claimant argued that the award should be entirely set aside and referred to a new tribunal.[304]

The TCC noted that the Act allowed the courts to set aside an award if remittal was inappropriate, on a case-by-case basis. The burden for establishing such circumstances is on the party arguing that the award should not be remitted.[305] The TCC then explained the relevant elements of the analysis:

> What the Court needs to do in deciding whether to remit or set aside is to consider all the circumstances and background facts relating to the dispute, the award, the arbitrators and the overall desirability of remission and setting aside, as well as the ramifications, both in terms of costs, time and justice, of doing either. A review of 'appropriateness' encompasses a pragmatic consideration of all the circumstances and relevant facts to determine what it is best to do but it necessarily covers the interests of justice as between the parties.[306]

[297] ibid.
[298] ibid, [31].
[299] ibid, [43–6].
[300] ibid, [47].
[301] ibid, [57].
[302] ibid, [59].
[303] *Secretary of State for the Home Department v Raytheon Systems Ltd* [2015] EWHC 311 (TCC).
[304] ibid, [1].
[305] ibid, [3].
[306] ibid, [4].

The Court decided the question from the perspective of a reasonable person in assessing the confidence in the arbitrator's ability to come to a fair and balanced conclusion on the issues if remitted.[307] Akenhead J concluded that it was necessary to find an objectively real risk of the arbitrator acting unfairly following a remission.[308]

Finally, the Court considered the fact that the cost of setting aside an award was higher than a remission:

> The costs of remission compared with the costs of a new tribunal looking at the case in the context of the overall amounts in issue must also be a factor which may go towards establishing the appropriateness of the one course of the other. The passage of time may also be a factor, because if a sufficiently long time has passed since the tribunal heard the evidence, it may, in relative terms, matter not much whether the tribunal is a new one because the old tribunal would in any event have to spend considerable time, effort and indeed cost in researching the evidence again.[309]

A mere finding of serious irregularity under section 68 was insufficient to set the award aside. It was, however, a relevant factor in the overall assessment: the more serious the irregularity, the more likely the award will be set aside.[310]

The main point was to ask whether the arbitrator could afford justice to the parties, following remittal of the award.[311] Accordingly, the Court held that the award ought to be set aside, rather than remitted.[312] In this case, the following were relevant:

(a) the section 68(2)(d) grounds were towards the more serious end of the spectrum of seriousness in terms of irregularity;
(b) it would be invidious and embarrassing for the tribunal to be required to try to free itself of all previous ideas and to re-determine the same issues. Doing so would create own undesirable tensions and pressures;
(c) it is unlikely that there will be any significant re-drawing of the issues in the new arbitration;
(d) much of the factual and expert evidence, adduced before the current tribunal, would be re-deployed before the new tribunal. There had already been substantial disclosure and little if any further disclosure would be required. This would contribute to reducing costs;
(e) the current tribunal was unlikely to recall the evidence regardless, due to the significant time lapse of almost three years.[313]

[307] ibid, [5], [8–9]. Applying the test in *Lovell Partnerships (Northern) Ltd v AW Construction plc* (1996) 81 BLR 83, 99E.
[308] ibid, [11].
[309] ibid.
[310] ibid, [3].
[311] ibid, [4].
[312] ibid, [32].
[313] ibid, [23].

G. Challenging an Award on a Point of Law

Under the Act, parties may appeal the award on the ground that the tribunal was wrong on a point of English law[314] pursuant to section 69 of the Arbitration Act. This section, unlike sections 67 and 68, is non-mandatory. In fact, many leading arbitration rules exclude it.[315]

This ground for challenge is highly controversial with some arguing for its abolishment, while others noting its value as a way of ensuring the development of English contract law that would otherwise be confined to arbitration.[316]

Leave to appeal. Section 69 requires either that all parties agree to the appeal or the leave of the court. If the appellant requires permission from the court, the criteria listed in section 69(3) must be met. The court must be satisfied that:

> (a) the determination of the question will substantially affect the rights of one or more of the parties,
> (b) the question is one which the tribunal was asked to determine,
> (c) on the basis of the findings of fact in the award—
>   (i) the decision of the tribunal on the question is obviously wrong, or
>   (ii) the question is one of general public importance and the decision of the tribunal is at least open to serious doubt, and
> (d) that, despite the agreement of the parties to resolve the matter by arbitration, it is just and proper in all the circumstances for the court to determine the question.

The Court discussed the criteria for granting leave to appeal in *Morris Homes (West Midlands) Ltd v Keay*.[317] The underlying dispute related to the construction of a medical centre on land that the claimant purchased from the respondent.[318] Following completion of the construction, the land would be leased back by the respondent. A dispute arose and the claimant was found in breach of contract following an arbitration. The claimant sought to appeal the award on the grounds of the arbitrator's errors in his interpretation of due diligence/best endeavours clauses and his assessment of the respondent's losses.[319]

The Court declined to give permission to appeal,[320] noting that the application was a summary one.[321] Therefore, it should be decided on paper only or, if an oral hearing is necessary, following a brief hearing.[322] However, the Court recognised

[314] *Schwebel v Schwebel* [2010] EWHC 3280 (TCC). Only issues of law, not fact, can be the subject-matter of an appeal: *Surefire Systems Ltd v Guardian ECL Ltd* [2005] BLR 534 [21]; *Majorboom Ltd v NHBC* [2008] EWHC 2672 (TCC) [8].

[315] See, eg, ICC Arbitration Rules, Art 28.6; LCIA Arbitration Rules, Art 26.9.

[316] See discussion in Departmental Advisory Committee on Arbitration, 'DAC Report on Arbitration Bill 1996' (DAC February 1996) [284–92]; J Paulsson, 'Arbitration-Friendliness: Promises of Principle and Realities of Practice' (2007) 23(3) *Arbitration International* 477.

[317] *Morris Homes (West Midlands) Ltd v Keay* [2013] EWHC 932 (TCC).

[318] ibid, [4].

[319] ibid, [17–21], [28].

[320] ibid, [49].

[321] ibid, [27].

[322] ibid, [23].

that such applications might not be determined within merely 'half an hour or so', which was the test suggested in the earlier case of *CMA CGM SA v Beteiligungs KG MS Northern Pioneer Schiffahrtsgesellschaft mbH & Co.*[323] The TCC observed that it would not always be possible to decide the matter so briefly.[324] Instead, the Court followed the seminal case *Pioneer Shipping Ltd v BTP Tioxide Ltd (The Nema) (No.2)*[325] and held that the appellant must demonstrate that they have a 'clear-cut' case that the conditions for granting leave are met.[326]

In the case at hand, the disputed conditions were those under section 69(3)(c) and (d). First of all, following *The Nema*, the Court held that while due diligence/best endeavours clauses were widespread in construction contracts, the facts of the case were highly unusual so that it could not be said that the case was one of general public importance. Rather, it was a one-off case. The appellant, therefore, had to make out a clear-cut case that the arbitrator had been obviously wrong. In the instant case, the claimant had failed to do so.[327]

In *White Young Green Consulting v Brooke House*,[328] the TCC confirmed that the mere fact that an error of law relates to a standard form contract does not automatically mean that the issue is of general public importance. At the very least, there would have to be some uncertainty, either in publications or elsewhere, which indicates that the issue is not just a matter of importance because it arises under a commonly used clause, but it is a matter of general public importance.[329] The Court also took the opportunity to reaffirm the conclusion in *Kershaw Mechanical Services Ltd v Kendrick Construction Ltd*,[330] that a section 69 appeal might prompt the court to consider documents external to the arbitral award. For example, such external evidence could be used to demonstrate that the question of law raised in the appeal was one of general public importance under section 69(3)(c)(ii).[331]

The TCC applied section 69(3)(a) in *Shaw v MFP Foundation & Pilings Ltd*.[332] The section 69 appeal was based on the allegation that the arbitrator applied an incorrect measure of damages in the award. In fact, the arbitrator rejected figures provided by the claimant, finding them unreasonably incurred.[333] The Court found that the reasonableness of the claimed sums was indeed not the right legal test. However, the TCC noted that these sums only amounted to a few hundred pounds so it could not be said that the rights of the parties were substantially affected within the meaning of section 69(3)(a).[334]

[323] *CMA CGM SA v Beteiligungs KG MS Northern Pioneer Schiffahrtsgesellschaft mbH & Co* [2003] 1 WLR 1015.
[324] *Morris Homes (West Midlands) Ltd v Keay* [2013] EWHC 932 (TCC) [27].
[325] *Pioneer Shipping Ltd v BTP Tioxide Ltd (The Nema) (No.2)* [1981] 7 WLUK 184, 742–43.
[326] ibid, [22–7].
[327] ibid, [31].
[328] *White Young Green Consulting v Brooke House* [2007] EWHC 2018 (TCC).
[329] ibid, [27].
[330] *Kershaw Mechanical Services Ltd v Kendrick Construction Ltd* [2006] EWHC 727 (TCC).
[331] *White Young Green Consulting v Brooke House* [2007] EWHC 2018 (TCC) [26].
[332] *Shaw v MFP Foundation & Pilings Ltd* [2010] EWHC 1839 (TCC).
[333] ibid, [53].
[334] ibid, [56].

Although section 69 is non-mandatory and hence often excluded, the Court will not hastily conclude that the parties have so intended. In *Essex CC v Premier Recycling Ltd*,[335] the contract related to the provision of services to a local authority. A dispute arose and the parties agreed to refer it to an arbitrator to obtain a 'final and binding decision'. The arbitrator found in the appellant's favour. The defendant sought to appeal the award under section 69 and the issue arose whether the parties had contracted out of section 69 when they agreed that the award was 'final and binding'.[336] The Court held that phrase 'final and binding' does not in isolation suffice to exclude the right to appeal and could have merely referred to the award being final and binding but subject to the Act. In fact, the same wording is used in section 58(1) of the Act.[337] On the other hand, an express mention of section 69 is not required for the appeal to be excluded.[338] Further, the courts would only grant leave to appeal if it was just and proper to do so under section 69(3)(d). In this case, reference to the award as final and binding, the dispute being referred to an expert and the requirement of a quick procedure weighed against granting leave to appeal. The parties could not have intended a protracted appeals procedure.[339] This focus on party intention under section 69(3)(d) resonates with the later TCC decision in *White Young Green Consulting v Brooke House Sixth Form College*.[340] Ramsey J held that the parties could not have intended a protracted review by the court since they named an arbitrator in their arbitration agreement.[341]

Can the Court consider documents other the award when deciding whether to grant leave to appeal? In *HOK Sport Ltd (formerly Lobb Partnership Ltd) v Aintree Racecourse Co Ltd*,[342] the Court noted that the parties submitted unnecessarily voluminous evidence to support it. The Court said: 'it should now be clear to experienced practitioners in the TCC that extraneous materials are not to be referred to in arbitration appeal leave applications'.[343] The Court, nevertheless, granted leave to appeal.[344]

The issue of what documents, other than the award, can be considered on a section 69 appeal arose again in *Kershaw Mechanical Services Ltd v Kendrick Construction Ltd*.[345] Jackson J noted that the principal document for the purposes of section 69 is the award itself. However, if the question of law related to some external documents and the award made a reference to them, the Court will have

[335] *Essex CC v Premier Recycling Ltd* [2006] EWHC 3594 (TCC).

[336] ibid, [1–2].

[337] ibid, [16].

[338] ibid, [23]. This is important as many arbitration rules exclude any right of recourse or appeal against the award insofar as such a right can be waived under the applicable law, without specific reference to section 69: see, eg, ICC Rules of Arbitration 2017, rule 35(6) and LCIA Rules 2020, rule 26(8).

[339] ibid, [28].

[340] *White Young Green Consulting v Brooke House Sixth Form College* [2007] EWHC 2018 (TCC).

[341] ibid, [28–30].

[342] *HOK Sport Ltd (formerly Lobb Partnership Ltd) v Aintree Racecourse Co Ltd* [2002] EWHC 3094 (TCC).

[343] ibid, [18].

[344] ibid, [59].

[345] *Kershaw Mechanical Services Ltd v Kendrick Construction Ltd* [2006] EWHC 727 (TCC).

to consider these documents as well.[346] In this case, the appellant's appeal turned on the construction of correspondence between the parties that had the effect of amending the contract. Jackson J thus rightly considered the approach in *HOK Sport* to be too restrictive. To determine the appeal, the Court did have to consider the correspondence amending the contract on the construction of which the questions law of turned.[347]

Appeals decided on the merits. The TCC has decided a number of appeals on the merits. In *Fence Gate Ltd v NEL Construction Ltd*,[348] the HHJ Thornton QC considered an appeal against an arbitrator's award that both parties should bear their own costs relating to appellant's counterclaim. In reaching this conclusion, the arbitrator considered the appellant's unreasonable conduct in the performance of the contract and departed from the costs-follow-the-event approach.[349]

The Court first noted that the appellant did not require leave pursuant to section 69(2)(b) of the Act because the arbitration agreement consented to either party bringing such an appeal on a point of law. Hence, the proceedings fell within section 69(2)(a).[350] The case is remarkable in setting out the principles that apply to a challenge of an award of costs. The Court noted that the Arbitration Act 1996 clearly sets out the arbitrator's powers as to costs. Therefore, the requirement, developed under the Arbitration Act 1979 and the Arbitration Act 1950, that, in awarding costs, arbitrators had to act 'judicially', no longer applied.[351] The Court also commented that an award of costs which is within the arbitrator's jurisdiction can be challenged for serious irregularity under section 68 or appealed on a point of law under section 69. In principle, if a question of law arises out of the award, the proper remedy should be an appeal on points of law, otherwise the restrictions on such appeals would be circumvented.[352] Turning to the merits, the Court allowed appeal and ordered that the award be varied under section 69(7)(b).[353] The arbitrator was found to have committed four errors of law, namely: (i) he erroneously concluded that the magnitude of the counterclaim had a deterrent effect on early settlement and took that matter into account in his decision on costs; (ii) he failed to have regard to offers to settle; (iii) he considered the appellant's conduct during the performance of the contract relevant to the decision on costs; (iv) he failed to consider any intermediate solution, such as awarding to the appellant only a proportion of its costs.[354] The Court varied the award and allowed the appellant to recover only a part (determined at 65 per cent) of their costs.[355]

[346] ibid, [45].
[347] ibid, [44–5].
[348] *Fence Gate Ltd v NEL Construction Ltd* [2001] 12 WLUK 100. Decision considered or applied in *Maurice J Bushell and Co v Born* [2017] EWHC 2227 (Ch); *Newfield Construction Ltd v Tomlinson* [2004] EWHC 3051 (TCC).
[349] ibid, [1–2].
[350] ibid, [2].
[351] ibid, [22–9].
[352] ibid, [31–2].
[353] ibid, [137].
[354] ibid, [86].
[355] ibid, [137].

Another case where the section 69 challenge was successful was *HOK Sport Ltd (formerly Lobb Partnership Ltd) v Aintree Racecourse Co Ltd*.[356] The appellant sought permission to appeal the tribunal's award of damages under section 69(2)(b), arguing that the tribunal failed to ascertain the correct scope of the duty the breach of which caused the recoverable loss. On the merits, the appellant argued that the tribunal applied the 'but for' test for causation when he should have considered foreseeability instead. The result of the two was that the arbitrator erroneously calculated loss.[357] The TCC upheld the appellant's appeal,[358] holding that the losses should have been attributed to the respondent's failure to warn the appellant of the potential losses, making them foreseeable to the appellant.[359] The Court then varied the award on the point of causation and then remitted it to the arbitrator to allow for findings of fact.[360]

H. Duties of Experts in Arbitration

The TCC contributed to clarifying the law on the duties of experts who act in an arbitration for a party in the case *A Company v X and Others*,[361] known, on appeal, as the *Secretariat* case. The claimant in this case had engaged Secretariat Consulting Pte Ltd to act as delay experts in an arbitration against a subcontractor in a project. The claimant was also involved in a dispute, concerning the same project, against the project manager. The project manager engaged as experts Secretariat International UK Ltd. The claimant sought an injunction to restrain Secretariat International UK Ltd from acting for the project manager. The second arbitration concerned the same delays as the first, resulting in a significant overlap of issues. O'Farrell J granted the injunction, holding that the relationship between an expert and its client was fiduciary in nature, noting that the test is nonetheless a case-by-case one,[362] and the fiduciary duty does not apply to all experts by default.[363] O'Farrell J placed particular emphasis on the terms of the experts' retainer which provided for extensive assistance to the claimant in conducting the arbitration.[364] The outcome could have been different if the experts' role had been minimal. O'Farrell J added, applying earlier authorities, that the duty of loyalty extends to the entire organisation, not just the individual expert.[365] Even internal 'Chinese walls' would not prevent the application of the fiduciary duty to the entire organisation. Her Ladyship noted, however, that the same would not apply

[356] *HOK Sport Ltd (formerly Lobb Partnership Ltd) v Aintree Racecourse Co Ltd* [2002] EWHC 3094 (TCC).
[357] ibid, [30].
[358] ibid, [90].
[359] ibid, [83].
[360] ibid, [89].
[361] *A Company v X and Others* [2020] EWHC 809 (TCC).
[362] ibid, [11].
[363] ibid, [50].
[364] ibid.
[365] ibid, [55].

to barristers' chambers that consist of self-employed practitioners, rather than an organisation where individuals share profits.[366]

The decision of O'Farrell J was upheld on appeal, albeit on a different basis.[367] The Court of Appeal acknowledged that there was no earlier authority in English law on the fiduciary duties that experts owed to their clients.[368] However, Coulson LJ held that the conflicts of interest clause in the retainer was sufficient in determining the scope and content of the experts' duties in the case and there was hence no need to investigate the existence of a freestanding fiduciary duty of loyalty.[369] Through the retainer, Secretariat undertook to avoid conflicts of interest for the duration of the contract.[370] The Court upheld the finding that there was a conflict of interest on the facts.[371]

V. Conclusion

This chapter identified and analysed the most significant decisions of the TCC on arbitration rendered between the Court's inception in 1998 until May 2022. The Court has made significant contributions in almost all aspects of arbitration law:

- in defining what is and what is not an arbitration agreement, bearing in mind that in the construction industry other forms of dispute resolution, such as expert determination, are also widespread;
- in putting forward a strong pro-arbitration approach to the principle of competence-competence, which, however, has being significantly constrained by the subsequent case law;
- in clarifying the principles of incorporation of arbitration clauses;
- in developing the principles that apply to the construction and enforceability of multi-tier clauses and conditions precedent;
- in examining the interaction between adjudication and arbitration;
- in clarifying the law on the enforceability of arbitration clauses between businesses and consumers;
- in the area of interim injunctions and the interaction between the court's powers under section 44 and emergency arbitration;
- in developing the law on impartiality of arbitrators;
- with respect to sections 67, 68 and 69 of the Act;
- in the field of the duties of experts in arbitration.

[366] ibid, [58].
[367] *Secretariat Consulting PTE Ltd & Ors v A Company* [2021] EWCA Civ 6.
[368] ibid, [35–9].
[369] ibid, [65–6].
[370] ibid, [69].
[371] ibid, [87–9].

The analysis in this chapter shows that, in relation to arbitration, the TCC has served the construction industry well. While the Act, and generally arbitration law, are a set of rules that apply across all industries, there are undeniably issues that are specific to construction, from the definition of what is an arbitration agreement as opposed to expert determination clauses to multi-tier clauses and conditions precedent, from the interaction of adjudication and arbitration to determination of substantive appeals under section 69. The TCC case law in these areas is of fundamental importance to the development of English arbitration law in a way that is responsive to the commercial reality and dynamics of the construction sector. But also in areas where, inevitably, the TCC's contribution to English arbitration law has been less closely linked to the Court's specialism, such as, for example, with respect to sections 67 and 68 of the Act or the duties of experts, the TCC has been instrumental in developing the law and has adopted novel approaches that have been followed elsewhere in the High Court and have been upheld by the higher courts.

11

The TCC and Developments in Technology and Innovation

DR STACY SINCLAIR AND SIMON TOLSON

Not only has the TCC shown itself to be at the forefront of procedural reform and innovation, but it too has been a pioneer and leader in the use of technology and digital innovation.

Other chapters in this book have highlighted the TCC's revolutionary approach over the years to procedural reform and innovation: for example, from its outset in 1873 when Lord Selborne introduced the concept of the Official Referees, to the early 1900s when Sir Francis Newbolt implemented his 'Scheme', which is considered to be an early form of case management, aiming to aid settlement. Further examples, to name just a few, include Official Referee George Alexander Scott's development of the Scott Schedule in the 1920s, the establishment of statutory adjudication in late 1990s, the introduction of the Construction and Engineering Pre-Action Protocol in 2000, and the Jackson Reforms in 2013 which included such measures as cost reforms and indeed 'hot-tubbing' (the simultaneous given of evidence by two or more witnesses), which was first trialled in the TCC, having previously been a feature of Sir Walker Kelly Carter's courtroom in the 1960s.

In 1996, Richard Susskind,[1] a pioneer in the emerging field of information technology and the law and IT advisor to the Lord Chief Justice, identified that the challenge 'is to investigate and devise innovative techniques for the provision of legal information, guidance, knowledge, and expertise; to develop new ways of meeting clients' needs'. A decade later, Mr Justice Jackson of the TCC demonstrated that there was willingness to innovate through the creation of a new court, with a new constitution of judges. A further ten years on, this innovation has rightly been credited with success.[2]

In addition to these prominent procedural innovations, the TCC was, and is, the vanguard in its use of technology and the digital transformation of the

[1] R Susskind, *The Future of Law: Facing the Challenges of Information Technology* (Oxford, OUP, 1996).

[2] I Collett, 'Sir Rupert Jackson and the TCC' (2018) 34(5) *Construction Law Journal* 392, 393.

courts. The TCC encouraged the use of email, was the first court to produce a protocol for the preparation and use of electronic bundles, has actively developed and supported procedures in respect of eDisclosure, was one of the first courts to implement the CE-File (electronic filing) in 2014 and, most recently, was at the forefront of deploying and utilising technology for virtual hearings during the COVID-19 pandemic.

Not only has the TCC adopted a proactive approach to digital transformation in respect of its internal operations and case management, it also has been resilient over the years in its response to the dynamic, digital developments of technology in the construction, energy and technology industries. Since the 1980s the Court has adapted from reviewing evidence of hardcopy blueprints and programmes, to electronic 2D AutoCAD files and excel spreadsheets, to today's Building Information Modelling (BIM): 3D federated models which include not only geometrical design information, but also construction information and other parameters, which have the potential to link time, cost and asset management software.

This chapter highlights some of the TCC's digital transformations and innovations from the 1990s to the present day, through its own adoption of technology, its ability to address and incorporate new technological developments in dispute resolution and its agility to hear cases concerning issues relating to new and rapidly evolving technologies in both the construction and wider technology industries.

I. Technology and Digital Innovation: A Timeline

Since the 1990s, the TCC consistently has addressed, adopted and spearheaded issues relating to technology and digital transformation. The following maps some of these important notable events and innovations, ranging from the use of technology in its operation and case management, to the implementation of guidance and reforms and the hearing of disputes in relation to new technological developments and advancements.

A. 1980s: Setting the Scene

Sir Terence Etherton, in his 2017 Lord Slynn Memorial Lecture on the Civil Court of the Future, stated:

> Since the 1990s there has been one reform after another. From Woolf to Jackson to Briggs, to Briggs again, and then once more to Jackson. Civil justice reform is a subject that never rests …[3]

[3] Sir Terence Etherton, Master of the Rolls, *The Civil Court of the Future, The Lord Slynn Memorial Lecture* (14 June 2017), www.judiciary.uk/wp-content/uploads/2017/06/slynn-lecture-mr-civil-court-of-the-future-20170615.pdf (accessed 17 October 2022) 1.

A subject that never rests: the same can be said of Microsoft updates and Apple iPhone releases (though of course at a much more exponential rate) as well as the technological reform and advancement in the TCC. Similar to the starting point for the civil justice reforms,[4] the starting point for the digital transformation certainly goes as far back as Civil Justice Review in the late 1980s.[5]

To begin, earlier in the 1980s, the Information Technology and the Courts Committee (ITAC) was formed, with eight delegates from the Lord Chancellor's Department, the Home Office, the Bar and the Law Society. The ITAC's first chairman was Lord Justice Neill, its first meeting took place in December 1985 and its purpose was 'to improve the running of the courts and to reform the costs of legal services by establishing better chains of communication between government departments and the legal profession'.[6] In February 1986 the ITAC set up a small working group to respond to the Civil Justice Review's consultation paper on personal injuries litigation. The ITAC working group considered the use of expert systems to help high street litigation solicitors, the establishment of legal information databases, the implementation of computerised judicial case control and the widespread use of electronic communications. In July 1986 the working group submitted two papers to the Civil Justice Review suggesting 'all the different ways in which technology could help solve some of the issues with which the review team was grappling in the field of personal injuries litigation', and a year later it advocated 'greater investment in debt recovery systems and in list, case management and management information systems'.[7] The Civil Justice Review's final report included recommendations for the use of computers to manage court listings and that a major programme should be mounted with the aim of improving the quality and quantity of management information available to both judges and administrators.

Sir Henry Brooke, a member of the ITAC who championed the introduction of technology into the judicial process since the 1980s and was more involved than anyone in the long struggle for digitisation of the courts,[8] noted that 'very little was done to implement either of these recommendations, so far as the judiciary was concerned'.[9]

[4] ibid, 2.

[5] Sir Maurice Hodgson, *Civil Justice Review, Report of the Review Body on Civil Justice*, 1988.

[6] H Brooke, *Technology and the Judicial Process*, in 'Essays in Honour of Sir Brian Neill: The Quintessential Judge' (London, LexisNexis UK, 2003). Also available on Sir Henry Brooke's website, sirhenrybrooke.me/2015/10/25/my-2002-essay-on-technology-and-the-judicial-process/ (accessed 17 October 2022). The essay provides a detailed history of the efforts to introduce technology into to the courts from 1985–2002.

[7] ibid.

[8] Etherton (n 3).

[9] ibid, Brooke (n 4). Brooke also recounts a time when he met with Lord Justice Neill, ITACS then second president, in his room in the Law Courts. Lord Justice Neill said that: 'he thought he had joined the movement far too early. Since 1973 the cause of technology and the law had gone backwards almost as often as it had gone forwards, particularly with one over-ambitious project … He said, however, that things were now going forward again. He had nearly persuaded the Lord Chancellor (Lord Hailsham) to approve the creation of a joint committee of civil servants and practising lawyers who would study the place which technology could play in our court system …'

Then, as Sir Henry Brooke notes, in February 1989, a working party of the Society for Computer and Law (SCL) prepared a paper advocating the use of computers in the Official Referees' courts. He highlights that the Official Referees 'were chosen for special treatment because the six Official Referees were all housed together in a newly refurbished court building, and the courts' clientele contained many for whom the use of modern technology in their businesses was a commonplace'. The message in the SCL paper is summarised as:

> We conclude that the computerisation of the administration will:
>
> (i) provide the court with the ability to monitor and report on the state and progress of all cases in the Official Referees' list, and take appropriate early action;
> (ii) improve trial listing performance;
> (iii) encourage early settlement of cases by monitoring compliance with orders such as a costs estimate order, or other orders requiring action to be taken which is directed to be notified to the court;
> (iv) speed up the production of formal orders and certificates;
> (v) cater for cashless payments of fees;
> (vi) remove the need for stamping of documents to be carried out in the Royal Courts of Justice;
> (vii) automate accounting procedures.
>
> Further, if the proposed computerisation of the administration is linked to an external network accessible to solicitors, this would:
>
> (i) provide for electronic issue of writs;
> (ii) provide for the electronic issue of summonses, and the fixing of dates for the hearing;
> (iii) enable electronic communication with court staff or court clerks, to supplement the use of the telephone and fax.

It certainly was the case that the users of the Official Referees' Court were already using modern technology and were well-placed to be leading and contributing to technological reform in court. For example our firm, Fenwick Elliott LLP, a London law firm established in 1986 specialising in construction, engineering and energy law, was one of the Court's clientele at that time – a frequent visitor in the Official Referees' corridor. By 1986 Fenwick Elliott had rolled out the use of networked computers across the firm including accounts. We used *fast fax*, large format, 24-inch daisy wheel printers for printing programmes and plans. In 1989, we even used a mobile fax machine to transmit an image from the outback in Australia to our office in the Strand. Our clients too were already using computers and other technologies for design, construction and communication. Blueprints and hardcopy drawings and documents were still in abundance; however, software for computer-aided design had been released for commercial use in the early 1980s[10] and by the early 1990s Fenwick Elliott was advising on and reviewing evidence contained in AutoCAD and MicroStation files (.dwg and .dgn files). By late 1996, a few clients were emailing us as we were one of the few firms to embrace

[10] Autodesk released the first version of AutoCAD in December 1982 (also known as AutoCAD 86) and Bentley released the first version of PseudoStation in 1985, the predecessor to MicroStation which it released in February 1986.

the internet and email. By 1997 we had announced to clients the progress we had made in our IT infrastructure.[11] The SCL was spot on: the use of modern technology in the businesses of the Court's clientele was commonplace.

Mr Simon Tolson, now Senior Partner of Fenwick Elliott, recalls:

> When I first started in the law, and at Fenwick Elliott, my initial introduction to construction was at the Official Referees' Court in a case before His Honour Judge Fox Andrews QC (then known affectionately in my firm as 'Foxy'): Stanor Electric Ltd v Mansell Ltd.[12] It was heard in the Official Referees' corridor on the third floor of the QBD within the RCJ, deep within the Gothic Revival cathedral of that building (one of George Edmund Street's last designs which cost nearly £1,000,000 with fittings, decoration and furnishings and required 11 years of construction). It was an interesting liquidated damages penalty case and Paul Darling OBE QC was then a very junior counsel.
>
> I remember ascending the stairs and using the old wire cage lift to leave, thinking nothing had changed for 100 years. The corridor was so tucked away in the RCJ that it took two or three excursions to commit to memory which dog legs to go down to safely return. It certainly was not the corridor with the red linoleum, which I learnt was the Judge's corridor!
>
> Whilst hardcopy documents were everywhere, we regularly received electronic files, including Primavera P3 data files, from our clients.

Again, with regard to the SCL's recommendations in 1989, Sir Brooke noted that 'very little came of any of this'. However, despite his disappointment, the SCL's recommendations 'formed part of the thinking behind the court modernisation plans developed by the Court Service a decade later',[13] as well as laying the foundation for improved technologies in the Official Referees' Court.

B. 1990: Improved Technology for the Official Referees' Court[14]

In 1990, following the Official Referees' Users' Committee request to the Information Technology Board for the Royal Courts of Justice, chaired by Lord Justice Neill,

[11] 'During the course of the last year, there have been a number of new developments at Fenwick Elliott on the IT front. The most significant has been the installation of a new file server (the firm's fourth) dedicated to managing Internet browsing and Internet mail for all members of our team. Every member of staff now has their own personal Internet email address and is able to gain access to the World Wide Web using our newly installed high speed ISDN lines. All the firm e-mail addresses can be found in the Firm Directory. We have now also recently developed our own web page, which includes personal profiles of our entire legal team. Our web address is www.fenwickelliott.co.uk. The ability to electronically search through vast quantities of case documentation continues to be a priority, with the ongoing development of our own in-house software, which in turn utilises a number of well-established software applications for document scanning, imaging and OCR. Today, as documents are produced by our word processors, they are automatically word-indexed for future reference.'

[12] *Stanor Electric Ltd v Mansell Ltd* (1988) CILL 399.

[13] Brooke (n 4).

[14] 'Improved technology for Official Referees' Court' (1990) 16(1) *Commonwealth Law Bulletin* 370.

the Lord Chancellor's Department agreed to fund a £20,000 project in the Official Referees' Court for improved technology. The project was to evaluate enhanced facilities for display and demonstration of expert witness charts, documents, sketches and models. Depending on the findings, other courtrooms would be equipped with similar technology, if proved successful. Whilst this was not the full computerisation of administration that the SCL had proposed, nevertheless a step in the right direction for a court whose cases and users were ripe for technological reform.

As it is a specialist court with, at that time, over 80 per cent of its cases involving the construction industry, the Official Referees' cases involved complex construction and engineering projects, typically involving references to documents with small detail, photographs and video-recordings as evidence. Handling these hard-copy documents and electronic files, whilst attempting to isolate the relevant detail, often resulted in a complicated and sometimes lengthy processes.

To address these issues, the pilot project, presided over by Judge Bowsher QC, involved installing closed circuit television monitors, with 'zoom' and video facilities, in courtroom number 8. This allowed for 'simultaneous display in colour of original documents to the judge, witness and parties to the case being heard', which cut down the time it took for all participants to have access to the exhibits.

The reference to 'zoom' facilities above of course is not reference to the video conferencing platform, 'Zoom', which was founded in 2011 and whose stock skyrocketed in 2020 in the COVID-19 pandemic, rising by more than 370 per cent.[15] The zoom facilities installed in courtroom number 8, rather, were those facilities that allowed small details on plans, photographs and models to be magnified and displayed on the screens. Presenting video-recordings also became more effective and efficient with these functionalities.

The new equipment aimed to speed up the process of referencing and examining expert evidence, which is frequent in these types of case, enabling, 'literally in seconds, all concerned have the same detail before them for consideration'. The project was also considering 'installing a computer interface so that not 'only computer graphics could be used but documents on litigants' computer disks could be offered in evidence more easily'.

In the early 1990s, the courts also saw the introduction and rise of LiveNote – software which revolutionised court recording and court reporting services globally. Graham Smith-Bernal, a British entrepreneur and inventor who left school at the age of 16, became a court stenographer by the age of 18 and before 30 had established his own 100-person court reporting company, developed a programme that instantaneously would turn oral evidence, the spoken word, into writing. This would allow lawyers and judges to view and annotate real-time transcripts

[15] S Klebnikov, 'Zoom Stock Skyrockets Over 40% After Blowout Quarter, And It Expects To Keep Rising' (*Forbes*, 1 September 2020), www.forbes.com/sites/sergeiklebnikov/2020/09/01/zoom-stock-skyrockets-over-40-after-blowout-quarter-and-it-expects-to-keep-rising/?sh=258674369f18 (accessed 17 October 2022).

of court proceedings.[16] Smith-Bernal's programme, LiveNote, was commercially available by 1991 and within three years 'had become a virtual standard on major litigation in the UK'.[17]

The Official Referees' Court, like a number of the courts, implemented LiveNote by the mid-1990s.

C. 1991: Official Referees' Solicitors Association IT Protocol

In September 1990, the Official Referees Solicitors Association (ORSA)[18] was formed to promote the interests of solicitors and their clients conducting business in the Official Referees' Courts and related domestic and international arbitration. In 1991, ORSA formed an Information Technology Sub-Committee. It aimed to promote the use of technology in litigation and arbitration and subsequently drafted the ORSA Protocol, Version 1.0. The purpose of the ORSA Protocol was to 'facilitate and encourage the exchange of information amongst users of the Official Referees' Courts through the use of information technology (IT)'. The Protocol envisaged that parties implement it as soon as possible after the start of proceedings and voluntarily, in the spirit of co-operation, complete and exchange Questionnaires, involving their respective IT managers or advisers.

The Court supported the Protocol, it was successfully used for several years, and was commended in Lord Woolf's Interim and Final Reports in 1995–96:

> To encourage greater usage within the professions, I would like to call on the energies and experience of the Society for Computers and Law, assisted, where appropriate, by ITAC (the Information Technology and Courts Committee) to build on the solid work of the Official Referees' Solicitors' Association which produced the ORSA Protocol. This is ORSA's set of standard formats which encourage opposing parties to agree compatible systems and, where possible, to share the costs of setting up these systems. I have in mind that an extended protocol might be developed for use across the entire civil justice system.[19]

Following Lord Woolf's Final Report, the Sub-Committee updated and revised the Protocol in April 1998 ('The ORSA IT Protocol, Version 2.0') taking into

[16] By 1997 Fenwick Elliott was informing clients in newsletters that Smith Bernal & Co. offers the facility of a transcript that is prepared in electronic form, virtually instantaneous: 'At the end of every day, they give us a transcript of the day's proceedings in hard copy and/or floppy disk form. Again, the latter will enable text retrieval systems to locate, within a few seconds, any occurrence of a given word. In a lengthy trial, where the transcripts will soon occupy several lever arch files, this facility we and counsel have found extremely useful.'

[17] *The Evolution of the Digital Courtroom*, Interview with Graham Smith-Bernal, 31 August 2016, legaltalknetwork.com/podcasts/law-technology-now/2016/08/evolution-digital-courtroom/ (accessed 17 October 2022).

[18] Now known as the Technology and Construction Solicitors' Association (TECSA), tecsa.org.uk/.

[19] Lord Woolf, *Access to Justice (Final Report)*, ch 21, Maintaining the Pace of Change, webarchive.nationalarchives.gov.uk/ukgwa/20060213223540/http://www.dca.gov.uk/civil/final/contents.htm (accessed 17 October 2022).

account changes in the use of technology by solicitors, barristers and the courts at that time. For those that remember, it is heart-warming to see references to the floppy disk, the CD ROM and PKZip. Version 2.0 referred to serving documents in 'Word 7.0 format', 'Word97', 'WordPerfect v8.1', checking all documents for viruses (with the recommendation to use Dr Solomon's virus checking software) and 'if any one documents is less than 1.4 megabytes, it should be served on 3 ½ inch high density floppy disk, without using any file compression technology'. Version 2.0 even provided guidance on OCRing:

- Once the image has been stored on the computer there are many packages that will attempt an OCR (optical character recognition) in order to identify the words on the page. Typically, the OCRing of clean printed pages is near perfect, but OCRing of manuscript text is more or less hopeless. Faxes or poor photocopies will result in some but not all words being correctly recognised.
- The OCRed text will, to be useful, need to be stored, but typically takes only about 1/20th of the disk space of the image.
- Once stored, OCRed text may be word searched by many standard packages, such that any occurrence of any word can be located automatically.

The extent to which the Protocol was used in practice is questionable, but nevertheless, it really was ahead of its time and began to tackle eDisclosure issues that we still see today.

D. 1995: First Use of CD-ROM Technology in Case Presentation – The First Paperless Trial?

The Court' s technology enhancements in 1990 paved the way for what is believed to be the first use of CD-ROM technology in the presentation of a case at trial[20] – a case which has become known as 'the first paperless trial'.[21]

John Mowlem & Company v Eagle Star and Others[22] concerned a dispute over the 580-home Carlton Gate complex in west London. It was a protracted, multi-party dispute, arising out of the termination of Mowlem's management contract with Carlton Gate Development in 1989. Having first started proceedings (unsuccessfully) against Carlton Gate Development,[23] and then successfully winning an arbitration, Mowlem ultimately commenced litigation proceedings against Declan Kelly Group, Eagle Star Insurance Co Ltd and the architect, PRP, for the £12 million the arbitrator had awarded Mowlem, but had not been paid. In 1993, Judge John Lloyd QC in the Queen's Bench Division, Official Referees' Business, first heard an

[20] 'Computer helps in Carlton Gate battle' (*Construction News*, 2 February 1995) www.constructionnews.co.uk/archive/computer-helps-in-carlton-gate-battle-02-02-1995/ (accessed 17 October 2022).

[21] See ch 5 in this volume.

[22] *John Mowlem & Company v Eagle Star and Others* (1993) 62 BLR 126, (1995) CILL 1047.

[23] (1991) 51 BLR 104.

application to strike out parts of Mowlem's claim,[24] a dispute that ended up in the Court of Appeal regarding a point of interpretation.[25] In 1995 Judge Bowsher QC in the Official Referees' Court then heard the substantive dispute (unreported).

At the time, the case was thought to be one of the biggest cases before the Official Referees in years. Given the length of the dispute, the number of parties involved and the complexity of the facts, the allegations and the evidence, legal costs had soared and the time required for trial was extensive given the amount of witness evidence.

From a technology perspective, the case is significant for two reasons. First, during the trial, the parties presented their case on-screen, using CD-ROM technology. This enabled exhibits to be presented quickly and efficiently, cutting down the time required for cross-examination of witnesses and experts. Second, it is believed that this is one of the first cases to use a degree of coding (or electronically categorising) of documents, which allowed the trial bundle to be operated from a large computer in the courtroom.

In addition, whilst not relating to technology, Judge Bowsher QC's case management was also procedurally innovative. Seemingly following the Lord Chief Justice's new Practice Direction of 24 January 1995 (Order 18 Rule 7 of the Rules of the Supreme Court), known as 'Cut the Waffle',[26] Judge Bowsher severely reduced the estimated trial timetable:

> … Mowlem's Leading Counsel Charles Falconer estimated 90 court days for cross-examination of the Defendant's 26 witnesses. Judge Bowsher has, however, guillotined cross-examination to one day each in respect of two of the witnesses, and one hour each for the rest, thereby reducing the 90 day estimate to about 10 days.[27]

In 1990, Jeremy Glover, now a Partner at Fenwick Elliott LLP, was an articled clerk at Fishburn Boxer, the solicitors acting for the architects, PRP. Mr Glover recalls:[28]

> Whilst it might seem run of the mill today, the Mowlem case certainly was remarkable in terms of its use of technology – something which was not typically used or available at that time. There was a significant amount of documents, and most, if not all were in hardcopy. The architect's documents literally were scattered in a house and the contractor's documents filled a shipping container. All of the documents were collected, scanned in and coded. There was a large computer in the courtroom, and the trial bundle was electronic. The operator was able to locate both the pleadings and exhibits 'relatively' quickly and display them on the monitors in the courtroom. This, combined with Judge Bowsher's directions to axe the time available to every party's Counsel to cross-examine witnesses, greatly expedited the timetable, leading to quite novel and innovative proceedings for its time – and indeed ahead of its time.

Mowlem v Eagle Star is an early example, if not the first example, of the TCC's use of technology for more efficient and cost-effective proceedings.

[24] (1993) 62 BLR 126.
[25] (1995) CILL 1047.
[26] *Editorial Comment*, (1995) CILL 1009.
[27] *The Guillotine Falls …*, (1995) CILL 1042a.
[28] Telephone interview with Dr Stacy Sinclair (October 2022).

E. The Late 1990s: Electronic Copies of Judgments

By the late 1990s, the pressure was building for electronic copies of TCC judgments to be made available. At that time a few construction law firms were sent WordPerfect file copies. As Fenwick Elliott edited the Construction Industry Law Letter (CILL), we were one such recipient. One interesting piece of ephemera from that time was a meeting on 31 March 1997. Our then Senior Partner Robert Fenwick Elliott wrote to fellow ORSA Committee Members saying:

> … I had a meeting with Judge Bowsher on Monday of this week in order to discuss the possibility of once again getting Official Referee's Judgments available in electronic form for our members. The meeting was attended by Paul Letman of 3 Paper Buildings, who has been appointed by ORBA. The Lord Chancellors' Department was invited, but did not turn up to the meeting.
>
> … I estimated that the total number of Official Referees cases which are either reported or made available for reporting is about 50 per year, and I estimated that the average length of these judgments is of the order of 30 pages (sometimes more sometimes less). It appears that on the Internet the standard unit of storage space is 5 megabytes, although of course one can buy more. However, in order to keep costs down, old judgments would have to be removed, and provided the cases are left on the Internet for 6 months or so, we saw no difficulty with that. Depending on costs, it may be sensible that there should be an editorial filter, provided by ORSA and/or ORBA, to cut out non-relevant cases.
>
> There is inevitably going to be a recurring charge … In principle, and on the assumption that ORSA and ORBA share the cost 50/50, do you think that we would be up for an expenditure of £750, plus a bit more for blank discs etc.?

1999 was quite a year for technology and the law. Following a 'Free the Law' meeting in November 1999 at Chatham House,[29] the SCL convened a UK Steering Group comprising Lord Saville, Lord Justice Brooke, Richard Susskind, Carol Tullo (Controller, Her Majesty's Stationery Office and Queen's Printer), Amanda Finlay (Lord Chancellor's Department) and Laurence West-Knights (barrister). The UK Steering Group succeeded in obtaining funding as well as permissions for the use of UK data in a free access service. That was the start of BAILII. It was established as an independent charity in order to make primary legal information from all the jurisdictions of the UK and from the Republic of Ireland freely available over the internet.

These pioneers saw the potential of online services and the need for a service free to users. Sir Henry Brooke, whose blog is still available and remains an inspiration,[30] wrote: 'From the time I joined the English Court of Appeal in 1996,

[29] The meeting was sponsored jointly by the Society for Computers & Law (SCL), the Information Technology and the Courts Committee (ITAC), the British and Irish Legal Education and Technology Association (BILETA), the British & Irish Association of Law Librarians (BIALL) and the Institute of Advanced Legal Studies (IALS).

[30] sirhenrybrooke.me/ (accessed 17 October 2022).

I was determined to establish a level playing-field in access to the law.' He quoted Ronan Keane, then the recently retired Chief Justice of Ireland, at the time of BAILII's fifth anniversary:

> [I]t is indeed extraordinary, and in some ways, I suppose, redeems one's faith in human nature that a project can be so successful when driven by nothing but the dedication and commitment of the people concerned … BAILII has come to its great success over these five years in having a … mission in life … to make sure that legal information is accessible to everybody who needs legal information; be they judges, be they lawyers, be they persons engaged in the teaching or research of law, or be they the ordinary citizen who wants to and is entitled to find out what the law is on any given topic.

In March 2000, the Solicitors Journal reported that in same week it saw the stock market flotation of a ridiculously overvalued 'dot com', it also saw the launch of a minimally funded 'dot org' whose value to the UK lawyer is likely to be immense. BAILII, the British and Irish Legal Information Institute, was launched at www.bailii.org and was the first website to provide free access to case law and legislation from numerous British and Irish courts and legislatures, with a single search engine and uniform data formats. At that point the site included 14 databases from five jurisdictions (UK, England and Wales, Scotland, Northern Ireland and the Republic of Ireland), comprising over 400 megabytes of legal materials. As it came to pass, BAILII was indeed a roaring success establishing itself as the go-to free electronic source of new case law.

F. 2009: The TCC Electronic Working Pilot Scheme

In 1996, Lord Woolf set out his vision for a new civil justice system in his report *'Access to Justice'*,[31] which included the introduction of a comprehensive IT system for the civil courts. Yet despite the introduction, improvements and state of the art technology implemented in the Court in the 1990s regrettably, even in the midst of a global information technology boom, the road to modernisation of the court service continued to be as long and arduous as it was in the last century.[32] By the early 2000s, the condition of the Court's IT infrastructure was less than ideal. Lord Justice Jackson regarded the Court's IT system as a 'patchwork quilt':

> Thirteen years have now elapsed since Lord Woolf published his final report. Ten years have elapsed since the introduction of the Civil Procedure Rules (the "CPR"). The courts still do not have an IT system which is adequate for the delivery of civil justice at proportionate cost. Instead we have a patchwork quilt of different IT systems which have evolved without proper co-ordination.[33]

[31] Lord Woolf, *Access to Justice (Final Report)*.

[32] 'Technology failures', *Law Society Gazette*, 13 May 2004, www.lawgazette.co.uk/news/technology-failures/42016.article (accessed 30 October 2022).

[33] R Jackson, *Review of Civil Litigation Costs Final Report (December 2009)*, ch 43, Information Technology, para 1.3, TSO, www.judiciary.uk/wp-content/uploads/JCO/Documents/Reports/jackson-final-report-140110.pdf (accessed 17 October 2022).

Lord Justice Brooke, then judge in charge of modernisation of the Court Service, drawing parallels, also lamented the fact that it had taken 20 years from the first polite request by judges during the First World War, for electricity to be installed in their chambers.[34]

The Court' s various IT systems had been installed over a number of years and were not compatible with each other – interoperability is not simply a new challenge of today's technology issues. Lord Justice Jackson considered that a new, holistic electronic system, that would save time and costs, was needed. He noted that one such system (under the Electronic Filing and Document Management (EFDM) project) had been planned in 2008 but was halted due to a lack of funding.[35] His final report on the Review of Civil Litigation Costs set out measures aiming to reduce significantly the 'paper mountains' at courts and therefore enable staff to concentrate on court administration.

Nevertheless, by the time Lord Justice Jackson's report was published, the TCC already had a pilot scheme for electronic working up and running which was proving successful.[36] Over the years the TCC has led the march on electronic working pilot schemes, with the 2009 pilot being the first.

On 20 July 2009 the TCC commenced the pilot scheme and started electronic working: all cases issued in the TCC were to be either issued electronically or be scanned in so that there was an electronic case file.[37] All proceedings, whether the claims were commenced electronically or by a paper claim form issued after that date, could take advantage of the electronic issuing and filing process (known as 'e-working' at the TCC):

> One of the main advantages of electronic working is that parties are able to issue a claim form and then take all further steps by issuing or filing documents on-line. There has been great enthusiasm for the scheme in the TCC. Where the claimant issues a claim form in hard copy, the TCC Registry then scans the document and provides the claimant with an electronic link which enables all the parties to continue those proceedings by electronic working as if the claim form had been issued on-line.[38]

This Electronic Working Pilot Scheme was introduced as a supplementary Practice Direction to CPR 5.5 and supported Part 7 claim forms, Part 8 claim forms and pre-issues applications. A few months after its introduction, HMCS hosted an 'e-Working Awareness Workshop' at the RCJ. Mr Justice Ramsey (the judge in charge of the TCC at that time) and representatives of several law firms who were using e-Working attended. Comments were positive, noting its simplicity, its speed and its telephone support service and HMCS reported that around 20 per cent of TCC cases were using e-Working. Despite some notable room for improvement

[34] 'Technology failures' (n 32).

[35] ibid, para 4.1.

[36] M Rousell, 'Electronic working in the TCC, is it e-working?' (*PLC Construction*, 21 October 2009), constructionblog.practicallaw.com/electronic-working-in-the-tcc-is-it-e-working/.

[37] *Annual Report of the Construction and Technology Court 2009–2010*, www.judiciary.uk/wp-content/uploads/JCO/Documents/Reports/tcc-ann-report-2010.pdf (accessed 17 October 2022).

[38] ibid, 7.

(eg, being able to pay the Court fee online), the pilot was deemed a success at that point in time.[39]

G. 2012 (20 April): Set-back in Electronic Working

Ultimately, however, the attempt at electronic working in the TCC between 2009 and 2012 was not wholly successful. It certainly was cutting-edge, leading the industry and moving the professions forward, though more time, training and technical advancement was needed.

Perhaps adoption proved challenging due to the inability for parties to pay online, the fact that parties could not access the Court case file, and/or the issues with acceptable file sizes and other technical issues. No doubt difficulties in changing existing mindsets and established practises were also factors (as often is the case when implementing new technology and software). At this point, only 10 per cent of cases were file electronically, but nevertheless, the Court was optimistic.

On 26 March 2012, Lord Justice Jackson delivered his thirteenth lecture in the Implementation Programme, '*Reforming the Civil Justice System – The Role of IT*'.[40] First Lord Justice Jackson opened with a quote from Steve Jobs, seemingly suggesting that simply because users currently are not able to use certain technologies, it does not follow that you should not implement that technology: 'When Apple first started out, people couldn't type. We realized: Death would eventually take care of this.'[41] His paper went on to emphasise the importance of IT for the future of the courts, its importance for specific reforms, and the need for an integrated court IT system. He stated that we cannot afford not to develop an integrated court IT system:

> I would respectfully suggest that **<u>we cannot afford not</u>** to develop an integrated court IT system. Britain has long been and must remain a major centre for international dispute resolution. In those circumstances there should be no question of allowing our own court IT to lag behind that of competitor jurisdictions. [Original emphasis by Lord Justice Jackson]

Despite this plea for support, on 20 April 2012, HM Courts and Tribunals Service (HMCTS) announced that the electronic working system introduced in the Rolls Building would be shut down.[42] The Royal Courts of Justice e-working mailbox

[39] Rousell (n 36).

[40] Lord Justice Jackson, *Reforming the Civil Justice System – The Role of IT*, 13th Lecture in the Implementation Programme, 26 March 2012, Society for Computers and Law, www.judiciary.uk/wp-content/uploads/JCO/Documents/Speeches/lj-jackson-lecture-13-it-society.pdf (accessed 17 October 2022).

[41] Steve Jobs, interview with Walt Mossberg at the first annual 'All Things D' conference, 28 May 2003.

[42] *Electronic working system shut down*, PLC Dispute Resolution, Thomson Reuters Practical Law.

was no longer available. HMCTS remained committed to delivering e-working, though there was no target date for implementation at that point.

Mr Justice Edwards-Stuart had opened the 2011 TeCSA/TECBAR annual joint conference, on the subject of '*E-disclosure and e-Working in the TCC*', with the following General Ferdinand Foch WWI quote:

> Hard pressed on my right. My centre is yielding. Impossible to manoeuvre. Situation excellent. I am attacking.[43]

Despite the setback and the less than ideal take up of e-working, not only was Lord Justice Jackson and Mr Justice Edwards-Stuart optimistic and prepared to fight back, so too was the TCC, as we see below.

H. 2012 (23 April): Introduction of Electronic Applications in the Central London County Court TCC

Despite the announcement on 20 April 2012 that electronic working would be shut down, all was not lost. Digital innovation in the TCC carried on – this time in the Central London County Court TCC.

On 23 April 2012 the Central London County Court TCC began a pilot scheme to see whether it should introduce applications by email.[44] The '*Protocol for TCC E-applications list*' was open for an experimental period, aimed to provide a simpler method of making applications and was open to any application where all parties were represented by solicitors.[45] The advantages were thought to be convenience to solicitors, the speed within which orders could be made (TCC list judges were aiming to deal with all applications within 10 days of receipt) and the reduction of administrative burden on the Court.

It is noteworthy that whilst the aim was complete electronic working, cyber security concerns even at that time continued to demand hardcopy submissions. The Protocol reminded solicitors that email was not a secure medium:

> Solicitors are reminded that e-mail is not a secure medium. In the unusual cases where it is necessary to include commercially sensitive information in the evidence in support of the application such evidence should be sent in hard copy marked 'For the immediate attention of the Judge in charge of the TCC list'.[46]

[43] L Collett, 'E-working in the TCC – a view from the Bench' (*Practical Law Construction Blog*, 6 July 2011), constructionblog.practicallaw.com/e-working-in-the-tcc-a-view-from-the-bench/ (accessed 17 October 2022).

[44] *Electronic applications in the TCC CLCC [Archived]*, LexisNexis PSL (Dispute Resolution, Key DR developments; Pilot schemes), www.lexisnexis.com/uk/lexispsl/disputeresolution/document/393750/55VR-T911-F18B-81FR-00000-00/Electronic-applications-in-the-TCC-CLCC-%5BArchived%5D (accessed 17 October 2022).

[45] *Protocol for TCC E-applications list*, 2012, LexisNexis PSL, Att_1666235005020.pdf (accessed 17 October 2022).

[46] ibid, para 8.

I. 2013: TCC Supports the TeCSA/SCL/TECBAR eDisclosure Protocol

Whilst electronic working in terms of filing and case management was proving difficult to adopt and implement, the TCC continued to take positive steps in terms of the electronic disclosure of documents and data ('eDisclosure').

In March 2013, in response to the introduction of the new Civil Procedure Rules and the Jackson cost management reforms, TeCSA,[47] TECBAR[48] and the SCL[49] jointly proposed and began to draft an eDisclosure Protocol.[50] They resolved to produce much-needed support for their members (along with other practitioners and court users) in handling eDisclosure and the many issues that it was raising.[51] The Protocol and its associated guidance underpinned the operation of the then newly introduced Practice Direction 31B and the new Disclosure Report and Electronic Questionnaire.

In October 2013, the incoming senior judge in the TCC, Mr Justice Edwards-Stuart, confirmed that the proposed TeCSA/SCL/TECBAR eDisclosure Protocol ('the Protocol') would have the support of the TCC Judges and would be incorporated into the TCC Guide in the future.[52] On 1 November 2013 the three organisations jointly launched the Protocol, as part of an 'eDisclosure Pack', which included an introduction, the Protocol, guidelines to the Protocol and a guide to eDisclosure.[53] The TCC adopted the Protocol on 1 January 2014 and included it in the TCC Guide. Paragraph 11.2.3 of the TCC Guide made it clear that the Protocol was not mandatory, but if the parties were not able to agree a suitable alternative, the Court is likely to order the use of the Protocol.[54] Version 0.2 of the Protocol was issued just over a year later on 9 January 2015, reflecting user feedback. In general, the industry positively received the Protocol and it was adopted on a number of cases, including the high-profile TCC case of *Accolade Wines v Volkerfitzpatrick and others*[55] in 2014, which involved six parties and raised both complex legal and technical issues.

The TCC's adoption of the eDisclosure Protocol was significant given the pivotal role evidence plays in the majority of construction, engineering, energy

[47] Technology and Construction Solicitors' Association, tecsa.org.uk/ (accessed 17 October 2022).

[48] Technology and Construction Bar Association, tecbar.org/ (accessed 17 October 2022).

[49] Society of Computers and Law, www.scl.org/ (accessed 17 October 2022).

[50] TeCSA formed a sub-committee comprising member of its full Committee, Marie-Claire O'Hara (then of Nabarro), Andrew Kennel (then of FTI Consulting) and Andrew Haslam (Allvision) who were instrumental in producing the draft.

[51] *Introduction to the TeCSA/SCL/TECBAR eDisclosure Protocol*, tecsa.org.uk/wp-content/uploads/2020/11/TECSA_eDisclosure_Protocol_Vr0.1_2013.pdf (accessed 17 October 2022).

[52] ibid, 2.

[53] *TeCSA/SCL/TECBAR eDisclosure Protocol Pack*, tecsa.org.uk/wpcontent/uploads/2020/11/TECSA_eDisclosure_Protocol_Vr0.1_2013.pdf (accessed 17 October 2022).

[54] *The Technology and Construction Court Guide*, 2nd edn, Issued 3 October 2005, third revision with effect from 3 March 2014 (HMCTS, 2014).

[55] Settled before trial. For further information on the feedback see: S Paradisi, 'The TCC e-disclosure protocol: a year on' (*Practical Law Construction Blog*, 14 January 2015), constructionblog.practicallaw.com/the-tcc-edisclosure-protocol-a-year-on/ (accessed 17 October 2022).

and technology cases. New types of data and evidence were emerging, new technologies were developing (both in terms of construction technology as well legal technology, such as eDisclosure review platforms) and the sheer amount of data and documents was increasing. More issues began to arise in respect of disclosure and TeCSA, SCL and TECBAR highlighted various disputes which concerned disclosure issues from 2007 to 2013.[56] In the TCC, Judge Ramsey heard claims for costs due to disorganised, irrelevant and duplicated documents, and errors in the review of these documents (*Vector Investments v J D Williams*[57] and *West African Gas Pipeline Company Limited v Willbros Global Holdings Inc*[58]), Judge Akenhead heard an application for an extension of time to deal with eDisclosure (*Phaestos and another v Ho*[59]) and Judge Coulson heard an application for an adjournment of a trial, one of the reasons being the unexpected amount of electronic disclosure (*Elliot Group v GECC UK*[60]).

The TCC was alive to the increasing issues of eDisclosure and the emergence of new types and sources of data, and was at the forefront of addressing them in case management and administration. For example, in 2015 the Guidelines to Version 0.2 of the Protocol[61] included a new paragraph 1.4 which recognised the rise of social media and the new types and sources of evidence that was yet to come:

> It is important to consider all possible sources of documentation or data, including 'non-traditional' sources such as social media (Twitter, Facebook, LinkedIn etc.), instant messaging, audio data and photographs including, where relevant, associated metadata. A decision can then be made about whether each source is likely to yield disclosable documents and, if so, whether on balance it is proportionate in terms of time and costs to collect such documents. Decisions made on each source should be documented in case a decision needs to be revisited and/or justified at a later date. *It should be noted that as new forms of communication emerge, the types of 'non-traditional' sources of documents will change and expand.* [Emphasis added.]

J. 2014: The CE-File – The Next Phase of Electronic Filing in the TCC

Although the electronic working system had been shut down officially in April 2012, in due course a new system was developed. On 10 November 2014, the TCC

[56] *eDisclosure Case Notes* (TeCSA, 2013), tecsa.org.uk/wp-content/uploads/2020/11/TECSA_eDisclosure_Case_Notes_Various_2013.pdf (accessed 17 October 2022).

[57] *Vector Investments v J D Williams* [2009] EWHC 3601 (TCC).

[58] *West African Gas Pipeline Company Limited v Willbros Global Holdings Inc* [2012] EWHC 396 (TCC).

[59] *Phaestos and another v Ho* [2012] EWHC 1996 (TCC).

[60] *Elliot Group v GECC UK* [2010] EWHC 409 (TCC).

[61] *Guidelines to the TeCSA/SCL/TECBAR eDisclosure Protocol*, Version 0.2, 9 January 2015, tecsa.org.uk/wp-content/uploads/2020/11/TECSA_eDisclosure_Guidelines_to_eDisclosure_Protocol_Vr0.2_2015.pdf (accessed 17 October 2022).

introduced a new pilot for electronic court filing procedures, known as the 'CE-File'. The new filing procedure applied to all claims, including adjudication enforcement claims and Part 7 claims, as well as Tomlin orders. The TCC gave guidance on how and what should be scanned and submitted electronically.[62] Payment on-line was possible and a number of technical issues worked out.

Again we see the TCC at the forefront – the remainder of the Rolls Building went live on the new Electronic Working Pilot Scheme on 16 November 2015, under the under Practice Direction 51O (PD 51O), with an original pilot period of one year. The pilot period was extended several times and ultimately, the use of the electronic working became compulsory in the Business and Property Courts on 25 April 2017. The current extension expires on 6 April 2023.[63]

Initially, within the first year or two, the uptake of the CE-File was still slow.[64] However, now, eight years on, surely there can be no turning back with the ambitions of today's digital world (despite the fact that PD 51O is still described as a 'pilot'). Solicitors are well-familiar with issuing claims online and the CE-File is part and parcel of issuing a claim and subsequent documents, including electronic bundles, as well as payment of court fees.

K. 2017: First Building Information Modelling Case in the UK, Heard in the TCC

Building Information Modelling (BIM) describes a method by which all relevant information for the life cycle of a building is coordinated, administered and exchanged among the project participants. A 3D federated model is at the heart of the method which includes not only geometrical design information, but also construction information and other parameters such as material characteristics, lifespan, fire resistance, carbon and acoustic values. It can also be linked to the programme (4D BIM) and cost estimate (5D BIM), and information can be issued for loading into facilities and/or asset management software.

In 2011, the government's construction strategy introduced the mandate that all government projects utilise a fully collaborative 3D computer model (Level 2) by 2016, with all project and asset information, documentation and data being electronic.[65]

[62] AES, *Electronic Filing in the TCC* (10 November 2014), view.officeapps.live.com/op/view.aspx?src=https%3A%2F%2Fwww.judiciary.uk%2Fwp-content%2Fuploads%2F2014%2F11%2FELECTRONIC-FILING-IN-THE-TCC-procedures-final.docx&wdOrigin=BROWSELINK (accessed 17 October 2022).

[63] *140th Update – Practice Direction Amendments* (Ministry of Justice, 2022), Update www.justice.gov.uk/__data/assets/pdf_file/0010/177256/cpr-140th-pd-update.pdf (accessed 17 October 2022).

[64] J Varley, 'Electronic working in the TCC: is the ball in our court now?' (*Practical Law Construction Blog*, 29 July 2015), constructionblog.practicallaw.com/electronic-working-in-the-tcc-is-the-ball-in-our-court-now/ (accessed 17 October 2022).

[65] *Government Construction Strategy* (Cabinet Office, May 2011), para 2.32, assets.publishing.service.gov.uk/government/uploads/system/uploads/attachment_data/file/61152/Government-Construction-Strategy_0.pdf (accessed 17 October 2022).

Whether it was a testament to its success or the lack of usage and implementation of BIM, it was not until 2017 that we saw the first reported UK BIM case: *Trant Engineering Limited v Mott MacDonald Limited.*[66]

Whilst the underlying dispute in *Trant v Mott MacDonald* actually was about what services Mott MacDonald was to provide and how much they were worth – rather than a dispute over defects or design issues with the BIM models or data – it is useful to set out the facts and arguments of the dispute to understand what issues can arise out of new technologies.

Here, the Ministry of Defence employed Trant in May 2016 to provide a new £55 million power generation facility at the Mount Pleasant Complex in the Falkland Islands. During the tender period for this project, Trant engaged Mott MacDonald to provide design consultancy services, including preliminary design, detailed design, design coordination, preparation and implementation of BIM and procurement support, principal designer responsibilities and the development of the DREAM assessment (an environment assessment throughout the design stage). Mott MacDonald intended to use an engineering project software programme called 'ProjectWise' to enable the design teams to manage, share and distribute design data on a single platform.

In July 2016, after Trant notified Mott MacDonald that they had been given the green light to go ahead with the project, Mott MacDonald emailed to Trant a proposed contract and schedules regarding its scope of services and terms of payment. Trant did not respond to Mott MacDonald's proposed contract, nor did it sign and return the contract. The relationship between Trant and Mott MacDonald eventually broke down. Ultimately, Trant did not pay Mott MacDonald the sums it considered were due. In June 2017 Mott MacDonald denied Trant access to the servers hosting the ProjectWise design data by revoking the passwords that had been issued to Trant.

The dispute between the parties concerned what services Mott MacDonald was to provide, the value of those services and what sums of money Mott MacDonald was entitled to receive. In addition, the parties disputed whether a contract existed and whether the terms of any such contract entitled Trant to access the design data Mott MacDonald had prepared which was stored on ProjectWise.

Ultimately Trant applied to the TCC for an interim injunction that Mott MacDonald should provide access to the design data on ProjectWise. Trant also sought an order entitling itself or other third parties in connection with the project to use that design data.

Trant argued that a contract did exist and that the terms of that contract included the obligation for the BIM preparation and implementation. The proposed contract also included an intellectual property provision which granted Trant a licence to use Mott MacDonald's intellectual property in connection with the project. Whilst it was agreed that Trant had not responded to Mott MacDonald's proposed contract in July 2016, Trant considered that it had accepted those terms and conditions by

[66] *Trant Engineering Limited v Mott MacDonald Limited* [2017] EWHC 2061 (TCC).

performance in making payments to Mott MacDonald. Furthermore, Trant argued that Mott MacDonald carried out its services in accordance with the schedules attached to that proposed contract.

Mott MacDonald argued that a contract did not exist. Mott MacDonald made the point that there was no express acceptance of the contract and that the fees payable, contract terms and scope of its services had not been finalised or agreed.

On the documents before it, the Court was not able to determine whether or not a contract existed between the parties – that was an issue to be decided at a full trial. The Court, however, was satisfied that there was a serious case to be tried, that damages would not be an adequate remedy and that there was a high degree of assurance that Trant was entitled to the design data that Mott MacDonald had already carried out and that was sitting in the public database area of ProjectWise. The Court noted that even if there were no contract, Mott MacDonald had already accepted payment on account in respect of the work that it had carried out.

The Court also had to consider the question of the balance of convenience and which course of action was likely to carry the least risk of injustice if it turned out to be wrong. Trant argued that without restoring access to the relevant database on ProjectWise, the project could not be progressed: Trant would be forced to start the project over again, losing a year of progress. Trant also argued that there would be little harm to Mott MacDonald in providing access to the design data that it had already provided, particularly in circumstances where Trant was prepared to pay compensation, whether by way of outstanding fees or damages that might subsequently be ordered.

Mrs Justice O'Farrell agreed and considered that the balance of convenience lay firmly in granting the injunction. She therefore ordered Mott MacDonald to make available the design data that had already been procured and completed to date. This would allow Trant to progress the project. Access was permitted only to the public folders which were intended for use by Trant.

This case only scratches the surface of issues we may well see with the new technologies of the future:[67] access rights, copyright/PI, right to terminate, etc. With the rise of digital twins, smart contracts, blockchain, AI, the Internet of Things and other construction specific technologies, issues surrounding interoperability, data privacy, data rights, cybersecurity, licensing, liability and insurance are on the horizon.

L. 2019: The Disclosure Pilot, eDisclosure and Technology Assisted Review (TAR)

On 1 January 2019, a disclosure pilot commenced in the BPC and included the TCC. Practice Directive 51U (PD 51U) covered the pilot, which initially ran for two years

[67] See, eg, *The Construction Playbook*, Version 1.1, HM Government, September 2022, assets.publishing.service.gov.uk/government/uploads/system/uploads/attachment_data/file/1102386/14.116_CO_Construction_Playbook_Web.pdf, and '*Procuring Net Zero Construction*', Kings' College London

and then was extended. The pilot ended with the introduction of the permanent regime under Practice Direction 57AD, which came into effect on 1 October 2022. In chapter eight, Mrs Justice O'Farrell covers the history and the detail of the regime, which we do not repeat here. Instead, we look at one important aspect included in the pilot, and the subsequent permanent Practice Direction, that is enabling a greater use of technology in dispute resolution: Technology Assisted Review (TAR).

TAR (or as some say CAR, Computer Assisted Review) 'includes all forms of document review that may be undertaken or assisted by the use of technology, including but not limited to predictive coding and computer assisted review'.[68] In short, one (or a few) highly qualified user(s) 'train' the software by identifying in a batch of documents those which are relevant, those which are significant to a particular topic and those which are privileged (sometimes known as a 'seed' set). This first round of training involves manually reviewing several hundreds or thousands of documents (the exact number of course varies in each case). The computer learns from the results and subsequent batches of documents are reviewed. Eventually the computer will suggest values/codes. The reviewer(s) correct these if necessary, and the computer refines its algorithm, again learning further each time. This is repeated until the computer is ready to process and run on its own. Continuous Active Leaving (CAL), the next generation in TAR, is now also available and has improved speed and quality if carried out correctly. Here there is no seed set, but rather reviewers begin coding documents while the computer learns in the background from their entries/tagging. The computer offers the review team what it believes are the most important documents, improving its understanding of the documents continuously as the team codes the data.

The pilot, and now Practice Direction 57AD, recognises the future of TAR in eDisclosure and the significant costs and time savings it can have where large volumes of documents are involved. Section 2 of the Disclosure Review Document (DRD), which is part of Appendix 2 to Practice Direction 57AD, requires parties to complete a questionnaire, if the parties are seeking an order for Extended Disclosure involving a search-based Disclosure Model (ie, Models C, D and/or E). Section 2 is to provide the Court with information about the data held by each party, including:[69]

(1) where and how the data is held;
(2) how the parties propose to process and search the data where a search-based Disclosure Model (Models C, D and E) is sought in relation to particular Issues for Disclosure); and
(3) whether there are any points that the parties have not been able to agree through discussions and which they therefore need the court to determine at the case management conference.

& Society of Construction Law, March 2022, www.scl.org.uk/sites/default/files/2022-03/Procuring%20Net%20Zero%20Construction%20Report%20for%20SCL%2018%20March%202022.pdf (both accessed 17 October 2022).

[68] Appendix 1 to Practice Direction 57AD, Definitions for the purpose of Section I.

[69] Appendix 2 to Practice Direction 57AD, Disclosure Review Document, Explanatory notes for Disclosure Review Document.

Question 9 of Section 2 demonstrates the Court's expectations in respect of TAR: where there is a significant amount of documents, particularly in excess of 50,000 documents, the use of TAR is anticipated. If the parties decide against it, they will need to explain to the Court:

> Technology / computer assisted review
>
> Parties are to consider the use of technology to facilitate the efficient collection of data and its further use for data review. This may include the use of some of the more sophisticated forms of technology / computer assisted review software (TAR / CAR / analytics). If the parties are in a position to propose the use of any technology or computer assisted review tools in advance of the CMC, those proposals should be set out in this section. *Where parties have considered the use of such tools but decided against this at this stage (particularly where the review universe is in excess of 50,000 documents), they should explain why such tools will not be used, particularly where this may mean that large volumes of data will have to be the subject of a manual review exercise.* Parties should update this form and draw any material updates to the attention of all parties and the Court if they later determine it would be appropriate to use such tools. [Emphasis added.]

Even prior to the Disclosure Pilot the courts were supportive of TAR. In February 2016 we saw the first time a UK court had approved the use of predictive coding for determining which electronic documents were relevant to the dispute: *Pyrrho Investments Limited & Anr v MWB Property Limited & Ors.*[70] More than three million documents had to be assessed and Master Matthews held that predictive coding would 'promote the overriding objective' of the Civil Procedure Rules. Amongst other reasons, he held that the CPR does not prohibit the use of predictive coding, the costs of the software was deemed proportionate and the parties had agreed both on the use of the software and on the way the software should be used, which the Master said, 'highlights the benefits that can result from parties collaborating early on disclosure and seeking to find common ground on how to proceed in a cost-effective by robust way'. A few months later, in May 2016, the Court again approved the use of predictive coding in electronic disclosure proceedings in *Brown v BCA Trading Ltd.*[71]

The TCC too has been instrumental in the administration of cases concerning TAR. In order for technology to be successful and trusted in applications such as TAR in eDisclosure, it needs to be properly understood, managed and used correctly. The TCC clearly has no issue with getting its hands dirty and taking a deep dive into the technicalities of TAR in order to understand the issues, both technical and procedural, and provide a solution for the parties. In February 2018, in the case of *Triumph Controls UK Ltd & Anor v Primus International Holding Co & Ors*,[72] Mr Justice Coulson did just that. The Defendants sought wide-ranging

[70] *Pyrrho Investments Limited (2) MWB Business Exchange limited v (1) MWB Property Limited (2) Rick Aspland-Robinson (3) Keval Pankhania (4) Ricard Balfour-Lynn (5) Jagtar Singh* [2016] EWHC 256 (Ch).

[71] *Brown v BCA Trading Ltd* [2016] EWHC 1464 (Ch).

[72] *Triumph Controls UK Ltd & Anor v Primus International Holding Co & Ors* [2018] EWHC 176 (TCC).

orders arising out of what they said were the fundamental deficiencies in the claimants' disclosure. The claimants had unilaterally departed from the agreed electronic disclosure process. Mr Justice Coulson reviewed the claimant's disclosure actions in detail and held that whilst some steps had been taken to reduce the data collected were sensible and proportionate, the claimants had used TAR in ways which were not transparent or satisfactory. They had not carried out the manual review it promised in its Electronics Documents Questionnaire nor had it made clear in its list of documents the nature of the sampling exercise undertaken, for example by reference to tolerances or rounds of sampling. It appeared that no senior lawyer had been involved in supervising the exercise and there was no explanation offered of how the claimant's TAR had been undertaken. He ordered the parties to agree a methodology by which a sample of previously excluded documents would be manually searched.

eDisclosure is a vast subject, one beyond possible to tackle as part of this chapter.[73] However, in the context of construction, engineering and technology disputes, eDisclosure can be pivotal in the case and the Court's case management is essential if the parties cannot agree. Imposing an efficient structure on electronic disclosure via the Practice Direction is welcomed and the wide consultation on the original pilot scheme has provided a good platform for the final drafting of PD 57AD. It is important, however, that feedback continues to be given and that the Practice Direction evolves in line with practical disclosure practice and new technology. Equally important is to ensure that all stakeholders, and particularly those parties who do not have to carry out the disclosure physically, are properly educated as to the time, complexity and cost of the processes involved. Without this common understanding there is a danger of a gap appearing between the requirements of the Court and the reality of practice, which in turn will impact the wider principle of access to justice for court users.

M. 2020: First Entirely Virtual TCC Trial

The COVID-19 pandemic accelerated society's digital upskilling. Virtually overnight, with the onset of the first UK lockdown in March 2020, companies were forced to consider how their employees could continue to work remotely from home, with the use of technology, if they wanted their businesses to survive. Whilst some companies were already well-placed, many were not and they, and their employees, quickly had to become familiar with the likes of Teams (or Skype for Business, as it was still around at that time), Zoom and a lack of easy access to quick, quality printing, which meant more electronic working. Dispute resolution

[73] For a detailed overview of eDisclosure, including its concepts, processes, techniques and tools, see Andrew Haslem's 10th and last edition of *The eDisclosure Systems Buyers Guide – 2022 Edition*, complexdiscovery.com/the-edisclosure-systems-buyers-guide-2022-edition-andrew-haslam/ (accessed 17 October 2022).

was no different and courts turned to remote video-conferencing, where possible and where appropriate.

As Mrs Justice O'Farrell DBE notes in chapter eight, the TCC's response to the COVID-19 pandemic in 2020 was 'swift' and one of 'resilience, agility and adaptability of the courts during challenging circumstances'. By 23 March 2020, the TCC had issued template orders for short adjudication enforcements, as well as longer trials, and had started organising remote hearings. By 26 March 2020, there was a Protocol for Remote Hearings for use across all jurisdictions of the High Court. But for a small number, almost all hearings in the TCC went ahead as originally listed, but of course as remote virtual hearings. At a webinar in May 2020, Mrs Justice O'Farrell DBE discussed the status of the TCC and its approach to virtual hearings in light of COVID-19 and confirmed that it was to 'keep calm and carry on' and that 'the TCC managed to continue business, pretty much, as usual'.[74] To achieve such a feat took true collaboration and coordination across all parties, and Mrs Justice O'Farrell DBE notes in chapter eight the 'impressive co-operation and flexibility was shown by the parties, legal representatives, judges and court staff to ensure that the wheels of justice kept turning'.

Whilst the beginning of the pandemic was extremely challenging on a number of levels, we again see the TCC at the forefront in its use of technology. It is considered that the first UK civil trial conducted entirely remotely using video-conferencing (Zoom) was in the TCC, in *Patel v Barnet London Borough Council & Others* (unreported). The claim concerned the repeated flooding of a family home. The dispute allegedly took four years to reach trial, and Mrs Justice Jefford rejected the defendant's application to adjourn the case because of the pandemic, instead ordering that it continue via video conference. Paul Darling QC carried out cross-examination virtually, commenting:

> Amongst the principal concerns when it comes to remote trials is the loss of visual cues. Any barrister will tell you that body language is invaluable in cross examination … What the trial has proved beyond reasonable doubt, however, is that none of the intimacy of the physical courtroom is in fact lost with a remote trial. Rather, *video sharing can in fact heighten our ability to dissect testimony, whilst opening up proceedings to the public.*[75]

The case ultimately settled; however, this set the scene for the 'virtual hearing', beginning to identify the pros and cons of the use of technology in dispute resolution.

[74] *Virtual Hearings & Virtual Mediations: the future of dispute resolution*, Fenwick Elliott Webinar, 28 May 2022, www.fenwickelliott.com/research-insight/webinars-podcasts/virtual-hearings-mediations (accessed 17 October 2022).

[75] *UK Court Settles Trial Via Zoom – But is this the Future We Want?*, 19 May 2020, www.artificiallawyer.com/2020/05/19/uk-court-settles-trial-via-zoom-but-is-this-the-future-we-want/ (accessed 17 October 2022). See also, www.newcivilengineer.com/latest/first-entirely-remote-construction-trial-sets-precedent-for-future-cases-20-05-2020/ (accessed 17 October 2022).

After over a year of virtual hearings, in September 2021 the TCC (and the Business and Property Courts) issued further guidance. For all hearings under half a day (including adjudication enforcement), the default position was that they take place remotely. The Court would consider a live hearing in such cases only if there was a particular reason why an in-person hearing was more appropriate. The approach for longer hearings and trials was, whilst parties would be asked to express a preference, a matter for the judge on the facts of each case. The guidance noted that remote and hybrid hearings may cover a full menu of options, from proceedings that are fully remote and accessible live to anyone who is in possession of a link, down to proceedings to which remote access is afforded to a single participant, everyone else being in court. Finally, the guidance noted that for: 'the foreseeable future, the default format for bundles will be electronic bundles'[76] The current BPC Protocol for Remote and Hybrid Hearings is attached at Appendix K to the October 2022 version of the TCC Guide.[77]

Amongst its other wide-reaching implications, COVID-19 has transformed the use of technology in dispute resolution: accelerating digital competency and shifting the industry to significantly more electronic working and remote hearings (where appropriate). The TCC saw this from the outset of the pandemic and was able to continue to provide access to justice in unprecedented times.

II. The 'T', the 'C' and the 'T&C' in TCC: The Future of Disputes in the TCC

As others in this book have referred, most of the disputes in the Official Referee's corridor concerned building and engineering disputes, until the arrival of the computer.[78] At this point, more complex technical litigation about both hardware and software emerged. The Official Referees were best placed for these technical disputes and accordingly their scope and caseload expanded. The TCC has seen an increasing number of disputes requiring technical input or which it is appropriate for the Court to deal with because of its experience in the type of dispute, including complex computer and IT infrastructure disputes and renewable energy disputes.

In addition to disputes over foundations, fire detection systems and refrigeration plants for ice-cream manufacturers (to name just a few), the Official Referees and the TCC have dealt with a number of technology disputes ranging from hardware and software failures, to project and IT infrastructure disputes to

[76] *Remote hearings guidance to help the Business and Property Courts*, 15 September 2021, www.judiciary.uk/remote-hearings-guidance-to-help-the-business-and-property-courts-2/ (accessed 17 October 2022).

[77] TCC Guide, October 2022, www.judiciary.uk/guidance-and-resources/technology-and-construction-court-tcc-guide-october-2022/ (accessed 28 October 2022).

[78] See ch 6 in this volume.

commercial, contract and software licensing issues – as well as claims relating to the design, supply and installation of computer systems, related network systems. For example, in 2000, *Watford Electronics Ltd v Sanderson CFL Ltd*,[79] Judge Thornton considered the interpretation of limitation of liability and entire agreement clauses in software licensing contracts for Mailbrain and Genasys products. In 2002, *SAM Business Systems Ltd v Hedley & Co*,[80] Judge Bowsher QC considered the definition and the legal status of a software 'bug'. In 2010, *De Beers UK (formerly Diamond Trading Co Ltd) v Atos Origin IT Services UK Ltd*,[81] Mr Justice Edwards-Stuart found an information technology supplier to be in repudiatory breach of a contract to supply a software system to support the diamond trader's diamond supply chain management. More recently, in 2021, *CIS General Insurance Ltd v IBM UK Ltd*,[82] Mrs Justice O'Farrell DBE heard a claim for wasted costs and damages following the technology supplier's failure to provide a new IT system, and in 2022, *Transparently Limited v Growth Capital Ventures Limited*,[83] a dispute over the completion of bespoke software, ending in the judge refusing to grant a mandatory injunction for the delivery up of the software, including its source code and underlying architecture to the claimant. These are but a few examples. There have been, and currently are, ground-breaking technology disputes in the TCC which have had wide-reaching effects on English law as a whole. The *Triple Point*[84] case, for example, started in 2018 in the TCC concerning a dispute in relation to a software contract. It reached the Supreme Court in 2021 resolving much-needed uncertainty on important points of law concerning liquidated damages for delayed works.[85]

With advancements in AI, blockchain, IoT, quantum computing, the Metaverse and other highly sophisticated, emerging technologies, no doubt the TCC can expect to see an even wider range and scope of disputes. In March 2022, at the Society of Computers & Law's Sir Brian Neill Lecture, '*The Future of Dispute Resolution: Horizon Scanning*', Sir Geoffrey Vos, Master of the Rolls, listed eight interconnected, technological changes which he considered are the current landscape and the existing direction of travel: blockchain, smart contracts, Internet of Things, Metaverse, Central Bank Digital Currency (CBDC), electronic trade documents (Bills of Lading & Bills of Exchange), decentralised autonomous

[79] *Watford Electronics Ltd v Sanderson CFL Ltd* [2000] 2 All ER (Comm) 984, reversed in the Court of Appeal, [2001] EWCA Civ 317.

[80] *SAM Business Systems Ltd v Hedley & Co* [2002] EWHC 2733 (TCC).

[81] *De Beers UK (formerly Diamond Trading Co Ltd) v Atos Origin IT Services UK Ltd* [2010] EWHC 3276 (TCC).

[82] *CIS General Insurance Ltd v IBM UK Ltd* [2021] EWHC 347 (TCC), followed by a successful appeal in the Court of Appeal in *Soteria Insurance Ltd (formerly CIS General Insurance Limited) v IBM United Kingdom Ltd* [2022] EWCA Civ 440.

[83] *Transparently Limited v Growth Capital Ventures Limited* [2022] EWHC 144 (TCC).

[84] *Triple Point Technology Inc v PTT Public Co Ltd* [2021] UKSC 29, [2019] EWCA Civ 230, [2018] EWHC 45 (TCC), [2017] EWHC 2178 (TCC).

[85] See also *Bates & Others v Post Office Ltd* (No 3) [2019] EWHC 606 (QB).

organisations (DAO) and quantum computing.[86] Each of these has the potential to raise new issues and create a very different disputing environment. Sir Geoffrey Vos noted:

> Technological change is also not new to the justice system. Even since the last major round of structural reforms to the courts in the 19th century, we have seen trains, planes, and derivative trading, to name but a few take off. The justice system has more or less successfully adapted to deciding new kinds of dispute.[87]

Technological change is not new to the justice system, and certainly not new to the TCC, as we have seen. It has taken on board technological change in its stride, and is well-placed for disputes around emerging technologies. In addition, the TCC is well-placed for the technological change and digital transformation of the construction industry. Whilst the pace has been somewhat glacial to date, momentum is building and technology is pervading all aspects of design, procurement, construction and operation – the whole-life cycle of both new buildings, assets and infrastructure, as well as existing. It is already proving to be the enabler and provider of solutions in the built environment to the very serious issues we face today; for example, climate change and connectivity and connection in the era of COVID-19. As the construction industry accelerates its digitisation and digitalisation,[88] and adopts more of the emerging technologies, no doubt we will see new types of disputes too.

Having said that, in the future, once digital processes are embodied in the construction processes, the distinction between 'construction' disputes and 'technology' disputes may not be so easy to define. This may not matter whatsoever, particularly as we have a specialist court that is experienced in and can address both the 'T' and the 'C', however, an interesting space to watch. The rise of smart contracts in the construction and energy industries is one such example: roughly speaking, the technology defines the construction contract.

A 'smart contract' is:

- a legally binding contract in which some or all of the contractual obligations are defined in and/or performed automatically by a computer programme;[89] or
- computer code that, upon the occurrence of a specified condition or conditions, is capable of running automatically according to pre-specified functions.[90]

[86] Sir G Vos, *The Future of Dispute Resolution: Horizon Scanning*, Society of Computers & Law, 17 March 2022, /www.judiciary.uk/wp-content/uploads/2022/03/MR-to-SCL-Sir-Brain-Neill-Lecture-2022-The-Future-for-Dispute-Resolution-Horizon-Scannings-.pdf (accessed 17 October 2022).

[87] ibid, para 36.

[88] The former being simply working electronically with all digital assets, but the underlying processes remain the same, and latter being the creation of new ways of working and new business models with the use of digital technologies that provide new efficiencies and new value-producing opportunities.

[89] *Smart Legal Contracts (Summary)*, The Law Commission, November 2021, 3, s3-eu-west-2.amazonaws.com/lawcom-prod-storage-11jsxou24uy7q/uploads/2021/11/6.7776_LC_Smart_Legal_Contracts_2021_Final.pdf (accessed 17 October 2022).

[90] *Smart legal contracts, Advice to Government*, Law Commission, Law Com No 401, November 2021, s3-eu-west-2.amazonaws.com/lawcom-prod-storage-11jsxou24uy7q/uploads/2021/11/Smart-legal-contracts-accessible.pdf (accessed 17 October 2022).

In other words: if X occurs, then execute Y. Nick Szabo, a computer scientist and legal scholar known for developing the concept of the smart contract in the 1990s, illustrated the smart contract by comparing it to a vending machine. An automatic transaction is executed when two conditions are met (the money is received and the snack is selected):

money inserted + snack selection = snack dispensed.

In the context of construction, an example might be: if the concrete lorry turns up on site with the correct amount/specification (which is monitored automatically by the use of sensors and other image recognition technology), payment of a pre-agreed sum is automatically deposited into the concrete supplier's bank account. Whilst this is a hypothetical example, we are already beginning to see some use of smart contracts/clauses in certain sectors, and research both in industry and academia is well-progressed.

For example, '*The Weather Ledger*' was a successful collaboration funded by Innovate UK which created a smart contract (clauses), with the use of distributed ledger technology (DLT) and the Internet of Things (IoT), to interpret and execute the weather-related Early Warning Notice and Compensation Event clauses in the NEC standard form of contract. If predetermined weather thresholds were reached, using sensors and connected databases, a notification was sent to the appropriate parties. After the Compensation Event is checked and verified, a compensation claim is raised with the client.[91]

Whilst there are a number of issues to consider for adoption and implementation of smart contracts, one perceived barrier was the legal status of a smart contract: is such a contract valid and enforceable? There has been some debate of this in the UK, and ultimately the government's LawTech Delivery Panel, along with the Law Commission, convened task groups to review, leading to the most recent findings in February 2022.

First, in December 2017, the Lord Chancellor asked the Law Commission to work on smart legal contracts. This was paused with the creation of the UK Jurisdiction Taskforce (UKJT), a task group under the government's LawTech Delivery Panel. In November 2019, the UKJT published its legal statement on cryptoassets and smart contracts.[92] It concluded that, in principle, smart contracts are capable of giving rise to binding legal obligations and are enforceable in accordance with their terms. Following this, the Ministry of Justice asked the Law Commission to undertake a scoping study on smart legal contracts, building on the findings of the UKJT legal statement.

[91] *The Weather Ledger*, Digital Catapult, May 2021, www.digicatapult.org.uk/wp-content/uploads/2021/11/Weather_Ledger_WP5_report-v2.pdf (accessed 17 October 2022).

[92] *Legal Statement on cryptoassets and smart contracts*, UK Jurisdiction Taskforce, The LawTech Delivery Panel, November 2019, 35z8e83m1ih83drye280o9d1-wpengine.netdna-ssl.com/wp-content/uploads/2019/11/6.6056_JO_Cryptocurrencies_Statement_FINAL_WEB_111119-1.pdf (accessed 17 October 2022).

In November 2021, the Law Commission published its advice to government.[93] It confirmed that the current legal framework in England and Wales is able to facilitate and support the use of smart contracts, without the need for statutory reform, and that current legal principles can apply to smart contracts in much the same way as they do to traditional contracts.[94] The Law Commission helpfully summarised smart contracts and identified that they can take different forms, albeit that regardless of the form used, the performance or execution of the contract (or a clause/obligation of the contract) is by code, ie, with the use of technology.[95]

The Law Commission set out the main features of a smart contract: (1) some or all of the contractual obligations are performed automatically by a computer programme; and (2) the contract is legally enforceable. In addition, it reviewed the formation, interpretation and remedies when dealing with smart contracts, and include a non-exhaustive list of issues parties may wish to provide for in their smart legal contract.

In February 2022, LawTechUK published '*Smarter Contracts*', a report documenting the outcome of its project which identified important examples of how technology is transforming contract use across various key industries. The report sets out case studies which demonstrate digital-first solutions to real-world problems: electronic signatures, contract automation and management, insurance, renewable energy, financial services, trade, sale of goods and services, logistics and transportation, the digital ownership of physical assets, sport sponsorship, home buying and selling and the digital company.[96]

In addition to addressing disputes which arise out of emerging new technologies globally, with the acceleration of the digital transformation of the construction industry, the 'T' in TCC will become ever more important to construction disputes. The construction industry is beginning to leverage machine learning, AI, and data analytics, and implement digital twins, smart cities, smart contracts and product platform approaches.[97] It is already using drones, design configurators, point cloud surveys and 3D/4D BIM. The volume of data in relation to construction is rapidly increasing – though is often fragmented and/or not easily accessible – and new issues of IP, interoperability, data rights and ownership are surfacing. Indeed, it is easy to see the TCC as home to the 'T', the 'C' and the 'T&C' disputes.

[93] *Smart legal contracts, Advice to Government*, Law Commission.

[94] ibid, and also see *Smart Legal Contracts (Summary)*, Law Commission.

[95] The three forms of smart contracts are: (1) natural language contract with automatic performance by code; (2) a hybrid smart contract; and (3) a contract recorded solely in code.

[96] *Smarter Contracts*, LawTechUK, February 2022, resources.lawtechuk.io/files/report_smarter_contracts.pdf (accessed 17 October 2022).

[97] *The Construction Playbook*, Version 1.1, HM Government, September 2022.

III. Conclusion

What is innovation? A recent McKinsey article defines 'innovation' as:

> the systematic practice of developing and marketing breakthrough products and services for adoption by customers.[98]

In 1994, a Law Society Gazette article noted that innovation was not a new concept to the Official Referees:

> The official referees have long been innovators … Official referees have also been able to carry out practical experiments with various forms of information technology and recording of evidence.[99]

We have seen that the TCC's principles and practices embody technical innovation and as Sir Peter Fraser stated, 'The TCC has always prided itself in being at the forefront of technical innovation.'[100] Since the 1980s, the Official Referees and then the TCC have led the march in their use and promotion of technology, the digital transformation of the Court and their ability to address new technologies both in the context of new types of disputes seen in the industry and new methodologies of processing disputes.

Given the pace of technological change, what does the future hold for dispute resolution? On 11 October 2022, an AI-powered robot named Ai-Da (named in honour of the nineteenth century pioneering female mathematician Ada Lovelace (1815–1852) by Aidan Meller, a specialist in modern and contemporary art) gave evidence to the communications and digital committee in the House of Lords, as part of an inquiry into the future of the creative industries in the UK and how AI might affect them. Ai-Da looks like a real human being (relatively), creates art and can answer questions. At the House of Lords, in response to questioning, she said:

> Technology has already had a huge impact on the way we create and consume art … technology can be both a thread and an opportunity …[101]

There was some criticism, it was noted that Ai-Da was providing evidence but was not a witness in its own right, and indeed Ai-Da's performance was not entirely successful,[102] but wow. Seeing this, it is not difficult to comprehend a future which

[98] *What is innovation?* (McKinsey, 17 August 2022), www.mckinsey.com/featured-insights/mckinsey-explainers/what-is-innovation (accessed 17 October 2022).

[99] 'Constructing solutions – the work undertaken by the London official referees' courts', (*The Law Society Gazette*, 6 January 1994), www.lawgazette.co.uk/news/constructing-solutions-the-work-undertaken-by-the-london-official-referees-courts-/19441.article (accessed 17 October 2022).

[100] Sir P Fraser, *Forward*, in A Constable QC, L Garrett QC and C Lamont (eds), *Litigation in the Technology & Construction Court* (London, Informa, 2018).

[101] A Hern, 'Typos and shutdowns: robots 'gives evidence' to Lords committee' (*Guardian online*, 11 October 2022), www.theguardian.com/technology/2022/oct/11/typos-and-shutdowns-robot-gives-evidence-to-lords-committee (accessed 20 October 2022).

[102] A Hern, 'Ai-Da the robot sums up the flawed logic of Lords debate on AI' (*Guardian online*, 14 October 2022), www.theguardian.com/technology/2022/oct/14/ai-da-robot-sums-up-flawed-logic-lords-debate-ai (accessed 20 October 2022). As the *Guardian* reported: 'Apparently overcome by the

involves robots from construction sites or off-site factories giving evidence before the TCC. In addition, given the increase in the use of video recordings either on 'wearables' and/or drone footage, perhaps we will see aspects of witness testimony being assessed with video assistant referee (VAR) tools, such as those used in the elite professional football industry.[103] Image recognition and classification of photos are already available and increasing steadily in their sophistication – VAR must be on the horizon. Given the TCC's resilience and forward-thinking approach to technology since the 1980s, we can only expect that the TCC would take robots-giving-evidence and the use of VAR in its stride.

Technology is transforming the way disputes are resolved.[104] The TCC (formerly the Official Referees) has lived through two industrial revolutions: the second revolution in the 1870s with the division of labour, electricity and mass production, and the third revolution in 1970s with the explosion of electronics, IT and automated production. Given the TCC's progressive and resilient nature in relation to technology, the Court is well-placed to face the onset of the fourth industrial revolution.[105] With its use of technology and innovative approach, we are confident the TCC will continue to be a global leader in dispute resolution.

stuffy atmosphere, the machine, which resembles a sex doll strapped to a pair of egg whisks, shut down halfway through the evidence session. As its creator, Aidan Meller, scrabbled with power sockets to restart the device, he put a pair of sunglasses on the machine. "When we reset her, she can sometimes pull quite interesting faces," he explained.'

[103] VAR was approved by The International Football Association Board (IFAB) on 3 March 2018 (IFAB 2018).

[104] For a further detailed reading on the subject, see R Susskind, *Online Courts and the Future of Justice* (Oxford, OUP, 2019).

[105] N Davis, 'What is the fourth industrial revolution?' (*World Economic Forum*, 19 January 2016), www.weforum.org/agenda/2016/01/what-is-the-fourth-industrial-revolution/ (accessed 17 October 2022).

12

Fire at the Palace: 150 Years of Fire Safety in Buildings

RACHEL ANSELL KC AND DR DOUGLAS MAXWELL*

I. Introduction

The one hundred and fiftieth anniversary of what is now the Technology and Construction Court (TCC) has coincided with the most far-reaching reforms of building safety in a generation. These reforms were enacted in response to the 2017 Grenfell Tower fire and the resulting review of fire safety in buildings.[1] Over the coming years, the regulation of fire safety in buildings will present many challenges for the TCC. However, the regulation of fire safety in buildings is not new.[2]

To demonstrate what has changed and remains constant, we have chosen to consider the last one hundred and fifty years through the prism of a single case. The fire at the Alexandra Palace in north London in 1873 (the same year as the Judicature Act 1873) was a real fire, and we have relied heavily on original sources to establish the relevant facts. However, we have filled in the gaps where information was missing and lost in time. To condense the changes into a manageable chapter, we have written four hypothetical opinions to the Alexandra Palace Company (the 'APC') in half-century increments: starting in 1873 and proceeding in 50-year increments

* Rachel Ansell KC (4 Pump Court) and Dr Douglas Maxwell (Henderson Chambers) would like to thank Professor Philip Britton (KCL), Toby Riley-Smith KC (Henderson Chambers), David Sawtell (39 Essex Chambers), and Anthony Ley (FRICS) for generously giving their time to discuss earlier versions of this chapter.

[1] For the purposes of this chapter, we use 'fire safety' as an 'umbrella term' to include, among other things, passive fire safety measures such as compartmentalisation, the use of fire-resistant or limited combustibility materials, the construction of party walls, and means of escape. Fire safety also encompasses active fire safety measures such as the use of fire extinguishers, staff training and sprinkler systems.

[2] P Bruner, 'The Historical Emergence of Construction Law' (2007) 34 *William Mitchell Law Review* 4: 'Since mankind first promulgated rudimentary principles of law to regulate human rights and obligations arising out of societal interaction, there have existed principles of law governing the built environment and the construction process.'

to 1923, 1973 and 2023. The style is intended to be informal and conversational.[3] We have peppered our four hypothetical opinions with cases and other contemporary sources to help demonstrate the challenges and changes that have occurred.

II. Fire at the Palace

The relevant facts for our four hypothetical opinions are based on a real fire that occurred in the same year as the Official Referees were established.

The Alexandra Palace Company began building the Palace in 1864 between Wood Green and Muswell Hill in what is now the London Borough of Haringey.[4] Designed in an Italian renaissance style, it extended 900 feet in length with a width of 450 feet and a 170 feet diameter with a 220 feet high dome. The Palace contained a large 3,000-seat concert hall and a theatre.

The architect for the Palace was the well-respected Mr John Johnson (1807–1878) of Meesom & Johnson, who had previously been involved in the Victoria and Albert Museum and the Albert Memorial. The main contractors were the equally well-respected Lucas Brothers, who, prior to the building of the Palace, had received much public acclaim for their many triumphs, including the Covent Garden Opera House (1858) and the Royal Albert Hall (1871).

On 9 June 1873, just two weeks after the Palace opened, plumbers were working on the roof of the dome. They were using an open fire called a brazier to heat their tools. Reports following the fire concluded that when the plumbers went for a break, they left the fire burning.[5] At some point, the fire ignited on the roof. *The Morning Post* reported that 'with remarkable rapidity to the other parts of the whole was soon irretrievably under the influence of the flame'.[6]

While there does appear to have been an unexplained delay, the Metropolitan Fire Brigade was eventually sent a telegram. *The Times* reported that Captain Shaw was 'speedily on his way', but 'by the time they reached their destination the ruins which had been effected in the meantime was well-nigh complete and irreparable'.[7]

[3] This chapter is not designed to give a comprehensive account of the history of building regulations in England and Wales. Readers in search of such an account should consult inter alia: A Ley, *A History of Building Control in England and Wales 1840–1990* (Coventry, RICS Books, 2000); A Ley, 'Building control: its development and application 1840–1936' (MPhil Thesis, Open University 1990); RH Harper 'The Evolution of the English Building Regulations 1840–1914' (PhD Thesis, University of Sheffield 1978).

[4] For the purposes of this chapter, we are ging to work on the fictional basis that the Alexandra Palace came within the jurisdiction of the Metropolitan Building Act 1855.

[5] 'Destruction of the Alexandra Palace', *The Times* (London, June 1873) 7.

[6] 'The Alexandra Palace has been destroyed by fire' *The Morning Post* (London, 10 July 1873) 4.

[7] 'Destruction of the Alexandra Palace', *The Times* (London, June 1873) 7; 'Tremendous Fire in London', *The Dundee Courier* (Dundee 10 June 1873) gave a slightly different account: 'There was but one engine on the premises, and although the engines of the Metropolitan Brigade – sixteen in all – were despatched by rail immediately on receipt of the telegram announcing the fire, the whole building was in flames within half-an-hour of the first alarm ….'

The principal supports for the dome were iron girders which contracted under the heat of the fire, causing it to collapse.[8] *The Times* reported:

> Yesterday, in mid-day, this stately edifice, which but a fortnight ago had been opened to the public under new and promising auspices, was destroyed by fire, with most of the valuable property it contained including many rare works of art, and nothing now remains of it but four bare, blackened, rootless walls, presenting a melancholy spectacle.[9]

The fire resulted in at least three fatalities. Two separate Coroner's Inquests were held in a local tavern within a week of the fire, returning verdicts of death by smoke inhalation, burns and crushing.[10] Several months later, then in the process of rebuilding the Palace, builders reported the discovery of 'a few charred bones, with a set of human teeth'.[11]

However, Victorian England could sleep slightly easier as *The Times* reported that despite the destruction and deaths, 'Mr Waterer's show of rhododendrons is still intact, and uninjured.'[12] The stiff upper lip appeared in much of the media coverage. *The Morning Post* noted that 'Much that has been destroyed can be replaced.' *Lloyd's Illustrated Newspaper* wrote, 'The directors of the company, headed by their chairman, Mr Gruning, came up during the Monday afternoon and witnessed the destruction of their hopes with a calm philosophy which was quite inspiriting to observers amid such a sense of desolation.'[13]

The Alexandra Palace Company had not procured sufficient insurance to cover the damage or to rebuild the Palace. There was notable criticism of the systems in place. *The Times* reported:

> Concerning the precautions against the possibility of fire … they seem to have been either *nil* or very insufficient. With a large reservoir and the New River at the foot of the hill, there does not seem to have been any arrangements for pumping it up in quantities. It is hardly too much to say that if a couple of steamers with a good supply of water had been on the spot when the fire was first discovered the mischief done would have been trifling.[14]

The fire resulted in much public consternation. The mood was reflected in an editorial in *The Morning Post*, reported on 10 July 1873:

> The fate of the Alexandra Palace once more points to the moral that we cannot make fireproof buildings. There seems always some weak point in every so called building that we erect. In this case brick, stone, iron and zinc were freely and principally used;

[8] 'Court and Official' *Cheshire Observer* (Chester, 22 November 1873).
[9] 'Destruction of the Alexandra Palace', *The Times* (London, June 1873) 7.
[10] 'The Fire and the Alexandra Palace', *The Daily News* (London, 13 June 1873); 'Summary of News' *The Standard* (London, 11 June 1973) 6; The Coroner's Inquest into the death of Thomas Larner in the Twyford Arms Tavern on 16 June 1873 'The Fire at the Alexandra Palace' *The Morning Post* (London, 17 June 1873).
[11] 'Another Shocking Discovery at the Alexandra Palace' *York Herald* (York, 27 September 1873).
[12] 'Destruction of the Alexandra Palace', *The Times* (London, June 1873) 7.
[13] 'Destruction of the Alexandra Palace' *Lloyd's Illustrated Newspaper* (London, 15 June 1873).
[14] 'Destruction of the Alexandra Palace' *The Times* (London, June 1873) 7.

> and yet we see that the enormous structure, in the space of some three hours or so, is destroyed almost so completely as it had been built of wood. It was the dome, we are told, that took fire first the dome was formed of iron ribs standing on brick and stone supports and covered in with zinc roofing. But then the zinc we presume, was laid on wood, and there were of course other wooden fittings to the dome and we have seen that there must have been a sufficiency of this inflammable substance to take and communicate fire. It may be that the task of making a building that practically would be proof against fire is beyond our skill and resources, though we hardly think that such is the case. But at all events it is certain that we are not very successful in our efforts to that end. Yet we have every inducement to discover the art. The loss of a building like the Alexandra Palace is a lesson as impressive and instructive as could be conceived. Here was a building, a great centre for attraction for a large district of London, a source of amusement and instruction to hundreds of thousands of people a vast depositary of valuables and various kinds, a means of converting an unprofitable into a prosperous property, yet it was, as has been proved, but in reality a great tinder-box, lying as an easy and ready prey to broad daylight. We have had many other such lessons, but where may we ask are the results of these lessons! Every great fire testifies to neglect …. What has happened must not happen again.[15]

The 'new' Alexandra Palace, built from the ashes, did not follow the original design. Notably, four 16,000-gallon capacity water towers were added, the steel girders were replaced, fire breaks were added, and much of the new building was made of fireproof brick. It took just two years to rebuild at the cost of £417,128 (£43 million today).[16] Another fire occurred at the Palace in 1980, and again it was rebuilt.[17] The Palace remains open in 2023 and is perhaps best known as the 'Ally Pally' to Darts fans.[18]

[15] 'The Alexandra Palace has been destroyed by fire' *The Morning Post* (London, 10 July 1873) 4; 'It is curious how many preventable evils we suffer from', *Huddersfield Chronicle* (West Yorkshire, 12 June 1873) 'To our list of preventable evils, we must add one which has just not been brought very prominently before us in London, or rather in one of the suburbs of the metropolis. We allude of course to fire, and to the terrible catastrophe which has just occurred at the Alexandra Palace. Once more the custodians of our public building, and indeed the community generally, have been taught a stern lesson; but since we have been many such and profited so little by them before, it would be perhaps utopian to expect us to become more sensible now. Over and over again we have pursued with horror the accounts of fire involve great damage to both life and property, and we have read also how to guard against and prevent such casualties. But still we find that we are obliged to add to the catalogue. Still we have to chronicle disastrous fires which with the commonest precautions would have been prevented …. As if to show up in higher relief the culpable carelessness of those who had charge of the Palace, the cause of fire was on which had happened only a comparatively short time ago at Canterbury Cathedral. Some plumbers were at work on the roof of the dome, and in order to head their soldering tools they had open braziers in use. Open braziers on an inflammable roof at an elevation where the wind was naturally powerful! What then was to be expected but fire? And, indeed, the only wonder if that the accident did not happen sooner. Then again, with water close to the Palace, there was an insufficient pressure, and here again we have an instance of neglect of precaution in the case of fire which would have suggested itself to a child. The whole affair is indeed pitiful when we remember how easily the calamity might have been prevented.'

[16] See 'In re The Alexandra Palace Company' *The Era* (London, 13 May 1882).

[17] See Appendix at the end of this chapter.

[18] This chapter is entirely hypothetical. We do not seek to comment on any legal issues resulting from the 1980 fire. This chapter is for academic purposes only.

III. Our Instructions

A. Assumptions for Our Advice

This chapter will take the real facts from the fire at the Palace and, with some artistic licence, make the following assumptions when drafting our four hypothetical opinions:

(i) in addition to comprising an exhibition space for housing artwork and artefacts, the Palace also incorporated an accommodation block for the curators and tour guides working at the Palace;
(ii) the design was defective in that it did not provide for sufficient structural fire precautions: it incorporated non-fireproof brick and timber (in our 2023 example, combustible/limited combustibility cladding materials), inadequate means to suppress the fire (the absence of the water towers and, in later years, inadequate fire sprinkler systems) and inadequate means of escape; and
(iii) the workmanship of the main contractors was inadequate because amongst other things they did not install the required fire breaks and the subcontractors used unsafe working procedures (the use of a brazier and, in later years, the failure to properly implement proper procedures when carrying out hot works).

B. Our Instructions

Each of our four opinions will be based upon the assumption that Counsel has been instructed by solicitors acting on behalf of the APC. With the passage of each half-century, our fictional instructions will remain broadly the same; but over the 150 years, the form and style of the drafting of our hypothetical instructions will have changed dramatically.

Under these instructions, we are expected to advise the APC in relation to:

(i) The relevant regulatory framework for fire safety.
(ii) Any claims the APC may have under statute.
(iii) Any recourse the APC may have against construction professionals, broadly defined to include individuals or entities such as architects, surveyors, and fire engineers.

We are not required to consider claims against the main contractors or subcontractors. The authors of this chapter have been unable to locate original copies of any contracts between the relevant parties involved in the construction of the Palace in 1873. In any event, this chapter is intended to focus on the developing role of the Official Referees' and building regulations. However, for the purposes of our hypothetical advice, we will assume the existence of direct contractual relations between the APC, the architects and builders, with a sub-contract with the roofers involved in the lead works on the dome.

In 1873, 1923, 1973 and 2023, we would refer to the fact that there may be potential claims brought against the APC for damages or destruction to the property of others in the Palace,[19] liability for fire spread,[20] and death or injury to persons.[21] It would not be until our advice in 1973, and the 1972 House of Lords decision in *British Railway Board v Herrington*, that the APC would have any duty towards trespassers.[22] However, such issues would be beyond the scope of the initial advice we had been instructed to provide. Further, to consider it here would add complexity beyond that which could reasonably be dealt with in a single chapter.

IV. Eighteen Seventy-Three

A. The Legal Scene and the Official Referees

Our first brief arrives in the aftermath of the fire in 1873. The legal world of Victorian England is slow and complicated.[23] Our hypothetical instructions will most likely be handwritten and arrive in Chambers tied in pink tape. For members

[19] *Vaughan v Menlove* [1835] All ER Rep 156 the defendant's haystack spontaneously combusted and it was alleged that he had 'wrongfully negligently and improperly kept his haystack so that it became liable to ignite' and so be a danger to the claimant's property. The jury were left to consider the question of negligence and that direction was upheld. Tindal CJ said: '... But there is a rule of law which says you must so employ your own property as not to injure that of another; and according to that rule the defendant is liable for the consequences of its own neglect; and though the defendant did not himself light the fire yet mediately, he is as much the cause of it as if he had himself put a candle to the rick; for it is well known that hay will ferment and take fire if it be not carefully stacked.'

[20] *Rylands v Fletcher* (1866) LR 1 Ex 265, 279 (Exch.); (1868) L.R. 3 HL 330 (HL); *Becquet v MacCarthy* (1831) 2 B & Ad 951 at 958 per Lord Tenderton CJ; *Collingwood v Home and Colonial Stores* [1936] 3 All ER 200 per Lord Wright at 204: 'Before [the Fires Prevention (Metropolis) Act 1774] if a fire spread from a man's premises and did damage to adjoining premises, he was liable in damage on the broad ground that it was his duty at his own peril to keep any fire that originated on his premises from spreading to and damaging his neighbour's premises.'

[21] *Parnaby v The Lancaster Canal Company* (1839) 11 A & E 223; *Mersey Docks and Harbour Board Trustees v Gibb* (1866) LR 1 HL 93; *Hodgman v West Midland Railway Company* (1864) 5 B & S 173, 122 ER 796, 802 Cockburn CJ 'it being now settled law that any one inviting the public to a given place for purposes of business is bound to take reasonable care that the place in question can be entered with safety'.

[22] *Robert Addie & Sons (Collieries) Ltd v Dumbreck* [1929] AC 358, 365 'Towards the trespasser the occupier has no duty to take reasonable care for his protection or even to protect him from concealed danger. The trespasser comes on to the premises at his own risk. An occupier is in such a case liable only where the injury is due to some wilful act involving something more than the absence of reasonable care. There must be some act done with the deliberate intention of doing harm to the trespasser, or at least some act done with reckless disregard of the presence of the trespasser' (Lord Hailsham). In 1972 the House of Lords in *British Railway Board v Herrington* [1972] AC 877 (HL) overturned its earlier decision in *Robert Addie & Sons (Collieries) Ltd v Dumbreck*.

[23] HC Deb 9 June 1873 vol 216, col 642 the Attorney General stated, '... it was beyond controversy, that in many instances our procedure was impracticable and inconvenient, for no one practically conversant with its details could deny that there were certain great defects in them which ought to be remedied'.

of the Bar, advertising one's services and fraternising with solicitors is prohibited: even if it was permissible, nobody would hold themselves out as a 'construction lawyer'. It will be over 100 years until the first Building Law Reports are published and one hundred and ten years until the Construction Law Reports will make it onto the shelves in Chambers.

Our sources are limited. Donald Keating would not publish *Law and Practice of Building Contracts including Architects and Surveyors*, until 1955.[24] While significantly older, Alfred Hudson's book *The Law of Building and Engineering Contracts* was not published until 1891.[25] If Counsel is lucky, they will have access to a copy of Humphrey Woolrych's *The Metropolitan Building Act*, published in 1856.[26]

As this book is concerned with the history of what would become the TCC, some artistic licence is required to run a case in the 1870s. The first Official Referees were not appointed until 1876, and even then, their powers were limited until the Judicature Act 1884 gave an Official Referee the power to make orders for costs and exercise the power of a High Court Judge.[27] The need for the consent of both parties was not removed until the Arbitration Act 1889.[28] While the Official Referees (and then the TCC) have come to assume specialist jurisdiction over all high-value technical cases, including cases involving the technical details of fire safety in buildings, the original role of the Official Referees was exceedingly limited.

As the case will most likely be heard in London, it will be important to remind our client in the 1870s that they were required to pay the Official Referees one guinea per hour of sitting time.[29] By 2023 the costs have increased with an issue fee of £10,000.[30] The Royal Courts of Justice (the 'RCJ') were not opened until 1882, but as far back as 1876, *The Times* was reporting that no room in the RCJ had been marked out for the Official Referees.[31]

B. Our Advice: The Regulatory Framework

i. *The Historical Development of Building Regulations*

The first recorded regulation of fire protection in England can be observed in the 1189 decree of FitzAlwyn, the First Lord Mayor of London, that 'all party walls

[24] D Keating, *Law and Practice of Building Contracts including Architects and Surveyors*, 1st edn (London, Sweet & Maxwell, 1955).

[25] A Hudson, *The Law of Building and Engineering Contracts* (Waterlow and Sons 1891).

[26] H Woolrych, *The Metropolitan Building Act* (V & R Stevens 1856). A copy of this text is still available in the Middle Temple Library. Where the legislation has been amended the librarian of the day has either hand written in the new text or scored the deleted text through in ink. See Appendix in this volume.

[27] Supreme Court of Judicature Act 1884, s 9; Order 36 Rule 48. RSC 1883; Order 36 Rule 50. RSC 1883.

[28] Arbitration Act 1889, s 14.

[29] E Fay, *Official Referees' Business*, 2nd edn (London, Sweet & Maxwell, 1988) 18.

[30] Civil Proceedings Fees Order 2008, SI 2008/1053, Sch 1.

[31] 'The New Law Courts' *The Times* (London, 11 January 1876) 3.

should be of stone; that every landowner should give up 1 ½ feet of land to enable a wall 3 feet thick and 16 feet high to be built at their joint cost'.[32] The focus of early building regulations was on preventing the spread of fire and infectious diseases.[33]

The Great Fire of London in 1666 had a profound effect on building safety. The 'Fire Courts' established under the Fire of London Disputes Act 1666 enabled judges to resolve thousands of disputes with notable speed to allow for the city to be rebuilt. The Rebuilding Act appears to contemporary observers to be London's first building code, which would eventually, develop into the much-copied London Building Act of 1774.[34] The primary focus of the regulations was on preventing fire spread with provisions relating to the construction of party walls, construction materials, the height of buildings and the width of streets.

In late Victorian England, there were no national building regulations. The decentralised approach continued: for example, by 1882 there were almost 1,000 urban authorities and 600 rural authorities with their own distinct building Byelaws. Larger towns such as London, Liverpool and Bristol had their own Building Acts, although these Acts were often inconsistent, and enforcement was patchy. Lord Normanby's unsuccessful proposal for a National Building Act in 1841 met stiff opposition. *The Times* reported in February 1841 the mood of many: 'This reckless and wanton invasion of property and liberty is proposed by a Liberal Government in the Nineteenth century, and in a country where every man's 'house' was formerly said to be 'his castle'.'[35]

The Alexandra Palace fire was just one of many notable fires in the late nineteenth century. In 1874 the large Pantechnicon warehouse, advertised as 'the largest, the safest and the most fireproof warehouse in the metropolis', burned down. Many of those storing valuable property in the Pantechnicon were Members of Parliament, which was not in session due to William Gladstone calling a general election. The fire at the Pantechnicon and the downfall of the government were reflected in Tom Taylor's satirical poem '*Fire-Proof*', published in *Punch Magazine* in 1874.[36]

[32] See M Webb 'The Design and Construction of Buildings in Relation to Fire Risks' (1933) 81 *Journal of the Royal Society of Arts* 242, 244. See also the later Commonwealth Act 1657 'No one should build houses save of brick and stone, and straight up.'

[33] For example, the Calais Paving Act 1548 set out the roofs were to be covered in slate and tiles rather than thatch.

[34] See discussion in Roger Henley Harper 'The Evolution of the English Building Regulations 1840–1914' (PhD Thesis, University of Sheffield 1978) 17.

[35] *The Times* (London, 16 February 1841) 4. Tensions between regulations and rights to property remain. For example, S Bright and D Maxwell, 'Extending limitation periods in the Defective Premises Act 1972: a breach of Article 1 of Protocol No.1' University of Oxford, Housing After Grenfell Blog (2 September 2021) blogs.law.ox.ac.uk/housing-after-grenfell/blog/2021/09/extending-limitation-periods-defective-premises-act-1972-breach? and D Maxwell *The Human Right to Property* (Oxford, Hart, 2022).

[36] T Taylor 'Fire-Proof' *Punch* (London, 28 February 1874) 92. Tom Taylor became the editor of *Punch* having previously practised as a Barrister, being called to the Bar of the Middle Temple in 1846.

"FIRE-PROOF"

(IN BUILDING AND CABINET-MAKING).

LOOK aghast at the fate of the pompous Pantechnicon,
Chicago and Boston to blazes assigned;
Spite of SHAW and steam-squirts, see the flames, without check, lick on,
And the stoutest of "fire-proof" to ashes calcined.

See the pillars, the beams, and the girders of iron,
The trust of the builder, writhed, wrenched, warped awry,
Till the stays that should hold what their framework environ,
Fire-twisted, tear down all 'twas hoped they would tie.

O, blind breasts of mortals! nor such the delusion
Of the builders of structures called "fire-proof" alone;
Wills of iron, in Cabinets set, work conclusion
As fatal as girders of iron in stone.

As I gaze on this ghastly Pantechnicon ruin,
Where the metal most trusted has brought the walls low,
I think of a Cabinet's recent undoing,
Which the means used to strengthen have helped to o'erthrow.

Such a girder was LOWE; such a pillar was AYRTON.
What a rending, and riving, and wrenching were seen,
Engendered by *their* rigid strain, and unfair tone,
Their resistance too stubborn, their tension too keen.

Nay, the tie-beam itself of the Cabinet building,
Had it shown but more equable force under flame,
Not yielded, at times when the worst thing was yielding,
Nor held out, when resistance to grief surely came.

We had not now sighed o'er a Cabinet sunken
From the zenith of power to the nadir of fall,
On high hopes collapsed, and on large promise shrunken,
Disunion for union, and gloom over all!

ii. The Metropolitan Building Act 1855

In 1873, the most important regulations were contained in the Metropolitan Building Act 1855 (as amended).[37] Much of the 1855 Act is a prescriptive list of what can and cannot be done in relation to matters such as the size, height, and materials to be used in party walls.[38] The rules on construction materials used in public buildings appear to have been guided by the discretion of the

[37] Metropolitan Building Act 1855; Metropolitan Building Act (Amendment) 1860; Metropolitan Building Act 1869. At this time section numbers in legislation were given in Roman Numerals. For ease we have used the modern method of Arabic numerals.

[38] Metropolitan Building Act 1855, ss 14–18.

District Surveyors.[39] Of particular relevance to the APC would have been section 19, which set out that:

> The roofs of buildings shall be constructed as follows; that is to say, 1. The flat, gutter, and roof of every building, and every turret, dormer, lantern light, sky-light or other incombustible material, except the doors, door frames, windows and window frame of such dormers, turrets, lanterns lights, skylights, or other erections.[40]

Similar rules on the mandatory requirement to use 'incombustible materials' can be seen in relation to chimneys and under an oven or stove used for trade or manufacture.[41] The Act was silent in relation to residential buildings, but in relation to public buildings, section 22 set out that:

> In every public building, and in every other building containing more than one hundred and twenty-five thousand cubic feet, and used as a dwelling house for separate families, the floors of the lobbies, corridors, passages and landings, and also the flights of stairs, shall be of stone or other fire-proof materials, and carried by supports of a fire-proof material.[42]

Decoration and external features such as 'cornice, facia, window dressing, portico, balcony, veranda, balustrade and architectural projection or decoration whatsoever' were to be constructed from 'brick, tile, stone, artificial stone, slate, cement or other fire-proof material'.[43] The First Schedule of the 1855 Act set out that:

> Every building shall be enclosed with walls constructed of brick, stone, or other hard and incombustible substances, and the foundation shall rest on the solid ground, or upon concrete or upon other solid sub-structure.[44]

The accompanying commentary in Glen and Glen, *The Metropolitan Building Acts 1855 to 1882* states that the provisions in the First Schedule 'amount to a prohibition against building the wall of wood or other combustible substances'.[45] This prescriptive rules-based approach can be contrasted with our later advice in which we will consider the standards-based approach of 'limited combustibility'.[46]

The District Surveyors had significant power and oversight.[47] They could give a builder 48 hours' notice for 'anything done contrary to the rules' of the 1855 Act to be remedied. If a builder failed to comply, a complaint could be made, whereon a Justice of the Peace would issue a summons and require the builder to appear before them.[48] To contemporary readers, the most notable provision of the 1855

[39] ibid, s 15.
[40] ibid, s 19.
[41] ibid, ss 20–21.
[42] ibid, s 22.
[43] ibid, s 27.
[44] ibid, First Schedule.
[45] W Cunningham Glen and R Cunningham Glen, *The Metropolitan Building Acts 1855 to 1882* (Shaw & Sons, 1883) 89 citing *Stevens v Gourley* 141 ER 752 (1859) 7 C.B. N.S. 99.
[46] See discussion below.
[47] Metropolitan Building Act 1855, s 31.
[48] ibid, s 46.

Act was section 47 (section XLVII in 1873), which set out that where an order of a Justice of the Peace is not complied with:

> … the Builder on whom it is made shall incur a Penalty not exceeding Twenty Pounds a Day, to be recovered before a Justice of the Peace, during every Day of the Continuance of such Noncompliance, and in addition thereto the District Surveyor may, if he thinks fit, proceed with a sufficient Number of Workmen to enter upon the Premises, and do all such Things as may be necessary for enforcing the Requisitions of such Notice, and for bringing any Building or Work into conformity with the Rules of this Act, and all Expenses incurred by him in so doing and in any such Proceedings as aforesaid, may be recovered from the Builder on whom such Order was made, in a summary Manner, before a Justice of the Peace, or may be recovered from the Owner of the Premises in the same Manner in which Expenses incurred by the Commissioners herein-after named in respect of dangerous Buildings are herein-after directed to be recovered from any Owner; and if the Owner cannot be found, or if, on Demand, he refuses or neglects to pay the aforesaid Expenses, the District Surveyor shall have the same Power of taking and selling the Building in respect of which the Order is made, and of applying the Proceeds, as is thereby given to the Commissioners.[49]

The contemporary equivalent in 2023 is the powers of removal or alteration of offending works in section 36 of the Building Act 1984 (the '1984 Act'), which provides:

> (1) If any work to which building regulations are applicable contravenes any of those regulations, the local authority, without prejudice to their right to take proceedings for a fine in respect of the contravention, may by notice require the owner—
>
> (a) to pull down or remove the work, or
>
> (b) if he so elects, to effect such alterations in it as may be necessary to make it comply with the regulations.[50]

Where a person fails to comply with a notice within 28 days, or such longer period as a magistrates' court may on his application allow, the local authority has the power to pull down or remove the work in question or effect such alterations in it as they deem necessary.[51] The local authority can recover the expenses reasonably incurred in the process.[52] Local authorities retain a power of entry for the purpose of ascertaining whether there is, or has been, a contravention of the 1984 Act, or of any building regulations.[53] Under the 1984 Act an individual who fails to comply with an enforcement notice can be liable on summary conviction to a fine not exceeding level 4 on the standard scale and to a further fine not exceeding £2 for each day on which the default continues after they are convicted.[54]

[49] ibid, s 47.

[50] Building Act 1984, s 36(1) and (2); There is only limited caselaw on s 36 demolition notices. See, *Lessees and Management Co of Herons Court v Heronslea Ltd* [2019] EWCA Civ 1423; [2019] 1 WLR 5849; *R (Bello) v Lewisham LBC* [2002] EWHC 1332 (Admin); [2002] EHLR 19; *R (Bello) v Lewisham LBC* [2003] EWCA Civ 353; 20 Const. LJ 89 (CA).

[51] Building Act 1984, s 36(3).

[52] ibid, s 36(3)(b).

[53] ibid, ss 95–96.

[54] ibid, s 99(2)(b).

iii. The Byelaws

Historically byelaws, guided by centrally drafted templates, most notably the 1875 Model Byelaws, played a major part in the regulation of buildings at a local level.

The Public Health Act 1875, section 157 required every urban authority to make byelaws with respect to inter alia 'the structure of walls, foundations, roofs and chimney of new buildings, for securing stability and the prevention of fires, and for the purposes of health'.[55] The Model Byelaws were exceedingly detailed and prescriptive. A 343-page version of the 1877 Model Byelaws, 'Issued by the Local Government Board for the use of Sanitary Authorities', published by George E. Eyre and William Spottiswoode, attests to their breadth.[56] To modern eyes, they encompass inter alia aspects of building safety, town and country planning and health and safety.

For present purposes, the most significant part of the Model Byelaws closest in time to the establishment of the Official Referees' Court is section 21, which sets out that 'Every person who shall erect a new building shall construct, in accordance with the following rules … walls built of good bricks, not less than nine inches long, or of suitable stone or other blocks of hard and incombustible substances ….' Further, section 22 states that external and party walls are to be built of '…. Good bricks, not less than nine inches long, or suitable store or other block of hard and incombustible substances, …'; and section 52 provides that 'Every person who shall erect a new building shall cause the flat and roof of such building, and every turret, dormer, lantern-light, skylight, or other erection place on the flat or roof of such building to be externally covered with slates, tile metal, or other incombustible materials, ….'[57]

C. Our Advice: Claims under Statute

In 1873 the APC will need to advise of the potential for public law actions being brought against the District Surveyor, architects, and builders if there has been a breach of the relevant byelaws.

We can draw the APC's attention to the absolute rule that a contract for the erection of a building in contravention of the provisions of the Metropolitan Building Act 1855 cannot be enforced.[58] In the 1859 case of *Stevens v Gourley*, a builder was unable to recover the contracted fee for constructing a building when it had instructed a sub-contractor to change the materials used in contravention of

[55] Public Health Act 1875, s 157.

[56] *Model Byelaws Issued by the Local Government Board for the use of Sanitary Authorities*' (London, George E. Eyre and William Spottiswood, 1877).

[57] See *Model Byelaws Issued by the Local Government Board for the use of Sanitary Authorities*' (London, George E. Eyre and William Spottiswood, 1877).

[58] *Stevens v Gourley* 141 ER 752 (1859) 7 CB NS 99.

the 1855 Act.[59] However, without further evidence, it will not be possible to advise on whether the relevant contracts are enforceable.

D. Our Advice: The Owner's Claims against Construction Professionals

Whether the design of the dome and other parts of the Palace complied with the regulations would need to be determined based on expert evidence. However, the information reported in the media suggests that the fire started in the dome and that whilst the principal supports for the new roof were made of fire-proof brick with iron girders, the zinc roofing was laid on wood and had other wood fittings.[60] If the dome contained wood, this may be contrary to section 19 and the First Schedule of the 1855 Act.

In 1873, an architect could be liable if the plans were defective because they: (1) did not comply with the instructions of the employer; (2) did not comply with the building law; (3) did not observe restrictions or limitations, public and private, on the use of the land; or (4) because there were 'faults of structure or plans forbidden by the science or art of architecture'.[61] Further, it was generally thought that when instructing an architect or builder, there was an implied term that the building and plans would be made in accordance with the Acts or Byelaws.[62]

The test for liability for breach of contract was articulated by Tindal CJ in the 1833 case of *Chapman v Walton*, where he observed that the question was 'whether other persons exercising the same profession or calling, and being men of experience and skill therein, would or would not have come to the same conclusion as the Defendant'.[63]

If it was established that the architects did not exercise ordinary skill and care, they would also forfeit wholly or in part the right to be paid under the contract. Relying on authorities decided before 1873, the first edition of *Hudson* noted that 'a person of skill cannot recover for services which are useless, and which, in the ordinary exercise of his skill, he ought to have known would be useless towards the object for which he was employed'.[64] Approval of a plan by the employer would not release the architect from liability for structural defects of defects in the plans.[65]

[59] ibid.

[60] 'Court and Official' *Cheshire Observer* (Chester, 22 November 1873).

[61] A Hudson, *The Law of Building and Engineering Contracts* (Waterlow and Sons 1891) 44.

[62] ibid 48.

[63] *Chapman v Walton* 131 ER 826 (1833), 10 Bing 57, 63; HHJ Emden, *The Law Relating to Buildings* (Knight & Co, 1895) 47 wrote that 'If an architect orders materials or does some act professing to contract for the employer, he impliedly warrants to the other contracting party that he in fact possesses the authority he assumes to exercise; and he becomes liable to an action for the breach of such warranty.'

[64] A Hudson, *The Law of Building and Engineering Contracts* (Waterlow and Sons 1891) 41.

[65] ibid 44.

In 1873, damages in such actions were not limited to the amount the architect would have been entitled to on properly discharging their duties.[66] An architect could potentially lose their right to remuneration, but also be held liable for the damage caused by the fire.

V. Nineteen Twenty-Three

A. The Legal Scene and the Official Referees

By 1923 our instructions are typed, but the Bar remains embedded in tradition. In May 1922, Dr Ivy Williams became the first woman to be called to the Bar of England and Wales, and in November 1922, Helena Normanton became the first woman to practise. As the world marvelled at the opening of Tutankhamun's sarcophagus, there are three Official Referees: Sir Edward Pollock, Sir Francis Newbolt, and Mr GA Scott, the inventor of the Scott Schedule. The Official Referees are now effectively doing the work of a High Court Judge, dealing with over 300 cases in 1922.[67] By 1923, the most recent edition of *Hudson* is now slightly out of date, published in 1914.[68] We may try, but finding published decisions of the Official Referees will be near impossible.[69] By 1923 there had emerged a backlash against the byelaws, particularly by some architects, who felt constrained and preferred the aestheticism and writings of such as John Ruskin.[70]

The Official Referees' Court is now regularly dealing with construction disputes. For example, in 1923, Sir Edward Pollock considered an action brought by a claimant who had contracted for the building of a bungalow. A newspaper article from the time reported that 'the Defendant verbally represented that the walls of the house would be 'as strong as the tomb of Tutankhamun''.[71] However, once the house was completed, it was found to be riddled with defects, which it was alleged that it would take £250 to repair. Sir Edward awarded the claimant £26.5.0 and made no award as to costs. He observed that it was an unfortunate case and that the statement that the house would be 'as strong as the 'tomb of Tutankhamen' did

[66] ibid 41.

[67] E Fay, *Official Referees' Business*, 2nd edn (London, Sweet & Maxwell, 1988) 24.

[68] A Hudson, *The Law of Building, Engineering, and Ship Building* (London, Sweet and Maxwell, 1914).

[69] See ch 13 in this volume.

[70] An article by RM Lucas FRIB entitled 'Anti -building by-laws, suggestions for reform' first published in 1905, cited in RH Harper, 'The Conflict Between English Building Regulations and Architectural Design 1890–1918' (1977) 6 *Journal of Architectural Research* 22, 28, Lucas lamented 'the splendid type of 17th or 18th century cottage with its thick walls … heavy oak timbers, oak or elm floors, tile roof and ample hearth … to a miserable thin walled 'brick box with a slate', as Ruskin called it, made generally to a stock pattern because any departure in design or material are apt to lead to wearisome explanations to a garrulous committee or to an official who, in some cases at least, combines the qualifications of a coster with the authority of a censor.'

[71] 'Bungalows' lives and the Pyramids' *Essex Chronicle* (Essex, 13 November 1925) 4.

not amount to much. It did not suggest that the house was going to last to the age of the Pyramids': at which point a rare moment of audible laughter was reported in the Official Referees' Court.[72]

B. Our Advice: The Regulatory Framework

i. *The London Building Act 1894*

Since 1873 the regulatory landscape has changed significantly. The London Building Act 1894 (the '1894 Act') suspended wholly or in part 13 Acts of Parliament affecting streets, buildings, and structures in the administrative county of London. By 1923 the 1894 Act had been amended 11 times.[73] Important changes to the 1894 Act were made in the London Building Acts (Amendment) Act 1905. William Woodward, commenting on the 1905 Act, in the *Journal of the Royal Institute of British Architects*, noted:

> Section 28 is marginally described as 'For Protection of Inns of Court,' and this is the only piece of real humour which I have detected in the Act, because it turns out that the Honourable Societies respectively of the Inner Temple, the Middle Temple, Lincoln's Inn, and Gray's Inn shall be exempt from the operation of the Act: in other words, the whole of the lawyers occupying these Inns may be left to be burnt to death under the sub-heading of 'Protection.'[74]

The establishment of the London County Council in 1889 was to impact the regulation of buildings significantly for the following 70 years.[75]

The standard of buildings and adherence to the relevant laws appears to have been lax. The Legal Pages of *The Builder* from the late nineteenth century offer many examples of builders failing to comply with the Byelaws and attempting to cut corners. For example, on 16 May 1891, it was reported that Alfred Margerison had been fined £3 and ordered to pay £2 in costs for using road scraping and horse manure for mortar while building four new houses in Sheffield.[76] In one instance, Mr Jukes, a builder of homes on Tewkesbury Road, near Seven Sisters, built houses with defective foundations. Before the local Magistrates in 1889, he pleaded: 'It will simply ruin me if I have to pull down these houses, as they are built up to the bedroom windows.' The Magistrate replied, 'You talk about ruining yourself if you

[72] ibid.

[73] See, London Building Act 1894, Amendment Act 1898; London Government Act 1899; London Building Acts (Amendment) Act 1905; London County Council (General Powers) Act 1908; London County Council (General Powers) Act 1909; London County Council (General Powers) 1915; London County Council (General Powers) Act 1920; London County Council (General Powers) Act 1921; and London County Council (General Powers) Act 1923.

[74] W Woodward, 'Notes on the London Building Act (Amendment) Act 1905' (1905) 13 *Journal of the Royal Institute of British Architects* 74.

[75] Local Government Act 1888.

[76] Road-Scrapings for 'Mortar', *The Builder* (London, vol 60, 15 May 1891) 399.

have to pull the houses down, but what about ruining the purchaser?' Mr Jukes responded: 'When a man buys a house he is supposed to do so with his eye open, and if he is ruined that is his business.'

The period between 1873 and 1923 has seen the population of London explode from 3.8 million to over 7.3 million. Technological change is having a profound effect on the construction industry. By 1923, steel-frame construction and the use of reinforced concrete, pioneered in the US, and once impossible under the prescriptive Byelaws, are starting to be used in London.[77] Still, the relevant regulations struggle to keep up. Giving a lecture in 1933, Architect Maurice Webb noted that

> Since 1894, building methods, through the introduction of steel and reinforced concrete, have undergone possibly the greatest revolution known in building at any time since the Romans substituted an arch for the Greek lintel, and as a result of this the present Building Act is hopelessly out-of-date and the L.C.C, are in the course of revising it now to meet modern requirements.[78]

Other means, such as the use of sprinklers, which had become a common and proven fire safety measure in the US, remain off the regulatory agenda due to perceptions about the cost.[79] By the 1930s, fire safety was being talked about in terms of national security as the fear of a 'great war in the air' was eventually proven correct during the Blitz.[80] While the Munich Beer Hall Putsch took place in 1923, the nightmares of the Blitz and the Second Great Fire of London were not realised for nearly another 18 years.

Challenges interpreting the regulations remain. In 1901 Messrs, Weary & James builders were summonsed by Mr McLachlan, the District Surveyor, for installing a shop front on 169 Fleet Street without serving the required notice under section 145 of the London Building Act 1894. The builders alleged that the forms had not been served because they could not state the 'intended occupation' because the shop was already in occupation. In response to this apparent lacuna in the Act, Sir Henry is reported to have stated: 'The Act may have been drawn by some philosopher, who sat in his closet and thought it was a theoretical accomplishment, but I look upon it as impractical and worthless.'[81]

One significant development since 1873, following a series of tragic fires in factories and theatres, was the introduction of rules relating to reasonable means of escape.[82] Nevertheless, under the London Building Act 1930, any residential

[77] JC Lawrence, 'Steel Frame Architecture versus the London Building Regulations: Selfridges, the Ritz, and American Technology' (1990) 6 *Construction History* 23.

[78] M Webb 'The Design and Construction of Buildings in relation to fire risks' (1933) 81 *Journal of the Royal Society of Arts* 242, 247.

[79] M Webb 'The Design and Construction of Buildings in Relation to Fire Risks' (1933) 81 *Journal of the Royal Society of Arts* 242.

[80] ibid.

[81] 'An 'Impractical and Worthless' Measure' *The Builder*, vol 80 (London, 9 March 1901) 248.

[82] Factory and Workshop Act 1901; Factory and Workshop Act 1907; London Buildings Act (Amendment) Act 1905, ss 7 and 9.

building erected in 1905 or earlier which was occupied as a private dwelling house was made totally exempt from any requirement for the provision of means of escape in case of fire.[83]

The key provisions to consider are the limits on the methods of construction and the use of fireproof and incombustible materials. There remained a major focus on party walls: the 1894 Act, section 56(3) provided that 'A bond timber or wood plate shall not be built into any party wall and the end of any wooden beam or joist bearing on such walls shall be at least four inches distant from the centre line of the party walls.'

To add a new level of confusion, the 1894 Act used 'fire-resisting materials',[84] 'incombustible material',[85] and 'fire proof materials'.[86] The three expressions were not synonymous.

The Second Schedule of the London Building Act 1894 provided:

> The following materials shall for the purposes of this Act be deemed to be fire-resisting materials: -
>
> (1) Brickwork constructed of good bricks well burnt hard and sound properly bounded and solidly put together –
>   (a) With good mortar compounded of good lime and sharp clean sand hard clean broken flint grit or slag; or
>   (b) With good cement; or
>   (c) With cement mixed with sharp clean sand hard clean broken brick broken flint grit or slag:
>
> (2) Granite and other stone suitable for building purposes by reason of its solidity and durability:
>
> (3) Iron steel and copper:
>
> (4) Oak and oak and other hard timber when used for beams or posts or in combination with iron the timber and the iron (if any) being protected by plastering in cement or other incombustible or non-conducting external coating;
>
> In the case of doors –
>
> Oak or teak or other hard timber not less than two inches thick;
>
> In the case of staircases –
>
> Oak or teak or other hard timber with treads strings and risers not less than two inches thick:
>
> (1) Slate tiles brick and terra-cotta when used for covering or corbels;
>
> (2) Flagstones when used for floors over arches but not exposed on the underside and not supported at the ends only:
>
> (3) Concrete composed of broken brick stone chippings or ballast and lime cement or calcined gypsum when used for filling in between joists of floors:
>
> (4) Any materials from time to time approved by the council as fire-resisting.

[83] London Building Act 1930, s 30; 'Building Code for London' *The Times* (London, 11 December 1937) 19.
[84] London Building Act 1894, ss 64 and 67.
[85] ibid, ss 61, 64, and 72.
[86] ibid, s 74.

The materials in the First Schedule of the 1905 Act are not specifically declared to be either 'incombustible' or 'fireproof'. Compliance with the 'fire-resisting' materials standard can be achieved by using any of the materials mentioned in the schedule. The picture was slightly more complicated, as Cohen noted, 'not all materials mentioned there are incombustible or fireproof, e.g., it declares that oak, teak and other hard timber to be fire-resisting, but it cannot be said that timber is incombustible'.[87]

Conflicting guidance can be taken from the 1892 decision of *Payne v Wright*, where the Queen's Bench Division held that an 'incombustible material' was a material 'wholly incombustible'.[88] In *Payne*, it was held that a material consisting of woven iron wire covered with an oily compound was not an incombustible material.

The challenge of identifying the difference between fireproof and fire-resisting was raised before the Lord Mayor in 1897.[89] A builder had been summonsed under the 1894 Act for failing to comply with a notice of irregularity in relation to premises at 60 Cheapside. The District Surveyor noted that the question was whether certain dormer windows on the roof of the premises were 'combustible' within the meaning of the Act. The solicitor appearing for the owner of the premises argued that as the dormers were covered in lead, they were not combustible, but he did concede that lead melted by fire, exposing the wooden frames. The Chief Clerk said that the list of fire-resisting materials in the 1894 Act did not include lead. The Lord Mayor observed that it was 'a pity the Act was not more explicit' but directed that the notice be complied with, the remediation works were to be undertaken, and he granted 13 shillings in costs.[90]

C. Our Advice: Claims under Statute

While the relevant byelaws have been revised since 1873, the APC will still need to advise of the potential for public law actions being brought against the District Surveyor, architects, and builders if there has been a breach of the relevant byelaws.

In 1923, the principle in *Stevens v Gourley* remain good law.[91] However, as in 1873, without further information, it will not be possible to advise on whether the relevant contracts are enforceable.

D. Our Advice: The Owner's Claims

Our advice in relation to potential claims would not have changed significantly since 1873.

[87] A Cohen, *The London Building Acts 1894 to 1905* (Stevens & Sons 1906) 26.
[88] *Payne v Wright* [1892] 1 QB 104.
[89] 'The London Building Act' *The Builder*, vol 72 (London, 6 February 1897) 133.
[90] ibid.
[91] *Stevens v Gourley* 141 ER 752, (1859) 7 CBNS 99.

Applying the decision of the Lord Mayor in 1897 and *Payne v Wright*, it could have been arguable that the dome was not made from 'incombustible material' and fire that occurred is evidence that the materials used on the roof were not 'wholly incombustible'.[92] This would suggest the design was defective.

We would however also have to ask our client whether they had instructed a fire engineer. The principles would have been the same: a claim in contract, knowledge of the building regulations, and for 'negligence', albeit we might expect fire engineers to have greater knowledge of the fire safety regulations.

VI. Nineteen Seventy-Three

A. The Legal Scene and the Official Referee

Our third brief arrives in Chambers; working from home is not merely a faux pas, but nearly impossible. It comes via the solicitors' outdoor clerk, with further documents sent by the Royal Mail.[93] Our instructions are on folded A3 paper, typed in large font, double-spaced with a back sheet, and tied up with a pink ribbon. Hard copies of documents are provided in lever arch files or cardboard boxes as appropriate.

We will dictate our Advice (or Opinion, if we are a QC) and hope that the Chambers' typist has time to complete accurately our Advice (Opinion) today and that it is right the first time. Tippex may be used if we have time to spot a mistake. We will endorse the back sheet to our instructions with a 'γ', our name and the date, and our work will be returned via the outdoor clerks. Decimalisation in 1971 has changed how we are paid. In 1873 and 1923 we would have been paid in guineas, keeping a pound with a shilling for the clerk.

Outside of Court, we still speak about Official Referees, but the swots among us will note that the office was abolished at midnight on 31 December 1971. The work is now undertaken by senior circuit judges nominated by the Lord Chancellor to deal with Official Referees' business. In Court, we refer to the judges as 'His/Her Honour', as we have been doing since 1938.[94] In 1973 there are three 'Official Referees', namely Sir Norman Richards QC, Sir William Stabb QC, and Edgar Fay QC.[95] The Court still lacks original jurisdiction, necessitating an order from a Master of the Chancery or Queen's Bench Division referring each case to the Official Referees. For procedural points, we can consult the succinct five paragraph *Practice Notice (OR: Procedure)* [1986] 1 WLR 1425 drafted by Walker Carter.[96]

[92] *Payne v Wright* [1892] 1 QB 104.

[93] The DX is still in the future, because the DX Group does not start providing their services until 1975, following a number of strikes by the Royal Mail.

[94] The Official Referees were accorded the style and title by Royal Warrant.

[95] See ch 5 in this volume.

[96] *Practice Notice (OR: Procedure)* [1986] 1 WLR 1425.

From 1974, the Official Referees will be required to retain their notebooks and minute books records for a period of time. This will follow the intervention of Lord Denning in his role as Superintendent of the Public Records Office. However, as noted above, much of the surviving records are difficult to read or understand.[97]

Since our last hearing in the 1920s, the Official Referees have played a short game of musical chairs, moving in 1965 from the West Wing of the RCJ to Victory House in Kingsway (as of 2023, home to the Central London Employment Tribunal), before returning back to the 'Official Referees' Corridor' on the top floor of the West Block of the RCJ.

To assist us with our research, we have the tenth edition of *Hudson*,[98] and the third edition of *Keating*,[99] and such law reports as we can find in Chambers (including the cut-outs of the Times Law Reports put in a scrapbook by the Chambers secretary) or in the Inns' libraries. Even the first version of Lexis-Nexis, which will allow us to search for unreported cases online (for a small fortune per minute), will not be available until the 1990s.

B. Our Advice: The Regulatory Framework

i. The Building Regulations 1965

The Public Health Act 1961 (which amended the Public Health Act 1936) gave the Minister of Housing and Local Government and his successors (rather than local authorities) the power to make building laws. The first set of national building standards, the Building Regulations 1965, which replaced approximately 1,400 sets of local byelaws, were laid before Parliament on 22 July 1965 and came into force on 1 February 1966.[100] They covered England and Wales apart from Inner London Boroughs, where the London Building Acts continued to prevail.

The Building Regulations 1965 (like the previous Byelaws) set down mandatory and prescriptive standards that had to be followed. They contain 'deemed-to-satisfy provisions', which identify the British Standards and British Standard Codes of Practice which, if followed, would mean that the building was 'deemed to satisfy' the relevant regulation.

The Building Regulations 1965 run to 174 pages and apply to the erection of buildings, alterations and extensions to existing buildings and to buildings for which there had been a material change of use. Part E sets out the standards for 'Structural Fire Precautions' and includes, amongst other things, requirements for the provision of compartment walls and floors, fire resistance, external walls, separating walls, and roofs.

[97] M Reynolds, *Caseflow Management: A Rudimentary Referees Process, 1919–70* (PhD, LSE 2008) 34.

[98] IN Duncan Wallace, *Hudson's Building and Engineering Contracts*, 10th edn (London, Sweet & Maxwell,1970).

[99] D Keating, *Law and Practice of Building Contracts*, 3rd edn (London, Sweet & Maxwell, 1969).

[100] Building Regulations 1965, SI 1965/1373. Scotland had already beaten England and Wales to the mark and adopted national regulations in the Building (Scotland) Act 1959.

a. External Walls

Regulation E7 of the Building Regulations provides that external walls which are situated within a distance of 3 feet (90cm) of a relevant boundary (ie adjoining property) and any external wall of a building which is more than 50 feet (15 metres) in height and which is situated three feet or more from the relevant boundary is required to be constructed:

(1) *without any combustible material apart from*: (a) internal lining which complies with regulation E14; and (b) and *any external cladding not required by paragraph 3 of regulation E17 to be non-combustible*; and
(2) so that any required fire resistance is to be attained by the non-combustible part alone. [Emphasis added]

There are no specific requirements for external walls which are not situated within 3 feet of a relevant boundary and are less than 50 feet in height.

Regulation E7(3)(a) requires cladding on *any* external wall which is situated within a distance of 3 feet of the relevant boundary to be non-combustible.

The requirements set down in paragraph 3(b) of regulation E7 for external walls which are more than 50 feet in height (and more than 3 feet from a relevant boundary) are less stringent. They do not require the material to be non-combustible but rather require that the surface of the cladding complies with the requirements specified for 'Class 0'.

Class 0 materials are defined in regulation E14 of the Building Regulations 1965. They include:

(1) materials which are non-combustible throughout; *and*
(2) *products* comprising a base (or background) which is non-combustible and a surface not exceeding 1/32 inch thick *which has a spread of flame rating not lower than Class 1 (i.e. the best rating) when tested in accordance with clause 7 of BS 476: Part I: 1953.*[101] [Emphasis added]

Significantly, clause 7 (later referred to as the Part 7) BS 476 test is a small-scale test which measures the lateral spread of flame along the surface of the combined product and *not* the combustibility of the combined product when involved in a fire.

It appears therefore that the focus of regulation E7 in the Building Regulations 1965 was on preventing the spread of fire between buildings, as opposed to fire spread on external walls.

Notably, the Inner London Byelaws applicable in 1965 differed from the Building Regulations 1965 because they required external walls to be constructed with materials that had a fire resistance of 60 minutes.[102]

[101] Building Regulations 1985, SI 1985/1065, Regulation E14 also provided that materials comprising a base which was combustible but with any exposed face finished with a layer not less than 1/8 inch thick of non-combustible material and with the other face not exposed to air would also be classified as Class 0.

[102] Local Law (Greater London Council and Inner London Boroughs) Order 1965.

b. Roofs

The specific requirements for roofs are set out in Regulation E15 of the Building Regulations 1965.[103] They are set by reference to BS 476: Part 3 – 'External Fire Exposure Roof Test'. There are more stringent requirements for buildings with a capacity of more than 500,000 cubic feet like the Palace (and also for properties used for factories or for storage and for a house in a continuous terrace of more than two houses).[104] The roof (or rather the dome) of the Palace should therefore have been constructed so that: (1) it would not be penetrated by fire within 1 hour; or (2) it would not be penetrated by fire in less than 30 minutes and could resist the spread of flame.[105]

c. Proper Means of Escape and Fire-Fighting Measures

The Building Regulations 1965 contained no specific provisions relating to the provision of a proper means of escape or for fire-fighting measures.

The omission of any provisions relating to a proper means of escape in the Building Regulations might be explained by section 60 of the Public Health Act 1936. Section 60 applied to all buildings which exceed two storeys in height and in which the floor of any upper storey is more than 20 feet above the surface of the street and which is: (i) let in flats or tenement dwellings; or (ii) is used as an inn, hotel, boarding house, hospital, nursing home, boarding school, children's home or similar institution; or (iii) is used as a restaurant, shop, store or warehouse and has sleeping accommodation on an upper floor for employees.[106] Section 60(1) gives the local authority the power to require modifications to be made to existing and proposed buildings to which section 60 applies, if it appears to the authority that any building or proposed building is or is not going to be provided with such means of escape in case of fire as the local authority deems necessary.

There were no equivalent provisions for other types of buildings in the Public Health Act, although section 59 gave the local authority power to reject plans for certain public and other buildings[107] including, any theatre, hall or other building or other place of public resort (like the Palace), certain shops and licensed clubs, which 'do not provide means of ingress and egress and passages or gangways as the

[103] Building Regulations 1965, SI 1965/1373.
[104] Building Regulations 1985, SI 1985/1065, Regulation E15.
[105] Designations AA, AB, AC, AD, BA, BB, and BD were permitted by Regulation E15 with the first letter giving the fire penetration classification (A=specimens which have not been penetrated within 1 hour; B=specimens which are penetrated in not less than 30 minutes; C=specimens which are penetrated in less than 30 minutes; D=specimens which are penetrated in the preliminary flame test) and the second letter giving the spread of flame classification (A=specimens on which there is no spread of flame; B=specimens on which there is not more than 533mm, (21 inches), spread of flame; C= specimens on which there is more than 533mm, (21 inches), spread of flame; D=specimens which continue to burn for 5 minutes after the removal of the test flame or with spread of flame more than 381mm, (15 inches), in the preliminary test).
[106] Public Health Act 1936, s 60(4).
[107] ibid, s 59 lists the buildings to which the section applies in s 59(5).

authority deem satisfactory'.[108] However, this provision was not obviously directed to escape in the case of fire.

However, factories have been required, under the Factories Act 1937, to have a proper means of escape in case of fire and a (what we would now consider basic) fire certificate and have since 1948 been required to have 'necessary equipment and facilities for extinguishing fire'.[109] However, that legislation proved to be inadequate. Amendments remained reactive rather than proactive.

A fire at the Eastwood Mills, Keighley, Yorkshire in February 1956 resulted in eight deaths as workers became trapped following the collapse of the only staircase (fire escape).[110] In response the Factories Act 1961 gave the Fire Authority rather than the District Council the power to inspect factories for fire safety, and fire certificates were required to cover not only means of escape but also provisions for fire-fighting, and structural fire separation.[111]

A fire in June 1960 at the William Henderson & Sons department store in Liverpool resulted in the death of ten people who were trapped on the fourth floor. Another man fell to his death whilst assisting others to safety from a window ledge.[112] This led to the Offices, Shops and Railway Premises Act 1963, which extended the protection of workplace health, safety and welfare under the Factories Act 1961 to other employees in Great Britain. Like the Factories Act, it required offices, shops and railway premises to have fire certificates covering means of escape, provision for fire-fighting, and structural fire separation.[113]

In May 1961, there was a fire at the Top Storey Club in Bolton in which 15 people died in the building; four were killed after jumping out of windows and falling to the ground.[114] This tragedy occurred although the Chief Constable had sent a letter to the owners of the club on 5 April 1961 warning them that the use of the building as a club was unauthorised and that if planning permission was granted he would require the owners to carry out alterations, including providing an external fire escape.[115] Again reactive amendments were made, this time to the Licensing Act 1961. The fire at the Rose and Crown Hotel, Saffron Walden in December 1969, in which eleven people lost their lives,[116] was one of a number of fires in hotels which prompted a further review of the fire safety legislation.

[108] Public Health Act 1936, s 59(1).

[109] Factories Act 1937, s 34 and Factories Act 1948, s 38.

[110] 'Eight feared dead in fire', *The Times* (London, 24 February 1956) 'About 10 of 15 people working on the top floor were unable to escape … As a fireman prepared to re-enter the building the staircase collapsed and the first floor fell through to trap the seven employees still on the top floor.'

[111] Factories Act 1961, ss 40–52.

[112] 'Store Fire Damage Estimated at £1m' *The Times* (London 24 June 1960) 'It is believed the fire started in the stoor room on the third floor near a stone staircase. The victims trapped are through to have asphyxiated before the flames reached them.'

[113] Offices, Shops and Railway Premises Act 1963, ss 28–39.

[114] 'Blind Panic in blazing club as lights went out' *The Times* (London, 3 May 1961) 8.

[115] ibid and 'Club Landlords were told of fire risk' *The Times* (London, 3 May 1961) 12.

[116] 'Eleven die as fire sweeps holiday hotel' *The Times* (London, 27 December 1969) 1 'The alarm was raised by the hotel manager, Mr Emil Landsman …. Mr Landsman ran up the fire escape with one of the hotel porters to try to help. They found glass in the windows was red hot. A senior Essex fire officer

The result was the Fire Precautions Act 1971. This gave the Secretary of State the power to: (1) issue building regulations imposing requirements ensuring a proper means of escape (to cover new builds and extensions/alterations); and (2) designate types of premises required to have fire certificates confirming that the premises has proper means of escape, provision for fighting fire, and structural fire separation (which was applicable to existing buildings).

In 1972, hotels and boarding houses were the first premises to be designated as requiring a fire certificate under the Fire Precautions Act 1971.[117] A designating order was also made for factories, offices, shops and railway premises in 1976.[118] However, no further premises required a fire certificate.

ii. The Building Regulations 1972

The Building Regulations were updated in 1972 and amended in the Building (First Amendment) Regulations 1973. These included an amended Part E, which (as before) stipulated requirements for structural fire precautions; and a new Part EE, which stipulated requirements in relation to means of escape in case of a fire (as permitted by the Fire Precautions Act 1971).

a. External Walls

Regulation E7(3) of the Building (First Amendment) Regulations 1973 requires any external wall which is situated within 1 metre from any point on the relevant boundary and any external wall of a building which exceeds 15 metres in height to

(1) *be constructed of non-combustible materials apart from any external cladding which complies with regulation E7(4)* or any internal lining which complies with regulation E15; and
(2) be so constructed that any fire resistance required by the regulations is attained by the non-combustible part alone.[119]

The requirements for external cladding on a building which is situated within 1 metre from the relevant boundary and external cladding on a building which exceeds 15 metres in height are the same under Part E of the Building (First Amendment) Regulations 1973. They are required to be Class 0. As such, the requirements for external cladding on buildings which are situated within 1m of the relevant boundary have been 'relaxed'.

said that he found the glass box containing the key to the escape unbroken, and added that from the position of the bodies nearby it was clear that the man had got to 3ft of the box before flames overcame him. Mr Landsman said that although the room alarm was designed to continue ringing once the circuit had been activated he did not believe it had rung long enough to wake any of the guests. Trust House officials suggested that the wiring circuit might have been burnt through.'

[117] Fire Precautions (Hotels and Boarding Houses) Order 1972, SI 1972/238.

[118] Fire Precautions (Factories, Offices, Shops and Railway Premises) Order 1976.

[119] Building (First Amendment) Regulations 1973, SI 1973/1276.

Regulation E15(1)(e) states that a reference to a surface being Class 0 is a requirement that the material of which the wall (or ceiling) is:

(1) non-combustible throughout; *or*
(2) has a surface *material* or, if it is bonded throughout to a substrate the surface material in conjunction with the substrate) *which would 'pass' the test set out in BS 476: Part 6: 1968.*[120] [Emphasis added.]

The Part 6 BS 476 test is a small-scale test which provides a comparative measure of the combined product's contribution to the growth of fire. Like the Part 7 BS 476 test it does *not* test the combustibility of the materials when involved in a fire.[121]

The Inner London byelaws applicable in 1975 again differed from the Building Regulations, requiring external walls to be constructed with materials having a fire resistance of 60 minutes.

b. Roofs

Regulation E7 of the Building (First Amendment) Regulations 1973 set out the requirements for roofs – the same as in the Building Regulations 1965.

c. Means of Escape

Part EE (Means of Escape in Case of Fire) applies to flats and maisonettes with a floor above 4.5 metres, shops (except for a shop having a sales floor area not exceeding 280 meters^2 per floor on not more than three storeys, one of which may be a basement storey) and offices (except for an office having more than four storeys, including any basement storey or storeys, served by only one stairway).[122]

Part EE therefore applies to the accommodation block. It does not apply to the Palace.

Regulation EE3 requires all buildings to which it applies to have means of escape consisting of exits and escape routes as was reasonably required in the circumstances of the case to enable the occupants to reach a place of safety in the event of the fire and such other works (other than by means of fighting fire) as might be necessary for securing that such means of escape could be safely and effectively used at all material times.[123]

Regulation EE4 states that the requirements of Regulation EE3 will be deemed to be satisfied if the building complied with the relevant recommendations of the British Standard Code of Practice CP3, Code of Basic Design Data for the

[120] ie, had an index of performance (I) not exceeding 12 and a sub-index (i_1) not exceeding 6.

[121] Building (First Amendment) Regulations 1973, Regulation E14 also provided that materials comprising a base which was combustible but with any exposed face finished with a layer not less than 1/8 inch thick of non-combustible material and with the other face not exposed to air would also be classified as Class 0.

[122] Building (First Amendment) Regulations 1973, Regulation EE1.

[123] Building (First Amendment) Regulations 1973, Regulation EE3.

Design of Building ('CP3').[124] Chapter IV of CP3 1971. CP3 1971 allowed flats to be served by a single common stair where flats were separated from the stair by a protected lobby and each flat entrance door was no more than 15 metres from the protected stair door.[125]

d. Firefighting Measures

The Building Regulations 1972 contain no specific provisions relating to the provision of fire sprinklers. The provision of fire-fighting measures is (still) regulated by the Fire Precautions Act 1971. However, the use of sprinklers (with water towers) in factories, mills and theatres is becoming more common because insurers require their installation.

iii. The Building Act 1984 and the Building Regulations from 1985

We would not have known in 1973 (but do now) that the Building Regulations would be further amended in 1974 to include an amended Part F, setting down new requirements for insulation to provide for better energy conservation. As a result, the use of plastic materials and cladding on buildings increased. This was permitted provided (as described above) the surface or the surface and substrate of the material met the Class 0 requirements.

Again, we would not have known in 1973 (but do now) that the Building Act 1984 would bring a fundamental change to the building regulations regime. The prescriptive standards in the Building Regulations (1972), as amended (set out over 306 pages), were trimmed down to just 28 pages and replaced by functional performance standards in the Building Regulations 1985, which were supported by statutory guidance in the Approved Documents.[126]

The Building (Inner London) Regulations 1985 amended the Building Regulations 1985, meaning that from 6 January 1986 the Building Regulations also applied to Inner London.[127]

Part B of the Building Regulations 1985 set out the functional performance standards in respect of fire. However, the new drafting was notably opaque. For example, Requirement B1, dealing with means of escape, said no more than

[124] The relevant provisions of CP3 were Chapter IV; Part I 1971 (Flats and maisonettes), Part 2: 1968 (Shops and departmental stores) or Part 3 1968 (office buildings).

[125] The earlier versions of the CP3 Code of Practice which had applied from 1948 provided that it was acceptable for residential blocks of flats to be served by a single protected stairway. Individual flats were also to be provided with an 'escape balcony' provided that no balcony was higher than 14 yards (12.8m) above ground, which was the then height of fire brigade ladders. Corridors giving access from flats to the single protected staircase could be over 12m in length. Blocks of flats had become taller during the 1950s and 1960s, but CP3 was not updated until 1971. As a result, a number of high rise buildings built in the 1950s and 1960s had corridors as long as 24m. This included Lakanal House which caught fire on 3 July 2009.

[126] Building Regulations 1985, SI 1985/1065.

[127] Building (Inner London) Regulations 1985, Sch 2, para 1(1).

'[t]here shall be means of escape of fire from the building to a place of safety outside the building capable of being used safely and effectively used at all material times'. Requirements B4(1) and B4(2), which dealt with external walls and roofs said no more than the external walls and the roof of a building 'shall offer adequate resistance to the spread of fire' over the walls or the roof and from one building to another 'having regard to the height, use and position of the building'.

a. External Walls

The first edition of Approved Document B relating to Parts B2 (internal fire spread (surfaces)), B3 (internal fire spread (structure)) and B4 (external fire spread) of Schedule 1 to the Building Regulations 1985 was issued in 1985 ('ADB 1985').

The guidance concerning external cladding was essentially the same for all types of buildings. ADB 1985 stated that cladding to an external wall that was required to be constructed of material of 'limited combustibility' could be combustible if it was not being relied upon to contribute to the fire resistance of the wall *and* met the provisions set down for external cladding in ADB 1985.[128]

The provisions for external cladding provided that buildings which were less than 1m from a relevant boundary were required to have class 0 external materials, ie, they were required to be:

(1) composed throughout of materials of 'limited combustibility'; or
(2) to be a Class I surface spread of flame material in accordance with the BS 476 Part 7 test *and* to have 'passed' the BS 476 Part 6 test for fire propagation.[129]

There was no provision for cladding on buildings which were less than 15 metres in height and more than 1 metre from a relevant boundary. Buildings which were over 15 metres in height and more than 1 metre from a relevant boundary were required to have class 0 cladding 15 metres or more above the ground.

The provisions of ADB 1985 were therefore similar to the prescriptive provisions set down in Regulation E7(3) of the Building Regulations 1972.[130] However, as stated above, from 1985, the Building Regulations applied to buildings in Inner London. This meant that at a stroke of a pen, hundreds of high-rise blocks in London became subject to less stringent conditions.

The issue was highlighted in the findings of the Assistant Deputy Coroner, Her Honour Frances Kirkham, a former TCC Judge, in the Lakanal House Inquest.[131] Lakanal House was built in the late 1950s. Works including window replacement had been undertaken in 1978–1979, and a further substantial refurbishment which

[128] ADB 1985, paras 1.9, 1.3 and Table 1.2 (Dwellinghouses), paras 2.9, 2.3 and Table 2.2 (Flats), paras 3.9, 3.13 and Table 3.2 (Institutional), paras 4.9, 4.13 and Table 4.2 (Other residential), paras 5.9 and 5.15 and Table 5.2 and Table 5.2 (Assembly) and paras 6.9 and 6.13 (Offices, etc), and 6.2.

[129] ie, have a fire propagation index (I) of nor more than 12 and a sub-index (i1) of not more than 6.

[130] Building Regulations 1972, SI 1972/317.

[131] Her Honour Frances Kirkham retired from the TCC in 2011.

included the installation of panels, had taken place in 2006–2007. On 3 July 2009, there was a fire in which three adults and three children were killed, and at least 20 people were injured. One of the issues which arose during the Inquest was whether the composite panels in the window sets installed as part of the 2006–2007 refurbishment were required to be class 0 under the Building Regulations 2000 and the guidance contained in Approved Document B (2000 edition incorporating 2000 and 2002 amendments) *and* fire resistant as had been required by the Inner London byelaws which had been applicable at the time of the original construction of and first set of refurbishment works.[132] The Coroner determined that at the time the 2006–07 refurbishment works were completed there was no legal requirement for the panels to be fire resistant, they only had to be Class 0.[133]

Following the Lakanal House Inquest, the Coroner wrote to Eric Pickles MP, the then Secretary of State for Communities and Local Government, under Rule 43 of the Coroners Rules 1984 (as amended).[134] In her letter dated 28 March 2013, the Coroner raised a number of concerns, including a concern that Approved Document B was 'a difficult document to use' and noted that reference had to be made to additional documents 'in order to find an answer to relatively straightforward questions concerning the fire protection properties of materials to be incorporated into the fabric of the building'. The Coroner recommended its review in order to ensure that it provided 'clear guidance in relation to Regulation B4 … with particular regard to the spread of fire over the external envelope of the building and the circumstances in which attention should be paid to whether proposed work might reduce existing fire protection'.

Mr Pickles replied by a letter dated 20 May 2013. Insofar as his response to the concerns raised in respect of Approved Document B, he said:

> I can assure you that my Department is committed to a programme of simplification. However the design of fire protection in buildings is a complex subject and should remain, to some extent, in the realm of professionals.

Mr Pickles referred to the fact that further research had been commissioned, and that would lead to a new edition of Approved Document B in 2016–17. The Grenfell Tower fire occurred on 14 June 2017, before the results of that research had been published or a new edition of Approved Document B had been issued.

[132] Building Regulations 2000 (SI 2000/2531).

[133] See Frances Kirkham, 'Decision concerning fire resistance of composite panels' Lakanal House Coroner Inquest (4 April 2013) available online www.lambeth.gov.uk/sites/default/files/ec-decisions-on-fire-resistance-of-composite-panels-4April2013.pdf (accessed 14 October 2022). Judge Kirkham's reasons for directing the jury in the Lakanal Inquest were that there was no legal requirement for the panels installed in 2006–2007 to be FR60.

[134] Coroners Rules 1984, SI 1984/552, Rule 43 (as amended), applicable at the time, provided: (1) Where (a) a coroner is holding an inquest into a person's death, (b) the evidence gives rise to a concern that circumstances creating a risk of other deaths will occur, or will continue to exist in the future, and (c) in the coroner's opinion, action should be taken to prevent the occurrence or continuation of such circumstances, or to eliminate or reduce the risk of death created by such circumstances the coroner may report the circumstances to a person who the coroner believes may have power to take such action.

b. Roofs

The guidance for roofs (other than roofs passing over separating walls or compartment walls) was in essentially the same terms as the prescriptive requirements in the Building Regulations 1972 (as amended).[135]

c. Firefighting Measures

The provision of fire-fighting measures is (still) primarily regulated by the Fire Precautions Act 1971. ADB 1985 did not include express guidance on sprinklers. However, it contained provisions that could be varied if they were 'unnecessarily onerous'. This required a consideration of the fire safety of the building as a whole, including a number of factors, including whether 'compensatory features' such as sprinklers or automatic fire detection systems were installed.[136]

C. Our Advice: Claims under Statute

In 1973, our advice concerning the possibilities of claims which the APC could make pursuant to statute will be brief: there are none. The Defective Premises Act 1972 does not come into force until 1 January 1974 and only applies to work taken on after that date.[137] In any event, it only imposes duties upon persons taking on work for or in connection with the provision of a dwelling (whether the dwelling is provided by the erection or by the conversion or enlargement of a building) and so would only be relevant to the accommodation block.

However, whilst our Advice on a potential cause of action under the DPA 1972 will be brief, that will not be the case in later years. The Official Referees and later the judges of the TCC will be instrumental in developing the law regarding the application of the DPA 1972.

Those taking on works for the purposes of the DPA 1972 includes contractors, subcontractors, suppliers, sub-suppliers, construction professionals and developers who have houses built for sale. The duty imposed is:

> to see that the work which he takes on is done in a workmanlike or, as the case may be, professional manner, with proper materials and so that as regards that work the dwelling will be fit for habitation when completed.

The law, as it stands at the time of writing this chapter in 2022, imposes a single obligation whereby a failure to do the work in a workmanlike or professional manner or with proper materials is actionable only if the dwelling is not fit for habitation.[138]

[135] ADB 1985, Tables 1.3, 2.3, 3.3, 4.3, 5.3 and 6.3.

[136] ADB 1985, para 0.34.

[137] This was confirmed by the Court of Appeal in *Alexander v Mercouris* [1979] 1 WLR 1270, per Buckley LJ at 1274.

[138] Defective Premises Act 1972, s 1. The source of that 'single obligation' line of authority is the Court of Appeal decision in *Alexander v Mercouris* [1979] 1 WLR 1270, followed by HHJ Esyr Lewis QC in

The Official Referees and the TCC have to some extent moderated the stringency of treating the duty at section 1(1) as a single obligation through their decisions on what is or what is not a defect affecting fitness for habitation. There are multiple judgments from the Official Referees and the TCC which illustrate that fitness for habitation is a question of fact, which obviously allows for decisions to be based on the merits of the case. Lists of criteria which may be relevant in determining the fitness of a dwelling have been set out by HHJ Toulmin CMG QC in *Bole v Huntsbuild*[139] and by Edwards-Stuart J in *Rendlesham Estates Plc v Barr Ltd.*[140] Given the subject matter of this chapter, it is pertinent to note that Edwards-Stuart J held that:

> [F]or a dwelling to be fit for habitation within the meaning of the Act, it must, on completion (without any remedial works being carried out): (a) be capable of occupation for a reasonable time without risk to the health or safety of the occupants ….

D. Our Advice: The Owner's Claims against the Construction Professionals

In 1973 we will advise – much as we did in 1873 and 1923 – that to succeed in a claim against the architects or the fire engineer and in the absence of any express contractual duty imposing a higher duty, the APC will need to show that the architect or fire engineer failed to act with reasonable skill and care when preparing the design for the Palace. We will (again) refer to the test in *Chapman v Walton,*[141] which re-appears in both the tenth edition of *Hudson*[142] and the third edition of *Keating.*[143] We would also refer to the further explanation provided in *Keating*:[144]

> If the majority of such persons would, under the circumstances, have done the same thing as the architect this normally provides a good defence, for 'a defendant charged with negligence can clear himself if he shows that he acted in accord with general and

Thompson v Clive Alexander & Partners (1992) 28 Con LR 49 and Ramsey J in *Harrison v Shepherd Homes Ltd* [2011] EWHC 1811 (TCC), 156 Con LR 158. However, in *Bole v Huntsbuild Ltd* [2009] EWHC 483 (TCC), 127 Con LR 154, HHJ Toulmin CMG QC seemed to take a different view, pointing out that the terms of the Law Commission Report (Law Com No. 40) which led to the enactment of the Defective Premises Act 1972 indicated that s 1 imposed three separate duties to carry out the work in: (1) a workmanlike or professional manner; (2) with professional materials; and (c) so that the dwelling will be fit for habitation. Ramsey J went further in *Harrison*, stating that if he was not bound by *Alexander v Mercouris* he would, (on the basis of the Law Commission Report and the decisions in *Hancock v Brazier* [1966] WLR 1317 (CA), *D&F Estates Ltd v The Church Commissioners* [1989] AC 177 (HL), *Murphy v Brentwood* [1991] AC 398 (HL), and *Batty v Metropolitan Realisations Ltd* [1978] QB 554 (CA)) have found that s 1(1) imposed a threefold duty on builders.

[139] *Bole v Huntsbuild Ltd* [2009] EWHC 483 (TCC) 127 Con LR 154.

[140] *Rendlesham Estates Plc v Barr Ltd* [2014] EWHC 3968 (TCC), [2015] WLR 3663.

[141] *Chapman v Walton* (1833) 131 826, 10 Bing 57.

[142] Duncan Wallace (n 98) 124.

[143] Keating (n 99) 217.

[144] ibid.

> approved practice,' or where there is no one accepted practice if he acted in accordance with a practice accepted as proper by a responsible body of architects.

The main duties of the construction professionals remain to provide a design which is 'skilful, effective to achieve [the employer's purpose] within any financial limitations imposed or made known, and comprehensive in the sense that no necessary and foreseeable work is omitted'.[145]

The tenth edition of *Hudson* differed from the earlier editions in that it did not say in express terms that a plan or specification will be defective if it does not comply with 'building law'. However, Counsel in 1973 will probably note that it does say (as must be the case) that a building 'designed without regard to any relevant public legislation, byelaws … may, while being structurally a well-planned design be quite useless to the employer, since the work may be prohibited, or if carried out may expose him to fines, demolition orders or litigation'.[146] The third edition of *Keating* says

> If his working drawings, plans or directions result in a building which contravenes the by-laws or building regulations which apply to it, this is, it is submitted, some but not conclusive evidence of breach of duty.

Prior to receiving expert input in 1973, Counsel may venture to suggest that the fact that fire took hold as quickly as it did and destroyed the Palace suggests that the design was defective and did not comply with the Building Regulations 1972/the applicable Inner London byelaws.

However, such advice will be qualified by reference to the conclusions of the Griffiths Inquiry into the gas explosion on 16 May 1968 in the 22-storey tower block Ronan Point, London. The explosion in a kitchen on the 18th floor led to the collapse of an entire corner of the building, causing four deaths and 17 injuries. The Griffiths Inquiry concluded that the building was not acceptable because it did not have sufficient 'anti progressive collapse'[147] measures but noted that it had been designed to comply with the standards in the Newham byelaws, which were in all material respects identical to the current Building Regulations. The Inquiry concluded this was 'so manifestly an unsatisfactory state of affairs',[148] which it clearly was.

The issue had arisen because whilst the building was designed to comply with the byelaws and relevant Codes of Practice, there was no Code of Practice specifically relating to the (new) large panel construction which had been used for Ronan Point. Furthermore, Ronan Point had been designed to comply with CP3: Chapter V on wind loading, which was 15 years old and did not take account of more recent research that suggested high-rise buildings may have to withstand greater wind

[145] Duncan Wallace (n 98) 124.

[146] ibid (under the sub-heading 'Knowledge of legislation, building regulations, by-laws and rights of adjoining owners').

[147] Progressive collapse occurs where local failure of a primary structural component leads to the collapse of adjoining members which in turn leads to additional collapse.

[148] *Report into the Inquiry into the Collapse of Flats at Ronan Point, Canning Town* (1968) 55 (para 194).

forces than the Code of Practice had envisaged – meaning they could suffer structural damage which could contribute to progressive collapse.[149]

The Inquiry concluded that whilst the general approach of the Building Regulations was right, ie having functional requirements and 'deemed to satisfy' provisions relating to British Standards and Codes of Practice, the system would only work if the British Standards and Codes of Practice were kept up to date, and new ones promulgated as necessary.[150]

In 1973 a claim in professional negligence against the construction professionals could, like the claims against the contractor, be heard by an Official Referee. The Court of Appeal had held in *Osenton v Johnston*[151] that claims for professional negligence were not to be referred to an Official Referee because there was no right of appeal on fact from an Official Referee.[152] Parliament promptly conferred a right of appeal in such cases,[153] and negligence actions against architects, engineers and surveyors became (and remain) a major section of Official Referees' work. Guidance can be taken from the tenth edition of *Hudson*, which says:

> … even in long building cases the sums involved on a per diem basis are often substantially greater than in other classes of case which are tried without question by High Court judges, with the result that it must be said that in England the High Court Bench is often seriously handicapped by lack of experience of the factual background of building contracts and disputes when such cases do become before them. Furthermore building disputes almost invariably involve difficult questions of construction of the contracts used, which are notoriously diffuse and imprecise, which also makes a trial judge desirable.

The fire having occurred so shortly after construction of the Palace means that Counsel in 1973 will not have to worry about claims in tort because the six-year limitation period for breach of contract claims (set down by section 2 of the Limitation Act 1939) will not have expired. That is, to say the least fortunate because the 'latest word' in 1973 on the question of whether a construction professional, more particularly, an architect had concurrent duties in contract and in tort was (notwithstanding the decision in *Hedley v Byrne*) a firm 'no'.[154] The tenth edition of *Hudson* states, 'the duty owed by an architect or engineer to his employer arises in contract and not in tort'[155] and *Keating* confirmed that actions had to be brought from the date of the breach of duty which is consistent with a claim against an architect arising only in contract.[156]

However, the position changed in 1976, following the decision of the Court of Appeal in *Esso Petroleum Co. Ltd v Mardon*,[157] applied in a construction context

[149] ibid, 61 (conclusions 1(8) and 1(9)) 61.
[150] ibid, 65 (conclusion, paras 37–38).
[151] Duncan Wallace (n 98) 126–127.
[152] *Ostenton & Co v Johnston* [1942] AC 130 (HL).
[153] Order 58, rule 5 of The Supreme Court Rules.
[154] *Bagot v Stevens Scanlan & Co. Ltd* [1966] QB 197 at 204D-E.
[155] Duncan Wallace (n 98) 123.
[156] Keating (n 99) 229.
[157] *Esso Petroleum Co. Ltd v Mardon* [1976] QB 801.

in *Batty v Metropolitan Property Realisations Ltd*,[158] but we had to wait until 1994 for the position to be confirmed by the House of Lords in *Henderson v Merrett Syndicates Ltd.*[159]

VII. Twenty Twenty-Three

A. The Legal Scene and the Technology and Construction Court

Our fourth brief arrives by email, which is helpful as most in chambers appear to have absconded in favour of working from home. We may be lucky enough to receive detailed electronic instructions with a tabbed and paginated bundle. However, our instructions may just comprise a series of email threads with the promise of a virtual conference (or consultation), leaving us unsure whether this is progress. Pink ribbons have not been seen for years, although an older member of Chambers swears he saw one just before the first lockdown. Any conference (with a junior) or consultation (with a KC) is unlikely to take place in person. While in our previous three opinions, we were prohibited from marketing or advertising, times have changed: thankfully, we are too busy to attend events or write long, forever unread, chapters.

This advice will be the first time in our story in which the TCC has original jurisdiction. In 1982 litigants were given the right to start their actions in the Official Referees' Court. This right moved to the TCC, when it was formed in 1998, and is now well established. The TCC has been part of the Business and Property courts since 2017.

The judges of the TCC are all held in the highest esteem. In 2023 they comprise Mrs Justice O'Farrell DBE (Judge in Charge), Mr Justice Fraser, Mrs Justice Jefford DBE, Mr Justice Waksman and Mr Justice Pepperall, together with the High Court Judges who may hear TCC cases when necessary[160] and the judges in the TCC regional centres.[161] Three former TCC judges are now sitting in the Court of Appeal: Lady Justice Carr, Lord Justice Coulson, and Lord Justice Stuart-Smith.

There are many eminent TCC alumni. Lord Dyson, the Judge in Charge of the TCC from 1998 to 2001, was a Justice of the Supreme Court from 2010 to 2012,

[158] *Batty v Metropolitan Property Realisations Ltd* [1978] QB 554.

[159] *Henderson v Merrett Syndicates Ltd* [1995] 2 AC 145 (HL).

[160] Mrs Justice Cockerill DBE, Mr Justice Kerr, Mr Justice Choudhury, and Mrs Justice Joanna Smith DBE.

[161] Her Honour Judge Sarah Watson (Principal TCC Judge) (Birmingham), HHJ Russen KC (Principal TCC judge) (Bristol), HHJ Keyser KC (Principal TCC Judge) and HHJ Jarman KC (Cardiff), HHJ Nick Parfitt and HHJ Alan Johns KC (Central London), HHJ Siobhan Kelly (Principal TCC Judge), HHJ Davis-White KC, HHJ Andrew Saffman, HHJ Klein, and HHJ Claire Jackson (Leeds), HHJ Graham Wood KC and District Judge Baldwin (Liverpool), His Honour Judge Stephen Davies (Principal TCC judge), HHJ David Hodge KC, HHJ Mark Halliwell, HHJ Cawson KC, HHJ Cadwallader, HHJ Richard Pearce, HHJ Nigel Bird and District Judge Andrew Bartley (Manchester) and HHJ Kramer (Principal TCC judge) (Newcastle).

and Master of the Rolls from 2012 until 2016. Lord Justice Jackson was the Judge in Charge of the TCC between 2004 and 2007 and a Lord Justice of Appeal between 2008 and 2018.

Again, there have been some musical chairs. In 1988 the Official Referees moved to St Dunstan's House on Fetter Lane, which 'was not a wonderful building, but it was important that it was also occupied by the Commercial Court'.[162] In 2011 the TCC moved (with the Commercial Court and the Chancery Division) to the plush interiors of the Rolls Building.

However, we will now advise the APC that it has the right to have its claims determined by an adjudicator (pursuant to the Housing Grants, Construction and Regeneration Act 1996) and that it should consider using that dispute resolution process before issuing proceedings in the TCC.

In order to assist us with our research, we have the fourteenth edition of *Hudson's Building and Engineering Contracts*,[163] the eleventh edition of *Keating on Construction Contracts*,[164] and the ninth edition of Jackson and Powell[165] (the first edition having been published in 1982). We have access to every case we could possibly need (and many we do not) through the numerous online resources: Google is perhaps overused.[166]

The TCC has become known for its practical advice. In *Sahib Foods Ltd v Paskin Kyriakidies Sands* a claim was brought against a firm of architects, following a fire which had destroyed most of a food factory. The fire started when a gas flame heating a pan in the vegetable preparation area was not switched off.[167] The use of combustible panels in a kitchen would have been contrary to the Metropolitan Building Act 1855, section 21, and a claim could have been brought against the architect in 1873. However, this claim came before the TCC in 2003. In 2003 the judge decided to note the following:

> On the day in question, he worked from 6 a.m. until 8 p.m. At the end of the day, he was responsible for turning off the gas supply to the bratt pan. There may be many women

[162] Lord Dyson, Keating Lecture 2015 '*The Contribution of Construction Cases to the Development of the Common Law*' 24 March 2015.

[163] A Chambers, *Hudson's Building and Engineering Contracts*, 14th edn (London, Sweet and Maxwell 2020).

[164] *Keating on Construction Contracts*, 11th edn (London, Sweet and Maxwell, 2021).

[165] *Jackson and Powell on Professional Liability*, 9th edn (London, Sweet and Maxwell, 2022).

[166] Our research into hot works will bring us across *National Trust v Haden Young Ltd* (1994) 72 BLR 1, (1994) 41 Con. LR 112. In 1989 the National Trust carried out extensive repairs on Uppark House in Sussex. During the course of those works, the main contractor sub-contracted Haden Young Ltd to carry out lead works on the roof. The negligent use of naked flames on the roof resulted in a fire that destroyed the stately home. The litigation that followed focused on the question of contractual interpretation as Hadden Young Ltd unsuccessfully contended that despite the negligence of their employees, the contractual arrangement between the National Trust and the main contractor meant that the risk of such damage had been assumed by the National Trust. We would also be reminded of the fire at the Mandarin Oriental Hotel in 2018. The cause of the fire at the luxury hotel in London was reported by the London Fire Brigade as: 'The fire is believed to have been caused by the by-product of arc welding landing on the felt lining of the planting façade.'

[167] *Sahib Foods Ltd v Paskin Kyriakidies Sands* [2003] EWHC 142 (TCC), 87 Con LR 1 at para 22(b). This part of the decision was not the subject of the appeal to the Court of Appeal (*Sahib Foods Ltd v Paskin Kyriakidies Sands* [2003] EWCA Civ 1832).

> who work hours like that in their own homes and kitchens, but Mr. Reynolds agreed that it was not sensible to employ a man to work those hours and rely on him to perform an important task like turning off the gas at the end of the day. Mr. Singh did not turn off the gas supply or the pilot light. The gas burners were left on in the maximum position. In that failure, Mr. Singh was negligent, though in the circumstances one could only sympathise with him if he were here to accept that sympathy. His employers, Sahib, were not only vicariously liable for his negligence, they were independently negligent for relying on him to perform a responsible (though simple) task after working such long hours.[168]

We do not know whether the same advice would have been given in 1873.

B. Our Advice: The Regulatory Framework

Our advice in 2023 will be shaped by the terrible events on 14 June 2017, when 72 died, and many more were injured and displaced as a result of the fire at Grenfell Tower in London.[169] The Grenfell Tower fire has had a profound effect on the regulation of fire safety, particularly in high-rise residential buildings.[170] As Matthew Bell noted, the fire resulted in a realisation that 'the regulatory regime, overseeing the myriad of activities and motivations which collide in the construction of dwellings, is inadequate to ensure the safety of those dwellings' occupants'.[171] Dame Judith Hackitt concluded in May 2018:

> The current system of building regulations and fire safety is not fit for purpose and … a culture change is required to support the delivery of buildings that are safe, both now and in the future. The system failure identified in the interim report has allowed a culture of indifference to perpetuate.[172]

Dame Judith Hackitt identified six 'key reasons' why this was the case, the first of which was that the '[c]urrent regulations are complex and unclear'.[173]

While the fire at the Palace resulted in calls for regulatory reforms, the importance of fire safety in public and political consciousness following the

[168] *Sahib Foods Ltd v Paskin Kyriakidies Sands* [2003] EWHC 142 (TCC) 87 Con LR 1 at para 22(b). This helpful advice was not the subject of the appeal to the Court of Appeal (*Sahib Foods Ltd v Paskin Kyriakidies Sands* [2003] EWCA Civ 1832).

[169] See A O'Hagan, 'The Tower' (London Review of Books, 7 June 2018) www.lrb.co.uk/v40/n11/andrew-ohagan/the-tower.

[170] Minister of Housing, Communities & Local Government, *Building a Safer Future: Proposals for Reform of the Building Safety Regulatory System* (June 2019) 10 'The Grenfell Tower fire represents the greatest loss of life in a residential fire in a century. It shattered the lives of many people and shook the trust of countless more in a system that was intended to ensure the most basic human need of having a decent and safe place to live.'

[171] M Bell, 'How is that even possible? Raising construction regulations from the ashes of Grenfell Tower' *The Society of Construction Law* (London, 8 May 2018) 4.

[172] Secretary of State for Housing, Communities & Local Government (n 6) 11; Secretary of State for Communities & Local Government, *Building a Safer Future Independent Review of Building Regulations and Fire Safety: Interim Report* (Cm 9551, 2017) 9.

[173] Dame Judith Hackett DBE FREng, *Building a Safer Future Independent Review of Building Regulations and Fire Safety: Interim Report* (OGL, 2017) 9.

Grenfell Tower fire appears to have been unmatched since the Great Fire of London in 1666. The fire resulted in many calling for fire safety measures such as external fire escape, sprinklers and a thorough inquiry quickly following the Grenfell Tower fire.[174] The government responded by setting up an Independent Review of Building Regulations and Fire Safety (the 'Hackitt Review') in July 2017 chaired by Dame Judith Hackitt. The Hackitt Review published an interim report in December 2017 and a Final Report in May 2018.

The government also set up the Grenfell Tower Inquiry, chaired by Sir Martin Moore-Bick in June 2017. The report on Phase 1 of the inquiry (focusing on the events on the night of 14 June 2017) was issued on 30 October 2019 (following hearings between 21 May 2018 and 12 December 2018). As of writing this chapter in 2022, the report on Phase 2 (dealing with the causes of the events on 14 June 2017, including how Grenfell Tower came to be in the condition which allowed the fire to spread in the way identified by Phase 1) has not been published. The hearings in Phase 2 took place from September 2020 to February 2022 with closing submissions in late 2022. The Grenfell Inquiry has taken significantly longer than other public inquiries.[175] This is not surprising given the scope of the Inquiry. Phase 1 alone had 581 core participants and required consideration of some 400,000 documents.

Our advice in 2023 will be shaped by the provisions of the Building Safety Act 2022 (the 'BSA 2022') and related regulations and materials.[176] What became the BSA 2022 was first announced in the Queen's Speech on 19 December 2019: 'to ensure residents are safe in their homes, we will bring forward measures to implement the most urgent recommendations from the first phase of the Grenfell Tower Public Inquiry. We will also publish a draft Building Safety Bill to implement the recommendations of Dame Judith Hackitt's review of building regulations.'[177]

The BSA 2022 received Royal Assent on 28 April 2022 and makes sweeping changes to the Building Act 1984 and many others, including the Architects Act 1997, the Housing Act 1996, and Regulatory Reform (Fire Safety) Order 2005. The establishment of the Building Safety Regulator within the Health & Safety Executive with oversight, including the ability to prosecute offences and issue compliance notices, takes on a role not too dissimilar from the District Surveyors

[174] D Kennedy, 'Calls for external fire escapes' *The Times* (London, 16 June 2017) 7; S O'Neil, 'Sprinkler system would have kept blaze in check' *The Times* (London, 16 June 2017) 9; P Collins, 'Judge must work fast to give answers' *The Times* (London, 16 June 2017) 11.

[175] For example, the inquiry into the 1966 Aberfan disaster was published in August 1967. Mr Justice Popplewell's report on the May 1965 Bradford City Football ground fire was published in January 1986. Lord Justice Taylor published an interim report in August 1989 and a final report in January 1990 after the Hillsborough disaster.

[176] D Maxwell 'Building Safety Still Under Construction' (2022) 172 *New Law Journal* 11.

[177] Prime Minister's Office (PMO), 'The Queen's Speech and Associated Background Briefing, On the Occasion of the Opening of Parliament on Monday 19 December 2019' at assets.publishing.service.gov.uk/government/uploads/system/uploads/attachment_data/file/853886/Queen_s_Speech_December_2019_-_background_briefing_notes.pdf, 11.

in 1873.[178] However, the standards and researched scientific approach today are not comparable to the lax approach in 1873. For example, as part of a strategy to avoid enforcing the model byelaws in 1870, the City of Sheffield deliberately appointed a surveyor who could not read or write.[179] Unsurprisingly, compliance was limited.[180]

Much of the BSA 2022 seeks to provide greater protection to leaseholders in high-rise buildings. The limited ability of leaseholders to obtain full redress can be observed in the TCC decision in *Zagora Management Ltd v Zurich Insurance Plc.*[181] In *Zagora Management Ltd*, the freeholder and leaseholders partially succeeded in showing that the remediation of major defects fell within the scope of insurance protection under warranties supplied by Zurich, but the policy wording appeared to limit recovery to the original purchase price of each relevant flat (or, as the Court of Appeal later decided, of all flats in the development). However, the leaseholders failed in their claim of deceit against the company, which had certified the building as complying with the building regulations.[182]

i. *Building Regulations 2010 and Approved Document B 2013*

We will refer – by way of background – to the fact that new Building Regulations had been issued in 1991, 2000 and 2010. The Building Regulations 2010 came into force on 1 October 2010 and applied to amongst other things, the erection or extension of a building and the material alteration of a building.[183]

Requirements B1 and B4 in the 1985 and 2010 Building Regulations were in substantially the same terms, but Requirement B1 in Schedule 1 to the 2010 Building Regulations required not only appropriate means of escape but also appropriate provisions for the early warning of fire.

The Approved Document B ('ADB'), which was in force at the time of the Grenfell Tower fire was the 2013 Approved Document B (which was the 2006 edition incorporating the 2010 and 2013 amendments) ('ADB 2013'). It included guidance on Parts B1(Means of warning and escape), B2 (Internal fire spread (linings)), B3 (Internal fire spread (structure), B4 (External fire spread) and B5 (Access and facilities for the fire service) of Schedule 1 to the 2010 Building Regulations. It was in two volumes. The first volume dealt with dwelling houses and the second volume dealt with all other types of building covered by the

[178] Building Safety Act 2022, Pt 2; D Maxwell and M Bell '(How) Can a Building Safety Regulator Help Cure the UK's Defects Crisis? Analysing the Current Proposals in Light of Australia's Experience' (2020) 2 *Construction Law Journal* 3–17.

[179] Cited in A Ley, 'Building Control UK – An Historical Review'.

[180] ibid.

[181] *Zagora Management Ltd v Zurich Insurance Plc* [2019] EWHC 140 (TCC).

[182] *Zagora Management Ltd v Zurich Insurance Plc* [2019] EWHC 140 (TCC) (HHJ Stephen Davies); See also *Zagora Management Ltd v Zurich Insurance Plc* [2019] EWCA Civ 2163; 187 Con LR 62.

[183] Building Regulations 2010, Reg 3.

Building Regulations. The second volume ('ADB(2) 2013') contains the provisions relevant to the Palace.

Like its predecessors, ADB 2013 was issued for the 'purpose of providing practical guidance'[184] and included guidance, which if followed should have resulted in satisfaction of the Building Regulations.[185] Alternative approaches were permitted[186] including taking a fire safety engineering approach, ie, appointing a fire safety engineer to prepare a full fire strategy for the building (using BS 7974 *Fire safety engineering in buildings* and supporting published documents).[187]

a. External Walls

Since the Building Act 1984, there has been a principle-based regulatory approach where the focus is on outcomes that can be contrasted with the prescriptive rules cited in relation to 1873 and 1923. Paragraph 12.5 of ADB(2) 2013 (which was concerned with Requirement B4) stated that the external envelope of a building should not provide a medium for fire spread and noted that the use of combustible materials in the cladding system on tall buildings could present such a risk. Paragraph 12.5 of ADB(2) 2013 went on to say external walls should either meet the guidance given in paragraphs 12.6 to 12.9 (commonly referred to as the 'Linear Route') *or* meet the performance criteria given in the BRE Report *Fire performance of external thermal insulation for walls of multi storey buildings* (BRE 135) for cladding systems using full scale test date from BS8414-1:2002 or BS8414-2:2005.[188]

Insofar as the requirements for the 'Linear Route' were concerned, paragraph 12.6 of ADB(2) 2013 stated that the external walls were required to meet the provisions in Diagram 40. The requirements set down in Diagram 40 were very similar to those in the ADB 1985 and still used the 'Class 0' classification which had been first introduced in statute in 1965. In summary, Diagram 40 provided:

(1) any building (whatever its height) which is less than 1m from a relevant boundary is required to have external surfaces or walls which are: '*Class 0 (national class) or class B-s3, d2 (European class) or better*';
(2) 'no provision' for buildings which are less than 18m high and less than 1m from a relevant boundary unless they are an assembly or recreation building of more than one storey; and
(3) any building which is more than 18 high and is no more than 1m from a relevant boundary is required to have material with '*Index (i) not more than*

[184] Approved Document B (herein after 'ADB 2013(2)', para 0.1.
[185] ADB 2013(2), para 0.21.
[186] ibid.
[187] ADB 2013(2), para 0.30.
[188] An additional way of achieving compliance was introduced by BCA Technical Guidance Note 18, Issue 1 (June 2015) which provided that if no actual fire test data existed for a system, the client could instead submit a desktop study report from a suitably qualified fire specialist stating whether, in their opinion, BR 135 criteria would be met by the proposed system.

> *20 (National class) or Class C-s3, d2 or better (European Class)*' up to 18m and '*Class 0 (National class) or clause B-s3, d2 or better (European class)*' 18m from the ground.

As explained above, Class 0 products are products which have been shown by a BS 476 Part 7 test to be Class 1 for surface spread of flame materials and 'pass' the BS 476 Part 6 test for fire propagation. The classification class 0 is therefore based on the surface spread of flames on the material, rather than combustibility of the materials.

The reference to a 'European Class' is a reference to the Euroclass system which, using the results of defined tests,[189] categorises products into seven reaction-to-fire classes ranging from A1 (non-combustible) to F (the worst performing) and provides additional classification relating to smoke production and flaming droplets. The Euroclass classification is therefore based on the combustibility of the materials.

Euroclass B-s3,-d2 materials are combustible materials which make a very limited contribution to fire (B), have a high intensity smoke emission on combustion (s3), and result in a high level of droplets during combustion (d2). Euroclass C-s3, d2 materials are combustible materials which make a limited contribution to fire (C), have a high intensity smoke emission on combustion (s3), and result in a high level of droplets during combustion (d2).

Given the basis of the Class 0 classification and the basis of the Euroclass classifications are different it is difficult to understand how they could properly have been given as alternative routes to determining the appropriateness of the materials for use on external walls or surfaces. However, leaving aside that issue, what is clear is that the guidance in ADB 2013 suggested that combustible materials were not prohibited from use in external walls or surfaces.[190]

Paragraph 12.7 of ADB(2) 2013 – which was introduced for the first time in volume 2 of the ADB 2006 – provided that in a building with a storey 18m or more above ground level 'any insulation product, filler material … used in external wall construction should be of limited combustibility'. Materials of limited combustibility were defined as non-combustible or materials (of density 300/kg/m') which when tested in accordance with BS 476, Part 11: 1982 (a test which unlike the tests under Parts 6 and 7 tests the combustibility of the product) does not flame and results in a temperature rise of not more than 20°C (national class) or are classified as A1 (non-combustible) or A2-s3, d2 (limited combustibility/very limited contribution to fire) or better.[191]

[189] The tests applicable to construction products other than flooring are BS EN ISO 1182: 2019 (Non-combustibility test), BS EN ISO 1716 (Determination of the gross heat of combustion (calorific value)), BS EN 13823 (Single burning item (SBI) test) and BS ENISO 11925-2

[190] Non-combustible materials are classified as Class A1 and materials of limited combustibility, ie, make a very limited contribution to fire are Class A2.

[191] ADB 2013(2), Appx A, para 9 and Table A7.

There has been some debate as to the scope of paragraph 12.7 in ADB 2013 and more particularly whether it applied to the core in composite panels.[192] However, within days of the Grenfell fire, the Ministry of Housing and Local Government confirmed that the core material of cladding panels was required to comply with paragraph 12.7 of ADB 2013.[193]

b. Roofs

The advice concerning roof coverings is set out in section 14 of ADB(2) 2013. Insofar as the Palace (including the accommodation block) is concerned the recommendations made in ADB(2) 2013 were in similar terms to the advice given in ADB 1985.[194]

c. Means of Escape

Section 1 of volume 2 of ADB(2) 2013 dealt with Requirement B1 and set out details of the fire alarm and detection systems which were required and included guidance on the means of escape from flats (and other buildings). The maximum length of the corridor between the entrance to a flat and the protected stair had been reduced to 7.5 metres.[195]

d. Firefighting Measures

ADB 2013 contained more detailed guidance on the use of sprinkler systems. ADB(2) 2013 confirmed (as the commentators in 1873 and insurers had recognised) that firefighting measures, be that water towers or sprinkler systems, can reduce the risk to life and reduce the degree of damage to property caused by fire.[196] ADB(2)2013 confirmed what had been said in ADB 1985, namely that sprinkler systems could be used as a compensatory feature when the provisions of ADB(2) 2013 were varied[197] and also identified circumstances in which the installation of a sprinkler could be used to comply with the Building Regulations.[198] More significantly, ADB(2) 2013 provided that sprinklers were to be provided in flats within blocks of flats exceeding 30 metres in height.[199]

[192] P Apps, '*The Paper Trail: The Failure of Building Regulations*' Inside Housing (London, 23 March 2018).

[193] Letters from the Department for Communities and Local Government to Local Authorities and Housing Associations dated 18 and 22 June 2008.

[194] ADB 2013(2), Table 16.

[195] ADB 2013(2), Diagram 7.

[196] ADB 2013(2), para 0.16.

[197] ibid.

[198] See, eg, ADB 2013(2), para 2.16 which provided that there were four acceptable approaches to planning a multi-story flat which did not have its own external entrance at ground level and had a floor more than 4.5m above ground level. One of those approaches (para 2.16(d)) was to provide a protected stairway, a sprinkler system and a smoke alarm.

[199] ADB 2013(2), paras 4.29 and 8.14.

ii. Building Regulations 2010 (as Amended) and Approved Document B 2022

The Building Regulations 2010 and Approved Document B have been amended following the Grenfell Tower fire.[200] The current version of the Approved Document B was issued in June 2022 (amending the 2019 edition incorporating the 2020 amendments). It is also in two volumes. Again it is the second volume which deals with buildings other than dwellinghouses which is relevant to the Palace ('ADB(2) 2022').

The introduction to ADB(2) 2022 is in different terms to the ADB(2) 2013 stating that whilst it covers common building situations, compliance with the guidance set out in ADB(2) 2013 does not provide a guarantee of compliance with the requirements of the regulations. It notes that there may be other ways to comply with the requirements than the methods set out in ADB(2) 2013 but does not expressly refer to the 'fire safety engineering approach'.[201]

a. External Walls

The advice in respect of external walls and surfaces has been rewritten. No reference is made to Class 0. All requirements are defined with reference to the Euroclass System. The requirements in respect of 'relevant buildings' as defined by Regulation 7(4) of the Building Regulations 2010 (as amended) are set out in Regulation 7(2) of the Building Regulations 2010 (as amended) and are prescriptive. All other external walls are required to 'follow' the provisions in paragraphs 10.5 to 10.9 of ADB(2) 2022 *or* meet the performance criteria given in the BRE report BR 135 for external walls using full scale test data from BS 8414-1 or BS 8414-2.[202] A desk top study or fire safety engineering approach is no longer advised.

Regulation 7(2) of the Building Regulations 2010 (as amended) states that all building works 'shall' be carried out so that materials which become part of an external wall of or specified attachment to a 'relevant building'[203] defined as a building with a storey at least 18 metres above ground level which contains one or more dwellings, an institution[204] or a room for residential purposes are of limited combustibility (Class A2-s1, d0) or better, ie non-combustible (Class A1).[205]

[200] Building (Amendment) Regulations 2018, SI 2018/1230.
[201] ADB(2) 2022, i.
[202] ADB(2) 2022, para 12.3.
[203] 'Relevant Buildings' as defined Building Regulations 2010 as amended by Building (Amendment) Act Regulations 2018 and Building etc (Amendment) England Regulations 2022, SI 2022/603 Regulation 7(4)(a).
[204] Building Regulations 2010, Regulation 2 states that an 'institution' is 'an institution (whether described as a hospital, home, school or other similar establishment) which is used as living accommodation for, or for the treatment, care or maintenance of persons – (a) suffering from disabilities due to illness, old age or other physical or mental incapacity, or (b) under the age of five years where such persons sleep on the premises'.
[205] Building Regulations 2010 as amended by Building (Amendment) Act Regulations 2018 and Building etc (Amendment) England Regulations 2022, Regulation 7(1).

Paragraph 10.5 and Table 10.1 of ADB(2) 2022 sets out the requirements for the reaction to fire performance of the external surface of the walls for buildings other than 'relevant buildings'. The external surfaces of external walls of all other residential buildings that are more than 11 metres are required to be of limited combustibility (Class A2-s1, d0) or better (Class A1). The requirements for assembly and recreation buildings like the Palace are less stringent. Such buildings require materials that make only a very limited contribution (Class B) or a limited contribution to fire (Class C). Different requirements are set for buildings with a height above 18 metres and those with a height less than 18 metres and for those buildings which are less than 1 metre from a relevant boundary and those which are more than 1m from a relevant boundary.[206]

Paragraphs 10.6 and 10.7 of ADB(2) 2022 state that in buildings with a storey of 18 metres or more in height and buildings that include a residential purpose with a storey of 11 metres or more in height, any 'insulation product, filler material (such as the core materials of metal composite panels, sandwich panels and window spandrel panels but not including gaskets, sealants and similar) etc.' used in the construction of an external wall 'should be' of limited combustibility (class A-2, s3, d2) or better (class A1).

Any ambiguity in ADB(2) 2013 has therefore been removed.

b. Roofs

The guidance relating to the fire spread over roof coverings is set out in section 12 of ADB(2) 2022. Express reference is made to separate requirements for roofs that are part of means of escape, rooflights and for roofs passing over a compartment wall and roofs where there is a requirement for space separation.

c. Means of Escape

The guidance in relation to Requirement B1 (Means of warning and escape) are much more detailed and now spans some 46 pages. Single escape stairs are no longer permitted in new buildings more than 11 metres above ground.[207]

[206] Assembly and recreation buildings which are within 1m of the relevant boundary are required to have external surfaces of external walls which are classified as Class B-s3, d2 or better. Assembly and recreation buildings which are more than 18m high and more than 1m from the relevant boundary are required to have external surfaces of external walls from ground level to 18m which are classified as Class C-s3, d2 or better and from 18m in high and above which are classified as Class B-s3, d2 or better. Assembly and recreation buildings which are less than 18m high and more than 1m from the relevant boundary are required to have external surfaces of external walls up to 10m above ground level which are classified as Class C-s3, d2 or better, up to 10m above a roof or any part of the building to which the public which are classified as Class C-s3, d2 or better, and from 10m in height and above no minimum performance.

[207] ADB(2) 2013, para 3.3.

d. Firefighting Measures

The guidance in ADB(2) 2022 regarding sprinklers is in similar terms to the guidance in ADB(2) 2013 save that the 'trigger height' for sprinklers in flats is now 11 rather than 18 metres.[208]

iii. Regulatory Reform (Fire Safety Order) 2005

We will ask APC to confirm that it had complied with the Regulatory Reform (Fire Safety Order) 2005 which was implemented following a review of the fire safety legislation, which found that circa 80 Acts of Parliaments dealt in whole or part fire safety. We will note that the fact that the relevant legislation is now in one place is an improvement noting that if the APC had come to us 50 years ago, we would have had to spend hours trying to find the relevant legislation.

The Regulatory Reform (Fire Safety) Order 2005 differs from previous legislation because it is based on the concept of risk assessment rather than prescriptive codes, and so we will need confirmation that the client has carried out a proper risk assessment. We will ask this question with reference to the HM Government Guide 'Safety risk assessment large places of assembly' (which is when compared to some of the other documents we have considered easy to understand).[209]

C. Our Advice: Claims under Statute

Insofar as statutory claims are concerned, the Building Safety Act 2022 ('the BSA') is a 'game changer'.

Section 38 of the Building Act 1984 was due to be brought into force in line with the BSA 2022, although at the time of writing this has not yet happened. It provides a statutory cause of action to a party who has suffered personal injury or property damage as a result of a breach of the building regulations applicable at the time.

The BSA also brought in significant amendments to the Defective Premises Act 1972. A new section 2A imposes a duty on a person who takes on work after 28 June 2022 in relation to any part of a relevant building (ie, a building consisting of or containing one or more dwellings).[210] Previously, a duty was only imposed when work was taken on for or in connection with the provision of a dwelling.

Prior to the passing of the BSA 2022, HHJ Eyre QC struck out a claim under the DPA in *Sportcity 4 Management Ltd and other companies v Countryside Properties (UK) Ltd*.[211] Such cases are less likely to be struck out by the TCC in the future

[208] ADB(2) 2022, Table B4 (as amended in 2020).

[209] HM Government, *Fire safety risk assessment large places of assembly* (2006).

[210] Building Safety Act 2022, s 134.

[211] *Sportcity 4 Management Ltd and other companies v Countryside Properties (UK) Ltd* [2020] EWHC 1591 (TCC), 192 Con LR 131.

as the time limit for bringing actions under the DPA has been extended from six years to 15 years from the date on which the action accrued.[212]

The time limit for bringing actions under section 1 of the DPA, ie, actions against persons who took on work for or in connection with the provision of a dwelling, which accrued prior to 28 June 2022, has been extended to 30 years albeit that a claim which would have otherwise been statute-barred must be dismissed if the Court is satisfied that it is necessary to do so to avoid a breach of the defendant's Convention rights.[213]

The BSA has introduced two new causes of action which can be brought by persons with a relevant interest in a dwelling or a building containing more than one dwelling in respect of liability 'relating to construction products' (section 148) and liability for 'past defaults relating to cladding products' (section 149).

A claim can be brought if four conditions (A to D) are met, namely:

(1) Condition A – at any time after 28 June 2022 for section 148 and any time before 28 June 2022 for section 149: (i) a person fails to comply with a construction product requirement in relation to a construction product (s 148) / a cladding product (s 149); (ii) a person who markets or supplies a construction product (s 148) / a cladding product (s 149) makes a misleading statement in relation to it; or (iii) a person manufactures a construction product (s 148) / cladding product (s 149) that is inherently defective);
(2) Condition B – the construction (s 148) / cladding (s 149) product is attached to or included in the external wall of the building;
(3) Condition C when the works are completed a dwelling is unfit for habitation; and
(4) Condition D – the facts referred to in Condition A were the cause or one of the causes of the building or dwelling being unfit for habitation.

If all four Conditions are met the claiming party is entitled to recover damages for personal injury, damage to property, and economic loss.[214] Any term of an agreement purporting to exclude or restrict liability under section 148 or section 149 of the BSA is void.[215]

The rights of action under sections 148 and 149 accrue on the date on which the construction of the building or the works were completed.[216] The limitation period for a claim under section 148 of the Building Act is 15 years from the date on which the action accrued.[217] The limitation periods for a claim under section 149 in respect of which the cause of action accrued before 28 June 2022 and for which the cause of action accrued on or after 28 June 2022 are 30 years and 15 years respectively.[218]

[212] Building Safety Act 2022, s 135(1).
[213] ibid.
[214] Building Safety Act 2022, ss 148(6) and 149(6).
[215] ibid, ss 148(7) and 149(7).
[216] ibid, ss 148(8) and 149(8).
[217] ibid, s 150.
[218] ibid, s 150.

The BSA also contains provisions which, if brought into force, will enable the TCC to make a building liability order, providing that any relevant liability (defined as a liability incurred under the DPA 1972, section 38 of the Building Act or as a result of a building safety risk) is a liability of not only the original body but also of an 'associate' of the original body.[219]

D. Our Advice: The Owner's Claims against the Construction Professionals

As in 1873, 1923, and 1973, the position in 2023 remains broadly the same. In the absence of any express contractual obligation imposing a higher duty of care, the APC would need to show that the architects or the fire engineer failed to act with reasonable skill and care when preparing the design for the Palace. The only difference is that the implied term to that effect was given statutory expression in the Supply of Goods and Services Act 1982.[220]

Whilst there have been numerous cases in the last 50 years dealing with claims against construction professionals in which the standard of care which a construction professional is required to exercise has been considered, the standard of care required is essentially the same as it was in 1973. Notably, paragraph 14-027 of the eleventh edition of *Keating*[221] is in very similar terms to the equivalent section in the third edition of *Keating* (albeit it no longer refers to *Chapman v Walton*). It states:

> An error of judgment may or may not amount to negligence. If the majority of professionals of the relevant discipline would, under the circumstances, have done the same thing this normally provides a good defence, for a 'defendant charged with negligence can clear himself if he shows that he acted in accord with general and approved practice. Where there is no one accepted practice, professionals will not be negligent if they acted in accordance with a practice accepted as proper by a responsible body of that profession, even if another body of competent professional opinion considered the practice wrong.

That statement is now subject to the caveat that any such professional opinion must be capable of withstanding logical analysis because a judge is entitled to hold that the body of opinion is neither responsible nor reasonable.[222]

In 2023 it is unlikely that Counsel would give a preliminary view on liability. The fact that the fire at the Palace took hold quickly, destroying the building and

[219] ibid, s 130–132.
[220] Supply of Goods and Services Act 1982, s 13.
[221] *Keating on Construction Contracts* (n 164) 432–433.
[222] *Bolitho v City and Hackney Health Authority* [1998] AC 232 at 243B-C (HL) referred to Chambers (n 163) 249 (para 2-106) and *Keating on Construction Contracts* (n 164) 433 (para 14-027). See also the application of this principle by Edwards-Stuart J in *199 Knightsbridge Development Ltd v WSP UK Ltd* [2014] EWHC 43 (TCC) at paras 101 to 120.

resulted in the deaths of three people (suggesting there was no proper means of escape) points toward the design being defective. However, Counsel cannot simply assume that was in breach of the Building Regulations which as we now know are, at least in some respects, not fit for purpose.[223]

The law has developed, and Counsel would as above advise that a claim could be brought in tort for the breach of the common law duty of care. By 2023 it is well established that architects and fire engineers owe concurrent duties in contract and tort.[224]

It is now beyond doubt that the TCC is the correct forum to hear the claims for professional negligence involving fire safety, and indeed a number of cases dealing with issues arising following the Grenfell Tower fire are before the Court. The first judgment dealing with such issues was handed down by HHJ Stephen Davies on 14 July 2022 in *Martlet Homes Ltd v Mulalley & Co Ltd*[225] (in which the judge noted, amongst other things, that BRE 135 (1988) is 'not a masterpiece of clarity'[226] and that BRE 135 (2003) 'could have been clearer'[227]). Further guidance from the TCC can be expected in the coming years.

VIII. Conclusion

In writing this chapter and attempting to step into the shoes of Counsel approaching the regulation of fire safety over the last 150 years, we have come to seven central conclusions:

(i) Our regulatory system's ability to adapt to change has been and remains a problem that persists. Whether it was responding to new developments such as electricity, internal gas pipes, steel structures, the use of concrete or new forms of insulation and cladding, the regulatory system has persistently lagged behind technological change.

(ii) Fire safety requires a holistic approach far beyond what contemporary legal discourse would consider the domain of 'construction law'. Planning, housing, environmental, product liability, and much more play equally important roles. The compartmentalisation of legal practice over the last one hundred and fifty years and the resulting silos have limited our ability to face the challenges head-on. Going forward, practitioners in this area should remain mindful of the broad context and importance of effective fire safety. The continued high quality of TCC judges and their technical expertise in

[223] Secretary of State for Housing, Communities & Local Government (n 6) 11; Secretary of State for Communities & Local Government, *Building a Safer Future Independent Review of Building Regulations and Fire Safety: Interim Report* (Cm 9551, 2017) 9.

[224] Chambers (n 163) 243–244 (para 2-011).

[225] *Martlet Homes Limited v Mulalley & Co Limited* [2022] EWHC 1813 (TCC).

[226] ibid, para 116.

[227] ibid, para 136.

relation to the complexities of fire regulations and building safety should not be underestimated.

(iii) There has always been a tension between 'individual' rights (most notably the right to property) and the regulation of property through fire safety regulations. However, the last 150 years have seen society and individuals become far more accepting of regulatory interference.

(iv) Compliance was and remains fundamental, yet history shows us the extreme ends individuals and entities will go to avoid compliance and its perceived costs.[228] As such, effective methods of redress before the TCC will remain a key forum for interpreting and aiding in enforcing the regulation of fire safety.[229]

(v) The development of 'construction law' as a distinct area of legal practice has been a relatively recent development. Further, within the sphere of what is now considered to be construction law, there is a significant gap and lack of appreciation of the historical role of the Official Referees due to what David Sawtell describes as a 'lacuna in reporting of construction disputes in general, and the decisions of the Official Referees in particular'. It was not until 1974 that Official Referees were required to retain their own records. Nevertheless, what remains is of limited use. After surveying the available records of the Official Referees from 1919 to 1970, Michael Reynolds noted that the archives and particularly the judges' notebooks '[w]ith the exception of Eastham's notebooks, the other referees' notebooks and correspondence were barely legible and could only be read with some difficulty or computer aided enhancement.'[230] The limited citation of decisions from the Official Referees, particularly in relation to our opinions in 1873 and 1923, partially reflect the limited role of the Official Referees, compared to the contemporary work of the TCC. The lack of significant documentary evidence and reported cases should not be taken as meaning that this role was not important.

(vi) The regulation of fire safety in buildings has been – and remains – exceedingly complicated. Over the last 150 years, there has come into being a patchwork quilt of rules and regulations relating to fire safety. While practitioners' texts have sought to rationalise these rules, and there are a large number of reported decisions from the TCC and other courts, the overall picture always feels dishearteningly out of reach. The authors of this chapter have come to

[228] The most peculiar example we found of this was that when constructing their own County Hall, the London County Council (the 'LCC') found enforcing their own rules too demanding, so they created an exemption for themselves.

[229] However, it is worth noting that the majority of reported cases concerning the criminal side of Building Regulations are in the Divisional Court of the King's Bench Division. These will be reformed in 2023 when the Fire Safety (England) Regulations 2022 come into force.

[230] M Reynolds, 'Caseflow Management: A Rudimentary Referees Process, 1919–70' (PhD, the LSE 2008) 34.

the conclusion that one needs the super-human skills comparable to Ronald Dworkin's hypothetical Judge Hercules to first identify and then master all of the relevant legal principles.[231]

(vii) Finally, perhaps most significantly, the regulation of fire safety in England and Wales is – and always has been – a reactive process.[232] Regulatory reforms invariably follow tragedy as the importance of building fire safety has oscillated in and out of public and political consciousness. The Grenfell Tower fire of 2017 appears to have been on a scale only comparable to the Great Fire of London in 1666 in terms of effecting regulatory change.

The challenges of the past and how the law has sought to respond offer valuable insights to help inform the future. The resounding narrative of this chapter is the increased importance of the TCC in this sphere from a limited onlooker to the central arbiter of disputes concerning fire safety in England and Wales.

To mark the 150th anniversary of the TCC, this chapter has sought to look back on the Court's evolving role in the regulation and resolution of fire safety disputes. For the first 50 years, the role of the Official Referees remained limited. Many sources point toward the Court having a relatively poor reputation, and the work appears to have been restricted.[233] Edgar Fay noted that 'the limit on their powers to try parts of cases tended to diminish their status in the judicial hierarchy'.[234] The full picture remains lost in time as there are only limited surviving records from the first 50 years of Official Referees' Business. The regulation of fire safety in the 1870s was highly prescriptive. Rules were set down in the byelaws and local Acts. The approach courts took to compliance was often based on a rudimentary assessment of the oral evidence of a District Surveyor. Detailed expert evidence and expert evidence on the causes of fire and fire spread were largely unknown. By modern standards, the resolution of disputes or the use of public law remedies and criminal law to deal with breaches of the regulations lacked any form of critical review. It did, however, have the advantage of speed.

As the Court approached half a century, a high proportion of its work concerned construction and engineering disputes. Newspapers from the time are peppered with stories of the Official Referees' Business as it gained a notable reputation for its technical expertise. The Court still lacked original jurisdiction, and the available records are patchy, and where they do exist, they are difficult to comprehend.

[231] See R Dworkin, *Law's Empire* (Oxford, Hart, 1998).

[232] In making this conclusion it should be noted that our common law system is in effect a reactive system. This has the obvious benefit of flexibility. The epitome of the alleged failure of government to act without a significant fire can be observed in P Apps, *Show me the Bodies: How we let Grenfell happen* (London, Oneworld, 2022) 76–79.

[233] For example, G Alexander, *The Temple of the Nineties* (William Hodge and Company, 1938) 102 notes in relation to GW Hemming QC, 'as an official referee he was so bad that nobody would let his case get into his life if he could possibly help it … Daily he [Hemming Q.C.] had to listen to things which he did not understand, but he was always determined to master them; if he could not comprehend he got irritable and angry with the witness or counsel who failed to make him understand. The result was an inordinate amount of time wasted'.

[234] E Fay, *Official Referees' Business*, 2nd edn (London, Sweet & Maxwell 1988) 17.

In the last 50 years, the Official Referees Court has transformed into the Technology and Construction Court. The reputation of the TCC, and its judges is known around the world. The TCC is well placed to interpret and apply new legislation such as the Building Safety Act 2022 and to interpret and understand the highly technical and scientific challenges that arise in relation to fire safety in buildings.

Appendix

A photograph showing the devastation at the Alexandra Palace in 1873.

13

The Contribution of the Official Referees' Court and the TCC to the English Common Law

DAVID R F SAWTELL

I. Introduction[1]

The Judicature Act 1873, which established the first Official Referees, did not directly contemplate the establishment of a specialist construction court.[2] By the 1910s, however, the majority of its work was connected with building or engineering works. When the Official Referees' Business was formally reconstituted as the Technology and Construction Court (TCC) in 1998, the Lord Chancellor stated at the Court's formal opening that the work done was 'by any standards, exacting and economically very important work, calling for an elite corps of specialist judges'.[3] What this chapter will consider is how the adjudication of specialist construction law by the Official Referees and the TCC has contributed to the English common law.

The first part of this chapter will define the subject matter. Construction law, as a distinct subject, is taught as a postgraduate course in a number of law schools across the world. Practitioners, neutral decision makers such as arbitrators and specialist courts deal with construction law as a recognisable practice area. It is less obvious, however, that it is taxonomically identifiable as a legal category in the same way as, for example, tort law or family law. This part of the chapter will set out why and how it has been recognised as a distinct category.

[1] An initial draft of this chapter was presented at the Society of Legal Scholars annual conference at King's College, London in September 2022: the author is thankful to the participants at the conference for the resulting insights and discussion. The author of this chapter is extremely grateful to Professor Anthony Lavers, and to Richard Wilmot-Smith KC and Paul Darling KC, for their feedback.

[2] Section 57 of the Judicature Act 1857 set out that the subject matter of the new procedure was to include 'any such cause or matter requiring any prolonged examination of documents or accounts, or any scientific or local investigation which cannot in the opinion of the court or a judge conveniently be made before a jury or conducted by the court through its other ordinary officers …'.

[3] Hon. Mr Justice Forbes, 'Adjudication – the first 1,000 days – a general overview' (SCL Paper, December 2001) 1.

The second part of this chapter will consider, through a small number of case examples, how the decisions of the Official Referees and the TCC contributed to the broader development of the English common law. The cases selected were all decided, at first instance, by an Official Referee or a judge of the TCC. This part will consider how the nature of the disputes and the way in which they were treated at first instance affected the overall outcome and conclusion.

This part broadly breaks down into two sections, the first dealing with contract, and the second with negligence. The first case, *RTS Flexible Systems Ltd v Molkerei Alois Müller GmbH & Co KG* ('*Müller*') considered the question of contract formation.[4] The second, *Young and Marten Ltd v McManus Childs Ltd* ('*McManus Childs*') examined implied terms in contracts for the supply of goods and services.[5] The second section considers the cases of *Governors of the Peabody Donation Fund v Sir Lindsay Parkinson & Co Ltd* ('*Peabody v Sir Lindsay Parkinson*'),[6] and *Murphy v Brentwood* ('*Murphy v Brentwood*').[7]

The third part of this chapter will turn the focus around, returning to the themes of the first part of the chapter. It will consider the extent to which the Official Referees and the TCC contributed to the development of construction law as a distinctly identifiable category of English law. By 2001, it was considered that this court was 'unique in the world in producing a specialised jurisprudence which is now systematically and enthusiastically reported'.[8] The extensive reporting of decisions of a specialist construction court, supported by a vigorous textbook tradition, is commonly considered to be one important limb in the recognition of construction law as a distinct category. This part of the chapter will examine the underlying merit to this assumption by analysing the Building Law Reports and the Construction Law Reports from the 1970s to 1999, together with the textbook tradition that had developed since the late nineteenth century. It will identify that there is evidence that the growth in reporting of building and engineering cases through specialised law reports did greatly contribute to the development of construction law as a subject.

The Official Referees and their Business (subsequently reconstituted as the TCC) which form the subject of this chapter underwent considerable transformation during the period under analysis. The Judicature Act 1873 did not give the Official Referees their own jurisdiction: instead, a question arising before the High Court or the Court of Appeal could be referred 'for inquiry and report' to them.[9] This position was later changed so that the whole matter could be tried before

[4] *RTS Flexible Systems Ltd v Molkerei Alois Müller GmbH & Co KG* [2010] UKSC 14, [2010] 1 WLR 753.

[5] *Young and Marten Ltd v McManus Childs Ltd* [1969] 1 AC 454.

[6] *Governors of the Peabody Donation Fund v Sir Lindsay Parkinson & Co Ltd* [1985] AC 210.

[7] *Murphy v Brentwood* [1991] 1 AC 398.

[8] J Uff QC, 'Are we all in the wrong job? Reflections on construction dispute resolution' (SCL Paper, July 2001).

[9] Judicature Act 1873, s 56.

an Official Referee.[10] The Arbitration Act 1889 codified the Official Referees' trial jurisdiction,[11] while by 1892 they were given their own premises in Portugal Street behind the Royal Courts of Justice, and moved again in 1900 to the west wing of the Royal Courts of Justice until 1988, save for a short period in the 1960s.[12] The Official Referees were technically abolished by section 25 of the Courts Act 1971. By the same section, Circuit Judges were appointed to hear 'Official referees' Business'. They continued to be referred to as 'Official Referees'. For ease, this chapter will refer to these judges as 'Official Referees' consistently throughout until the formation of the TCC, notwithstanding their official abolition. Before 1 October 1982, all cases had to begin in the Chancery Division or the Queen's Bench Division, before being 'referred' to the Official Referees' courts. This could be on the application of the parties, or by the masters or judges themselves.[13] Since then, it has been possible to start cases directly in the Official Referees' Business list, and then in the TCC.

II. What is Construction Law?

> We need to adopt a very different approach to the regulatory framework covering the design, construction and maintenance of high-rise residential buildings which recognises that they are complex systems where the actions of many different people can compromise the integrity of that system.[14]

Few would argue with Julian Bailey's definition of the subject: 'Construction law is the law that applies to and in respect of the undertaking of construction and engineering projects.'[15] Likewise, the identification of a 'fundamental characteristic' and distinguishing feature of construction contracts set out in the latest edition of *Hudson's Building and Engineering Contracts* that 'as the work proceeds and becomes fixed or attached to the land of the owner, it progressively and irretrievably becomes the property of the Owner, whatever the financial rights or obligations of the parties may be at the time' is uncontroversial.[16] Construction law, therefore,

[10] Supreme Court of Judicature Act 1884, s 9. Originally this was only with the consent of all the parties before this position was repealed by the Arbitration Act 1884.

[11] Arbitration Act 1889, s 14.

[12] E Fay, *Official Referees' Business*, 2nd edn (London, Sweet & Maxwell, 1988) 20–2, 27.

[13] This was given effect by a change to the Rules of the Supreme Court Order 36, r 2(1). After 1 October 1982, a plaintiff who wished to have the proceedings they were commencing treated as 'Official Referees' Business' would mark this in the top left hand corner of the writ or originating summons: J Newy, *Official Referees' Courts: Practice and Procedure* (London, Butterworths, 1988) 6. In practice, this absence of an original jurisdiction meant that the Commercial Court might hold on to cases that turned on points of law, but refer factually or technically complicated disputes to the Official Referees.

[14] Dame Judith Hackitt, *Building a Safer Future – Independent Review of Building Regulations and Fire Safety: Final Report* (May 2018, Stationery Office, Cm 9607) 6.

[15] J Bailey, *Construction Law*, 3rd edn (London Publishing Partnership, 2020) Vol I, 4.

[16] *Hudson's Building and Engineering Contracts*, 14th edn (London, Sweet & Maxwell, 2019) para 1-001.

is defined by its subject matter, as opposed to any doctrinally distinct principles of law.

On one level, therefore, it is not part of a doctrinal legal taxonomy, instead falling into what Peter Birks described as an area of the law lacking a 'unity of concept of event', such as labour law or company law. As he acknowledged, however, the function of such contextual categorisation is that it collects aspects of doctrinal law which would otherwise be kept apart.[17] While Blackstone was trained, practised as, and published as an architect, his taxonomy of English law did not include construction law as a distinct category, despite his use of construction scenarios.[18] Instead, if construction law exists as a taxonomically separate subject, there must be some purpose or utility in its identification as part of a rational ordering system.[19] As Lord Dyson reflected, 'When I came to the Bar in 1968, construction law was regarded as a rather dull, specialist subject, in some respects hardly worthy of being considered as proper law at all.'[20] The question, therefore, is the extent to which construction law is recognised to be a categorically separate area of the law, as distinct from broader contract, tort and commercial law.

There is a long and documented history to the use of construction contracts. It is possible to identify contracts with detailed specifications and express provisions as to quality, both in England on the continent, from at least the 1350s.[21] The outlines of modern construction law can probably be traced from the late to mid-nineteenth century. Philip L Bruner, in his magisterial study of the emergence of construction law in the US, identifies the origins of construction law in the emergence of the architect's profession as well as other professional specialisation after the Civil War, the adoption of standard form contracts, and the enactment of mechanic's lien statutes in different states and the federal Heard Act in 1894 placing requirements as to surety bonds on contractors to protect against the performance risk.[22] There is no comparable study of English construction law. Unlike other common law jurisdictions, England never saw the adoption of builder's or mechanic's lien legislation, but in the late nineteenth and early twentieth century it is possible to trace similar developments in the creation of a textbook tradition, the emergence of recognisable construction professions, and by 1939 the adoption of a standard form of building contract.[23] The growth of construction

[17] P Birks, *An Introduction to the Law of Restitution* (Oxford, Clarendon, 1985)73–4.

[18] W Prest, 'Blackstone as Architect: Constructing the Commentaries' (2003) 15 *Yale Journal of Law & the Humanities* 103–133.

[19] D Sheehan and TT Arvind, 'Private Law Theory and Taxonomy: Reframing the Debate' (2015) 35(3) *Legal Studies* 480, 485–88.

[20] Lord Dyson, *Justice: Continuity and Change* (Oxford, Hart, 2018) 179.

[21] G van Tussenbroek, 'Building Contracts in the Low Countries. Provisions Concerning Form and Quality Control in the Construction Industry (1350–1650)' (2017) 32(1) *Construction History* 1. See also the discussion of building contracts in F Salzman, *Building in England down to 1540* (Oxford, Clarendon Press, 1952) 51–2, and the building contracts in Appendix B.

[22] PL Bruner, 'The Historical Emergence of Construction Law' (2007) 34(1) *William Mitchell Law Review* 1, 4–7.

[23] The first RIBA form, produced in agreement with the Institute of Builders and the National Federation of Building Trades Employers of Great Britain and Northern Ireland, was produced in 1903, and was revised in 1939. The Joint Contracts Tribunal was formed by RIBA in 1931, with later

law as a specialised area of legal practice emerged after the Second World War.[24] The 1970s, in particular, represented a watershed moment, with the adoption of different arrangements of standard form contracts, the growth of disputes, and increasing specialisation in legal practice.[25]

Construction law does not stand apart from normal common law principles of contract, tort, property, unjust enrichment, and other doctrinal areas. The first edition of Donald Keating's book on construction contracts made this point clearly: 'The law of building contracts is a part of the general law of contract and is not governed by any codifying statute.'[26] In the important House of Lords case of *Modern Engineering (Bristol) v Gilbert Ash*, the suggestion that a construction contract should be interpreted as a *sui generis* form of contract was squashed.[27] The case involved the then commonly used RIBA Local Authorities 1963 edition form. The case turned on certification: the earlier Court of Appeal authority of *Dawnays Ltd v F. G. Minter* had considered that it was not possible to raise a set-off against a certified sum.[28] In the Court of Appeal in *Gilbert Ash*, Lord Denning MR applied *Dawnays*, holding that, 'There must be a 'cash flow' in the building trade.' Lord Morris refused to interpret the contract so as to give effect to the 'especial' importance of cash flow in the building industry, and considered that the contract did not prohibit set-off.[29] Lord Diplock, likewise, regarded the decision in *Dawnays* to have turned on the particular wording of the instant contract, rather than setting down any general principle applicable to building contracts.[30] Ultimately, the law as to certification underwent considerable reform so as to provide for mandatory payment notices and provisions in construction contracts in Part II of the Housing Grants, Construction and Regeneration Act 1996, which recognised the

editions published in 1939, 1963, 1980 and 1998. The Joint Contracts Tribunal Limited commenced in May 1998. The development of a textbook tradition is discussed further below. This can be compared to the American Institute of Architect's Uniform Contract: the first edition was published in 1888: J Sweet, 'The American Institute of Architects: Dominant actor in the Construction Documents Market' [1991] *Wisconsin Law Review* 317.

[24] Dyson (n 20) 179; TJ Stipanowich, 'Reconstructing Construction Law: Reality and Reform in a Transactional System' (1998) 2 Wisconsin Law Review 463, 491.

[25] EW Cooney, 'Innovation and Contracts in the Postwar British Building Industry' (1987) 3 *Construction History* 115; Mr Justice Jackson, 'The Tower of Babel: what happens when a building contract goes wrong' (SCL Paper 136, March 2007) 3. IN Duncan Wallace QC, in his preface to the eleventh edition of *Hudson's Building and Engineering Contracts* (London, Sweet & Maxwell, 1995), pointed to the 'huge increase' in construction litigation since 1970, with specialist judiciaries formed or expanded, and almost every major commercial firm of lawyers having professional construction expertise. CR Seppala has also pointed to the 'boom in international construction in the oil producing countries' since the 1970s, which created the conditions for the FIDIC forms of contract to achieve wider currency: 'Contractor's Claims under the FIDIC International Civil Engineering Contract' [1986] *International Business Law* 14, 179.

[26] D Keating, *Law and Practice of Building Contracts including Architects and Surveyors* (London, Sweet & Maxwell, 1955) 1.

[27] *Modern Engineering (Bristol) v Gilbert Ash* [1974] AC 689. See also the comment of Lord Salmon in *Mottram Consultants v Bernard Sunley* [1975] 2 Lloyd's Rep. 197 that '… there has never been anything special about construction cases'.

[28] *Dawnays Ltd v F. G. Minter* [1971] 1 WLR 1205.

[29] 707–08.

[30] 718.

policy impetus for cash flow recognised in the Court of Appeal in *Gilbert Ash*. In its essentials, therefore, a construction contract has been recognised as being no different from any other contract.[31]

There is, therefore, no doctrinal rule set unique to construction law save for limited statutory exceptions, such as those created by Part II of the Housing Grants, Construction and Regeneration Act 1996 and sections 1 to 2A of the Defective Premises Act 1972. Instead, the characterisation of construction law as an 'umbrella term' covering multiple legal principles, is appropriate.[32] The field has also been described as a 'kaleidoscope of complex legal and factual issues inherent in the construction process itself'.[33] Construction law contains a number of features that are, in combination, particular to the subject matter. It is generally concerned with the procurement and contractual processes leading to the creation of the built environment through the incorporation of materials into real property, in the course of a medium-term project with multiple project participants in the conception, design, procurement, and construction phases; and dispute resolution is often through third-party specialist dispute resolution such as adjudication or arbitration, as opposed to court-based litigation. In recent history, as well, it has also become clear through the Grenfell Tower disaster in June 2017 that construction law must take into account the post-construction, occupational phase of a building's life cycle, including issues of building safety. The quotation from the Hackitt Report at the start of this section is both a demonstration of the importance of construction law, and the critical need to keep in mind the fact that the product of construction operations must be safe for use and occupation.

Construction law, therefore, is economically important, reflecting the significance of the construction industry to the UK economy. It is also thematically important, affecting how the built environment comes into existence and is then enjoyed. It is also, however, a subject that is locked into the common law's doctrinal rule sets. The extent to which construction law has contributed to the development of and our understanding of those rule sets will be considered in the next part of this chapter.

III. Contribution to the Development of the Common Law

This part of the chapter will focus on a selection of case studies taken from the decisions of the Official Referees and the TCC and their subsequent appellate history which identify how they have contributed to the development of the

[31] Dyson (n 20) 181.

[32] P Gerber, 'The Teaching of Construction Law and the Practice of Construction Law: Never the Twain Shall Meet?' (2010) 20(1/2) *Legal Education Review* 59, 60.

[33] Bruner (n 22) 14.

common law in general. There is some overlap with the cases selected by Lord Dyson in his 2015 Keating Lecture, especially in relation to implied terms and duties of care.[34] The approach below differs in it will focus on the specific contribution of the first instance decision, as opposed to the final appellate conclusion. Many important construction cases have shaped the common law without being dealt with at first instance by the Official Referees or the TCC.[35] This entry point illustrates the importance of the construction issues faced by the Court, alongside the more general issues of law the cases raised.

A. Contract Formation: RTS Flexible Systems Ltd v Molkerei Alois Müller GmbH & Co KG (UK Production)

It is not uncommon for pre-construction design and consultancy and construction operations to commence before the execution of the final contract. The instruction to proceed often takes the form of a letter of intent, requiring the designer, consultant or contractor to start work. The form of such a letter of intent can vary immensely, from a simple request to commence without any stipulation as to payment, to a detailed document imposing a cap on liability and creating detailed contractual obligations and procedures. The letter may also set out the form of contract that the parties intend to contract upon. The instruction to proceed may also take the form of an order, which may or may not refer to more detailed contractual terms. It is not unusual for the tendering contractor to include its own standard terms and conditions as part of its quotation, or to refer to them in subsequent correspondence. Even if the parties settle on the form and terms of the contract, it is not rare for one or both parties to fail to sign the agreement, which can often take the form of a deed in order to take advantage of the extended limitation period associated with such an instrument. It is not unknown, when executing a contract, for a party to handwrite different terms or particulars on to the instrument after the first party has executed it.

As a result, it can be difficult to establish if the parties have entered into a contract at all if a classic offer and acceptance analysis is applied, let alone to ascertain what the terms of any such contract might be. A number of the doctrinally important cases in this field, therefore, have arisen either from the supply of

[34] Reprinted in Lord Dyson, *Justice* (n 20) ch 11.

[35] For example, *Ruxley Electronics and Constructions Ltd v Forsyth* [1995] 3 WLR 118, which considered different approaches to the measurement of contractual damages for defective works, came before Judge Diamond QC at the Central London County Court at first instance; and *Williams v Roffey Bros* [1991] 1 QB 1, a significant case on consideration, was dealt with by a then assistant recorder, Mr Rupert Jackson QC, sitting in the Kingston-upon-Thames County Court. See M Chen-Wishart, 'The Legacy of *Williams v Roffey*: Death Knell for Consideration or Infusion of New Blood?' in J Bailey (ed), *Construction Law, Costs and Contemporary Developments and Contemporary Developments: Drawing the Threads Together: A Festschrift for Lord Justice Jackson* (Oxford, Hart, 2018) 144: she notes that the first instance decision has disappeared and that no copy of it can be located.

construction materials or the engagement of construction operations. In *British Steel Corporation v Cleveland Bridge and Engineering Co Ltd*, Goff J (as he then was), sitting in the Queen's Bench Division (Commercial Court) determined that no contract was, in fact, concluded.[36] British Steel delivered 137 cast-steel nodes and other related goods. Before the nodes were manufactured, they sent a telex providing an indicative price and specification. Cleveland Bridge sent a letter of intent, asking British Steel to proceed immediately with the works pending the issuance of a sub-contract. The parties continued to negotiate, however, and no final form of contract was entered into. Goff J held that, while both parties anticipated that a contract would be entered into, the work carried out was not referable to any contract.[37]

It is noteworthy that the claim was commenced in the Queen's Bench Division; it could not, of course, have been issued directly for hearing as Official Referees' Business. Goff J, in the opening paragraph, noted that initially it had been contemplated that he would only deal with certain issues, with quantum most likely being decided by an Official Referee: he regarded this division of the case into different parts unsatisfactory. Ultimately, as the parties had agreed quantum, he was able to deal with the entire case.[38]

The dispute in *Müller* came before Mr Justice Christopher Clarke in the TCC at first instance.[39] The hearing was listed to determine, as preliminary issues, what the terms of the contract constituted, in part, by the letter of intent were; whether that contract came to an end; whether it was replaced by another contract; and if so, what its terms were.[40] The existence of a contract at all was not disputed at first instance. He opened his judgment on a cautionary note: 'This case is another example of the perils of proceeding with work under a letter of intent.'[41]

The defendant, well known as 'Müller', was a leading yoghurt manufacturer. The claimant, RTS, was a supplier of automated machines for product handling in the food industry. Müller had a problem that its existing system for packaging pots of yoghurts could not process twin pots of yoghurts without wasting the original trays that held them: RTS was lined up to design, manufacture and install a solution. Discussions between the parties proceeded for years. RTS submitted a number of quotations, which referred to its terms and conditions.

On 21 February 2005, Müller sent a letter of intent to proceed with an offer by RTS. The letter of intent was expressed, however, to be subject to contract: 'Prior to agreement on the full contractual terms, only Müller shall have the right to terminate this supply project and contract.'[42] It was set out in the letter that the full terms of the contract would be finalised, agreed and signed within four weeks

[36] *British Steel Corporation v Cleveland Bridge and Engineering Co Ltd* [1984] 1 All ER 504.
[37] ibid, 511.
[38] ibid, 506.
[39] [2008] EWHC 1087 (TCC).
[40] ibid, [1].
[41] ibid.
[42] ibid, [27].

of the date of the letter. RTS, however, responded by confirming that they had commenced work on the project, subject to two points, effectively revising parts of the letter of intent.[43]

At first instance, the parties set out competing submissions as to the construction of what was styled the 'Letter of Intent contract'. RTS submitted that Müller accepted the whole of its quotation, including its terms and conditions, which operated as an offer to contract. While the letter of intent contemplated that the final contractual terms would be agreed and signed within four weeks, it did not provide that it would automatically come to an end in four weeks. Müller submitted that the letter of intent was a counter-offer to the quotation, and that it did not incorporate any of the terms in the quotation. That counter-offer was, itself, met by a further counter-offer by RTS, which was then accepted either by Müller's conduct in allowing RTS to continue, or by a further letter extending the four-week period. Müller also submitted that, following the period of four weeks or any agreed extension, the agreement would come to an end: RTS would not be under any obligation to continue working, and Müller would have no obligation in relation to work performed after that date.

Christopher Clarke J concluded that the quotation was an offer to carry out the work specified in it on the terms set out in that quotation, including RTS' standard terms. The letter of intent was a counter-offer. This was responded to in RTS' letter, which accepted the letter of intent subject to the two qualifications contained within it. RTS' letter was, itself, a counter-offer, which was accepted, at the latest, by Müller's letter.[44] He rejected the conclusion that there was no contract: the reference in the letter of intent to the right to terminate the project and contract, and the statement that it would be governed by English law, militated against this, while he recorded that the parties were agreed that they had entered into a contract of some sort.[45]

The judge went on to determine the terms of the contract and the remaining preliminary issues. He recorded that, after the letter of intent had expired, RTS continued to build and deliver the equipment, and were partly paid for it. He noted that, 'In those circumstances the court strongly inclines to concluding that the parties have entered into some contract even though such a contract cannot be spelt out by a classic analysis of the sequence of offer and acceptance.'[46] He held that,

> The natural inference is that their contract was that RTS would carry out the agreed work for the agreed price. It was not essential for them to have agreed the terms and

[43] ibid, [28]–[30].
[44] ibid, [33].
[45] ibid, [34].
[46] ibid, [65], citing at [66] the judgment of Steyn LJ (as he then was) in *Trentham v Archital Luxfer* [1993] 1 Lloyds LR 25 that, 'it is true that the coincidence of offer and acceptance will in the vast majority of cases represent the mechanism of contract formation. It is so in the case of a contract alleged to have been made by an exchange of correspondence. But it is not necessarily so in the case of a contract alleged to have come into existence during and as a result of performance ….'

> conditions and they did not do so. In this respect they continued after the expiry of the Letter of Intent just as they had before, i.e. calling for and carrying out the work without agreement as to the applicable terms.

The contract did not, however, contain the MF/I conditions that the parties had been negotiating. Clause 48 of those conditions stated that, 'This Contract may be executed in any number of counterparts provided that it shall not become effective until each party has executed a counterpart and exchanged it with the other.' As no counterparts were executed or exchanged, it was held that this clause prevented the MF/I conditions from being incorporated. Instead, the contract contained more sparse terms contained in a number of documents identified by the judge.[47]

Christopher Clarke J handed down a detailed judgment, running to 141 paragraphs. The issues involved were, on one level, comparable to those considered by Goff J in *British Steel Corporation v Cleveland Bridge*, which was notably heard in the Queen's Bench Division (Commercial Court) and not by an Official Referee. In the course of his judgment, Goff J referred to the earlier decision of Mr Edgar Fay QC, one of the Official Referees, in *Turriff Construction Ltd v Regalia Knitting Mills Ltd*: initially it was not fully reported, appearing in the *Estates Gazette*; the specialist Building Law Reports only started some years later, where it was subsequently reported.[48] If *British Steel Corporation v Cleveland Bridge* had been heard in 2010, it most likely would have been commenced in or transferred to the TCC, given the nature of its subject matter, where it would have been heard by a High Court Judge. The first instance decision in *Müller* was not officially reported, but it is accessible on BAILII and other legal case law databases. The comparison between these two cases, therefore, gives an indication of the changes in the nature of construction law reporting and jurisprudence between the 1970s and the 2010s. Even unreported cases were now far more accessible. Heavier construction disputes were listed in the TCC.

RTS appealed to the Court of Appeal. The nature of their case changed. Whereas both parties had argued before Christopher Clarke J that their primary position was that there was a contract, RTS now submitted that there was no contract; the Court of Appeal allowed them to make this argument. The decision of the Court of Appeal is reported, in the Construction Law Reports, as well as in the Commercial All England Reports.[49]

RTS' main argument on appeal was that no contract was concluded; any entitlement that they had to receive payment would be on a quantum meruit.[50] The comparison was made with *British Steel Corporation v Cleveland Bridge*, and Robert Goff J's reasoning as to why there was no contract in that case: this passage had not been cited to Christopher Clarke J.[51] They relied heavily on clause 48 of the

[47] ibid, [67]–[77].

[48] *Turriff Construction Ltd v Regalia Knitting Mills Ltd* (1971) 202 EG 169. It was reported in the Building Law Reports over a decade later: (1979) 9 BLR 20.

[49] [2009] EWCA Civ 26; 123 ConLR 130; [2009] 2 All ER (Comm) 542.

[50] ibid, [48].

[51] ibid, [56] per Waller LJ.

general conditions of the contract. Waller LJ held that this clause was a 'complete answer', and that it prevented a contract from coming into being.[52] Moses and Hallett LJJ agreed without giving substantive judgments.

The Court of Appeal refused permission to appeal to the House of Lords. Permission to appeal was, however, granted by the House of Lords, and the case was heard by the newly constituted Supreme Court on 2 and 3 December 2009, with judgment being handed down on 10 March 2010.[53] The decision of the Court of Appeal was reversed.

Lord Clarke JSC, giving the judgment of the Court, noted that, 'The moral of the story to is to agree first and to start work later.'[54] He set out principles that, he stated, 'apply to all contracts, including both sales contracts and construction contracts', and which had been clearly stated in *Pagnan SpA v Feed Products Ltd*.[55] Whether there is a binding contract between the parties and, if so, upon what terms, depends upon what they have agreed:

> even if certain terms of economic or other significance to the parties have not been finalised, an objective appraisal of their words and conduct may lead to the conclusion that they did not intend agreement of such terms to be a precondition to a concluded and legally binding agreement.[56]

There was not, however, a conflict between the *Percy Trentham* case,[57] cited by Christopher Clarke J, and *British Steel Corporation v Cleveland Bridge*: each case depends upon its own facts.[58] As the parties had agreed a price, and it was unrealistic to suppose that the parties did not intend to create legal relations, the 'no contract' solution was unconvincing.[59] The Supreme Court noted, in particular, that the parties had agreed practically everything save for the provisions in relation to a parent company guarantee and items which were not necessary to complete.[60] Given the extent of the agreement, the parties had agreed to waive the 'subject to contract' clause at clause 48: 'Any other conclusion makes no commercial sense.'[61] It was held that 'we do not think that the reasonable honest businessman in the position of either RTS or Müller would have concluded … that there was no contract between them or that there was a contract on some but not all of the terms that had been agreed'.[62]

[52] ibid, [56] per Waller LJ.

[53] The jurisdiction of the House of Lords was transferred to the Supreme Court pursuant to s 57 and Sch 10 to the Constitutional Reform Act 2005 on 1 October 2009.

[54] *RTS v Molkerei* (SC) (n 4) [1].

[55] *Pagnan SpA v Feed Products Ltd* [1987] 2 Lloyd's Rep 601: Bingham J (as he then was) and in the Court of Appeal.

[56] *RTS v Molkerei* (SC) (n 4) [45].

[57] *Trentham (G Percy) Ltd v Archital Luxfer Ltd* (1993) 63 BLR 44, where the Court of Appeal held that the governing criterion as to contract formation was the reasonable expectations of 'honest men', although the coincidence of offer and acceptance would represent the mechanism of contract formation in the vast majority of cases.

[58] *RTS v Molkerei* (SC) (n 4) [54].

[59] ibid, [58].

[60] ibid, [84].

[61] ibid, [86].

[62] ibid, [87].

The case falls squarely into the debate about how a 'battle of the forms' should be resolved. At the same time, it positions the threshold where a contract will be found, as opposed to leaving the parties with a restitutionary claim (if they have any claim at all).[63] The parties' own precondition as to whether or not a contract would be entered into was waived by the Supreme Court on the grounds of commercial sense and the reasonable expectations of the parties. It has been suggested that, while the conclusion is practical, it does not provide a clear guide as to whether or not a contract has been formed.[64] This may well be inevitable: as Paul S Davies correctly observed, 'Deciding when the die was cast and the parties intended to be bound on the negotiated terms may not be easy.'[65] As the Supreme Court acknowledged, the question is highly fact sensitive. Given this, it is appropriate for the Court determining the issue to have considerable experience in the area of specialism, as is the case with the TCC. It would be highly unusual for the parties to simply agree a 'reasonable sum' with no other terms in respect of construction operations: the very fact that these disputes arise is because the terms of the contract are so important to both parties. While Davies, perhaps, goes too far in suggesting that the course taken in *British Steel* should be 'sidelined', there is considerable weight in the Supreme Court's conclusion that it is generally unrealistic to hold that there is no contract where the parties intend to create legal relations, have agreed a price and, in particular, have begun to perform.[66]

B. Implied Terms: Young and Marten Ltd v McManus Childs Ltd

While considerable quantities of construction materials may move through the construction supply chain and be incorporated into the land pursuant to a construction contract, they are not contracts for the sale of goods, but are interpreted for these purposes as contracts for work and materials. Whereas the law as to sale of goods was effectively codified by the Sale of Goods Act 1893, there was no such legislative action in respect of contracts for work and materials until the Supply of Goods and Services Act 1982 nearly a century later. It was not inevitable that the implied terms for construction contracts as to quality and fitness and purpose would mirror those for sale of goods. While most standard form contracts adopt express terms in respect of these points, these implied terms form an important starting point or presumption. Furthermore, bespoke subcontracts and less detailed contracts, such as contract orders, can fail to include such provisions. The outcome of the case of *McManus Childs* confirmed that there was no

[63] J Morgan, *Great Debates in Contract Law*, 2nd edn (London, Bloomsbury, 2015) 15–29.
[64] J Morgan, *Contract Law Minimalism* (Cambridge, Cambridge University Press, 2013).
[65] PS Davies, 'Anticipated Contracts: Room for Agreement' (2010) 69(3) *Cambridge Law Journal* 467, 474.
[66] ibid 474.

artificial distinction between construction contracts and contracts for the sale of goods when it came to quality and fitness for purpose. The conclusion had ramifications for subsequent cases, such as those in respect of the fitness for purpose of design and build projects, and influenced the Law Commission in its proposals for what became the Defective Premises Act 1972.

At the outset, it should be noted that the first instance judgment of the Official Referee, His Honour Norman Richards QC, was not reported. The case was not an insignificant one, notwithstanding its relatively low value;[67] the case had been transferred from the Bloomsbury County Court for trial by an Official Referee of the Supreme Court, and, as set out above, the issues involved were relevant to many other disputes. The Court of Appeal decision was reported in the All England Reports.[68] The lacuna in reporting of construction disputes in general, and the decisions of the Official Referees in particular, in this period will be discussed in the following sections.

The construction contract was for the erection of a dwelling house in Gerrards Cross in Buckinghamshire. The employer was Peter Prior; the builder was McManus Childs Limited. The Official Referee found that Mr Saunders specified the use of 'Somerset 13' tiles for the roof. McManus Childs subcontracted the roofing works to Young & Marten as roofing subcontractors to supply and fix the 'Somerset 13 tiles'. They, in turn, subcontracted the supply of the tiles and the works to the Acme Roofing Co (London) Limited, who purchased the 'Somerset 13' tiles from the manufacturer. In fact, the tiles were not suitable for their purpose: they required replacement, and it is probable that they were not manufactured according to their usual standard due to a problem with the supply of raw materials at the manufacturing stage. Before the Official Referee, it was conceded that the tiles were not merchantable, and that the suppliers would be liable if section 14(2) of the Sale of Goods Act 1893 applied; but it did not: this was a contract for work and materials.

From the report of the Court of Appeal, it appears that the Official Referee found for Mr Prior as against McManus Childs, but found in favour of Young & Marten, leaving the whole loss with the main contractor.

In the Court of Appeal, Sellers LJ noted the following:

> A contract to supply a named commodity, being future goods, specified by the building owner does not relieve the builder from supplying material of the quality specified. The contract itself imposes the obligation. On the other hand, if a building owner expressly specifies material, which, properly manufactured or supplied without defect in accordance with the contractual description and quality, proves inadequate and unsuitable for its purpose, the builder will have performed his contract unless the contract and the circumstances establish that reliance was placed on the builder to supply material fit for its intended purpose.[69]

[67] The construction contract was for the construction of a single dwelling house for the contract sum of £3,350. The judgment sum at first instance was £3,694.

[68] [1967] 3 All ER 451.

[69] ibid, 454.

The Official Referee relied upon *G H Myers & Co v Brent Cross Service Co*, where it was held that a person contracting to do work and supply materials warrants that the materials which he uses will be of good quality and reasonably fit for the purpose for which he is using them, unless the circumstances of the contract are such as to exclude any such warranty.[70] That decision, however, was not altogether satisfactory: it concerned the repair of a car, and both Sellers LJ and Russell LJ expressed some caution about different parts of it. Sellers LJ also cited *Stewart v Reavell's Garage*.[71] The Court of Appeal must have regarded the case as being of some significance, however, as leave to appeal to the House of Lords was granted.

The House of Lords dismissed the appeal by Young & Marten. Lord Reid stated that the precise issue in respect of material supplied by a contractor under the contract was whether that contractor warrants the material against latent defects, as well as those which would have been detected on a reasonable inspection.[72] Lord Reid answered the question in the affirmative. Any loss could be passed down the construction supply chain: if the employer could not claim against the contractor, it would be left without a remedy, but if it could, the contractor could bring a claim against the seller under the Sale of Goods Act.[73] If this chain of liability was broken (such as where one party excluded their liability, as in *Gloucestershire County Council v Richardson (trading as W. J. Richardson & Son)*,[74] this was nothing to do with the employer and should not deprive it of its remedy. Furthermore, he observed that many contracts for work and materials resemble contracts of sale: it would be 'strange' if the fact that the seller also agreed to install it made all the difference.[75] Lord Pearce observed that the cases that preceded and crystallised in the Sale of Goods Act 1893 did not demonstrate a clear difference of principle between a sale of goods and a contract for labour and materials.[76] Lord Upjohn, as well, could not see any logical distinction.[77]

Lord Reid observed that there was not very much authority in respect of the issue raised in *McManus Childs*. This is, on one level, surprising: the question of whether the materials supplied by a builder are fit for their purpose (despite being in accordance with the specification) is a relatively common one in construction disputes. Both in the Court of Appeal and the House of Lords, some doubt was expressed about all of the obiter reasoning contained in the *G. H. Myers* case. It is striking that such an important issue took so long to be resolved definitively,

[70] *G H Myers & Co v Brent Cross Service Co* [1934] 1 KB 46 at 55, per DuParcq J, sitting with Swift J in the Divisional Court.

[71] *Stewart v Reavell's Garage* [1952] 2 QB 545 at 550.

[72] [1969] 1 AC 454, 465.

[73] ibid, 466.

[74] *Gloucestershire County Council v Richardson (trading as W. J. Richardson & Son)* [1969] 1 AC 480. This case was heard just after *McManus Childs* was decided, and was reported in the same volume of the ICLR Appeal Cases reports. Counsel for the Respondents were Donald Keating and Patrick Garland, as discussed below.

[75] ibid, 467.

[76] ibid, 470.

[77] ibid, 473.

requiring a consideration of pre-1893 case law. The question of why this should be the case will be considered in the following sections.

C. Tortious Duty of Care: Governors of the Peabody Donation Fund v Sir Lindsay Parkinson & Co Ltd and Murphy v Brentwood

The House of Lords decision in *Anns v Merton London Borough Council* ('*Anns v Merton*'),[78] and the subsequent retreat from the test set out in that case as to when a duty of care would be recognised which concluded in the decision in *Murphy v Brentwood*, is familiar to all students of English law. What is less well appreciated is the fact that these two cases, as well as the important case of *Peabody v Sir Lindsay Parkinson*, were building cases that began at first instance and were heard as Official Referees' Business. At first instance in *Anns v Merton*, Judge Edgar Fay QC held that the lessees' claims for damages arising from defects to their properties in a two-storey block against the defendant local authority (which was the successor to the body which had approved the developer's plans) were statute-barred on the grounds of limitation. This was overturned by the Court of Appeal. The local authority appealed, and was also given leave to argue whether they came under a duty of care at all. The House of Lords held that a local body, in carrying out the inspection, came under a duty of care in private law to take reasonable care to ensure compliance with the byelaws. If the local authority came under such a duty of care, then the contractor whose primary fault it was also found themselves subject to a duty of care to subsequent owners.

In so doing, Lord Wilberforce set out a more generalised two-stage test as to whether a duty of care would arise in a particular situation:

> First one has to ask whether, as between the alleged wrongdoer and the person who has suffered damage there is a sufficient relationship of proximity or neighbourhood such that, in the reasonable contemplation of the former, carelessness on his part may be likely to cause damage to the latter – in which case a prima facie duty of care arises. Secondly, if the first question is answered affirmatively, it is necessary to consider whether there are any considerations which ought to negative, or to reduce or limit the scope of the duty or the class of person to whom it is owed or the damages to which a breach of it may give rise.[79]

The decision in *Anns v Merton* substantially adopted the judgment of Lord Denning MR in *Dutton v Bognor Regis Urban District Council*.[80] As Lord Bridge noted subsequently in *Murphy v Brentwood*, the decision in *Dutton* was without precedent and

[78] *Anns v Merton London Borough Council* [1978] AC 728.
[79] ibid, 751–52.
[80] *Dutton v Bognor Regis Urban District Council* [1972] 1 QB 373.

was widely regarded as judicial legislation.[81] *Anns v Merton* expanded the law both in respect of negligence and in respect of economic loss: the lessees' claim was for the cost of remediating the buildings, as opposed to damages for physical injury to the lessees themselves. The House of Lords did not refer to the recently enacted Defective Premises Act 1972, either, which created a statutory liability for those involved in the construction of new dwellings.

The first instance decision in *Peabody v Sir Lindsay Parkinson* of Judge Oddie, sitting as a deputy Official Referee, was not reported. Given the importance of the case, both at first instance and on appeal, this is a point of interest. The Governors of the Peabody Donation Fund brought a claim in respect of serious defects at their housing development at Knight's Hill in Lambeth. The claim was brought for breach of contract in respect of the builders, Sir Lindsay Parkinson & Co Ltd, for negligence or breach of duty by Austin Vernon and Partners as the architects, and negligence against Lambeth Borough Council. While the original plans lodged with and subsequently approved by the local authority had provided for a flexible system to allow for subsoil movement, the builder and the architect installed a different system without seeking approval from the local authority. The local authority failed to realise that the drainage system was different from that approved. Before the development was completed, the drains failed, leading to three years of delay.

Judge Oddie held that the local authority owed a duty of care to Peabody, and that they were liable in negligence for the failure of their drainage inspector in carrying out his duties. The local authority appealed to the Court of Appeal, arguing that the judge was wrong to hold that, under Schedule 9 of the London Government Act 1963, they had power to ensure that the drainage installed complied with the original drainage system approved by the council, and that the damages (consisting of extra sums for delay and expense paid to the builder) were recoverable from them.[82] The Court of Appeal allowed the appeal. Peabody themselves came under a statutory obligation as building owners to construct the drains to the satisfaction of the local authority, which they had breached: in those circumstances, the local authority did not come under a duty of care to Peabody to ensure that a defective system was not installed.[83]

The House of Lords dismissed Peabody's appeal.[84] Lord Keith stated that the 'temptation' to treat Lord Wilberforce's remarks as to a two-stage test as to whether a duty of care would be stablished should be 'resisted'; it was also necessary to take into consideration whether it was just and reasonable that such a duty should be recognised.[85] A Court of Appeal decision which had applied Lord Wilberforce's

[81] *Murphy v Brentwood* (HL) (n 7) 473.
[82] [1983] 3 WLR 754.
[83] ibid, 760 per Lawton LJ; 763 per Fox LJ; 767–68 per Slade LJ.
[84] [1985] AC 210.
[85] ibid, 24041.

speech without appreciating his reasoning was overruled.[86] The decision in *Anns v Merton* was therefore limited.

The first instance decision in *Murphy v Brentwood* was reported in the Construction Law Reports.[87] It was heard by His Honour Judge Esyr Lewis QC, sitting in the Queen's Bench Division (Official referees' business). The facts were relatively straightforward (and were not even reported in full). The plaintiff claimed damages against the local authority following subsidence to his house. It had been built in 1969; the plaintiff had purchased it from the builders in 1970; he sold it in July 1986. The developers had submitted the design of the foundations to the local authority, who approved them under section 64 of the Public Health Act 1936.[88] Before they were approved, the local authority submitted them to independent consultant engineers, who approved them without making any independent judgment on their suitability. It was the local authority's defence that, by submitting them to consultant engineers, they had discharged their duty under section 64. Serious cracks became apparent in 1981. The foundations were inadequate, and the judge at first instance held that the consultant engineers were negligent in considering their design. The claim was for the diminution in value of the house.

It had been accepted by the local authority that, because of the decision in *Anns v Merton*, they owed the plaintiff a duty of care. Its submission that they were entitled to rely on a competent independent contractor was rejected: it was held that section 64 imposed a non-delegable duty of care.[89] Further, the plaintiff had no cause of action until the state of the house was such that it became an imminent danger to safety.[90] The learned judge held that this occurred in 1981: the claim was therefore within limitation.[91]

When the case went to the Court of Appeal, the issues were similar to those before the Official Referee, whose decision was affirmed.[92] Ralph Gibson LJ referred to the decision in *D&F Estates*,[93] and in particular, the comparison in the development in the law represented in *Anns v Merton* and the legislative development contained within the Defective Premises Act 1972.[94] The subsequent

[86] *Acrecrest Ltd v W. S. Hattrell & Partners* [1983] QB 260.

[87] (1988) 13 ConLR 96.

[88] Section 64(1) read: '(1) Where plans of any proposed work are, in accordance with building byelaws, deposited with a local authority, the local authority shall, subject to the provisions of any other section of this Act which expressly requires or authorises them in certain cases to reject plans, pass the plans unless they either are defective, or show that the proposed work would contravene any of those byelaws, and, if the plans are defective or show that the proposed work would contravene any of those byelaws, they shall reject the plans.'

[89] ibid, 99.

[90] *Anns v Merton London Borough Council* [1978] AC 728 at 759 per Lord Wilberforce.

[91] (1988) 13 ConLR 96, 100.

[92] [1990] 2 WLR 944.

[93] *D&F Estates Ltd v Church Commissioners for England* [1989] AC 177. This was another case that had proceeded from the QBD (Official Referees' Business) ((1985) 7 ConLR 40), before being heard by the Court of Appeal ((1987) 11 ConLR 12). The House of Lords considered that the cost of remediating defective plasterwork was pure economic loss and was not recoverable.

[94] ibid, 950.

enactment of the Building Act 1984 was accepted to be irrelevant to the issues on appeal. He noted, as well, that *Anns v Merton* remained binding on the Court of Appeal. The duty under section 64, however, could not be delegated, making reference to its purpose of ensuring that buildings are constructed which conform to the standards laid down by the byelaws.[95] Nicholls LJ went on to consider the tension between the decision in *Anns v Merton* and *D&F Estates Ltd*. The Court of Appeal, however, was bound by *Anns v Merton*.

The decision of the House of lords in *Murphy v Brentwood* requires little elaboration. The House of Lords departed from its previous decision in *Anns v Merton*. Lord Keith noted that the two-stage test set out in *Anns v Merton* had not been accepted as a universally applicable principle, and that reservations had been expressed about it in cases including *Peabody v Sir Lindsay Parkinson*. The House of Lords considered that the builder of premises was under a duty to take reasonable care to avoid injuries through defects in the premises to the person or property of those whom he should have in contemplation as likely to suffer such injury if care was not taken.[96] If, however, the defect was identified before injury was caused, the cost of rectifying it was considered to be pure economic loss.[97] The builder and, therefore, the local authority charged with inspecting the building, did not owe a duty of care to avoid putting a future inhabitant of a building in a position where money would have to be expended to rectify the defect where it was capable of causing physical injury.[98] As Sir Anthony May observed in the preface to the fifth edition of *Keating on Building Contracts*, 'The law of negligence has in general gone back to where it was in 1970.'[99]

Ultimately, however, whether or not liability should be imposed is a question of policy.[100] The Building Safety Act 2022 has moved the dial again, towards increasing the number of potential defendants in respect of a building which suffers from defects which affect its fitness for habitation. The basic nature of the test for liability in the Defective Premises Act 1972, however, remains in place, despite the fact that it probably does not reflect the original intent of the Law Commission.[101]

D. Conclusion

Sir Philip Otton, writing extra-judicially, commented that, 'The contribution of the construction industry to the development of the common law has indeed been

[95] ibid, 953–57, citing *Dutton v Bognor Regis Urban District Council* [1972] 1 QB 373.
[96] ibid, 461, per Lord Keith; 475 per Lord Bridge.
[97] ibid, 465–68, per Lord Keith; 475 per Lord Bridge; 484, per Lord Oliver.
[98] ibid, 468–71, per Lord Keith; 475, 479 per Lord Bridge; 489 per Lord Oliver.
[99] Sir A May, *Keating on Building Contracts*, 5th edn (London, Sweet & Maxwell, 1991) ix.
[100] See, eg, S Todd, 'The Negligence Liability of Public Authorities: Divergence in the Common Law' (1986) 102 *Law Quarterly Review* 370, 402.
[101] See, eg, DRF Sawtell, 'The Residential Leaseholder's Interest in Construction Operations' (2019) 11(2) *Journal of Property, Planning and Environmental Law* 108.

impressive; equally, construction law has often been innovative and dynamic in its responses to wider changers in the law.'[102] This part of this chapter has demonstrated that, more narrowly, the decisions of the Official Referees and the TCC also impacted on the development of the common law. As will be explored below, reporting of first-instance decisions before the 1980s and 1990s was limited. Furthermore, some of the points that would later become significant were not explored fully or at all at first instance. What these decisions demonstrate, however, is that the technical expertise and subject matter experience of the first-instance judge did carry through into the appellate decisions. They also disclose that construction law disputes can push the boundaries of contractual and tortious obligations, both doctrinally and in their overall policy importance.

IV. Contribution to the Development of Construction Law

This part of the chapter will consider how the Official Referees and the TCC contributed to the development of construction law. From an early stage in the history of their jurisdiction, a significant proportion of the work of the Official Referees was comprised of building disputes. It does not follow directly from this, however, that their decisions directly contributed to the growth of construction law jurisprudence. This part will set out to ascertain the influence and contribution of the Official Referees and the TCC to the development of construction law by considering two different sources. First, the contribution of the Official Referees to a textbook tradition in construction law will be reviewed, primarily through the lens of successive editions of *Hudson's Building and Engineering Contracts*. Second, the growth of specialist law reporting and the increased visibility and accessibility of their decisions will considered through an analysis of the Building Law Reports and the Construction Law Reports.

A. Contribution of the Official Referees to a Textbook Tradition

In this section, the extent to which the decisions of the Official Referees and the TCC fed into the development of a textbook tradition will be considered. The primary focus of this section will be *Hudson's Building and Engineering Contracts*, which has run in successive editions since 1891. This is not to discount the contribution or importance of other construction law textbooks, including in particular

[102] P Otton, 'The Contribution of Construction to the Common Law' in J Uff and MO de Zylva (eds), *New Horizons in Construction Law* (Construction Law Press, 1998) ch 4.

the successive editions of Donald Keating's textbook since 1955.[103] Hudson's work is chosen primarily because of its continuity, running through successive editions from the 1890s through to the modern day. The successive editions also contain clear expressions by successive authors and editors as to the state of construction law. While these views may not have always been universally held, they can be compared for accuracy with the actual state of law reporting considered in the following section of this part of the chapter.

A legal textbook or treatise is more than simply a practitioner's crib. It creates an interpretative framework into which legal authorities are selected and categorised.[104] By selecting what is, and what is not, included, it can assist in the definition of a legal area, with the implication that there is a unifying logic to that selection.[105] A legal treatise, therefore, represents an important source for legal historical research.[106] The nineteenth century saw the growth of legal treatise writing, with publications such as *Chitty on Contracts* and *Woodfall on Landlord and Tenant* emerging amongst a crop of other still recognisable names.[107] When Hudson's book was first published, there was already a corpus of legal text-books dealing with contract law.[108] His decision that there was scope for a book focussed on construction contracts and construction professionals reflects, in itself, an opinion that there was a market and need for a book in this field.

In this section, the way in, and extent to, which the decisions of the Official Referees fed into the successive editions of Hudson's book will be analysed. This will then lead into the second section of this part of the chapter, which will set out the changing state of law reporting of these decisions.

i. An Antecedent: *Emden's Construction Law*

Alfred Hudson's book was not, however, the first textbook that considered issues related to construction law. The first edition of *Emden's Construction Law* is informative in that it considered a number of areas that are not today considered to be part of the doctrinal core of construction law. It therefore demonstrates that

[103] D Keating, *Law and Practice of Building Contracts including Architects and Surveyors* (London, Sweet & Maxwell, 1955). This is discussed in more detail below.

[104] RA Danner, 'Oh, the Treatise!' (2013) 111(6) *Michigan Law Review* 821, 822; 833.

[105] TFT Plucknett, *Early English Legal Literature* (Cambridge, Cambridge University Press, 1958) 19; AWB Simpson, 'The Rise and Fall of the Legal Treatise: Legal Principles and the Forms of Legal Literature' (1981) 48(3) *The University of Chicago Law Review* 632, 633.

[106] MJ Horwitz, 'Part III – Treatise Literature' (1976) 69 *Law Library Journal* 460; C Tomlins, 'Commentary: Effects of Scale: Toward a History of the Literature of Law' in A Fernandez and M Dubber (eds), *Law Books in Action: Essays on the Anglo-American Legal Treatise* (London, Bloomsbury, 2012) ch 11.

[107] Simpson (n 105) 663. For an account of the origins of *Woodfall on Landlord and Tenant* from its first edition in 1802 to its transformation into a looseleaf format in 1978, see P Luther, 'The Foundations of *Elitestone*' (2008) 28(4) *Legal Studies* 574, 576–580.

[108] S Waddams, 'Nineteenth-Century Treatises on English Contract Law' in Fernandez and Dubber (eds) (n 106) ch 6; W Swain, *The Law of Contract 1670–1870* (Cambridge, Cambridge University Press, 2015) ch 9.

construction law, as a concept, had not crystallised in the form that we would recognise it today.

Alfred Emden gives his name to *Emden's Construction Law*, a looseleaf practitioners' work produced by Crown Office Chambers.[109] Alfred Emden himself was born in 1849 and was called to the Bar by Inner Temple in 1880. He was first appointed the registrar in companies winding up in 1892, before becoming a County Court Judge in 1894.[110] Alongside his work on construction law, he also wrote a treatise on company law.[111] The first edition of Alfred Emden's treatise, *The Law Relating to Building Leases and Building Contracts, the Improvement of Land By, and the Construction Of, Buildings* was published in 1882.[112] In its preface, it sought to emphasise that it would not deal with contract law or the law of landlord in tenant in general.[113] Instead, the focus was to be 'such matters only as are connected with building operations'.[114] At the start of the first chapter, Emden noted that there were four courses open to a person possessed with land who intended to build on it: (1) to enter into a building agreement and then to grant leases; (2) to let the land to the builder; (3) to convey the land to the grantee for building in consideration for a rentcharge; and (4) to sell the land with restrictive covenants to ensure that the houses built are uniform.[115]

The structure of the book follows the pattern set out in this introductory chapter. Sections dealing with landlord and tenant and real property issues (such as chapter three, dealing with agreements for building leases, and chapter sixteen, dealing with specific performance of both building contracts and agreements for building leases) are intertwined with chapters that would be recognisable in a modern textbook on construction law, such as chapter seven on the architect and his duties and liabilities, and chapter eleven on conditions as to the time for completion.

Emden's book is focussed on the owner of land who may go on to become the employer under a building contract or the lessor under a building lease. It is, therefore, procurement focussed, looking at the typical forms of procuring construction works in the later nineteenth century. Building leases and development agreements have almost entirely disappeared from modern construction law books and the syllabus of construction law programmes. Emden's first edition, therefore, while including the words 'building contracts' in its title, did not separate out land law and construction law in a way that is recognisable to modern construction

[109] LexisNexis, looseleaf.

[110] *Who Was Who* 'Emden, His Honour Judge Alfred' (Online edition, Oxford University Press, 2007) [accessed 4 August 2022].

[111] A Emden, *The Practice In Winding-Up Companies: A Concise and Practical Treatise Upon the Law and Practice Relating to the Winding-Up of Companies from the Commencement of the Winding-Up Proceedings to Dissolution* (William Clowes and Sons, 1883).

[112] (1st edn, Stevens and Haynes, 1882).

[113] ibid viii.

[114] ibid viii.

[115] ibid 1–2.

lawyers. Modern studies of construction procurement focus on the supporting contractual framework as opposed to the disposition of interests in land.[116]

ii. Hudson's Own Building and Engineering Contracts

Hudson, at the time of writing, is now in its fourteenth edition. Its current editors are Robert Clay and Nicholas Dennys QC, both members of Atkin Chambers, who now contribute the text to the work. It has a long and important history.

Alfred A Hudson practised from 5 Paper Buildings, Temple. He was a Bencher of the Inner Temple and became King's Counsel. He was appointed President of the Tribunal of Appeal under the London Building Acts from 1894 to 1908, alongside other appointments (including to the Panel of Referees under the Landlord and Tenant Act 1927).[117] Alongside his book on building contracts, he also co-authored *The Law of Light and Air*.[118] The preface to the first edition also confirms that he had qualified as an architect.[119]

The first edition of Hudson was published in 1891.[120] It confirmed, in the opening words of the preface, that 'This work is the result of an attempt by the author to apply his technical knowledge of building, gained as an architect, to the preparation of a practical treatise on the law relating to Building and Engineering Works.'[121] The focus of the book was on building and engineering contracts. Unlike Emden's work, it did not seek to include material in respect of the 'kindred subjects' of restrictive covenants, repair covenants, statutory enactments as to buildings, or easements.

The introductory first chapter starts by describing the 'peculiarity' of building contracts by making ten points. These can be summarised as follows.[122]

(1) The building owner or employer does not accurately know what they want. Instead, they engage someone to describe for them by plans and specifications what they themselves cannot describe.
(2) As the building owner does not know that this is what he actually wants, this process gives rise to variations and extras.
(3) The building owner does not know, when the work is done, whether the work is as described, or with proper workmanship and materials.
(4) The builder relies on the plans and specification of an architect or engineer.

[116] See, eg, D Mosey, *Early Contractor Involvement in Building Procurement: Contracts, Partnering and Project Management* (Chichester, Wiley-Blackwell, 2009); D Mosey, *Collaborative Construction and Procurement and Improved Value* (Chichester, Wiley-Blackwell, 2019).

[117] *Who Was Who* 'Hudson, Alfred Arthur' (Online edition, Oxford University Press, 2007) [accessed 4 August 2022].

[118] AA Hudson and Arnold Inman (*Estates Gazette*, 1905).

[119] IN Duncan Wallace traced Alfred Hudson's life in 'Alfred Hudson QC – a Man of hat Parts?' (2005) 21(3) *Construction Law Journal* 197.

[120] A Hudson, *The Law of Building and Engineering Contracts and the Duties and Liabilities of Engineers, Architects, Surveyors, and Valuers*, 1st edn (Waterlow and Sons Ltd, 1891).

[121] ibid vii.

[122] ibid 2–3.

(5) The plans themselves, however, give insufficient detail, giving rise to claims for extras.
(6) The performance of building contracts is subject to immense detail, as well as various risks and contingencies.
(7) Due to the cost of obtaining estimates for the work, a quantity surveyor is often employed.
(8) The architect or engineer, the agent of one side (almost always the employer), is put in the position of valuer and decider of all questions to prevent disputes. He is described as 'more powerful than any judge, and may do practically what he pleases, and his negligent or incompetent decisions or valuations are binding on builder and employer'. Some disputes give rise to a right to refer to arbitration.
(9) No acceptance or approval of work can be implied from the possession of the property on which the work is done, so that if the builder does not do what he contracts to do, he cannot recover, though the work done be as good or better than that specified. Further, the builder cannot take away what he has built on to the property of the owner.
(10) The building contract is drawn up by the engineer or architect, consisting of conditions which have been handed down for numerous years.

Many of these points, including the separation between employer, designer and contractor; the importance of risk, change and cost; reliance on construction professionals; the incorporation of building materials as part of the land during the construction process; the use of construction contracts; and the use of arbitration or other non-litigation forms of dispute resolution, are recognisably parts of modern construction law. Importantly, Hudson attempted to identify the reason why the building contract represented a distinct form of agreement that was suitable for separate study, as opposed to simply one emanation of general contract law.

Appendix B to the work began a practice that continued until the fourth edition of including otherwise unreported decisions. As Hudson noted, these were 'decisions which either have not been reported at all, or have not been fully reported or made accessible, but which seem to the author to be decisions of great interest and importance.' The first edition contained 19 unreported cases. Most of them were decisions of the Queen's Bench. Only one decision of the Official Referees, *George Smith v the Howden Union Sanitary Authority*, was included, but only because the report of Edward Ridley, the Official Referee, was subject to an application to set aside, which was granted by Vaughan Williams J (as he then was) and Lawrance J.

The book itself contains very limited references to decisions of the Official Referees. It was noted that complicated accounts for damages for termination were usually sent before an Official Referee.[123] The authority given for this is *In re Taylor: Turpin v Pain*, a decision of Chitty J, which gives an insight into the

[123] ibid 372.

procedure to be adopted by an Official Referee in the 1890s.[124] The subject matter of the case was, however, an inquiry into and an account of a testatrix's estate, as opposed to a building dispute, giving an indication as to the wide scope of the Official Referees' work at that time.

The book includes a number of references to American and what were described as 'colonial' reports.[125] It was noted that the American law reports contained a number of references to cases arising from building disputes. This was alongside the unreported cases in Appendix B. These features betray a shortage of material in the form of reported English construction cases.

Hudson did call for a specialist 'building court': 'it would seem that the large interests at stake, and the peculiarly technical nature of building and engineering contracts, would justify the formation of a 'Building Court', presided over by a judge with assessor'.[126] He did not, in this section, refer to the Official Referees, but instead to the power under section 56 of the Judicature Act 1873 to call in assessors. He therefore recognised that there was a gap in the way that complicated construction disputes were being decided.

The second edition (published in 1895) saw the work enlarged to two volumes, with the appendices containing unreported cases and precedents being split into the second volume.[127] This time, 36 cases were reported. The title now included reference to ship building contracts as well.

The third edition (published in 1907) expanded again.[128] This time, 53 cases were reported in the second volume. It contained a new chapter, on nuisance and negligence.[129] The description of the unique qualities of building contracts, as well as the calls for a specialist building court, remained.

The fourth edition, published in 1914, is probably the apogee of Alfred Hudson's work.[130] It remained in two volumes. Hudson himself was now King's Counsel. Some chapters had been entirely re-written. In particular, another new chapter, on building leases and agreements, was now included.[131] This illustrates the moveable interface between the mode of procuring construction operations and the construction contract itself reflected in Emden's treatise.

The second volume of the fourth edition is historically and practically important, in that it contains the only reports of a number of highly significant construction

[124] *In re Taylor: Turpin v Pain* (1890) 44 ChD 128 at 137.

[125] ibid, 4–6.

[126] ibid, 7–8.

[127] AA Hudson, *The Law of Building, Engineering, and Ship Building Contracts and the Duties and Liabilities of Engineers, Architects, Surveyors, and Valuers*, 2nd edn (Waterlow and Sons Ltd, 1895).

[128] AA Hudson, *The Law of Building, Engineering, and Ship Building Contracts and the Duties and Liabilities of Engineers, Architects, Surveyors, and Valuers*, 3rd edn (London, Sweet & Maxwell Ltd, 1907).

[129] ibid ch 14.

[130] AA Hudson assisted by CS Rewcastle, *The Law of Building, Engineering, and Ship Building Contracts and the Duties and Liabilities of Engineers, Architects, Surveyors, and Valuers*, 4th edn (London, Sweet & Maxwell Ltd, 1914). The preface to the eighth edition, written after his death, described the fourth edition as 'a locus classicus on the subject': v.

[131] ibid ch 16.

cases, such as *Bottoms v York Corp.* on ground conditions.[132] The decision in *Bush v Whitehaven Port and Town Trustees*, where the conditions of the contract were so completely changed that the contractual provisions dealing with time of possession were set aside, entitling the builder to a *quantum meruit*, was cited at all levels in the important case on frustration of *Davis Contractors Ltd v Fareham UDC*.[133]

The second volume of the fourth edition, however, only preserved a handful of decisions of the Official Referees, which are only reported as the basis for a subsequent appeal. In *Saunders and Collard v Broadstairs Local Board*, the verdict and judgment of the Official Referee was upheld on appeal;[134] in *Cunliffe v Hampton Wick Local Board*, Mr E Ridley QC's decision was appealed before being remitted back;[135] in *London Steam Stone Saw Mills v Lorden* the decision of the Official Referee was appealed;[136] as was the decision of Mr Verey, the Official Referee, in *Sattin v Poole*.[137] The decisions of the Official Referees, therefore, being unreported and essentially invisible save to the parties themselves, did not contribute substantially to a jurisprudence of construction law.[138]

Hudson died on 21 August 1930. The fifth,[139] sixth,[140] and seventh editions,[141] published in 1926, 1933 and 1946, omitted the second volume and the collection of unreported decisions. The chapters on nuisance and building leases were also removed, together with the introductory chapter on the exceptionality of building contracts. There is no real evidence for any increased influence of the decision of the Official Referees themselves in these volumes.

By the late 1940s and early 1950s, *Hudson* was in severe need of updating. In particular, there was no available commentary on the then-dominant RIBA form of contract (now the JCT forms of contract). Donald Keating, therefore, took up the challenge of writing over the course of two years the first edition of his book on building contracts, which was first published in 1955. He used a card index of case law that he had built up together with his notes on a series of lectures he had given on construction contracts.[142] The book was successful, being re-reprinted in 1956,

[132] (1892) *Hudson's Building Contracts* (4th edn) Vol 2, 208.

[133] (1888) *Hudson's Building Contracts* (4th edn), Vol 2, 122. In *Fareham*, the arbitrator had relied on this principle, which went on appeal to Lord Goddard CJ, and then to the Court of Appeal ([1955] 2 WLR 388) and to the House of Lords ([1956] AC 696).

[134] (1890, QBD, Mathew and Grantham JJ) *Hudson's Building Contracts* (4th edn), Vol 2, 164.

[135] (1892 QBD; 1892 CA; 1893 QBD) *Hudson's Building Contracts* (4th edn), Vol 2, 250.

[136] (1900) QBD (Lord Alverstone, CJ and Kennedy J) *Hudson's Building Contracts* (4th edn), Vol 2, 301.

[137] (1901) KBD (Bruce and Phillimore JJ) (4th edn), Vol 2, 306.

[138] Ian Duncan Wallace observed that 'Official Referee decisions are incidentally mentioned but not reported' (2005) 199–200.

[139] AA Hudson assisted by Lawrence Mead, *The Law of Building and Engineering Contracts and the Duties and Liabilities of Engineers, Architects, Surveyors, and Valuers*, 5th edn (London, Sweet & Maxwell Ltd, 1926).

[140] A Inman and L Mead, *The Law of Building and Engineering Contracts and the Duties and Liabilities of Architects, Engineers and Surveyors*, 6th edn (London, Sweet & Maxwell Ltd, 1933).

[141] L Mead, *The Law of Building and Engineering Contracts and of the Duties and Liabilities of Architects, Engineers and Surveyors*, 7th edn (London, Sweet & Maxwell Ltd, 1946).

[142] Discussion with Paul Darling KC, August 2022. The collation and collection of judgments (often unreported) by barristers in practice, as well as by law firms, is a feature that has continued to date.

and followed by the second edition in 1963 and the third edition in 1969. It is, however, noteworthy that, in 1955, Donald Keating's practice was still in landlord and tenant, crime and other work; he made his name in arguing *Gloucestershire County Council v Richardson (trading as W. J. Richardson & Son)* leading Patrick Garland (later Mr Justice Garland) to the House of Lords, where he was ultimately successful.[143] After the fourth edition, Sir Anthony May took over, and the book became a collective effort of the members of Keating Chambers.[144]

iii. Ian Duncan Wallace's Editions

A transformational moment in the history of *Hudson* came with the eighth edition, and the new author team of EJ Rimmer and Ian Duncan Wallace, in 1959.[145] The preface was not slow in criticising the state of law reporting when it came to construction law, and its consequential effect on the subject.

> Secondly, the specialised law of building contracts has, most unfortunately, been to a great extent truncated in its growth, by reason of the rapid spread of the use of independent arbitrators for settling building disputes, which began in earnest after the First World War, and also of the practice of the High Court in referring virtually all building cases to the Official Referees. These developments have reduced to a mere trickle the number of reported cases, despite the substantial amount of litigation which arises annually in this field. Nor has the situation been assisted by the attitude of law reporters, who, with certain honourable exceptions, appear unwilling to report even cases on the current standard forms of contract.[146]

The authors, therefore, saw the growth of the Official Referees as having a harmful, not positive, effect on the state of construction law as a subject on account of the lack of proper reporting of their decisions. The authors took pains, however, in the body of the work to make it clear that this was not due to the lack of expertise or experience of the Official Referees: they observed that trial by Official Referee was often cheaper and more expeditious in settling disputes than arbitration, while noting the limits on their jurisdiction when it came to fraud or professional negligence.[147]

[143] *Gloucestershire County Council v Richardson (trading as W. J. Richardson & Son)* [1969] 1 AC 480, distinguishing *McManus Childs*. See the obituary of Donald Keating, QC 1924–1995 written by J Uff in (1995) 11(5) *Construction Law Journal* 329. Uff recalls that, 'Ironically, he never approved of the term Construction Law: he considered building contracts to be an integral branch of commercial law and indeed to have become the major generator of commercial law in the last decade' (332).

[144] Paul Darling KC relayed to the author that he, with a number of other then-juniors, would work to a rigid schedule, with the team working until 3am on Monday morning on occasion. Sir Anthony May then thanked the contributors to the 5th edition with a superb dinner party that he hosted: conversation with Paul Darling KC, August 2022.

[145] EJ Rimmer and IN Duncan Wallace, *Hudson's Building and Engineering Contracts including the Duties and Liabilities of Architects, Engineers and Surveyors*, 8th edn (London, Sweet and Maxwell, 1959).

[146] ibid v.

[147] ibid 478; RSC Ord 36A, r 8.

The criticism of the lack of proper law reporting was continued in the ninth edition in 1965, which was now solely the work of Ian Duncan Wallace.[148] He strikingly observed that, 'When it is also remembered that literally hundreds of millions of pounds worth of work are carried out annually under such contracts, the reluctance to report building cases, which unhappily has no shown no sign of improvement since the last edition, is difficult to understand.'[149] He reflected that this no doubt explained why Hudson himself had to report the cases that he did in volume 2 of the fourth edition. This, the writer explained, was the reason why such value was given in that edition to the Commonwealth cases in the book: there were no reports of English cases to deal with those points of construction law.[150]

This criticism was diluted in the tenth edition, published in 1970, by the fact that two critically important construction law cases had been reported: *Hancock v Brazier (Anerley) Ltd* and,[151] of course, *McManus Childs*.[152] There was, however, still a dearth of reporting of construction cases. The fourth edition of Donald Keating's *Building Contracts* (which now included a commentary on the ICE conditions of contract by John Uff), did not express in such strident tones any disappointment as to the state of law reporting: but it was observed in the preface that Commonwealth authorities were of assistance in filling the gaps in English law.[153]

The eleventh edition of *Hudson*, however, saw a change of tone.[154] Published in 1995, some 25 years after the previous edition, Ian Duncan Wallace noted that the field of construction law had changed. Instead, he gave especial praise to the Building Law Reports in England and the Australian Construction Law Reporter, which he 'found particularly helpful'.[155]

This was the last substantial edition that Ian Duncan Wallace was involved in. A new editorial team, of Nicholas Dennys QC, Mark Raeside QC, and Robert Clay, were responsible for the twelfth edition, when the book assumed the current one-volume format.[156]

[148] IN Duncan Wallace, *Hudson's Building and Engineering Contracts including the Duties and Liabilities of Architects, Engineers and Surveyors*, 9th edn (London, Sweet and Maxwell, 1965).
[149] ibid viii.
[150] ibid ix.
[151] *Hancock v Brazier (Anerley) Ltd* [1966] 1 WLR 1317.
[152] IN Duncan Wallace, *Hudson's Building and Engineering Contracts including the Duties and Liabilities of Architects, Engineers and Surveyors*, 10th edn (London, Sweet and Maxwell, 1970).
[153] D Keating, *Building Contracts including a commentary on the JCT Standard Form of Building Contract* (London, Sweet & Maxwell, 1978) viii.
[154] IN Duncan Wallace, *Hudson's Building and Engineering Contracts including the Duties and Liabilities of Architects, Engineers and Surveyors*, 11th edn (London, Sweet and Maxwell, 1995) (2 volumes).
[155] ibid p xx.
[156] N Dennys, M Raeside and R Clay, *Hudson's Building and Engineering Contracts*, 12th edn (London, Sweet and Maxwell, 2010).

B. Reporting the Decisions of the Official Referees

There are currently two main law reports specialising in construction law: the Building Law Reports, which began in 1975; and the Construction Law Reports, which began in 1983. As the successive editions of *Hudson's Building Contracts* point out, before the Building Law Reports began, construction cases were rarely reported, and there was almost no reporting at all of the decisions of the Official Referees.[157] This substantial gap in construction law jurisprudence was, to a limited extent, filled by citation of US and Commonwealth decisions. It undoubtedly, however, limited the growth of English construction law in general, and the impact of the Official Referees on construction law more specifically. Even important decisions with widespread impact and limited earlier authority, such as *McManus Child*, were not reported at first instance. Construction law as a field was kept within the close confines of reported appellate decisions.

This section of this part of the chapter will quantitatively analyse the Building Law Reports and the Construction Law Reports from their inception to 1999. This cut-off date is chosen as it includes the first decisions of the TCC as well as the early decisions in respect of adjudication and the payment regime under Part II of the Housing Grants, Construction and Regeneration Act 1996. By the early twenty-first century, the criticisms as to the lack of reporting of construction cases had largely fallen away. As well as more systematic law reporting, written judgments of the TCC were, by this time, being recorded online on BAILII and on legal databases.[158] The period chosen, therefore, reflects the change in the volume of decisions which were made accessible to the legal profession and academics.

In order to break down the law reports into more informative periods, they have been divided into five-year time segments, starting with 1975–79. The cases are allocated according to the year that they were reported, as opposed to the actual judgment date. Both the Building Law Reports and the Construction Law Reports, especially in their earlier volumes, reported historic cases, which were sometimes grouped together thematically. This study is not concerned with the volume of cases reported each year, however, as the potential influence of and importance given to the courts from which they emanated. A decision of an Official Referee which had been handed down some years previously could be given prominence by the fact that it was now being reported.

The Building Law Reports and the Construction Law Reports will not be aggregated together for the obvious reason that the same decision might well be reported in both law reports. Furthermore, as the discussion below demonstrates, the two law reports have different and distinct patterns of reporting.

[157] A case law search of the LexisNexis legal database for 'official referee' between 1 January 1965 and 1 January 1975 produces only one case which is a judgment of an Official Referee: *Turriff Construction Ltd v Regalia Knitting Mills Ltd* [1972] EGD 257, reported as a digest, subsequently reported in full in the Building Law Reports, discussed above (on remuneration for work carried out pursuant to a letter of intent).

[158] The British and Irish Legal Information Institute (BAILII), based at the Institute of Advanced Legal Studies, was incepted in 2000.

Table 1 Building Law Reports

	First instance?		Court		
	Yes	No	OR	TCC	Total number of cases
1975–1979	25	66	4	0	91
1980–1984	49	64	12	0	113
1985–1989	76	74	46	0	150
1990–1994	76	76	49	0	152
1995–1999	64	77	38	17	141

Table 2 Construction Law Reports

	First instance?		Court		
	Yes	No	OR	TCC	Total number of cases
1980–1984	26	6	26	0	32
1985–1989	104	52	99	0	156
1990–1994	112	58	95	0	170
1995–1999	97	81	55	32	178

i. 1975–1979

In the first period, from 1975–79, only the Building Law Reports were available. Of 91 cases reported, 25 were first instance decisions, and only four were decisions of an Official Referee. This was a very low figure. By contrast, there were eleven decisions of either the Queen's Bench Division or the QBD (Commercial Court). 45 cases, more than half, were decisions of the Court of Appeal. By contrast, the Building Law Reports did report historic decisions of especial importance. For example, the 1841 decision of the Court of Exchequer of *Mondel v Steel*, which was an important milestone in the development of the defence of abatement, was reported.[159] The troubling decision of *London Borough of Hounslow v Twickenham Garden Developments Ltd* of Megarry J in the Chancery Decision from 1970 was reported, together with a hostile commentary on the decision in comparison to commonwealth case law.[160] The initial impact of the Building Law Reports on the visibility afforded to the Official Referees was therefore very limited, but it was a start.

ii. 1980–1984

The next period shows a limited increase in the number of reports of Official Referees in the Building Law Reports, which now reached twelve out of a total of 113 cases. The overall proportion of first instance decisions also crept up.

[159] *Mondel v Steel* (1976) 1 BLR 106.

[160] *London Borough of Hounslow v Twickenham Garden Developments Ltd* (1978) 7 BLR 81; it was compared unfavourably with *Mayfield Holdings Ltd v Moana Reef Ltd* [1973] 1 NZLR 309.

By way of contrast, the bulk of the reporting of the Construction Law Reports was of the decisions of the Official Referees, a total of 26 out of 32 reported cases.

iii. 1985–1989

This period saw a large jump in the number of decisions of Official Referees being reported in the Building Law Reports, 46 out of a total of 150 reported cases. To put this in context, in this period 57 decisions of the Court of Appeal were reported.

The Construction Law Reports grew significantly in scope, with 156 cases being reported. Of those, 99 cases were decisions of Official Referees. In respect of the report of *Design 5 v Keniston Housing Association Ltd*, it was recorded in a note that, 'His Honour Judge David Smout died on 7 May 1987. His premature death at the early age of 63 was a great blow to the scientific development of construction law and to the editors and producers of these reports, to whom he was consistently helpful and encouraging.'[161]

By the late 1980s, therefore, there had been a complete change in the accessibility of decisions of the Official Referees. It was now possible to point to a run of reports in both the Building Law Reports and the Construction Law Reports which were accessible to practitioners, academics, and text-book writers.

iv. 1990–1994

The first half of the 1990s saw a continuation of the pattern seen in the second half of the 1980s. In the Building Law Reports, of 152 cases reports, 49 were decisions of the Official Referee. This is in comparison to the Construction Law Reports, where 95 of the 170 cases reported were such decisions.

By the mid-1990s, therefore, there was a significant corpus of reported decisions of Official Referees.

v. 1995–1999

The pattern substantially continued into the last period under consideration. In the Building Law Reports, of 141 cases reported, 55 came either from the Official Referees or the TCC. In the Construction Law Reports, of 178 cases reports, 87 came from either the Official Referee or the TCC.

vi. Analysis

The Official Referees and appeals to the Court of Appeal were not the only sources of reportable cases for these two law reports. The Building Law Reports, in particular, maintained a tradition of reporting important or useful commonwealth or US cases

[161] *Design 5 v Keniston Housing Association Ltd* (1986) 10 ConLR 123.

throughout the period. The Queen's Bench Division and the QBD (Commercial Court) provided a source of important construction cases, as well as decisions which were relevant to arbitration practice. For example, the first instance and Court of Appeal decision of *Tate & Lyle Industries Ltd v Davy Mckee (London) Ltd* determined that Order 36, rule 1 of the RSC empowered a Commercial Court Judge in construction industry cases to direct that applications for leave to appeal on questions of law arising out of an arbitrator's award be heard by an Official Referee.[162]

The growth of reporting of decisions of the Official Referee and, subsequently, the TCC, meant that the conditions were set to allow an English construction law jurisprudence to grow. Alfred Hudson considered it necessary to include, as part of his textbook, a compilation of unreported cases. From the 1950s to 1970s, despite the growing importance of the Official Referee's list as a forum for the resolution of construction disputes, their decisions were not being reported unless, tangentially, they were appealed to the Court of Appeal. This dearth of case reporting continued notwithstanding the reconstitution of the judge's work as a fully integrated part of the High Court in the Courts Act 1971. The start of the Building Law Reports, and then the Construction Law Reports, corrected this imbalance. For the first time, decisions of the Official Referees were readily available, facilitating the growth of a construction law jurisprudence.

There were, as well, other factors at work. The jurisdiction of the Official Referees grew from the 1920s, becoming fully fledged judges whose decision were appealed to the Court of Appeal, until by 1998 the TCC was established.[163] The prestige of the Official Referees grew as well. By the 1940s, it was recognised that their work was the same as a High Court Judge in a number of their cases.[164] In the 1980s and early 1990s, the Official Referees had developed a reputation for carrying out difficult work with excellent judges.[165] Without adequate reporting, however, this work could not achieve the visibility it merited.

The development of specialist law reporting of construction cases fuelled the development of construction law as a subject. While the use of case law from other jurisdictions remains a feature of English construction law scholarship, this is not to fill the gaps in the English jurisprudence but for comparative analysis. This contribution to the growth of construction law, in turn, enhanced the potential of that subject to feed into the English common law more generally.

V. Conclusion

The selection of cases in the second part of this chapter demonstrate the impact of construction law disputes on the development of the English common law in

[162] *Tate & Lyle Industries Ltd v Davy Mckee (London) Ltd* (1988) 16 ConLR 1 (QBD); (1989) 20 ConLR 137 (CA).
[163] Fay (n 12) 24–30.
[164] R Burrows, *The Official Referees* (1940) 56 *LQR* 506.
[165] P Coulson, 'Lord Justice Jackson and the Evolution of the TCC' in Bailey (ed) (n 35) 40.

shaping the limits of contractual and tortious liability. At one level, their subject matter is, undoubtedly, specialist. Claims for delay and loss and expense, as in *Peabody v Sir Lindsay Parkinson*, or disputes in respect of defective materials, design or workmanship, as in *McManus Childs* or *Murphy v Brentwood*, require subject matter expertise in order for cases to be adjudicated efficiently and consistently. On another level, however, these cases involved very significant issues of English contract, commercial and tort law which are still open for discussion today. Lord Dyson was undoubtedly correct to consider that construction law has been integrated into the mainstream.[166] At the same time, construction law issues, debates and decisions have fed into the English common law.

The growth of construction law as a subject, therefore, has represented a distinct contribution to English law more generally. Despite the fact, however, that the Official Referees conducted a great deal of the litigation that arose out of construction law, there was a breakdown between the decisions that were generated and construction law more generally, on account of inadequate reporting. We see that for a large part of the twentieth century the impact of the Official Referees was indirect, through decisions of the appellate courts. Instead, the successive authors of *Hudson's Building Contracts* had to turn elsewhere to identify the decisions that would support or illustrate the points of law under discussion. This limited the development of English construction law jurisprudence. Given the importance of the decision in *McManus Childs*, it is unlikely that the issue had not arisen elsewhere.

The inception of the Building Law Reports and the Construction Law Reports, therefore, represented an opportunity for the decisions of the Official Referees to begin to feed directly into the growth of construction law as a subject. By the 1990s, there was a significant corpus of decisions, together with two established law reports. By the time the TCC was constituted in 1998, there was already a construction law tradition that had grown out of the specialist reporting of first instance decisions. It was this combination of a specialist court, producing reported decisions, and an established textbook tradition, that fed into the establishment of construction law as an identifiable field in the English common law.

[166] Lord Dyson (n 20) 180.

14

Energy and the Environment: Future Litigation in the TCC

JUAN LOPEZ

This chapter explores incremental influences on the TCC in its adjudication of construction, engineering and technological litigation, originating from energy disputes and environmental principles and norms. This chapter overviews what is a fascinating and rapidly developing synergy, integrating with the workload of other specialist courts of the Business and Property courts of England and Wales, viewed in the context of renewable energy generation technologies, and key infrastructure typologies and storage capabilities which are destined to frontload future UK energy sector growth (headlined by nuclear, wind, solar and biomass – further to geothermal, hydrogen and tidal) as part of a graduated transition away from oil and gas dependency.

This chapter reflects upon the TCC's maturity of decision-taking in the light of defining statutory and policy instruments that are honing the UK industry's drive to maximise energy efficiency: including the Building Regulations and retained EU law objectives of the Energy Performance of Buildings Directive and Energy Efficiency Directive, decarbonisation (both, embodied and delivery), the net zero strategy, and sustainability in the engineering world. This chapter will also identify various sector-related jurisprudence from associated specialist courts, which is assisting the TCC to acclimatise to the growth of energy and environmental litigation, in response to rapid energy sector expansion.

This chapter will appraise, distinctly from important technological advances actively being promoted by the TCC through enhanced case-management practices addressed elsewhere in chapter eight, how TCC adjudication and the legal landscape more generally, is already being influenced – but also critiqued – by domestic energy transition, complex questions of energy security and intrinsically politicised environmental policy.

Following years of energy and environmental law transitioning, as well as much geopolitical and global commercial instability, should the present domestic and international arbitral systems, unmodified, prove unable to respond with full effect, or to provide a rigorous and sustainable platform for enabling the resolution of internal and cross-border energy-concentrated disputes, then the TCC – in synchronised tandem with the Commercial and Chancery courts – will inevitably inherit a sizeable increase in cross-border as well as state litigation.

This valuable and unique opportunity for the TCC will be strongly welcomed as but further reinforcement of its jurisdictional proficiency, and will not be misinterpreted as any sign that dispute resolution, be it negotiation, mediation, expert determination, or arbitration, or a hybrid combination, cannot provide for effective dispute resolution of complex and high-value energy and environmental disputes, whether between non-state or state actors. The increasing prominence of the TCC (and the Business and Property courts more generally) within the energy and environmental arenas, will therefore act to precedent-set and ultimately compliment, not compete with, principal dispute resolution mechanisms.

The extensive jurisdictional reach of the TCC in this energy and environmental context, is altogether unsurprising. It naturally reflects the inherent dexterity and versatility of the specialist judicial system, as exemplified not least by the ready availability of extensive interim and enforcement measures, active case-management, case expedition, breadth of technical expertise, and opportunity for implementing sector-specific rules, which together, will ensure that litigation remains an attractive forum for many.

It however seems likely over the immediate term at least that nuclear operations, and nuclear infrastructure and supply, will remain outliers in effectively opting out of this jurisdictional reach, instead preferencing the general confidentiality of arbitration.

Save therefore for this one, albeit important, industrial exclusion – at least for now – not one continent is untouched by the spectre for an enlargement of energy and environmental disputes or judicial challenges, directed at state financing (including government subsidy and investment schemes); contractual liabilities (including for defects and delay); or the regulation of energy production, operation, transportation or health and safety.

Given the expanse of principal dispute causes and typologies encountered within the energy sector, there is extended scope for the TCC to apply a purist approach when exploring staple contractual mechanisms and principles (eg, of contractual interpretation, performance, modifications, delivery and completion, termination, frustration, guarantees, and risk) albeit in the context of diffuse, highly-specialised and technically complex fields, projects and infrastructure.

One such recent illustration of such may be gleaned from the case of *Mott Macdonald Limited v Trant Engineering Limited* in which the TCC was tasked with considering the significance and effect, applying baseline norms of contractual construction, of exclusion and limitation clauses purporting to restrict liability for breach (including repudiatory breach) in the context of a settlement and services agreement (SSA) for engineering services, in connection with the construction of power generation infrastructure at an installation in the Falkland Islands.[1] The pivotal questions for consideration were conventional, and albeit set against a bespoke and sophisticated energy infrastructure project, did not in fact turn upon the specific dimensions of the project itself. Relevant questions were whether and to what extent, liability for any relevant breaches of the SSA, could either be excluded or restricted for deliberate or wilful repudiatory breach. The TCC's conclusions were perhaps immediately unsurprising in finding there to be no operative presumption against the exclusion of liability and no orthodox formulaic or special wording to effect the exclusion of liability, when reaching a combined conclusion, that where the language of an exclusion clause may only bear one meaning, effect must be given to that same meaning.

Elsewhere however, the TCC may be expected to extend the contractual interpretation exercise in order to acclimatise to the specific energy technologies and infrastructure typologies central to the particular dispute, whilst remaining mindful that, invariably, typologies will continually evolve as to potentially affect objective industry and science norms and the objective interpretational exercise. Indeed, some typologies to be explored by the TCC will be largely untested, if not entirely new, and unreported upon (eg, marine engineering or decarbonisation triggers and liabilities).

The recent Commercial Court case of *Apache UK Investment v Esso Exploration and Production UK* amply illustrates the newly tested complexities of energy sector decommissioning liabilities.[2] This case is understood to be the first to see explored, these liabilities arising explored specifically under the Petroleum Act 1998. The Court considered the nature and extent of contractual decommissioning requirements in conjunction with a subsidiary sale, extant licences held for hydrocarbon producing fields in the North Sea, viewed against statutory decommissioning obligations having been imposed on bodies which had previously participated in exploration activities involving field facilities, upon the end life of the subsea installations, and, in turn, decide the basis for quantifying a sales security indemnification consequently arising under a sale and purchase agreement intended to govern future liability for decommissioning expenditure.[3] Remotely from decommissioning-specific liabilities, the familiar potential for energy sector complexities may also be drawn from two distantly associated Commercial Court and Court of Appeal cases, arising in conjunction with declaration proceedings brought in the context of an agreement for the transportation and processing of hydrocarbons in connection with a North Sea pipeline system (*Apache North Sea Limited v Ineos FPS Limited*[4]) and in a claim arguing the construction of farmout and joint operating agreements under which an interest in a UK Continental Shelf

[1] *Mott Macdonald Limited v Trant Engineering Limited* [2021] EWHC 754 (TCC), 195 Con LR 74.

[2] *Apache UK Investment Limited v Esso Exploration and Production UK Limited* [2021] EWHC 1283 (Comm), [2021] 4 WLR 85.

[3] Under s 29 of the Petroleum Act 1998.

[4] *Apache North Sea Limited v Ineos FPS Limited* [2020] EWHC 2081 (Comm).

Licence had been sold, with attendant drilling rig charge liabilities (*Apache North Sea Limited v Euroil Exploration Limited*[5]).

Typically characteristic of energy disputes, integral factors upon which litigation may turn, will doubtless develop in their sophistication and draw upon commercial and technological advancements in equal measure, so further aligning the jurisdictional competences of the TCC, Commercial and Chancery Courts. Energy disputes commonly draw upon intricacies of market price volatility of materials, security of infrastructure and energy supply, other supply chain risk, finance and procurement, government subsidy and incentive schemes, technological enhancements, decommissioning, and regulatory sanctions. The onward consideration of energy transitioning, and of climate change implications, pollution controls and broader environmental concerns, have the obvious capacity to influence and further layer these intricacies. Examples which are commonly familiar to disputes involving renewable energy typologies, include contractual suspension and termination (including force majeure), design and performance, connectivity, regulatory permitting, materials pricing, finance, governance, the influence of joint venture agreements, frustration, and damages. A further example concerns basic energy technology failures, whether by way of defect or a standards breach, during either construction or operation phase, and as to cause project delay and disruption, cost overruns or another commercial injury.

Intricacies such as these inevitably are the more complex with regard to significant energy projects encompassing numerous state or non-state actors, investors, stakeholders and other interested parties, which, in turn, increase the contractual complexities of litigation. Joint ventures, or similar contractual relationships will also be common. Energy project and associated finance risk will also be high, for owners, main- or sub-contracting parties.

Energy and environmental complexities should not however lessen the TCC's familiarity or refined ability to engage with the full breadth of energy projects, including basic contractual arrangement for the specific project, and project delivery at design and construction phases.

The growing concentration of TCC cases that specifically involve renewable energy projects or financing has focused largely on either wind (both on- and off-shore), biofuels (biomass and biogas), solar energy schemes, and the renewable electricity market. Waste-to-energy infrastructure is an important and well-established sector in both permitting and planning terms, and will certainly grow in significance in cases before the TCC. The present reluctance of contracting parties within the nuclear sphere, to expose agreements to litigation and their preference for private arbitration solutions, may also be set for change. The Court's consideration of renewable energy disputes generally, has often brought into sharp focus, key energy and environmental norms and topical drivers, including climate change governance and net zero targeting. Instructive precedents are

[5] *Apache North Sea Limited v Euroil Exploration Limited* [2020] EWCA Civ 1397.

now beginning to emerge from both the TCC's and other specialist courts' consideration of renewables, as has been demonstrated by a series of cases highlighting the clear merit of judicial specialism, and as such, which have been heard by the Business and Property courts, notably since 2017.

In *Biosol Renewables UK Ltd v Lovering (R&A Properties (A Partnership))*,[6] three disputes encompassing contractual claims concerning the supply of biomass boilers, and against which RHI proved a significant background, had involved claimed misrepresentation, breach of warranty and breach of contract by virtue of delayed and defective installation, and unfitness for purpose (ultimately, the principal purpose having been income-generation under the RHI scheme). The claims extended to seeking recovery for boiler costs, ancillary works to facilitate installation (as well as for the supply of woodchip material) and loss of profit damages under separately argued liability for maintaining the boilers and supplying woodchip. Eligibility criteria under the RHI Regulations, had corresponded to installations of biomass heating, and was supportive in principle of the claim made for damages for lost profit on boiler maintenance and woodchip supply.

The case of *MT Hojgaard A/S v E.ON Climate and Renewables UK Robin Rigg East Limited*,[7] involved a contract for the construction of offshore wind turbines (intended for a lifetime of 20 years) and claim made for remediation costs. The Supreme Court upheld the liability of a contractor for the failure of turbine foundations, in finding that a contract that incorporated technical requirements for production in accordance with a prescribed design and criteria – whereby conformity with that design would necessarily mean that the product would not comply fully with the criteria – did not necessarily give rise to mutual inconsistency. In such circumstances, a contractor could be expected to improve upon the prescribed design or alternatively, treat one or more aspects of the prescribed criteria as applying only to design matters which were not in fact prescribed. It was observed that the courts will generally give full effect to a requirement for the item produced to comply with prescribed criteria, on the basis that the contractor could be expected to adopt the risk in circumstances where it had contracted to fulfil a design which would necessarily mean that prescribed criteria would not be met. In the context of the contract, more rigorous requirements under prescribed criteria would properly be treated as prevailing over inadequate, minimum requirements of prescribed design.

In *Clancy Docwra Ltd v E.On Energy Solutions Limited*,[8] the TCC held in declaration proceedings which had followed on from an adjudication, that an amended JCT sub-contract for works of installing a network of heating and cooling underground piping servicing residential development from a combined heat and

[6] *Biosol Renewables UK Ltd v Lovering (R&A Properties (A Partnership))* [2021] EWHC 71 (Comm), [2018] 2 All ER 22.

[7] *MT Hojgaard A/S v E.ON Climate and Renewables UK Robin Rigg East Limited* [2017] UKSC 59, [2018] 2 All ER 22.

[8] *Clancy Docwra Ltd v E.On Energy Solutions Limited* [2018] EWHC 3124 (TCC).

power plant, had excluded particular ground, subsurface and subsoil conditions, with the effect that as and when such adverse conditions were encountered (as underground conditions of brick and rubble were eventually encountered during installation works), the sub-contractor had been entitled to treat the work undertaken as amounting to a variation (in the light of what amounted to an addition to the sub-contract works as defined, to include a breaking of trench obstructions by hand-digging, and soft spots) and as to entitle the sub-contractor an extension of time, in the event of having received no variation instruction or adjustment in the sub-contract sum upon its correct interpretation. The claimant would also not be denied a claim for adjustment in the light of the variation.

In *Equitix ESI CHP (Sheff) Limited v Veolia Energy and Utility Services UK Plc*,[9] the TCC was invited to consider declaratory relief in respect of the procedure engaged for the resolution of a defects dispute, which had provided for the engagement of experts from the Chartered Institute of Arbitrators in adjudication, concerning the construction of a biomass energy plant and supply of biomass fuel, together with the operational impacts caused by the alleged defects. The claimant for the declarations had alternatively sought to engage an alternative dispute resolution procedure provided elsewhere in the contract concerning 'related agreements' with regard to the alleged defects engaging the engineering, procurement and construction contract. With regard to a requirement under contract that a specific standard of expertise in connection with biomass energy plants be held by the appointed adjudicator, being 'experts in the field of biomass energy plants', the TCC observed that the phrase 'in the field of' indicated something broader than a specific technical qualification or expertise, and was different to a requirement for an expert in 'biogas energy plants'. This interpretation would respect the reality that defects disputes may necessitate expertise over and above matters of a technical nature (for example, necessitating the consideration of health and safety implications or quantification of liquidated damages), was not however to be treated as excluding experts in dispute resolution. This interpretation would respect the distinction between this expertise and technical expertise, as well as reinforcing a matter of policy in discouraging inappropriate challenges made to the appropriateness of the adjudicator. In the circumstances, the appointment of a non-technical experts as adjudicators, had been permissible.

In *Gwynt y Mor OFTO plc v Gwynt y Mor Offshore Wind Farm Limited*,[10] concerning a defects claim in which reinstatement costs were sought, the Commercial Court held that an indemnity clause of a sale and purchase agreement (SPA) governing the transfer of sub-sea export electrical cabling (having suffered seawater corrosion) that sourced a wind farm from the National Grid, was confined to recovery in respect of damage caused during the period specifically between contractual execution and completion. Construing the indemnity

[9] *Equitix ESI CHP (Sheff) Limited v Veolia Energy and Utility Services UK Plc* [2019] EWHC 593 (TCC), [2019] 183 Con LR 129.

[10] *Gwynt y Mor OFTO plc v Gwynt y Mor Offshore Wind Farm Limited* [2020] EWHC 850 (Comm).

clause contextually within the SPA, the precisely framed indemnity against pre-completion damage was found to contemplate recovery for damage occurring within this period only, and no wider an indemnity. Separately, the term 'damaged', as construed against the operative clause, would not be limited to 'new damage' or 'damage caused by an extraneous event' but would also not include unobservable corrosion not adversely affecting asset performance. The Court found also that even had unobservable corrosion amounted to recoverable damage for the purposes of the indemnity, then impairment to the value or utility of the cabling, would have additionally been necessary.

In another defects case, *Toucan Energy Holdings Limited v Wirsol Energy Limited*,[11] the Commercial Court partially upheld the claim and awarded damages for instances of irremediably defective design and construction in relation to solar park infrastructure (including defective transformers, busbars, deficient capacity and defective circuit-breakers) built pursuant to engineering, procurement and construction (EPC) contracts which had been entered into with site leaseholder special purpose vehicles (SPV). The claim incorporated also one made in respect of diminution in value attributable to the failed investment, and loan refinancing as well as argued waiver of conditions subsequent. Of particular note, regarding the unsuccessful blight claim, the Court found it unlikely that any possible damage caused to commercial reputations by virtue of the arising defects would mean, in turn, a devaluation of the solar parks. The Court observed that devaluation would likely only be attributable to factors creating a real risk of future, impeding cash flow, and it could properly be assumed that damages for defects would remedy operational harm caused by those defects, meaning that argued reputational harm had become irrelevant. As regards refinancing, the established defects had not brought about any loss arising from the breach of the EPC contracts (which would likely have eventuated in any event) nor less commercially advantageous refinancing.

The formulation and application of state financing (including UK Government subsidy and investment) has also been a notable source of commercial litigation, as well as public law focus, so highlighting the scope for jurisdictional overlay between the TCC and the Administrative Court. Such cases should also prove instructive for concentrating the norms of good regulatory governance of energy matters. In *Havant Biogas v Gas and Electricity Markets Authority*,[12] the High Court considered a judicial review claim brought against the refusal by the Office of Gas and Electricity Markets (OFGEM) to register and grant the applications of SPV producers, of biomethane for injection, for a green energy subsidy scheme, the domestic Renewable Heat Incentive (RHI) (being a government-funded environmental programme which had been heralded by the then Department of Energy & Climate Change, to financially incentivise renewable heat uptake and

[11] *Toucan Energy Holdings Limited v Wirsol Energy Limited* [2021] EWHC 895 (Comm).
[12] *Havant Biogas v Gas and Electricity Markets Authority* [2021] EWHC 84, [2021] ACD 39.

attract institutional private and public investment, and which had been wound-up to entry in March 2022) pursuant to the Renewable Heat Incentive Scheme Regulations 2018 and Renewable Heat Incentive Scheme and Domestic Renewable Heat Incentive Scheme (Amendment) Regulations 2018 (RHI Regulations), made under the Energy Act 2008. OFGEM's evaluative judgment had been successfully challenged by claim of judicial review on public law grounds, targeting OFGEM's misunderstanding and misinterpretation of the scheme of regulations and guidance.

The case of *Havant Biogas* followed on from the earlier case of *Solaria Energy UK Limited v Department for Business, Energy and Industrial Strategy*,[13] where the Court of Appeal had held in favour of a supplier of solar panels whose claim had been struck out for wrongful interference with an existing supply sub-contract (arising from a reduction in the UK Government's subsidies payable under a feed-in tariff scheme for a typology of solar panels – which caused, in turn, the provider to reduce its sale price), that a part-performed commercial contract amounted to a 'possession' for the purposes of Article 1 Protocol 1 of the European Convention on Human Rights (ECHR). The Court found that this interpretation was not undermined by a limitation upon the assignment of the 'possession'. In particular, the factual analysis in *Solaria Energy* may be viewed as underscoring the Court's developed approach, consistent with an established line of authority, in scoping appropriate protections against the commercial risk that commonly arises from investment in energy infrastructure, especially given the proliferation of many and various public financing schemes.

Separately from renewable energy typologies, yet firmly within the energy generation infrastructure sector, are to be found energy from waste and recycling installations, in respect of which construction disputes will also see considerable growth, as this sector continues to benefit from sizeable investment interest.

In *Essex County Council v UBB Waste (Essex) Limited*,[14] in connection with a claim brought by a county waste planning authority for damages and declarations for breach of a private finance initiative contract governing the design, construction, operation and maintenance of a biological waste treatment facility (operating to produce waste for incineration and produce material for landfill), the contract was held to be a relational contract. This was a finding with regard to explicit, mutual environmental objectives and served by the treatment facility operations carried out. This therefore characterised a contract in respect of which a significant level of commercial cooperation and confidence of the parties was presupposed. Within such a contract, an implied term to act in good faith, cooperatively and exercise discretion accordingly, was properly to be implied. On the facts, in light of the duty implied and with regard to an inability of the treatment facility to

[13] *Solaria Energy UK Limited v Department for Business, Energy and Industrial Strategy* [2020] EWCA 1625, [2021] 1 WLR 2349.

[14] *Essex County Council v UBB Waste (Essex) Limited* [2020] EWHC 1581 (TCC), [2020] 192 Con LR 143.

satisfy throughput and output acceptances or requirements under the contract by the acceptance longstop date, the authority was not contractually required to renegotiate terms governing either requirement, and it would be unreasonable to imply a further term curtailing the authority's right of termination by reference to a requirement for promptitude. The associated operational and risk posed by the planning constraints under which the treatment facility operator was functioning, was one which the operator had adopted. The high environmental objectives underscoring the contract, which were not in argument, did not operate to extend the duty of good faith to require any such renegotiation on the part of the authority.

Within the context of resolving substantive issues in litigation that concerns energy generation facilities – including electricity or gas generation, or integral waste treatment processes and waste disposal (eg: composting, incineration or gasification) – and with increasing commonality, the TCC is being invited to consider how such facilities fall to be characterised statutorily. In *Engie Fabricom (UK) Limited V MW High Tech Projects UK Limited*,[15] the TCC considered whether the relevant 'primary' onsite operation (framed statutorily, as an 'activity') of an energy from waste facility – being the Energy Works Hull facility which had been processing and gasifying refuse derived fuel, and combusting syngas by product for electricity generation – was tantamount to 'power generation' rather than 'waste processing'. In *Engie Fabricom*, the answer would resolve a main trial issue of whether the facility operation was properly excluded from adjudication (by section 105(2)(c)(i) of the Housing Grants, Construction and Regeneration Act 1996) and, in the circumstances, render two, already concluded, adjudications unenforceable for want of adjudicator jurisdiction exercisable under the 1996 Act.

The TCC observed that section 105(1) defines 'construction operations' and that a list of ousted operations under section 105(2) includes plant or machinery installation on a site by which the 'primary activity' is 'power generation'. In turn, the principal engineering, procurement and construction contract (EPC) for the energy from waste facility, by which the 'overriding contractual requirement' was held to be the performance of the facility for energy production (not waste throughput) was considered to amount to 'very strong evidence' that the 'primary activity' was 'power generation'. This was compatible with signposting from a funding model estimation that the majority of revenue for the facility would source from electricity exports and subsidies. This finding meant, in turn, that the works the subject of the dispute were not qualifying 'construction operations' within the meaning of the 1996 Act. There being no statutory or contractual right to adjudication on the dispute, it followed that the relevant adjudications were unenforceable.

The case of *Engie Fabricom* ultimately reinforces an important subtext; that the TCC's characterisation of energy generation infrastructure within analogous statutory contexts, will intrinsically be a question of fact (*Laker Vent Engineering*

[15] *Engie Fabricom (UK) Limited V MW High Tech Projects UK Limited* [2020] EWHC 1626, [2020] 191 Con LR 19.

Limited v Jacobs E&C Limited [2014][16]). Distinguishing 'primary' from 'ancillary' operations at trial, will inevitably turn on factual analysis as well as expert evidence addressing wide-ranging factors such as: how all relevant operations of a specific facility are contractually defined, how such operations are defined statutorily under frameworks governing facility consenting, permitting and regulation, how operations are characterised by energy infrastructure policy, facility financing, and how operations are carried out onsite.

There will be capacity for expert evidence in TCC claims to address, just as in *Engie Fabricom*, on complimenting, albeit less construction law-centric matters, including: (i) planning and waste regulatory and policy frameworks – although there will likely be less room for forensic analysis of UK Government energy policy (see, eg: EN-1 (Overarching National Policy Statement for Energy) and EN-3 (National Policy Statement for Renewable Energy Infrastructure)) or detailed critique of development plan policy on energy infrastructure; (ii) the scope of the operative planning permission or development consent (if the facility constitutes a Nationally Significant Infrastructure Project, under sections 14 and 15 of the Planning Act 2008); (iii) the scope of an Environment Agency permit, including one granted under the Industrial Emissions Directive 2010/75/EU (IED) to regulate a waste incineration plant undertaking waste thermal treatment; (iv) onsite operations; and (v) the financial model for the facility, subsidies and grants.

TCC decision-making may even extend to the specific weighing of factors differentiating energy facility typologies, significantly exceeding conventional distinctions of power generation, waste processing, transmission and distribution. This would seem to coincide with TCC decisions, to which factual analysis has already proven central when considering definitional questions on energy generation facilities, or where there has been call for particular scrutiny of onsite operations when viewed contextually against the specific contract(s) governing matters such as design and manufacture. Generalities of expression embedded in layers of government policy that overviews consenting, permitting and regulatory frameworks, to lesser extent, will inform the 'primary activity' but even these will commonly achieve relevance in decision-making. The case of *Engie Fabricom* is an illustrative example, and importantly, within the energy from waste sector, being one experiencing considerable upscaling to incorporate various waste combustion generation processes, distinguishable from 'primary' waste treatment. Alongside this industry trend, the factual analysis critically underpinning the question of 'primary activity' – for the purposes of section 105 of the 1996 Act, and indeed beyond (the interpretative question being one also of environmental law) – will inevitably develop in sophistication. Anaerobic digestion and gasification plants are clear examples of integrated UK energy from waste facilities, and the upturn in their domestic construction signposts a likely direction of travel for the energy

[16] *Laker Vent Engineering Limited v Jacobs E&C Limited* [2014] EWHC 1058 (TCC), [2014] 154 Con LR 77.

generation industry alongside energy planning objectives, including those articulated through the British Energy Security Strategy.

The TCC's role becomes increasing daring as the government's energy-related national policy ages. As at 2022, EN-1 and EN-3 – albeit not interpretational instruments – have fallen behind energy sector growth and industrial technological advances, with neither offering specificity on defining 'primary activity' of an energy from waste facility.

The future significance of interpretive questions for the TCC will likely shadow that of other specialist tribunals, including the Planning Court. In *EFW Group Limited v Secretary of State for Business Energy & Industrial Strategy*,[17] the Planning Court considered whether specific EfW infrastructure could permissibly be cumulatively-assessed for development consent under a single – rather than dual – decision-making framework, under section 104 of the 2008 Act. Here, operative factors considered by the Court – albeit in answer to an altogether different interpretative and jurisdictional question than arises under section 105(2) of the 1996 Act – included facility generation capacity, facility impact on the 'waste hierarchy', capacity of waste fuel, and waste-fuel throughput. These were seemingly not instructive in *Engie Fabricom*. There would, however, be no good reason why such factors, where satisfactorily in evidence, should be excluded from the overall factual analysis of an energy from waste facility for the purposes of section 105.

The interpretative question discussed here serves only to underscore the critical importance of comprehensive, industry-informed, expert evidence in navigating the factual analysis necessary to identify the 'primary activity' of energy from waste facilities, and potentially other energy generation infrastructure.

The EU Waste Framework Directive 2008/98EC (transposed by the Waste (England and Wales) Regulations 2011) and environmental permitting under the Environmental Permitting (England & Wales) Regulations 2010, concern waste incineration and pollution control and treatment operations, and formulate only, a series of high-level waste operation generalities. The Directive addresses operations in terms of management, collection, treatment, recovery, recycling and disposal in the context of 'power generating' and 'waste processing'. The process of 'recovery' under the Directive (Annex II) may properly comprise a use defined 'to generate energy' and include incineration (of solid waste, etc) whilst similarly incorporating an identifiable waste process.

According to the UK Government,[18] infrastructure and the built environment is responsible for approximately 25 per cent of the UK's total carbon emissions, when taking account of construction (embodied carbon), use (operational carbon), and the whole life cycle (whole-life carbon), from materials manufacturing, up to building demolition. An almost hitherto pronounced focus within UK industry upon infrastructure and building operational emissions and daily build

[17] *EFW Group Limited v Secretary of State for Business Energy & Industrial Strategy* [2021] EWHC 2697.

[18] House of Commons Committee Report (First Report of Session 2022–23).

energy consumption, will fundamentally be reset, to incorporate a shared focus on embodied carbon emissions. Albeit in its infancy, UK Government policy is promoting increased regulatory assessment and control of embodied carbon and decarbonisation. Their statutory framework and regulation will soon follow, the precise parameters of which cannot be anticipated here. A significant component will however be the assessment and control of whole-life carbon impacting of infrastructure and buildings.[19] This will be further testing ground for the TCC, in parallel with other specialist courts in adjudicating upon claims involving failed or delayed infrastructure and built development.

Some precedent may be derived from considered action points now guiding future infrastructure improvements within the rail and road transportation industry.[20] The UK Government announced in 2020, a significant step-change to its pathway for the achievement of net zero transport emissions, encompassing all transportation infrastructure and embodied carbon, with general rationalisation targeting and the delivery of a net zero railway network by 2050. Network Rail Infrastructure Limited, as the lead UK rail infrastructure provider, adopted the Traction Decarbonisation Network Strategy and, with it, an intensified programme of electrification of much of the system's rail network, accelerated delivery of electric pathways, creation of battery and hydrogen trains, and increased line capacity for accommodating projected growth in net passenger uplift and freight demand, away from road and air.

Considerations far exceeding the energy performance of infrastructure and buildings, and extending to whole-life carbon impacting, will ultimately mean a renewed conceptualisation of net zero for TCC litigation. A primary focus for infrastructure and the built environment will therefore be the achievement of net zero carbon in both construction, and whole-life operation and consumption. The Building Regulations will also promote reduced energy demand alongside clean growth strategising to significantly reduce energy use, and ensure transparent operational energy performance for all infrastructure and buildings.

Existing inaccuracies over the statistical measurement of emissions and associated datasets, standards and targets beyond high level metrics, and compliance predictions, will however continue to mean complexities for UK Government policy, and for experts as well as professionals within this emerging discipline. Future net zero carbon construction, through to completion stage, will in turn also require the consideration of offsetting impacts onsite or procuring on-site renewable energy. This will require, and likely eventually see, the formulation of UK Government and Industry standards on typical performance, in conjunction with a workable framework of principles.

The expectation of decision-taking that is consistent with such frameworks, which are ultimately intended to guide the energy and environmentally-compliant

[19] Industrial Decarbonisation Strategy (BEIS), issued March 2021.

[20] This includes the railway, ever since publication of the Traction Decarbonisation Network Strategy (TDNS) Interim Programme Business Case (July 2020).

delivery of infrastructure and the built environment, is however far from a novel proposition. For example, the Infrastructure Act 2015 (Part 6: Energy) provides for an allowable solutions mechanism, and the establishment of carbon offset funding for both domestic and non-domestic buildings in conjunction with the 2015 Act, to provide for offset funds in respect of eligible and suitable building projects, to collect developer payments, has long been advocated, for example, with regard to London development[21] and London Plan carbon reduction targets.

Nonetheless, the judicial appreciation and application of more sophisticated net zero datasets, assessment criteria, standards and targets, established and enforced across new regulatory frameworks, will necessarily import an additional level of complexity for professionals – and, ultimately also – for the TCC, in their interpretation. This may only however prove a point of transitional inexperience. The TCC (and other specialist courts) have, for example, proven well-placed and forensically adept in grappling with established environmental law concepts, perhaps once considered unconventional within its jurisdiction, including 'the polluter pays', and off-setting in conjunction with operational energy performance. There is, therefore, no well-founded reason to doubt the TCC's jurisdictional competence in its extended application to complex energy or environmental implications of infrastructure and development construction.

The Climate Change Act 2008 was pivotal in formulating a statutory target for emission reduction and creating a legal framework for an accumulation of carbon reduction-focussed measures, in connection with the built environment. Separately from domestic statute, is a body of (post-Brexit, retained) EU law. The EU Energy Performance of Buildings Directive, concerning the energy performance of buildings (2002, revisited in 2010) was intended to develop the energy performance of buildings and reduce carbon impacting. This Directive, together with the Energy Efficiency Directive (2012) have long-served as leading EU legislation aiming to reduce the energy consumption of buildings, and promoting qualitative energy efficiency transparency by importing energy performance certification for the disposal of buildings, energy certification, 'nearly zero energy' buildings and energy rating.

Accompanying EU measures were at least partly intended to enable the review and reinforcement of supply and user contracts, to allow for greater modernisation and reinforcement of energy supply and in a way consistent with technological advances, as well as to minimise sector vulnerability to energy transitioning and reduce the capacity for commercially significant disputes to arise, especially within the oil and gas sector, but also within the renewables sector. Renewables demand is considered essential for reaching climate neutrality.

Within this context, reference may additionally be made of renewable or 'green' hydrogen, in the event that 'blue' hydrogen generation from fossil fuels, is eventually phased-out by the UK Government. Green hydrogen has been

[21] Carbon Offset Funds Greater London Authority guidance for London's Local Planning Authorities on establishing carbon offset funds October 2018.

promoted through an assimilation of strategy- and plan-making, and underscores also a potential for synergising multiple renewables, including through the harmonised siting of key infrastructure within a centralised location: for example, the installation of electrolysers in conjunction with other renewables project infrastructure. Similarly with other infrastructure and technologies required to support a hydrogen-supported economy, production plants, tank, cylinder and pipeline transportation, storage and dispensing facilities will be required. Their intricate construction, maintenance and eventual decommissioning must meet standards prescribed under statutory frameworks, including the Pipeline Safety Regulations 1996, Gas Safety (Management) Regulations 1996, and the Pressure Equipment (Safety) Regulations 2016.

Separately from decarbonisation, the Building Regulations 2010 provide, more generally, for minimum standards in England and Wales governing the performance of buildings, including Approved Document L (Conservation of Fuel and Power), setting minimum practical standards for building performance in the context of the conservation of fuel and power, so enabling the transition to 'nearly zero energy buildings'. Approved Document L includes criteria addressing the carbon emission rate, the Target Emission Rate, reasonable energy efficiency standards, energy trade-offs and the performance gap (between projected and actual performance). As with other Approved Documents, Approved Document L incorporates general guidance, including compliance in technology-specific, design, use, and scale terms. Approved Document L compliments the wider technical requirements[22] regulating individual aspects of building design and construction, promoting energy efficiency[23] of buildings.[24]

The 2008 Act has introduced a legally binding framework, which includes a statutorily defined target for the UK to achieve net zero carbon emissions by 2050 (the section 1 obligation) with regard to targeted greenhouse gases (GHGs). This target has full application to the UK, and so includes its construction and technology sectors. The 2008 Act separately compliments subsequent commitments made by the UK Government on climate change initiatives. The UK's Sixth Carbon Budget requirement is for a reduction in carbon emissions by 78 per cent, by 2035 (in comparison to 1990s levels) albeit there has been a subsequent commitment to a 68 per cent reduction by 2030 on this same comparative basis.

Climate change litigation, whether strategic, individual or project-targeted in nature, is typically founded in public law, and commonly pivots on a challenge made to the implementation or effect of UK Government policy and the implications for project decision-making. Other climate change litigation has seen challenges made to public investment into projects contended not to satisfy

[22] See, eg, Table 7.1; Vol 1 of the Manual to the Building Regulations.

[23] Paragraphs A12(d)–(f), A14(f)–(h), A22, A23, B2(c) and F24 of Vol 2 of the Manual.

[24] See, eg, heat pump requirements (paras 6.49 to 6.53 6.36) and heat pumps of a prescribed output, pursuant to Commission Regulation No 2016/2281 eco-design standards applicable to cooling and chiller units.

established climate change standards or safeguards, or a contended failure to properly adopt or otherwise apply policy. Other climate change litigation has however concentrated upon contended private commercial harms, which include claims brought for compensation for failures of implementation or contended climate change harms.

Modern UK climate change legal challenges should not however be strictly compartmentalised or be treated inflexibly. Discrete principles, potentially instructive to the TCC's consideration of possible climate change implications of a claim, do abridge public and private law orthodoxies. Hence, some instructive insights for TCC proceedings may be sourced from considered examples of climate change litigation. One example is the litigation in *R (on the application of Friends of the Earth Limited and Others) v Heathrow Airport Limited*,[25] concerning the UK Government's published policy statement[26] for increasing air passenger traffic capacity at Heathrow airport which was initially heard by the Planning Court and subsequently by the Supreme Court, in connection with any future consenting of a third (north-west) runway and the application of the UK Government's policy statement considering the expansion.

In the *Heathrow* case, the Court was required to interpret section 5(8) of the Planning Act 2008 and explore how the ANPS may properly account for UK Government policy promoting climate change mitigation and adaptation, in the context of section 10(3) and a duty of the Secretary of State to have regard to the desirability of such in exercising the wider decision-making function of whether to consent to airport expansion. In considering a contended breach of the EU Strategic Environmental Assessment Directive and adopting a comparatively narrow construction of climate change obligations,[27] the Court held there to have been no breach of these obligations, but pointed to other important requirements held to give effect to the 'legal significance' of climate change. The Court was particularly mindful of the indirect effect of climate legislation (for example, development consent order-making powers in respect of Nationally Significant Infrastructure Projects, including Environmental Impact Assessment, and compatibility with net zero by 2050 in conjunction with other climate change targets (reflecting the section 1 obligation of the 2008 Act). The Court also reflected upon both short- and long-term UK carbon targeting and UK carbon budgets (produced by the independent Committee on Climate Change) in the context of environmentally-focussed ministerial statements across various UK Government departments, including BEIS, and the Department for Transport.

In *R (on the application of Finch) v Surrey County Council*,[28] the Court of Appeal heard an appeal from the dismissal of a judicial review claim made for

[25] *R (on the application of Friends of the Earth Limited and Others) v Heathrow Airport Limited* [2020] UKSC 52, [2021] 2 All ER 967 (from June 2018 – December 2020).

[26] Airports National Policy Statement (ANPS).

[27] SEA Directive 2001/42/EC.

[28] *R (on the application of Finch) v Surrey County Council* [2022] EWCA Civ 187, [2022] Env LR 27.

planning permission for expanding an oil well, permitting 25 years of extraction. The Court considered (offsite and downstream) environmental impact assessment in respect of extraction GHGs which would exceed natural gas release, from oil hydrocarbons, and from future refined oil combustion. It was found acceptable for the EIA to have been confined to onsite GHGs assessment, having excluded the GHGs of 'end product' use/refined oil combustion. It was instead the assessment of whether the development would give rise to (indirect) likely significant effects on environment, which had been critical (Regulation 4(2) of the Environmental Impact Assessment Regulations 2017 (EIA Regulations)). In EIA terms, GHGs from future combustion were considered capable of constituting a (likely, significant) environmental effect, so necessitating EIA of the project This meant, in turn, that the decision-taker was not legally incapable of taking account of future combustion GHGs, albeit this inclusion was not mandated. The construction of 'project' and of 'proposed development' for the purposes of the statutory framework (principally, EIA Regulation 4(2)) included the 'during construction' and 'extraction' processes. The 'purpose' or 'project' neither defined project components, nor the potential (likely, significant) environmental effects of the project. The Court emphasised that EIA is an iterative process, and comprised an important component of development consent order-making, and that both direct and indirect (likely, significant) effects are potentially relevant to this function. Separately, the ultimate use of 'end product' combustion had not amounted to any identifiable part of the consented project, and any significant environmental effect of this combustion was outwith assessment.

Jurisprudence of the Environmental Court of Justice has found that an 'end-product' is not to be drawn so widely as to encompass consequences beyond those typically associated with the project outcome.[29] Also, considering *R (on the application of Squire) v Shropshire Council*,[30] the Court found there to be no requirement to assess the environmental effects of end consumption/use of the 'end product', seemingly on the basis that the environmental effects of successive, post-extraction, oil treatment phases were not properly comprised within the subject project.

The case of *R (on the application of Goesa Limited) v Eastleigh BC* concerned a judicial review of a decision to grant planning permission for developing a runway extension at Southampton International Airport.[31] Environmental Assessment addenda submitted in support of expansion had projected future operations, subject to sensitivity testing of future passenger growth. The application EIA had assessed that GHGs may prove significant, when comparing likely scheme emissions with UK carbon budgets, UK aviation forecasts and local zone emissions. The Court found the quality of baseline environmental information and policy

[29] Case C-142/07 *Ecologistas en Accion-CODA v Ayuntamiento de Madrid* [2008] (Third Chamber).

[30] *R (on the application of Squire) v Shropshire Council* [2019] EWCA Civ 888, [2019] Env LR 36.

[31] *R (on the application of Goesa Limited) v Eastleigh Borough Council* [2022] EWHC 1221 (Admin), [2022] JPL 1309.

assessment to be legally unassailable, noting the UK's recommended (fifth) carbon budget, (excluding international flight emissions), net zero policy (including these emissions), sector planning assumptions, and UK Government policy 'gaps'. There was also no basis to legally criticise the absence of in-combination assessment of the cumulative effects of GHG emissions in combination with regional airport expansion projects, which had been argued to be in breach of the EIA Regulations (including EIA Regulation 18(3)). The EIA requirement (EIA Regulation 18(3)(b)) had been that all likely significant effects should be described, and for all additional information relevant to: (i) specific characteristics of development (or development type); and (ii) environmental features likely to be significantly affected (EIA Regulation 18(3)(f); and Schedule 4), to be identified.

The Court identified that an environmental statement must include (EIA regulation 18(4)) information 'reasonably required for reaching reasoned conclusion' on significant effects of development on environment, accounting of current knowledge and methods of assessment; that (Schedule 4) categories of additional information, including 'climate' and GHGs (paragraph 5(f)) must be observed; and that the overall EIA process (including the environmental statement, consultation responses, and in/direct significant effects) is required; that the cumulation of effects with other existing and approved projects, should take account of existing environmental problems (Schedule 4(5)(e)); that climate impacts including the 'nature and magnitude of GHG emissions, and the vulnerability of the project to climate change' (Schedule 4(5)(f)) should properly be accounted for.

The Court left unresolved whether the phrase 'existing and/or approved' (Schedule 4(5)(e)) is capable of including unconsented, pipeline infrastructure proposals. It is to be recalled however that EIA regulation 18(4) requires no more or less information than is 'reasonably required …' (*Preston New Road Action Group v Secretary of State for Communities and Local Government*,[32] considering a fracking infrastructure proposal) and that 'significance' and 'adequacy' in the context of evaluative environmental judgments, are subject only to irrationality challenge (*R (on the application of Blewett) v Derbyshire County Council*;[33] and *Finch* at [15]). Separately, the Court reaffirmed that a substantial margin of appreciation applies to judgments founded upon scientific, technical or predictive assessments, typically undertaken by experts (*R (on application of Plan B Earth) v Secretary of State for Transport*[34]). The Court endorsed the summary appraisal of climate change statutory framework in *R (on the application of Packham) v Secretary of State for Transport* at [83–85] (being the judicial review of environmental impact of HS2, Phase 1;[35] argued failure to take into account GHGs in the light of CCA 2008 and

[32] *Preston New Road Action Group v Secretary of State for Local Government* [2018] EWCA Civ 9, [2018] Env LR 18.

[33] *R (on the application of Blewett) v Derbyshire County Council* [2003] EWHC 2775 (Admin), [2004] Env LR 29.

[34] *R (on application of Plan B Earth) v Secretary of State for Transport* [2020] EWCA Civ 214, [2020] JPL 1005.

[35] *R (on the application of Packham) v Secretary of State for Transport* [2020] EWCA Civ 1004, [2021] Env LR 10.

the Paris Agreement). The Court identified (*R (on the application of Spurrier) v Secretary of State for Transport* [2019][36]) that issues essentially depending on political judgment, will likely warrant a lower intensity of review and that the margin of appreciation is capable of enveloping environmental impact assessment impracticalities, underscoring public interest considerations.

It however remains unclear, in the application of the margin of appreciation, whether a 'nil' baseline (as to exclude associated emissions) for a construction site, should be adopted; how the assessment of GHGs, including of comparative data (at local, regional and national level) may permissibly vary; and how GHGs (whether aligned to the concepts of embodied and operational carbon) fall to be properly quantified in each given case, and in the absence of an absolutist standard.

Concluding Thoughts

It is certain that the TCC will continue to experience an upward trajectory in legal disputes arising from, or in connection, with the energy sector. The collaborative treatment of conventional contract law principles and energy norms, additionally with environmental standards, will similarly intensify. The complexity and magnitude of the commercial risk which commonly turns upon either the success or failure of any sizeable, investable energy project, makes this inevitable.

The ongoing refinement of alternative means of resolving energy disputes, other than through litigation, will mean that the TCC, synchronised with the wider jurisdiction of other specialist courts of the Business and Property division, will remain mindful of both the scope and practical utility (or otherwise) of dispute resolution, when modified in its application to energy matters.

There is an evidently strong and comprehensive basis – justifiably borne from the confident and rigorous jurisprudence emerging from the TCC (and other specialist courts) since a notable uptick in 2017 – for concluding that the TCC remains well-placed to accommodate disputes engaging the transitioning technologies and infrastructure typologies that make up today's UK energy sector. Judicial consideration of litigation involving renewables projects, their financing and their contractual compliance, offers but one significant endorsement. Albeit the nuclear sector has, up until now at least, elected to principally remain remote from the orbit of the TCC, this may also be induced to change in lockstep with the UK Government's repositioning on the need for greater domestic nuclear infrastructure.

This judicial aptitude has unsurprisingly been much guided, to date, by the TCC's confident exploration and application of conventional contractual mechanisms and principles, coupled with appropriate resort to expertise, whenever

[36] *R (on the application of Spurrier) v Secretary of State for Transport* [2019] EWHC 1070 (Admin), [2019] JPL 1163.

merited on the factual and textual analysis. Properly characterised therefore, the TCC's accommodation of energy disputes signposts an exciting jurisdictional extension, rather than any sea-change.

The terrific influence of fundamental environmental norms and standards underlying energy efficiency, energy security, recycling initiatives, energy from waste, pollution control and climate change litigation, still remains largely unchartered ground for the TCC. There is significant ground to be covered. The jurisprudence of the Administrative Court is however already providing an important permeating influence upon the determinations of outwardly commercial claims. There is additionally, therefore, justification for some modification of approach by the TCC, but, again, this may be viewed as extension rather than redirection. The appropriateness of this, furthermore, will necessarily vary, in response to the peculiarities of the individual energy dispute. There will perhaps eventually arise a need, as such, for modification, also. Questions inevitably arise over the precise future direction of energy and environmental litigation, the parameters of the practical expectations of parties before the TCC regarding litigation remedies, as well as the dexterity and jurisdictional competence of the Court to satisfy commercially-driven demand for bespoke forms of relief, including interim relief.

This all serves to underscore the unique and compounding importance of the TCC in respect of litigation that encompasses energy or environmental law dimensions. Albeit a role that raises considerable scope for intervention and challenge, it is conspicuously one also that is resounding of the demonstrable specialism of the Court.

Appendix: Official Referees and Judges of the Technology and Construction Court 1876–2004

DR ELIZABETH NORTON; WITH SIR FRANCIS NEWBOLT KC BY DR MICHAEL REYNOLDS

James Anderson QC 1876–1886

James Anderson QC has the distinction of being appointed as the first Official Referee, accepting the full-time appointment on 15 February 1876. He was the eldest son of David Anderson Esquire of Bellfield, near Edinburgh and was educated at the High School in the Scottish capital, before studying at Edinburgh University. He began a long and distinguished career in law by becoming a member of the Faculty of Advocates in June 1828, which allowed him to practice in the Scottish courts. Although he would later move his practice to England, he retained a reputation as an authority on Scottish legal affairs. For example, he was called to give an opinion before the Select Committee on the Appellate Jurisdiction of the House of Lords in 1856 on the question of whether a Scottish judge should sit as a permanent member of the House of Lords (Anderson considered 'my opinion is that, practically, the introduction of a Scotch Judge is not desirable', a view shared by other Scottish lawyers consulted). He also had parliamentary ambition, twice standing unsuccessfully as a candidate for Parliament for seats in Scotland. The election for Ayr in 1868 was particularly close, with Anderson losing by 91 votes.

Anderson moved his practice to London early in his career. He became a student member of Lincoln's Inn on 20 April 1835 and was called to the bar at Middle Temple on 7 June 1839. He became a QC 12 years later in July 1851, before being appointed as a bencher of Middle Temple on 12 January 1852. In 1868 he became the treasurer of Middle Temple. Throughout his career Anderson was active in the Inns of Court, serving as one of the Members of the Board of Examiners for the admission of Students to the Inns of Court in 1866, for example.

In 1873 James Anderson was appointed as an Examiner in the Court of Chancery by the then Lord Chancellor, Lord Selborne, on the understanding that this would lead to his appointment as an Official Referee. This agreement which, as the next Lord Chancellor Lord Cairns noted in a letter dated 14 March 1876, was one in which 'I was in no way bound', served to draw attention to Anderson as a candidate, with Cairns considering 'it so advantageous to the public service that I had no hesitation in confirming it'. Anderson, who was Lord Cairns' first appointee as Official Referee, had impressed the Lord Chancellor, with Cairns considering him 'a gentleman of long standing, high reputation, and considerable practice at the Bar'.

Anderson married later in life, wedding Minnie, the daughter of George Upward Esquire of Blackheath, in August 1871.

George Dowdeswell QC 1876–1889

Lord Cairns' second appointment as Official Referee in 1876 was George Morley Dowdeswell, QC. Dowdeswell, who was born on 5 September 1809, came from a legal family, with his father, William Dowdeswell of Ewell in Surrey, himself a barrister of the Inner Temple, who had served as Recorder at Bombay. George Dowdeswell studied at Pembroke College, Oxford, graduating in 1830. He became a student member of Inner Temple in June 1831, at the age of 22 and was called to the bar three years later on 6 June 1834. Dowdeswell was a member of 1 Harecourt Buildings throughout his practice, while he was also appointed as a Recorder for Newbury from 1854. He became a QC on 15 December 1866 and was appointed as a bencher at Inner Temple the following month. In 1869 he was appointed to act as Chief Commissioner to enquire into corrupt practices at Norwich.

Dowdeswell was a prolific legal author. In 1846 his *The Law of Life and Fire Insurances* was released, while a decade later he published his *The Merchant Shipping Acts, 1854 & 1855, with a Readable Abridgment of the Former Act, and an Explanation of the Law Relating to It*. He was also the editor of *Smith's Mercantile Law*, *Starkie on Evidence* and *Bayley on Bills*.

Dowdeswell was a member of the Garrick Club. He married Mary, the daughter of the Reverend John Neville Freeman of Hayes, Middlesex, in April 1865. He remained a busy practitioner well into his later years, being appointed as a magistrate for Sussex in 1886, while still sitting as a Recorder for Newbury and as an Official Referee. He died at his home of Rogate Lodge in Petersfield, Hampshire, on 2 December 1893 at the age of 84.

Charles Roupell 1876–1889

Charles Morris Roupell, was appointed by Lord Cairns as the third Official Referee in 1876. He was born in 1813, the sixth son of George Boone Roupell of London and Kent, who was himself a barrister and had formerly served as a Master in Chancery. The Roupells were a legal family, with two of Charles Roupell's elder brothers, Robert Prioleau Roupell and John Stuart Roupell, becoming prominent at the bar. Charles Roupell was educated at Eton College and then Trinity College,

Cambridge, graduating in 1840. He was admitted as a student member of Lincoln's Inn on 11 November 1836 at the age of 23 and was called to the bar just over five years later on 26 January 1842.

Roupell's practice was notable for his work as an equity draftsman and conveyancer, while he also frequently acted as a special examiner in equity suits. On 15 February 1860 he was appointed as the senior captain for Lincoln's Inn of the Inns of Court Rifle Volunteer Corps. Like George Dowdeswell, he was recommended to be appointed as one of the Official Referees by Lord Coleridge, with Lord Cairns supporting Roupell's appointment since he was 'well known to him before, and whom he believed to be in every way fitted for the position'.

Roupell was active in the Athenaeum Club, which he joined in 1859. Herbert Spencer, the philosopher and political theorist, recalled being there with Charles Roupell in the late 1880s when Roupell remarked to him 'that to play billiards well was a sign of an ill-spent youth', a saying that – to Spencer's chagrin – later became firmly attributed to him. Charles Roupell, who lived at 21 Sackville Street in London, was a lifelong bachelor.

Sir Henry Verey 1876–1920

The fourth Official Referee to be appointed, Sir Henry Verey, would go on to sit for more than 44 years, something which was described by Lord Birkenhead, who was the Lord Chancellor at the time of his death, as likely to be a record in the annals of judicial appointments. His was a longstanding and successful term, with *The Times* noting in his obituary that the occasions in which his appointments were reversed on appeal 'can be counted on one's fingers'. Such longevity and success in the role is all the more remarkable given the highly controversial circumstances of his appointment.

Verey was considerably younger than the other three Official Referees with whom he originally served. He was born in 1836 as the eldest son of Henry Verey of Bridge House, Twyford in Berkshire, which later became his own residence. A relative latecomer to the bar, he studied mathematics at Trinity College, Cambridge, graduating in 1859. He then took up a position in a solicitor's office, spending three years working in the firm of Messrs Crowden and Maynerd. On 19 November 1862 he joined Inner Temple as a student member, before being called to the bar in 1865. This just permitted him to fulfil the minimum requirement of ten years in practice when he was unexpectedly nominated to become one of the Official Referees in 1876 by Sir Fitzroy Kelly, Lord Chief Baron of the Exchequer.

Verey's appointment was highly controversial, being referred to as a 'public scandal' in Parliament. Indeed, it was strongly hinted during a debate over the appointment in the House of Commons on 26 May 1876 that his selection was due to the personal favour of Sir Fitzroy Kelly, with the Attorney-General himself forced to state in the chamber 'that the previous charge was one of nepotism against the Lord Chief Baron. But he had no hesitation in saying that there was not a word of foundation for the charge of nepotism'. The primary charges against Verey's appointment were that he was comparatively young and inexperienced and that he had continued to seek private practice work even after his appointment. His career up until that date had also been undistinguished, with it strongly noted that other – apparently more qualified – individuals had applied for the role. Indeed, even the Attorney-General, who was prepared to support Verey was scathing in Parliament, reading out a letter from Messrs Fearon and Clabon, with whom Verey had worked and who praised the fact that 'he was quiet and clear-headed'. To this, the Attorney General joked that 'it was, perhaps, because he was quiet that his want of success at the bar was to be attributed'. Lord Cairns, too, publicly supported the appointment, telling the Commons that while 'Mr Verey was not known personally to him (the Lord Chancellor), but he had very marked concurrent testimony in his favour, and he believed him to be well qualified for the office.'

The controversy continued even after Verey's appointment was confirmed, with the *Law Times* from 2 June 1876 noting that 'it was absolutely necessary that the Government should defend the appointment of Mr Verey, but it is admitted on all hands that a process of selection for important judicial offices which passes over prominent members of both branches of the Profession, and elevates a person hitherto absolutely unknown, is not only unusual but vicious in the extreme'. It was an inauspicious start, particularly when one of Verey's judgments was almost immediately overturned on appeal on the grounds that he had not given any reasons for his decision. Nonetheless, Verey, who had been called by one supporter in the Commons 'a gentleman of very considerable powers', quickly developed into his role. His 44 years in office would see considerable change in the business of the Official Referees, not least in the fact that the venue of the court and its offices moved on more than one occasion.

Sir Henry Verey married Henrietta Maria, daughter of Edward Williams Hasell of Dalemain in Cumberland and had one son and one daughter. He was knighted shortly after his retirement in 1920, but enjoyed the honour for a few days short of six months, dying on 4 December 1920. Years before, during the debate over his appointment in the House of Commons, one Mr Herschell had very succinctly summed up the feelings of many by arguing that 'if a young lieutenant were to be suddenly made a general he might happen to turn out a very good good man for the post, but would anybody say it was a proper appointment to make?', something that caused cheers in the house. Sir Henry Verey did indeed turn out to be a successful and authoritative member of the Official Referees, in spite of the controversy of his appointment.

Rt. Hon. Sir Edward Ridley 1886–1897

Sir Edward Ridley was particularly well-connected, a fact that did not go unnoticed in his judicial career. He was born in August 1843, the second son of

Sir Matthew White Ridley, Baronet. He was educated at Harrow and then Corpus Christi College, Oxford, before becoming a fellow of All Soul's College, Oxford. Ridley became a student member of the Inner Temple on 27 January 1865, when he was 21 years old and was called to the bar in June 1868. He also served as the member of Parliament for South Northumberland from 1878 until 1880.

Ridley became an Official Referee at a relatively early stage in his career, only taking silk six years into his appointment. He was, by most accounts, successful in the role. On 31 March 1897 the Lord Chancellor wrote to the Prime Minister, the Marquess of Salisbury, suggesting four names as possible candidates for a vacancy on the High Court bench and favouring Ridley, considering him 'a very experienced and excellent lawyer … an excellent scholar and a man with a very considerable university record. He is also a poet and has translated Lucan but these I do not insist on as judicial qualifications'. There were two objections raised to Ridley in the letter: that 'he has been for several years Official Referee and he is the brother of the Home Secretary [Sir Matthew White Ridley]'.

While both the Lord Chancellor and the Prime Minister felt these objections were surmountable, the legal profession as a whole and the general public certainly did not. The *Law Journal* argued that 'the appointment can be defended on no ground whatsoever. It would be easy to name fifty members of the Bar with a better claim', while the *Solicitors' Journal* considered the appointment to be a 'grave mistake'. The *Law Times* considered him barred by his earlier role as an Official Referee, stating that 'no one will believe that he would have been appointed to the High Court Bench but for his connections … Such an innovation, we repeat, was only possible where the hard-working official, the bearer of so many heavy burdens of the High Court judges, was highly connected. This is Ridleyism. Let it be known hereafter as Ridleyism'.

Ridley's tenure on the High Court bench continued to be controversial. He was almost universally unpopular as a judge, with Lord Justice MacKinnon dubbing him 'the worst judge I have appeared before', with 'a perverse instinct for unfairness'. He was not alone in his opinion. At Ridley's death, Sir Frederick Pollock considered him to be a 'good scholar, Fellow of All Souls, successful, *sicut dicunt*, as an Official Referee, and by general opinion of the Bar the worst High Court judge of our time, ill-tempered and grossly unfair: which is rather a mystery'.

Given Ridley's acknowledged intellect and largely successful tenure as an Official Referee, the opprobrium he drew on the High Court bench was indeed mysterious. He married Alice, daughter of William Bromley-Davenport MP on 29 July 1882 and was survived by two sons. He died 14 October 1928, having retired from the bench in 1917.

George W. Hemming QC 1889–1905

George Wirgman Hemming was born on 19 August 1821, the second son of Henry Keene Hemming of Gray's Hall in Essex. Hemming was educated at Clapham

Grammar School and then St John's College, Cambridge, becoming Senior Wrangler in 1844 as the highest achieving mathematics student in his final year. Unsurprisingly, due to his stellar academic results, he was elected to a fellowship at St John's in 1844. He became a student member of Lincoln's Inn in 1844, but retained a strong interest in mathematics, publishing his *Differential and Integral Calculus* in 1848. Hemming was called to the bar on 3 May 1850.

Hemming enjoyed a successful career at the bar, serving as standing counsel to Cambridge University from 1875 and as junior counsel to the Crown between 1871 and 1875. Known for his continuing involvement with academia, he was also appointed as a Commissioner under the Universities Act of 1877. Hemming published widely, serving as the editor of the equity portion of *Law Reports* and as joint editor of *Johnson and Hemming's Reports (Vice-Chancellors' Courts)* in (1860–2) and *Hemming and Miller's Reports* (1862–65). Early in his legal career he published *A Just Income Tax: How Possible*, which was a review of the evidence reported by the Income Tax committee, as well as looking at the principle of taxation. Hemming took silk in 1875, becoming a bencher of Lincoln's Inn the following year.

Hemming showed an early interest in the Official Referees, publishing his *Thoughts on the Fusion of Law and Equity* in 1873. He became an Official Referee in 1887, serving until his death on 6 January 1905. In his later years he was also notable for applying his undoubted mathematical ability to the popular game of billiards, publishing his work in 1899 in *Billiards Mathematically Treated.* While Hemming considered that 'the problem of the motion of the two balls after impact involved the determination of the important constants', which he identified as the coefficient of elasticity and friction, not everyone was quite as convinced. One reviewer considered that the book might be 'useful to the amateur billiard player who has a competent knowledge of mathematics, though not, perhaps, to the very accomplished player who may have attained to excellence by natural gifts of eye and hand, and by long practice without theory'. The book, however, was published in more than one edition.

Hemming married Louisa Annie, daughter of his cousin, Samuel Hemming, of Merrywood Hall in Bristol and had four sons and four daughters.

Sir Edward Pollock 1897–1927

Sir Edward Pollock, who was born on 1 February 1841, came from a legal family. He was the eighth and youngest son of Sir Frederick Pollock, Lord Chief Baron of the Exchequer, with four of his older brothers, William, Walter, George and Charles all following their father to the Bar. Surprisingly, Sir Edward Pollock was initially intended for a different future, studying medicine at King's College London and becoming a fellow of the Royal College of Surgeons in 1868. Two years later, on 11 January 1870 he joined Inner Temple as a student member, being called to the bar on 18 November 1872 at the age of 31.

Pollock was appointed as an Official Referee in 1897, serving for 30 years before his retirement in 1927. The Pollock family were, unsurprisingly, widely known at the Bar, with Sir Edward Pollock co-editing Russell's Treatise on the Power and Duty of an Arbitrator with his relative, HW Pollock.

Pollock was a member of the Union Club. He married Alice Georgina, the daughter of Warren de la Rue in 1871. He died on 14 April 1930. For further details on Sir Edward Pollock, see chapter three of this volume.

Montague Muir-Mackenzie 1905–1919

Montague Johnstone Muir-Mackenzie was born on 29 September 1847, the fifth son of Sir John William Pitt Muir-Mackenzie, baronet, of Delvine in Perthshire. He was educated first at Charterhouse, before studying at Oxford. He was a fellow of Hertford College, Oxford between 1874 and 1888.

In his youth, Muir-Mackenzie was a sportsman of some note, playing cricket and football at Charterhouse as a schoolboy. As an adult, he was selected to play for the Scottish football team in a match played against England on 24 February 1872. He spent much of the match, which was lost 1-0, in goal. The Scottish team were considered the underdogs, with one report recording that 'the Scotchmen all worked hard throughout, and considering the difficulties under which they laboured, their play did them infinite credit, although it must be stated that the slippery state of the ground favoured them more than their heavier opponents'.

Muir-Mackenzie became a student member of Lincoln's Inn on 11 January 1869 and was called to the bar on 27 January 1873. He rapidly secured an appointment as secretary to Lord Chief Justice Coleridge, a position that he held until 1877. He was also appointed as Recorder of Deal in 1892 and Recorder of Sandwich in 1894, the same year in which he became a bencher. He acted as Standing Counsel to the Board of Trade. Muir-Mackenzie published widely during his career at the Bar, including *Mackenzie on Bills of Lading, Chalmers and Mackenzie on the Judicature Acts, Mackenzie and Lushington on the Laws of Registration* and *Mackenzie and Clarke on the Bankruptcy Acts.* He was joint editor of Wilson's *Supreme Court of Judicature Acts and Rules.*

Muir-Mackenzie was known for his interest in music. He was the joint author, along with Edmund Macrory, of *Notes on the Temple Organ*, which was published in 1911. He was a member of the honourary council of the Royal College of Music for a number of years and is remembered as a supporter of the college. The College's museum collection still holds a painting of Muir-Mackenzie, painted by his daughter, in which he is depicted playing the cello.

Montague Muir-Mackenzie married the Honourable Sarah Napier Bruce, the daughter of Lord Aberdare, in 1888. He resigned his Recorderships in 1905 in order to take up his position as an Official Referee, remaining in office until his death in April 1919.

Sir Francis Newbolt KC 1920–1936

Like Lord Selbourne, Newbolt came from a religious background being the second son of the Vicar of St Marys in Bilstone, born 21 November 1863. He was educated at Clifton, and later at Balliol College Oxford where he read Natural Science (Chemistry) obtaining honours in 1887. He read law with Sir Thomas Wilkes Chitty, his brother-in-law, and a leading authority on Common Law procedure. He was called to the Bar by the Inner Temple in 1890 and joined the Western Circuit. He remained in Wilkes Chitty's Chambers for 10 years but did not enjoy an extensive practice. He took Silk in 1914. While at the Bar he continued his interest in science and gave over 1,000 experimental science lectures in board schools. He became Recorder of Doncaster in 1916, and a Chancellor of the Diocese of Exeter and Bradford and Chairman of the Devon Quarter Session. He became a referee after Sir Henry Verey's resignation in 1920. He was President of the Norwegian Club from 1920 to 1926 and an honorary member of the Land Agents Society. He was also an accomplished etcher and the author of a number of books in law, art and literature.[1]

His role as a referee was remarkable. On taking his appointment he found a court in the backwoods of the civil justice system. His status as a Referee was prescribed by the Judicature Acts and despite an extension of their judicial powers, they ranked below County Court Judges. As Anthony Burrows has suggested they were judges without jurisdiction.[2] The status was a bone of contention as was the number of judges then appointed three instead of four during most of his tenure. The problem was that in 1919, England had emerged from the Great War as a creditor to its allies but as a debtor to the US and was suffering from a global pandemic whose economic effects made a difficult situation much worse. Another problem was that in those days there seemed to be no appreciation for the importance of their cases involving complex technical issues and increasingly difficult issues of law.

His legacy may be that his contribution to the process of civil justice demonstrated the advantage of macro-case management by judicial delegation. His procedural micro-case management experiments indicated the benefit of informal proceedings at an interlocutory stage with a judge who readily understood the technical issues in the case. In certain circumstances that placed him in a unique position of discussing with solicitors on a directions hearing how best to proceed so that a fair and just resolution could be achieved without unnecessary waste of time or money in certain cases. In taking Lord Birkenhead's wise advice not to compromise his role as a judge he was able to procure settlement with the consent of the parties. This was easier for him, as a subordinate judge. Undoubtedly much court time was saved by such means as he pioneered. In this sense he was an innovator and an activist who was the father of modern case management many decades before it came into fashion. His approach of 'friendly discussions in chambers' was

[1] *The Times* 9 December 1940, 7; Issue 48794: col. E.
[2] R Burrows, 'Official Referees' (1940) 56 *LQR* 504, 506.

something I experienced as a solicitor when I had often appeared in directions hearings in the 1980s. Little did I know then its origin.

(Dr MP Reynolds)

George Alexander Scott 1920–1933

George Alexander Scott was born on 14 May 1862. He was educated at Worthing House in Worthing, before moving to Repton. He studied Classics at Pembroke College, Cambridge, graduating in 1883 and was called to the bar at the Inner Temple in 1887. He became an Official Referee in 1920, remaining in office until his death on 29 March 1933.

Scott had a keen interest in fishing, writing articles on his hobby for the *Daily Telegraph* and other periodicals. He was married twice. First to Alice, daughter of the author and journalist Daniel Faucon, with whom he had one son and, secondly, to Florence, the daughter of Ellis Williams of the Stock Exchange.

For further information on George Alexander Scott, who famously invented the Scott Schedule during his 13 years as an Official Referee, see chapter three.

Sir William Hansell 1927–1931

Born on 2 December 1856, Sir William Hansell came from an ecclesiastical family. He was the eldest son of the Reverend Edward Halifax Hansell, the rector of East Ilsley in Berkshire and his wife, Mary Elizabeth, daughter of Reverend David Williams, Warden of New College, Oxford. Hansell was educated first at Charterhouse and then Christ Church College, Oxford, where he took his BA in 1880 and MA in 1892. He became a student member of Inner Temple in 1877 and was called to the bar on 17 November 1880. He became a bencher at Inner Temple in 1912 and served as treasurer there from 1933. He took silk in 1927.

As befitted his family background, Hansell frequently took on ecclesiastical roles. He became Chancellor of Oxford Diocese in 1912, then of Gloucester and Birmingham Dioceses in 1920, of Coventry Diocese 1921 and of Lincoln and Southwark Dioceses in 1923.

In his practice, Hansell acted as Counsel to the Board of Trade in Bankruptcy between 1905 and 1927. He was also assistant editor of Vaughan Williams' *Law and Practice in Bankruptcy.* Hansell was appointed as Recorder of Maidstone in 1917, resigning this post in 1927 when he became an Official Referee. In the year after his resignation as an Official Referee in 1931, he became Commissioner of Assize on the North Easter circuit.

Sir William Hansell was a member of the Conservative Club. He married Edith Mary Maude, daughter of Admiral Sir Erasmus Ommanney in 1886. He died on 18 April 1937. For more information on Sir William Hansell, see chapter three.

Sir Ronald Bosanquet 1931–1954

Sir Samuel Ronald Courthope Bosanquet was born on 6 September 1868, the eldest son of Samuel Courthope Bosanquet of Dinestow Court, Monmouth. He was educated first at Eton, before studying at Trinity College, Cambridge. While at Cambridge, he served as president of the Union in 1891. He was called to the bar at the Inner Temple two years later, in 1893 and became a bencher there in 1930. He took silk in 1924.

Bosanquet became Chancellor of the Diocese of Hereford in 1928 and had ambitions outside the law, standing as the Unionist candidate for Stafford in the 1906 election, for example. As a lawyer, he acted as Recorder of Ludlow between 1919 and 1928 and of Walsall between 1928 and 1931. On resigning this recordership in 1931, he took office as an Official Referee, retiring in 1943. He continued to sit as Chairman of the Quarter Sessions and as a Justice of the Peace for Monmouthshire until 1950. Bosanquet was the lead author of *A Magistrate's Handbook*, which was published in 1929. He also wrote *The Burden of Neutrality: Notes for Onlookers in Time of War* in 1904, which discussed the legal implications of neutrality in war.

In his later years, Bosanquet wrote a memoir, *The Oxford Circuit*, which was published in 1951. In it, he devoted an entire chapter to what he considered to be 'the most sensational case in which I figured'. Bosanquet acted as part of the defence counsel on a particularly notorious criminal trial in 1922, involving a solicitor from Hay on Wye, Major Herbert Rowse Armstrong, who was accused of murdering his wife with Arsenic, as well as poisoning a rival solicitor, who survived. Bosanquet had, in fact, known Armstrong professionally for many years on the Oxford Circuit, while the pair had attended Cambridge at the same time. Indeed, Bosanquet recalled that Armstrong, who appeared detached and calm throughout his trial, repeatedly reminisced with him about their Cambridge days, on one occasion telling his counsel that 'you won't remember me, Bosanquet, but I remember you because I used to see you in the chair at the Union when I was a fresher'. On the first day of the trial, during a break, Armstrong chatted about Cambridge Union news, saying 'Bosanquet, I can tell you something that will interest you very much. A Cats man is president of the Union for the first time this term.' Bosanquet was the last visitor that Armstrong received before his execution in May 1922: he was the only solicitor to ever be hanged for murder.

Bosanquet was a member of the Athenaeum Club. He married Mary Acland Anson in 1911. The couple's only son was killed on active service in 1944, leaving their three daughters to survive them. Sir Ronald Bosanquet died on 5 November 1952. For more information on Sir Ronald Bosanquet, see chapter three.

Charles Pitman KC 1933–1945

Charles Murray Pitman was born on 8 January 1972, the seventh son of Frederick Pitman of Edinburgh. He was educated at Eton and then at New College, Oxford. Pitman was called to the bar in 1897, becoming a bencher of the Inner Temple in 1926. In 1924 he became a Recorder of Rochester and Judge Advocate of the Fleet, holding these roles until 1933 when he became an Official Referee. He retired as an Official Referee in 1945, in the same year that he also retired as Chairman of the Berkshire Quarter Sessions, a role that he had held since 1927.

Probably more famous as a rower than a lawyer, Charles Pitman came from a famously sporty family. The eight Pitman brothers (of whom he was the seventh) formed a winning rowing eight comprised only of themselves at Eton, while his elder brothers enjoyed significant rowing success. Charles Pitman was himself Captain of the Boats at Eton and a fixture in their first eight in 1890 and 1891. While at Oxford, Pitman won more than one event at Henley Royal Regatta. He also rowed in either the stroke or the seven seat for Oxford in the Oxford and Cambridge Boat Race in 1892, 1893, 1894 and 1895, all of which Oxford won with notably fast times. In 1895 he also served as president of the Oxford University Boat Club, giving an interview to *Vanity Fair* where he spoke of his hopes of again watching 'eight Cambridge galley-slaves toiling in his wake for most of the distance between Putney and Mortlake'. He was, it was considered, 'a typical young barbarian of the better sort', as well as 'a cheerful, wholesome boy, full of pluck'. Charles Pitman was so renowned as a rower that *The Times* described him in his obituary as 'one of the most distinguished oarsmen of his time'. He continued to follow rowing long after he had put down his oar, publishing a volume entitled *Rowing* with his co-author Reginald Percy Pfeiffer Rowe in 1901 and *The Record of the University Boat Race 1829–1909* with George Gilbert Treherne in 1909.

Charles Pitman married Hilda Mary Donkin in 1909. In keeping with his strong interest in rowing, he lived at Rememham Lodge in Henley-on-Thames. He died on 13 October 1948.

Sir Tom Eastham KC 1936–1954

Sir Tom Eastham was the third son of James Cook Eastham of Hadfield in Derbyshire and was born in 1879. He was educated at Manchester Grammar School, before studying at Owens College, which later became Victoria University in Manchester. Eastham studied medicine, becoming resident medical officer at the Royal Boscombe and West Hants Hospital in 1902. He rapidly changed careers and was called to the bar at Lincoln's Inn in 1904. He became a bencher there in 1927 and treasurer in 1948.

Sir Tom Eastham was appointed as Recorder of Oldham in 1924, holding the role until 1936 when he became an Official Referee. In his later life, he served as a justice of the peace for Surrey from 1947 until 1948, as well as holding the office of Deputy Chairman of Surrey Quarter Sessions from 1940 until 1954. He was Chairman of the Dorking Petty Sessions from 1943 until 1954.

Eastham also had political ambitions, standing as the Conservative candidate in the 1925 Stockport by-election which followed the death of the Conservative MP William Greenwood. He was unsuccessful, losing to Arnold Townend of the Labour party who won 36.5 per cent of the vote to Eastham's 32.3 per cent.

Sir Tom Eastham married Margaret Ernestine Smith, the daughter of a justice of the peace in 1911 and had three sons and two daughters. He lived in Hove in Sussex and died on 11 April 1967.

John Trapnell KC 1943–1949

John Graham Trapnell was the son of Caleb Trapnell of Stoke Bishop, Bristol. He was educated at Harrogate College and then King's College, Cambridge. He was called to the bar in 1903 and joined the Western Circuit. Trapnell took silk in 1931, before becoming Recorder of Plymouth in 1932, an appointment which he held until 1943. He was Judge Advocate of the Fleet, supervising the court-martial system in the Royal Navy from 1933 until 1943, while he was also a member of the Royal Navy Reserves. Trapnell resigned his appointments in 1943 when he became an Official Referee, a post that he held until his death.

John Trapnell led the prosecution team in the trial of Dorothy O'Grady, who was the first person to be found guilty under the Treachery Act 1940. Acting as a Nazi saboteur, O'Grady had cut telegraph wires and made detailed – and highly accurate – maps of the Isle of Wight defences. She was initially sentenced to death before this was commuted to penal servitude on appeal, with Trapnell involved in both the original trial in the Hampshire Assizes at Winchester and the appeal in London.

John Trapnell was a member of the RAF Club. He married Ethel Gardiner and had two sons, one of whom was the surveyor and ecologist Colin Trapnell, who was a co-founder of the Oxford University Exploration Club and spent most of his career surveying lands in Africa before turning to conservation ecology in his later years. John Trapnell died on 3 November 1949.

Herbert Samuels KC 1945–1947

Herbert David Samuels was born in 1880. He was called to the bar at Lincoln's Inn in 1908, becoming a bencher there in 1937. He took silk in 1933 and served as a Recorder of Bournemouth from 1944, resigning this post in 1945 when he was appointed as an Official Referee. He remained as an Official Referee until his death.

Samuels was a member of the Union Club. He married Beatrice Annie Smith of Nottingham in 1911 and had one daughter. He had homes both in London and in Farnham Common in Buckinghamshire and died in his London house on 11 December 1947 at the age of 67.

Sir Brett Cloutman VC, QC 1948–1963

See chapter four.

Sir Lionel Leach QC 1948–1956

Sir Alfred Henry Lionel Leach (known as Lionel Leach) was born on 3 February 1883, the eldest son of Robert Alfred Leach of Rochdale and Southport, who was himself a barrister. He was called to the bar at Gray's Inn in 1907.

Leach spent much of his career in British Burma and India. In 1933 he became a judge of the High Court of Rangoon, before becoming chief justice of the High Court of Madras between 1937 and 1947.

Leach had a reputation as a hard-working and successful judge in Madras, improving the standard of work and ensuring that the backlog of cases reduced. He had a reputation for stoicism. When his residence, Brodie Castle, which stood on the banks of the River Adyar, flooded in October 1943, for example, a number of lawyers from Madras would later recall that they had imagined him sitting in his high-backed chair commanding the river to rise no more. He worked well with his colleagues and was particularly focussed on ending conflicting rulings, something which was to 'the great enhancement of the prestige of the court' as one colleague put it. This was particularly the case with The Madras Agriculturalists Relief Act IV of 1938, which caused a torrent of new legal cases. Leach was concerned that conflicting judgments would render the law 'chaotic' and considered that 'the task of interpreting the new act consistently and prescribing a procedure was going to require continuity and specialised knowledge'. He therefore created a special bench, under the oversight of his fellow judge, Sir Sidney Wadsworth, to hear these matters.

Leach was involved in the defence of Madras, with Sir Sidney Wadsworth, a fellow judge there, recalling in his memoirs that on 13 April 1942 while leading the managers, clerks and translators from the High Court's office down to the General Hospital to give blood, he received a telephone call from Leach, 'speaking with great earnestness', to inform him that 'a large Japanese fleet with transports had been sighted, heading for the Madras coast, and that it was expected to land somewhere between Madras and the extreme south not later than the following Wednesday morning'. As a result, the civil government and courts were evacuated, officially beginning the summer vacation two weeks early. During his time in India, which included the Second World War, Leach served in the Indian Defence Force and the Indian Army Reserve of Officers.

Sir Lionel Leach returned to Britain after retiring from his post in 1947. The following year he became an Official Referee, serving until 1956. He also took silk in 1949. He continued to be considered an authority on Britain's colonial possessions, chairing the Singapore Riots Inquiry Commission in 1951, for example.

Leach was a member of the Carlton Club, the Flyfishers' Club and the Madras Club. He married Sophia Hedwig Kiel, the daughter of Professor Dr Heinrich August Kiel in 1908 and had one son. His wife died in 1954 and he died on 26 January 1960.

Sir Hubert Hull 1949–1950

Sir Hubert Hull was born on 10 September 1887, the second son of Robert Hull of Preston, Lancashire. He was a devout Catholic all his life, being educated at the leading Catholic boarding school, Stonyhurst College in Lancashire. Clement Attlee, who became mayor of Stepney in 1919, knew Hull, recalled that 'we were fortunate to have as leader of the council and chairman of the Finance Committee a very able barrister, Hubert Hull, who lived in a Catholic Settlement in Wapping'. For most of his adult life, Sir Hubert Hull would serve as the honorary legal advisor to the Catholic Record Society.

Hull was called to the bar at the Inner Temple in 1910, becoming a bencher there in 1945. During both World Wars he served as a temporary member of the civil service, being awarded a CBE after the Second World War, during which he had served as Assistant Procurator-General. He was a junior counsel to the Ministry of Agriculture and Fisheries and Commissioners of Crown Lands between 1939 and 1945, a role that presumably interested him, since he was the author of the fourth edition of *Oke's Fishery Laws*, which was published in 1924. Hull served as Official Referee only briefly, between 1949 and 1950, before becoming president of the Transport Tribunal in 1951, a role he retained until 1962.

Sir Hubert Hull was a member of the Reform Club. He married Judith Stokes, the daughter of a barrister, in 1915 and had two sons and four daughters. He lived in Kensington and died on 24 March 1976.

Joshua Casswell QC 1951–1959

Joshua David Casswell was born in 1886, the son of Joshua Joyce Casswell. He was educated as King's College School and then Pembroke College, Oxford, where he studied Classics, graduating in 1907. He was also sporty, representing Oxford three times in the Long Jump. He was called to the Bar in 1910, becoming a bencher at Middle Temple in 1947. In 1914 he became an Assistant Commander in the Special Constabulary, while he served as a major during the First World War, being wounded in 1917. He became a Recorder of Salisbury in 1938, holding the position until 1941 when he became a Recorder of Southampton. He resigned this post to become an Official Referee, remaining in office until 1959. Between 1954 and 1961 he was Deputy Chairman of the Surrey Quarter Sessions.

Casswell was a well-known figure at the bar, being renowned for his excellent knowledge of the law, gift for rhetoric and his ability to remain calm and unruffled. He famously acted for some of the bereaved families of passengers on the *Titanic* in 1913, obtaining £100 each in damages for many of them in a case against *The Oceanic Steam Navigation Company*, which was owned by the *White Star Line*.

He was able to persuade the jury to return a verdict of negligence on the part of the *Titanic's* captain.

Casswell was also famed for his involvement in the defence of a number of infamous murder cases. He acted as defence counsel for 40 people accused of murder and kept all but five of his clients from the gallows. Casswell often accepted fees so low that they barely covered expenses in these cases, later claiming that he 'always made a point of accepting these briefs whenever [he] was available, not only because they provided [him] with a challenge of a stimulating kind … but because [he] considered them an essential part of [his] professional duties'. Celebrated cases included that of Neville Heath, who was accused in 1946 of two particularly unpleasant murders. When Casswell questioned his client's decision to plead guilty, Heath replied 'all right, put me down as not guilty, old boy'. Casswell relied on a defence of insanity for Heath, choosing not to call him to give evidence The defence fell apart when his expert witness, a criminal psychiatrist admitted to being a drug addict, under the influence of morphine in the witness box. Neville Heath, who was executed on 16 October 1946 was a rare failure in Casswell's role as a defence counsel in cases of murder.

Casswell published his memoirs, *A Lance for Liberty*, in 1961, which give a detailed account of his life and practice. He gave his recreational interests to 'Who's Who' as 'odd jobs'. He was a member of the Royal Wimbledon Club and lived in Wimbledon. In 1919 he married Irene FitzRoy Hutton and had three sons and one daughter. He died on 15 December 1963.

The Later Official Referees

The lives of later Official Referees are detailed in chapter five of this volume.

Sir Walker Kelly Carter QC 1954–1971
Percy Lamb QC 1959–1969
Sir Norman Richards QC 1963–1977
Sir William Stabb QC 1969–1985
Edgar Fay QC 1971–1980
Lewis Hawser QC 1978–1990
John Newey QC 1980–1993
David Smout QC 1983–1987
Esyr Lewis QC 1984–1998
John Davies QC 1984–1993
James Fox-Andrews QC 1985–1994
Peter Bowsher QC 1987–2003
John Hicks QC 1993–2000
Sir Thayne Forbes 1993–2009
Humphrey Lloyd QC 1993–2005
Richard Havery QC 1998–2007

Anthony Thornton QC 1994–2009
David Wilcox 1996–2012
John Toulmin QC 1997–2011
Richard Seymour QC 2000–2005
Sir Peter Coulson 2004–2018

(Judges in Charge: Lord Dyson 1998–2001; Sir Rupert Jackson 2004–2007).

INDEX

www.ingramcontent.com/pod-product-compliance
Ingram Content Group UK Ltd.
Pitfield, Milton Keynes, MK11 3LW, UK
UKHW020229290926
15470UKWH00002B/440

9 781509 964178